The Story Of Our Generation

The Story Of Our Generation

FROM MONARCHY TO DEMOCRACY

———

*Matei Cazacu, Ioana Crețoiu
and Ladislau G. Hajós*

Translation: Ioana Poenaru and Maria Rizoiu

Photographs by: Decebal Becea

Cover: From the bottom, left to right: Rodica Peligrad-Tinca, **Ioan Berindei,** Constatin Cernat, **Englentina Vlasie**, followed by: Monica Diaconu-Bottez, Ioana Crețoiu-Casassovici and Florin Seimeanu; Patricia Filip and Roland Filippi; **Domnica Sufana**, **Felicia Badescu** and **Mircea Sebastian**; Ana Zsoldos-Atari, Gabriela Vasilescu-Iacobescu and Adrian Stoica; Niculae Ene, Serban Manolescu and Mihail Andreev

ISBN-13: 9781543184839
ISBN-10: 1543184839

Printed in the United States of America

Library of Congress Cataloging-in-Publishing Data

Hajos, Ladislau, Cazacu, Matei, Crețoiu, Ioana, 1. Iron Curtain, 2. Soviet Union, 3. Communism 4. Political Revolution, 5. Regime Changes

Table of Contents

Foreword – Ladislau G. Hajos

———

IN THE WINTER OF 2014, the Spiru Haret class of 1964 decided to organize a meeting to celebrate our 50th year of graduation. Half of our colleagues were scattered throughout the world including Israel, USA, France, Germany, United Kingdom, Spain, Switzerland and Australia. I discovered the addresses of 54 individuals, and launched the invitation to meet in Bucharest in May of 2014.

Since I am an engineer, I created various spreadsheets with names, name changes after marriage and/or immigration, email addresses, country of residence, phones numbers and nicknames from school. I asked my classmates to write what they had accomplished in the last 50 years. Each autobiographical note was to be accompanied by two photos: one from high school and the second photo from present day.

I received 41 presentations, which made it possible to meet again and more importantly recognize each other at the reunion, since most of us had not seen each other for 50 years. The collection of those biographies is included in Part III of this book. Some individuals requested not to be included in the book for various reasons. I also created a slide show with all the imagines that were gathered, as well as photographs from our school years. I provided each participant with a memory stick containing all the information I collected.

The idea of this book was conceived at the reunion, with Matei Cazacu as the originator. Ioana Crețoiu and myself joined immediately.

The concept of the book was to include all biographical information placed in the context of the social/political history of our birth and school years. A partnership was developed between Matei Cazacu (France), a published author and historian, Ioana Crețoiu (Romania), an architect and also an author and myself, Ladislau G. Hajos (USA), an electrical engineer and an author. We worked very closely together in a triangle from Bucharest to Paris to West Palm Beach for over two years. Ioana living in Bucharest handled all the hard work with the publisher, Editura Corint, for the Romania version of the book.

Matei obtained the sponsorship of The Institute of Investigation of Communist Crimes and the Memory of the Romanian Exile (IICCMER) for the publishing of the Romanian version of the book. The official release occurred at our school in Bucharest on December 12, 2016. This book is a very well documented and precise history of the time period that can be used by students and researchers in schools and universities.

We are all very happy with our accomplishment. However, something was missing, an English version. Some of us have spouses, children, family and friends that are not familiar with the Romanian language. We felt that they should have the opportunity to read this book. We wanted to provide a format for non-Romanian readers to understand our lives and the time period in which we lived. As stated by Andrei Plesu in the preface "Reading Matei Cazacu's study will offer, especially to the younger audience, a complete and unnerving view of those times; one that differs from their parents' and grandparents'. It is the time, as the author says, of "the last generation born in the Kingdom of Romania."

I pushed very hard for the English version and took it upon myself to coordinate and manage the translation and the publication. Based on my previous experiences in publishing, I started the fund raising work and found the right publisher. I researched the possibility of translating the book into English. With help from our colleague Georgiana Gălățeanu, presently a professor at UCLA, we found two translators, Ioana Poenaru and Maria Rizoiu. They did a phenomenal job translating the book into English. More importantly they put up patiently with my demands. Dr. Linda Edelstein, my wife, helped with editing the many portions of the book. Some of our colleagues did their own translations.

The financing was supported by most of the graduates. Specials thanks go to Gabriela Vasilescu-Iacobescu for her generous contribution.

Also, I want to mention our official photographer, Decebal Becea.

After six months of hard work, the English translation of the book is ready for sale. It is available for purchase on many major sites, such as Amazon.com and Barnes and Noble. "Tot înainte tovarăși!" This roughly translates to mean: "Go forward commrades!"

Ladislau G. Hajos
West Palm Beach, Florida, USA
May 2017

**Bucharest December 12, 2016, Romanian book
release at the Spiru Haret Highschool.**
From left to right: Nicolae Serban Tanaşoca, Ladislau G. Hajos, Matei
Cazacu, Ioana Creţoiu, Andrei Pleşu and Prof. Alexandru Constantinescu

**Bucharest December 12, 2016, Romanian book
release at the Spiru Haret Highschool.**
From left to right Ladislau G. Hajos, Ioana Crețoiu and Decebal Becea

Preface - A place of destiny – Andrei Pleșu

─────

HIGH SCHOOL ISN'T JUST A place of discipline and neatly organized study. It also inevitably becomes a place of *memory*. We all reminisce, especially when we are at the age of pre-senile nostalgia. We all feel the need to share our stories with the younger generation. Using the "Once upon a time" scheme, we tell them about our spectacular pranks, our feats of camaraderie, our timid romances, our severe or otherwise laughable teachers, our adolescent dreams and escapades, all the while expressing a rather foreseeable fondness to these distant memories. But once they all come together, once we begin to see them less as singular episodes and more as an interconnected web of events, the space in which they all took place becomes more than a place of memory, it becomes a place of destiny. We begin to perceive memories, as they truly are, as formative events, decisive encounters, existential coincidences that do not belong in an old and withered scrapbook, but are instead part of our biography, indistinct from its enduring fiber. Every place of memory, any space of encounter can become a place of destiny. A common knowledge and sense of belonging to the same historical design is needed; the persistence through time of events one has experienced together, in short, a common and burning interest pertaining to past events.

I may be wrong, but I am of the opinion that in this regard, "Spiru Haret" high school was such a place of destiny. I suppose all high schools, especially the ones with tradition, have the habit of reuniting past graduates. All generations celebrate the anniversaries of their graduation. But, as far as I am concerned, the "spirists" do not play into the monotony of the general rule. Four years ago, my generation (we graduated in 1966) decided to publish their memories. The resulting volume proved that a great number of ladies and gentlemen that "parted ways" almost fifty years ago and spread across the world have kept in touch. They kept seeing each other, exchanging ideas and holding the occasional get-together. And by that, I don't mean regular reunions but rather lively encounters that go beyond their times and circumstances. In the preface of our volume, we comment on this destiny driven survival of the group: sometimes, "a community of people turns into an aggregate; a unitary organism, a creature of some kind. All its individuals become absorbed by a wholeness of being, a unitary soul, it becomes a spiritual field that is greater than the sum of its parts". This is what I believe has happened with the volume we have before us; it documents a generation that has not merely lived through its adolescence, but treasured it, turned it into an assumed destiny.

The book is not only about the history of a generation. Through the ample and consistent introduction written by Matei Cazacu, the reader witnesses one of the dramatic periods in this country's history: the first two decades after World War II. It is a period for which we do not have an informative compendium today and that does not seem to draw a lot of public interest. Reading Matei Cazacu's study will offer, especially to the younger audience, a complete and unnerving view of those times; one that differs from their parents' and grandparents'. It is the time, as the author says, of "the last generation born in the Kingdom of Romania." It is about the hard times of famine, financial instability, and soviet occupation, a time of arrests, centralization, food rationing and other restrictive measures. We are offered the results of erudite research into the matter, by means of rigorously verified data, vast statistics and cited sources but also accompanied by remembrances and reconstructions that could only be delivered to the contemporary reader by an informed witness. It also includes the detailed and picturesque history of the epoch: the old names of the streets, their notorious inhabitants, buildings that survived and buildings that were lost, what was allowed and, most of all, what was forbidden, and the mix of tragedy and absurdity in which people were forced to live back then. ("A mix of I. V. Stalin and I. L. Caragiale" – in the words of Belu Zilber, tenacious communist yet at the same time a victim of the system).

The collected memories of my other colleagues also illustrate this epoch accurately, often by evocations rich in atmosphere and lush cultural and political retrospectives. For example, Adrian Irvin Rozei reminds his colleagues of the melancholic ambiance in which we could all survive, despite the circumstances. He talks about the Festival of the Youth in 1953, held in the "Timpuri Noi" cinema, where, in exchange for one leu and twenty bani as the price of admission, you could sit indefinitely through performances by artists and seductive singers such as Mircea Crişan, Arkadi Raikin, "Trio Armonia", "Trio Grigoriu", Sergiu Malagamba, Aida Moga, Vico Torriani and Domenico Modugno, Dorina Drăghici and Luigi Ionescu, "Los Paraguayos", madam Bulandra, Jules Cazaban, Fory Etterle or Lazăr Vrabie and many others.

At first, the honor of writing the preface for this book seemed too much to me. As I was born in 1948, I don't belong to the same generation as Matei Cazacu. But afterwards, I gradually came to the realization that the idea of destiny itself governs the part I will play in this volume. I have crossed paths, in various ways, with quite a few people belonging to the "spirist universe" – beginning in 1957, when I entered my third grade in school with Vasile Ghineţ as a teacher. Still "green" back then, I grew up admiring "the boys" from the older generations: Petru Popescu, for example, who would amaze us with his "relations" with the literary world (Geo Bogza, Radu Tudoran, etc.), and later Nicolae-Şerban Tanaşoca, now a great byzantinologist. Matei Cazacu was younger than they were and he was one of my uncle's favorites. My uncle, Vladimir Niculescu, taught French at the same high school (He was the one that had spoken fondly to me of Ionică Bruckner and Dan Cheţa, who were both later to become distinguished doctors). Years later, Matei would come again into my life through a confession by Andrei Scrima about his father, Niţişor Cazacu, who was a priest of the Batiştei Church and a secretary to the Justinian Patriarch. Father Cazacu had accompanied Andrei Scrima to the airport in 1958 when he had embarked on an unhoped for and, I could say, providential journey towards the West.

"Spiru Haret" is also the high school attended by some of my mentors: Constantin Noica, Alexandru Paleologu, and Nicu Steinhardt. After 1989,

I would come to the realization that, by the hand of destiny, both those in power and those in opposition at that time, Ion Iliescu and Octavian Paler had graduated from the same high school. Moreover, the father of Ioana Casassovici (Crețoiu), also present in this volume, was the brother of Adina Juvara (the wife of the great surgeon) and cousin to Mr. Noica. I ran across Zamfir Dumitrescu (Firu) because he and I shared the same professional sphere, he as a painter and I as an art critic. But I remember him from back then, when I would hear him during recess, blonde and joyful, caught up in recounting his numerous feats to his colleagues, some more believable than others.

In the pages of this book, I unexpectedly came across a small detail pertaining to my own biography, one I had not known about until now. One of the authors relates how he met a certain "delightful young miss" named Crenguța Munteanu who became the mother of his daughter, Ilinca. Miss Munteanu had also previously been the mother of my eldest son, Mihai. If this is not the hand of fate, I don't know what is.

A lot of teachers also have a part to play in the "place of destiny" called "Spiru Haret". They were the enduring glue that has kept numerous generations of students together. They were grand, fit to teach in universities, still having the benefit of the high standards of education present in the interwar period. They have all been mentioned in the following pages. One of them, Ion Voiculescu, our biology teacher, was known as "Cell" due to his stature and field of study. But he had also taught my father! I could not believe it when I first found out about this. The nicknaming policy was different when my father was a student. "Cell" had been nicknamed "Ionică Dor-Mărunt", by association with the town with the same name in Călărași county (My father attended high school in Turnu Măgurele, which was close to the town in question).

And so here I am, "affiliated" through multiple connections to the community that expresses itself in between the covers of this book. I am part of its constellation and I live through its evanescence. I would point out that what this book offers vastly exceeds the chapter of one's private life or one closed group. It is, as I have mentioned earlier, a nutritious slice of national history, an illuminating insight into the epoch from which our parents have tried to shield themselves, but which has become part of their underlining fiber, even if they do not fully acknowledge it.

I have learned that there is a crater on the Moon, discovered in the last century by astronomers, that bears the name of Spiru Haret, as a tribute to his scientific career. We, the "spirists", may not be the center of the world, but we are, by way of our symbolic "patron", an immovable "crater" on the surface of South Eastern Europe. From this point of view, the following book may very well be the beginning of an adventure...

Andrei Pleșu
Bucharest, Romania
2016

Part One - The Story of Our Generation (1946 - 1964) - Matei Cazacu

—

Introduction

——

THIS BOOK IS THE WORK of an historian who specializes in medieval and modern history. Moreover, it encompasses contemporary accounts, personal memories and extracts from important works, both recent and old. This offers the book a more composite character but I believe it also makes for an easier read. I have tried, on one hand, to understand the time in which I was born and lived in and on the other, to make my contemporaries reflect on their life in Romania between 1950 and 1960. We all lived in Romania during its first decades under the communist regime and we all have special memories of this period. They were good times for some, for others they were mediocre at best and nightmarish still for a few of us. We form an age group born after World War II, during a time when a whole world was crumbling down as a new one was rising. An old Chinese curse goes something like this: "May you live in an interesting epoch." And it truly was interesting, the epoch of our childhood and adolescence, although we were too young to understand much of it. Some may have understood it faster than others.

During the aforementioned decades, Romanian society undertook a double process of destruction followed by reconstruction on all its facets: the political, the economic, the social, and the cultural. The model that was imposed on it was that of soviet communism as Lenin, Stalin and their comrades had used it during 1920 through 1930. The Utopia in power, applied forcefully by the coercing utopians, brought forth a *pastoral* or *biopower* (Michel Foucault) type of regime in which the state seizes all functions and forces the individual from birth to death into an ever more

3

constraining mold. This system proved itself to be more effective than all the autocracies and totalitarian regimes known up until now due to the technological means that were at its disposal and the authoritarian methods that were put to use. Under the wooden fist of the Ottoman Empire domination over Moldavia and Țara Românească, and later the iron fist of Austrian administration in Transylvania and Russian administration in Bessarabia, Romanians had created the modern state of Romania (1859-1944), led by a local oligarchy, with its constitutional monarchy slowly evolving towards parliamentary democracy, in spite of its patriarchal mentalities and economic and social inequalities. The Russian Revolution of 1917, followed by the Italian one in 1922 and its German counterpart in 1933 shook the entirety of Europe and prevented Romania's evolution towards parliamentary democracy. Modern historians have had passionate debates over Ernst Nolte's thesis[1] about the European civil war carried out between 1917 and 1945 and the appearance of Italian fascism and German National Socialism as reactions of the bourgeoisie towards the communist threat of declaring war on all governments and its prophesizing of the world wide revolutionary victory. However things may actually be, the alliance of western democracies in World War II wiped out the extreme right-wing dictatorships with the price of leaving Eastern and Central Europe to fall under Soviet domination. Here, the Red Army and NKVD (descendant of CEKA and a predecessor to KGB) were the harbingers of a new political system, copied after the one in USSR, which was deemed to be flawless. We find ourselves in front of an exported revolution, in the words of Stalin and Lenin, and not the result of an internal organic evolution. The consequences of this grafting, made with such brutality as is not yet fully recognized by history, were on one hand, the demise of any political opposition, and on the other, the enrollment of millions of people towards the realization of this sought after utopia. Utopia is being defined as a society without classes and exploitation, a resplendent future of human kind. Yet this project failed, or is about to fail, in all the places it has been implemented. This is neither the time nor the place to discuss the causes of this disastrous failure, which caused tens and hundreds of millions of victims and unimaginable damages to the economy.

I have more profoundly reflected over the meaning of this experience that took place under the sign of modernity induced by the communist dictatorship. I have asked myself, as any historian would, whether this process's influence was positive or negative and whether the utopia in power was able to eliminate the injustices of the past and instill justice and equality in society, turning it into a meritocratic democracy in which the individual can affirm himself and perfect his role in society as a worker and as a citizen. History is a witness that the industrial revolutions of the past, in England, France, Germany and the United States, all took place with the price of great suffering and transformation in which a part of the rural community had to relocate to the city and become the industrialized working class. The industrial revolution in USSR, as was the case in Romania, had a peculiar character to it due to the ideology's monopoly, this intellectual activity with a purpose other than discovering the truth. Through its very nature, ideology is incompatible with democracy, with justice, and finally, with the industrial revolution itself. This is because industrialization and modernization naturally and inevitably lead to specialization and thus inequality between individuals. Ideology tends to level individuals, with a few privileged exceptions, namely the nomenclature, which represents an infinitely small minority comparable only with the aristocracy of the Old Regime and the true bourgeoisie (as defined by Mihail Manoilescu[2]), amounting to between 1.5 and 3% of the entire population. In other words, "You get up so I can sit down." as I recall some reactionaries would say in my childhood. Where was the legitimacy then for this new minority in comparison with the old one, who was destroyed with such hatred that is still not understandable to me? It is not its origins, the occupation by the Soviet military and the imposed model of Stalinist dictatorship, but the flaunted expectations to forcefully impose happiness on the population through industrialization and the collectivization of agriculture in an accelerated fashion and by any means – even terror.

A distinguished Romanian political scientist Daniel Barbu engaged with this subject a few years ago, and came to the following conclusion:

Data available today suggests that repression seems to not have played the important political role that has been attributed to it. After 1948, surveillance, arrest, trial, condemnation, conviction and incarceration did not evolve into social practices capable of defining the nature and objectives of power.[3]

In aid to his thesis, Barbu points out an important series of numbers. People were "affected by repression in varying degrees." More precisely "no more than 1,500,000 people, amounting to a maximum of 8% of the total population" were impacted by repression. By comparison, "the percentage of people for which communism brought a positive change to their lives, with stable income in continual growth, ever growing access to superior education and a closer bond with the state ranges from 20% to 70%". By approximating both of those numbers, we conclude that, according to Barbu, 6% (little over a million) of the Romanian population were repressed in varying degrees (some directly and others indirectly, through their family and close ones), while 45% (7.65 million) were the beneficiaries of the communist regime: farmers who migrated from rural areas to the city, wage earners and pensioners, college and high school students. In total, almost half of the population reaped the benefits from the communist experience and 6% suffered from it.

These statements need a more in depth analysis. First of all, we must pose the question: what happened with the 49% of the population who are not represented in this statistic? Mr. Daniel Barbu does not mention the fate of the others, whether it was worse or better than before, so we must presume that, in his opinion, it was neither. We shall soon see what to believe about this opinion.

Talking about the 6% of Romanian citizens who suffered the "penal rigors of the regime", Daniel Barbu takes only a part of the reality of the communist era into account. To these numbers, one has to add the victims of political assassinations – 60,000 only between 1946 and 1947[4] and several thousand during the subsequent years. Applying the family coefficient of 4.5%, we reach the number of 270,000 additional victims just for the period between 1946 and 1947. We must then add the number of those assassinated between 1948 and 1964, those killed in the times of agricultural collectivization (unearthed by Marius Oprea and his team), the tens of thousands of peasants who were forced into collective farms as a result of inhuman pressure enacted upon them by party activists about which Constantin Turturică talks in his book *Nu este nevoie sa mori tâmpit. Mărturia informatorului* (*You Don't Have to Die an Idiot. Confessions of an informer*, Eminescu publishing house, Bucharest, 2000).

Usually, one only sees the numbers confessed by Gheorghe Gheorghiu-Dej and acknowledged by Nicolae Ceaușescu: 80,000 arrested, out of which 30,000 were publicly trialed. By all means, the exiled and the illegal emigrants, over one million people – Jewish people, Transylvanian Saxons and other minorities, people with family members in other countries which were ransomed in dollars between 1944 and 1989 – they must also be considered victims of the communist regime, because they didn't flee the country for pleasure, but out of various reasons with cumulative effects. In 1982, The Securitate's Third Division of Counterespionage claimed that, between 1941 and 1982, "42,262 people have fled the country illegally"[5], numbers that were grossly smaller than reality, as the author of the book from which I have extracted the information admits. Securitate is the Romanian Communist Secret Police the equivalent of the Soviet KGB at that time. Each communist country had such an institution.

Another number that must be altered is the number of people condemned to mandatory residence (with the acronym d. o., secretly known as "diplomat olandez[6]"). In this case, Mr. Daniel Barbu writes about 60,000 people, but the most recent (and the only one) synthesis of the problem, which we owe to Mrs. Nicoleta Ionescu-Gură (2010), brings additional insight: "The result is that 73,239 people were uprooted and forced to relocate during the Gheorghe Gheorghiu-Dej regime. The number is 13,239 higher than the one existing in the securities documentation. Yet we should consider that even this number (73,239 people) is not close to reality, because the documents do not mention people who were relocated upon refusal to pay their quota to the state, the families of the resistance fighters up in the mountains, the people who opposed agricultural collectivization. The archives keep no clear records of these people, only sporadic data, during certain periods. If we would add to those numbers the people who were reallocated due to the systematization of territories and rural areas during the Nicolae Ceaușescu regime, we would get several tens of thousands of people who were the victims of such drastic measures."[7].

Another category of victims due to extra-economic constraints (terror) were the young generations of college and high school students who were unable to attend their studies due to their "unhealthy" social origins, the thousands of people "exposed" between 1958 and 1959 (students, workers, functionaries, etc.), "parasites" or "malagambists"[8]"[9] chased on the streets by the police, monks and nuns sent away from their monasteries during the same period of time. In December 1957, for 323,207 "elements of the enemy" (if we apply the coefficient of 4.5% we come to approximately 1,500,000 people) the Ministry of Internal Affairs held "compromising information" provided by those in charge of apartment buildings and street committees in collaboration with the more than 150,000 informants (numbers taken from records back in 1958; by 1965, the number of informants would rise towards 400,000 people, according to the work of Cicerone Ionițoiu). They should also be considered victims of the regime – both effective and potential ones, although sometimes the two categories would converge, the same individual being both "element of the enemy" and informant in order to save himself and his family.

The numbers and percentages given to us by Mr. Daniel Barbu ignore a whole category of victims of the communist regime who did not go to prison (and thus did not suffer "the penal rigors of the law") – I am referring to the victims of "economic constraint", about whom I have spoken more profusely throughout my contribution to this volume. Here, we are not dealing with hundreds of thousands, but with millions of people ruined by the two monetary "stabilizing" movements in 1947 and 1952, when peasants (78% of the country's population) sold one year's worth of crops for 250 new lei (an equivalent of 1.67 dollars with the official exchange rate and 0.50 dollars on the black market), functionaries, wage earners and pensioners saw their earnings reduced to 150 lei (an equivalent of 1 dollar with the official exchange rate and 0.33 on the black market), and people "outside the work field" got a mere 75 lei (0.5 dollars or 0.15 on the black market). Through this reform, salaries were fixed between 300 and 500 lei, at a time when a pair of shoes cost 150 lei and a meter of canvas was 255 lei. Taxes were raised as well, in comparison with the year 1938: 500% for agricultural incomes, 793% for commercial incomes, 350% for professional incomes and a small lowering on salary taxation (94%). Tax evasion became assimilated and was considered a crime of sabotage to the economy, and became punishable with prison to lifetime forced labor – in 1949 it was changed to the death sentence. This measure was especially applicable to peasants who couldn't pay their quota to the state – an organized theft that lasted for years and that ruined this social-economic category, explaining the massive urban exodus (estimated at about 3.5 million people, approximately 20% of the population). This segment is exactly the one referred to by Daniel Barbu as being "mesmerized by the civilization of the factories".

The nationalization of the country's economy by the state in 1948 and the expropriation of landowners who had up to 50 hectares of land in 1949, the seizing of buildings and houses belonging to the dignitaries of the "old regime" in 1950 (they were in the hundreds of thousands throughout the country), and the bankruptcy of thousands of merchants and entrepreneurs created a great number of unemployed and people without any social or political standing (after the Soviet model written in the 1918 Constitution) – "elements of the enemy", people without rights to food rationing cards, condemned to starve to death.

The same thing happened during the "stabilization" of 1952, another "legal theft" during which the state seized approximately 80 to 90% of the Romanians' small sums and 95% of the big sums. We will further discuss about the reduction and even withdrawal of pensions that ruined thousands of pensioners. If we were to add all these numbers, we would come to the conclusion that many millions of people have fallen victims – and this is only during the Gheorghe Gheorghiu-Dej era, the period to which Mr. Daniel Barbu refers exclusively. The 6% of victims of the "penal rigors of the regime" represent a mere fraction of the total number of victims of the economic and extra-economic constraints during the 1945 to 1964 period. It vastly exceeds the number of beneficiaries of the 8 square meters per person apartments (this was all that was permitted at this time in regards to living space, imitating the Soviet model of *komunalka*), of measly salaries and pensions, of hard and alienating work, chaotic dietary habits, lack of heating and multiple other "privileges" that were the primary source of their constant lamentations.

In conclusion, I will cite Boris Bajanov[10], an ex-Soviet communist and secretary to the Central Committee of the Communist Party in the Soviet Union and to Stalin between 1923 and 1926. Here are his conclusions in regards to the philosophy and Marxist-Leninist practices in the Soviet Union and, by imitation, in Romania:

> *I quickly realized all nuances in the attitudes of the communist leaders in regards to Marxist theory. As practitioners and pragmatists in leading the state, they perfectly understood the utter uselessness of Marxism in regards to the comprehension and orchestration of economic life – as such, they had adopted a rather skeptical and ironic attitude towards the "learned Marxists". However, they greatly appreciated the explosive emotional force of Marxism that had brought them to power in Russia and was about to bring them to power in the whole world (as they were rightfully hoping). To resume in a few words: as a science, Marxism was nonsense, but as a method of manipulating the masses towards revolution, it was an irreplaceable weapon.[11]*

By writing these lines, I am aware of the risk I am taking of being called a reactionary by some, or a nostalgic who regrets the past, the monarchy or perhaps civil and military dictatorship. I do not regret them at all; I merely see them as steps within a historical process, endowed with both positive and negative aspects. In my present work, I have concerned myself with the period of time between 1944 and 1964, the time of our childhood and adolescence. It is true that I have done this by using the experiences – of my family, of the people I met and, to some extent, of my own – as a starting point, but I didn't limit myself to my own memory – I perused all I could find, such as confessions, articles, documents from the archives, historical synthesizes about this epoch not only in Romania, but also in Hungary and Bulgaria.

Using the excellent synthesis of Mr. Radu Preda, president of the Institute for the Investigation of the Crimes of Communism and the Memory of

Romanian Exile, reproduced in the following lines, I hope I was successful in avoiding the traps set by only appealing to the memory of one individual: "Just as in literature or art we cannot find pure instances of style, so is memory incapable of limiting itself to solely one period. To be in the possession of one separate memory, in fact, of one single instance of the present dilated and limited to a single space of reference is to have no memory at all. Such an existence refuses projection, out of lack of horizons, but it refuses introspection as well, out of lack of depth. The incapacity of comparing times keeps us in such captivity as resembles the artificial spaces in which plants grow without the touch of sunlight. Simply put, the memory – singular – is inevitably a coalescence of other memories. In other words, our memory is a meeting place for memories. Thus, by self-comparison and moreover by comparison to others, the appeal to memory is never equivocal. In regards to communism, it is true that we all went through the same epoch, but did so differently. So differently, that our remembrances are absolutely different. Facing scrutiny, memories can clash, and this is the reason for which such a variety of types exists in regards to what the historical unleashing of evil meant for us: from the nostalgic to the cynical and from the resolute anti-communists to the apathetic, from the disconsolate victim to the ones that practice relativism. Thus we reach a worrisome conclusion: history cannot be written based solely on memory, both singular and plural. As we can see in polls, as well as spontaneous discussions, the positive memories – apartment buildings, factories and plants, secure jobs and holidays – is systematically and programmatically confronted with the negative memories – labor camps, assassinations, deportations, discrimination. From this confrontation comes the tendency to find a false compromise in discussing communism. The perverse effect this tendency for compromise has is seen in the warm exegesis – only pretending to be objective – when stating something along the lines of 'communism was a good idea, but its application was faulty' or that 'capitalism has its faults as well'. What is frequently forgotten is that totalitarianism, communist or otherwise, is evil through its very nature. Crimes cannot be symbolically negotiated nor can they be ethically justified as being inevitable or 'faults in manufacturing'. As much as some would wish it, it cannot be said that the intentions are all that matter or that the road towards happiness somehow deserves over a hundred million victims. … The reconciling of memories in order to avoid the risk of amnesia has to begin with a few rules: we have different memories which are not mutually exclusive; memory is generally preferred to forgetfulness; our maturity depends on how much we own up to what we have lived personally or through others; the common denominator of all memories about communism or from that period is the acknowledgement of the negative impact it had, no matter what its intensity in our memories. We didn't have to be related to political prisoners, executed or deported, to understand the criminal nature of a regime that used such tactics. In the same way, we don't need to feel guilty because we lived wonderful moments during the communist era, because we loved, because we met friends, or because we were filled by the joy of the first steps of our children, memories we would never want to forget. The sun rises each and every day in North Korea, and when the season comes, the cherry trees blossom. Having had normal moments only makes the abnormality of dictatorship shine through. It is not the presence of normality but its absence that demands an explanation. "[12]

Matei Cazacu

---

1. Ernst Nolte (1923 - 2016) – German philosopher and historian, professor at the Freie Universitat in Berlin, author of several controverted analyses about fascism and communism. The book cited appeared in Romanian as *"Războiul civil European (1917 - 1945). Național –socialism și bolșevism"*, preface by Florin Constantiniu, translated by Irina Cristea, Bucharest, Runa, 2005

2. Mihail Manoilescu (1891-1950) – engineer, inventor, economist and political person, minister of external affairs, an adept of corporatism and protectionism, author of many works, including *Rostul și destinul burgheziei românești* (The purpose and destiny of the Romanian bourgeoisie), Bucharest, 1942

3. Daniel Barbu *"Destinul colectiv, servitutea involuntară, nefericirea totalitară: trei mituri ale comunismului românesc"*(The collective destiny, involuntary servitude and totalitarian unhappiness: three myths of Romanian communism) apud Lucian Boia, *Miturile comunismului românesc,* București, 1942.

4. Ghiță Ionescu, *Communism in Rumania (1944-1962)*, London, New York, Toronto, 1962, pp. 131-132. All works in the introduction have been cited in the text of my contribution to this volume, so I will only mention the title and page in these notes.
5. Mihai Pelin, *Opisul emigrației politice* (The archives of political emigration), pp. 7-10.
6. Dutch diplomat
7. Nicoleta Gură-Ionescu, op. cit., 2010, pp. 381-382.
8. Malagambist – frivolous person, preoccupied with their attire and fashionable events. The word defines a young individual between 1940 and 1960, dressed to the height of fashion and with a non-conformist attitude.

10. Boris Bajanov (1900-1982) – although he held positions of power in the Soviet inner circle, he defected in 1928. After he fled the country through Iran, he was offered political asylum in France. He was "chased" by the soviet regime's secret agents, but escaped with his life. In 1930, he published his memoirs about the period he spent in Iosif Stalin's entourage.
11. Boris Bajanov, *Bajanov revele Staline. Souvenirs d'un ancien secretaire de Staline*, Paris, Gallimard, 1979, p. 111.
12. Radu Preda *"Dupa 25 de ani. Pentru reconcilierea memoriilor"*(After 25 years. For the reconcilement of memories.), in *Memoria. Revista gândirii aresta te*, no.89 (4/2014), pp. 5-7.

CHAPTER 1

The Cold War Generation

——

THE STORY OF OUR GENERATION is intertwined with the history of post war Romania. The majority of those of us passing the baccalaureate at "Spiru Haret" high school in 1964 are born in 1946 (77 people out of a total of 119). The year 1964 was the year of one of the most ravaging droughts of the 20th Century, but also one of the best years for wine in the last one hundred years. The other 43 graduates, representing approximately a third of the total, are born in 1947 (23 of them), 1945 (14), 1944 (4) and 1943 (1). We can thus conclude that we represent the generation that was called *the baby boomers* in the West – children born in great numbers after the war, out of the joy of living, coming as one of life's natural reactions following the immense massacres on the fields of war and in the death camps. Yet the concept of *baby boomers* remains purely American, as post war Europe had been transformed in what an English historian recently called *the Savage Continent*[1], and Eastern Europe had remained the *blood lands*, as defined by Timothy Snyder[2]. As such, we are the first generation of children born during the Cold War.

We started our first grade in school in September 1953, a few months after the death of Stalin – it was the beginning of a period of relative relaxation of internal politics, considered to be a true destalinization; in any case, the regime had become less fearful in comparison with the previous years. This was also the beginning of one of the harshest winters of the century (more than 5 million cubic meters of snow falling between the 30th of January and the 3rd of February 1954). I finished high school in 1964, in the midst of the euphoria of so called freedom caused by the Declaration in April, through which the Working Party of Romania refused to take part in the Sino-Soviet conflict and was ideologically stating its equidistance towards the two colossi. In actuality, this declaration was never about any sympathy towards the Chinese – it was a counterweight towards soviet power. Mao would publicly condemn the "high-powered chauvinism" and Stalin's seizing of Bessarabia. The country's opening towards the West and the cessation of jamming "enemy" radio stations, the freeing of political prisoners and the renunciation of persecution policies of former elites and especially their children, who were finally permitted to access higher education were all signs of a normalization of public life for a society who had underwent another "glaciation" between 1958 and 1962. It was the beginning of the decade of liberalization that would end in 1971 or 1974 (historians are still debating the subject)[3] – an epoch of respite for which some still yearn today. The personal conflict between Gheorghe Gheorghiu-Dej and Nikita Hrușciov was seen as a cooling of relations with the *Big Brother* in the East, when in fact it was – as in the later conflict between Nicolae Ceaușescu and Mihail Gorbaciov – the Romanian leader's resistance towards the chaotic reform projects proposed by their homologue from Kremlin. The forced retirement of Hrușciov in October 1964 and the death of Gheorghe Gheorghiu-Dej in March 1965 would set the stage for the Ceaușescu-Brejnev-Gorbaciov confrontation and the transformation of national-communist Romania from the *maverick*[4] of international politics into a *rogue state*[5].

All observers agree that Romania had less to suffer than Poland, Hungary, Yugoslavia and Greece from the ravages of war – Bulgaria being the most privileged region in this respect. Romanian cities – especially Bucharest, Ploiești and Iași – were subjected to bombings of considerable proportions between April and August 1944, but incomparable to Warsaw (93% destroyed), Belgrade or Budapest (75% destroyed) – not to mention German cities. Likewise, the mass ethnic cleansing in Central and Western Europe after 1944 that especially reached the German population (approximately 12 million people), the Ukrainian population in Poland, the Polish population in Ukraine, the Magyar population in Slovakia and so on, did not reach similar proportions in Romania: the Red Army deported approximately 70,000 German ethnics in 1945 and "hunted down" the Bessarabian and Bucovina refugees that had settled here in 1940-1941 and after 1944. Several thousand Hungarians, relocated to Northern Transylvania by the Magyar administration (1940-1944), left Romania, although it seems that many have stayed, and others from Hungary sought refuge here, as have many Polish and Czechoslovakian Jewish people[6].

In order to limit ourselves to Romania, for the moment, it suffices for us to quote from a French study published in November 1948, based on the reports of the International Red Cross Committee, an organization that was doing a lot of fieldwork at the time:

> *The state of the Romanian populace in 1947 is hard to imagine: famine ruled over entire regions of the country; in certain parts of the country, people ate grass and the bark of trees, sometimes even clay. It is estimated that approximately 6 million people were left in the care of the government (for food) in 1947-1948. Here are some of the consequences of famine and squalor present in this country: 1. The disappearance of small children in some regions; infantile mortality has reached 80%[7]; 2. The rapid growth in the number of deceases and mortality; bodies were thrown into the waste trenches in the back of the houses; 3. Generalized poverty has facilitated the rapid spread of sexually transmitted diseases. According to some recent studies done by the Ministry of Health, one person in twelve suffers from syphilis[8].*

For the period between 1946 and 1947, statistics signal 300,000 people dead of starvation and epidemic typhus in Romania and at least 200,000 in Bessarabia, mostly children (see the following). Over one million people were relocated between 1940 and 1947; numerous women and girls were raped in 1944 and the following years by the soldiers in the Red Army, crimes for which we do not have precise numbers, but which can be compared with the similar situation in neighboring countries: between 50,000 and 200,000 in Hungary[9], 87,000 in Vienna and in Austria and approximately 2 million people in all of Germany (110,000 in Berlin only) – this also explains the spread of sexually transmitted diseases in these countries, thus in Romania as well.[10]

We are a generation of survivors who had the fortune of having, within our families, the proper conditions to live a relatively normal life, despite the extremely difficult circumstances; yet we are far from truly knowing the suffering our parents and grandparents endured during those years.

We are the last generation born in the Kingdom of Romania (although in 1958 or 1959 we were all declared "the children of the republic"). At the end of high school we lived in the People's Republic of Romania (RPR), which would one year later become the Socialist Republic of Romania (RSR). The few of us who didn't leave the country or came back afterwards now live in Romania, a republic under parliamentary democracy, with a president elected by universal vote and a member of the EU and NATO. I have lived, entirely or partially, under four or five political regimes: constitutional monarchy, "people's democracy", the proletariat's dictatorship – which was in fact communist dictatorship of Bolshevik design (the Gheorghe Gheorghiu-Dej era), afterwards followed by national-communist dictatorship (the Nicolae Ceaușescu era between 1965 and 1989), and finally the "original" parliamentary and presidential democracy. During all this time, the national flag (with the colors red, yellow and blue becoming horizontal as they were once vertical) and Romania's coat of arms (with or without the crown, with or without the star, with tractors, oil wells, pine forests and ears of wheat, with a vulture nowadays) changed five times, as well as the national hymn (*Trăiască Regele, Zdrobite cătușe, Te slăvim, Românie, Deșteaptă-te Române*). Romanian orthography was modified three times, and the names of streets in Bucharest – not all of them, fortunately – changed several times: in 1949 "just" 1,345 out of 3,541 streets were renamed! Hardly could we fathom any other generation in Europe who had to handle so many political and social revolutions; a generation marked by so many changes in regimes, and of such a varied nature: political, constitutional, judicial, military and educational. "Burn down what you have adored and adore what you have burned down!" in the words of Saint Remi addressing Clovis, the king of Franks, at his baptism (in 496). "The new man" and "the enemy[11]" were "the magic key to the existence of communism". On one hand, "hatred of the classes" coupled by "Who is not on our side is against us" and "The Americans are coming!" on the other – these were the circulated currency and practically became the mottos of those decades[12]. Our childhood and adolescence passed under the sign of revolution and progress: the communist revolution following the soviet model[13] meant a clean break with the past, the end of the "bourgeoisie and landowners" regime and the proclamation of RPR, the fast and continuous evolution process towards a class-less society, situated on "the highest stages of civilization"[14]. But Romanians had lived, alongside the entirety of Europe, through several other revolutionary moments back in 1848 and progress was more or less the key word of all political parties before 1944, with the notable exception of the Conservative Party, extinguished in 1925! In conclusion, we will have to look elsewhere for the novelty of our experience

1. Keith Lowe, *Savage Continent. Europe in the Aftermath of World War II,* Picador, London 2013.

2. Timothy Snyder, *Bloodlands : Europe between Hitler and Stalin*, Basic Books, New York, 2010. Romanian translation: *Tărâmul morții.Europa între Hitler și Stalin*, Humanitas, Bucharest, 2012.

3. Mircea Malița and Dinu C. Giurescu, *Zid de pace, turnuri de frăție. Deceniul deschiderii: 1962-1972,* Compania Publishing House, Bucharest, 2011.

4. A person who shows independence through thought or action.

5. A state which threatens world peace, through the restriction of human rights, terrorist liaisons and the use of weapons of mass destruction. At present, the list of such states is short. According to the USA, the rogue states today are: Iran, North Korea, Sudan and Syria.

6. Dumitru Şandru, *Mișcări de populație în România (1940-1948),* Editura Enciclopedică, Bucharest, 2003.

7. For comparison, infantile mortality rate in Budapest was 45% in the autumn of 1945, and in November on the same year, 823 births and 2,108 deaths were registered.

8. „Étude sur la santé de la population dans plusieurs pays européens touchés par la guerre", in *Documentation française*, Paris, 19 noiembrie 1948, apud Ygael Gluckstein, *Les satellites européens de Staline*, Les Iles d'Or, Paris, 1953, p. 142. A Moldavian peasant described an almost identical situation: "A Russian division stopped at Negrilești… 'How was it?' I asked Costică

Pristavu, the former horse thief, former hero from Doaga, former mayor of the village. Costică was sincere, as you seldom see men to be: 'What can I tell you, sir? The entire village fed from the soup cauldrons. You would see the common Russian sitting on the porch, small child in arms. They were mild, generous, they sang very beautifully… until they got to the moonshine. Then, I pitied our women… If they were to only leave them with child, that wouldn't be a problem, but they got a lot of them sick. A lot of women died."', Gheorghe Jurgea-Negrileşti, *Troica amintirilor. Sub patru regi,* Second edition, Cartea Românească publishing house, Bucharest, 2007, pp. 78-79. Also the memories of Theodor Pallady, p. 20. "During those times, syphilis was worse than '*le mal napoletain*' in the Renaissance. It spared no one. From the last gypsy to the first minister, it killed them all." The only difference is that, in 1944, the cauldrons of soup were offered by the Romanians, as seen in the writings of Mihail Gramatopol.

9.   The women – it has been confirmed at a much to large scale to be considered unverified information or inaccurate memories – were raped to an extent almost equal to the rapes during the war: behind closed doors, caught in cellars, stalked from high roofs and terraces, attacked violently during the day and in crowded places." Hal Lehrman, *Russia's Europe*, D. Appleton-Century Company Inc., New York, London, 1947, p. 176.

10. Keith Lowe, *op. cit.*, pp. 68-73. The situation was made more dire by the fact that penicillin was not yet available.

11. For Bulgaria, about the *enemy mania*, see Georgi Markov, *The Truth That Killed*, Weidenfeld and Nicolson, London, 1983, p. 14.

12. For other examples, see chapter "Noul vocabular" in LiviuDorin Bîtfoi, *Aşa s-a născut omul nou. În România anilor '50*, Compania Publishing House, Bucharest, 2012, pp. 181–185.

13. In an interview at the end of his life, Leonte Răutu declared without hesitation that "communist Romania was entirely built after the soviet model." Apud Vladimir Tismăneanu and Cristian Vasile, *Perfectul acrobat. Leonte Răutu, măştile răului*, Humanitas, Bucharest, 2008, p. 37. This fact was already visible in 1949: "In no other country outside the USSR is the domination of the communist party more absolute than in Romania. In no other country does the communist party so blatantly bow to the Russians. In no other country

does the state show such utter contempt for the public opinion." See Vernon Bartlett, *East of the Iron Curtain*, Latimer House, London, 1949, p. 174.

14. The atrocities committed in order to bring forth the "radiant future" were justified by the Jesuit adagio: "The ends justify the means" or, in communist language, "you can't make an omelette without breaking some eggs". And yet, in 1922, Romain Rolland, a sympathizer of the Bolshevik revolution, would bring the following to the attention of Henri Barbusse, another fellow traveller of the communists: "It is not true that the ends justify the means. The means are more important for true progress than the ends. Because the ends (rarely reached and always incompletely) only modify the external relations between people, while the means meld the spirit of man, and set it either on the path towards justice, or on the path towards violence". Nagy Imre spoke of the same truth during his detention, in a letter addressed to Valter Roman on the 6th of April 1957: "Let us not be Jesuits; let us rather be communists and recognize that the ends do not justify the means!" Liviu-Dorin Bîtfoi, *op. cit.*, p. 481.

CHAPTER 2

The Sovietization of Romania: starvation, pauperization and terror

———

WE WERE BORN IN A country allied with the Soviets, but occupied, in reality, by the Red Army[1] for 14 years – the first paradox in a long series of Russian occupations in the 18th and 19th Century (1736-1739, 1768-1774, 1787-1792, 1806-1812, 1828-1832, 1848-1849, 1854-1855, 1877) which all ended up with extensive destruction and pillaging, the result of Russian-Austrian-Ottoman wars largely fought on the territory of Moldavia and Muntenia. As a result of these confrontations, Moldavia lost half of its territory, Bessarabia and Northern Bucovina, provinces occupied by Russia and Austria, respectively. Romania was a country, which paid dearly for the enterprise represented by the war in the East, when it allied itself with Hitler's Germany. Its purpose was noble and legitimate – the recovery of the provinces of Bessarabia and Northern Bucovina, forcefully seized through an ultimatum that resembled a declaration of war. Romania complied because it was not like Finland, which opposed using armed forces, resisting the Soviet assault for months, and because King Carol the second was no Marshal Mannerheim[2]. The collaboration between Marshal Antonescu and Hitler placed Romania in the enemy camp facing the Western Allies after Romanian troops stepped over the border delimitated by the Nistru River and continued their military operations in the East[3]. The solely military endeavor of the "Conducator" – in order to take back the provinces, the war must be fought until the utter destruction of the adversary – did not hold in the face of Allied unity and they let Romania fall under the USSR's sphere of influence[4]. Marshal Antonescu used to say that, from the moment in which he took over, he "donned the garb of death" (repeating the words spoken by Tudor Vladimirescu in 1821). What he could not foresee was that the entire country was to do the same, as his actions would leave hundreds of thousands of people dead, injured, invalid, imprisoned and deported. After four years of war in the East and West, the victims would represent a *first installment* of the blood and gold tribute that was to be paid for two decades.

The *second installment* was quick to follow – the raiding, destruction, requisitioning, and raping of the occupying army, starting in the spring of 1944 and continuing throughout the entire country after the 23rd of August, when Romania surrendered. Consequently, 130,000 Romanian officers and soldiers (which were ordered not to oppose allied forces) were taken prisoner and snt – often on foot, in restraints – to the USSR. The entire military fleet and the bigger part of the commercial fleet, enormous quantities of oil drilling materials (pipes, engines, drills and spare parts representing 6 months' worth of imports from before the beginning of the war, half of the entire reserve of train cars (25,000) and locomotives (227), all goods held in customs and all automobiles (including the one belonging to the PM General Constantin Sănătescu[5]) were taken away as spoils of war. Then came the assassinations[6], the plundering, the destruction and the raping (of girls and women of ages 9 to 75) done by soldiers individually or in groups[7]. Apart from their well-known passion for nibbling on sunflower and squash seeds, a pastime brought here as early as 1916[8], Soviet soldiers were utterly captivated by clocks and watches, in all shapes and sizes, for which they would exchange anything and even murder. They would take great pleasure in wearing watches on both arms, as seen in the photograph of the soviet soldier planting the red flag on Reichstag in Berlin (the photograph was later retouched[9]). Comedian Constantin Tănase accurately portrayed the spirit of the time during one of his performances when he would enter the stage in long trousers and a sleeveless overcoat, covered by watches and wearing a clock around his neck while reciting:

It was bad with der, die, and das
But now it's worse, with davai watch!

From the Tisa to the Don
Davai watch, and no coat on!
Davai watch and davai land
Harasho my comrade grand!

Similar occurrences have taken place in all countries occupied by the Red Army and have been documented at the time by first hand witnesses, so Tănase cannot be accused of primary or visceral anticommunism[10].

A few examples from Hungary between 1945 and 1946: *"The devoted children of the Revolution proved to be even the Russians that solitarily plundered us through the fact that they were absolutely indifferent towards the meaning of private property. It was more than indifference: they were absolutely ignorant of the concept itself. On the other hand, they disappointed the Kremlin because they made no difference between the 'fascist rulers' and the 'democratic masses'. The mother of a worker who dug trenches and the daughter of a reactionary aristocrat were equal candidates for rape. The overcoat of a high ranking communist from town, as well as the mattress off the bed of a simple factory worker were taken as well, alongside the limousines and the Rembrandt paintings of the fallen magnates. Russians were in awe of all small commodities of western civilization. In Budapest, I watched three infantry men enthusiastically pushing a rotating door. After they dismantled it and carried it in the middle of the street, they could not understand why it had stopped working. Bicycles and clocks, especially watches, fascinated soldiers coming from the countryside. The Russian word for 'watch' became known in all languages as an exchange currency. Soldiers would strap all their watches to their arm, going down towards their elbows. They taught all of occupied Europe the meaning of the word davai. It means 'to give', 'to shell out' or 'to hand everything over'. Threatening gestures with their pistols or Kalashnikovs to shout out the word, almost as a barking command, followed their usual technique. Later, this davai became very well known as davai-chitara. Stalin was honored as the Davai Lama. The bitterness of people grew to such degrees that even the large stone monuments the Russian placed to honor their fallen men were irreverently known as 'The Monument of the Unknown Watch Thief'"*.[11]

The *third installment* started on the 12th of September 1944, with the signing of the Armistice Convention in Moscow[12]. Summoned by the

Ministry of Foreign Affairs Viaceslav Molotov in the presence of English and American ambassadors, Romanian delegates were invited to sign an act they saw for the first time. It was to be expected: what Romanians considered – some still consider this today – an Armistice Convention was, in the eyes of the Allies, an unconditional surrender with no additional conditions (a new paradox in our history)[13]. In actuality, that is what it was, because the clauses in the convention (let us call it that) were a mix of military, economic, and political directives (as a side note, it was a German contrivance from the First World War already imposed on Romania in 1918) that were vastly exceeding the boundaries of an armistice that simply demands ceasefire.

This surrender not only shaped relations with our eastern neighbor for two decades, but laid the foundations of the life we lived, basically up until our baccalaureate, in 1964. Romania was forced to pay reparations worth 300 million dollars (at their exchange rate in 1938)[14] in goods and resources on a six year plan; to return all goods taken from the USSR during the three years of military campaigns; and finally, to ensure the upkeep and transport of Soviet troops (between 800,000 and 1.5 million men, officially, at different times) on Romanian territory during the war; to disband all "fascist" organizations (actually, all organizations that were not communist or were anti-communist, including the extreme right wing), to cleanse the state of war criminals and introduce democracy to the country. There is no need for us to delve here into the methods by which the conquerors (*Vae victis!*) calculated all these reparations and obligations[15], it suffices to say that in 1944 Romania became a colony of the Soviet empire[16]. We have known all the mechanisms of economic exploitation the great totalitarian empire applied to the territories it occupied – a massive subordination in both form and foundation[17]. I remember now how back in 1964, party activists organized countrywide meetings to inform the population on the Romanian-Soviet relations in the past 20 years. They came to our high school as well. Their message was that Romania had paid their war debt towards USSR tenfold (a percentage of 1,000%). It was an unnecessary lie, because up until 1946 only, Romania had paid 1,785,000,000 dollars in goods and resources, representing more than four times the war debt calculated with the exchange rate in 1938! In all fairness, several additional obligations came into play here: war reparations, the restitution of USSR goods from the three years of war (even if some had been bought and paid for) and the expenses of feeding and housing soviet troops during the war – but in actuality, up until 1958.

A spectacle described by an eyewitness spares us any further comments:

The Red Army's inclination towards violence was the first and most grotesque characteristic observed in the Eastern and Western Europe. In my chapter on Hungary I have had the occasion to refer to the inclination of Russians towards crime. They also had a predilection towards stealing both valuable and valueless objects. Such operations were inspired by the example of the Red Army itself. The official pillaging reached such proportions, that it seemed they were supplying the whole Soviet Union. Months after the arrival of the Russians, the most common sight in Central and South Eastern Europe was the long line of convoys, automobiles, trucks and horse drawn wagons filled to the brim with kitchen pots, toilet seats, lathes, presses, calipers, tubs, furniture, old clothes, microscopes and many other items. Even the department of information within the army worked for this project. Officers in charge with these detachments of robbers had the buildings' schematics, lists of valuable objects belonging to the families inside and places where they were hidden[18].

Some of the magic of bourgeois civilization probably attracted the Russians, because Russian propaganda was doing its best to find and antidote'. Radio Moscow vehemently declared itself against those who, by enrolling in the army and getting to see the western world would deplore the primitive character of their existence back in the Soviet Union. ... Obviously, many Russians welcomed the life offered to them by the incursion of the Red Army into the west with joy and awe. But the people under occupation would rarely see this. What they actually saw was that Russians would break all they could not carry with them, out of the pure joy of breaking things or because they did not understand the purpose and value of some objects. Wooden kitchen chairs were triumphantly carried away as war trophies, while at the same time vases, porcelain figures and fine glassware were thrown through the closed windows. They amused themselves with cutting up paintings and shooting out the eyes of family portraits. They adored throwing rare tapestries and old books into the fire.

The manner in which Russian soldiers and officers as well, lived in the houses requisitioned from the population was utterly shocking. Only a poet, laureate of verses written on the walls of latrines could accurately describe what was happening. To resume, indulgently, we can say that Russians held an Olympian disdain for the toilets of the bourgeoisie. [19]

———

One of the questions posed by those specialized in the history of communist countries was whether Stalin wanted to colonize (or even *Sovietize*) them from the very beginning, or whether this operation was initialized during the Cold War, in 1947-1948. Our opinion is that the first hypothesis is correct: on the 9th of October 1944, English Prime Minister Winston Churchill and Stalin would sign a secret pact, scribbled on a piece of paper in Moscow which would grant the Soviet Union 90% influence (*predominance*) in Romania over 90% English influence in Greece. From that moment on, Stalin felt he had the right to introduce the Soviet model in Romania and the other occupied countries, which he considered to be spoils of war, as he declared to Tito, in April 1945: "This war is not like the wars of the past. Anyone who occupies a territory has to impose his own social system. Each one imposes his own social system up to where he marches his army too. It cannot be otherwise"[20].

The methods used by the empire to *Sovietize* and turn Romania into a satellite, to radically morph the political system and Romanians' mental system were, in my opinion, three: *starvation, pauperization* and *terror*. These methods – first applied to Soviet Russia, beginning with 1917 – were used all at once and within a tight inter-dependency, because the first two could not succeed if they were not sustained by the continuous and generalized terror.

Starvation was produced by the utter disorganization of agriculture, starting with the counties in North Moldavia, occupied by the Red Army in the spring of 1944[21], then through the agricultural reform in the March of 1945, a reform with a strong social and political character, not an economic one[22]. The main goals of the reform were "the crushing of the old ruling class and the neutralization of the peasantry while the war for power was conducted within the cities"[23]. The political character of this reform – introduced in all east-communist states at about the same time – was all the more obvious as it was to be performed within 10 days and in the absence of Romanian soldiers, positioned on the western front, and who could not benefit from it. In actuality, the expropriation operations were to last for over an year, in a tense atmosphere, of local uprisings and anarchy, of endless trials between the new and the old landowners (in June 1947, courts were still conducting such trials). In consequence, sowing could not occur on time and a great famine broke out, especially in Moldavia and Bessarabia, on the grounds of an unimaginable drought and the epidemic of typhus transmitted by the lice brought by the Soviet troops[24]. The combination of all these factors led to the deaths of approximately 300,000 people in Bessarabia and Moldavia, according to the Red Cross[25]. There were recorded cases of cannibalism and the exodus of thousands of children, either sent away by their parents or orphans, leaving their villages in order to survive in other parts of the country, where they were adopted by other families.

The famine and typhus epidemic were eradicated due to the help received from the Red Cross International, the United States of America (6 million dollars out of the total of 10 million), Switzerland, Denmark and Sweden[26].

In the light of what we know today about the famine organized by Lenin and Stalin between 1919 and 1920, in the Volga region, and between 1931 and 1933 in Ukraine, it becomes evident that the Bolsheviks exercised the famine between 1946 and 1947[27]. The main cause has roots back to the utter disorganization of agriculture due to the seizing of the great estates and farm lands with good equipment and seeds – the only ones capable of producing the surpluses needed by the market – without any form of compensation. One single 1,000-hectare domain could wield many times more produce than 1,000 one hectare parcels, which couldn't even provide sustenance for their new owners[28]. The same thing happened after the agricultural reform from 1918-1921 (when peasants had been given, on average, 2.7 hectares, compared with 1945, when they only received about 1.3 hectares). Agriculture in Romania would take several years before being able to produce surpluses for export, as it had been in the period before the war[29]. Even so, in 1938, Romania had fallen to the rank of country with the smallest production per hectare (with a value of 1,000 lei) and lowest yield of grain per hectare (860 kg). For the same period, Germany's production per hectare valued 15,000 lei and had a yield of 2,070 kg of grain per hectare. Such a massive reversal in the order of things was doomed to end in catastrophe, because Romanian communists did not seek the aid of the more wealthy peasants (stigmatized as "exploiters and kulaks"), the only ones capable of ensuring a steady supply to the cities – on the contrary, they overwhelmed them with extensive taxes and fees which ultimately led to their ruin[30].

The only response the authorities had in this situation was the introduction of ration cards for bread and an entire range of products that the populace was lacking[31]. We now quote from the memories of Annie Bentoiu:

I have previously mentioned stringencies, but I have not gone into detail. The simplest way to illustrate the spirit of those times is to reproduce the data found in a table in the Scanteia newspaper under the title of 'Days in which we get bread and days in which we get corn flour". Five types of ration cards are presented (they would remain as such for many years): A (for miners), B (hard labor), C (regular family of workers, functionaries and such), D1 and D2 (family members) and E (unemployed population). Bread quantities are as follows, in the same order: A. 700 grams, every day; B. 500 grams, every day; C. 350 grams, but only from Wednesday to Sunday; D1 and D2 250 grams from Thursday or Friday to Sunday; E 250 grams only once per week, on Thursday. On days without bread, corn flour was distributed, in daily rations of 250 to 350 grams[32]. For the better understanding of the situations, some details need to be addressed: first of all, there were numerous people who did not have the right to have a ration card – until the nationalization in 1948, some privately own mills and baker shops still existed, where bread was available 'without restrictions', but at a higher price. More and more people would bake bread at home. … When nationalization came, bread and flour disappeared completely for those who did not have a ration card. Soon, bread would no longer be made out of regular dough, but instead it would become a brownish paste poured into molds after a soviet recipe (it was not bad). Second of all, it is important to mention that Romulus Zăroni, Minister of Agriculture in 1946 had then declared that "Ration cards will be obsolete by the next year's harvest", and people had believed him. It was true; the country had extensive war debts to pay to the USSR. It is probably impossible to clarify nowadays which aspects of the stark poverty of that time was due to the debt being paid and which were the consequences of the brutal transformation of the social and political systems. The only thing I am trying to do is remember. Ration cards remained valid for years on end, with the same quantities in regards to bread and continually rationing more and more products (cooking oil, meat, sugar, pasta and biscuits). Moreover, ration cards for clothing were introduced. Years after the war, ration cards were the only way to get food and clothing. Without the worker canteens existing in factories and institutions (a means for some members of the family to get a hot meal, but not the elderly, the unemployed and the children), most people would not have survived. … The availability of meat was an extremely rare occurrence, and massive crowds and truly hysterical scenes always followed it.[33]

Another period of artificially created famine was the so-called "Stalin's fast", or the fast of the World Festival of the Youth, in March to August 1953[34]. In order to showcase Romania as a prosperous country to foreign visitors, large quantities of basic goods were withdrawn from the market by the communists, causing a mass panic among the less privileged population:

Certain goods such as food, wine and beer are already hard to come by. Basic goods are rapidly disappearing altogether. Even bread, given only based on the Population ID and only at the local Bread Center, has become scarce. The already enormous queues have become incommensurable. They are three or four hours long, at a minimum. Women borrow small children between themselves to cut to the front; there are already rumors of children dead at their posts, suffocated by the crowd. There is a huge sugar crisis; it is only procured after long queues and hard battles. People do not understand why there is a shortage in sugar… Shops are empty, canteen rations have been cut[35], and restaurants have very little food and no beer or wine. The famous Zissu terrace bar and restaurant, on Batiștei street, where every evening people come to dance (Jean Ionescu plays the violin, accompanied by Alexandru Imre on clarinet), has changed its menu to dishes prepared with fish heads, bird wings and veal knuckle – the so-called 'cutlery'. And their salads have no cooking oil.[36]

A study appearing in France published the estimations of the government – thus, official numbers – in regards to the annual food ration for Romanian citizens: meat – 6.5 kg[37]; fish – 7 kg; milk – 2 liters; bread – 39 kg; pasta – 850 grams; cheese – 500 grams; sugar – 4.5 kg[38]; canvas and various textiles – 7.8 meters; wool – 260 grams; shoes – a pair every two years; firewood – 500 kg.[39]

Food restrictions reappeared in the last decade of communist government, during the Nicolae Ceaușescu regime, but they are out of the scope of the essay at hand. It suffices to say that the alimentation of Romanians was a complicated issue all across communist rule, another paradox for a country with so many resources and such fertile lands as Romania. Massive food exports and the dramatic drop in the number of livestock due to the repurposing of pastures, as with the dwindling of fresh water fish supplies due to the desiccation of lakes formed by the Danube, all caused alterations in the population's food habits – it led to a massive increase in pork consumption (80% in total, as I was informed by an Italian business man) and to the introduction of many food substitutes such as the famous soy salami. The citizens of communist countries perfectly understood this state of affairs by experiencing it first hand – from this, many jokes appeared: "If communism would ever reach the Sahara desert, people would be forced to import sand!"[40] Or another one, which can be found in USSR as well: "What are the biggest enemies to agriculture? Mainly four: spring, summer, fall and winter".

The *pauperization* ("economic constraints", in Marxist terms) of the country and its entire population was put into practice, following the extensive and much more chaotic plundering of the first months of occupation, through the much more direct and efficient exploitation settled in on the 16th of January 1945 by the signing of the Soviet-Romanian Convention that set the quantities of goods that Romania was to supply the Soviets with as war reparations[41]. We have previously seen how the conquerors had calculated the prices for these goods: it suffices to say that for at least 8 years (from 1945 to 1953), Romania paid USSR in goods representing approximately 63% of its national income.

The legal frame for this extensive theft was the Convention signed on the 8th of May 1945, which set up the ensemble of economic relations between the two countries[42]. A special protocol mandated that several Soviet-Romanian companies be opened – they were called Sovrom and their purpose was to "make the most out of Romania's resources"[43]. Moscow held 50% of the stocks and of the results of exploitation. The Soviet contribution was actually based off the former German properties in Romania, most of which were originally French, Belgian and Dutch goods seized by the Germans during the war and considered "goods of the enemy"[44] by the communists. Romania contributed with its ground and underground resources, its existent machinery, its personnel and financial means. Between 1945 and 1952, 16 such Sovroms were created, in all industrial fields, in the field of transportation, banks and insurance. Their simple enumeration is enough for us to understand the extent of this operation: Sovrom Insurance (all Insurance companies), Sovrom Bank (initially controlled 40% of all deposited capital, 95% of exports and financed 75% of all major transactions[45]), Sovrom Coal, Sovrom Chemistry, Sovrom Construction, Sovrom Naval Construction, Sovrom Film, Sovrom Gas, Sovrom Wood (produced 50% of all wood cut in Romania), Sovrom Metal (especially the factories of Max Auschnit; established in 1950, it held all gold and silver mines in Romania and exported their annual production of 2 tons of gold and 8 tons of silver to the USSR), Sovrom Petrol (the first to be established, in 1945, it controlled 75% of all petrol production which extracted between 3.5 and 4 million tons annually; after 1948, it controlled 100% of production)[46], Sovrom Quartz (established at the end of 1952, it extracted uranium), Sovrom Tractor, Sovrom Transport (which managed to obtain a 30 year lease on the bigger part of all wharfs, silos and buildings, elevators and cranes, as well as the four main shipyards, the entire state owned ship fleet and 220 ships, privately owned but seized by the state)[47], Sovrom Petrol Extracting Equipment and TARS air company, which held monopoly over the air. After the nationalization of the whole economy in 1948-1949, Sovroms presided over all of Romania's economy.

Sovroms functioned until 1954-1955, when Romanians bought Soviet stocks for double their price, through a financial artifice of revaluating the leu in regards to the ruble (the monetary reform on the 31st of January 1954)[48]. At this time, 14 of the Sovroms were bought, while two still remained active: Sovrom Quartz (which ceased to exist as late as October 1956, but, through a new treaty, Romania would give the USSR no less than 85% of its uranium production) and Sovrom Petrol, which were bought at an unknown time[49].

In July 1955, the Central Committee (CC) of the Communist Party of the Soviet Union (PCUS) discussed, among other issues, the relations with countries under people's democracies based on a report presented by Anastas Mikoian, who insisted on the subject of mixed companies. His conclusion was the following: "These companies are an inadmissible form of meddling into the internal economic affairs of the people's democracies. They are contrary to the spirit of the proletarian internationalism and are a sign of high powered chauvinism"[50].

The epilogue to this story unfolds rather tragicomically, in 1964, told by Mihai Gramatopol, epigraphist and excellent numismatist – back then he was a functionary in the Numismatic Cabinet of the Romanian Academy Library:

The numismatic collections of the Cabinet have also increased due to the communist seizing of private riches. In 1964, I. Gh. Maurer had negotiated the renewal of commercial exchanges between Romania and the West. Naturally, he required the Romanian state pay reparations for nationalized foreign investments (industrial and petrol extraction equipment, for instance). As Romania had been once again robbed of all its interwar wealth, it did not possess any foreign currency or other monetary reserves. The Department of State Securitate, on the other hand, as soon as it had begun arresting high political personalities, the bourgeoisie and other wealthy landowners, had not only seized their goods, but had also spoliated their personal jewelry – ornaments which were often true masterpieces of immeasurable value, heirlooms passed on and collected through multiple generations. Romania's great agrarians before the Ferdinand-Brătianu reform had bought them from other countries[51], when they owned tens of thousands of hectares of land. Especially after the passing of the Law of Gold which mandated that all gold coins be turned over to the state, with the exception of historical gold pieces which had to be registered with the National Bank by their collectors who would become their sole custodians, the Department of State Securitate, aided by the police force gathered – through endless abuse – a considerable quantity of jewelry with precious stones set in high value materials, naturally keeping a part of the spoils. In any case, the hoard gathered in Marmorosch Blank manor (in an impressive oval hall, donned with vaults on two levels) had taken such grand proportions – it had gold pieces of all qualities (even the chains of gold coins have been seized from the wealthy peasantry who were either deported or sent to prison) – that the ruling communists decide to pay the reparations of nationalization (claimed by means of a list opened in Haga) with it. They were thus turning the last speck of treasure that Romanians had – their last fragile independence from that piece of dry bread that the communists would throw their way – into currency. Jewelers from the Benelux region were summoned to help with the evaluation and selling of the jewelry. They bought all the precious stones in their exquisite gold or platinum settings by the kilogram, for an extremely low price. Their motivation was that all that precious treasure was merely rough material, that the settings would have to be melted down, that the stones would need to be cut in a more modern manner, thus more than halving their carats. These were lies told to a desperate seller: the thief was stealing from the double thief. The jewels were sumptuous masterpieces, modern and elegant in aspect, with corundum stones (an 8 on the Mohl scale of hardness), of an uncommon size and clarity. The ideological whim of nationalization that ruined industry in Romania was paid dearly with what multiple generations of this country had accumulated as ornaments.[52]

Apart from gold and jewelry, the goods that were of special interest to the Red Army, as in the case of Germany in 1945 and in all other occupied countries, were the automobiles, the weapons and ammunition, the radios and cameras, the typewriters and printers (the last two categories were not seized, but their ownership had to be declared)[53].

Another measure taken for the massive pauperization of the populace, an incredibly vast plundering of monetary reserves and of the majority's savings – one that reshaped society as a whole[54], was the monetary reform ("stabilization") in August 1947. The apparent purpose of this reform was the elimination of inflation, which had reached formerly unknown proportions. The cost of living coefficient had gone up from 100 in August 1939 to 944 in August 1944 – a normal trend, considering that Romania had suffered a series of grave territorial and population loses, followed by three years of war in the East and nine months in the West. The occupation and plundering (chaotic at first, and subsequently becoming more organized) of the Red Army and soviet administration caused the coefficient to rise to 3,678.7 in 1945, 46140 in December 1946, 440,869 in April 1947 and 525,688 in July 1947[55]. This meant that it had grown over 5,000 times, a similar situation to that of Hungary, which had been subjected to the same "treatment". The entirety of circulating currency, which had been 212 billion back in June 1944 had reached, on the 14th of August 1947, the staggering sum of 48,451 billion. The exchange rate for dollars, an important indicator of the phenomenon, had kept rising from 2,500 – 3,000 lei in August 1944, to 20,000 lei in October 1945, to 190,000 at the end of 1946, to 2 million in June 1947 and finally over 4.2 million in august 1947[56].

Ghiță Ionescu writes: "The introduction of state terror was coupled by the loom-ing threat of economic bankruptcy, growing ever more closely by 1945. In the summer of 1947, economic chaos reached levels never before seen in the Kingdom of Romania … In the summer of 1947, the situation in Romania was more reminiscent of the economic crisis and inflation that had occurred in Germany and Hungary in 1919"[57].

It was true that, in 1946, the country's agricultural yield represented a mere 59% of the average in the years 1934 to 1938, industrial production in 1947 was down to 47% of that in 1938, and the annual budget in 1947 and 1948, the last correctly reported years, would note that more than 46.4% had gone into "international obligations" – clearly, as exports towards the USSR[58].

A profound reform of the economy and its currency was urgently needed. Yet, the manner in which this reform was conducted is radically different from the manner in which similar reforms have been carried out in other civilized countries, as it was the work of No. 1 soviet economist (of Magyar origin) Eugen S. Varga, member of the academy and director of the Institute of World Economy of the Science Academy[59].

Here is the way these reforms were described by French economist Henri Prost, who spent 20 years living in Romania (1931-1950) and was a first-hand witness to these events:

"In 1947, destitution becomes generalized[60]. *No family budget can cope with food expenses. The normal salary varies between 2.5 and 3.5 million lei per month, while expenses at the discount stores*[61] *would amount to 4.5 million, evaluated at the official prices at which products are sold to workers – these products, bought on the black market, cause factories to lose over 10 million lei for each worker. On the 14th of June 1947, Gheorghiu-Dej passes a plan made by the communist party for the rehabilitation of the economy. This plan foresaw the rise of industrial production, the consolidation of the agricultural reform, the balancing of the national budget, the establishing of trimestral bud-gets, control over all commercial operations, and control of the National Bank over all credits granted and finally, the stabilization of currency. On the 12th of July, factories that had not been allowed to license personnel without being authorized since Antonescu was in power are now suddenly all authorized to do so. The excess of personnel will be redistributed to work force deficient factories;*

thus, all workers are rationally distributed. Immediately, syndicate committees impose the licensing of non-communist workers and technicians, who had, of course, ran out of other places to work. In some societies, would, out of their own initiative, expel their head personnel. Similar measures are taken by state authorities who must license 30% of their budgetary effects. The ones who show dignity and independent spirit are the ones who suffer. Under the pretext of budgetary cuts, a great political cleansing was in effect. On the 12th of August 1947, every citizen was summoned to declare his or her money within 72 hours. People are seized by panic and sought to rid themselves of liquid assets by any means possible. Storeowners receive the order to keep all stores open; some shops are cleared in a matter of hours. Markets are only supplied with immediately perishable produce; for a few days, the urban populace feeds on tomatoes, cantaloupe, honeydew, and grapes alone. The state services rush to pay all suppliers, sometimes writing antedated checks; a few weeks earlier, all obligations pertaining to internal debt have been mandatorily reimbursed. People rapidly begin to buy foreign stocks and gold; the exchange rate for the dollar reaches 7 million lei, and the one for the French gold coin (louis d'or) reaches 50 million (in July 1944, the Romanian 'Rooster' valued 10,000 lei). On the 15th of August, the decrees containing the measures for the monetary stabilization are published. The new leu currency is worth 20,000 old lei; it represents the value of 6.6 gold milligrams of 900/1,000 purity, the price of a kilogram of gold being 168,350 lei. The exchange rate for the dollar is fixed at 150 lei, the one for the French gold coin, at 977 lei, and 1.25 lei for the French franc. The exchange of old currency for new is authorized for the maximum sum of 5 million old lei for peasant families (250 new lei), 3 million for functionaries, salary earners and pensioners (150 new lei), 1.5 million for people 'outside the work force' (75 lei). Factories can exchange sums equal to paid salaries, the soviet army can exchange sums equal to monthly pay, diplomatic missions can exchange sums equal to the former months' worth of stocks exchanged at the National Bank. Currency not being exchanged will be deposited at the National Bank, in locked accounts – we need to mention that it will never be exchanged into new currency. This was done in order to cull fiat money (money that is not backed by gold or any other precious commodity stored in the treasury) and bank deposits. Under the penalty of 25 years in prison and a 500% fine, orders go out for all foreign assets and gold coins to be presented to the National Bank within 15 days, in order for them to be paid for according to the official exchange rate. Despite threats and numerous house searches, the total of recovered assets is worth no more than 10 million dollars. In regards to foreign assets, none are to be transferred to the National Bank, due to the fact that foreign banks had already locked them. The newly fixed salaries vary: between 3,192 and 14,035 lei technical personnel and between 2,525 and 9,662 lei for administrative personnel. The new prices are fixed as well. Salary increases are between 20 and 40 times their value in old currency, and the increase in prices of up to between 2 and 3 times for agricultural produce, between 3 and 5 times for manufactured goods and up to 30 times for public service fees. Material assets have not been spared either. On the 7th of August, all factories were forced to balance the entirety of their tax debt within 5 days; after the given period, they could only be acquit said debts by the exchange of goods valued at their official rates – which is the method most factories were forced to turn to. On the 12th, 13th and 14th of August, stores remained open; their wares were mostly converted to currency that, on the 15th of August, had next to no value. On the 12th of September, an exceptional 10% tax is set for all wares; seeing as their liquid assets had been depleted, all tradesmen and manufacturers were forced to pay this tax in goods. In the end, with all credits being revoked, all pawned assets had to be ceded to the creditor, meaning the issuing bank. Without any currency available and stripped of most of their goods, left in the impossibility of paying their workers at the exchange rate fixed by legislation, many factories are forced into declaring bankruptcy. Industrial factories benefit from loans issued by the National Bank, because it was in the interest of the state for them to continue their production. Commerce is abandoned to its fate, due to no credits being granted to keep it afloat, and state owned stores rise from its ruin. These stores gradually replace discount stores; they will benefit from several privileges, especially the monopoly of selling rationed produce, meaning all basic goods. The goods seized from free commerce by the means described earlier would become their first stock. The backlash of the law issued on the 15th of August hits farmers as bad as in the case of the merchants. The farmers were the category that held the biggest liquid assets in the old currency. During the weeks that preceded the monetary reform, they had to give away a part of their grain to the state; all requisitions were fully paid before the 15th of August. Thus, farmers lose up to 60% of their harvest. Functionaries and salary earners are the ben-eficiaries of this reform. Salaries have been revalued in a comfortable manner; ration cards awarded to workers allow them to buy produce cheaply from state owned stores. These advantages will be short lived, as the new currency will not hold its buying power for long. On the evening of the 15th of August, the black exchange market sold dollars with 450 lei (three times the official exchange rate) and promised to deliver them on the 15th of October. On the 30th of September, the exchange rate for dollars was 450 lei, and it reached 575 lei by the end of October. The price of goods rose under the same proportions as the exchange rate of bonds. This monetary stabilization would be, in consequence, rapidly com-promised, although we are inclined to believe that it was only a pretext for the government to drastically and swiftly instate a countrywide economic and social revolution. Through this monetary operation, a great step was made towards the centralization of all privately owned factories and towards the inclusion of all their owners into the proletariat. [62]"

Another specialist, Radu Plessia, emphasizes the pauperization of entire groups of the population deemed "unproductive": the newly unemployed, the people who were not issued ration cards, all those considered to be "enemies to the regime" – which were under the same treatment as in the USSR, through the July 1918 Constitution (This was an entire part of the population utterly stripped of their rights, under the new name of *lishentsy* – *"stripped of his rights"*)[63]. Plessia also measured the general pauperization of the populace through an ingenious method:

From the total of 48,500 billion old lei in circulation on the 14th of August 1947, only 27,500 billion were exchanged into new currency. The extent of this theft becomes apparent when we think that the last sum also included the total of fiat money owned by the government and Soviet authorities. This number also included vast quantities exchanged by the members of the Soviet occupational force and high-ranking com-munists. Thus, by deducting all these vast sums from the total, we can see that the portion of currency exchanged for the Romanian people was almost insignificant. In fact, this operation meant the seizing of all

*currency existing in Romania. Communist leaders would shamelessly
declare to the public that the monetary reform had been dictated by the
necessity "of ending inflation and getting back the money accumulated
by the bourgeoisie and the wealthy landowners."[64]*

In addition, Plessia proved and precisely exemplified the fact that taxes grew
eightfold after the reform, and rent had a 100 to 200% increase: the difference here was not given to the landlords, which only had the right to 16
up to 25%, but it was taken by the state, who would take the rest. Here are
some more examples of the increase in the price of living, as exemplified by
the same author:

*At the same time, prices for all public services increased. Train tickets
were 40 times more expensive, telephone calls were 8 times more costly,
and public transport costs were increased 12 times. Prices of goods rose
up as well: the new prices for meat was 2.6 times higher, milk was
100% more expensive, and textiles were 160% more expensive. Gas
had skyrocketed to being 2,400% more costly ... the general increase
of prices for staple commodities was 100% in comparison with prices
back in 1938.[65]*

Another contemporary observer would note that after the reform, salaries
were set between 300 and 500 lei, at a time when a pair of shoes cost 150, a
meter of canvas cost 255 lei, a kilogram of butter was 21.50 lei, a kilogram
of veal (on third was only bones and sinew) cost 7.5 lei and a kilogram of
sugar cost 2.3 lei.[66]

But the pauperization of the population did not stop with these measures, and here is what Henri Prost writes about those days, during which
he was present in Bucharest:

*In order to complete the destruction of private wealth, the govern-
ment will employ a weapon that had up until then been seldom used
in Romania: taxes[67]. As soon as he became head of the Ministry of
Finances in November 1947, Vasile Luca passed a law, which stated*

that tax evasion was a crime of economic sabotage. The law decree issued in October 1946 defined such crimes as punishable by up to life long forced labor. Taxes have been raised to such proportions that they no longer correspond to any income; this is clearly about seizing capital funds. Due dates are very tight and as soon as they are not met, the person in debt is wanted for sabotage. If he is unable to pay his taxes, he is sentenced to one day in jail for every 100 lei. Vasile Luca does not stop at only receiving taxes for the current tax year. He demands accounts for the last 10 years be checked and verifies if all those taxes have been paid fully and in a timely manner. Past debts are reevaluated into the new currency, according to the date until which they had to be paid: for the debts due immediately before the reform, the reevaluation coefficient is not of 20,000 but of 3,000 old lei for one new leu. Debts are to be paid tenfold and additional crushing fines are to be applied. Every citizen must accurately declare all acquired sums for the last 10 years. If one forgets even the smallest amount, one becomes wanted for sabotage. People are at the mercy of one denouncement coming from the secretaries or accountants. As tax laws have always been complicated and suffered change constantly, people had come, with all good intentions, to different interpretations of the laws. In the case of a retroactive audit, the government can condemn any former director or administrator of a factory who had to manage any assets. The people most affected by this abusive tax collection are the agricultural landowners.[68]

A few numbers are needed in support of these affirmations: between December 1947 and May 1948, the monthly rate amounted to between 9.8 and 11.8 billion lei for a total circulation of 25 billion. In consequence, taxes represented 40-47% of all currency in circulation, compared to 8.5% in 1938. To more accurately understand the enormous pressure of taxation, it suffices to remind the reader that, if in 1938 taxation index was 100, it had risen to 344 in 1947 and 414 in January 1948. Agricultural income taxes had become five times higher and commercial income taxes were raised eightfold (an index of 793). Professional income taxes were 3.5 times higher, salary taxes alone representing 94 (compared to 100 in 1938)[69]. It can be observed that the more heavily taxed socio-professional classes were, in descending order, merchants, farmers, and freelancers – known in communist terms as "the bourgeois-landlords", although in agriculture, most of the tax payers were peasants. The favored classes were the salary earners – functionaries and people who had jobs.

Fiscal pressure only became greater and, in April 1948, the Minister of Finances, the same Vasile Luca, issued a series of decrees that equaled tax evasion with economic sabotage, a crime punishable by forced labor for life. According to specialists, between 1947 and 1948 alone, 80,000 trials for economic sabotage took place, and more than 200,000 people were sentenced to prison or sent to labor camps, after receiving between 6 months and 15 years punishment. Finally, on the 12th of January 1949, the government reinstates the death penalty for treason and economic sabotage. Romania was the first communist country to apply the death penalty for economic crimes.[70]

But what exactly constitutes economic sabotage[71]? A contemporary journalist clarifies the issue:

In Romania, you become a suspect for economic sabotage if you have a liter of cooking oil, if you give somebody a higher salary than the ones fixed by the General Confederation of Work (the sole syndicate) or, if you bought an extra liter of milk or another loaf of bread. This lax law can send to prison thousands of people deemed to be unwanted by the regime. Every day, on the streets of the capital or in provincial cities, you can see people walking under the supervision of the members of the Patriotic Defense committee, carrying signs that read "I hid a liter of oil", "I kept a loaf of bread hidden in my house", "I gave bigger salaries than is permitted by law". In order to easily reach their goals, The Romanian Communist Party have created the tax police under the jurisdiction of the Ministry of Internal Affairs. Under the pretext of a denouncement, the tax police can search houses at any given moment: a few kilograms of flour or sugar, few liters of cooking oil, a few family jewels, old coins, a sum of money, it does not matter. The victim easily becomes a perpetrator. Once arrested, one is informed that one will be released under the condition that one gives his assets towards "public assistance". And most victims bear and accept this government autho-rized blackmail.[72]

The landowners and the bourgeoisie take one final blow. Firstly, the bour-geoisie is struck, on the 11th of June 1948, when the nationalization of all industrial and commercial factories is proclaimed, followed by laboratories and pharmacies. The landowners (several thousand people[73]), after being allowed to farm 50 hectares, were expropriated on the night between the 1st and 2nd of March 1949. They were forcefully taken out of their homes, permitted to take only a few personal belongings, clothes and the maximum sum of 5,000 lei (less than 10 dollars) with them before being loaded onto trucks and deported in several provincial town outside the county where they are forced to find lodgings and a new way of subsistence under the close surveillance of the police, who forbid them from ever leaving[74]. Their land is nationalized – 342,319 hectares – to be transformed into state owned farms, precursors of the state owned agricultural farmstead.

On the second day (3rd to the 5th of March 1949), the CC plenum of the Romanian Workers' Party decide for the "socialist transformation of agriculture" through the creation of the collective farms to which peasants would later refuse to adhere, starting what can be described as a "civil war" in the countryside. Georghiu-Dej would state that this agricultural revolu-tion resulted in the arrest, trial and sentencing of over 80,000 peasants, out of which 30,000 had been sentenced in public trial; sadly, the communist leader did not also specify the number of victims assassinated on the out-skirts of villages and buried furtively in the woods or thrown in ravines – their remains are in the course of being discovered at present by Marius Oprea and his team of researchers.

After the nationalization of factories and plants, of stores and artisans' shops, followed by the last bits of land left for former landowners, naturally, there came a time for the nationalization of housing. Here as well, Henri Prost will be our guide:

"There is one form of property which was not subject, up until the spring of 1950, to any generalized form of plundering: urban real estate properties – but

the situation of their owners is not at all enviable. Many urban houses were requisitioned, especially in Bucharest. The ever multiplying public services, their functionaries, the countless sections of political parties, the diverse communist organizations, as well as the clubs and canteens of functionaries and workers, student housing, kindergartens, new schools[75] — there was dire need for buildings in which to place them all. On several streets in the capital, all houses were seized, even if not all are occupied. In upscale neighborhoods, the most beautiful villas are granted to the important people of the regime. The requisitioning is done without warning, the occupants of the property sometimes have only a few hours to leave and take their furniture along with them — or as much of it as is permitted[76]. The owner and the people affected by the relocation do not receive any reparations. They are usually relocated towards the outskirts of the city, in a house as miserable as the one they have been expelled from was comfortable[77]."

The owner who managed to escape requisition is not however free to use his house as he sees fit. For several years, the tenants have been protected by laws that defend them from getting thrown out and limit any increase in rent. From this point of view, the Romanian landlord is no different from his French counterpart[78] — the problem is somewhere else. In December 1948, rent offices were created; these offices hold absolute power in regards to real estate distribution. No one can decide what to do with their house without their prior consent. Commissions are constantly in search of available space. Tenants imposed by the rent offices pay little rent and often refuse to pay their share of utility bills, which become the sole burden of the landlord or previous tenant. A law passed in February 1949 brings living space under regulation: a single person cannot occupy more than one room; a single room is also granted to a couple, even if they have three children under 11 years, two children of the same sex older than 11 years; additional rooms are granted to state dignitaries, to state decorated persons, to doctors, to scientists, to writers and artists — it is to be understood that only the intellectual class recognized by the regime received such privileges. In certain cases, these norms, albeit severe, are not even applied and often enough three or four persons huddle together in the same room, sharing the kitchen and lavatory with all other tenants.

The owner can of course sell his apartment, but because of the servitudes created by legislation, it would be fairly difficult to find a buyer, even for prices 20 times lower than its actual value. Even if such buyer is found, the seller would have to pay tax as calculated to the real estate worth as valued by the tax collection office, not the price of sale. Thus, the tax may be fairly higher than the price of the house. And even if such exchange does come to profit the seller, he will be immediately prompted to donate the bigger part of his money to fund Free Greece, for Korea, for Vietnam or for other communist charity missions. Urban real estate owners receive their final blow through the nationalization decree on the 20th of April 1950. According to the decree, the state now owns:

1. *All urban estates formerly owned by 'former grand industrialists, former grand landowners, former bankers, former grand merchants and all other elements of the bourgeoisie';*
2. *Rented estates;*
3. *All hotels, with all their apparel;*
4. *All real estate that was formerly under construction and is now abandoned, with all construction materials needed for their completion;*
5. *All real estate damaged by the November 1940 earthquake or 1944 bombings and that have not been repaired.*

All real estate belonging to workers, functionaries, small artisans, 'working intellectuals' and pensioners is exempted from nationalization – granted that they are not part of the bourgeoisie[79]."

Over 9,170 owners (who stayed or fled the country) were thus deposed of their apartments or houses, of damaged or unfinished real estate, of 16 hotels and 5 baths. Among them we find people who owned 30 apartments in new built apartment blocks (Architect Arghir Culina for example), and so the estimated total is somewhere among the hundreds of thousands of seized houses and apartments[80].

On the last month of 1950, authorities announced that, starting with the 1st of January 1951, all citizens of Bucharest who were not part of the 'workforce'[81] were going to be forced to leave the city and be relocated outside the capital. Finally, in March 1952, the government informed the population that, in conformity with the law to clear up industrial centers and main cities, approximately 200,000 people from Bucharest (of a total of 1.1 million) would be relocated to cities and villages located at least 100 kilometers away from the capital[82]. From our knowledge, Henri Prost is the only author who wrote about the manner in which this decree was applied:

"In order to find housing for the industrial labor force surplus needed in order to fill the five year quota, for the Russians arriving in increasing number, to eliminate the unnecessary mouths to feed from the capital and at the same time expel unwanted elements from the populace, halfway through February, the government decides to deport the following people from Bucharest: first of all, the families of people convicted on political grounds, deported and people who chose to emigrate – through the term family we understand spouses, children, siblings and parents; secondly, military personnel who had been discharged from the army, former magistrates and lawyers, former land proprietors who had owned more than 10 hectares and pensioners under the age of 70. The first category of deported people only have the right to carry 50 kilograms of personal belongings with them – if they are found fit to work, they are brought to the construction sites of the Danube-Black Sea Canal and the Bicaz hydropower plant, in the Moldavian Carpathians[83]; women, children and the elderly are deported to the Bărăgan steppes, where they are crammed into shacks. The second category of deported people may bring all their belongings with them and are allowed to choose their new home, with the condition that it is at least 50 kilometers further than their former one, and it is outside strategic or industrial areas and is not adjacent to the state border. After a few weeks, similar operations take place in Brașov (now named the City of Stalin, the source of the contemporary saying that Stalin's work is also 'brasovs[84]') and other industrial cities throughout Transylvania and on the course of the Danube River. However, these measures are not enough to put an end to the housing crisis and consequently a new decree limits the rights of occupation to 8 square meters per citizen; some of the privileged are allowed up to 20 square meters."[85]

I have become personally acquainted with many cases in which people and entire families were thrown out of their homes; the most impressive story has been told to me by the protagonist himself: it is the case of archeologist Dinu V. Rosetti, grand-son to C. A. Rosetti, the political figure and 1848 revolutionary, who was thrown out of his own house on 5 General Berthelot Street, following this decree. Dinu V. Rosetti, nicknamed Vinu D. Rosetti[86] was not only a grand specialist – he had been the first director of the Museum of the Municipality of Bucharest and had discovered the Tei archeological culture – but also a kingly drunkard and a man of great courage and even greater sense of humor. Without much hesitance, he had settled at the feet of his illustrious predecessor's statue (erected in 1903, the work of sculptor W. Hegel) in the middle of the plaza that bore his name (finished in 1907) and repeatedly raised his bottle of wine while vigorously shouting: "in your honor, grandpa". Passersby glanced at him in astonishment, and one policeman hurried towards him to arrest him for public disturbance. Upon questioning, Rosetti plainly replied that he had come to live with his grandfather because his house had been taken away. Authorities were informed that the descendant of the only "good" 1848 revolutionary (among Bălcescu, Magheru and Ana Ipătescu, extensively celebrated in 1948) was making a scene in public and hurriedly offered him a room in the attic of his old home, as a French military attaché had occupied the rest of the house[87].

The Colonel and hero Radu Miclescu, left invalid from the First World War, and his wife, Elza, born Florescu, were also thrown out of their fabulous house on 35 Kiseleff Road, but they didn't let themselves be intimidated (even if the colonel had been brutally beaten down at the Police Station) and took to living in their old garage – this is where I met them in 1968. Elza looked after a goat that provided them with milk and mowed their lawn perfectly[88].

Dorin-Liviu Bîtfoi writes about yet another category of victims of pauperization:

"Up until 1949 several institutions were in place, such as the General Pensions Fund, The Central Social Insurance Fund, the CFR Pensions Fund, and other over 1,000 pension funds belonging to former privately owned factories. In 1949, they were all absorbed into the State Social Insurance (afterwards, the Worker's Cooperative Social Insurance Central Fund, the Lawyers' Insurance Fund, artistic and literary funds and so on were created). Yet authorities conclude that current legislation does not sufficiently promote the class criterion in setting pensions, even though article 4 in Decree no. 102/16 July 1948 allows its application. Through this article of law, many citizen's right to receive pensions were annulled – during 1947 to 1949, 'the revision

of pensioners done by a committee organized by the Ministry of Finance' was carried out – as declared by the Minister of Labor and Social Planning, Lothar Rădăceanu, during the meeting of the Council of Ministers. Thus, the categories deprived of pensions were the 'enemies' of the working class and of RPR, the former landowners and capitalists who were expropriated under seizing and nationalization laws, those who obtained revenue from industrial or commercial ventures, if they used workforce to do so, agricultural terrain owners in the same situation, landlords who rented their real estate or lands and made an annual profit exceeding 18,000 old lei, former functionaries that held 'repressive, oppressive or confining' offices, former functionaries with leading or managerial positions within privately owned factories that have been nationalized and many others – practically, all the old world people who, starting with 1950, found themselves aging and without any means to get by... It is also the case of regular poor people, such as the women with many children, widowed by the war and now left without pension. Such is the case of Ana Roza from Mediaș, decorated and praised in her work, a widow with six children that 'cannot send to school because she can't afford to clothe them all'. Even if the life of pensioners had become extremely hard, if not almost impossible, at the beginning of 1950 the Council of Ministers discusses a new decree for 'revising pensioners' in order for a part of them to be 'excluded from the right to receive pensions', because 'the empowering of the fight against class could not take place without considering the issue of pensions', in the words of comrade Rădăceanu."[89]

Finally, on the 28th of January 1952, a new monetary reform took place due to the constant depreciation of the leu currency – in almost 4 and a half years, it had lost one third of its value. This time, no further discriminations were made. All citizens equally exchanged the old currency for the new one that had been aligned to the ruble. The exchange rate was set to 2.8 lei for one ruble: 1 new leu for 100 old lei for the first 1,000 lei exchanged, 1 for 200 for the next 2,000 and 1 for 400 for any sums greater than this amount. Economies deposited at the CEC were exchanged at a higher rate. And yet, prices continued to rise and the whole operation, called "legal theft" by experts, returned between 80 and 90% of small sums and over 95% of big sums back to the state.

Bucharest Radio justified the reform thus: "The goal of the reconversion was to fortify the nation's finances by striking capitalist speculators who, by means of the funds they had accumulated, had become a threat to the social order in Romania".[90]

Nobody has ever written a better description of the atmosphere during those days than Pericle Martinescu, unemployed writer who survived only due to his wife's salary and translations commissioned by publishing houses:

"The 12th *of February 1952. For more than two weeks, our entire country is desperately trying to go back to 'normal' after the 'monetary reform' initiated on the 28*[th] *of January 1952. This 'reform' was actually, a veritable revolution, in the Marxist meaning of the word. First of all, the Romanian leu, about which everyone had been complaining for 30 years that it has continually dropped in value, has suddenly made a spectacular leap, regaining the value it had before the beginning of the First World War. Our parents had often told us of the times when a loaf of bread cost 25 bani or a suit of clothes was 80 lei. We never hoped to live to see such times come again. They were too beautiful and too distant to fathom. Yet, often, you happen to come upon exactly what you have not hoped for. After we had lived through different periods, during which the leu would oscillate from one thousand to one million, losing all worth, until 1947, the year of the 5,000,000 banknotes, new and beautiful, but worthless, and after the times when, for almost five years, we had become acquainted with a living standard of approximately 10,000 lei on a monthly basis, a period during which one leu had no value, and the standard exchanging unit was the twenty or the hundred, suddenly, one leu has become the equivalent of 100 bani – an important currency. Overnight, due to a simple decree issued by the government, the country was flooded with coins worth 1 ban, 3 bani, 5 bani, 10 bani and 25 bani, by comparison with which 1 leu seemed like a 'sum'. We could not believe our eyes! It was as if we were back to the times of Carol the First, or before; we carried 'small change' in our pockets, for tram tickets, for cigarettes, for bread – we kept the leu for more important matters. It was as if the 'good times' of our parents had returned. They had almost forgotten how to think of merchandise – as small and insignificant as it might be – in terms of lei and bani; we were all accustomed to calculating everything using hundreds and thousands. Now we were back to fractions of the leu, to 'small change'. 'What a blessing!' someone*

who only hears about this would say. 'What a curse!' say the people who are forced – and by this, I mean the whole populace – to bear with such a 'blessing'. The specter of 'stabilization' that haunted the entire public opinion has finally reared its ugly head. With all the assurances of the minister of Finances, Vasile Luca, who has been trying ever since 1949 to deny 'the rumors' set in motion by 'the enemies of our nation', Anglo-Saxon imperialists, who 'rave on' (as he put it in his report for the 1950 yearly budget) about a new stabilization, firmly making promises that our currency will never have the need for a new stabilization (after the one done on the 15th of August 1947), here we are with this very thing happening, without a word from the country's vault keeper. What has to be admitted is that the new stabilization was made with the tactics and the masterwork worthy of the greatest stock specialists known in history, from Law to Varga. Events unfolded in the following manner:

During the month of January, the masses had started spreading the rumors of stabilization more and more avidly. Yet, it seemed than no one truly believed them. No manner of inflation was felt, and the majority of people were eagerly waiting for their 'chenzine[91]' to cover their daily expenses. Around the middle of the month, the rumor gained strength, because after the 20th, the public picked up on clues that this time 'it was serious'. The assault on stores, markets and shops began. All sorts of stories are told: peasants who were buying perfume by the canister, city folk who heavily invested in axe handles and anything else they could get a hold of. Everyone has similar stories, but when asked where one saw such happenings, one replies that one does not know precisely, that one has 'heard' such stories from friends and other similar excuses. The truth is that people, alarmed, raced to buy all they could, but found that there wasn't really anything they could buy – stores and markets were empty. Some of them, more prudently bought everything they could come by – but not in an exaggerated fashion – in order to invest the little money they had into something more durable. On the other hand, the government had adopted the same tactic, and had consequently and purposefully taken all goods off the market. It was truly captivating to watch – this blind battle between the government and the population for the accumulation of products. This household battle was, alas, over in an instant.

On the night of the 24th of January, the government issued a press release through which it announced that all stores throughout the country will be closed during the 25th and 26th of January, in order to recalculate and reduce prices. Good. An announcement like any other, said the citizens. On the following day, on Friday, all stores – with the exception of pharmacies, which were only filling out 'emergency prescriptions' – were in fact closed. No restaurant, no tobacco shop, absolutely no kind of commercial enterprise existed anymore. Citizens would walk around with money in their pockets, but couldn't spend them anywhere. Only theaters, cinemas and public baths (three in all of Bucharest) were open – the baths were impossible to access, due to them being filled to capacity. It was as if everyone had been suddenly reminded that they need a wash and thousands of citizens have discovered an establishment they had never known existed. Utility bills could not be paid, even though the citizens, suddenly seized by patriotic zeal, had rushed to pay all their debts to the state. The city was thrown in extraordinary fits of anxiety: the populace, exasperated into silence, kept glancing towards the closed booths and shops, not knowing what to do with their money. Some would ride the tramway, from one end of the line to the other, taking it as an occasion to get acquainted with all the neighborhoods and slums of Bucharest – mainly because the tramway was the only place they could use money in order to buy a ticket. This situation lasted for three days: Friday, Saturday, and Sunday. On Sunday evening, the bomb finally dropped: the Scînteia newspaper came out, containing the decision of the party in regards to the monetary reform. The newspaper was snatched out of the sellers' hands, moreover, there were cases in which people broke their legs and arms overwhelmed by the rushing crowd, fighting for a slither of newspaper. After three days of 'total fasting', the population was in its right to manifest curiosity towards the government's declaration.

The declaration announced the 'monetary reform'. The currency changes and new currency is introduced. Old money is exchanged at a rate of 200 for 1 for sums of money up to 3,000 lei, and a t a rate of 300 to 1 for sums exceeding this value. Citizens' rights will be paid by the state following the same rate, while the debts of citizens towards the state will be paid at a rate of 20 to 1. It is announced that on the following day, Monday, the exchange of money would commence. On the 28th and 29th of January (Monday and Tuesday), old money would only be accepted to pay for tramway and theater tickets, but their prices will increase tenfold. Stores and everything else – with the exception of theaters and cinema, where people no longer flocked – were closed on Monday as well, up until evening, and so the population could not buy anything – and a great deal of them, those that didn't cook at home, had nothing to eat for four whole days. All the while, store windows were stocked full of goods, like in the most cherished old days of prosperity: mountains of butter, loads of eggs, immense quantities of fish and salami, lemons, oranges and many other such delights. People stopped and stared in front of them, half of them believing they were dreaming. This had been the government's intention all along: for more than two months – even during Christmas and New Year's – it had held on to all products, in order to release them all to the market now, all at once, creating the illusion of a fascinating luxury.

People were starving after being patient for four days. Every one of them thought that once they get their hands on the new currency, they will march straight into a grocery store and spend them all on the spot. They all wanted to secure their place at the front of the queue to be sure they will get their share of produce. But the government was careful enough to avoid fights breaking out on the streets, and planned the exchanges in such a way as to not have people assault stores all at once. Exchange centers were scarce, and exchanges were made in alphabetical order; the whole process took approximately four days. Citizens with names starting with the letters A, B, C, and D were lucky enough to get the money first, but this happened late on Monday evening. Even so, buyers began to pour into stores in the evening. How proud they were of themselves as they exited the store holding 2 or 3 small packets in their bag, and how they victorious they strode through the city! At around 5 o'clock I saw a worker who was very pleased with exchanging his money and who had bought a loaf of bread which he carried as one would carry one's cane, as he went down the Boulevard, conscious of being the first citizen to appear with a loaf of white bread in hand and being fully aware of what that meant at that time. With the new money, you could hardly buy anything. Prices had fallen, they were in fact 20 times lower for any product. But to what use? For 1,000 old lei you would only get 5 lei. With 1,000 old lei you could have previously bought an entire basket of food, while with 5 new lei you could barely afford half a kilo of butter or one kilo of cheese. In this manner, the government only offered the starving population – who had been so eager to see the stores open after four whole days of 'fasting' – a small appetizer. Each and every one of them spent one month's salary in one day – without really buying much – because 10,000 lei were exchanged for 37 new lei, which was the price of a wholesome meal, paid with a month's worth of work. This was the monetary reform. In one single night, all people – be they rich or poor, hardworking or lazy, intelligent or idiots – were reduced to being equal, because no one had more than any other, and those who had more had lost everything. There were cases of people saving money for years to buy a house, or others that had just sold their house; both lost everything. More aptly put, the state had taken everything from both. In general, each citizen had at least one month's salary taken from them – but no one said anything, not a single peep.

Of course, the motivation behind the laws that facilitated this theft spoke of 'speculators' and of 'capitalists', of 'the war against classes' and so on – but who were the speculators, the capitalists, and the enemies to the class after four years of people's democracy?! If I were to trust this discourse, they would be the people struck by this 'reform', meaning the working class itself, the ones said to be protected by the regime. A lot was also spoken in regards to the peasantry – namely that peasants had money, and the reform wanted to get the money out of the peasants' grasp. This was merely a pretext, in order to justify the theft and find a scapegoat. The truth was that the peasantry had the least money. The peasantry which had nothing to eat, no clothes and no shoes, the peasantry who had no gas to light up their households with and which was more abused than back in the times of the Fanariot preceptors – this peasantry was once again found guilty. Moreover, the peasantry took the heaviest blow in this reform. City workers were able to get a part of their salary after 10 to 15 days and managed to cover their expenses, but peasants didn't get anything, and were forced to sell everything they had around the house: pigs, chickens, eggs, or milk, thus flooding the market which the state could no longer supply. And who would believe that peasants were able to buy anything with money taken for the little food they had? Only those who do not know the suffering and the tragedy in the lives of our peasants today would believe so. With the money from what they were forced to sell, peasants cannot afford to buy the urgently necessary clothing and shoes, because they are forced to pay their taxes with them. And the government announcement and the article published in Scînteia have the audacity to demonstrate that the monetary reform is made to benefit the peasantry 'as well', and that this reform strengthens the alliance between the working class and the peasantry! With 'alliances' such as this, they are one million better off without any!

Today, two weeks after the 'reform', people are still hungry, and are still staring at the store windows that have gradually began to empty. The state is constantly delaying the payment of salaries for its workers, in an attempt to prolong the illusion of prosperity – which was an illusion to begin with, and one that rapidly dissipated. If people were to receive all their small salaries, the market could not withstand the demand, and so the state chooses to delay payments, while citizens get by as they can, stomachs grumbling. Who is the winner and who is the loser in this whole affair? The press, throughout this country – I was just about to say the press owned by the government, but I forgot that this is the only kind of press we have been left with today! – had immediately announced 'the people' that this reform was done for their benefit, to the benefit of the working class. But after its application, the working class realizes that they have been mugged. Moreover, they are still being mugged and will continue to be so, in the name of the law. Who is the winner? The next calculation is clear: one ruble was worth 30 lei before the reform. Afterwards, it was worth 2.8 lei. According to the exchange rate, it should have been worth 1.9 lei. A soviet functionary – and good Grace if there aren't thousands of them in our country – who is paid 1000 rubles, received in RPR, prior to the reform, a salary of 38,000 lei per month. Now he receives, for the same amount of rubles, a salary of 2,800 lei. All the while a Romanian functionary, who would formerly receive 38,000 lei per month, now only gets 1,900 lei – 900 lei less than his Russian counterpart. In the same manner, a commercial business between RPR and the USSR with a value of, let's say, 38 million old lei is now paid 2,800,000 lei instead of 1,900,000 lei – a difference of 900,000 lei in the USSR's advantage. If we would calculate the entire volume of payments the USSR receives from RPR, we will come to the conclusion that the USSR wins fabulous sums following this reform. We have identified the thief!

As I have mentioned earlier, the working class continues to be mugged after the reform has ended. Many people – workers, writers, artists, and so on –had supplied the state with certain works: exceeded norms in factories, works of literature, works of art and others such as these. Four months or so, the state did not pay for these works, the money being withheld at the State Bank. No one knew why the money was withheld and they eagerly waited for their work to be compensated. Then came the reform. Rumors started circulating that all debts would be paid at a very high exchange rate. It was normally 20 to 1 or 200 to 1. It should have been paid 20 to 1, meaning that for the sum calculated in the old currency the equivalent in new lei would be paid. Finally, the state concluded that it had postponed these people long enough and decided that all payments that should have been made before the 28th of January – the state does not mention why they were not made – will be paid at the rate of 200 to 1. And so, a worker who toiled at the price of his health to earn an extra 20,000 lei, a writer or artist who had worked for one month to earn 20,000 lei, they would all receive 100 lei. With 20,000 old lei, you could feed a family for an entire month, or you could buy yourself three meters of good canvas from 'Romarta'. With 100 new lei, you could feed a family for two days or buy ¼ of the same canvas. This is how the monetary reform helped the working class! Moreover, in some cases, citizens receive their sums exchanged at the rate of 200 to 1. However, taxes for these sums are calculated using the 20 to 1 rate. For example, a functionary that had not received his salary of 14,900 lei for the month of December would now receive it in the new currency. Before the reform, he would receive 13,300 lei, and the remaining 1,600 lei would represent taxes. Today, he receives 74.5 new lei, out of which 75 lei are taxes, meaning that the citizen must pay an additional 0.5 lei. Such cases are numerous: workers on leave, functionaries that had to travel and could not receive their salaries on time, people of the arts, and many more now suffer similar 'recalculations'.

We have found the victim! And still, no one expresses their discontent. But patience has its limits!"[92]

The last monetary reform, which passed without being observed but had great consequences in the pauperization of the whole country, took place on the 31st of January 1954: it was dictated by external affairs. Through this measure, the Romanian leu, which had been formerly set to the value of 2.8 rubles in 1952, would now be fixed at 1.5 lei per ruble, without any changes made to banknotes or coins and without any official increases in prices. Economist Radu Plessia is the only person who managed to solve this mystery:

The 1954 monetary reform did not seek to plunder the Romanian population individually as was the case with the previous two reforms. Its purpose was the plundering of the entire country in favor of the USSR.[93]

The matter at hand was, in other words, the breaking down of the previously mentioned Sovroms and the buying out of soviet stocks (50% in total), that had been announced in Moscow on the 24th of September 1954, through a joint decree, signed by Miron Constantinescu, the head of the State Council for Planning (who gained the completely undeserved fame as a "patriot" and great economist, because Romania was in the process of once again buying (back) half of its industry, transports, insurance and raw materials from the Russians that had seized them after the war and had been profiting from them for more than 9 years)[94].

Here is the manner in which Radu Plessia understood the entire operation:

"In Moscow, it was decided that all Soviet capital must be transferred from Romania. But, as I have mentioned before, the Soviets did not invest any capital in Sovroms – the contribution of the Soviet Union was self-attributed. By doubling the value of the leu, this so-called capital, calculated in rubles, would also double. If we consider that the prices of Romanian products exported to the USSR are calculated in rubles and do not take Romanian production costs into consideration, the extent of the organized theft of Romanian goods achieved by reevaluating the foreign exchange rate of the leu becomes clear. Taking into account the fact that the vast quantities of Soviet capital that needs to be transferred to the USSR will be calculated at double its value, it becomes clear that Romania will be forced to send the greater part of its exports to the USSR and receive next to nothing in return."[95]

What could the thousands of people who had been thrown out of their houses, expelled from their jobs ("cleansed") and left without secure properties and valuables (gold, stocks, jewelry), with no hope of joining the "workforce"[96] and deprived of ration cards do to get by? The state offered them the possibility of selling their last valuable objects (such as paintings, rugs and furniture) through the creation in 1949 of stores called "Consignatia[97]".

Here are the observations made by Pericle Martinescu – the most trust-worthy witness of these times – in October 1950:

"More and more 'Consignația' stores started opening, each more luxurious than the other. I have asked myself many times whether these kinds of luxury items were not a contradiction of the regime's values. By pondering the subject more deeply, I have come to the conviction that this commerce is no more than another ingenious manner in which the state sought to strip the bourgeois of their last rare goods and valuables. Because the state was not able to find a method of seizing all the rugs, jewelry, vases, furniture, paintings and art still in the possession of certain people, it devised this official action of voluntary expropriation, after the model of the Russian 'talcioc'. In general, the owners of such goods have been forced out of society. They are left to live off what they can sell, and they are constrained to sell all they have left at a very small price, to the consignment store.

In this manner, the state can easily make all valuables surface, from the most hidden corners, without even looking for them. But once they are bought by the consignment store, what happens to these valuables? They usually take one of two possible routes: they are either bought by institutions (rugs, paintings, and similar goods), which use them as decorations or they enter into the pos-session of the regime's privileged, who had rapidly succeeded in exchanging the hammer and the grinding stone for the gold watch and the pork skin travelling case – valuables change sides: from the people who had painstakingly collected them to the ones who have recently become entitled to them and who pay for them with the money they take out of the country's coffers. Through consignment stores, one class strips the other of possessions – so to speak, using terminology that has become popular nowadays, even if it is not a question of social classes, but of people who exchange places with others, of proles who become true bourgeois overnight! – In the most peaceful fashion possible: without evacuating houses, without nationalization, without involving the police. This peaceful degrading of the bourgeoisie is not very Marxist at all, but in spite of this, it continues to take place, because it benefits all parties involved: the owner, who is satisfied with selling an object for a tenth of its worth in order to get by for another month, the buyer, who pays double the price but is satisfied with spending some of the money that keep pouring into his pockets twice a month, and the state, because it pockets the difference between the buying and selling price plus taxes. Before this, a place called the Mountain of Piety existed. Downtrodden people would take their possessions there and pawn them for a fixed amount of time. The Mountain of Piety was taken over by 'Consignația'. It changed in name only. The sole difference is that 'the stock exchange of strife' – as the urban news reporters named it – has now become a state institution under the government's patronage. And some people say we don't have real progress!"[98]

For the people who refused to give 90% of their selling profit on goods they were selling in order to stay alive to the state, the last solution was the "talcioc"[99]. This Russian word ("tolcioc" means "knock", "collision", "a hit executed with the shoulder" or "the action of making your way through a crowd by use of your elbows") described a vast outdoor bazaar[100] held in the outskirts of Bucharest, at the end of Colentina Drive, in the hole of a former excavation site for bricks. Writer George Călinescu compared it to one of the Circles of Hell from Dante's Inferno[101], this place would fill every Sunday with tens of thousands of people who would buy and sell the most diverse range of objects. Sellers laid their wares on the ground, sprawling over entire hectares.

Our guide in this new Inferno is Pericle Martinescu, the writer who visited the flea market on the 22nd of October 1950:

"TALCIOC. Today I went for the first time to the famous flea market held in Colentina, about which all of Bucharest has been talking. It is truly a sight worth seeing! The market is open only on Sundays. But in order to get there, you need to fight your way through the trams. Special trams without numbers are supplemented from the Sf. Gheorghe station – they keep rolling in, count-less, at short intervals of time. Not even on the 'Day of the Scînteia newspaper' could you see so many vehicles being put into circulation. Despite all this, many citizens make their way to Colentina on foot, incapable of boarding the trams that leave the station filled to capacity, and with clusters of people hanging from doors like ripe bushels of grapes. People carrying suitcases, packages, and bags fill Calea Moșilor and other streets that lead towards Colentina Drive –and especially this street –, as if Bucharest is being evacuated. The end of the line for tramway no. 1 is the last stop of this exodus and here you get off into a constant bustle of fantastic proportions. Although the flea market is still some way off,

all the streets in this neighborhood are crowded. Beggars line the edge of the streets – blind and emaciated – they sing and wail, imploring for the mercy of the passers-by. But can anyone stop and throw a coin into the tin can of these poor downtrodden people? Once you are in the moving crowd, you are forcefully pushed forward by the masses of people, and it becomes impossible to stop or to change course. This formidable stream runs straight into the sea of people in the flea market.

The market is held in an enormous hole in the ground – its massive surface of several hectares is completely covered. This hole is surrounded by tall walls of earth, about 4 or 5 meters high, on the edge of which other streams of people attempt to negotiate a path down into this compact hell, because the only entrance – a large wooden board gate – is completely packed with people. Over the walls of the hole, you can see the vast and empty plum orchards, their leaves turned to gold by autumn – an enchanting bucolic scene, that doesn't catch the interest of anyone. Towards midday, the orchards begin to be frequented by people in search of places to do their business away from the eyes of the public. As seen from above, the flea market looks like a squalid concentration camp in which tens of thousands of people have been crammed together. The masses are so tightly packed, that any distinct movement is not observable, and no sounds are distinguishable from the general rumor – although the tens of thousands of people constantly walk from one seller to the next, speaking all languages and talking about all manners of things. Former capitalists, evacuated landowners, ex-merchants, Jewish people, gypsies, professors, artists, and writers – people of all categories have gathered here. You can hear English, French, German and Yiddish being spoken around you and, generally, these are the languages used by those who sell, discussing with each other over what prices to ask for while the client sits in front of them, examining an object, trying out an article of clothing, some boots, a hat or an umbrella. Here you can buy everything human fantasy has ever been capable of creating over the course of centuries, from Persian rugs to sewing thread, from radios to rusty nails, from porcelain statues and irrigation pumps to undergarments and pencils. Valuable objects from the houses of the rich lie net to the most insignificant things, whose sole value is the fact that you can't find them in the city anymore. Here, you can find old notes sold by a former bank director or by a former landowner, treasured by those who haven't seen them in stores, where notebooks and any kind of stationery are available only with a special permit from school – for students – or from the institution, for functionaries. In regards to their social origins, most sellers represent the former 'uptown people', and most buyers are people who have just left their cellars and attics in search of goods to make their life more bearable: some are buying blankets, some furs; some spend their money on binoculars, some spend it on plates and cutlery. Among the buyers there are some people who are interested in investing their money into valuable objects, predicting a time when they would have to resell them on future market days. Some buy things from one side of the market and sell them, on the same day and for double the price, on the other side of the sea of people. It is a stock exchange for the miserable and the shrewd, where the cunning and the naïve take their chances at every moment, where the avaricious tendencies of former exploiters and the unhealthy greed of the newly well off clash, confront each other and roll around in silent battle, gentle only in appearance, fierce in actuality. This fight unfolds throughout the flea market.

Out of the bustling hive of people you can hear commercial advertising in all its forms, and you see all sorts of improvised merchants or buyers who don't seem to be in much of a hurry. A landlord is selling his leather saddle, atop which he had so often surveyed his endless fields of wheat. His wife is at his side – I can imagine her now at the manor, cheerfully administrating incredibly vast fortunes – now selling her sleave scarf and silk traditional dress. Between the two, their children, dressed in high fashion, the uptown boy with studies completed abroad and used to the most expensive bars, the girl, raised in the most sophisticated boarding schools – they stand still and upright like wooden mannequins with coats and pairs of shoes in their hands and merchandise draped on their extended arms, towards the curious public. Next to them, the former travelling merchant, the gypsy of the slums, seems to have more experience in the business: 'Come one, come all, come if you have money, I'll put shoes on your feet!'. The principle that advertisement is the soul of commerce is quickly adopted by 'the elites'. From time to time, a lady – you could tell by her eyes that she had seen better times – learned a few artifices from her gypsy 'comrade' and tries her own twist on his words: 'If you have the money, I have good quality goods!'. While the gypsy's phrase has an exotic ring to it that tickles the ear, hers voice sounds coarse and it becomes irritating.

Somewhere else, a painter sold ladies' underwear, a former antiquarian (Mișu Pach himself[102]) was looking for a bolt nut, a writer (Jebeleanu[103]) was examining a Persian rug, a newly instated 'director' was buying silverware, a former minister was selling his silk shirts and a former University professor was selling his library. There are books as well at the flea market. Moreover, often enough, you can find the most interesting ones, not yet confiscated by the cultural flayers from Book Control. Progressive books and forbidden books, valuable books and dirty books (both figuratively and literally) – all of them laid down in the dirt or on top of old newspaper, containing hand written dedications offered by parents to their children, by uncles to their nephews, by boyfriends to their girlfriends, full of dust, with broken spines, with tattered covers, books in French, English, German, old and new, good and bad, all are sold here with varied prices. They represent the least important article for sale, and consequently sellers have not come to an agreement in regards to a general rule of price. They give the books away for any price they can get, as long as they get rid of them. In the dust that chokes the entire atmosphere of the market, you can find Goethe's works next to The Red Mask, Mircea Eliade's Hooligans next to Nicolae Moraru's Essays, writings by Iorga next to Mihail Roller's brochures, Marx next to Conan Doyle and Stalin – written in big letters on the cover – lost among a wide range of novels and precious prints predating the war. But buyers are either too pretentious or too vulgar. Mediocrity attracts no one. On the covers of Stalin, for example, are only touched by the dust of the market. A student buys Aristotle's Politic (80 lei), and women stops to by Mud by Octav Dessila (120 lei). You gladly watch the moment when a young man's intelligent eyes linger on Philosophical Works by Vasile Conta and you turn away in disgust when you see the seller charge 200 lei for a Vicky Baum novel. No one even glances in the direction of progressive literature!

After several hours of wading, literally wading through the masses of people, with lungs filled with muck and eyes red from the dust, with sore feet from the long hours of walking around, some other shouts seem to catch your ear: 'If you have money, my brothers, come here and have something to eat!'. A pair takes out meatballs, large loaves of bread and peppers out of a big wicker basket and lay them down at the feet of the passers-by. It is lunchtime – time to leave this Inferno. We will come back next Sunday, because the flea market is a wonderful occasion to get acquainted to life in all its immensity and depth, in all its cruelty and gentleness. The flea market is the 'achievement' of the regime. Like all other achievements of the regime, this too was imported from Russia, or more accurately, imported from the communist regime in Russia. It has become the most popular manifestation of the masses, an aspect for which communists regard it rather 'a contre coeur', without having the courage to make a move against it. All political and social regimes have such specific achievements that mirror their structure. The regime before the war, in our country, had created the Maglavit, while the current regime has created the Talcioc. The only difference is that while people looked towards the Maglavit seeking redemption, they now look towards the talcioc in order to earn their daily bread. The Maglavit was the result of the spiritual exploitation of the people. The talcioc is the result of economic exploitation. Both of these manifestations are oriental in nature, and both engage entire masses of people while becoming instruments fallen into the hands of the most horrid dictators. In our country, masses have let themselves be dragged towards disaster – entire generations pass until they are capable of realizing this. It happened so in the era of the Maglavit, and it is happening now in the era of the Talcioc."[104]

Terror ("economic constraint", in Marxist terminology) was introduced to Romania by the Red Army and NKVD (become MGB in 1946 and KGB in 1954), which thus terminated the short-lived euphoria produced by the act of 23rd of August 1944[105]. Here as well, the USSR rulers have great expertise: the "red" terror (Trotsky), followed by state terror, planned, systematic, applied to all of society, it crushes entire social groups, being directed at social classes whose members were called *bâvşie liudi*, translated into Romanian as "the formers"(former landlords, former directors, and so on)[106]. "The alliance between utopic promises and unwavering mass terror was the explosive mixture that allowed the Bolsheviks to secure their victory" in the Russian civil war between 1918 and 1920.[107] Terror became the order of day for Soviet citizens in the 30's, when it made millions of victims not only among the population, but also in the ranks of the communist party, the army and the secret services[108]. Under the umbrella of the Allied High Command[109], the Soviets and their protégées (The Romanian Communist Party - PCR) began to destroy old society through the action of "defascization" of the country, which was carried out through the arrest and deportation to concentration camps[110] and even to the USSR of tens of thousands of Romanian citizens accused of destroying the country and numerous other war crimes (such as the participation in the war against the Soviet Union): military personnel, public functionaries, Magyar and German ethnic groups (out of which almost 70,000 were deported to Donbas in January 1945)[111], political figures and members of left wing parties. Article 2 of the 24th of April 1945 law-decree identified no less than 15 categories of guilty citizens or, in the words of experts, "any person proven to have been part of any military unit that had fought on Soviet lands or which had subscribed to the mandatory wartime loan from which weaponry was made and sent to the Eastern front" could have theoretically been accused of the crimes described by the decree[112]. This explains why war veterans injured on the Eastern front did not receive any pensions – they were reserved only for those injured and maimed on the Western front.

The first 36 concentration camps were created in "democratic" Romania for all these categories of "suspects": Târgu Jiu (over 5,000 prisoners in December 1944), Slobozia Veche, Ciurel-București, Timșul de Sus and Timișul de Jos, Lugoj, Pitești, Vulcan (Hunedoara county), Caracal (2,500 prisoners)[113] and Turnu Măgurele[114]. This was just the beginning of mass terror initiated under the Allied High Command (Soviet), and it would be finished and perfected by the communist institutions in Romania[115]. This have all been accurately synthesized by Teohari Georgescu, the Minister of Internal Affairs, during this period (1945-1952), during the inquiries following his arrest:

While my work for the Ministry was not without its mistakes, I certainly was never found lacking hatred of classes. The party would have never permitted me to remain the head of the Ministry of Internal Affairs for one year, let alone seven, were I not to have great hatred of classes and were I to surrender to the enemy. In seven years, the Ministry of Internal Affairs had difficult tasks to carry out ... From the 6th of March 1945 to the 26th of May 1952, the enemy within and the enemy without sustained numerous blows. During these seven years, over

100,000 bandits were arrested and sentenced for conspiring against our regime. This meant hundreds of terrorist organizations, groups who sought to create diversions, and espionage groups discovered and neutralized. The entire bourgeois oppression contingent (Siguranta), The Special Bureau of Intelligence, The Military Counterintelligence Bureau) was arrested. All identified legionary personnel who held high ranking positions, the legionary police, the former central and county heads of bourgeois political parties, former chiefs of staff, former ministers, prefects, senators, deputies from 1920-1944, as well as other categories of elements considered to be the enemy were also arrested. All this could not have been done without hatred of classes.[116]

The confession of Teohari Georgescu spares us of going into further detail in regards to the terror enforced by the regime against democratic parties – The National Liberal Party (PNL), the National Peasant Party (PNȚ), and the Social-Democratic Party (PSD) – during the election campaign in 1946 and in all subsequent years[117]. The result was the disbanding of PNȚ, the arrest, trial and sentencing of its leaders, starting with Iuliu Maniu and Ion Mihalache; the disappearance of PNL who disbanded itself at the end of the year 1947 or the beginning of 1948; the disbanding of the Independent Social-Democratic Party – Titel Petrescu and the arrest of its leaders; finally, the engulfment of PSD by PCR and the apparition of The Romanian Workers Party (PMR) in February 1948[118]. And, as a finishing touch to all these efforts, King Mihai – the last obstacle in the way of the dictatorship of the proletariat – abdicates his throne and RPR is proclaimed on the 30th of December 1947. From this moment on, Romanian communist could entirely support and agree with the affirmation made by the Soviet syndicate leader Mihail Tomsky (1880-1936) during the 11th Congress of PCUS in 1922: "Foreign powers have accused us of having a single party regime. Such claims are false. We have numerous parties. But, unlike other foreign countries, in our country one party is in power and all the others are in prison."[119]

As a simple observation, I will say that state induced terror was exercised upon all political groups and parties considered to be hostile towards

PCR, but it has been exercised more upon PNȚ and legionaries[120], as well as against "partisans" (the official term used for them was "bandits") and members of guerilla fighters in the mountains, who were hunted down and assassinated up until 1958[121]. Apart from them, arrests were made on thousands of people accused of being members of Freemasonry[122], Zionists[123], "titelist" social-democrats (followers of the social-democratic party founded by Titel Petrescu, who refused to ally himself to the communist during 1946 elections), Greek Catholics (as a consequence to the disbandment of the Romanian Church United with Rome in 1948), ministers and secretaries of state active between 1920 and 1944[124], Catholics (priests, monks and even legate Monsignor O'Hara and his collaborators)[125], journalists (the first round of trials took place on June 1945), free syndicates (trials taking place in July 1945), gendarmes and policemen, former mayors and prefects, peasants who refused to enter collective farmsteads (89,000 people)[126], those in possession of stocks and gold coins, those in possession of collection weapons and regular weapons ("gunslingers"), those who criticized the system ("matists" – this term is derived from the national swear words addressed to mothers), those who spread rumors ("rumorists"), those who told political jokes, those who attempted to flee the country ("frontierists" – the law would sentence them to between 2 and 5 years of prison and the confiscation of their possessions and wealth), those singing forbidden songs or in possession of books and publications listed in the *Forbidden Publications Index* issued in 1945, 1948 and subsequent years (the lists contained, aside from Hitler and Goebbels, works written by Churchill and General Charles de Gaulle), those who listened to foreign radio stations, these accused of "mysticism" and espionage (the group called "Rugul Aprins" – the lit stake – 16 people arrested in August 1958 and prosecuted in October[127]), those writing protest letters to political people and journals, pensioners who formed ministries on the benches in Cișmigiu Park, those who possessed typewriters without registering them to the Police[128], those who admired "decadent" Western culture and denigrated the USSR (which was the case of the Noica group, resulting in 23 people prosecuted in February 1960)[129], stamp collectors who exchanged stamps depicting Marshal Antonescu or King Carol the Second (17 people arrested in July 1961), Romanian functionaries working in the American, English[130], French[131] and Italian Cultural Institutes, those who visited the aforementioned institutes' libraries, titoists (accompanied by, of course, "imperialist spies"), the families of political prisoners[132] and even their children[133].

Estimated statistics published in France in October 1950 offered the following numbers for the period between 1945 and 1950: 200,000 people in work camps and prisons for economic sabotage, 14,282 detained without due process, 1,852 people condemned in political trials, 4,346 people executed or missing[134]. In most cases, the severity of the sentence was not set depending on the severity of the crimes committed by the defendant as much as it was set by diligently following the principle stated by Soviet prosecuting attorney Andrei Ianuarevich Vîşinski: "We do not judge actions, we judge people!"[135]. Until 1989, the number of victims of the communist regime in Romania is estimated to have amounted to between 500,000 and 2,000,000 people[136].

For comparison, we mention that in Hungary, a country of less than 10 million people, 1,3 million people were arrested and prosecuted between 1948 and 1953, out of which 700,000 (over 7% of the entire population) were officially sentenced[137]. In Poland, a country with a larger population than Romania, at least 200,000 people were arrested between 1945 and 1956, out of which 6,000 were executed[138].

Deportation was itself another form of terror, imitating the Soviet and Tsarist Russian model, although not to the same extent: in Romania, it was mainly practiced against "the land owning bourgeoisie": 60,000 people had mandatory residence (with the acronym d. o., from which the ironic formula "diplomat olandez[139]") in 1949. This was also imposed for 44,000 Serbian peasants, foreign colonists in Banat and Transylvania and Romanians situated on the border with Yugoslavia, all deported to the Bărăgan Field in 1951, when preparing for war with Tito and his "clique"[140], 9,000 people in 1952 and 890 in 1953, and the process continued primarily for prisoners freed after 1954[141].

Finally, "work units", as work camps[142] were known and special military units where soldiers with unhealthy social origins[143] were sent to, the so called "Tiribau" or "Diribau" (from the name of the former German-Romanian construction company called *Deutsch Rumänische Bauunternehmung* or Derubau for short), which amounted to over 22,000 people in 1950 and 1954[144].

Another form of terror was the "cleansing" of institutions, factories and socio-professional associations, begun in 1945 and continued for several years. It started in the army and administration, proceeding to strike the industry, commerce, syndicates, the Bar (in Bucharest, only 2,000 lawyers of the previously existing 10,000 would remain to be organized in boards), the medical field, pharmacists (manifesting masses, forced by PCR to shout mobilizing mottos, first confused them with … fascists) who were stripped of their pharmacies, laboratories and medical supply storehouses in 1949, engineers, accountants and many other categories. Those cleansed would lose their right to practice their profession, the right to ration cards and would be forced to search for the most diverse sorts of unqualified labor[145].

In the long list of cleansing activities to which the Romanian justice system was constrained after 1945, there is only one exception: communists were never judged in public trials as it happened in the USSR between 1936 and 1938, in Bulgaria (the Traicio Kostov trial), Hungary (László Rajk), and Czechoslovakia (the Slánský trial). In our country, communists resolved their conflicts in a manner similar to the mafia, furtively, behind closed doors, starting with the assassination of General Secretary of the Party, Ștefan Foriș, and including Lucrețiu Pătrășcanu and Remus Koffler, the "antipartizan Ana Pauker – Vasile Luca – Teohari Georgescu group", Iosif Chișinevschi and Miron Constantinescu in 1957. We are not aware of any satisfactory explanation for this secrecy, but we find it truly telling of the siege mentality of PCR leaders who were fully aware of the fact that they are not popular with the populace and who preferred to wash their laundry inside the family, to avoid revealing the ferocity of power struggles and their total dependency on Moscow to the public. This was also a general characteristic of the communist movement about which one specialist writes the following: "Communism is the only movement in modern history that has assassinated its own leaders, functionaries and members in larger number than its enemies ever could have."[146]

A special addendum must be made in regards to *political assassinations,* an essential component of the terror in that period. Political violence, especially exercised by the communists, made numerous victims throughout all of postwar Europe, in the East and West (especially France and Italy). There were several assassinations of notable political adversaries that had become uncomfortable, crimes called *omicidi eccelenti* in Italian and *cadavres exquis*[147] in French. In Romania, only for the period between 1946 and 1947, the number of "missing" people – executed without trials – was evaluated by Ghiță Ionescu, a political science specialist who was contemporary with the events and who had communist convictions in his youth, to be approximately 60,000![148] Sometimes, their bodies would be left bloodied and mutilated on the streets, guarded by policemen, as it happened in 1954-1955 – the official explanation was that they were "shot thieves"[149].

The society's reaction to these aggressions had a multitude of forms: *the resistance army in the mountains, passive resistance, and most of all, exile*[150], and *legal emigration* rose constantly during 1945-1952. Legal emigration was the emigration of Jewish people to Palestine, which started during the war and was accelerating in 1944, when others joined Romanian Jewish people from Bessarabia, Northern Bucovina, Hungary and Poland. At the end of year 1944, Romanian authorities had already received 70,000 applications for passports for the emigration to Palestine and the movement was only increasing due to the fact that numerous people immigrated to other countries or did so illegally. In June 1947, 150,000 applications were filed and 70,000 passports were issued for *alia*[151]. According to official numbers published by the state of Israel (founded in 1948), between 1948 and August 1952, 128,609 people came into the country legally and many more ("a considerable number") did so illegally (some sources cite 160,000 people)[152]. Finally, on January 1953, we can observe that emigration from Romania to Israel suffered a 85% decrease in 1952 (23,370 people) in comparison with 1951 (173,901)[153]. In August 1952, legal emigration to Israel was stopped: 146,264 Jewish people still lived in Romania, barely 20% of the numbers of Jewish people living in 1939. Emigration will start again in September 1958 – 20,000 departures out of 100,000 applications – then stopped again for five months and restarted in 1960, through Vienna (25,000 departures in 1965 alone) during the entire Ceaușescu era[154].

---

1.   For a wider perspective over the matter, see Constantin Hlihor, *Armata Roșie în România. Adversar, aliat, ocupant (1944–1948)*, vol. I, Academia de Înalte Studii Militare, Bucharest, 1996; Flori Stănescu and Dragoș Zamfirescu, *Ocupația sovietică în România. Documente (1944–1946)*, Vremea, București, 1998; Aurel Sergiu Marinescu, *1944–1958: Armata Roșie în România*, 2 vol., Vremea, Bucharest, 2001.

2.   Carl Gustaf Emil Mannerheim (1867–1951) – the president of Finland (1944-1946), commander of the Finnish army during World War II.

3.   In 1916, Prime Minister I.C. Brătianu affirmed that Romania was only declaring war against Austria-Hungary, not against Germany; 25 years later, Marshal Antonescu declared that Romania was hostile towards the Soviet Union, neutral towards Great Britain and favorable towards the USA in their conflict with Japan. Curious mentality, similar to Finland: "In 1941, the Finns took advantage of Hitler's attack of the USSR and declared war. They wanted to fight against the Russians." See Vernon Bartlett, *op. cit.,* p. 182.

4.   Alexandru O. Teodoreanu, known under the nickname of Păstorel (Little shepherd), said that in 1944 he had heard the following from the Minister of France in Bucharest, the writer Paul Morand: "Today, Europe is divided in two: one part is occupied by Russians, and the other is preoccupied by the Russians." See G. Jurgea-Negrilești, *op. cit.,* p. 317.

5.   This theft (*carjacking*) had an illustrious predecessor: in March 1918, Lenin himself had been the victim of this operation of "expropriating the expro-priators" that he had begun, while cruising Petrograd in a superb Delaunay-Bellevile which had belonged to Tsar Nicholas the Second (Lenin had also confiscated two Rolls Royce automobiles, for personal use). After this, the ruler of the proletarian revolution used a Rolls Royce, which had belonged to Great Duke Michael, according to Douglas Smith, *Former people. The last days of the Russian Aristocracy*, Pan Books, London, 2013, p. 139. An American journalist adds that 21,000 automobiles were confiscated, the only ones still left in Romania from a total of 44,000(Hal Lehrman, *op. cit.,* p. 239).

6. For assassinations in Budapest, see Hal Lehrman, *op. cit.*, pp. 176–178. In September only, over 1,998 assassinations were documented! Many were the work of deserters and bandits clothed in Russian uniforms. According to a soviet general, during the first month of occupation in Romania – between August and September 1944 – the Red Army had been confronted with approximately 100,000 desertions, while the Americans had, in all of Europe, fewer than 10,982 such cases. Robert Bishop and E.S. Crayfield, *Russia astride the Balkans*, Evans Brothers Limited, London, 1949, p. 96.

7. Hal Lehrman perfectly illustrated the atmosphere in Hungary, very similar to Romania, after the "freeing": "A year after the 'freeing', all social classes in Hungarian society lived in a sort of Russian style Wild West, completed by armed attacks during the night, burglaries and murders." (Hal Lehrman, *op. cit.*, pp. 176). For the period between 1944 and 1948, also see the extraordinary account of Sandor Marai, *Mémoires de Hongrie*, Albin Michel, Paris, 2006. Remembering the liberation of his country in 1945, a Hungarian told an English journalist: "We do not want another war, but if such a war is necessary, we surely do not want another liberation!" (Vernon Bartlett, *op. cit.*, pp. 76–77). In March 1945, in Bucharest, singer Maria Tănase would tell of the latest joke in Romania: "An old peasant woman comes to Bucharest and is in awe of the great portraits of Stalin everywhere. Confused, she asks a passer-by: 'Who is this man?' to which the citizen replies: 'He is Stalin, the great man who freed us of the Germans.' 'God bless his heart, then, he will surely free us of the Russians as well!'" (*Wolfgang Bretholz, Ich sah sie stürzen. Bericht über die Ereignisse in Ost- und Südosteuropa in den Jahren 1944–1948*, Verlag Kurt Desch, Viena, München, Basel, 1955, p. 165). Another version of this joke was published by e Sorana Gurian, *Ochiurile rețelei*, Jurnalul Literar, Bucharest, 2002, p. 196.

8. Contemporary confessions of Nicolae Iorga, *Supt trei regi. Istorie a unei lupte pentru un ideal moral și național: România contemporană de la 1904 la 1930*, second edition., Bucharest, 1932, p. 232 ; idem, *Orizonturile mele. O viață de om. Așa cum a fost,* vol. II, Editura N. Stroilă, Bucharest, 1934, p. 270; Constantin Argetoianu*, Memorii. Pentru cei de mâine: amintiri din vremea celor de ieri*, Second edition, revised and complete, scientific editor, Vol. III–V, Machiavelli, Bucharest, 2008, pp. 150 and 236. Americans used chewing gum.

9. The photograph appeared in the May 1950 edition of the magazine *Union Soviétique* (formerly URSS *en construction*). The magazine was taken out of circulation worldwide and, two months after its apparition, was replaced with a new version. The reason behind this operation? One of the contemporaries, writer Pericle Martinescu, explains: "In one of the photographs published on the occasion of the anniversary of five years since the surrender of Germany, the very famous photograph, to be exact – this time authentic – in which the first soviet soldier to plant the red flag in the ruins of Berlin appeared, the whole world could see that this soldier – the bearer of the new civilization upon earth – wore a watch on each wrist…" (Pericle Martinescu, *7 ani cât 70. Pagini de jurnal (1948-1954),* Vitruvius, Bucharest, 1997, p. 139). See Alexander and Alice Nakhimovsky, *Witness to History: The Photographs of Yevgeny Khaldei*, Aperture Foundation, New York, 1997.

10. See, among other accounts, those belonging to General Constantin Sănătescu, *Jurnal*, ed. Simona Ghițescu-Sănătescu, Humanitas, Bucharest, 1993, *passim*, and Ulrich Berger, *Misiunea Ethridge în România,* Fundația Academia Civică, Bucharest, 2000. For Hungaria, see Sandor Marai, *op. cit.*, pp. 32, 41–42. No watches could be found in Czechoslovakia, an industrialized country, in 1948, after the passing of soviet troops, see Jan Stransky, *East Wind Over Prague*, Hollis & Carter, London, 1950, pp. 28–29. In Austrian territories occupied by soviets, a Viennese functionary would tell an American journalist in 1948: "The tractors in our area, as well as the watches, all went towards East." (Sam Welles, *Profile of Europe*, Harper & Brothers Publishers, New York, 1948, pp. 286–287). For all examples in Germany, see Keith Lowe, *op. cit.*, pp. 123 and 220–221, as well as historians who described the Berlin battle (Cornelius Ryan, Anthony Beevor etc.). After this spectacle, Constantin Tănase disappeared and it is said that he was brutally murdered by police, see Zoltan Rostas, *Chipurile orașului. Istorii de viață din București. Secolul XX*, Polirom, Iași, 2002, p. 169.

11. Hal Lehrman, *op. cit.*, pp. 294–295 ; Sandor Marai, *op. cit.*, p. 55 which register the term *zabra* to describe the chaotic plundering, from the Russian verb *zabrati*, "to take".

12. Maria Duțu, „*Aspecte ale obligațiilor financiare impuse României prin Convenția de armistițiu din 12 septembrie 1944*", in Revista Istorică, V, 1994,

pp. 899–905; Ulrich Burger, *Misiunea Ethridge în România..., op. cit.*, pp. 116–117, 217–218; Dinu Zamfirescu, Dumitru Dobre, Veronica Nanu, *România la Conferința de pace de la Paris (I)*, Bucharest, Caietele INMER, 2007; Dinu Zamfirescu, Ion Calafeteanu, *România la Conferința de pace de la Paris (II)*, Editura Enciclopedică, Bucharest, 2011.

13. A German journalist described it as "the second Diktat", after the one in Vienna, in 1940, through which Romania would lose Northern Transylvania to the benefit of Hungary, Wolfgang Bretholz, op. cit., pp. 97–98.

14. Considering the value of the US dollar in 2014, reparations represented exactly 3,975,258,614.38 USD. A sum of 200 million was imposed on Hungary as well (plus an additional 200 million owed to Czechoslovakia and Yugoslavia), which in reality paid over one billion dollars at its 1938 value, see László Borhi, *Hungary in the Cold War (1945–1956). Between the United States and the Soviet Union,* Central European University Press, Budapest, New York, 2004, p. 184; Hal Lehrman, *op. cit.*, pp. 223–228. In turn, soviet occupied territory in Germany (the future Democratic Republic of Germany), with population equivalent to Romania, paid approximately 14 billion dollars (at its 1938 value) between 1945 and 1953, see Hermann Weber, *Geschichte der DDR*, Deutscher Taschenbuch Verlag GmbH & Co. KG, München, 2004, p. 33. In the case of Austria, during the Potsdam Conference, Stalin demanded reparations in value of 250 million dollars, but was refused by Western Allies. Until 1948, the soviet army and administration in occupied territories had seized goods and equipment worth at least 255 million USD and still demanded 175 million USD cash, on a two year plan, 2/3 of petrol production for 50 years and total control over Austrian traffic on the Danube River. See Sam Welles, *op. cit.*, p. 282; Hal Lehrman, *op. cit.,* pp. 307–309.

15. See Reuben H. Markham, Rumania under the Soviet Yoke, Meador Publishing Company, Boston, 1949, pp. 504–537, describing the Red Army's ten varieties of plundering and gives the sum of 2 billion dollars as being paid between 1944 and 1940. In 1944, a dollar had the purchasing value of 13.39 USD in 2014. In July 1948, General Nicolae Rădescu, Romanian prime-minister between 1944 and 1945, would mention that to these sums, an additional 735 million dollars were added, having being previously paid, see Henry L. Roberts, *Rumania. Political Problems of an Agrarian State*, Yale

University Press, New Haven, London, 1951, p. 317, note 24; details of exports to the USSR between 1944 and 1949, by a D.G.R. Serbanesco, *Ciel rouge sur la Roumanie*, SIPUCO, Paris, 1952, pp. 284–285 (1.515 milion dollarsas communicated by a functionary of the Romanian Reparations Comission). For Hungary and Bulgaria, Hal Lehrman, *op. cit.*, pp. 223, 226–227, 275–276.

16. Both Tito in 1953 and Mao ten years later, accused the USSR of being an imperialist state, which practiced "high power chauvinism", see François Fejtö, *op. cit.*, vol. , pp. 268–270. For the description of the neo-colonialist regime, see Kenneth Jowitt, *Revolutionary Breakthroughs and National Development. The Case of Romania*, 1944–1965, University of California Press, 1971, pp. 53–55, 90–91 and Stelian Tănase, *Elite și societate. Guvernarea Gheorghiu Dej (1948–1965)*, Humanitas, Bucharest, 1998, pp. 26–32, in which proprieties intrinsic to Romanian communism are described.

17. A Polish socialist perfectly summarized the nature of economic relations with the USSR: "Our commercial treaty with Moscow states that Russia gets our coal and we give them our textiles in exchange!" (Sam Welles, Profile of Europe…, pp. 222–223.) A functionary in Sofia declared: „In politics, the Russians hail us as comrades and Slav brothers, but when it comes to business they never let us forget that we are 'ex-enemies'" See Hal Lehrman, *op. cit.,* pp. 275–276, with details for Bulgaria; for Hungary, also see Sandor Marai, *op. cit.,* pp. 59–61.

18. Hal Lehrman, *op. cit.*, p. 294. Also see pp. 296–299, for the value of human life for the soviets and their behavior, also applied in the case of Romania, in houses seized from Hungary; Sandor Marai, *op. cit.*, pp. 77–78; Ruben Markham, *op. cit.*

19. Hal Lehrman, *op. cit.,* p. 297.

20. Milovan Djilas, *Conversations avec Staline*, Paris, Gallimard, 1961, p. 153. Also see the reserved opinions of Vladimir Tismăneanu, which he presents in chapter „Stalinismul în Europa de Est", in his volume *Despre comunism. Destinul unei religii politice*, Humanitas, București, 2011, pp. 50–73. However, the idea was not as new. Napoleon I, who overturned all previous regimes in Europe, particularly in Germany or Austria, had the habit of saying "Une armée au dehors, c'est l'Etat qui voyage", see Ygael Gluckstein, *op. cit.,* p. 133. The comments of Hendry L. Roberts still hold today, see his book *Rumania. Political Problems of an Agrarian State*, Yale University Press, New Haven,

London, 1951, pp. 264–273. As with debates sprouting from the opinion of Isaac Deutscher – "Stalin had no master plan but a number of self-contradictory intentions". Regarding the entrance of Eastern European countries in the sphere of USSR influence, comments were also documented from American agent Robert Bishop, who issued precious information (over 600 messages) from Bucharest, gathered from Romanian Secret Services, see Anthony Cave Brown, Wild Bill Donavan. *The Last Hero*, Times Books, New York, 1982, p. 680. The idea of Sovietizing Hungary, Romania and Czechoslovakia is documented to appear in Lenin's work, in a letter addressed to Stalin in July 1920. See Richard Pipes (scientific editor), *The Unknown Lenin: From the Secret Archive*, Yale University Press, New Haven, London, 1996, p. 90.

21. Mihai Gramatopol very pertinently notice that "the Russians' wish to plunder was first of all based off the famine which continually ruled over them", because the Red Army, during the summer and autumn of 1944, only secured them their black bread. See Mihai Gramatopol, *Gustul eternității, vol. I*, Meridiane, Bucharest, Brașov, 2006, pp. 52–54. The 1946 famine in Moldavia was due "not only to a terrible regional drought, but most of all to the plundering of grain reserves by the occupants, constituting the first spoils of war for Russians", writes Gramatopol.

22. The model of terror through starvation had been applied in Ukraine between 1931 and 1933, with results beyond imagination, amassing approximately 6 million casualties. See Robert Conquest, *Recolta durerii. Colectivizarea sovietică și teroarea prin foamete*, Humanitas, București, 2003.

23. François Fejtö, Histoire des démocraties populaires, vol. I, L'ère de Staline: 1945–1952, Éditions du Seuil, Paris, 1952, pp. 145–146. The text of the law had "striking parallels" with that of the reforms performed on the German territories occupied by the soviets, see Henry L. Roberts, *Rumania...*, p. 298; Ghiță Ionescu, *Communism in Rumania*, 1944-1962, Oxford University Press, London, New York, Toronto, 1964, p. 111. The author speaks of "an universal plan for the entire region"; Stelian Tănase, *Elite și societate...*, pp. 86–96; Stephen K. Wegren, *Land Reform in Former Soviet Union and Eastern Europe*, Yale University Press, London and New Haven, 2009. A final synthesis for Romania is owed to Dumitru Șandru, *Reforma agrară din 1945 în România*, Editura Enciclopedică, București, 2000.

24. Moldavia had a similar situation in 1916-1917, when lice brought by Russians caused the break of a terrible epidemic of typhus, which targeted bodies weakened by famine and with poor immunity. An eye witness, the doctor Constantin Argetoianu, writes a horrifying description of the times: "Those who did not witness the state of the city of Iași in the winter and spring of year 1917 cannot even fathom to understand how things were. An entire book on the subject could not cover the suffering of a drained population, plagued by illness, which underwent such violence, as the world has never seen. The epidemic flared up with the coming of winter, and because nobody was prepared to face it, spread everywhere within a few days, like the plague ... Typhus was our real enemy; we fought it more than we fought the Germans – it killed three quarters of the 800,000 people – over 10% of the population of Romania in 1914 – people sacrificed in order to reunite our nation. It was a cruel and futile sacrifice which will certainly go down in history, and we can only hope that it will be seen as a dark lesson for future generations." See Constantin Argetoianu, *Pentru cei de mâine. Amintiri din vemea celor de ieri,* vol. 4 (1916–1917), ed. Stelian Neagoe, Humanitas, București, 1992, pp. 86–92.

25. Nicolas Penesco, *op. cit.,* p. 87; Dorin-Liviu Bîtfoi, *Așa s-a născut omul nou. În România anilor '50*, Editura Compania, București, 2012, p. 297.

26. Horrifying details coming from D.G.R. Serbanesco, Ciel rouge..., pp. 290–299. The author reproduces the discourse of General Secretary to the Ministry of Health, comrade Costăchel, during a meeting dedicated to taking action against typhus: "The louse is the enemy of the Revolution, as our great Lenin has previously said, in one of his works. Thus, this campaign in not a sanitary operation, it is a political campaign!" (p. 294). More recently, Dumitru Șandru, „*Seceta din 1945–1947 din România și consecințele ei asupra țărănimii*", in *Arhivele totalitarismului*, No. 14/1–2, 2006, pp. 39–58; Nicolae Ionescu, *Moldova în anii 1944–1947*, Polirom, Iași, 2005.

27. The 1947 famine also hit the inferior Volga region, Central Russia, Ukraine and Crimea. The causes were similar to Romania: the drought and the seizing of crops by soviet authorities. See Michel Heller and Aleksandr Nekritch, *L'utopie au pouvoir...*, p. 390. Vadim Guzun, *Imperiul foamei. Foametea artificială din URSS și impactul asupra spațiului românesc (1921–1922, 1931–1933, 1946–1947)*, Filos, Bucharest, 2014.

28. Henri Prost, *Destin de la Roumanie (1918–1954)*, Berger-Levrault, Paris, 1954, p. 203: "It is known that in Romania, a piece of land correctly farmed by an owner produces two or three times more in comparison to a similarly valued land exploited by a peasant." – translated from the original book.

29. The reform demonstrated very clearly that a piece of land under 3 hectares could not even feed the family who worked it. In 1948, lands under 3 hectares represented over half of the total, see Henry L. Roberts, *op. cit.*, pp. 292–299; Ghiţă Ionescu, *Communism in Rumania…*, pp. 111–112. Details pertaining to the manner in which the agrarian reform was performed, see Robert Bishop and E.S. Crayfield, *Russia Astride the Balkans*, Evans Brothers Limited, London, 1948, pp. 205–220 (including the assassinations of owners).

30. The same process took place in Hungary and in Bulgaria, which was not at war with the USSR. In 1947, "a sad joke [circulated] among simple and peaceful folk in Bulgaria, that their country was indeed the garden of Eden because everyone walked around naked and ate apples" (Hal Lehrman, *op. cit.*, pp. 273–274). The same things in other countries: "Russians knew that the only way to make Austria kneel was through economic strife. This was told to me by Chancellor Leopold Figl. (...) They offered us bread in exchange for the heart of our nation." (Hal Lehrman, *op. cit.*, p. 309).

31. The model was soviet, from June 1918, and came from Lenin, who would issue and order in December 1917, regarding the "necessity of distributing food rations by the principle of class". On the 27th of September 1918, *Pravda* published information by which "The People's Commissariat for Social Securitate confirms the need to forbid all bourgeois elements, both rural and urban, of their food rations. These would be then used towards raising the rations of the poor" (Michel Heller and Aleksandr Nekrich, *op. cit.*, pp. 52–53).

32. In November 1945, in the German territories under soviet occupation, six types of ration cards were introduced. See Hermann Weber, *op. cit.*, p. 74; the same in Bulgaria, see Vernon Bartlett, op. cit., p. 61. In Romania, six types of ration cards were also introduced.

33. Annie Bentoiu, *Timpul ce ni s-a dat*, vol. II, Editura Vitruviu, Bucharest, 2006, pp. 74–75. For details, see pp. 271–273; Dorin-Liviu Bîtfoi, *op. cit.*, pp. 297–306. The cards were discontinued on the 27th of December 1954, except for bread and sugar, see Ghiţă Ionescu, *Communism in Rumania, 1944–1962*,

p. 234; Ioan Lăcustă, *„Acum 50 de ani"*, in *Magazin istoric*, decembrie 2004, p. 74.

34. Ioana Gosman and others, „Despre Congresul Mondial al Tineretului și Festivalul Mondial al Tineretului și Studenților", in *Caietele Echinox*, No. 7, 2004, pp. 145–214.

35. Anne Bentoiu describes what a portion consisted of in the *Zorile* factory in Jilava, that made rubber: "The monthly subscription cost about a third of my salary. The menu was always the same: a vinegar soured soup, which was refused by most workers (their wives were waiting for them at home with a more consistent meal); after it came a 'stew', meaning an onion sauce with tomato paste in which small pieces meat had boiled with sinew, skin, bones, and along which potatoes, cabbage, pasta or 'rice splinters' were laid on the plate. The last course was a stew as well, made from rice crushed during deshelling and eliminated when the rice was sifted. This would contain some rice, but it had a lot of impurities with it, out of which most was birdseed. As for desert, it surfaced about two times a week and it came in the form of bad apples or moist pretzels which were highly appreciated. Anyway, this was my main meal." (Annie Bentoiu, *Timpul ce ni s-a dat*, vol. II, p. 271).

36. Dorin-Liviu Bîtfoi, *op. cit.*, p. 370. Actualy, the lack of food in Romania was chronic during the 50's, see information and party and state documents presented by Dorin-Liviu Bîtfoi, *op. cit.*, pp. 115–124. Same in Bulgaria, cf. Georgi Markov, *op. cit.*, p. 45.

37. For comparison, I shall add that, between 1926 and 1935, annual consumption of meat per capita was of 2.87 kilograms in rural areas (80% of the population), as to 52.159 kilograms in urban areas, see Ioan Claudian, *Alimentația poporului român*, Fundația pentru Literatură și Artă „Regele Carol al II-lea", București, 1939, p. 140.

38. Between 1926 and 1935, the annual consumption of sugar per family was, in rural areas, of 1.5-2 kilograms, see Ioan Claudian, *op. cit.*

39. *La Nation roumaine*, no. 35 from the 1st of January 1950, reproduced by D.G.R. Serbanesco, *op. cit.*, p. 229. Another source indicates slightly different numbers: 4.65 kg of meat, 40.92 kg of bread, 5.16 kg of sugar, according to Gheorghe Parusi, *Cronologia Bucureștilor*, 20.09.1459– 31.12.1989, Compania, Bucharest, 2007, p. 664. At the same time, the salaries of qualified

and unqualified workers ranged between 3,550 and 6,260 lei, and those of specialists were between 7,737 and 9,168 lei, whereas expenses for basic food and goods were od 6,970 lei per month, according to D.G.R. Serbanesco, *op. cit.*, p. 228.

40. "Agriculture has been communism's greatest failure" (see Ghiță Ionescu, *op. cit.*, p. 300). For Bulgaria, an agricultural country, see Georgi Markov, *op. cit.*, pp. 45–48.

41. During the same phase, a common saying circulated through Hungary, and was written down by an English journalist: "At first, they ate us up like wild beasts, but now they have begun to use cutlery!" (H. Lehrman, *op. cit.*, p. 227).

42. See Henri Prost, op. cit., p. 206: "On the 8th of May, the Ministry of Finances signed – the documents were never translated from Russian – several conventions regarding the delivery of various raw materials, especially cotton, and the creation of Soviet-Romanian mixed societies. These will be the Sovroms.".

43. The USSR created the Sovs, based on the same principles, in Hungary (Sovmagyar), Bulgaria and in Yugoslavia, see Nicolas Clarion, *Le Glacis soviétique, Somogy*, Paris, 1948; Fr. Fejtö, *op. cit.*, p. 154, pp. 435–437; Hal Lehrman, *op. cit.*, pp. 224–225; Gordon Shepherd, *Russia's Danubian Empire*, William Heinemann Ltd., Melbourne, London, Toronto, 1954, pp. 207–208. Polish communists refused this formula, see the considerations of Jakub Berman, published by Teresa Toranska, Oni. *Des Staliniens polonais s'expliquent, Flammarion*, Paris, 1986, p. 297. In soviet occupied Germany, soviet authorities nationalized industry in general, through the 31st of October 1945 reform. The greater part of heavy, light and extraction industries (over 200 factories having monopoly) was transformed in SAG (Sowjetische Aktiengesellschaften – stock based companies) see Hermann Weber, *op. cit.*, p. 91; Stefan Creuzberger, *Die Sowietische Militaradministration in Deutschland (SMAD), 1945–1949*, Melle, 1991; Volker Koop, Besetzt: *Sowjetische Besatzungspolitik in Deutschland*, Berlin, 2008. For Stalin's demands and the reality of "reparations" in eastern countries in general, see Anne Applebaum, *Iron Curtain. The Crushing of Eastern Europe, 1944-1956*, Doubleday, New York, 2012; French translation: *Rideau de Fer. L'Europe de l'Est écrasée, 1944–1956*, Paris, Grasset, 2014, pp. 78–83.

44. Ulrich Burger, *op. cit.*, pp. 204–206; Robert Bishop and E.S. Crayfield, *Russia astride the Balkans*, pp. 188–204 (chapter „The Sixth Column in Action"). After the Potsdam conference, Italian goods in Romania were added.

45. "Sovrombank was created through the merging of five Romanian banks, their German, Italian and Hungarian capital turning into its capital according to the Potsdam convention" (Hal Lehrman, *op. cit.*, p. 240).

46. To Sovrom Petrol, the Russians brought, as "former German goods", the petrol rich territories in Columbia, Concordia and others owned by French and Belgians and taken from Germans during the war. The soviets added some equipment consisting of bores and pipes, some plundered from Hungary, Austria and Germany, the rest of them being taken from American and British petrol fields from Romania. In accordance to communist ideas, not only did the government waive exploiting taxes for Sovrompetrol, but also ceded 75% of exploit rights belonging to the state and other companies. In February 1947, this raised the state's rights by 100%, adding the crude oil that the other companies paid as taxes. Sovrompetrol was privileged, receiving new prospects, while all the other companies were eliminated." (Hal Lehrman, op. cit., p. 240).

47. "Under Russian leadership, the company charged three times as much as western naval transporters and double as much as Russian companies. With Sovromtransport, the cost of shipping a Citroen from Marseille to Constanta cost as much as the car. One branch office functioned in Romania for almost all road transports." (Hal Lehrman, *op. cit.*, p. 240).

48. Explained for the first time by Radu Plessia, "Financial Policy", in his volume edited by Alexandre Cretzianu, *Captive Rumania. A Decade of Soviet Rule*, Praeger, New York, 1956, pp. 113–115.

49. The same happened in Hungary, see Gordon Shepherd, *op. cit.*, pp. 208–209.

50. Quoted from Fr. Fejtö, *op. cit.*, vol. II, Seuil, Paris, 1969, pp. 18–19; also see the study made by the CC of PMR in 1965, harshly criticizing the Sovrom, Stelian Tănase, *op. cit.*, p. 127; Florian Banu, *"Pași spre autonomia Republicii Populare Române. Desființarea sovromurilor"*, in Analele științifice ale Universității Al. I. Cuza din Iași, Istorie, Nr. 44–45, 1998–1999, pp. 133–150. The issue of compensating such extensive plundering was never addressed.

51. Here we have a soviet precedent, as was the case of the American ambassador Joseph Davies's wife, who was permitted to buy jewelry from a secret safe in

Moscow, see Douglas Smith, *Former People...*, p. 327. Also see the confessions of Simina Mezincescu according to which the wives of communist dignitaries had the right to buy "the seized jewelry, for next to nothing, from the National Bank", see Stelian Tănase, *Anatomia mistificării. 1944–1989*, Humanitas, Bucharest, 1997, p. 225.

52. Mihai Gramatopol, *Gustul eternității...*, vol. al II-lea, pp. 87–89. You can also find there information regarding the gold and silver items from accidental archaeological discoveries, deposited at the "office for precious metals" (a euphemism for the cesspool of country robbers), and bought *in extremis* by the Numismatic Cabinet of the Library of the Academy.

53. The soviet general Bersarin's order from the 4th of May 1945, in Georges Castellan, D.D.R., *Allemagne de l' Est, Seuil*, Paris, 1955, p. 30; Robert Bishop and E.S. Crayfield, *Russia astride the Balkans*, Evans Brothers Limited, London, 1949, p. 19.

54. The same happened in Bulgaria and Hungary: "The years 1945-1946 marked the total ruin of Magyar bourgeoisie" (Hal Lehrman, *op. cit.*, p. 176).

55. Henry L. Roberts, *Rumania...*, p. 317; Radu Plessia, *art. cit.*, p. 103.

56. Henri Prost, *op. cit.*, p. 207-208. The record on this matter was set by Hungary ("The most catastrophic inflation of modern times", Hall Lehrman, op. cit., p. 175), where the dollar had reached, on the 31st of July 1946, the value of 4,600,000 quadrillion pengo (a quadrillion is a number followed by 24 zeros), so 46 followed by 29 zeros! (P. Kenez, *Hungary from the Nazis to the Soviets. The Establishment of the Communist Regime in Hungary, 1944–1948*, Cambridge University Press, Cambridge, 2006, p. 125.) An English officer, member of the Allied Commission for Control in Austria, writes: "I remember that, during those times, housewives in Budapest went shopping with two baskets – one for all the groceries they could find, and the other to carry the billions upon billions of money representing the cost of daily sustenance. By the end of July, the sums that would have apparently previously bought a castle surrounded by a thousand hectares of land could now barely cover the cost of a tramway ticket" (Gordon Shepherd, *op. cit.*, p. 214, nota 1; Sandor Marai, *op.cit.*, p. 199).

57. Ghiță Ionescu, op. cit., pp. 136–139.

58. Henry L. Roberts, op. cit., pp. 315–316; Ghiță Ionescu, op. cit., p. 225.

59. The same soviet ideas were followed in the case of the "stabilization" in March 1947 in Bulgaria, tragi-comically described in detail by Hal Lehrman, op. cit., pp. 273–275.

60. Strife was generally present in all countries occupied by the Red Army, although it was not evenly distributed. In 1948, at the end of the Ministry of External Affairs Conference regarding Austria – which ended unsuccessfully – a functionary announced the exit of dignitaries by shouting: "[Call] the Rolls Royce of Mr. Bevin, the so called comrade Molotov, the Cadillac of General Marshall and … the shoes of Mr. Gruber (the Austrian Minister of External Affairs)!" (Sam Welles, *op. cit.*, p. 282).

61. Created in May 1945, the economy stores are mandatory for factories and must provide the salary earners, at official prices, with food and clothing. But the official prices are a sham, and factories must acquire goods by buying them on the black market, which brought ruin upon most of them, according to Henri Prost, *op. cit.*, p. 205.

62. Henri Prost, *op. cit.*, pp. 208–211; Costin C. Kirițescu, *Sistemul bănesc al leului și precursorii lui*, vol. III, Editura Academiei RSR, Bucharest, 1971, pp. 101–138. (the author considers that the reform had "positive" consequences, that it was "an innovation in the interests of the masses of working class citizens", which resulted in the disappearance of privately owned capital, and "a new distribution of national income between social classes", leading to "the abolishment of reselling tendencies").

63. Michel Heller and Aleksandr Nekrich*, op. cit.*, pp. 52–53.

64. Radu Plessia, *art. cit.*, pp. 106–107. The same discourse was held in the USSR, where the monetary reform was introduced at the end of the year 1947, according to Michel Heller and Aleksandr Nekrich, *op. cit.*, p. 386.

65. Idem, pp. 108–109.

66. René Théo, *La Roumanie sous la botte soviétique*, Editions B.I.R.E, Paris, 1952, pp. 14–15; D.G.R. Serbanesco, *Ciel rouge…*, pp. 167–173.

67. The model was, of course, soviet. Romanians had discovered it in Bessarabia and Northern Bucovina back when the Russians had occupied these territories (1940-1941).

68. Henri Prost*, op. cit.*, pp. 231–232.

69. Radu Plessia, *art. cit.*, p. 124.

70. Decree 83 was first published in *Scînteia* on the 14th of June 1949 and was reproduced by Annie Bentoiu, *op. cit.,* vol. II, pp. 170–173. Article 1 refers to spying, escaping the country and all manner of "conspiring" against the internal or external order of the state. Economic crimes are the subject of Article 2. Articles 4 and 5 condemn the accomplices of the aforementioned acts, in which we can find the crime of "not denouncing a plot", which strikes in all the family members of the accused, even the children (this was the case for Mihai D. Sturdza, arrested when he was 18 years old). We must also mention Decree 6, emitted on the 13th of January 1950, which set administrative punishment of up to 5 years. MAI and party representatives executed this procedure, inspired by the soviets. Sentences were usually forced labor in camps, see Annie Bentoiu, *op. cit.,* vol. II, pp. 313–314.

71. Robert Conquest considers that sabotage was "a frequent theme in soviet mythology" and "a political weapon" invoked by the famous prosecutor Vîşinski on the 26th of November 1936, in order to revise and worsen punishments (La *grande terreur...,* p. 553).

72. René Théo, *La Roumanie dans les griffes du communisme (Quatre ans de dictature rouge),* Chez l'auteur, Paris, 1949, pp. 36–37; examples in Dorin-Liviu Bîtfoi, *op. cit.,* pp. 65–66; for Bulgaria, see Georgi Markov, *op. cit.,* p. 48.

73. Numbers given by Dorin-Liviu Bîtfoi, op. cit., p. 40. Other authors speak of 15,000-17,000 families, numbers which are hard to believe. Nicoleta Gură-Ionescu gives us, following archived documents, 6,675 cases of "displacement" of former owners. („*Începutul colectivizării agriculturii în România*", in Revista Istorică, year 13, no. 5–6, 2002, pp. 41–68). A few accounts of the victims of these operations have been kept. The philosopher Constantin Rădulescu-Motru (born in 1866, he was 83 and had gone blind!) writes: "On the 2th of March 1949 I began my years as a beggar" (*Revizuiri şi adăugiri,* vol. VII, Floarea Darurilor, Bucharest, 2001, p. 50.; Stefan Fay, *Caietele unui fiu risipitor. Fragmente de jurnal,* Humanitas, Bucharest, 1994, p. 33; Annie Bentoiu, *op. cit.,* vol. 2, pp. 162–170.

74. The model was soviet, of course, as in the case of the entire code of law which struck the "enemies of class", see Douglas Smith, Former People..., pp. 271–272 (Decrees from March 1925, completed between January and August 1926).

75. In a similar manner, an entire nine story apartment building, inhabited by 50 families was evacuated, in order to move the offices of the newspaper *Scînteia* in the opposite building – where Pamfil Seicaru's newspaper *Curentul* had formerly been. The following is the account of philologist Mihai Gramatopol, a victim of this requisition: "In the absence of any nationalization law or disposition of requisitioning, all inhabitants are issued – through the guardian at the gate – the order of evacuating the building within 24 hours, without offering any housing in exchange. Seized by the confusion and fear caused by the abdication of the King, nobody even thought of asking about the 'legal' (how ironic!) grounds on which this evacuation was being performed. All people obediently conformed like lambs taken to the slaughterhouse, just as the victims of Hitler had been taken to the gas chamber. A decade later, we would find out that, after *Scînteia* had constructed its Stalinist manner palace near Herăstrău, the building we had lived in had been given back to the state and considered to be 'abandoned'." (Mihai Gramatopol, *Gustul eternității*, vol. I, 1940–1962, pp. 6–7).

76. A friend, Radu Otetelesanu, whose parents lived on 35 Aleea Alexandru, told me that they were taken outside by a woman commissary and two armed soldiers in less than one hour. His grandparents, who lived in a nearby house at no. 33, suffered the same fate, and their house became the headquarters of the Party Husbandry. In the rushed evacuation, only one of the houses was nationalized, while the other remained the propriety of the family – in name only – who was made to move into an apartment building in another neighborhood instead. There are more accounts of such evacuations, almost identical in nature, signed by Annie Bentoiu, Dorina Potârcă, Despina Skeletti-Budișteanu, Stefan Fay, Sanda Stolojan, who's family had to move in an old bakery, and others; Dorin-Liviu Bîtfoi, *op. cit.*, pp. 39–43; Radu R. Florescu and Matei Cazacu, *Draculas Bloodline. A Florescu Family Saga, Lanham*, Hamilton Books, 2013, pp. 211–212, 217. Also see Mihai Gramatopol, *Gustul eternității*, I, p. 123, for the evacuation of former landowners from their houses on the Driveway.

77. Writer Pericle Martinescu would write in this journal, on the 26-27th of August 1948: "A current problem: evacuations. The happy inhabitants of the Capital who live in the most beautiful, central, and comfortable apartment buildings

are now dealing with intense feelings of panic. Any day now, they risk being taken out of their houses and left on the streets. The great apartment buildings are being evacuated one by one: firstly – in the last weeks – the Dragomir building was evacuated (in order to house the Ministry of Internal Affairs); at present, the buildings around Cişmigiu Park are being evacuated, and rumor has it that Wilson building will be evacuated next. Last evening, I was passing by Wilson building when I overheard a fragment of conversation between two ladies who live in the building. 'I would prefer to go to the camps, over there they give you food, a roof over your head and you want for nothing' one of them would say regarding to the rumor that they are to be thrown in the street." (Pericle Martinescu, *7 ani cât 70. Pagini de jurnal (1948–1954)*, Bucureşti, 1997, p. 68). For examples from the Wilson building, see Victor Ieronim Stoichiţă, *Oublier Bucarest. Un récit, Actes Sud,* Paris, 2014, pp. 78–79.

78. This is regarding a law issued in 1948 which maintained very low fixed rent fees for apartments in Paris and other urban centers with the purpose of repopulating cities. These rents were set to remain constant throughout the tenant's entire life.

79. Henri Prost, *op. cit.,* pp. 237–239; Dorin-Liviu Bîtfoi, *op. cit.,* pp. 39–43, quotes Gheorghiu-Dej in his intervention during the 24th of February meeting of the CC Secretariat of PMR: those expropriated are to only take "their pillows, their blanket and their personal clothing".

80. See http://lege5.ro/Gratuit/geztcnrxgy/lista-imobilelor-naționalizate-din-20041950.

81. A law issued on the 17th of January 1949 classified all persons, of both sexes, with ages between 15 and 55, who could not present any evidence of employment by the state as being "vagabonds". According to calculations by specialists, Romania had approximately 2.5 million "vagabonds" and one million unemployed in all social categories, out of a total population of 17 million people. The law was reissued at the end of the 50's, when the crime was renamed as "parasitic living" and was punished with forced labor on construction sites. A similar law from 21st of July 1948 was passed in Bulgaria; see Vernon Bartlett, op. cit., p. 61. Also see the declaration of a Magyar worker turned unemployed in 1949: "Of course, I know that I own the state, and that's very nice. But I had never foreseen that I should give myself the sack!",

see Vernon Bartlett, *East of the Iron Curtain*, p. 96; cf. Anne Applebaum, *op. cit.*, pp. 557–568).

82. The idea also came from the USSR, where the exile and deportation of "formers" (*bâvșie liudi*) had taken proportions comparable with the vastness of the territory; see Douglas Smith, Former People, pp. 336–344.

83. On the 13th of January 1950, Decree 6 issued during the Grand National Meeting created the labor units for "the reeducation of the elements of the enemy", to which approximately 80,000 people were sent, according to Marius Oprea, *Banalitatea răului. O istorie a Securității în documente, 1949-1989*, Polirom, Iași, 2002; DorinLiviu Bîtfoi, *op. cit.*, pp. 85–90.

84. *Brașoave* in Romanian – lies, false statements, jokes

85. Henri Prost, *op. cit.*, p. 259; Nicoleta Ionescu-Gură, *Dimensiunea represiunii din România în regimul comunist. Dislocări de persoane și fixări de domiciliu obligatoriu*, Editura Corint, Bucharest, 2010, pp. 381–382, found a number of 72.239 people officially registered in this situation, although, in actuality, the author considers that their number amounts to several hundred thousand. Among the people thus deported was philosopher Constantin Noica, forced to settle in Câmpulung Muscel. He was alone, as his wife and children lived in England. However, a case known to me is that of Serban Oteteleșanu, who was over 60 years old and was also deported there, while his wife, the painter Otilia Oteteleșanu (born Mihail), who was "in the labor field", had continued to live in Bucharest, sharing an apartment with other tenants, because she had been thrown out of their house on Aleea Alexandru. See, along with the works cited above, the account of Dorinei Potârcă, *Amintirile unui „element dubios"*, Fundația Academia Civică, Bucharest, 2011.

86. Wordplay; in Romanian, Vin – wine

87. For other humorous moments in his life, see Mihai Gramatopol, *op. cit.*, vol. I, pp. 149–153 (the heroine of the story was actually Letiția Lăzărescu-Ionescu).

88. For other cases, see the accounts collected by Doina Tudorovici, *Amurgul nobililor*, Editura PRO, Bucharest, 1998.

89. Dorin-Liviu Bîtfoi, *op. cit.*, pp. 35–36.

90. Henri Prost, *op. cit.*, pp. 257–258; Radu Plessia, *art. cit.*, pp. 110– 113; Ghiță Ionescu, *op. cit.*, p. 203; Costin C. Kirițescu, *op. cit.*, pp. 261 268; Dorin-Liviu Bîtfoi, *op. cit.*, p. 356.

91. Wages received every fifteen days; from the French word *quinze, quinzaine,* meaning fifteen.

92. Pericle Martinescu*, op. cit.*, pp. 237–244.

93. Radu Plessia, art.cit., p.113.

94. His competence as an economist was non-existent, because he had no other studies apart from Sociology and had never in his life undergone any activity in commerce or production. More qualified than him was his Bulgarian homologue, who spoke about his competences to an American journalist in 1947: "Dobri Terpeşov, the jolly and party goer leader of Bulgaria's Committee of Economic Planning, presented his professional achievements thus: 'Firstly, I was a peasant paid for plowing the field with oxen, and this is how my official education began. Then I worked a small piece of land, where I learnt agriculture. Later, I opened a shop and I specialized in commercial studies. Finally, I set into motion a small factory of soda and lemonade, where I mastered all the problems of industry and economy'" (Hal Lehrman, *op. cit.*, p. 276).

95. Radu Plessia, *art. cit.*, pp. 113–115; Costin C. Kiriţescu*, op. cit.*, pp. 268–270. (The author concludes that the reform – the growth of gold reserves backing the leu currency – was determined by "the tendency manifested by other socialist countries [the USSR] to raise the exchange rates in question". In 1965, a study conducted by the CC of PMR reached the same conclusions, according to Stelian Tănase*, op. cit.*, p. 127).

96. For some (Maria Florescu Mavrocordat, nicknamed Marie Flo), who managed to find work (as a heater painter), see the extraordinary evocation of Silviei Colfescu, *Mătuşi fabuloase şi alte istorioare bucureştene*, Editura Vremea, Bucharest, 2013, pp. 15–22 (chapter „Prinţi şi vopsitori"); Dorin-Liviu Bîtfoi*, op. cit.*, pp. 305–306. And examples could continue: the ones in better physical condition would unload freight trains in Gara de Nord (Dinu Odobescu), others were time clerks on construction sites (Dinu C. Giurescu, Paul Cernovodeanu), some were walk-on actors in movies, others sold their blood, see the accounts of Stefan Fay, Annie Bentoiu, Ioana Berindei, Dinu C. Giurescu, Şerban Papacostea, Dorina Potârcă, Despina Skeletti-Budişteanu etc., in Doina Tudorovici, *Amurgul nobililor...*

97. Consignment

98. Pericle Martinescu, *op. cit.*, pp. 150–151; in volume *La Roumanie sous la botte soviétique*, pp. 17–18, René Théo describes a scene that took place in 1951 in front of a "Consignația" store: "An elderly lady … enters the store holding a porcelain object and exits promptly, tears in her eyes, exclaiming: 'Only 25 lei for a Sevres vase, they are mocking me! I'd rather smash it to pieces!'. Finishing her words, she tossed the vase on the pavement, where it shattered under the awestruck gaze of all the people lining up a long queue in front of the shop".

99. Flea market

100. The Romanians discovered it in the USSR, during the Eastern campaign. See the account of Dr. Demostene Gramatopol, in Zoltan Rostas, *op. cit.*, pp. 303, 306.

101. George Călinescu, Scrinul negru, Editura pentru Literatură, București, 1968, pp. 28–53, with a proper description of the talcioc.

102. Known antiquary from Bucharest, one of three brothers, all of them antiquaries. George Potra, Din Bucureștii de ieri, vol. II, Editura științifică și enciclopedică, București, kindly reproduces his portrait 1990, pp. 287–288.

103. Poet Eugen Jebeleanu was an enthusiastic collector of antiquities; see his very acid description written by Mihai Gramatopol, *op. cit.*, vol. I, pp. 185–186.

104. Pericle Martinescu, *op. cit.*, pp. 160–164; also see Dorin-Liviu Bîtfoi, *op. cit.*, pp. 306–308. A precise example in Victor Ieronim Stoichiță, *Oublier Bucarest*, pp. 109–118; Doina Tudorovici, *Amurgul nobililor*, pp. 167–173.

105. The old governing method in the Russian Empire, illustrated as early as 1839 by the Marquis of Custine: "In Russia, fear replaces, by means of paralyzing thought; this feeling, which dominates unchallenged, cannot produce anything but the shallow appearance of civilisation. … Fear will never represent the core of a well organized society; it is not order, it is a veil over chaos, and nothing more: in the absence of liberty, there is no soul and no truth to be found." (*La Russie en 1839*, ed. Pierre Nora, Paris, 1960, p. 180). Philosopher Edmund Burke (1729-1797) had also remarked "no passion does so radically deprive the spirit from its faculties of acting and rationing as does fear". American Journalist Hal Lehrman concluded that fear was the "engine" deeply rooted in the behaviour of soviet soldiers and officers, both in their relationships with westerners and among themselves, see H. Lehrman, *op. cit.*, pp. 299–300, 304.

106. Here is what Maxim Gorki wrote in *Pravda* and *Izvestia*, on the 15th of October 1930: "Opposing us, we have all who have lived their time, the time given to them by history, and this gives us the right to always consider ourselves as taking part in civil war. Thus we reach the natural conclusion: if the enemy does not surrender, we destroy him!" (Michel Heller and Aleksandr Nekrich, *op. cit.*, p. 194). For the USSR see Douglas Smith, *Former People. The last days of the Russian Aristocracy*, Pan Books, London, 2013.

107. Michel Heller and Aleksandr Nekritch, *op. cit.*, pp. 72–74.

108. Robert Conquest, *The Great Terror*, second edition, 1990, translated into French: *La Grande Terreur. Les purges staliniennes des années 30*, Robert Laffont, Paris, 1995; Timothy Snyder, *Bloodlands: Europe between Hitler and Stalin*, Bodley Head, London, 2010.

109. Members of this commission included representatives of England and the USA, lacking any rea authority in countries occupied by the Red Army. An American journalist characterized them as "monuments of concentrated frustration" (Hal Lehrman, *op. cit.*, p. 191).

110. Concentration camps for civilians were an invention of the Bolsheviks in Russia, the orders regarding their creation and population date back from between the 4th and 26th of June 1918 (Troțki), the 9th of August 1918 (Lenin) and the 5th of September 1918, when Sovnarkom (The soviet of the People's Commissaries), the soviet government, emitted an official resolution regarding the matter (Michel Heller and Aleksandr Nekrich, *op. cit.*, pp. 54–55). In 1918, 56 camps existed with 24,000 prisoners, and in 1919 the newly created work camps for women and men were functioning with 60,000 prisoners. It was the creation of the Gulag which preceded the Nazi concentration system by two decades, and which had long surpassed it in terms of the number of victims. Some historians searched for the origin of these camps in the American Civil War, in Cuba, under Spanish domination in 1890 and in South Africa, in the time of the war with the Burs. All the aforementioned documents referred to internment camps that were disbanded after the war, whereas the Gulag still exists today (see the memories of the Russian billionaire Hodorkovski and the protesters from the band *Pussy Riot*).

111. Numbers taken from Ilie Schipor, *"Pagini dramatice din istoria României: prizonierii de război, persoanele deportate, persoanele condamnate de către tribunalele*

sovietice și emigranții politici din Uniunea Sovietică", in In memoriam Acad. Florin Constantiniu, Bucharest, Editura Enciclopedică, 2013, pp. 573–594.

112. This is how composer Antonin Ciolan was arrested, considered to be a war criminal because he had been the director of the Odessa Opera House, similarly to theater director Aurel Ion Maican, the director of the Odessa National Theater! The former was freed after the pleas of his former colleagues and Russian subordinates.

113. Camp described by Barbu Niculescu, the former secretary of General Rădescu, in the book written by Reuben H. Markham, *op. cit.*, pp. 436–438, especially about the subordination of Romanian police to the NKVD who, in concentration camps, would "forsake any subterfuge and came directly among the prisoners, to abuse them and threaten them with deportation". Also see Onisifor Ghibu, *Zile de lagăr: Caracal–1945*, Editura Albatros, Bucharest, 1991.

114. See Dumitru Șandru, *"Comisia Aliată (sovietică) de Control și regimul de detenție din România"*, in Analele Sighet, No. 1, 1994, pp. 61–85; idem, *Comunizarea societății românești în anii 1944-1947*, Editura Enciclopedică, Bucharest, 2007, pp. 224–242, chapter „Implicarea Comisiei Aliate (Sovietice) de Control și arestările din România în primii ani de după constituirea ei". In the future RDG, soviet authorities managed to intern within 13 camps (many of which were already functioning during the Nazi period, such as Buchenwald and Sachsenhausen) between 160,000 and 260,000 people, out of which between 65,000 and 80,000 died, resulting in approximately half of the total prisoners, see Hermann Weber, *op. cit.*, pp. 84–86. For camps in Bulgaria, see Hal Lehrman, *op. cit.*, p. 269, which describes tortures applied here and which are described by survivors: "I was put in touch with enough survivors to establish the fact that Gestapo techniques were much admired by the camp faculties with new refinements such as 'the telephone conversation with Churchill' (holding an electrified receiver in each hand for fifteen minutes) or 'the trip to New York' (squatting in a tub of cold water for three days)". To which moral tortures were added, see Georgi Markov, *The Truth That Killed*, Weidenfeld and Nicolson, London, 1983.

115. Works on this subject that have appeared previously, especially prior to 1989, are vast and varied. For a general overview, see Dennis Deletant,

Teroarea comunistă în România. GheorghiuDej și statul polițienesc, 1948-1965, Polirom, Iași, 2002. For concentration camps and prisons, I shall quote one single synthesis which contains all the bibliography crucial in the matter: Andrei Muraru (coord*.), Dicționarul penitenciarelor din România comunistă (1945-1967)*, Polirom, Bucharest, Iași, 2008.

116. Marius Oprea, *Banalitatea răului*, pp. 255–256; reproduced by Dinu C. Giurescu (coord.), *in Istoria României în date*, Editura Enciclopedică, Bucharest, 2003, pp. 530–531. For the fundamental role of "class hatred" as a psychological support, see the extraordinary account of Bulgarian journalist Gheorghi Markov, assassinated in London by the KGB with the famous "Bulgarian umbrella", *The Truth That Killed*, Weidenfeld & Nicolson, London, 1983, p. 16; reproduced by Keith Lowe, *op. cit.*, p. 403. The model was of course, soviet; see articles from *Komsomolskaia Pravda*, no. 191 from the 28th of August 1935, signed by Maxim Gorki and Ilya Ehrenburg on learning class hatred (Douglas Smith, *Former People*, p. 325).

117. An incomplete list of series of people arrested and prosecuted during these years in Cicerone Ionițoiu, *Memorii. Din țara sârmelor ghimpate*, Polirom, Iași, 2009, pp. 112–113.

118. An operation found in all Eastern countries which started through the creation of SED (Sozialistische Einheitspartei Deutschlands) in 1946, by means of force and oppression (and even assassinations) on territories occupied by the soviets, see Hermann Weber, *op. cit.,* pp. 93, 106.

119. Quote by Boris Bajanov, *Bajanov révèle Staline. Souvenirs d'un ancien secrétaire de Staline*, Gallimard, Paris, 1979, p. 20.

120. In the beginning, in 1945, the legionaries were advised to enter PCR, which needed for their physical confrontations with the bourgeoisie; it was a decision inspired by the soviets, because similar operations were performed in Hungary as well, where the members of the "Arrowed Crosses" fascist party adhered to communism *en masse*. Documents have been kept to prove their adherence, and communist leaders such as Matyas Rakosi stated that the fascists were "good" boys that had lost their way, and that it was simpler to enlist 600,000 people into the party than to stuff them into prisons, according to Hal Lehrman, *op. cit., pp.* 186–187.

121. Cicerone Ionițoiu, *Rezistența anticomunistă din munții României 1946-1958*, Editura Gândirea românească, Bucharest, 1993.

122. The freemasons were abolished in 1948. See an example of questioning done to freemasons in D.G.R. Serbanesco, *op. cit.*, p. 259; for Poland, see Anne Applebaum, *op. cit.*, pp. 381–385.

123. They were arrested in the second half of the year 1950, see the memoirs of Rabi David Safran and the account of Dr. Th. Lavi, *Nu a fost pisica neagră (Amintirile unui asir țion din România),* Editura Bronfman, Tel Aviv. In December, other 13 Zionist leaders were arrested, see A.L. Zissu, *Sioniști sub anchetă. Declarații, confruntări, interogatorii. 10 mai 1951–1 martie 1952,* Edart–FFP, București, 1993. Another trial took place in November 1959, when 200 people, all of them Jewish, functionaries of the Ministry of External Commerce, were accused of Zionism, stock trafficking, the spread of fake news, attempts at endangering state Securitate, and other such crimes. Among them was Mr. Andrei Csendes, high functionary and the father of our colleague, Ivan Csendes.

124. They were arrested and held without due process 5-6 years in Sighet, see C. Giurescu, "*Cinci ani și două luni în penitenciarul de la Sighet*", in Amintiri, editor Dinu C. Giurescu, Editura ALL, Bucharest, 2000, pp. 333–469, and the list of deceased persons annexed within.

125. See *Procesul unui grup de spioni, trădători și compLotiști în slujba Vaticanului și a centrului de spionaj italian – București,* the 10–17th of September 1951, Bucharest, 1952.

126. Numbers given by Nicolae Ceaușescu in Stelian Tănase, *Elite și societate…*, p. 69.

127. Marius Oprea, *Adevărata călătorie a lui Zahei. V. Voiculescu și taina Rugului Aprins*, Humanitas, Bucharest, 2008. Party militants were informed that the members of this group, who would hold meetings in Antim Monastery in Bucharest in order to discuss philosophy and theology, were actually American spies who would hide their messages within a crucifix in the church! Comrade Nicolau, the geography teacher and head mistress of my class, had the lack of prudence (the insolence?) of repeating this nonsense in our class in front of my father – for the first and the last time of my life, I saw him absolutely beside himself with rage and protesting against such outlandish claims.

128. Decree issued on the 3rd of June 1950, see Pericle Martinescu, op. cit., p. 149: "After the registration of typewriters with the Police, after the deposition that the owner of a typewriter – be it an institution or a private person – could only buy supplies for it with a special authorisation from the Police…" The law was passed again in 1959, and for the last time in 1983. In RDG, in 1950, "in order to buy colors and paints, artists needed to have a fiscal number issued by the Artists' Union and a member card confirming this number." (Anne Applebaum, op. cit., p. 432).

129. For additional details, see Stelian Tănase, *Anatomia mistificării…*

130. For this case, see the article of Şerban Rădulescu-Zoner, "*Procesul bibliotecilor engleză şi americană*", in Analele Sighet, No. 7, Fundaţia Civică, Bucharest, 1997, pp. 321–336; Dennis Deletant, "*Condemned but not Forgotten: the Fate of pro-British Activists in Romania, 1945–1964*", in Istoria: utopie, amintire şi proiect de viitor. Studii de istorie oferite profesorului Andrei Pippidi la împlinirea a 65 de ani, Universitatea „A.I. Cuza", Iaşi, 2013, pp. 458–473; Douglas Dunham, *Zone of violence*, Belmont Books, New York, 1962 and the memoirs of Annie Samuelli, *The Wall Between*, Robert B. Luce, London, 1967.

131. Micaela Ghiţescu, „*Am făcut parte din «lotul francez»*", in Memoria, No. 7, 1992, pp. 36–42; the confession of academy member Şerban Papacostea in Gazeta facultăţii de Istorie, I/4, iunie 2006, pp. 1–4; Gavin Bowd, *La France et la Roumanie communiste*, L'Harmattan, Paris, 2008, pp. 109–125.

132. See Dorina Potârcă, *Amintirile unui „element dubios"*, Fundaţia Academia Civică, Bucharest, 2011, p. 6: "On the night between the 14th and the 15th of April 1952, 50 people were arrested (other sources mention one hundred people), members of the families of former dignitaries, accused of being 'dubious elements'(decisions 533/1952). For these persons, Decree 6 of the 14th of January 1950 and HCM 1554 of the 22nd of August 1952 had been issued, ordering the creation of units (colonies, battalions, mandatory establishments) of labor for 'those who by their deeds or behaviour, directly or indirectly, endanger or seek to endanger the regime of popular democracy'. Ioana Berindei was thrown in the same category when she was arrested on the 29th of July 1950, for being the daughter of University professor Ion Hudiţă, leading man in PNT, arrested back in October 1947. Consequently,

the professor's three brothers and one sister were arrested, followed by
Ioana's father in law and mother in law – Alexandru and Dina Balş – and,
finally, the professor's wife, and mother of Ioana." See Lavinia Betea, *Am
făcut Jilava în pantofi de vară. Convorbiri cu Ioana Berindei*, Compania,
Bucharest, 2006, pp. 117–124.

133. Lăcrămioara Stoenescu, *Copiii-duşmani ai poporului,* Editura Curtea Veche,
Bucharest, 2007; Ion Varlam, *Pseudoromânia. Conspirarea deconspirării.
Interviuri cu Liviu Vălenaş*, Editura VOG, f.l., 2004, pp. 15–23; Oana
Orlea, Cantacuzino, *ia-ţi boarfele şi mişcă*, Interview by Mariana Mihai,
Editura Compania, Bucharest, 2008.

134. *B.I.R.E. (Buletin informativ al românilor din exil)*, Paris, 1978, p. 29.

135. For example, see the declaration of Noica's prosecutor from 1960: "I chose
people, not deeds!" (Stelian Tănase, *Anatomia mistificării*, p. 326).

136. *Comisia Prezidenţială pentru Analiza Dictaturii Comuniste din România,
Raport final*, Humanitas, Bucharest, 2006, p. 634; Marius Oprea, *Chipul
morţii: dialog cu Vladimir Bukovski despre natura comunismului*, Polirom,
Iaşi, 2006, p. 84, amounts to the number of 651,087 victims registered
as such in documents, not taking into account victims who's papers were
destroyed or were simply not registered in any.

137. Keith Lowe, *op. cit.*, p. 374; Stelian Tănase, *Elite şi societate...*, p. 69 (in
Czechoslovakia, in 1952, 100,000 people had been arrested and sentenced).

138. Tony Sharp, *Stalin's American Spy*, Hurst & Company, Londres, 2014, p. 255.

139. Dutch diplomat

140. Smaranda Vultur, *Istorie trăită – istorie povestită. Deportarea în Bărăgan
(1951–1956)*, Editura Amarcord, Timişoara, 1997.

141. Stelian Tănase, Elite şi societate, pp. 68–69; Nicoleta IonescuGură, op. cit.
See the case of historian C.C. Giurescu and other former prisoners from
Sighet, during 1955-1956, as the case of Paul Goma and other students
arrested after the Hungarian Revolution in 1956.

142. See the account of Dorinei Potârcă, *Amintirile unui „element dubios"* and
the work of Ioana Berindei, *op. cit.*

143. This was also the case, as with many others, for composer Pascal Bentoiu,
guilty of having had a lawyer and a liberal politician as a father, and, closer
to our times, the case of Radu Oteteleşanu, recruited in the army in 1972,

sent home on account of bad social origins and recalled an year later in such an unit. This happened although working units had been officially disbanded back in 1954, according to Stelian Tănase, *Elite și societate*, p. 122. During Ceaușescu's era, the whole Romanian army, as was the case once with the Roman army, was one huge labor unt on the construction sites of the motherland.

144. Stelian Tănase, op. cit., pp. 68–69.
145. A few examples in D.G.R. Serbanesco, op. cit., p. 265.
146. Hermann Weber and Ulrich Mählert (coordinator), *Terror. Stalinistische Parteisäuberungen, 1936–1953*, Paderborn, 1998; Hermann Weber, *Geschichte der DDR*, p. 33, in which other characteristics particular to this movement were also described: the evolution of parties in the Stalinist epoch progressed in reverse compared to modern organizations, more precisely the direction of "orders" (military or religious) hypercentralized and structured in a military fashion; disciplined functionaries outwardly displayed attitudes of courage and certitude towards others opposing their views or towards adversaries, going as far as making the ultimate sacrifice. Inwardly, however, inside the party, they behaved as humble subjects and were the perfect receptacles of orders issued by superiors. Communist parties copied the soviet model after 1945 and adored Stalin as an idol (in what was named as "personality cult"). Also see the affirmations made by a Czcchoslovakian citizen in a restaurant in Prague in 1949 and written down by an American journalist: "There never was another party in which so many of its members were also its bitter enemies" (Vernon Bartlett, *East of the Iron Curtain*, p. 123).
147. Keith Lowe, *op. cit.*, pp. 310–329; p. 150 for other countries; for Hungary, see Sandor Marai, *op. cit.*, p. 217.
148. Ghiță Ionescu, *Communism in Rumania, 1944–1962,* pp. 131–132; D.G.R. Serbanesco, *Ciel rouge...,* pp. 83–84, 120–121. In 1946, Emil Bodnăraș and a group of technicians who came from Moscow organized a school for officials in Târgoviște in order to secure the victory in upcoming elections. Politicial assassinations are planned here – about 1 or 2 in every county capital city (Șerban Milcoveanu, *Memorii (1929– 1989), Pământ,* București–Pitești, 2008, p. 501). Today, Marius Oprea is the historian who most

closely follows this phenomenon in Romania. In Yugoslavia, Tito killed over 250,000 people in mass massacres, death marches and concentration camps, solely in the period between 1945 and 1946 (Noel Malcolm, *Bosnia. A Short History,* Macmillan, London, 1994, p. 193). For political violence, see Timothy Snyder, *Sketches from a Secret War*, Yale University Press, New Haven and London, 2007, p. 210.

149. See the account of Cicerone Ionițoiu, *Memorii*, p. 187 (autumn 1954); Dorin-Liviu Bîtfoi, *op. cit.,* p. 431. Ionițoiu comments: "It was like we were in the time of Alimănescu, in 1945-1946, when peope were shot, especially near Floreasca … only now it was in the middle of Bucharest, in front of a shop window, and the person had no shoelaces, and 'thus was a convict'".

150. Mihai Pelin, *Opisul emigrației politice. Destine în 1222 de fișe alcătuite pe baza dosarelor din arhivele Securității,* Compania, Bucharest, 2002; Florin Manolescu, *Enciclopedia exilului literar românesc, 1945-1989,* Compania, Bucharest, second edition, 2010; for Hungary, Sandor Marai, *op. cit.,* p. 238.

151. Alia (or *aliyah*) – the emigration of Jewish people from the Diaspora into Israel.

152. Radu Ioanid, *Răscumpărarea evreilor. Istoria acordurilor secrete dintre România și Israel*, Polirom, Iași, 2005.

153. I have studied this issue in article *"Les Juifs de Roumanie au XXe siècle"*, in the Historical Yearbook, No. VI, 2009, pp. 137–160, especially p. 157. Also see Ghiță Ionescu, *op. cit.,* pp. 183–184; Gabriele Eschenazi and Gabriele Nissim, *Ebrei invisibili. I sopravissuti dell'Europa orientale dal comunismo a oggi*, Arnoldo Mondadori Editrice, Milano, 1995; Hildrun Glass, *Minderheit zwischen zwei Diktaturen. Zur Geschichte der Juden in Rumänien, 1944–1949*, R. Oldenbourg, München, 2002.

154. Matei Cazacu, art. cit., p. 158. Also see the episode told by Rabi Moses Rosen (*Primejdii, încercări, miracole. Povestea vieții șef rabinului Dr. Moses Rosen*, Hasefer, Bucharest, 1991) about the conversation with prime minister Ion Gheorghe Maurer on this subject and the parable of the Rabi and the fish enthusiasts; Ion Mihai Pacepa, *Red Horizons. Chronicles of a Communist Spy Chief,* Regnery Gateway, Washington D.C., 1987, p. 72.

CHAPTER 3

The Communists in Power

———

AT THE TIME WHEN STALIN was presenting Tito with the sovietisation politics for countries occupied by the Red Army, Romania had a "largely concentrated democratic" government, imposed on King Mihai through audacious
pressures made by Molotov's adjunct, Andrei Ianuarevici Vîşinski, a former
now reformed Menshevik who had made a name for himself through the
brutality of his conduit as prosecuting attorney during the times of the great
political trials in Moscow between 1936 and 1938, when Stalin eliminated
the old communist guard on account of fantastic accusations[1]. The Prime
Minister – back then it was called the President of the Council of Ministers –
was Petru Groza, an old fellow traveller of the communists, former minister in the Averescu government, alongside Octavian Goga. Groza was the
president of the Ploughmen's Front, a civil organisation that was active only
in areas surrounding Deva County, the place of origin of its leader, and
had managed to name friends of his and even his former coachman (the
ineffable Romulus Zăroni)[2] as ministers. The other ministers belonged to
different organizations of the Front, manipulated by communists that hid
under the label of the National Democratic Front, the liberals of Gheorghe
Tătărescu and finally the communists lead by Gheorghe Gheorghiu-Dej,
Lucreţiu Pătrăşcanu and Teohari Georgescu[3].

The instatement of this government on the 6th of March 1945 was considered to be an historical act that laid the foundation for a new historical
era[4]. Several years ago, I have published an article in which I demonstrated,
I think, that the end of the old regime in Romania did not take place back
then – it happened on the 21st of August 1945, when Petru Groza refuses

King Mihai's request of resignation[5]. Through this action, the president of the Council of Ministers tore down the constitutional pact – more precisely, Act 88 of the 1923 Constitution[6]. This was, in my opinion, the real breaking point; and I have found an indirect confirmation of this from a moment in the history of the USA that is seldom discussed – the retirement of President John Adams when his first term ended in 1801 and when he lost the race by which he had hoped to obtain a second term[7].

No matter where the truth lies, what happened then was the beginning of an entirely novel experience for the vast majority of Romanians. And where was the novelty, the originality of our experience? I will resume myself to the phrase "utopia in power", used by two historians to describe the history of the USSR. The Marxist-Leninist utopia produced a form of government based on, in theory, the dictatorship of the proletariat, the dictatorship of workers whose only fortune were their children (the Latin word for children, *proles* – from whence the name). But the proletariat was a minority class in 1917 Russia (1% of the population) as it was in Romania in 1945 (under 3% of the total population) and thus was incapable of effectively taking part in this dictatorship. That is why its avant-garde, as the communist party self-identified itself as, is summoned forth to exercise the power in its stead. For Lenin, dictatorship is too much of a serious business to be put into the hands of the proletariat[8]. In conclusion, the dictatorship of the proletariat is a system that rejects parliamentary power, the separation of legislative and executive powers, and is a fusion between legislation and administration: "The scientific definition of dictatorship is a power that is not limited by any law, or bridled by any rule and that directly supports itself on coercion… When we are accused of exercising the dictatorship of a party, we say 'Yes, the dictatorship of a party! We adhere to this and cannot renounce it'. It was Lenin as well who said that he despises and rejects the bourgeois concept of 'the will of the majority': 'What is important, he said, is to be the stronger force, to rise above all others at the right time, in the right place.' "[9]

Beginning with 1920, after the failure of communist revolutions in Central and Western Europe, "the Russian Communist Party was nothing more than a small number of individuals. Its members thought then that they did not really represent the existing Russian proletariat as much as they represented the future and its actual interests. They did not draw their justification from actuality, but rather from a prophetic vision. The source of their loyalty and solidarity sprung from themselves and the ideas brought forth by their leaders." (Robert Conquest).

The Bolsheviks thus became "coercive utopists", the descendants of those from the 18th Century, who carried on, as Vladimir Bukovski says, "a war fought for two centuries against the individual, his rights, his dignity and his sovereignty, by the power thirsty elite, *the coercive utopists*"[10]. Their motto was: "If you don't know how, we will teach you. If you can't, we will help you. If you don't want to, we will make you!"

From the moment in which the utopia was brought to power, began the immense contradiction between ideology[11] and modernization, between the ideal of a society without classes and the stratification of society that is the inevitable result of modernization. All the persecutions and massacres initiated by Lenin, Stalin and their imitators in Eastern countries were futile, because the material reality, as Marx had already concluded, is stronger than the ideological structure layered over it. The result was the failure of the utopia that was defeated by the necessities of modernization it practically imposed on itself[12]. But let us not get ahead of ourselves and return to the year 1945.

This is the more profound meaning of the Bolshevik revolution that was transplanted into Romania and the other Eastern European country through the brutal force of the Red Army and the political police (NKVD, MVD, KGB) led by Beria and his successors. The revolution would come after four years of legionary, followed by military dictatorship under Marshal Antonescu (1940-1944), which had replaced the dictatorship of King Carol the Second (1938-1940). In fact, from 1919 on, Great Romania had lived, with the exception of a few years, under the regime of siege due to the nearby Soviet Union, "The Evil Empire" to which it had declared war in 1918 (the year Bessarabia joined the motherland) and which constantly threatened Romania by various means: the infiltration of secret agents, terror and terrorist attacks such as the one that happened at the Senate in 1920, the spreading of manifestos, incidents at the frontier, sabotage, and the Tatar

Bunar revolt (1924) which was meant to be the prelude to a full military intervention[13]. This also explains the outlawing of the Communist Party in Romania - the Romanian section of the Third International (Comintern) with its headquarters in Moscow[14]. Adopting the views in Kremlin (the true leader of the Comintern), the communists considered Romania to be an "imperialistic" state, an artificial construct formed by occupying "foreign" territories such as Transylvania, Bessarabia, Bucovina and Dobrogea, which should have gone back to their former masters or become independent[15]. It thus comes as no surprise that they were persecuted, arrested and prosecuted in military courts which judged and severely punished hostile propaganda that threatened the unity of the state. Romania was, along with Poland and the Baltic countries a sanitary barrier that prevented Soviet expansion in Europe. These countries not only confronted Moscow propaganda, but had also felt Bolshevik violence: in 1919, Romania was attacked in Transylvania by communist Hungary, ruled by Bela Kun, which threatened to ally with the Bolsheviks from Ukraine and Bessarabia. Romanian troops had occupied Budapest following a successful campaign that was also revenge for the humiliation and plundering endured during occupation by the Central Powers in 1916 to 1918. Poland had declared independence and had been attacked by the Red Army, which it managed to stop, at the price of an immense effort, in what is known as "the miracle from Vistula" (1920).

It was just the beginning. Because they were direct neighbors of Soviet Russia, Romanians had sheltered thousands of refugees that had escaped the land of communism and would tell stories that made your hair stand: midnight arrests, mass executions, generalized misery and omnipresent terror, the transformation of 4 million people in *lishentsy*, people without rights, non-existent persons, who only had the right to die of starvation, the concentration camps up in the Gulag Archipelago, in Siberia and the Polar region[16]. And finally, they told of the common daily life with indescribable restrictions, the apartments crowded by entire families thrown out of their own homes, the atmosphere of constant fear that froze the mind (this was a constant state of affairs in Russia remarked by Marquis Custine as far back as 1839). Next came the Romanian and Ukrainian peasants that crossed the Nistru River in 1931-1933 due to the famine produced by the forceful collectivization of agriculture (6 million victims according to specialists), escapees hunted down like animals on the frozen Nistru River by Soviet border patrols[17]. Their accounts shocked Romanians, yet most of them could not believe such terrible atrocities were possible, and thought that the "Slav spirit" tends to exaggerate and fantasize.

From 1929, the voice of a great Romanian writer would join the accounts of the refugees – Panait Istrati. Enthusiastic communist who had lost all his illusions following a trip to the USSR, Istrati published the book *Vers l'autre flame*, written in collaboration with Boris Souvarine, another ex-communist, in which they accused Stalin's dictatorship of terrible crimes. A few years later, Andre Gide also published his impressions following his visit to the USSR, adding to the long list of accounts of the gulags and Bolshevik terror that had begun to surface in 1918-1919. Under these circumstances, even if they did not fully believe the horrors the survivors spoke of, Romanians were far from believing the illusions of the soviet regime and rejected any communist propaganda: intellectuals could not conceive the absence of freedom of thought and speech, the peasants were profoundly individualistic and rejected the idea of collectivization, the bourgeoisie and the landowners were not too enthusiastic of a regime that directly targeted them, and workers, the most prone to be seduced by communist discourse, were not very excited of a regime that proclaimed them to be the rulers of society but would in reality treat them like slaves. The majority of people who joined the communist movement were members of ethnic minorities who did not adhere to the idea of the Romanian Nation State, especially Hungarian industrial workers, Ukrainian and Russians, Jewish workers and intellectuals, frightened by the rise of antisemitism in Europe but there were also Romanians among them, the adversaries of Nazism and fascism that exalted the race and nation, contrasting with the "internationalism" of the 1917 Russian Revolution.

The account of a leading legionary, Nistor Chioreanu, published in Iași, 1992 (*Morminte vii*), includes a very important detail about this situation. In 1948, Chioreanu was arrested along with other 5,000 legionaries and sympathizers of the Legionary Movement; he was prosecuted and sentenced to many years in prison[18]. After some time, he was brought to Bucharest for further inquiries pertaining to some other affairs and he offered important information, to the satisfaction of Inquiries Department of the Secret Services and its boss, Colonel (and later General) Mişu Dulgheru. Taking advantage of the Colonel's good disposition, Chioreanu was bold enough to ask the feared inquirer: "Colonel, sir, please tell me honestly, why do you hate us so much? Generally, you show us unbridled hate, although we did not do anything to you. All in all, we legionaries didn't fight communists that much. We fought the rich bourgeoisie in this country more than we fought you. And during the times when we were locked into battle with the bourgeois, you didn't even exist in this country, or, in any case, you were so very few. What have we done to you? Why do you hate us so much?" Dulgheru replied with a somber and menacing voice that they have eliminated all "historical" parties and let them die a good death, but that they will never forgive the legionaries because they seduced and took the youth and the workers from them, the communists: "You see, Mr. Chioreanu, that is precisely the greatest sin of the legionaries. There were so very few of us because you took the youth and the workers away from us. And both these forces should have been ours. For this, we shall never forgive you. The bourgeois parties will die of inanition; we occasionally help them along to quicken their demise. As for the legionaries, we will have to destroy them and compromise their very virtues. And we will destroy them and their reputation in such a way, that history will have no choice but remember them with horror."[19] He could have added that the peasantry had also been won over by the legionaries, who spoke especially against the Parliament and corrupt politicians who, from their point of view, protected the Jewish people and other enemies to the nation. Religion was, of course, another important issue: communists professed their militant atheism and the USSR had destroyed the Orthodox Church and all other cults against which it had lead a fierce battle on all fronts, from publications and anti-religious museums, the closing of churches and monasteries turned into warehouses, cinemas or cultural centers, to arrests, convictions, deportations and the assassination of bishops, priests and monks. In contrast, one of the main characteristics of legionary movement was orthodoxy, the fanatic practice of religion (and at the same time, the death cult), which attracted sympathies with the peasantries, the absolute majority of Romanian population (78% in 1948) – as well as other social groups (the unemployed intellectuals and the lumpenproletariat). Finally, the Jewish people with revolutionary ideas who would thus distance themselves from family tradition – a phenomenon common in all European countries, often adopted atheism[20].

Diplomatic relations between Romania and the USSR were reestablished in 1934, but communist subversion did not cease even after this date – the trials against the communists in 1935 and 1936 stand as evidence for this claim. In 1940, Stalin practically declared war against Romania, forcing it, under armed threat, to give up Bessarabia and Northern Bucovina (also the Herța territory, occupied by accident). The Comintern plan of disbanding Great Romania was thus created and carried on in the same year by the other neighboring countries, Hungary and Bulgaria[21]. Romania followed the order, and waited for an opportunity for revenge to arise; it came in 1941. During the war on the Eastern front, Romanian soldiers, most of them peasants, saw the communist paradise and the miserable state in which the rural population lived, forced to work in collective farms like slaves on plantations: Mitrea Cocor, Mihail Sadoveanu's hero was a very atypical hero, a purely ideological creation. That is the reason why, in 1945, the majority of Romanians dreamed of the democratic regime promised to all by the Western Allies, an idea backed by Stalin as well, who told Romanians they needed to "become democratic" without delay, unless they want to endure the dire consequences. An English soldier, contemporary to the events, concluded thus: after the 23rd of August 1944 event, and especially after the 6th of March 1945, in Bucharest, the word "democrat" described anyone who agreed with the regime instated by the Soviets and "fascist" meant anyone who sympathized with Great Britain, with the United States of America or with parliamentary democracy[22]. Romanians were about to find out what Soviets meant by "democracy"[23]

The majority of Romanians thought that constitutional monarchy and parliamentary democracy based on the 1923 Constitution, reestablished after the 23rd of August 1944, could be the answer to the imperatives of the time, freedom, and democracy: the separation of state powers, free elections, the freedom of the press, freedom of speech, of manifestation and organization, the respect for private property, and friendly relations with Western Allies and the USSR. The legislative activity of governments lead by Sănătescu and Rădescu between the 24th of August 1944 and February 1945 was heading in that direction. But were those hopes compatible with the real situation of Romania during those times? They were not, because once in power, the communists were reluctant to step down (George Orwell wrote that for them "power is not a means, it is a purpose") and used all available resources to discredit and then eliminate, in a political and sometimes even physical way, all their adversaries and even some of their partners[24]. But who were those communists in March 1945? According to Lenin, Stalin and Trotski, communists declared themselves to be "the avant-garde of the working class", "the organized detachment of the working class", "the highest form of organization of the proletariat", "a new order of samurai", "a new sort of order of the Teutonic Knights"[25]. Roman Werfel, the ideologist-in-chief of the United Working Class Party of Poland (PMUP) between 1944 and 1959 (the equivalent of Iosif Chișinevschi in Romania), would openly declare that by the year 1944 "out of the old communist party, only scraps were left; we were all scraps, third rate personnel of the PMUP[26]", a situation found in all countries where the "popular democracy" was introduced[27]. Romanian communists were no exception to the rule, as their main leaders had been assassinated in the USSR in the 30's. On the 23rd of August 1944, the communist party had 83 members in Bucharest (number given by Pericle Martinescu, who knew them well) and several hundred throughout the country[28]. One of those "on the inside", the philosopher Herbert (Belu) Zilber (1901-1978), party member and one of the few intellectuals, wrote them a fine portrait:

"Such is man, this curious animal, made: he loves play. It is enough for him to don a new coat, and the game irresistibly commences. The most characteristic costume of man is the ideological suit. It fits all heads, by size, it has prestige, and it is cheap. I have as well, as so many others, played with ideology in my youth. The ones who came to make decisions for the whole country after the 23rd of August, all within a two hour meeting, had been party activists, now dressed in the costume of Bolshevik leaders. In 1917 in Russia, the Bolsheviks first imagined a socialist constitution, and afterwards built an industry and formed

an industrial proletariat, imposing the will of a revolution the likes of which humanity has never seen before. They fought, they suffered, they sacrificed, but they remained alone. No one helped them. Even if they have, quite a few times, made rash decisions, they have never played. Their acts bore the grandeur of the epic poem. Those that took superficial measures in Bucharest after the 23rd of August had done nothing or next to nothing to get to where they were. They had been born in a country where, for the past century – maybe even more – all ideas sown would bear but one fruit: comedy. Nothing could endure on this blessed land… Those who decided upon the fate of this country are the work of Ion Luca Caragiale… The new leaders were born and raised in this climate, but were Bolsheviks – members of a new type of party. Before the war, they were not many – a thousand, at most. I myself was a communist and I have lived among them in Bucharest and in prison. The few that came towards us were guided by the most varied motivations, from simple curiosity towards a mysterious organization, glorified by its partisans and cursed by its enemies, to the intellectuals convinced that here were the representatives of a glorious future, proven more geometrico, including the multitude of those unsatisfied of factories, of the state, of their families, or in the slums. Hungarians and Bulgarians who wanted to be separated from Romania, Jewish people terrified by antisemitism, the unemployed who lacked a specific profession or mediocre professionals, unfulfilled politicians and politicians who couldn't achieve anything in other parties, ugly housewives and children sick of study; this is the world from which party activists were recruited before the war. Each and every one of them felt marginalized in one way or the other and cheated out of their dreams. Attracted by the mystery of a world locked in their conscience, they wouldn't just join a political party, they would enter a new life. The first step was, for example, a small favor done for a friend, such as offering the house for a meeting with an unknown person, giving money to help some people who were unfairly imprisoned, the carrying of an envelope or small package from one city to another, or maybe sheltering an innocent man wanted by the police – an unanimously detested institution. These and other similar favors – asked for in hushed voices, under utmost secrecy – would give the small artisan, the housewife, the young man who was sick of school and eager to set out on adventures, the small functionary, the feeling that a doorway was opening before them, offering them a great and invisible power to them, trusting them with important secrets – them, the people who never got such attention before. They would become important to their own conscience, and began to see themselves as heroic. They could escape from their role of the downtrodden, to take on the role of an important character, a keeper of great secrets. (Constanța Crăciun, back when she looked like a saint from a Flemish painting, back when she was not a minister and knew how to laugh, confessed to me that she was once given a rusty set of keys for safekeeping just for the sake of feeling like she was keeping a secret!). After this initiation came an issue of the illegal Scînteia newspaper, read in a hushed voice and commented upon by the emissary of the unseen power, followed by significant articles written by ideologists in Clopotul, Manifest or Bluze Albastre, that told of heroic actions, full of sacrifices, of the grandeur of the five year plan and magnificent victories. As the person being manipulated would isolate himself from the people around him due to the secrets he held and the knowledge of his secret importance, more and more tasks would follow, until their entire schedule was completely occupied. Overwhelmed by the importance of their new identity, without the habit of individual thought and lacking any other substantial reading, the party's theses, administrated under the veil of conspiracy, would become a treasure trove of truths, entrusted upon a man who is not only serious, but truly a hero he could admire in his personal mirror. The last truths were the ones revealed in The History of the Party (short course), typewritten on yellow pages, passed from person to person. Through controlled memory, the phrases would adhere to the mind; they became part of the new man's fiber, which not only had the heroic status, but also held the keys to the universe. No one could fathom that there were other teachers besides Stalin and the party.

The critical autobiography completed the initiation. By the use of ironclad logic, the candidate would be convinced that the profound illegality in which the party found itself, surrounded by people who constantly tried to destroy it, directly obligated the candidate to confess everything done and thought by each and every new tenant, each new party member. First of all, the party needed to know the heinous crimes, the foulest secrets that cannot be confessed to the closest of friends or even family (assassinations, rapes, frauds, false witness, hidden vices, and thefts). Not only those done by the candidate had to come to light, but also those within their closed circle, family, and friends. This was the only way *in which the party could defend itself, and the candidate had to trust the party more than he trusted himself. Some would hesitate or lie. The majority of people would turn everything over to the party. They denounced themselves, their family, and their friends under the apparent safety of a false name. Passionate of his achievements, the frustrated candidate would cease to be anything more than a part of the great mystery. He had given himself to the Lord. He had no family, no friends. He would begin a new life, without love, without mercy, and without thankfulness. He had entered a community that could throw him away or burn him at the stake. A denouncement under an ideological pretext, or a mission to Moscow could end any liability.*

The new personality of the citizen become party member would rapidly consolidate through actions with whose purpose was only known by the mysterious party leadership. He was put to responsible actions such as sticking "flyers" on the tramway posts (which consisted of small papers on which words such as "Down with fascism!" and "Long live the Soviet Union!" were written), a fleeting meeting in front of the factory, the sabotage of social-democratic meetings, or joining peasant organizations and cooperatives. Such tasks were called activities of mass organization. Politically, the only repercussions such activities could have were arrests. But arrests constituted the motive for other activities of mass organization for helping those being arrested – which in turn, resulted in more arrests. They were the exams of the future activist. Upon passing them, he became responsible for others; he would organize meetings and would forward and issue orders. He who had no profession his entire life was now given one, while the ones who had professions quickly forgot them and 'qualified for the new workplace'. He was accustomed to a variety of ideological recipes, the rules of conspiracy, he knew how to organize a criminal group, how to control the activities of others, how to receive and issue orders, how to eliminate contestants and opposing forces, how to behave towards his superiors and to his inferiors, when to talk and when to remain silent. He administrated people; he had other lives in his hands. Even if before joining the party he had been one of the people who rallied against injustice and misery, and even loved his fellow men, his profession as an activist had gradually atrophied his moral senses and his peers had since become objects. Something fundamental would change in the party members' being. Their soul was veiled with a thick layer of insensibility towards people, ideas and feelings. They became somber, quiet, ruthless and unforgiving. Their laughter would change into a hypocritical smirk, their humor into sarcasm, their critique into derision. Dominican monks, prepared to send entire nations to the heavens in order to save their souls and ready to be sacrificed themselves as heroes in order to accomplish such redemption – these were the professional revolutionaries. I cannot recall one single street protest in Bucharest, sometimes comprised of only several tens of participants, that was ever anything more than a curious spectacle to the passers-by[29]. Yet all such public protests resulted in arrests and the prosecution of activists. Many suffered the long prison sentences with stoicism. They were suffering, but they were heroes.

Once the activist was steadily advancing up the hierarchy, he would escape a wide number of immediate risks, as it was forbidden for the leadership of the party to be put in any danger. Life would become more secure, more enjoyable, threatened only by intrigue and inter pares operations, as 'the interests of the working class' demanded. The transfer to Moscow sometimes ended the climb. There, Stalin was at the top, and no one could take his place.

These were the people taught to build a world of happy people. Professing no interest for abstractions and the esthetic, malicious by birth and hardened by life, voluntaries, lacking professional skills, thinking exclusively in stereotypes – no matter what social standing they came from, they all felt frustrated by open society. The party gave meaning and Securitate to their lives, as the Church had previously done. All they had was a small store of ideological recipes; the duty to hate, to denounce, to control minds and souls gave them the impression of having succeeded in life, having obtained power, having become what they had always dreamt of being: the bearers of noble ideas and sentiments – important people.

As in biblical times, not all called forth would be chosen. Power has its iron laws. Some lost patience, some were too vain, and many would have to settle for the lowest ranks in order for others to climb higher. There were cases of people who could not bear all the absurdity and stupidity. They disappeared[30]. Only the ones disowned by spirit and obsessed by power remained. This race of people has always existed, like the Neanderthal people, before they were discovered. Yet, they did not surface to become a feared force until the creation of this new type of party offered them the proper ideological climate and the right man to call them into action. The party imagined Lenin. Stalin called upon them for organization and discipline; he gave them power. He became their leader and their symbol – and they become the New Man. As Stalin and for Stalin"[31].

Belu Zilber was a true communist and had suffered during the trials and the long years of imprisonment in the most terrible prisons in communist Romania. This is why his account can be considered "subjective" – an adjective that meant, in communist language, heretical and thus, condemnable. That is why I will also quote a characterization made by a British observer who spent eight years living in Vienna, as an officer for the Allied Control Commission, and as a journalist:

"We must not forget that, after the war, the occupants of the ministerial seats in Prague and Budapest, Sofia and Bucharest, were communists who were not politicians, coming to occupy them again after a short period in the opposition. The vast majority of them were men and women who, for more than twenty-five years, had stoically endured different forms of persecution and had remained faithful to the cause. No matter what can be said against these people, their personal courage and loyalty towards their ideals cannot be put into question. Some, such as the Hungarian communist Mátyás Rákosi, spent more than 16 years and prison for political reasons between the two wars, sometimes for activities that would have just warranted a fee with the London police. All of them lived, for one generation, in a world of falsified passports and illegal crossing over the frontier, passwords and police spies, meetings set in isolated rooms and 'inquiries' held in prisons. At the end of this bitter battle came the exile to Moscow during the war, when 'freedom' plans were made and unmade as fronts shifted from one side to the other. From here resulted, first of all (ubiquitous to any form of refugee policy), inevitable sentiments of personal hatred and quarrels, followed by the immense impact of joy given by power and luxury in their own country. Those who had been hunters and the hunted for the past twenty five years, as rabbits in farms, became, almost overnight, owners over the domain. It is not at all surprising that, humanely speaking, the fights that broke out between them over these office seats as for the fruits that had been forbidden for so long were of unprecedented brutality, hard to imagine in western democracies. It is remarkable that there were some who indeed had the character to resist them, while

many others, such as Árpád Szakasits[32] in Hungary or Ana Pauker in Romania, were weak and succumbed to these temptations.

Whether they were personally corrupted by the luxury with which they were not accustomed to or not, all communists were engaged in a constant battle with what corrupted them completely: political power. The importance granted to the 'monolithic unity' of different communist parties was meant to hide internal battles until they were either lost or won, and the public, in general, was left to estimate the extent of the conflicts by the punishments applied to the defeated side. The moment of announcing the victory, along with the name of the victor, was of course a decision reserved for Moscow: in this sense, local intrigues were mere cogwheels in the mechanism of soviet politics.

The same rule applied to a secondary factor of local significance: the need to constantly produce scapegoats for the faulty leadership of various communist regimes and for the general decline of the standard of living. It is no coincidence that the majority of cleansing acts and Cominform[33] style trials take place in a period plagued with dire economic difficulties in the development of satel-lite-villages. In Bucharest, the victims were guilty of inflation and the lagging behind of agricultural production that weakened the Romanian economy while, in the Prague trial, all who had defended themselves were found guilty for all the shortcomings of Czech industry and external commerce – in reality, the fault lied with the total subjugation of the country to Russia. The year 1952, the year of the first burst of 'antizionism' in Cominform was also the first year of general crisis – the first year when the economic difficulties of the Eastern bloc became so severe, the effects were not only felt in the consumer goods market of civilians, but also in the state rationed supply of basic goods. The communist were not stupid enough to imitate the Nazis and blame the entire race of Jewish people for their economic failures. On the contrary, they proved to be much more cunning and won popularity through their politic: people were not being encouraged to hate each other more, but to work more. As for the 'Zionists', the fall of all the other traitors was also the reason for demanding greater production, and thus the political trial was also used in the second direction, for economic purposes. Not only was it detracting from the harsh realities of soviet exploitation, but it also served as a slogan through which the very purpose of exploitation was achieved more efficiently.

A final factor must be considered, one that has stood at the foundation of everything the Kremlin ever undertook, and also the satellite governments: the cleansing within communist power ranks was not only the natural law of life, but it was the foundation of political life. The stability and continuity rooted in tradition had no usefulness for the common people of the communist world. They live, have lived and would live in a continuous state of strife and uncertainty – a situation that spoke volumes of their mental sanity. Moreover, communist ideology does not recognise value, and its system knows no justice apart from the justice of the party. Add the fact that the 'loved leaders of the party' don't have the slightest chance of appealing to the people who did not in fact elect them, and you have a clear image of what having a 'career in politics' actually meant in communism. In the West, office experience and contracts with the business world are appreciated attributes, valuable for a mature state official, and respected as such. In communism, a veteran is usually a source of suspicion, because he has had a longer exposure to the dangers of 'contamination'. We shall see that, during the internal strife in satellite-countries, the names of unknown youth, who received their education in Moscow, sometimes surface along with the ones existent in the hierarchy, silently occupying a place among the victors. They would, in due time, become leaders in Cominform, but they can undoubtedly also be replaced, after some time, when others shall be promoted. This system of planned rejuvenation keeps functioning despite foreseeable needs and without regards for the loyalty or capacity of the named leaders. It is an instinctive and periodic process of expansion which communists could not stop, as the salmon instinctively finding its way up the river to the place of its birth.[34]

It is also worth mentioning the analysis of the three types of Marxists made by an American journalist in 1947:

"Why then are there so many communist Europeans? It is because Marxism simultaneously offers both exalted reactions and rituals that captivate them, the feeling of belonging to a cause and a blessed relaxation from individual thought, individual action and responsibility being a source of unbearable stress in most of Europe nowadays. Faced with harsh conditions, democracy demands a lot of initiative, courage, conviction and the moral equivalent to the nourishment in the stomach. These qualities are demanded even in the easiest of circumstances, such as in the case of America. Marxism presents an emotional attraction to a

wide variety of personalities: progressive people, genuinely moved by humanism and merciful towards their fellow men; introverted people who pity themselves or are filled with hatred and eager to seek revenge for the unfairness they have been subjected to, be it real or imagined; and cunning people, devoid of feeling and enamored with power.

The first type of Marxists, for example, the socialists in Scandinavia and England, and even some of the communists, are people with which America can collaborate. A Danish communist I have met was well indoctrinated by Marxism, but he was also much more eager to discuss the unjust and wrong distribution of vegetables in Copenhagen. When such communists are confronted with the harsher aspects of their doctrine, they usually quickly give up communism, given that they live in a country where they can afford doing so. With the second type of Marxists, it is very difficult to cooperate. And the third type of Marxists is the most difficult type of them all."[35]

Specialists have identified three groups that formed PCR (The Communist Party of Romania, renamed the Romanian Communist Party after the October 1945 National Conference) in 1945: the "inner" circle, divided into two categories – those who were still at large, starting with their leader general secretary Ştefan Foriş, Lucreţiu Pătrăşcanu, Constantin Pârvulescu, Emil Bodnăraş and Remus Koffler, and the group who was imprisoned, with their leader Gheorghiu-Dej, Chivu Stoica and Teohari Georgescu; finaly, there was the muscovite group, come from exile, led by Ana Pauker and Vasile Luca[36]. The "Muscovites" dominated the leadership of the party up until 1952, when Ana Pauker and Vasile Luca, but also Georgescu, were eliminated; the first group had been liquidated earlier, starting with Foriş, followed by Pătrăşcanu and Koffler, in operations carried out by Pârvulescu and Bodnăraş, who became Gheorghiu-Dej's most trusted allies. A motto circulating in 1945 accurately described the hierarchy of the party and of the state: "Ana, Luca, Teo, Dej all agree/ Striking down the bourgeoisie".

The Romanian communists were not alone, as a large numbers of their comrades who had sought refuge in the USSR joined them shortly after the 23rd of August 1994; Bessarabian and Transniestrian communists, all qualified and instructed as soviet party activists sent from Moscow to prepare for the transfer of power and the transformation of Romania into a satellite country[37]. First of all, the replacement of the government led by Sănătescu was necessary, as its usefulness after the signing of the armistice Convention was zero. On the 26th of September, PCdR published the project for the National Democratic Front (FND), the first "fictive coalition" orchestrated by the Moscow emissaries[38]. Immediately, street protests for the instauration of a new FND government began – a political government (although the country was still at war), as General Sănătescu accounts:

> *The 9th of October 1944. Rumors of a government crisis start spreading, as left wing newspapers continue to attack the government's actions in order to induce chaos. The communists follow the well-known plans applied in Russia and probably an orchestrator was sent from Moscow to lead the entire operation – moreover, none of the communists here have a lot of experience. After seeing the street protests, I immediately compare the situation to what I saw in Moscow in 1940 and I find numerous similarities, including the words written on the signs carried by the protesters[39]. I came to the conclusion that everything was controlled by the Russians, unlike Maniu, who still thinks that Russians do not meddle in internal affairs. Manifestations occur every day in which people cry: "We demand a democratic government!"*[40]

Aside from the invalidation of the entire legislation of "dictatorial and anti-popular governments", the cleansing of fascist elements and other democratic measures, the FND program also included the agricultural reform, the nationalization of the National Bank and other 18 banks. It was a modest program, but the protests continued and General Sănătescu, after a second government (November to December), ceded the presidency to General Nicolae Rădescu, a person tolerated by the communists, who considered him to be more compliant. Especially because the Red Army had pushed the Romanian army out of North Ardeal, which had been recently reconquered, thus keeping a valuable hostage and an efficient means of pressuring the government. But General Rădescu proved not to be compliant at all and firmly requested, among others, the disarming of the Patriotic Guard (the work of Emil Bodnăraș), in the same way General de Gaulle would request in France. After Gheorghiu-Dej and Ana Pauker's visit in Moscow (the 31st of December 1944 – 16th of January 1945), PCdR and its allies recommenced their assault against the government, this time led by Rădescu. Law 52 for the organization of syndicates, backed by socialists and communists, and passed on the 21st of January, marked the beginning of the domination over the working class through the General Confederation of Work, the unique syndicate throughout the country and for all activities (26-30th of January). The patriotic guards, syndicalist workers and, later, the majority of the Iron Guard, thus constituted the mass of maneuver for PCR, which expanded to encompass a large part of salary earners and functionaries: they were used to organize public protests, the attacks of prefectures and town halls, the dividing of land during the agricultural reform, and many other such activities.

But let us not anticipate: on the 6th of March 1945, the government led by Petru Groza swears loyalty to the king, the epilogue of one month and a half of manifestations and psychodrama in which General Rădescu became, through communist and socialist propaganda, public enemy no.1. His fall and the rise into power of the government led by Groza coincided with the civil war in Greece, where the English army openly sided with the anticommunists (25th of December 1944) and also with an attempt by the legionaries on the Western front to achieve a "23rd of August in reverse" in Hungary and Transylvania (January to February 1945)[41].

What interests us the most in this series of events is the program of the new government in Bucharest – not the official program, but the long term plans (3 plus 5 years) brought by soviet emissaries and rendered onto PCdR representatives, Ana Pauker, Constantin Pârvulescu and Constantin Doncea on the 7th of March 1945. The secret plan was transmitted by the Office of Strategic Services (OSS, the predecessor of CIA) in condensed-form by an American agent, Theodore (Teddy) Negroponte[42]:

The source [AD-201] could not obtain a copy, but details important aspects of the 3 year plan from memory: a) accomplishing the agricultural reform by seizing the vast proprieties and ruining the landowners; b) the disbanding of the army in its current form and the creation of a new armies from divisions "Tudor Vladimirescu" and "Avram Iancu" (the second division still in Russia), as well as all officers currently serving on soviet territory; c) the dissolution of all banks through attacks against the National Liberal Party, whose members are the owners of most banks; d) the small farmsteads must be dissolved in order to strip the peasantry of their lands, cattle, and machinery. This action will ease their integration in the collectivist system; e) the abdication of the king and the exile of the royal family; f) the gradual annihilation of all import-export businesses that deal with the United States of America and Great Britain and the orientation of Romanian exports towards the USSR and countries under soviet domination; g) the annihilation of historical parties through the arrest, assassination and kidnapping of their members; h) the creation of a police organization, based on "the people's militia" and similar to NKVD; j) turning the rural population towards industry. The development of industrial enterprises in Romania; k) forbidding any foreigner, with the exception of countries under soviet rule, to enter Romania.[43]

All the above directions were followed meticulously between 1945 and 1949, with a substantial acceleration of reforms following the 1946 November elections won through massive fraud[44] paradoxically similar to interwar practices, when the party in power would organize elections and would always win them almost unanimously, while their adversaries, who had obtained similar ratings one or two years prior, would plummet under 10% or less. In December 1937, during the last elections before the ones in 1946, the liberal party in power won the majority of votes but could not obtain the 40% that would have automatically granted it absolute majority (through the majority bonus). We do not know what the 5 year plan was entirely, as it only reached us in a condensed form, transmitted by Douglas Dunham, the director of the United States Information Service, the American cultural institute, following the meeting with a Romanian communist (possibly Belu Zilber), who came to visit him in December 1947:

"The man announced he wished to tell me of the project to activate Russian policy in Romania. Honestly, I did not believe him. I believed it was a trap, bait, but I decided to hear him through nonetheless. The man was an author

on economic subjects and I had heard of him by name. He was Jewish, about 40 years old, bald and spoke excellent English. 'I have come to tell you what will happen to this country... You don't know me. I had a deal with your predecessor and it is not very healthy to be seen talking to Americans too often these days. I have come to you because my time has come for me to disappear; I am programmed to be removed in approximately six weeks. I know too much about the country's economy and I will probably be sent somewhere in Siberia to work in a salt mine.' I watched the bald man and I couldn't see the slightest hint of emotion on his face. ... 'You look at me as if you do not believe me, he said to me. I know they will get rid of me and there is nothing to be done in this respect. I could try to escape, I could try, but I am under close surveillance. I think Americans should know of what is going to happen here. I don't think the United States of America will stop the events from occurring, although your country represents a moral force in the world capable of defeating this slavery, I am Jewish. I have already suffered for my country during Nazi occupation and I have suffered in vain. The friends of the invaders are still friends of the invad- ers, and the enemies of the invaders, are, also, still enemies of the invaders. This is the irony of the situation in Romania'. And can't you avoid this future (the arrest)... what you think (is about to happen) is only your case? I asked him. 'I saw the list, he replied. I know who is going to leave. You would be amazed. But we are only individuals. Those do not matter. The masses, the society strata mat- ter. The plan is final and inevitable. Masses of people will be transported from cities into the countryside, from the countryside into the cities, from Romania to Russia and from Russia to Romania. All industry will be taken over by the communists, and its owners will be left penniless, to die of starvation as soon as possible. Anyone who thinks for himself will be annihilated or destroyed. Work camps will spring up in all of Romania and they will be filled with people stripped of their wealth. Ruffians will be forced to join the party and will be given power over the educated ... this will make the country easier to dominate by the Russians. The ignorant and the poor will be given the bare minimum in order to survive. Some advantages will be created for them, not many, and only if they are party members. The country will not benefit from this change; it will become a vassal to an Eastern power. And any Romanian who will become any sort of leader will eventually be exterminated.'"[45]

As we have seen in the previous pages, all the events foreseen in December 1947 came to be during the first "five year plan" (1948-1952) put into practice by the communist leaders[46]. The second phase of the revolution could now commence: transitioning from the "people's democracy" (1945-1947) to the "dictatorship of the proletariat". The party had greatly expanded: from one thousand members in August 1944, it reached 52,253 members in the spring of 1945, 256,863 members (in October 1945), 325,000 members (on the 1st of January 1946), 417,264 members (1st of May 1946), 703,000 (1st of July 1947) and finally, 799,351 members at the end of year 1947. After "swallowing" PSD in the new workers' party, on the 21st to 23rd of February 1948, the roster of PMR officially counted 1,057,428 members[47]. However, on the 21st of November, the action of verifying party members began: until 1954, over 250,000 "careerists" were excluded, "elements of the enemy infiltrated in the party", former legionaries and former social-democrats who sympathized Titel-Petrescu, "right wing deviants" and other such members were culled, and no new members were added until 1952. Also prosecuted were several "illegalists"[48], former fighters in the international brigades in Spain, and others. Alone in power and without any internal opposition, the party did not wish to "share the pie" with many who had become members in 1945-1947, more accurately with the peasants who had gotten proprieties and would also receive a red card, legionaries who had been enticed from the beginning to join by the prospects of forming battalions of hooligans and terrorizing the bourgeois, arrivistes and all sorts of opportunists[49]. PMR was led by a Secretariat of 5 full members (Ana Pauker, Vasile Luca, Teohari Georgescu, Gheorghe Gheorghiu-Dej and Lotar Rădăceanu, the former being active for a short time) and five acting members, a Political Bureau comprised of 13 members (which included the Secretariat members, 11 from PCR and 2 from PSD), and a Central Committee comprised of 41 full members (31 from PCR and 10 from PSD) and 16 acting members[50]. The most important members of these structures, apart from those mentioned earlier, were Chivu Stoica, Gheorghe Apostol, Iosif and Liuba Chișinevschi, Alexandru Moghioroș, Gheorghe Vasilichi, Iosif Rangheț, Constantin Pârvulescu, Pintilie Bodnarenco, Constanța Crăciun, Petre Borilă, Miron Constantinescu, Alexandru Drăghici, Ion Vințe, Dumitru Coliu, Leonte

Răutu, and Ștefan Voitec, names which will appear during the whole period of proletariat dictatorship until the death of Gheorghiu-Dej (1965). Behind them, in the shadow of apparent power, were a considerable number of Soviet consultants, who played a decisive role in the transformation of society and the application of policies dictated by the interests of Moscow.

The largest part of the representatives of the new political "elites" were workers, with studies consisting of four years of school and sometimes technical professions; only a few of them were intellectuals, such as: Lucretiu Pătrășcanu (arrested in 1948 and assassinated six years later), Ana Pauker, Constanța Crăciun, Miron Constantinescu (born out of wedlock to the geographer Gheorghe Murgoci, had sociology studies), Grigore Preoteasa, Leonte Răutu (had finished high school and had some unfinished college studies), Petre Constantinescu-Iași (mediocre historian, he too was born out of wedlock to a magistrate from Iași), Belu Zilber, people younger than Silviu Brucan, Gheorghe (Gogu) Rădulescu, Gheorghe Gaston Marin and Alexandru Bârlădeanu, finally, the former socialist Ștefan Voitec (who only had the role of representative, and had no decisional powers). Their scientific prowess was limited, as proven by their extremely modest, if not without any merit, "work". Some did have, however, a PhD (although without passing the baccalaureate, without a Bachelor's Degree or any Master's studies). And yet a decision of the Political Bureau of CC of PMR on the 15th of December 1954 reveals the truth. More precisely, "the presentation by 5 comrades (Barbu Zaharescu, Ștefan Voicu, Mihai Frunză, Silviu Brucan and Ion Rachmuth) of a doctor's thesis, without passing exams beforehand for the title of candidate of sciences and the presentation by 4 comrades (Leonte Tismăneanu, Paul Niculescu-Mizil, Grigore Kotovschi, Constantin Borgeanu) of dissertations without any kind of candidacy examination[51]". Their example was followed by many other party activists and agents of the secret services who became intellectuals "using the point system", or using their card, as they said back then, culminating of course with Nicolae and Elena Ceaușescu (four years of primary schooling each), a true triumph of imposture. It was clear that these people with next to no culture and who had no experience in governing had to employ the help of specialists; beginning with the Soviets and gradually moving towards Romanians specialized in technical and scientific domains[52].

Historian Florin Constantiniu, one of the most in-depth documenters of this period of Romanian history, defined the four pillars on which the communist system stood: *the party*, about which we have discussed, *the Secret Police, planned economy* and *the nomenclature*[53].

In order to "defend democratic conquests and to secure RPR against the conspirators of enemies from within and without", The General Directorate for the Securitate of the People (DGSP) was created as part of the Ministry of Internal Affairs, according to Decree 221 issued on the 30th of August 1948. The director-general was lieutenant-general Gheorghe Pintilie (born Timofei Bodnarenko), vice-minister of Internal Affairs; his adjuncts, Alexandru Nicolschi and Vladimir Mazuru, were, as were their bosses, agents of the Soviet secret services who represented the model for similar institution in all Eastern countries[54]. In 1950, the Secret Police (formerly known as "the Siguranta") had 3,973 employees and 42,187 informers. Six months later, on the 23rd of January 1949, the Directorate for Militia (who had 40,000 employees in the next four years) and the Directorate for Securitate Troops were created, institutions that were also part of the Ministry of Internal Affairs. In March 1958, the Secret Police had over 30,000 employees, both military personnel and civilians (30,268 more precisely), and the Securitate Troops had 57,185 employees. Between 1954 and 1957, a somewhat relaxed period, over 6,211 arrests took place for activities directed "against state Securitate". Their numbers will rise to 10,125 in 1958 and 17,613 in January the next year (with the mention that 47,643 people had been investigated), 37,893 in 1959 and 21,176 in 1960[55]. In 1960, the Ministry of Internal Affairs kept 323,207 "elements of the enemy for which compromising materials have been collected" under surveillance, out of which 84,261 legionaries, 48,997 PNȚ members and 32,346 PNL members. These numbers indicate entire families, friends, neighbors and sympathizers, a horrifying reality that our generation – we were about 14-15 years old back then – could only barely understand.

The surveillance of the populace had been made ever since 1948 through apartment building managers and street committees (32,000 back then[56]) who collaborated with the "sectorists", police agents[57] tasked with searching the houses of suspects and peruse the building's books (an invention of the dictatorship of Carol the Second, in 1938)[58] to register the names of people living there, to check identity cards, and even count the beds in order to calculate how many people were living in one apartment.[59]

The *planned economy* was inaugurated on the 2nd of July 1948, through the creation of the State Planning Committee (CSP), led by Gheorghiu-Dej, party secretary and the minister of National Economy. Structured according to the Soviet model (Gosplan), this institution, created simultaneously in Hungary and Bulgaria, was meant to coordinate the entire country's economy after the nationalization of industry and commerce (11th of June 1948), according to the exigencies formulated by COMECON, in Romanian CAER (The Council for Mutual Economic Assistance), officially created by the soviet bloc in January 1949, in response to the Marshall Plan[60]. In April 1949, the CSP leadership was entrusted to Miron Constantinescu, the youngest member of the Political Bureau (he was 32 years old), who will be removed in 1955 and accused of authoritarian leadership and the falsifying of statistics in order to conceal the errors and failures of the institution. An identical situation can be found in the USSR, where Gosplan produced, for decades on end, what French soviet specialist Alain Besancon (who wrote a book on the subject, entitled L'*Anatomie d'un spectre: l'économie politique du socialisme réel*) described as a pseudo-economy based on falsified numbers on all levels, meant to illustrate the constant progress and unparalleled growth in production and quality of life. The main purpose of the CSP was the forced industrialisation of Romania, with emphasis on heavy industry and machinery. It was, of course, made following the Soviet model of 1929, which was in turn inspired by the European industrial revolution during the 18th and 19th Century; its ambition was to compete with the American model, to which it could compare due to the sheer vastness of geographic space and resources available. Ultimately, the plan failed due to numerous causes – especially due to the incompatibility between the utopia (ideology) and the need for modernization, which we have mentioned earlier.

In essence, the CSP had to transform itself into the patron of the entire economy – the campaign for the collectivization of agriculture begins in

1949 – and to organize the management of funding, raw materials and qualified workforce needed in order to achieve the first annual plans and, in 1951, the first five year plan[61].

The problems regarding the proper instruction of technical and scientific personnel and qualified workers proved to be quite challenging for Miron Constantinescu and his collaborators who put together, with the help of the people's councils (created in 1949), a the list of economical, industrial, political and administrative director seats, directly occupied by party members (*the nomenclature*). Happily, such a list has been preserved, found in the HCM no.139 from the 17th of January 1953. Published and discussed by Ghiță Ionescu[62] since 1956, it doubtlessly represents a translation from the soviet original document (which has been kept secret), as can be concluded from Michael Voslensky's book, *La Nomenklatura. Les privilégiés en URSS*, published in 1980 in the Federal Republic of Germany and translated into French in the same year[63]. Called "the new class" by Milovan Djilas, "the class of the newly privileged", "the red aristocracy" or "the administrative class", this superior class of bureaucracy now has unprecedented power, because it is the state itself. Together with party activists[64], members of the party nomenclature, this new class represented, according to Michael Voslensky, less than 1.5% of the USSR's entire population: it had declared itself "the leading force and the guide of the country", "the intelligence, honor and conscience of our era", "the organizer and inspiration of all victories of the Soviet people", and "the representatives of the entirety of progressive humanity"[65].

A document issued by the CC secretariat of the PMR in 1954 and titled "The Nomenclature of the Central Committee of PMR", discussed by Stelian Tănase, marks 5,243 job posts comprising the high ranking nomenclature, "that part of the apparatus where decisions are taken which impact the whole of society", invested and controlled by the Political Bureau (286 people) and the CC Secretariat of PMR (4,957 posts)[66].

Compared to Romania, which followed the soviet model in this regard as well ("let us proceed as they do", was the common expression), these percentages – 1.5% of the entire population, meaning 100,000 positions and if we add the personnel in the party, with their families, approximately 250,000 to 300,000 people – are very similar to the ones represented by the former bourgeoisie, and before that, the boyars[67]. We may observe the fact that we are confronted with the presence of a very select elite of privileged citizens[68], which justifies the often heard definition of the communist revolution: "You get up so I can sit down!"

Here is the list of positions occupied by the communist economic, industrial, and administrative nomenclature, "the medium and low rank nomenclature, the party and government personnel", as it was in 1953:

a) Directors of state institutions, organizations, factories and cooperatives.
b) Managing directors, directors and chiefs of independent departments within the ministries, institutions and factories, cooperative and public organizations and other positions similar to them.
c) Technical directors and chief engineers.
d) Accountants-general.
e) Construction site and production department chiefs.
f) Judges, prosecutors and state arbiters.
g) Leaders and chief administrators in scientific, educational and artistic institutions.
h) National and regional inspectors attached to the units mentioned in paragraph a).
i) State Committee regional delegates for the collection of agricultural products.
j) Department chiefs attached to the executive committees of the regional, urban and district people's council.
k) Jurisconsults of ministries and other central agencies of the state administration; chiefs of juridical departments.
l) Editors-in-chief, associate editors-in-chief, and district editors-in-chief.
m) Secretaries-general of press agencies.
n) Directors of medical institutions.
o) Pharmacy administrators.
p) Elected salary earners who occupy positions paid by the organizations that elected them.
q) Secretaries of the cabinets and deputy ministers.

r)   The station agents of main railroad stations.

s)   Ship captains on the commercial fleet.

t)   Chiefs, administrators and directors of economic sections, departments and similar units, of canteens, workshops and all other subunits organized on the principle of independent management.

u)   Administrators of state owned stores and cooperative commercial enterprises.

v)   Chiefs of Securitate and firefighting brigades.

w) The adjuncts or legal replacements of the people with all aforementioned responsibilities."[69]

I have reproduced this list of political, administrative, economic and industrial nomenclature in order to more accurately illustrate the socio-economic status of our parents, as well as their children after 1970 – in essence, ours, the graduates of "Spiru Haret" high school. In regards to the party nomenclature (the active)[70], we have one indication to help us identify it in public and school documents (class books): the girl (born in 1951) of Gheorghe Pintilie, the first director general of the secret police and deputy minister in the Ministry of Internal Affairs, writes that, on the first day of school, her father told her:

"My dear girl, I wish you good luck. During roll call, they will ask you the profession of your mother and father. By profession, your father is a worker and your mother, a mathematician." No job positions. My father considered his position to be uncertain – what is today may not be tomorrow.[71]

Pintilie's considerations were not original, nor were they the expression of excessive modesty: they belong to communist practices in which your profession and your job position are never tied to one another. Gordon Shepherd perceived this reality perfectly when he wrote:

It is clear that everything that matters within this system of power is not what title a leader holds, but his influence within the party or, in other words, the fame he has in Moscow. It is essential to find yourself in the

> *inner circle, the position does not matter! A syndicate leader inside this*
> *magic circle holds more power than a Prime Minister from a constella-*
> *tion separated from Moscow.*[72]

The interaction of these pillars of power led to the installation of totalitarianism, a regime which sought "to embrace everything", in the words of
Mussolini – all aspects of society. Or, in the words of Mihai Gramatopol:
"By seizing everything, and euphemistically calling it nationalization, or col-
lectivization, the state becomes not only paternalistic, but also a wet nurse to
its people. Until deaths do us part! The state raises the individual, takes him to
kindergarten, washes him, cuts his hair, sells him food and toilet paper, tends to
his health, 'chides' him, educates him, retires him and buries him in the sacred
ground of his beloved country. Left without the goods by which he used to live
and help other live beside him, the individual tells himself: the state took them,
let the state feed me; he then proceeds to work as much as he shall see fit[73]. …
The problem of working without any goal and implicitly the inefficiency of such
work (aside from the utmost chaos produced by the utmost planning) had to be
resolved by introducing a work hierarchy. By the means, the work itself becomes
an end. Egomania morphs into socialist competition and the egomaniacs become
heroes of socialist labor. But even this hierarchy was proven to be insufficient.
An attempt was made to introduce hierarchy within the individual labor ini-
tiative, but the result turned out to be even more counterproductive. Novelty is
a dangerous thing. It gnaws away at the sanctity and tyranny of the status quo,
that fundamental ne varietur of communist totalitarian dogma. Novelty must
be approved from above. Facing the necessity of 'democratic centralization',
which functioned slowly, novelty would become obsolete by the time it would
trickle down the line of approval. Only the party could be prime movers, and
critique was only applied from high above to lower down, never in reverse – to
the lowest of ranks, the only critique left was self-critique, a continuous scolding
of the individual ego. And thus, the situation led to general disinterest as a final
victory towards the conclusions drawn by the working people: they pretend to
pay us and we pretend to work! Aurel Baranga, as a dramatic whim, considers
the opposite as being the real state of affairs and the cause for the stagnation of
both society and power – general interest.[74]

From the failed sanctification of labor, tendencies quickly turned to the sanctification of the party, seeking to make its members into entities meant to stimulate production by being both human and exemplary, common and sacrosanct, and invested with supreme (communist) moral authority. But the millions of prototypes who attempted to embody the new man turned out to be more man than new man. The suspending of historical ascension and immobility made a middle class flock out of them instead – materialistic and vulgar, the party members compromised the sanctity and 'prestige' of the party as abstraction, through their small interests and privileges, their petty goals and abject methods of fulfilling them. Then, the name of "dictatorship of the proletariat" was abandoned, and it was declared that socialism had come out victorious due to the monolithic unity of the whole nation coming together around the party. Like the Duke, the communist party was always right. Its mistakes, admitted out of necessity and without assuming blame, were almost welcome, for they served to indicate the right path. The party was courageous, good, wise, cautious, full of love, and probably a hermaphrodite, seeing as it satisfied the needs of all, men and women."[75]

Anne Applebaum extended her analysis for all communist countries: "In a sense, all these countries have remained very close (similar): none of the regimes ever seemed to have realized just how fundamentally unstable they were. They would stagger on from crisis to crisis, not because they were incapable of adjusting their economy, but because the communist project itself was faulty. Wanting to control all aspects of society, the regimes made a source of potential protest out of each one of them. The state had dictated high quotas for workers: due to this fact, the strike of Eastern-German workers (June 1953) rapidly escalated into a protest against the state.[76] The state dictated what artists could paint and write, and thus an artist who painted or wrote differently would automatically also become a political dissident. The state had decreed that people were not allowed to form into independent organizations: anyone who created such an organization, as innocuous as it might have been, also became an adversary to the regime. And when people joined an independent organization en masse - for example, when 10 million Poles joined the Solidarnosc syndicate – the existence of the regime itself was suddenly in danger. But communist ideology and

Marxist-Leninist economic theory also contained the seeds of their own destruction in other regards. The legitimacy claims of the East European governments were based on the promises of future prosperity and high standards of living, guaranteed by the 'scientific' Marxism. The armbands and the banners, the solemn discourses, the newspaper articles and finally, the television show all spoke of the acceleration of progress. If there ever was progress, it was never as powerfully visible as propaganda sought to illustrate it. The standard of living never rose as fast and as spectacular as in Western Europe – a fact that was impossible to conceal for long. In 1950, Poland and Spain had similar GDP. In 1988, Poland's GDP had grown 2.5 times, while Spain's GDP was 13 times higher. Broadcasts from Radio Free Europe, travels and tourism permitted an empirical observation of this inequality, which would only increase due to the acceleration of technological evolution in Western Europe. Cynicism and disillusion progressed in the same rhythm, even with those who had at first believed in the system. … Even if some Eastern Europeans later felt a certain nostalgia for the idealism and ideas of communism, we must draw attention to the fact that no political party after 1989 ever tried to reinstate communist economy."[77]

1. For this individual, see his biography, signed by Arkadi Vaksberg and presented by Vladimir Tismăneanu, *"Marele inchizitor: Andrei Vîșinski și pseudojustiția stalinistă"*, în volume *Irepetabilul trecut*, second ed., Humanitas, Bucharest, 2008, pp. 160–165. Also, see the confession of a former prisoner from Siberia; his soviet prosecutor would tell him: "A dangerous element has not done anything, but is capable of doing anything."(Quote by Marius Oprea, *Adevărata călătorie a lui Zahei*, p. 219)

2. This naming has been described by Alexandru O. Teodoreanu (Păstorel) – the king of the Romanian epigram – as such: "Caligula Imperator/ Has made a horse senator/ Yet Groza was more sinister/ He made an ass minister"

3. A joke that circulated throughout Bucharest went like this: "Those who wanted to avoid prison took shelter in the Groza government." (Wolfgang Bretholz, *op. cit.*, p. 163)

4. See the volume *6 martie 1945. Începuturile comunizării României*, Editura Enciclopedică, Bucharest, 1995, in which are the works presented at the „*6 martie 1945 – Guvernul Petru Groza și comunizarea României*" symposium on the 3rd to the 5th of March 1995 at the "Nicolae Iorga" Institute of History in Bucharest, The exaltation of this date is the work of the "Muscovite" group (Ana Pauker, Vasile Luca) from PCR, who criticized the participation of "national" ("internal") communists at the 23th of August act – participation which, they thought, made them lose the opportunity to get rid of all political adversaries in one fell swoop, achieving *tabula rasa* with the occupation of the Red Army (Ghiță Ionescu, *op. cit.*, p. 107, and Gheorghiu-Dej's speech at the Meeting in 29 noiembrie– 5 decembrie 1961, ibidem, p. 334). This reproach was expressed for the first time by Andrei Jdanov to Lucrețiu Pătrășcanu in Moscow in September 1944, see the memoirs of Șerban Milcoveanu, *Memorii (1929–1989)*, Pământ, Bucharest-Pitești, 2008, p. 445; also, see the confession of Ana Pauker communicated by her daughter to Lavinia Betea, *Povești din cartierul Primăverii*, Curtea Veche, Bucharest, 2010, pp. 104–105.

5. M. Cazacu, "*Sfârșitul Vechiului Regim în România: 21 august 1945*", in Revista Istorică, XX, 2009, pp. 519–531.

6. Romania became an example of the method of brute force unaided in the imposing of a communist government by the Soviets. See the considerations of Gordon Shepherd, *Russia's Danubian Empire*, London, 1954, pp. 4–6. The other methods were force combined with fraud in the case of Hungary and sheer political blackmail in the case of Czechoslovakia.

7. Here is what Alan Ehrenhalt writes about the subject: "Much can be said about the moment in which American democracy manifested itself. I am not speaking of 1776 or 1787, as it is unanimously assumed, but of 1801, on the day when President John Adams, defeated in the elections, quietly packed his bags and went home. It was only then that the Americans knew for sure that the system was working exactly how they had been assured it would. The transfer of power is perhaps not the most impressive trait of democracy, but it is by far the most important. It sets America apart from most of the countries in which it could not be achieved. Admitting the fact that you have

been defeated and going home, or staying in minority and letting the majority govern – they are not only signs of good manners, but also of genuine sportsmanship … They are the essence of patriotism itself… There is nothing shameful of priding yourself with sticking to the rules.", *International Herald Tribune, 22 December* 1998.

8. And yet, in one of his previous works, *The Stateand the Revolution,* Lenin wrote: "Only an incurable ignorant and a bourgeois scoundrel could claim that workers are incapable of correctly governing the state." (Michel Heller and Aleksandr Nekrich, *op. cit.,* p. 51). It was him as well who claimed than even a kitchen lady could govern the state. It wasn't the first nor the last contradiction in his thinking, see Vladimir Bukovski, *Et le vent reprend ses tours*, Robert Laffont, Paris, 1978, pp. 99–102; Sandor Marai, *op. cit.*, p. 250.

9. Michel Heller and Aleksandr Nekrich, *L'Utopie au pouvoir. Histoire de l'URSS de 1917 à nos jours*, Calmann-Lévy, Paris, 1992, p. 51

10. Vladimir Bukovski*, Jugement à Moscou. Un dissident dans les archives du Kremlin*, Robert Laffont, Paris, 1995, p. 555. The phrase belongs to Rael Jean Isaac and Eric Isaac, *The Coercitive Utopians. Social Deception by America's Power Players*, Regnery Gateway, Chicago, 1983.

11. A good definition of ideology goes like this: "Ideology is an intellectual operation which does not seek to reveal the truth."

12. Stelian Tănase, *Elite și putere*, p. 244. Ideology is incompatible with democracy and more precisely, with the law, see conclusions of Vladimir Boukovsky*, Jugement à Moscou.*, pp. 145–146.

13. Gheorghe Tătărescu*, Internaționala a III-a și Basarabia*, in a speech held in Parliament in 1925, vol. *Mărturii pentru istorie*, ed. de Sanda Tătărescu-Negroponte, Editura Enciclopedică, Bucharest, 1996, pp. 75-109; Major D. Stancov, *Acțiunea subversivă sovietică*, n. ed., Bucharest, 1941.

14. The Comintern "was a declaration of war against all existing governments" (Richard Pipes, quote by Anne Applebaum, *op. cit.*, pp. 84–85).

15. Decision taken at the Fifth Congress of Comintern in 1924, see Henry L. Roberts, *op. cit.*, p. 252–253; Vladimir Tismăneanu, *Stalinism pentru eternitate. O istorie politică a comunismului românesc*, Humanitas, Bucharest, 2014, p. 85

16. Golfo Alexopoulos, *Stalin's Outcasts: Aliens, Citizens and the Soviet State*, 1926–1936, Ithaka, New York, 2003; Douglas Smith, *op. cit.*, p. 236

17. The first detailing of such atrocities appears in Nicolae P. Smochina's article: *"Din amarul românilor transnistrieni. Masacrele de la Nistru"* written in 1933 and published *in Moldova Nouă. Revistă de studii transnistriene, VI,* 1941, pp. 239–295. Also see the 25 horrifying photographs that accompany the article.

18. He was part of the group called "the group of conspirators, spies and saboteurs" (12 people, including Max Auschnitt, Admiral Horia Măcelariu, University professors Gheorghe Manu and Nicolae Mărgineanu, the industrialist Ioan Bujoiu and many others). The trial was held in October to November 1948, see *Procesul grupului de compLotiști, spioni și sabotori*, The State Publishing House, Bucharest, 1948.

19. Nistor Chioreanu, *Morminte vii*, Marius Cristian Publishing, European Institute, Iași, 1992, pp.168–169.

20. See Yuri Slezkine, *The Jewish Century*, Princeton University Press, New Jersey, 2004; French translation *Le siècle juif*, La Découverte, Paris, 2009, p. 151

21. King Carol the Second was aware of this plan even before 1940, see Gheorghe Jurgea-Negrilești, *Troica amintirilor*, second edition, Cartea Românească, Bucharest, 2007, pp. 326–327.

22. Ivor Porter, *Operation Autonomous. With the S.O.E. in wartime Romania*, Chatto and Windus, London 1989, pp. 243–244.

23. In order to understand what Stalin meant by "democracy", see Anne Applebaum, *op. cit.*, p. 262. We must also mention the reply given by Stalin in 1937 to an English aristocrat, Lady Astor, who "asked Stalin, twenty years after the Bolshevik revolution: 'How much longer do you intend to keep killing people?' Stalin replied: "As long as it is necessary.'" (Sam Welles, *op. cit.*, p. 7)

24. Stelian Tănase, *op. cit.*, p. 205; Vladimir Tismăneanu, *"Comunismul ca formă mentală"*, in vol. Irepetabilul trecut, second edition, Humanitas, Bucharest, 2008, pp. 172–175: communists want nothing else more than power ("the mad search for power") in an "attempt to establish a permanent despotic hierarchy, profoundly hostile to the values and merits of individuality."

25. Michel Heller and Aleksandr Nekrich, *op. cit.*, p. 108 ; Michael Voslensky, *La Nomenklatura. Les privilégiés en URSS*, Paris, Belfond, 1980, p. 118.

26. Interview taken by Teresa Toranska, *op. cit.*, p. 111.

27. A Yugoslavian communist who lived in the USSR between 1926 and 1935, Ante Ciliga, wrote a book that synthesizes the atmosphere within Comintern administration and the intellectual level of its functionaries: "In the midst of this rushing torrent of Soviet life, the Comintern seemed to me like an unimportant institution. Although I did not yet understand Soviet Russia and the actual role played by the Comintern, I clearly saw from the beginning that there was a truly great divide between reality and the grand discourse on 'the headquarters of worldwide Revolution'. The importance of the Comintern in Moscow was smaller than that of a People's Commissariat. It was nothing more than a department of propaganda under the direct command of the propaganda service of the Central Committee. The people I met – permanent collaborators with the Comintern – seemed to embody the mediocrity of the institution and the grey of the building that housed it. They had no vision, no profound ideas and not independence of thought. I was expecting giants and all I saw were dwarves. I had hoped to reap the teachings of venerable maestros and all I could find were lackeys." (Ante Ciliga, *Dix ans au pays du mensonge déconcertant*, Champ Libre, Paris, 1977, p. 24) The "thousands of parasites" of the Comintern (which Stalin would mockingly call *lavocika*) which consumed the soviet budget, are also dismissingly portrayed by General Walter Krivitsky, *J' étais l' agent de Staline*, Nouveau Monde Editions, Paris, 2015, p, 62. The book was written in 1940.

28. Specialists give out numbers generally ranging from 700 to 1,000 members. Şerban Milcoveanu talks of one thousand and mentions that 700 were Jewish, 150 to 200 were Hungarians, 50 Slavs and 100 Romanians (*Memorii*, pp. 264, 303, 313, 448). All numbers are based on approximations: the first one was given by Emil Bodnăraş when he was asked, prior to the 23rd of August, how many people were in the communist party and could oppose the Germans. I perfectly remember a visit of General Emilian Ionescu, former royal adjutant, at the "Nicolae Iorga" Institute of History in 1970-1971 when he talked about

these events and about the decisive role of the Romanian army (more than 1,400 dead, both soldiers and officers) in the neutralization of German troops around Bucharest (with the help of American Air Forces!). I asked him then how many weapons did the Army" distribute to the "patriotic guard" led by Bodnăraş , as he would later boast that him, alongside the whole party had solely taken down the Germans. "Exactly 200!" was the honest reply of the General, after which a long and profound silence followed in the auditorium full of "specialists" – they continued to remain silent over the decisive role of the army, and also of the fighters who were not part of the communist party. Moreover, in 1944-1945, Ana Pauker would confirm the number of 800 communists, first advanced by Rică Georgescu, see Ivor Porter, *Operation Autonomous*, p. 226. Also see Nicolas Penesco, *op. cit.*, p. 74. The round number of 1,000 seems to me to be copied from the number of Garibaldi's "red shirts".

29. This reminds me of a blanket maker who worked at the customer's home during the 50's and told us – mother and me – how he had been trained in the 30's in the communist movement: he was told that there will be a workers' protest to which he came as well, and modestly joined the crowd. As the crowd advanced down the street, he began to notice that his place in it was constantly moving towards the first line. When he understood that the "leaders" in front were gradually escaping through side alleys, leaving the innocent masses (the "helpful idiots", as Lenin put it) to occupy the first line, he also disappeared and never participated in any such protests ever again. Let us not forget that the first Chief Secretary of PCdR was Gheorghe Cristescu-Plăpumaru (blanket maker)!

30. Here is what Heda Margolius Kovaly, a Czechoslovakian communist wrote: "It is unthinkable to entertain the thought that in Czechoslovakia, after the rise of the communists in 1948, people were once again brutally beaten, if not tortured by the police and that the labor camps had been reopened; not only did we ignore such matters, but if someone would have told us the truth, we wouldn't have believed him. When we heard such acts described on foreign radio stations, such as Radio Free Europe and the BBC, we would unhesitatingly dismiss them on account of being 'imperialist' lies and we saw in them

further proof of this. We had to endure the impact of the crushing Stalinist terror of 1950 in order to open our eyes. It is easy for a totalitarian regime to keep its people in ignorance. Once you give up personal liberty in favour of state rationality, in order to submit to the state or the regime, for the greater glory of the mother land or for any kind of convincing ideas as such, you renounce your right to the truth. Beginning from then, your life starts escaping you, little by little, as if you had opened your veins; you have involuntarily condemned yourself to helplessness." (Heda Margolius Kovály, *Le premier printemps de Prague. Souvenirs*, 1941–1968, Payot, Paris, 1991, pp. 19–20) An exemplary case of a communist who analysed Marxist doctrine and soviet practice from the inside and using his own experience, came to the only sound conclusions is Boris Bajanov. See *Bajanov révèle Staline. Souvenirs d'un ancien secrétaire de Staline, Gallimard*, Paris, 1979.

31. Herbert (Belu) Zilber, *Actor în procesul Pătrășcanu.*, Humanitas, Bucharest, 1997, pp. 24–28. See the similar conclusions for Bulgaria, by Georgi Markov, *op. cit.*, pp. 137–148.

32. Árpád Szakasits (1888-1965) – president of Hungary (1948-1949)

33. Cominform – the International Communist Bureau, created in 1947, on the occasion of the Szklarska Poręba Conference in Poland. It was a forum meant for the coordination and leadership of the international communist movement.

34. Gordon Shepherd, *op. cit.*, pp. 38–40.

35. Sam Welles, *op. cit.*, pp. 6–7.

36. Vladimir Tismăneanu, *Stalinism pentru eternitate*, p. 134. Ana Pauker had been an important agent of the Comintern in France and apparently in the United States of America. She was sent to Romania to organize the 'people's front' imagined by Stalin in order to oppose Nazism, was arrested and sentenced to ten years of prison in 1935. She returned to Moscow in 1941 (as Vasile Luca did), as part of an exchange of prisoners. This explains how the two survived longer than Marcel Pauker and all PCdR leaders, who were executed in the 30's, under the accusations of "Trotskyism", "deviationism" and other "isms". In order to understand the differences between the two groups, see Henry L. Roberts, *op. cit.*, pp. 259–260. For the role of the Muscovites in the installment of eastern communist dictatorship, see Anne Applebaum, *op. cit.*, pp. 89–112.

37. Şerban Milcoveanu reproduces the conversation had in 1965 with an ex-commissary from the Capital Police Prefecture, Marius Gropoşilă. This former commissary told him: "On the 6th of March 1945 I was a commissary of the Capital Police Prefecture and, for one year, I was the leader of the Register Office Service. During these 12 months I issued, without any kind of inquiry, 1,000,000 IDs for people who had no connections with Bucharest". Milcoveanu commented: "Obviously, they were Jewish people from the USSR and Bessarabia, who gathered all in Bucharest, some with plans to create the Jewish Socialist Republic, some with plans to emigrate further, to form the Asian Israel". (Ş. Milcoveanu, *Memorii*, pp. 506, 562) The number has been obviously exaggerated, but the Jewish people would come in large numbers from Poland, Hungary and Germany in order to emigrate into Palestine.

38. The expression belongs to the English historian Hugh Seton-Watson, who elaborated a periodization of the installment of communist regimes in Europe in three phases: the authentic coalition, the fictive coalition, the monolithic regime (*The East European Revolution*, London, 1956, p. 167; Florin Constantiniu, *De la războiul fierbinte la Războiul Rece*, Editura Corint, Bucharest, 1998, p. 115). Gordon Sheperd described that, from 1954, the three phases of the exertion of power by the communists through the internal party politics, and alliances, see *op. cit.*, pp. 15-17.

39. In Iaşi, there were protesters with signs that read: "We want to live in apartment buildings!". For the role of the Red Army in supplying the communists in Hungary with money, cars, trucks with radio, gas, publications, all of which was transported by train in 1945, see Hal Lehrman, *op. cit.*, pp. 183–184. It happened similarly in Romania.

40. Constantin Sănătescu, Jurnal, pp. 173–174. To be compared with the declarations of Stalin made during the same period to the leaders of the communist government in Lublin, Poland, in the work of Florin Constantiniu, *Doi ori doi fac şaisprezece. A început Războiul Rece în România?*, Eurosong & Book, Bucharest, 1997, pp. 114–115.

41. Florin Constantiniu, *Doi ori doi...*, p. 78

42. Arrested by the Soviet secret services, he was prosecuted in Moscow and sentenced to 25 years in a camp in Siberia. He returned after 9 years, full of stories,

see Petre Pandrea, *Memoriile mandarinului valah*, Albatros, Bucharest, 2000, pp. 348–349; the accounts of his sister-in-law, Sanda Tătărescu Negroponte is found in the book written by Victoria Dragu Dimitriu, *Povești ale doamnelor din București*, Vremea, București, 2004, p. 341.

43. Ioan Chiper, Florin Constantiniu, Adrian Pop, *Sovietizarea României. Percepții anglo-americane*, Iconica, Bucharest, 1993, pp. 136–140; Florin Constantiniu, Mihail E. Ionescu, „*Planul sovietic de comunizare a României (martie 1945)*", in Revista Istorică, no. 4, 1993, pp. 657–66

44. Fraud was present in the Bulgarian elections on the 27th of October 1946, where communists turned to a wide variety of maneuvers, including the enlistment of deceased citizens on voting lists, to which people reacted thus: „the electoral lists were nicknamed 'tombstone registers'" (Hal Lehrman, *op. cit.*, p. 267). The Hungarian elections of August 1947 used the same methods, see Christopher Felix, *A Short Course in the Secret War*, Madison Books, Lanham, New York, Oxford, 2001, p. 232-234.

45. Douglas Dunham, *Zone of Violence*, Belmont Books, New York, 1962, pp. 105–106. To our knowledge, this account has not been used by any historian of the period.

46. The most complete reconstruction of this period is written by Nicoleta Ionescu-Gură, *Stalinizarea României. Republica Populară Română (1948–1950). Transformarea instituțională*, ALL, Bucharest, 2005.

47. Dorin-Liviu Bîtfoi, *op. cit.*, p. 37. These numbers, however, beg a few questions: if PCR had approximately 800,000 members at the time of the "unification", it is known that PSD had 560,201 members, plus approximately 193,011 members in its women and youth organizations, which, when added to the numbers of the communists, give out a greater total number than the one stated officially. See Ghiță Ionescu, *op. cit.*, pp. 149–151; and more recently, Nicoleta Ionescu-Gură, „*Crearea P.M.R.*", in Revista Istorică, XIV, 2003, no. 3–4 (May-August), pp. 255–290.

48. Their numers had grown, as shown in the statement belonging to the journalist Ghiță Dinu (known as Stephan Roll): "They were few, now many are left." (Vlaicu Bârna, *Între Capșa și Corso*, second edition, Polirom, Iași, 2014, p. 393)

49. The most famous of them must be mentioned: Mihail Sadoveanu, former president of the Senate and a venerable grade 33 in the Romanian Masonry, who coined the motto: "Lumina vine de la Răsărit" (*the light comes from the East*) – a paraphrase of Voltaire, who, enthusiastic about the cultural plans set in motion by Empress Catherine the Second, said: "Today, the light comes from the North". See Adrian Cioroianu, *"Lumina vine de la Răsărit. «Noua imagine» a Uniunii Sovietice în România postbelică, 1944–1947"*, in Lucian Boia (coord.), *Miturile comunismului românesc*, Nemira, Bucharest, 1998, pp. 21–68; Philosopher Mihai Ralea, former minister of Labor under Carlist dictatorship, when he introduced the fascist salute to official manifestations, who said, in 1944: "The Red Army is a caravan travelling through the dessert. Those who join it will not die of thirst and hunger"; publicist N.D. Cocea, who said, from 1919: "It is easy to sell your conscience, but it is difficult to find a good buyer for it. If all offered consciences would find buyers, we would no longer have any economic problems" (Gh. Jurgea-Negrileşti, *Troica amintirilor. Sub patru regi*, second edition, Cartea Românească, Bucharest, 2007, p. 254). See Lucian Boia, *Capcanele istoriei. Elita intelectuală românească între 1930 şi 1950*, Humanitas, Bucureşti, 2011. For Poland, see Czesław Miłosz, *La pensée captive. Essai sur les logocraties*, Gallimard, Paris, 1953; for Hungary see Sandor Marai, *op. cit.;* for Bulgaria, Georgi Markov, *op. cit.*

50. Ghiţă Ionescu, *op. cit.*, pp. 150–151; Nicoleta Ionescu-Gură, *"art. cit."*

51. Nicoleta Ionescu-Gură, *Stalinizarea României*, p. 353, note 110. The lack of a PhD did not stop any of them from occupying posts as university professors on Marxism and Leninism ever since 1949-1950, see Vladimir Tismăneanu, *Lumea secretă a nomenclaturii*, p. 81. Similar incidents occurred at the Faculty of History with Mihai Roller, Barbu Câmpina, Saşa Muşat, Eugen Stănescu, Solomon Ştirbu, Alexandru (Sami) Vianu, Zamfir Zorin and many others – see Radu Constantinescu, *100 (una sută) de istorioare adevărate cu istoricii epocii de aur povestite de...*, FIDES, Iaşi, 1997; Florin Constantiniu, *De la Răutu şi Roller la Muşat şi Ardeleanu*, Editura Enciclopedică, Bucharest, 2007.

52. I cannot resist the temptation of giving the reader two illustrative examples for the intellectual level of these people. The first is taken from Vernon

Bartlett: "I do have some form of sympathy towards the Romanian minister who interrupted a speech held by a westerner over some undemocratic issues in a rather mocking manner, by unbuttoning his shirt and revealing his back, deeply scarred by the former secret police." (Vernon Bartlett, *op. cit.*, p. 203.). The second example dates back from 1948-1949, and is written by English General Roy Redgrave, born in Romania to an English father and a Romanian mother from the family of General Capșa: "In Romania, Ana Pauker, a protégée of Russia, uneducated and coarse, managed to increase the number of party members by offering jobs and promotions to her friends and many uneducated and uncivilized opportunists. My sister, Ioana, who visited Romania as part of Lord Thompson's entourage, told me of a story that happened at a banquet held in Bucharest, in honor of the Lord's visit. Ana Pauker addressed one of the recently named ministers, telling him: 'Dimitri, your feet smell. Leave the table, leave the saloon and change your socks.' He left the table discreetly and returned to his place five minutes later. However, the smell obviously was still with him, and so she told him again: 'Dimitri, I told you to change your socks'. Profoundly injured by her suspicion of not obeying orders, he raised his voice and replied: 'And I have done so. Look!' He then reached into his pocket and produced the pair of socks in question." See Roy Redgrave, *Balkan Blue: Family and Military Memories, Leo Cooper, London*, 2000, p. 137.

53. For the definition and forms of totalitarianism (word coined in 1923 by Giovanni Amendola, an adversary of Mussolini, who adopted the name in 1925), see Applebaum, *op. cit.*, pp. 19–23. Carl J. Friedrich and Zbigniew Brzezinski identified five traits common to all totalitarian regimes: a dominant ideology, a single party in power, a political police organization meant to rule through terror, the monopoly of information and planned economy; see Carl Joachim Friedrich, Zbigniew K. Brzezinski, *Totalitarian Dictatorship and Autocracy*, Harvard University Press, Cambridge, Mass., 1956.

54. Dennis Deletant, *Teroarea comunistă în România. GheorghiuDej și statul polițienesc, 1948–1965*, Polirom, Iași, 2001, p. 96; for other communist countries, see Anne Applebaum, *op. cit.*, p. 117.

55. Stelian Tănase, *Elite și societate. Guvernarea Gheorghiu-Dej (1948–1965)*, Nemira, Bucharest, 1998; Dennis Deletant, *op. cit.*; Marius Oprea, *Banalitatea*

răului. O istorie a Securității în documente, 1949–1989, Polirom, Iași, 2002. In 1954, the Polish political police had compiled a list of 6 million people grouped in 25 categories of "enemies" who were going to be arrested, prosecuted, and sent to camps and prisons; Anne Applebaum, *op. cit.*, p. 357.

56. D.G.R. Serbanesco, *op. cit.*, p. 129, who also mentions the fact that those put in charge of streets were all communists, armed and with military training. Each one of them had a list with all the people they would have to neutralize in case a war started, so that all opponents to the regime would disappear. The same system was in place in Budapest, from 1945, of course, following the soviet model; Hal Lehrman, *op. cit.*, p. 186.

57. We also had one on General Praporgescu street; he often came along with comrade Florescu, the president of the Women's Street Committee (we called it the committee of street women!). The "sectorist" (I forgot what rank he was) disappeared at some point. I met him again years later; he was dressed in civilian clothes, in a coffee store in the Patria building, where he was arresting a store clerk for selling with faulty weights. He then presented himself as prosecuting attorney! He had advanced in his career.

58. Another invention of Carlist dictatorship was the identity card introduced on the 10th of February 1938; on the 18th of Januart 1941 the government led by Marshal Antonescu would instate the book of records for job attendance; Șerban Milcoveanu, *Memorii*, p. 326.

59. From Annie Bentoiu, *op. cit.*, vol. 2, pp. 277–278 and personal memory. Another scarecrow was the tax inspector named Hilote, a sort of sad clown but extremely perverse, who also made unannounced home visits to check for any signs of illicit earnings. It is true; he was only concerned with freelancers.

60. The first political reaction of the USSR towards the Marshall Plan was the creation of the Cominform, in September 1947 – Anne Applebaum, *Rideau de Fer*, pp. 292–296. The reaction on the economic level was the creation of COMECON (CAER, in Romanian). On the other hand, Henry L. Roberts rightfully noticed that annual and five year plans in communist countries all tended towards the creation of heavy industry and machinery as a solution to the lack of development and to absorb the overpopulation of agricultural personnel in the industry. This was in stark contrast with Nazi Germany politics

towards South-Eastern Europe which was destined to become the supplier of raw materials for the Reich, a solution also proposed by the counsellors of Hrușciov in 1958-1959. This led to tensions within CAER and the "rebellion" of Romania in regards to "socialism work division" and "the Valev plan". (Henry L. Roberts, *op. cit.*, p. 327; Stelian Tănase, *Elite și societate*, p. 206).

61. As to how the CSP managed to undertake these tasks, it can be observed in examples given by Dorin-Liviu Bîtfoi, *op. cit.*, pp. 142–157.

62. Ghiță Ionescu, *"The Pattern of Power"*, in Alexandru Cretzianu, *Captive Rumania,* p. 405.

63. On page 99 more precisely, where he discusses the secret lists in which the posts are found.

64. During the CC meeting of PMR on the 19th to 20th of August 1953, Gheorghiu-Dej announced the creation of a party "active" (soviet terminology) of 80,000-100,000 people, an accomplishment that was successfully carried out by Ceaușescu (Ghiță Ionescu, *op. cit.*, p. 229). In 1960, the party active consisted of over 150,000 people, according to Ghiță Ionescu, *op. cit.*, p. 318. A joke circulating back then illustrates the situation: "Gigel, what does your father do for a living? He's an activist. And your mother? She too doesn't work." (Mihaela-Viorica Constantinescu, *Umorul politic românesc în perioada comunistă. Perspective lingvistice*, Editura Universității din București, Bucharest, 2012, p. 241). Mihai Gramatopol called this social class the *"proțopindada"*, a word formed out of "protipendada" and "țoape".

65. Michael Voslensky, *op. cit.*, p. 125; Sandor Marai, *op. cit.*, p. 252 ; Georgi Markov, *op. cit.*, pp. 47–48, 154–159.

66. Stelian Tănase, *Elite și societate*, pp. 133–136, complete with the lists of job posts and the organizations they worked under. This author does not know of the document commented upon by Ghiță Ionescu, and thus the two works complete each other. Also see the fundamental work on this theme, Nicoleta Ionescu-Gură, *Nomenclatura Comitetului Central al Partidului Comunist Român*, Humanitas, Bucharest, 2006.

67. In 1831, the privileged class represented a total of 1.3% of the population of Tara Românească, and in 1858, the year of the ending of privileges, titles and ranks of the boyars, it was about 2%, see Paul Cernovodeanu and Irina

Gavrilă, *Arhondologiile Țării Românești de la 1837,* Istros, Brăila, 2002, pp. 4–5. In Moldavia, the numbers were slightly higher, see Gheorghe Platon and Alexandru Florin Platon, *Boierimea din Moldova în secolul al XIX-lea. Context european, evoluție socială și politică (Date statistice și observații istorice),* Editura Academiei Române, Bucharest, 1995. For the period before 1918, see the writings of Constantin Argetoianu: "The country is the one hundred thousand people who are in politics." *(Pentru cei de mâine. Amintiri din vremea celor de ieri, vol. I, Ed. Stelian Neagoe,* Humanitas, Bucharest, 1991, p. 120). Gheorghe Jurgea-Negrilești talks about the 300 (instead of one thousand) families who "ruled over feudal Romania", meaning the old kingdom *(op. cit.,* pp. 234 and 414). In 1942, Mihail Manoilescu found 125,000 bourgeois in Romania (out of which 101,000 pseudo-bourgeois in the service of the state or in liberal professions, and just 22,500 true bourgeois: big industrialists, bankers, big agricultural owners, engineers who occupied private economic functions, economists who did the same and the renters of the six categories) to a population of 20 million. However, proprietors and owners totalled 3,326,600 people, while salary owners of any kind were a mere 1,091,015, almost a third of the number of proprietors *(Rostul și destinul burgheziei românești,* Cugetarea, Bucharest, 1942, pp. 104–124). Thus, the bourgeois and proprietors represented approximately 17-18% of the entire population. But not all proprietors can be considered privileged, because there are differences between different proprieties and their value, thus the percentage of total privileged people in the era of the bourgeois was closer to the one from the former times than this 17-18%. Also see the observation made by Petre Pandrea who had noticed that in Bucharest (so in Romania), between 1924 and 1958, "only approximately 300 people govern." (Memoriile mandarinului valah, p. 159).

68. In Hungary, there are 71,000 positions, out of which 24,000-25,000 are superior in rank, according to Stelian Tănase, *op. cit.,* p. 135; Sandor Marai talks about 100,000 people forming the nomenclature, *op. cit.,* p. 252. For RDG, see Hermann Weber, *op. cit.,* pp. 201–202.

69. See the note above; reedited by Ghiță Ionescu, op. cit., pp. 167–168. Other lists, such as academicians and many others, written by Nicoleta Ionescu-Gură, *Nomenclatura,* pp. 204–226, as well as the detailed discussion of privileges;

for USSR in the 30's see Douglas Smith, *Former People*, pp. 326–330; for Bulgaria, see Georgi Markov, *op. cit.,* pp. 154–159. One of the most significant privileges of this group, also belonging to the ones aspiring to join it and set on the right track, was the blue "envelope" containing money, which only the most deserving comrades would receive at the end of the month. Another aspect borrowed from the soviets, where the "envelope" was called "a package" (Michael Voslensky, *op. cit.*, p. 224). For Romanians, the customs that came "packaged" were the ones received from the "formers" in the West. For other privileges and the life style of this elite, see Vladimir Tismăneanu, *Lumea secretă a nomenclaturii. Amintiri, dezvăluiri, portrete,* Humanitas, Bucharest, 2012. We also had a colleague whose father, a professor at Politehnica called Dumitru (Mitu) Dumitrescu was an academician and even a secretary to the Academy, which permitted him to amass a great art collection, for which see details in Mihai Gramatopol, *op. cit.*, vol. 2, pp. 82–85.

70. A person occupying a post in the nomenclature has no decisional power unless they are a party member as well: this was the case for professor Tudor Vianu, the director of the Academy Library, who had decisional power (to hire functionaries) only after he joined the party. The story appears in Mihai Gramatopol, *op. cit.*, vol. 2, pp. 7.

71. Lavinia Betea, *Povești din cartierul Primăverii*, Curtea Veche, Bucharest, 2010, p. 154. Her mother was Ana Toma, born Grossman, who was adjunct minister in MAE and a close collaborator to Ana Pauker (1947-1952), afterwards she was adjunct minister of Exterior Commerce and finally, adjunct minister of Interior Commerce. Between 1955 and 1965, she was acting and full member of the CC of PMR. Personally, my memory is contradictory: in the 1964 class book, my father's profession was written as "functionary to the Patriarchy", which was only half true, but the other way around: my father was first of all a priest for Batiștei church and we avoided saying that (even if it was widely known) in the hopes (an illusion) that it sounded more neutral.

72. Gordon Shepherd, *op. cit.*, pp. 14–15, 18. This explains the large number of "workers" in communist statistics: the activists were registered as workers, because most of them had been recruited from this social category, according to Stelian Tănase, op. cit., p. 220. An author wrote that to consider activists such as Ceaușescu or his wife to be workers was like considering an American

millionaire that had worked in the factory or sold ice on the street as a boy to be a worker. Let us remind the reader of a scene that took place in East Berlin in 1953, when a group of protesters from working sites was met in the front of the Ministry building by the Minister of Industry, Fritz Selbmann, who said to them: "My comrades! (Whistles of disapproval) We are not your comrades! But I am a worker as well! You have long forgotten what work means! Raising his arms, he said to the crowd: Workers! Look at my hands! Your hands are plump and beautiful, they said." Afterwards, Selbmann left in the discontented roar of the crowd. (Georges Castellan, *op. cit.*, p. 192) It is very probable thet the miners in Valea Jiului thought the same while listening to Ilie Verdeț in 1977.

73. In this sense, it is worth quoting the opinion of the chancellor Bismarck, who defined Marxism and its political system, which, back then in 1878 was a mere utopia, thus: "As every man must have his share of existence imparted from above, our existence becomes a sort of prison in which each of us is at the mercy of the wardens. But, in our modern prisons, the warden is at least an officially named person, against which a complaint can be filed. In the great socialist prison, who are the wardens? As for filing any complaint against them, it is out of the question, because they shall be the most merciless tyrants the world has ever seen, and the rest shall be the slaves to these tyrants." (Quoted by Sam Welles, *op. cit.,* p. 6).)

74. See the conclusions of Georgi Markov on the same matter in the case of Bulgaria, in *op. cit.*, pp. 22–44.

75. Mihai Gramatopol, „*Totalitarism și hieratism*" (1994), in *idem, Morfologia dezastrului*, Editura Orientul Latin, Brașov, 2005, pp. 37–39. Also see Anne Applebaum, op. cit., p. 492: "In the 50's, the biggest part of East European citizens worked for the state, occupied housing owned by the state and sent their children to state schools. They depended on the state for their health and bought food from state owned stores. It is understandable that they hesitated in confronting the state except in dramatic circumstances: most of the time that was not the case, because during peace time it is rare that circumstances are dramatic."

76. Strikes were permitted in USSR until 1937, when the criminal code banned them, the strike participants being punishable by death, and later by 20 years

of prison. In communist countries, strikes were declared to be reactionary and criminal. In Romania, Decree no. 138 from 1949 banned strikes, declaring them "economic aggressions" and punished it with up to 12 years in prison and a fine ranging from 10,000 to 100,000 lei, according to Ygael Gluckstein, op. cit., pp. 94–97.

77. Anne Applebaum, op. cit., pp. 571–572. Daniel Barbu identified this regime as "a pastoral type of power", a "biopower" (Michel Foucault) in which the power "takes over the vital functions of the social corpus, and the individual is "fed and nurtured in a sort of social maternity" (*„Destinul colectiv, servitutea involuntară, nefericirea totalitară: trei mituri ale comunismului românesc",* in *Lucian Boia (coord.), Miturile comunismului românesc,* Nemira, Bucharest, 1998, p. 191).

CHAPTER 4

Our Neighborhood

———

As FIRST GRADE STUDENTS, IN September 1953, we did not know or understand much of what had happened to our country over the past nine years, which had been decisive for the evolution of Romanian society. However, ancient philosophers and modern teachers believe that at the age of seven, the child reaches the age of reason, at which point our memories began filling out the outlines of this historical tableau whose evolution over the past year and a half had been dramatic. In February-March 1952, the CC of PMR publicly condemned three of the most prominent Communist leaders, who were deposed from office, arrested, put on trial and sent to prison. They were the very same people referenced in the slogan I mentioned earlier: "Our Ana[1]", "the most powerful woman in the world" or "the Balkan Passionaria", which is a nick name given to Ana Pauker in memory of the Spanish communist and civil war fighter Dolores Ibarruri, Luca (Vasile), Teo (Teohari Georgescu), people mentioned alongside Marx, Engels, Lenin and Stalin in the 1950 spelling book! They were being made responsible for every failure in economy, finance, agriculture, and last but not least, they held the blame regarding the purity of a party who had let all sorts of reactionaries join their ranks. Gheorghiu-Dej was the one who took their place, having gained Stalin's approval to eliminate his opponents. But there were some mixed signals: on the one hand, August saw the end of the so-called 're-education' program at Gherla prison, an atrocious invention of the Romanian prison system which began in 1949 in Pitești[2]. On the other hand, in August-September there were two massive public trials involving the 'saboteurs' at the Dunăre-Marea Neagră Canal, the largest (forced) labor camp in Romania (over 40,000 prisoners) - the leaders took their inspiration from the White Sea-Baltic Canal - destined to become "the graveyard of the Romanian bourgeoisie"[3]. 25 people were put on trial, "the subversive band lead by [engineer] Frangopol Nicolae", and were sentenced to death (three of them, including engineer Aurel Rozei-Rozenberg), to forced labor for life (Eng. Nicolae Frangopol) and to 8-25 years in prison (construction of the Canal would cease in 1953). Finally, on November 13th, 1952, the CC of PMR and the Council of Ministers announced the beginning of an ambitious plan to rebuild and organize the major cities in the country, particularly the capital, a plan that was well-received by the public opinion (despite the fact that it meant tens of thousands of "non-productive" people would be expelled from the city). Also in 1952 (in August), Jews' emigration to Israel was blocked, dealing a dramatic blow to the heart of this minority. This last measure, dictated by Moscow, showed the aggravation of Stalin's anti-Semitic paranoia, culminating in "The Doctors' plot", through which a group of Jewish doctors were accused of wanting to assassinate Communist leaders Andrei Jdanov and even Stalin himself. The death of the "Generalissim", officially announced on March 5th, 1953 (a numerical combination - 5.3.53 - that the late Stalin would have appreciated, wrote a contemporary), elicited a sigh of relief from everyone, along with the understanding that a new era was approaching[4]. This was followed by the arrest and execution of Lavrentiy Beria, Stalin's main henchman and Minister of the Interior, as well as Nikita Khrushchev's victory as the elected Chief Secretary of the CC of PCUS introduced a series of reforms in the history of the USSR and its satellites.

Gheorghiu-Dej and the other Communist leaders understood it was time for a *detente* and for de-Stalinization, a fact that is evident from the new Chief Secretary's speech at the CC of PMR plenum on August 19th-20th, 1953. He announced a "new course" for the state and party politics, something which all satellite states would share, based on a critique of excessive industrialization, on growing people's standard of living, abandoning forced collectivization in agriculture and a *detente* in international relations. The PMR's role as leader was strongly reaffirmed, as was the necessity of collective ruling and, most importantly, creating a party active of

80,000-100,000 members[5]. In the following years, the internal and external *detente* became even more real after the Geneva Conference (July 18th-23rd, 1955) where the Ministers for Foreign Affairs from the four superpowers met. One of the consequences was that states from the Eastern Bloc were allowed into the UN, in December: it was a package deal, through which 16 countries were admitted, including Spain, Italy and Finland from the West. As a gesture of good faith, Romanian authorities pardoned a few thousand political prisoners between September 1955 and 1957. Finally, the second PMR Congress which took place between December 23rd-28th, 1955, proceeded to make some changes at the head of the party, eliminating the three Communist leaders that had been forced to step down in 1952, as well as Constantin Doncea[6], and notably, they decided to bring Petre Borilă, young Alexandru Drăghici (Minister of the Interior) and Nicolae Ceaușescu into the political bureau.

The XXth Congress of the PCUS followed, where Khrushchev, in a report that made waves throughout the world, denounced Stalin's "cult of personality" and firmly assumed a reforming course based on an internal and international *detente*. The Romanian delegation (Gheorghiu-Dej, Miron Constantinescu and Petre Borilă) each drew the appropriate conclusion, the only difference being that Dej put the blame on his opponents, who had been eliminated in 1952, while Miron Constantinescu personally attacked Gheorghiu-Dej, whose responsibility for the errors and crimes of the past was obvious and ultimately lead to his own "downfall", together with Chișinevschi, in 1957[7].

As for education, it was still on the course set by Law 175 regarding the educational reform, from August 3rd, 1948, which set out to eradicate illiteracy and educate youth "in the spirit of popular democracy"[8]. Education was to be administered by the state, the Church and the schools would become separate, private and confessional schools would be suppressed, preschool (kindergarten) and a unified school system would be introduced - the first seven years of school were mandatory, plus another three (and later four, from 1956) of high school or trade school, like the Soviets had, and the tsarist system before that, who in turn had adopted the XIX century German system. Moreover, the concept of "class struggle" would become the focus:

children must be taught, as early as kindergarten, to hate and despise "the bourgeois", "the capitalists", "the kulaks", who are seen as "beasts". They should also combat "mysticism", an esoteric concept covering a large ideological sphere, from fighting against old superstitions to religion. Many teachers were fired and replaced with "new teachers", who lacked any serious training or qualifications[9]. Russian was introduced in fourth grade, three classes per week, which the lawmaker thought would ensure a perfect command of the language after eight years of study (some of my classmates, however, didn't even know the Cyrillic alphabet in the eleventh grade). In 1949, the pioneers were founded, their slogan being "Fight on, for Lenin and Stalin's cause!" The Government gave them the Cotroceni palace, hosting various useful and interesting clubs, like the one called "deft hands". Many children had the privilege of going on summer camps, to the mountains or to the sea, an opportunity which poor children didn't have before the war, and which the authorities saw as having the advantage of socializing and developing children's life skills while engage in group activities[10].

"Spiru Haret" high school was suppressed, like many other high schools (after 1948 there were only 153[11] out of 315 left in the country, as well as 1,700 schools out of 3,100), and in its place came "Lazăr" high school, called "L.B. 9"[12] (Boys' high school no. 9)[13], that became "L.b. 12" in 1954, then "Middle school" and finally, in 1956, it became "Mixed middle school no. 12". Students attending this school had to live in the I.V. Stalin district (renamed "30 Decembrie"[14] in 1962), although the high school was situated at the border with the "1 Mai"[15] district. Its People's Council (the old mayoralties had been replaced by People's Councils in 1949) was across the street from Batiştei church, on the corner of General Praporgescu street and Alexandru Sahia street, while the People's Council from the I.V. Stalin district was much farther, in 30 Decembrie Square, later renamed Amzei Square. This constraint meant that every year, those of us who lived closer to the boulevard (on Batiştei street no. 1-19) had to file a special request to be admitted to a school which was essentially five minutes away from our home. Despite this territorial division, many students were admitted into "Spiru Haret" from the Batiştei neighborhood, which stretched roughly from the Brătianu Boulevard (inaugurated in 1928 and finished in 1943), called Bălcescu and Magheru today, and the University Square to C.A. Rosetti Street (near the Scala cinema) to the West and the North, Vasile Lascăr up to Calea Moşilor to the East, and the Republicii Boulevard (the former and actual Carol I, previously known as Mareşal Tolbuhin) to the South. The alternative was "Dimitrie Cantemir" high school, in the North-West (high school no. 4 and no. 13), "Mihai Viteazul" in the North (L.B. 12) or "Matei Basarab" in the East (L.B. 2). Later, "Lazăr" high school was reopened and "Mihail Sadoveanu" high school was opened on Dacia Boulevard.

The history of this neighborhood is very interesting, and I know it well because in 1959 I entered a competition organized by the Bucharest History Museum called "Know your neighborhood" (or something like that). I wrote a paper and won Second Prize (the Grand Prize was for factory and plant monographs) and a diploma, which made my mother, who had insisted that I participate[16], very proud indeed. Since "Spiru Haret" was first of all a middle school for this neighborhood (the primary school was "Clemenţei", on C.A. Rosetti Street, formerly Clemenţei Street; there had been a middle school on Rotari Street, called I.L. Caragiale today), some information about the past of this part of Bucharest could be welcome[17].

"One of the neighborhoods that remind me of Western cities is the one called Batiştei," wrote Ulysse de Marsillac. "It is Bucharest's Saint-Germain suburb[18]. Here, the streets are almost straight and somewhat clean. There are few shops, but no factories or workshops; most houses are nestled between a garden and a backyard. The gates are shielded by metal grating or, baring that, wooden fences. It would have been primarily an aristocratic setting, were the great families not reunited in the more privileged Calea Mogoşoaia (Calea Victoriei). As it is, I firmly dislike Batiştei because it is completely unoriginal. It is a mere imitation of our Western cities, nothing more: plaster and *papier mâché* instead of marble and carved stone."[19]

This first description of our neighborhood, dating back to 1869, is important for understanding the setting in which we, the "Spiru Haret" students, developed between 1953 and 1964. The testimony of Ulysse de Marsillac, a French professor living in Bucharest, captures the transformation of a neighborhood, which, only a few decades prior, had been a "suburb"(mahala) largely populated by craftsmen, royal and noble servants, merchants etc. In 1852, the area between Carol Boulevard, Calea Moșilor, Maria Rosetti and Jean-Louis Calderon Streets was 83% green (in 1948, the green area was merely 0.5%)[20]. Batiștei's main feature was its aquatic nature, due to a large web of streams and ponds, flowing from "the Icoana pond" (also called "Bulindroiului Lake") It measured 2,5 hectares, stretching across what we know today as the "Grădina Icoanei" park (the name comes from a nearby church that had a miracle-working icon), Ioanid Park (called Ion Voicu today, after the famous violinist who lived nearby), Alexandru Sahia Square (former and actual Gogu Cantacuzino) and the area nearby. This lake and the lights that could be seen at night on its surface feature in a short story by Mihail Sadoveanu, published in the book "Bordeienii", about the death of a young, brave man who drowned, together with his horse, *in illo tempore*, because of a beautiful naiad who lured people in.

From the Icoanei pond sprang a stream called Bucureștioara (Gârlița, Bucureștianca, even Căcaina, like the one in Iași, and Căcata) which collected all "household, professional and human foulness" (as a historian called it), and weaved its way along the narrow streets, through people's yards or green fields for 2,5 kilometers: it formed a pond on the corner of Dionisie Lupu Street and C.A. Rosetti street, near a park with a statue of Constantin Dobrogeanu-Gherea; then it went along Jean-Louis Calderon Street, behind Batiștei church, across Republicii Boulevard (former and actual Carol I), behind Colțea Hospital, where it formed a lake called Balta Cucului[21], because there you could hear the cuckoo's song. Then it went on towards the Dâmbovița river, meeting it near the Forensic Institute (The Morgue, which Ceaușescu tore down).

Many different craftsmen settled on Bucureștioara's banks and in the nearby area between the 17th and 18th centuries, especially butchers who used a large uninhabited area (this shows up on city maps from 1770 and 1787-1789)[22] as a cattle pen for the cows they cut on "chairs"[23], or large tree trunks; from their fat, soap makers[24] would make soap, and these two guilds lent their names to the nearby churches neighborhood, "Scaune" and "Săpunari"[25]. There were also fishermen, skinners, chandlers, royal and noble servants, as well as some lower-rank noblemen. All sorts of dirt would carelessly be disposed of in the water (as was the case with Dâmbovița as well[26]), causing the drains to clog up frequently and the people to complain to the administration and to the lordship[27]. After 1830, some streets were paved with stone, causing the Batiștei suburbs to become flooded and the residents to remain in their homes or travel by boat.

The pavement of the streets and the great fire of 1847 completely reworked the urban landscape of this neighborhood: the streets were drawn straight, the buildings were aligned, some of the ponds were drained. But this was a recurring problem, as Alexandru Tzigara-Samurcaș (1872-1952) mentioned, an art historian who was born in the neighborhood and only left in 1880: "At the edge of the old city, at what today is no. 25 and 27, Icoanei Street, was my grandfather's vineyard, that could only be reached by carriage, because you had to cross the marshes on Crinului Street, on Sălciilor Street, going through the great bogs which today make up Grădina Icoanei and the huge building of the Girls' Middle School ["Școala Centrală", built by the architect Ion Mincu]. After the area was drained, the vineyard was taken up by the low buildings, which made up the Samurcaș Inn...[28]"

In fact, the mayoralty drained the Icoanei pond completely in 1873 and the following years, and in its place came the Gogu Cantacuzino Square, Icoanei Park and Ioanid Park, the latter named after an editor, Gheorghe Ioanid, who planted many different species of trees and plants here[29], then Strada Nouă (called Dumbrava Roșie Street today) and Bulevardul Nou (today Dacia Boulevard, inaugurated in 1910). The resulting land was allotted and sold to rich people who couldn't find available plots on Calea Victoriei and the nearby area, where the most luxurious residences of the most fashionable people were concentrated. This remained the most sought-after neighborhood until the 1930s, when the economic crisis lead to new neighborhoods being build in the North, the so-called Filipescu Park (owned by the Filipescu family), where the new bourgeois and later communist elites took up residence[30].

The sophisticated nature of Batiștei is hinted at by the presence of foreign delegations following the 1877 Independence and the 1881 Kingdom. Thus, in 1882 we find the English legation, and later, in 1887, the English consulate (at no. 46, Scaune Street)[31], the Belgian legation (at no. 6, Italiană Street, moved in 1890 to no. 9, Scaune Street, and the Minister Plenipotentiary at no. 69, Scaune Street), the Imperial German legation at no. 14, Polonă Street (called Calderon today), then in 1887, at no. 15, and in 1890, at no. 25, the same as Bernard von Bülow, the Minister Plenipotentiary (no. 62 and 65, Scaune Street), and the Bulgarian legation on Clemenței Street. In 1940-1941, we find the United States legation at no. 9, Dionisie Lupu Street, the Slovak one at no. 47 (it will move to Oțetari Street, as the Czechoslovak embassy, the Slovak embassy of today), and the Swiss legation on Pitar Moș Street. In 1939, we can find the Grand Duchy of Luxembourg's consulate at no. 6, Batișteii Street, the British one at no. 2, Columb Street, and the Spanish one at no. 29, Robert de Flers (Luca Stroici).

Nearby, between 1882 and 1912, there was the City Hall in the Hagi-Mosco building, which has been since torn down but used to be in the small park between Colțea Hospital and the Ministry of Agriculture (architect Louis Blanc, 1894), facing the large Ion C. Brătianu statue erected in 1903 by the sculptor Ernest Dubois[32]. Before having its own building, the mayoralty rented various houses after 1912: in 1939, it was at no. 21, Nicolae Filipescu Street, with different Directorates at different addresses on Batiștei Street (Financial at no. 39, moved to 25 in 1941; Firefighters and the Municipal Library at no. 15), on Dionisie Lupu Street, at no. 48 (New Developments), on Vasile Lascăr Street, at no. 38 (Roads and Bridges), and on Vasile Boerescu Street, at no. 3 (Technical Development Control)[33].

There were several new, high-quality and important private and public schools in the neighborhood: "Luigi Geanelloni" Boarding School for Boys, on Vestei Street (Pensionatului, then Vasile Boerescu), between 1834 and 1853, then the Schewitz-Thierrin Institute (at no. 51, Scaune Street, which became no. 33), founded by professors Raoul de Pontbriant and Anton Schewitz in 1851, torn down in 1938, where many generations studied, some leaving printed memories (Al. Tzigara-Samurcaș, Alexandru Bilciurescu etc.)[34]. The resulting space was sold to the neighboring Girls' High School "Regina Maria" (at no. 6, Eugen Stătescu), and afterwards the whole space was used to build the Gas and Oil Institute.

In 1859, the Girls' Boarding School "Sfânta Maria" was opened (founded in 1848 as an Episcopal School), at no. 13, Pitar Moș Street, giving its name to the building. The school also had a chapel, and the teachers were German nuns from Nymphenburg, near Munich, and were part of the English Ladies of Bavaria Congregation (*Bayerischen Englischen Fräulein*), founded by Maria Ward. The school had 600 students in 1915 and 700 in 1919, entire generations of well-bred Romanian girls. This beautiful institution was disbanded through the Educational Decree from 1948, and in its place came, chronologically: the School of Sanitary Engineering, the "Maxim Gorki" Romanian-Soviet Pedagogical Institute and then The Faculty of Foreign Languages from the University of Bucharest, while the chapel was seized by the library belonging to the Ministry of Health[35].

Next is Clemenței School, one of the oldest in the city (built before 1857), also called School no. 1 because it was the first primary school in Bucharest[36]. Then there was "Mihai Bravu" Middle School, first, in 1882, at no. 9 Rotari Street (I.L. Caragiale) with 12 teachers, and then, eight years later, at no. 6, Italiană Street, with 16 teachers, including the French teacher Bonifaciu Florescu (Nicolae Bălcescu's son with Alexandra "Luxița" Florescu), and the Science teacher Nicolae Coculescu. The headmaster and History teacher was I. Mărescu[37]. In 1864, the Council of Ministers decided that a commercial school would be founded at no. 48, Batiștei Street, which was later moved to a different neighborhood. Finally, three Girls' Boarding Schools were opened: the first, belonging to Mrs. Beaumont (at no. 7, Polonă Street), the second, belonging to Mrs. M. Dobrescu, at no. 47, Scaune Street, and the third, called "Profesorii asociați"[38] (at no. 16, Polonă Street, and then at no. 18, Italiană Street). At no 16, Polonă Street (called Calderon today) there was the Fröbel School for Small Children, headmistress Regina Roth. In 1892-1894, there will be added the Central School for Girls on Icoanei Street, designed by the architect Ion Mincu (1852-1912)[39]. During or immediately after World War II, the Faculty of Pharmacy came into being at no. 17, Gogu Cantacuzino, where it can be found today.

It must be noted that, before having its current building, the first location of "Spiru Haret" high school was on Scaune Street (Nicolae Filipescu), between Batiștei Street and Carol I Boulevard, which was aptly described by Constantin Bărbulescu (*Viața mea, cu smerenie*, Vremea, Bucharest, 2015, pp. 55-57). It moved after World War I, because Alexandru Ciorănescu, a student between 1922-1927, still remembers "playing *oină*[40] or football on the street behind the school, where the National Theatre was built later"[41]. I don't know if this is the Hungarian Catholic Kindergarten and School for Girls, opened in 1903 at no. 10, Scaune Street, in a very stylish location. A school for boys was opened around the same time (at no. 25, Gogu Cantacuzino Street), which also belonged to the "St. Ladislaus" Association in Budapest, headed by the Archbishop of Kalocsa, Leopold Arpad Varady. Both schools were closed and confiscated by the Romanian state in 1918[42]. Another Hungarian school functioned before 1914 at no. 30, Gogu Cantacuzino Street, but it was later turned into a Romanian school[43]. Finally, at no. 72, Dionisie Lupu Street, there was a "Spiru Haret" Boarding House for Girls since 1905, with 175 spots, donated by Mrs. Cțlda Averescu, the future marshal's wife[44].

There were also two hospitals in the neighborhood, the "Sfânta Elisabeta" Sisters of Charity Institute (patroned by Queen Elizabeth) at no. 15, Clemenței Street (later moved to Filantropia Boulevard), whose head and mother superior was Alexandra Florescu, Bonifaciu Florescu's mother, and whose doctors in the neighborhood included Nicolae Kalinderu, who lived at no. 34, Scaune Street. There was also a hospital at no 41, Teilor Street (Vasile Lascăr

Between 1882 and 1890 there were also two drugstores (La Aurora, at no. 14bis, Batiştei Street[45], and Esculap, at no. 18, Dionisie Lupu Street), two pubs[46], two grocery stores, two carpenters, four cartwrights, a quilt maker, the famous beer maker Luther and the businessman M. Tonolla, all famous people of that age.

But most people were landowners, stockholders, politicians, magistrates, field officers and members of liberal professions, as well as aristocrats: this is who Ulysse de Marsillac referred to: Lord Steward Alexandru Samurcaş, whose house took up the corner of Italiană Street and Polonă Street (Jean-Louis Calderon), a huge space with a large garden, servants' quarters, stables and other outbuildings. In front of it was a huge green field where children would fly paper kites. Across the street, at no. 21, Polonă Street, Toma Tzigara, Samurcaş' son-in-law and the memorialist's father, built another large house in 1864, with a yard near the street and a garden in the back, next to some properties owned by the banker I. Hagi-Theodoraki[47] (or Tudorache, father-in-law to Emil Protopopescu-Pache, the mayor who inaugurated the boulevard named after him, who lived, at first, next to his in-laws) and a Mr. Porumbaru, where doctor Gerota's house would be, and where the Taxing District Office is today. In the place occupied today by the Faculty of Pharmacy and a block of flats, in the middle of a huge desolate garden, there was the House with the Red Rooster (the name came from the red weathervane) belonging to Count Scarlat Rosetti (1802-1872), an original figure, also a former Bucharest mayor[48]. Other imposing houses belonged to Retoridi, at no. 42, Colțea Street, torn down in 1894 to build "Grădinița" Restaurant and later the Intercontinental Hotel, both owned by the banker Christofi Zerlendi, a Bucharest Senator and a member of the Local Council (1888-1895)[49] since 1885. Behind them, on Batiștei Street, there is a mention in Major Pappazoglu's 1871 plans of a small house, where the revolutionary political figure C.A. Rosetti had his printing office.

About halfway down Batiștei Street[50], there was a group of three large houses, as grand as palaces, owned by Constantin Blaremberg (1839-1886)[51], the police prefect between 1873-1875 (no. 15, the former Municipal Library which later became Schiller House), next to which (at no. 13) his son-in-law built a house[52] in 1887 (the US consulate since 1976). He was the conservative politician Nicolae Filipescu (d. 1916), the mayor of Bucharest (1893-1895), the richest man in Romania after the death of Gh. Gr. Cantacuzino "the Nawab" in 1913 (he owned a house on Calea Victoriei, today the George Enescu Museum). Another one of Blaremberg's son-in-laws, the diplomat Edgar Mavrocordat (d. 1935), built a house at no. 5, Tudor Arghezi Street, where his son, Georgel, lived until his death in 1976. He was a former political prisoner who was forced to hide in the house's basement, where the kitchen used to be. The next house, at no. 9, a palace in itself, the banker Mauriciu Blank owned it (who first lived on Calderon Street). He was the founder of Marmorosch-Blank Bank. It dates back to the last decade of the 19th century: in 1940-1941, the American legation took up rooms here. Nicolae Filipescu's house had a gigantic back yard, along which many houses were built, on the street named after him, up to no. 40[53], which belonged to his son, Grigore, a journalist and a politician, who died in 1938 without leaving any heirs (in 1952, this was the Central Militia Department and today it is the Department of Religions). Across the street from the American legation, at no. 24, Dionisie Lupu Street, in 1882 there was General Dumitru Sallmen's house (1836-1923, a descendant of a Russian officer of Finnish descent), who was married to Elena Butculescu, whose parents owned houses on Clemenței Street. Behind the house, where the stables used to be, General David Praporgescu built his house, which can be found today at no. 17, Praporgescu Street. He was a World War I hero, married to Maria Sallmen, the General's daughter. We notice that family houses tend to group up in this neighborhood.

Accross the street from the former no. 12, Dionisie Lupu street), we reach a large block of flats, on the corner of Dionisie Lupu Street and Batiștei Street: in 1890, a Mr. C. Ianoși built his house here, designed by the same architect, A. Krause, as the neighboring house at no. 17, Batiștei Street, owned by M. Popescu[54]. Two houses were built in 1887 at no. 20 and 20bis, Dionisie Lupu Street: the first, built by architect P. Petricu, belonged to the Urlățeanu family, and the second (architect W. Gerabek), belonged to Anghel D. Solacolu. Today, there are two blocks of flats in their place, at no. 18 and 20.

Going East on Batiștei Street, after the church and its houses (today a bank), on the left, at no. 23, there is an old building designed by architect Leonida Negrescu in 1890 (a former Post office, today a drugstore), and at no. 25 A a huge house[55] owned by Minister Jean Th. Florescu (who died in prison in 1950), the former Tax Office (1941), the former District Office of the Party, which today is the Court House, followed by I. Procopie Dumitrescu's house, a former mayor and landowner, Ioana Celibidache's grandfather, the conductor's wife, today a pay clinic[56]. In the next house, which is actually two wagon-style houses, dating back to the end of the 19th century, lived the Ghica-Deleni family and the lawyer Victor Eustațiu, together with his brother (or son), dr. George Eustațiu, between 1950-1960. At no. 31, a somber building, erected at the beginning of the 20th century, belonged to prince Alexandru Callimaki, who was married to Maria Vernescu, the daughter of a very rich liberal politician, whose lush house at no. 127, Calea Victoriei, hosts today a casino; after 1948, the house became the Sovromchimie headquarters (another beautiful house, at no. 25, Thomas Masaryk, was the Sovromfilm, then the Film Archive) and was taken by the Secret Services in 1954, who built a large block of flats, with antennae piled on top, at no. 14-16, Maria Rosetti Street. Finally, the beautiful house at no. 33, at the corner of I.L. Caragiale Street, the Hungarian Cultural Office for many years, was built in 1944 for the Minister for Foreign Affairs Mihai (Ică) Antonescu, but he could never live in it[57]. Accross the street, at no. 24 A, there was Hermann Spayer's house (1900)[58], Mauriciu Blank's brother-in-law. The house was seized by the PCR for a special canteen, today the "21 Decembrie" association, and to its right, on Dr. Bacalogu Street, the party built a hotel for party members, which has since been privatized.

To the North, on C.A. Rosetti Street, three majestic houses (no. 33, 35 and 37) were owned by the Butculescu family (1887)[59], the great land-owner Sava Șomănescu (1900)[60], the Vietnamese Embassy of today, and the one from 1896 by doctor Constantin Cantacuzino (1849-1920)[61], Sabina Brătianu's husband, the sister of Ion I.C. (Ionel) and Vintilă Brătianu. Today it is a military unit.

Going towards the boulevard, between C.A. Rosetti Street and Pitar Moș Street, next to the block of flats on the corner of Dionisie Lupu Street, a Catargi house has gone through many changes. I quote from Emanoil Hagi-Mosco:

> The land this house was built on was split in two. Next to the building on the corner of the street was a two-story house that served for some time as a diet restaurant, a fashion boutique and a state institution. In the back yard, the old, quite large Catargi outbuildings remained. On the remaining piece of land, doctor Botez Moscu (1882-1941), who used to work at the Brâncovenesc Hospital, married to one of the Catargi girls, who had the land as dowry, built a house (which shared a dead wall with the one next door), with a heightened first floor, a top floor and ceramic decorations. As for doctor Moscu, his patronym is Casasovici, of Macedonian origin. His grandfather or even his father was nicknamed "Moscu", hence the doctor's surname.[62]

Accross the street, where the Scala building is now, there was a house where General Ion Argetoianu used to live in 1884 and the following years, whose son, Constantin Argetoianu (1871-1954), the politician, was also a formidable memorialist. Here is what he wrote:

"Thus I discovered Heaven on Earth. It was in 1884, in the Fall, when my parents moved from Dorobanți Street to Clemenței Street (now called C.A. Rosetti), in Nicu Negri's houses, leaving us with a quite sizeable garden, half-abandoned and out of order. Negri's houses and especially the garden were cleaved to make way for the Brătianu Boulevard: a piece of the house where the "Regina Elisabeta" Sisters of Charity used to stay and a strip of garden are still visible as I write these lines[63]*... Our garden, disdained by the parents and left to me and Lică Odobescu, my closest companion in adventures and in learning, had once been lovingly cared for, because in it you could find anything you needed. The garden was fenced on three sides by high walls, while towards the yard there was a low wooden picket lined with privet hedges. Towards the back, separated from the wall by a narrow footpath, there was a sizeable octagonal pavilion, all solid brick, with a bolted door and a window (double-glassed, since the walls were thick) on each of the other seven sides of the building. Towards the center of the garden, a little to the right, there was a mound with a narrow footpath going round it up to the top. On the other side of the courtyard, opposite the mound, there was a dried-up pond, overrun by herbage and sprouts, which couldn't even hold rainwater. There were vestiges of abandoned alleys, whose straight or sinewy paths disappeared under piles of dried leaves and all sorts of weeds that grew unchecked. The untrimmed trees took liberties and grew tangled, making up a maze of branches you could hardly walk through. A wet, cool shadow, the specter of a place where no-one has set foot, loomed over this forgotten place in the middle of the city. Before being ours, this slip of Heaven belonged only to beasts, bugs, crickets, moles, lizards, and lost or lovesick cats. The sleepy, forgotten garden on Clemenței Street was, for a long time, the source of daily delights to us; through its bushes and hollows we sought to bring to life the pranks of our imagination, often whipped and puzzled by pointless readings. After making our way through the brushwood, like the explorers in central Africa, we made new paths, we dug drains, we built tiny bridges, we built cities - we even made a port, carrying buckets of water, and started a railway with what we could get from toy stores. Our connection to this*

beloved plot of land changed over the years, as we grew up, but it was never severed until the last moment of our childhood, when my family left the house and we left Bucharest. After it stopped being our whole world, the decrepit garden went on to be a place of peaceful relaxation and sensual delight. We had known for some time that the back wall stood between us and the nuns in Pitar Moș, and as we grew older, more knowledgeable, and our thoughts drifted to other sorts of games, we spent hours climbing trees along that wall, watching the groups of blonde and brunette girls who couldn't see us. We each chose one - like Turkish Pashas - and our imagination did the rest. A source for other, more serious activities was the pavilion, the air-locked pavilion. We learned that it was closed because inside it there was the Romanian Athenaeum Library (!!); back then, where the magnificent Athenaeum stands today, there were only the abandoned ruins of a monumental circus that Sașa Blaremberg had wanted to build, but he hadn't managed to fulfill his wish. The Athenaeum held conferences and concerts in a musty hall near Cișmigiu, where the Lyric Theatre was later built. Costică Esarcu begged "spare one leu for the Athenaeum" and, as he couldn't get other rooms, Nicu Negri (another supporter of the cause) gave him the garden pavilion to store a rather impressive library and a three-legged spyglass - honored gifts made by some glorious enterprise. This treasure seemed to have been forgotten by people and by God, because nobody had bothered to look after it for years. Together with my friends, we decided to take care of it, and since some of the windows had been broken over time, through patented instruments resembling fishing rods, we managed - with great difficulty, but all great deeds require sacrifice - to fish a few tomes that were nearest to the windows. Bookshelves lined the walls, there were some stacked on the floor, overseen by the ever-watchful eye of the three-legged spyglass; the difficulty was catching one of the tomes on the shelf, because we soon noticed that the ones stacked on the floor were worthless. The ones on the shelves were mostly old editions; one day, we even fished a beautiful Arabian book. Of course, everything we fished went to the antiquarians, and later, when I became a bibliophile, I was overcome with regret, thinking about our foolish behavior - and the loss of some rare pieces which I would have done better to keep, rather than sell for a small amount of money. I should add that neither Esarcu, nor the Romanian Athenaeum were ever made aware of the sizeable tithe we imposed on their patrimony."[64]

Going back to C.A. Rosetti Street, at no. 36, on the corner of Jean-Louis Calderon Street, there is the house of philanthropic industrialist Constantin Vasiliu-Bolnavu (1920), today Țiriac Bank (former Bulgarian legation turned clinic). At the next intersection there is the building erected in 1934, designed by architect Marcel Locar. Across the street from it there was "the small, wagon-style house, with only a few rooms, occupied by Maria Cartianu, the midwife of Bucharest elite. Fat and stout, she had a framed board on her bedroom wall with baptism medals from all the children she'd brought into this world. There were hundreds, perhaps more. In 1884, she started filling in for Szilagy, another famous midwife in her time."[65]

Further North, we reach Dionisie Lupu Street and the two large houses: Liebrecht-Filipescu (1864), which I already spoke about, and across from it, dr. N.N. Turnescu, built in 1893-1895 by the French architect Albert Galleron, who also designed the Romanian Athenaeum; the houses in Gogu Cantacuzino Square were mostly owned by *new money* people of the 1930s, one of whom was Minister Mihail Ghelmegeanu, and on Armașului Lane, an oasis of elegance and prosperity, we find Octavian Goga's house, a poet and former Prime Minister. On the corner of Armașului Lane and Dionisie Lupu Street there is a house built in 1882 by architect Grigore Cerkez, and at no. 17, N.N. Șoimescu's house, built in 1891 by architect P. Petricu[66]. On Columb Street we find houses Sclia (architect Grigore Cerkez, 1891) and Zoe Ionescu, at no. 1 (architect Joseph I. Exner, 1886). If we add, to the West, on Pictor Verona Street (former Mercur Street), the houses of Dimitrie A. Sturdza, President of the Liberal Party and Prime Minister (today Cărturești bookstore), and that of his Conservative opponent, Alexandru Marghiloman (today ARO building, architect Horia Creangă, 1931)[67], then Richard Franasovici's house, Minister and Ambassador in Paris, at no. 20, Pitar Moș Street, we have a pretty clear image of the socio-professional and economic profile of those living in the Batiștei neighborhood overall.[68]

Finally, on General Praporgescu Street, we find a beautiful house at no. 24, today Clinic no. 11, a mysterious name for a clinic belonging to the Party and later to the Diplomatic Corps[69], who also had a special store on Dianei Street. Also on Praporgescu Street, the penultimate house on the left (today a lawyer firm) belonged to the Ministry of Foreign Affairs during the communist era, and Vice-Minister Vasile Gliga used to live there, among others.

A large category of people living in this neighborhood were M.D.s - over 20 of them in 1890 alone - many of whom were University Professors, such as the famous Nicolae Kalinderu (nicknamed "Wonder Doctor"), Maria Cutzarida-Crătunescu (1857-1919), the first female doctor in Romania, a primary care physician at Filantropia Hospital, who specialized in "female illness" and childcare (she lived at no. 11bis, Teilor Street, and moved to no. 21 in 1910); surgeon C. Dimitrescu-Severeanu (born in 1840, considered to be the greatest doctor in the country in 1890), at no 2, Batiştei Street, G. Nanu, chief at Colţea Hospital (at no. 25, Polonă Street), Mihail Petrini-Galaţi, primary care physician at Colentina Hospital (no. 27, Clemenţei Street), Wilhelm Kremnitz, Titu Maiorescu's brother-in-law, doctor at Brâncovenesc Hospital, whose house at no. 23, Calderon Street held the Junimea Society meetings etc. From 1914, at no. 33, Sălciilor Street (later at no. 31, Thomas Masaryk Street, architect Ion D. Berindey) we find dr. Ioan E. Costinescu (1871-1951), mayor of Bucharest (1922-1928), Minister for Health, the last president of the Romanian Red Cross, arrested during the communist regime, who died in prison, most likely in Caransebeş[70]. Finally, on the same street, at no. 27, there lived doctor Gheorghe Marinescu (1863-1938), the famous neurosurgeon, a member of the Romanian Academy and of other scientific societies, author of an important scientific paper on neural disease. His house was turned into a museum in 1954, but was reclaimed by his heirs after 1990 and became private property. We also find four veterinarians (1882) and an impressive number of midwives (19 around 1889-1890). Another well-represented category was engineers (7 in 1882, but over 30 in 1890).

The most numerous were lawyers and magistrates, rather fluid categories, since a number of them, especially lawyers, were also politicians: at least 59 in 1890, including Barbu Ştefănescu-Delavrancea (at no. 56, Dionisie Lupu Street, in the same house as Senator Petre Borş)[71], Constantin Nacu, a Professor at the Faculty of Law (the one after whom that street was named, he lived at no. 24, Teilor Street), Nicolae Fleva, Petre Grădişteanu, Constantin Dissescu, Emil Protopopescu-Pache (the future Bucharest mayor, first on

Polonă Street, then at no. 6, Scaune Street), Constantin Stoicescu, also a Minister (no. 2bis, then no. 9, Batiştei Street), two of the Brătianus (Ion and Toma, both on Dionisie Lupu), V.D. Polizu-Micşuneşti (no. 14, Batiştei Street), President of the Appeal Court, as well as Nicolae Predescu (no. 22, Scaunelor) and many others.

There are also several professors, namely the French Frédéric Damé, journalist and statistician, author of an excellent Romanian-French Dictionary (at no. 79, Polonă Street), journalists (eight in 1890, including Constantin Mille, at no. 1, Polonă Street, and Delavrancea), and, in 1890, a large number of field officers, including the chief of the Bucharest Garrison, Adjutant General Constantin Barozzi (no. 38, Polonă Street), Alexandru Candiano-Popescu (no. 14, Batiştei Street), the President of the ephemeral Republic of Ploieşti (1870), Royal Adjutand and memorialist, even two Police Commissioners. There were also several executive officers, like Al. Degrea, the President of CFR's managing board (at no. 38bis, Polonă Street, in 1890), bankers and senators (brothers Dimitrie and Menelas Ghermani, descendants of Metropolitan Dionisie Lupu, who lived on the Metropolitan's old estate; he'd built a chapel here, at no. 62 and 68, Dionisie Lupu Street), the poet Alexandru Macedonski (in 1887 he lived at no. 88, Dionisie Lupu Street), Constantin Esarcu (1836-1898), Professor, Minister and diplomat, founder of the Romanian Athenaeum, for which he raised money all his life (he invented the slogan „spare one leu for the Athenaeum" - they were gold coins!), at no. 9, Calderon (Polonă) Street, five members of the aristocratic Brăiloiu family (no. 14, Dionisie Lupu Street and no. 23, Polonă Street), whose descendant, Constantin (he lived in a house on Dionisie Lupu Street that later became the Folklore Archives), would become one of the greatest Romanian musicologist and folklorist, Iuliu N. Seculici (no. 48, Polonă Street), the administrator of the Royal Domains, father of theosophist Bucura Dumbravă (nee Fany Seculici, 1868-1926), the printer and folktale collector Petre Ispirescu (1838-1887), who lived at no. 17, Sălciilor Street, and others.[72] We must not overlook the more peculiar figures, such as "Madame Laurethe nécromancienne", who lived in 1887 at no. 22, Batiştei Street, or the tenants on Minervei (Vasile Conta) Street, about whom Emanoil Hagi-Mosco wrote a few delicious lines:

Next to Săvescu House, on Minervei Street, there is a house - now
torn down - with a demi-basement and one story, occupied by two
beautiful women, the sort of ladies whom the French elegantly refer
to by the Greek name *hétaïre*, renowned and sought for on account
of their *sui generis* activities. One was nicknamed Lina Magazia, the
other Tincuța Colivia[73]. The gossip chronicles said that Alexandru
Battemberg of Bulgaria favored Lina, when he visited Bucharest.
The other had heirs.[74]

Among the houses whose interesting exterior matched their fascinating interior, we mention Lenș House at no. 23, Alecu Donici Street in 1893 (alle-
gorical figures were painted on the ceilings and doors), the Romanian style
house of Elie Radu, engineer (1853-1931), on the same street, at no. 40, on
the corner of Icoanei Street, designed by the architect Giulio Magni, with
interior paintings made by Italian masters, and finally, Matilda Villa (from
1897) at no. 2, Oțetari street, architect A.C. Clavel, interior decorations
made by the owner's cousin, the painter Ștefan Luchian.

We must pay special attention to a group of Art Nouveau buildings from
1900-1914. For instance, the tenement houses at no. 3 and 5, Hristo Botev
Street, as well as the one at no. 76, Vasile Lascăr Street (Hotăranu Drugstore
situated on the ground floor has gained back its old name), indicate a revival
of Neoclassicism, anticipating the 1925 style[75]. The tenement house at no.
1, Rosetti Square, on the corner of Tudor Archezi Street is inspired by Art
Nouveau, with its heightened first floor and mezzanine (often framed by
the same round, elliptical or *anse de panier* arch), with 4 or 6 stories and
"horseshoe hollows, atectonic shapes, rounded, sinuous lines, bow-win-
dows, distinctive ornaments etc."[76] Finally, there are, or were, four houses
influenced by the Viennese Secession style at no. 12, Maria Rosetti Street
(recently demolished)[77], no. 33, Speranței Street, and the corner of Sfinților
Street and Radu Cristian Street (former Melodiei Street)[78]. The fourth, torn
down in 1969, is the Aslan House (at no. 1, Tudor Arghezi Street, where the
National Theatre has been built), which a specialist described as being built
"in Joseph Hoffmann's reticular style, with geometric ceramic tiles similar
to Palais Stoclet in Brussels"[79].

An important means to know the people who lived in our neighborhood in the first half of the 20th century, especially the wealthy and/or the famos, is the *High-Life Calendar* (*Almanach du High-Life*), an annual French publication by *L'Indépendence Roumaine* newspaper, which to some extent replaced The Yearly Statistic of Romania and Bucharest, edited for three decades by Frédéric Damé. I consulted those from 1910 and 1924, the only ones that I own, and I noticed that in our neighborhood there are over 150 people or families thought to be "high-class". Of course, it is impossible to name all of them, but it is worth mentioning political figures such as Mihai Pherekyde (Ferechide) (1842-1928), former Liberal Minister and President of the House of Representatives, who lived at no. 7, Gloriei Street (Traian Vuia, Eugen Stătescu), where they later built a large block of flats with two access points, one on the Boulevard ("the Pherekyde Block"); Liberal politician Alexandru Constantinescu-Porcu (1859-1926), a well-known figure of the age, at no. 7, Rotari Street (in 1910); Prince Constantin Brâncoveanu-Basarab, a descendant of Constantin Brâncoveanu, at no. 22, Scaune Street (N. Filipescu Street); doctor Ioan Cantacuzino (1863-1934), founder of the Serum and Vaccine Institute that is named after him, which played a role in combating cholera in 1912 and camp fever in 1917, Doctor Ioan Cantacuzino lived at the end of Dionisie Lupu Street, in Lahovary Square, in a house that still stands today[80]; doctor Ion Nanu-Muscel (1862-1938), Professor at the Faculty of Medicine and Senator; dr. Dimitrie C. Gerota (1867-1939), a completely unusual figure, member of the Academy and founder of a clinic at no. 17, Gogu Cantacuzino Street (now a section of the street is named after him), journalist Constantin Mille (1861-1927), a Socialist, editor of *Adevărul* newspaper, political figure Dim. Nenițescu (1861-1930), at no. 4, Școalei Street, in a house his son, the great chemist and Professor C. Nenițescu, also lived in, architect Petre Antonescu (in 1910 on Crinului Street, today Praporgescu Street), architect George Mandrea, who worked for the Bucharest Mayoralty to build 14 primary schools (in 1914 he lived at no. 39, Gogu Cantacuzino Street), architect Duiliu Marcu at no. 21, Dionisie Lupu Street, also in 1914; Eugeniu Carada (1839-1910), one of the founders and pillars of the National Bank, the *éminence grise* of the Liberal Party (he was part of the "Occult", a term which signified the supreme, five-member leadership); journalist and political figure Andrei Corteanu (who died in 1959, at no. 4, Praporgescu Street), Constantin Garofild (1871-1942), one of the greatest Romanian agriculture specialists (at no. 35, Gogu Cantacuzino Street) and others. The first Jewish bankers mentioned in the neighborhood in 1910, Jacques Elias (no. 76, Polonă Street), Aristide Blank (no. 14, Sălciilor Street), his son, Mauriciu Blank (at no. 7, Tudor Arghezi Street), and Samuel Halfon and his wife, nee Mendel, at no. 23, Gogu Cantacuzino Street.

The elite politicians' predilection for our neighborhood can also be deduced from the fact that the most important negotiations for Romania's joining the war in 1916 and even the signing of treaties with Russia, France, England and Italy all took place in Ion G. Duca's office at no. 29, Caragiale Street, and at Vintilă Brătianu's house, the brother of Prime Minister Ion I.C. Brătianu, at no. 19, Aurel Vlaicu Street. And Romania's secrets were held for years in Constantin (Bebe) Brătianu's safe (the Prime Minister's nephew and Secretary) in the house at no. 7, Scaune Street. In order to be discreet, because Bucharest was full of the Central Powers' spies, the Prime Minister, who lived back then at no. 5, Lascăr Catargiu Boulevard, preferred to meet with allied Ministers at the house of a relative or a collaborator, such as Ion Procopiu, who lived at no. 5, Dumbrava Roşie Street.[81]

Between the two World Wards, many sturdy buildings appeared in our neighborhood: the blocks of flats on Batiştei Street, no. 1-7 (Miner's Trust in 1933, architect State Baloşin)[82], no. 11, 17 and 35 (Budişteanu Block, 1931-1933, architect Radu Stan), no. 35 and 48, Vasile Lascăr Street, as well as the one near Vasile Lascăr's statue, where our classmates used to live, the ones on Gogu Cantacuzino Street at no. 1 (it collapsed in 1977 because of the earthquake), no. 36 and 27, the latter was bombed in 1944[83] and rebuilt in 1960, the one on the same street as the Prosecutor's office, the ones on Praporgescu Street, no. 9 (the Costescu family) and 25 (where our older colleagues Andrei and Ghiţă Verona lived), the blocks on Dionisie Lupu Street, at no. 2 (N. Tabacovici Block, architect Duiliu Marcu 1935, collapsed during the 1977 earthquake), 11, 18 (on the corner of Batiştei Street), 20 and 38 (architect Jean Monda, 1936), others on Dianei Street, the beautiful Cernat House (no. 25, Italian Street) and the neighboring one,

on Gogu Cantacuzino, designed by Jean Krakauer, the Municipal Officials'
Association Palace (architect I.C. Roşu and Radu Culcer), which became
the Fantasio Cinema at no. 14, Batiştei Street, later ARLUS and now
ARCUB, and others on C.A. Rosetti Boulevard, on the corner of Dionisie
Lupu Street, at no. 36, Gogu Cantacuzino Street (where our older colleague
Nicolae-Şerban ("Nicki") Tanaşoca used to live), as well as the three large
blocks at the intersection with Maria Rosetti Street, at no. 8-10, and the one
accross from it, on the corner of Păcii Street (Schitul Darvari), where Chief
Rabbi Moses Rosen lived etc. Finally, the great industrialist Nicolae Malaxa
had his offices on Dionisie Lupu Street, at no. 19, and on Oţetari Street, at
no. 7. Two neighboring blocks deserve a special mention, the one at no. 65,
Dionisie Lupu Street (D.D. Bragadiru Block), on the corner of Lahovary
Square, designed by George Matei Cantacuzino and Vasile S. Arion (1935),
and the apartment block at no. 5A, on the same square, designed by Horia
Creangă and situated on Professor Barbu Dimitrescu's land (1933)[84].

Three of architect Marcel Iancu's buildings (1895-1984) are of extraordinary value: Juster Villa at no. 51 (75) Silvestru Street, the Clara Buildings,
on Caimatei Street (1931)[85], and Solly Gold at no. 34, Hristo Botev Street,
with bas-reliefs by Miliţia Pătraşcu[86].

In the first half of the 20th century, several symbols of Romanian culture lived in our neighborhood: Mateiu I. Caragiale (1885-1936)[87], after
marrying Marica Sion (1923) lived at no. 9A, Robert de Fleurs Street (now
Luca Stroici), a house later occupied by Titu Magheru, president of the
Court of Justice[88]; linguist Alexandru Rosetti-Bălăneşti (1895-1990) lived
his whole life in his parents' house at no. 56, Dionisie Lupu Street. A completely unique figure, writer Alexandru I. Teodoreanu (Păstorel) and his
wife Marta (who, thanks to the Communist regime, was a street sweeper![89])
lived at no. 38, Vasile Lascăr Street, which follows Batiştei Street, in a house
that was torn down after 1989. During his last months, suffering from a
gruelling disease, Păstorel was visited by his old friend Gheorghe Jurgea-
Negrileşti and told him the following:

Our religion says that the Almighty sends suffering. A priest came
by, you know. He tried explaining it to me. "Have you ever had a

toothache, father?" He had very good teeth. "No, ever." "That's too bad!" I said. "You would've seen for yourself how much of a sadist that guy is." "What 'guy'?" He asked incredulously. "The Almighty, of course." Without another word, the priest got up, crossed himself and took off! He never came around here again! Strange, isn't it?[90]

Another famous person in our neighborhood was the diplomat Nicolae Dianu (1889-1966) who lived in a small house (now replaced with an odd apartment block) next to a large apartment building on the corner of C.A. Rosetti and no. 57, Calderon Street. A career diplomat, he worked in Moscow between 1939-1941 and retired on May 1st, 1941, as a Minister Plenipotentiary, 1st class. Afterwards, he sought refuge in Paris, where he played a crucial role during the Peace Conference in 1946-1947, founding the "Pro Basarabia and Bucovina" organization, coming in conflict with Grigore Gafencu, whom he challenged to a duel on account of not bringing up the issue of the two regions during the conference. Nicolae Dianu stayed in Paris and became known in 1952, when, together with other esteemed refugees, a Bulgarian and a Pole, he sued writer Renaud de Jouvenel for slander. Together with communist journalist André Wurmser, he had written a despicable book, *L'Internationale des traîtres* (1949), in which he insulted agrarian leaders in Eastern Europe, namely Iuliu Maniu, Dimitrov from Bulgaria and Mikolajcik from Poland. The trial was held in Paris and made use of false witnesses brought from Romania in order to affirm that human rights were respected there and that democracy was blooming. The trial went in Dianu's favor and he later published a white paper, *Les communistes démasqués*, about this trial[91]. The problem was that he'd left his wife and daughter in Bucharest, two distinguished ladies, harassed by the Secret Services for years until the diplomat's death. They would come to our church sometimes, and my father would tell us about their troubles. In 1966 they were allowed to go to Paris, retrieve their inheritance left by Nicolae Dianu and restore their small house with the money.

Three other notable figures were Ministers in Antonescu's cabinets between 1941-1944; in alphabetical order: doctor Constantin Dănulescu (he lived at no. 17-19, Jules Michelet Street, see below), Ion Marinescu,

Minister for Economy and Justice (he lived at no. 16, Nicolae Filipescu Street), who died in prison, and Alexandru D. Neagu, Minister of Finance (between 1942-1944, no. 16, Batiştei Street). Finally, Virgil Potârcă (1888-1954, died in Sighet), politician, Representative and Senator in all legislators from 1920 onwards, Minister in several cabinets (1928-1931, 1932, 1937-1938), lived at no. 32, Maria Rosetti Street until 1948, when he was thrown out of his recently-nationalized home[92]. It is also worth mentioning Stelian Popescu (1873-1954), former Minister, owner of *Universul* newspaper, who lived at no. 10bis, Dionisie Lupu Street (the 1911 house designed by Paul Smărăndescu) until he left the country, and his daughter, Jana Şt. Popescu, married Popescu-Necşeşti, at no. 25, Gogu Cantacuzino Street[93]. Confiscated after Stelian Popescu was convicted for high treason and sentenced to forced labor for life, his fortune being confiscated during the journalists' trial, "guilty for ruining the country" (June 1945), his house was occupied by brigadier general Cortlandt Van Rensselear Schuyler, chief of the U.S. Army Task Force[94]. Around the same time, at no. 6, Italiană Street, there lived Eleonora Bunea de Wied, Queen Elizabeth's niece and King Michael's cousin, who had stayed in Romania and worked for the English Task Force and was arrested in 1949, investigated, tried and sentenced to 15 years in prison on May 5th, 1950, together with the other Romanian operatives[95].

Finally, at no 26, Popa Chiţu Street, there lived one of the greatest Romanian historians, Gheorghe I. Brătianu (1898-1953, died in Sighet), the son of Ion I.C. Brătianu, a Professor and a Liberal politician, a victim of the Communist regime, sentenced to three years of house arrest and then sent to his death in the Sighet prison, where he was incarcerated on May 6th, 1950, without trial, like many other former dignitaries between 1918-1944. Despite being under constant surveillance and being spied on during house arrest, Brătianu finished some of his greatest works, such as *Marea Neagră de la origini până la cucerirea otomană*, *Adunările de stări în principatele române*, *Întemeierea țărilor române* and others that appeared posthumously in France. The manuscripts were secreted away by his wife, who was allowed to go outside, entrusted to some of the Professor's faithful students and then sent to Paris in the French legation's diplomatic bag[96].

To end on a more original note, connected to our high school, a few words about an antiques store, well known between the two World Wars, about which I heard many stories in my childhood, when it had been turned into an upholstery co-op.

"Madam Batişte or the Old Dame from Batişte was none other than old Ghizela Popper who kept an antiques store on the corner of Batiştei Street and Alexandru Sahia Street (former Gogu Cantacuzino), across the street from Batiştei Church," wrote George Potra (1907-1990). This sizeable store, split in two sections, served both as a dwelling and as a shop; a thick curtain hanged on hoops that slid on a metal rod divided them. But there was more than old books in her store: all sorts of trinkets and things you'd never think about, like ornate cabinets, old-fashioned coats and dresses, buttons, ribbons, lace, post-cards, stamps in envelopes or glued on bits of cardboard by aspiring philatelists, young high school students, and many more. Although she had quite a few cus-tomers, mostly "Spiru Haret" students and those from "Regina Maria" Girls' School, the Schewitz Institute and others, students from other neighborhoods would often come and visit her, like those from "Gheorghe Lazăr" High School and "Sf. Sava" High School, and even "Matei Basarab" and "Mihai Viteazu", which were pretty far away.

They all came to sell and buy books. They could sell them for more than what they'd get from other traders and buy the ones they needed for cheaper, as for bargaining, the young customers were bolder and more daring when dealing with an old woman rather than a man who would scoff and bark at you if he saw you drove a hard bargain. With "Madam Batişte", the boys were too bold and even obnoxious, and for all her kindness and patience, sometimes she was so harrowed that she would tell off those who kept bargaining, saying "leave me the hell alone, go away, in God's name, and lay off." The most sought-after items for us students were stamps, but also corks for our cork guns, firecrackers, itching and sneezing powder, as well as prank candy (fondant candy with garlic fill-ing). For all these we were loyal customers of the Batiştei Street shop. (...) I don't know what "Madam Batişte" looked like when she was young, but when I knew her she was old and very wrinkled, although some features indicated traces of beauty, and on top of that she had no hair, which was why she wore a styled wig that sometimes fell to the side, and in trying to fix it up, she would ruin it even further, so that sometimes the back of the wig would sit in front or on the side. She was hilarious in these situations and it made us burst into laughter that was akin to an alarm bell for her, so she'd quickly go to the mirror and straighten it. "Madam Batiște" had a bad leg, swollen and much thicker than the other one. Because of this leg she couldn't walk well, it probably hurt a lot, too, so she often sat down and rested the sick leg on a king of pillowed stool.

As for her clothes, it was a display of old-fashioned rags. She always wore a different dress, each more ridiculous than the next, probably bought for a steal or received as a gift from the ladies in the neighborhood who didn't wear them anymore or who had them from their grandmothers. There was lacing on all of them, and the cut, width and length of them were altogether too much for the day and age when she wore them. She wore a rather long gold chain around her neck, with a diamond-studded gold watch. Ghizela Popper was incredibly scrimp, she always wanted to make money, as much money as possible, but for whom, we don't know, since she had no children. Her prices were low, but despite this, from the hundreds of items she had in her store she turned a profit and had savings, not by putting money away in some dark corner, but by lending it for a large interest and by pawning items much more valuable than the sum that was being lent. For this reason, word in the neighborhood was that "Madam Batiște" has a lot of money, that she was filthy rich, despite trying to pose as a poor woman. The truth was something else, and unfortunately the whole neighborhood found out, as well as some bandits who set out to murdered her one day and stole a large sum of money and the jewelry she had pawned."[97]

As you can see, calling it the Saint-Germain of Bucharest is very appropriate for the Batiște neighborhood in the first half of the 20th century[98]. After 1948, the neighborhood saw a profound change: the great landowners and their descendants were thrown out of their recently-nationalized homes or they were forced to huddle together in a single room, sharing the kitchen, bathroom and common areas with countless tenants, in the Romanian version of the Soviet *komunalka*. This phenomenon was seen in all cities in Stalinist Romania and it explains how many new people appeared in the neighborhood, usually important public officials those with liberal professions (mostly doctors), our colleagues' parents[99]. Referring to doctors, it is worth mentioning that all four doctors who in 1950 took care of Gheorghiu-Dej, members of the Political Bureau and the CC Secretaries of the PMR all lived in our neighborhood. Thus, the party leader's attending physician was dr. Leon Bercu from no. 55, Dionisie Lupu Street (in 1939 he lived at no. 21, Apolodor Street); doctor Alfred Brill (no. 18, Sfinților Street) was the attending physician of Gheorghe Vasilichi, Chivu Stoica, Al. Drăghici, Leontin Sălăjan, Gheorghe Florescu and Constantin Pârvulescu; doctor Leon Kaffè, described fondly by Ion Ianoşi in his memoirs (*Internaţionala mea*, Polirom, Iaşi, 2012), who lived at no. 6, Spătarului Street (in 1939, at no. 33b, Schitu Măgureanu Street), took care of Ana Pauker, Teohari Georgescu, Miron Constantinescu, Pintilie Bodnarenko and Gheorghe Apostol; finally, doctor Ernest Kahana from no. 29, Pitar Moş Street (in 1941 he lived at no. 62, Romană Street) took care of Vasile Luca, Vasile Vaida, Emil Bodnăraş, Lotar Rădăceanu, Petre Borilă and Avram Bunaciu[100]. Theirs was not an easy job, given the health of their patients as shown in confidential documents from 1950 and 1959[101].

The most important buildings were given to party and state organizations, the Finance Inspectorate (no. 25, Batiştei Street, later the Party District Office and now the High Court), the I.V. Stalin District Prosecutor's Office (at no. 6, Alexandru Sahia Street, then moved across the street), the Central Committee of Commerce and Co-op Workers' Unions (no. 11, Batiştei Street), the Ministry of Agriculture's Daycare and Canteen (no. 22, Italiană Street and no. 8, Nicolae Filipescu Street respectively[102]), the dorms of the "Andrei A. Jdanov" Social Sciences College (no. 2, Robert de Flers Street, which became Luca Stroici Street), the Department of Cults (no. 40, Nicolae Filipescu Street, former Militia General Office), the Diplomatic Corps Office (no. 9, Alexandru Sahia Street, then on Dianei Street), the kindergarten of the Ministry of Transport and Telecommunication (no. 4, Batiştei Street, later a Driving School), the Post Office (no. 23, Batiştei Street), various clinics (no. 18, Dionisie Lupu Street, no. 27, Batiştei Street, no. 24, Praporgescu Street (for the CC of the PMR, then for the Diplomatic Corps), a Girls Boarding House on the corner of Al. Sahia Street and Praporgescu Street (later the Popular Council of District I.V. Stalin) etc. Callimachi House at no. 31, Batiştei Street was a Sovrom, and after 1954 it was occupied by the Secret Services to monitor the activity of the Hungarian

Cultural Center next door, among other things. In fact, the presence of the American Embassy on Dionisie Lupu Street, Blanduziei Street, and the Ambassador's house on Nicolae Filipescu Street made up the pressure point of this neighborhood. Securitate members' families were set up in the neighboring apartment buildings, as well as espionage stations that patrolled day and night up and down Dionisie Lupu Street, Batiştei Street and Praporgescu Street, where parked cars were used to follow Americans and especially their cars (the Ambassador's driver was a very elegant gentleman, Dicu Massim, who lived on the corner of no. 30, Batiştei Street and no. 1, Oțetari Street, in the same house as our colleague, Lucian Moldoveanu). Right in front of the house at no. 1, Praporgescu Street (on the corner of no. 19, Batiştei Street), the place where I lived and from which I could watch their every move. This is why the wicked spread the rumor that "father Cazacu keeps getting new cars", as if they were ours! (and with a driver as well, the height of luxury). Another vantage point, at no. 13, Praporgescu Street, communicated through a yard with the apartment building at no. 20, Dionisie Lupu Street, and this is where Americans were more discreetly spied on, with directional microphones and telescopes. It was done so discreetly that the whole neighborhood knew about this hideout, thanks to the manicurist from the barbershop at no. 19, Batiştei Street, who lived there and was annoyed that she couldn't use those rooms. Other crews followed the Swiss (Pitar Moş Street), the Czechoslovaks (Oțetari Street) and, of course, the Hungarians (the Embassy on Alexandru Sahia Street at no. 67, after the intersection with Maria Rosetti Street). The icing on the cake was a radio jammer for those "malicious" frequencies (Radio Free Europe, The Voice of America, BBC) situated in a manor on Alexandru Sahia Street (Calderon) at no. 46, occupied more recently by the Palestinian Liberation Organization (PLO) so it was impossible for us to listen to them until the jamming was dropped after 1963.

From a cultural standpoint, our neighborhood was less gifted. At no. 14, Batiştei Street, on the corner of Nicolae Filipescu Street and Dionisie Lupu Street, there was a cinema called "Fantasio" (the building was originally the Palace of Municipal Clerks) that was closed after 1948, in order to make room for ARLUS, the association for Romanian Soviet Union relations (now ARCUB). Conferences would take place in the great hall, as well as Soviet movie screenings for the poor, mostly "has-beens" who took comfort in the red plush chairs and took advantage of the warmth to rest. During the summer, movies were shown in the garden on the corner of Dionisie Lupu Street, a chance for us to see them for free, because we had an excellent view from our roof. We were joined by those who lived in the apartment building at no. 17, Batiştei Street, who sat at the window or on the balcony and commented the movies with us. After a while, however, the poplar trees along the sides of the garden grew so tall that we couldn't see a thing; however, movies from the West started coming to Bucharest, so we unapologetically gave up on Soviet cinematography that was generally mediocre, but for a few exceptions such as *The Cranes are Flying* or *War and Peace*[103].

ARLUS had a very rich library and a reading room where you could flip through Soviet press and, interestingly, a satiric magazine from Chişinău printed in Cyrillic script called *Chipăruş*: it took a while for me to figure out it was actually "Pipăruş"[104]... Around 1959-1960, I was an avid reader of ARLUS history books and I kept a library card which proves I devoured them in just a few days. I must mention that I had already exhausted the municipal library's resources, which was across the street, in the old Blaremberg House at no. 15, turned into the municipal arts centre Friedrich Schiller of the GDR and then into a ballet school.

On the ground floor of the apartment building next to ours (no. 17, Batiştei Street, on the corner of Dionisie Lupu Street) was the only grocery store in the area, its competition being Glodeanu on the corner of Sahia Street and Iulius Fucik, then a barber shop and a mysterious store with a large sign that read "Ionel Jugastru". In the window there were green plants, various objects, dolls and even a frog skeleton, plus one or two miniature pairs of shoes, so nothing on the outside allowed you to guess the destination of that establishment. Only by stepping beyond its threshold did you realize it was a rather elegant shoemaker's workshop that had fallen from grace due to a lack of good leather and other noble materials. Ionel Jugastru was the only independent proprietor in the area, together with Costea the tailor at no. 28, Nicolae Filipescu Street, an old house where historian

Maria Holban also lived, a very distinguished person, the daughter of a general who lead Romanian troops in 1919 in Budapest[105]. Conversation with the two craftsmen had an inevitable dose of lamenting and swearing at tax inspector Hilote, whom I have mentioned before, and his extravagant taxes that choked the life out of them. Other quaint figures in the neighborhood were Mr. Luca, a glazier whom my parents often called on whenever my playmates from "Prapor" or I broke a window, Mr. Gheorghiță the tobacconist and news vendor, Glodeanu the merchant, mentioned above, who started a different business clearing houses infested by chinches and rats, a few women who made borsch, usually in their basements, a Russian countess who took refuge here around 1920 with her butler, a grouchy old man nicknamed "Ovța" (The Sheep), whom we taunted mercilessly, and he cursed at us in Russian, to our delight. Finally, an entire gallery of gentlemen and ladies from the old society, "has-beens" who came to church on Sunday dressed in 1920s-1930s fashion, the gentlemen wearing hats, gaiters, gloves and walking sticks, ladies in hat veils or turbans, worn fur coats, muffs and winter galoshes. Some had their own seats in church; their names written on brass plaques attached to the chairs, or simply on calling cards that were quite exotic back then. They disappeared one by one, and my father, who saw them to their graves, was the only one who remembered them sometimes, on his way back from a funeral, telling stories about them, often helped by my mother who had been born and had lived all her life at no. 19, Batiştei Street[106].

And, to finish on a more positive note, I will mention a few garden restaurant and sweetshops that gave our neighborhood a special air. The first one, Mon Jardin garden, opened in 1937, closed in 1948 (it was turned into a canteen for the unemployed), it reopened in 1955 and in 1972 it was destroyed, together with a restaurant next door, Poarta Albă, to make room for hotel Dorobanți, now Howard Johnson. The owner, a Mr. Papacostea, turned this venue into one of the merriest places in Bucharest in the 1940s when a police raid in 1944 ("The Mon Jardin Affair", "perhaps the last success of Antonescu's team") arrested some drunks, "many of whom went to Târgu Jiu (the camp) or to war". The only ones who escaped in *rocambolesque* fashion were George Jurgea-Negrileşti, who later told the story, and

Mr. Unterman, "a distinguished gemstone dealer, very well-liked by the Germans" and later by the Soviets[107]. In the 1950s, the "Monj" was considered to be the last stronghold of Romanian jazz music, where they played Cole Porter, samba and tango, and hosted performances by Jean Ionescu's orchestra, Sergiu Malagamba, Iancsi Körösi, Johnny Răducanu. In 1956 Yves Montard played here, a communist sympathizer at the time, on tour in Eastern countries[108].

The second establishment, another garden restaurant with music, was the one owned by Nicolae Zissu, at no. 10-12, Batiştei Street, opened around 1940-1941, then closed and reopened on October 6th 1952 under the name "Doina" Dining Room, between 4 pm and 2 am. This is where Jean Moscopol, Gică Petrescu and sometimes Maria Tănase would sing, Sile Vişan on the piano, Jean Ionescu's orchestra, Sergiu Malagamba, Imre Alexandru. In 1958, the "Diana" outdoor cinema was opened. Later, the garden closed and all that remained was the building turned into a canteen for the Oil, Gas and Geology Institute. Around the same time, its neighbor reopened, the "Mercur" steak restaurant[109]. This, too, disappeared along with the neighboring buildings when they did Hotel Intercontinental and the National Theatre (1966-1970)[110]. In Rosetti Square there was at that time a restaurant called "Peştera" or "La şapte craci"[111], seemingly because they had four waitresses, one of whom was crippled; it also disappeared after 1989.

Finally, I could mention the garden restaurant and must-cellar "Grădiniţa", on the corner of Bălcescu Boulevard and Batiştei Street, which disappeared when Hotel Intercontinental was built.

There were two sweetshops in our neighborhood, one of them was famous and the other not so well known, but just as good. The first was on the corner of C.A. Rosetti Street and Nicolae Filipescu Street, in the "Furnica" building, now a restaurant. Annie Bentoiu left us a few lines about it in her memoirs:

I must say that, thinking back to the decor of 1956-1957, that would forever be the most distinguished one we can remember, the symbol that comes immediately to mind is the window of Follas

sweetshop. The name belonged to a Greek who had been authorized to open a shop on C.A. Rosetti Street, very close to us, that
had the most exquisite cakes and pastries. Maybe they seemed
that way because we had been without such things for so long; but
truthfully, they were excellent. The light, fluffy, huge pastries from
Follas gave a sumptuous air to any meal. The chocolate cakes, three
times larger than the State-issued "amandines", were delicious and
unbelievably fresh, and the firm peaks of cream turned some of
them into dream-like castles. A cake from Follas turned any meager
family meal into a memorable feast. About a year later, there was
an article in the papers describing the so-called "unhygienic" conditions of the poor confectioner's lab, and when the shutters closed
over the window that had brought us such joy, I understood that it
had been just another social experiment, like so many others I had
known. Several years later, the same experiment would be repeated
on a national scale with the "mandated", in a small N.E.P. that
wished to select all those with commercial abilities, bravery and
talent: unable to navigate the maze of conflicting by-laws and punished with years of jail time, their example discouraged anyone who
would be tempted to imitate them for years to come[112].

I also knew Follas sweetshop and I completely agree with everything our
talented memorialist has evoked. However, in our neighborhood there was
also another Greek sweetshop that "Spiru Haret" students frequented in
that era : it was the small shop at no. 20, Batiştei Street, owned by Mr. and
Mrs. Gheorghe Scarvelis. Here you could also find extraordinary cakes, and
it was closed as well, but was able to function for a while as a dairy shop
with wonderful yoghurt and kanafah, with pastries like the ones at Follas.
The Scarvelis were a petite, very thin lady and a small, very fat man, who
suffered from diabetes and his doctor didn't allow him to eat cakes. I was
a regular customer and, talking to Mr. Gheorghe one time, he told me he
had permission (from himself) to eat "colivă"[113] and he proposed we made
a trade: I would bring him colivă from the church and he would give me
a piece of cake in exchange. Some days I brought him several servings of

colivă, but Mr. Gheorghe, being cheap, would always offer me a single piece of cake, no matter how much colivă I brought him. So I took notice and split the colivă in smaller portions that I would bring him one at a time, a few minutes apart. Mr. Gheorghe caught on and laughed, and we've been good friends ever since. Eventually he was forced to close his shop as well, to our great dismay, but he stayed in business: in an unsanitary building on Biserica Enei Street, he opened a collecting point for empty bottles and jars. There, in a high-ceiling room which seemed gigantic to me, lit only by a fire with a huge cauldron filled with water and washing soda hanging above it, young gypsies washed the bottles and jars they collected in a sack from all over Bucharest ("Empty bottles, we buy empty bottles, empty jars"), taking off their labels and giving them to a special center. Poor Mr. Gheorghe throned over this medley of humanity, making small talk with various people, including a good friend of his; I think he was also Greek, perhaps a nephew, a younger man wearing unbelievably eccentric clothes. Next to him, his wife withered away and died after a while. I felt very sorry for him and I brought him colivă a few times, one of the few joys he had left. He also vanished one day, like so many others, a great craftsman crushed by the steamroller of the Socialist revolution.

Among so many government buildings, Batiștei Church, with its large orchard over the former cemetery, a few crosses still visible, half-buried in the ground, was an island of calm and green that bothered the leaders of the time. Thus we were pressured by the Popular Council to give up a part of the orchard, so that clerks could relax there, and when those requests were denied by my father, we faced challenges during the most solemn time in the most important Christian celebration, on Good Friday during Passion Week: while the congregation and the priests carrying the epitaph (a symbol of Christ's dead body) went around the church on Batiștei Street, Gogu Cantacuzino Street and Praporgescu Street, an official car (in 1950 there weren't others) came speeding and ringing its horn to be let through. At first, the people muttered, but as the driver went on ringing his horn and racing the car, they surrounded him and would have surely lynched him (or pushed the car over) if my father hadn't calmed everybody down. I remember the most frantic of all was the Opera singer Șerban Tassian, whose family had lived in the neighborhood for almost a century. The incident was repeated twice or thrice, and I saw it unfold from the bell tower where I had the task of ringing the funeral toll. And Florin Seimeanu, my colleague and friend, who walked next to my father holding his arm, could get a much closer look at the congregation's outrage[114].

---

1. See also "Ana kicks ass/ For the working class!"
2. Virgil Ierunca, *Fenomenul Pitești*, Humanitas, Bucharest, 1990; Ilie Popa (coord.), *Experimentul Pitești. Reeducarea prin tortură*, Pitești, 2003; Mircea Stănescu, *Reeducarea în România comunistă (1945–1952)*, Polirom, Iași, 2010.
3. *Procesul bandei de sabotori și diversioniști de la Canalul Dunăre– Marea Neagră*, Editura pentru Literatură Politică, Bucharest, 1952. See also Andrei Muraru (coord.), *Dicționarul penitenciarelor din România comunistă (1945–1967)*, Polirom, Iași, 2008, pp. 199–252.
4. Communist countries proclaimed national mourning, priests were under an obligation to pray for the defunct, communists let their beards grow until the funeral, when all activities ceased, all trains and streetcars were stopped to hold a minute-long memorial. It is worth reproducing here Păstorel's reaction in an epigram: "I mourn dear Stalin, what a pity/ I'll tell you all a secret:/ I fear we'll soon be kissing ass/ For the entire Committee." (Stelian Tănase, *Anatomia mistificării*, p. 330).
5. Ghiță Ionescu, *op. cit.*, pp. 219-229. Activists had to be recruited from the ranks of the best party members, in factories and institutions, collective agricultural farms and state farms, and mass organizations. The activist had to collaborate with party leaders to "bring its policies to life" and to "strengthen the connection with the masses", connections which the unions and other organizations hadn't managed to sustain. Ghiță Ionescu's comment: "This decision surprised even the most skeptical observers of the party. It seemed unbelievable that a party with 600,000 members could not recruit 80,000 satisfactory "activists", but this was the way things were; and it would be long before the party managed to consolidate a group of activists that were entirely loyal."
6. Constantin Doncea, one of the people who lead the 1933 strike in Grivița, former mayor of Bucharest, had accumulated a huge fortune. After his death

in 1973, his first wife, a Russian who lived in the USSR, claimed some of his assets, and a group of experts were called in to evaluate it. One of them was Dan Cernovodeanu, who described Doncea's house (rehabilitated by Ceauşescu): it was like a warehouse, heaps of religious paintings stacked like bricks up to the ceiling, persian rugs piled like in a souk, scattered safes full of gold and silver coins, valuable stamp collections, jewellry, ornate cabinets etc., it was like Ali Baba's cave, and everything came from ransacking private homes in Bucharest around 1945; see Valentin Hossu-Longin's recent testimony, *Canalul Morţii. Martor*, Fundaţia Academia Civică, Bucharest, 2013, pp. 194-199. Art collectors, not of the realist-socialist kind, were Paul Niculescu-Mizil and Leonte Răutu, cf. Mihail Gramatopol, *op. cit.*, vol. II, pp. 86-87.

7.   It is worth reproducing Păstorel Teodoreanu's epigram after the XXth Congress: "The Kremlin's made a pass/ and this I know is true:/ For years we kissed the *genius'* ass/ But what good did it do?" For political context see Alina Tudor and Dan Cătănuş, *O destalinizare ratată. Culisele cazului Miron Constantinescu–Iosif Chişinevschi (1956-1961)*, Elion Pub., Bucharest, 2001.

8.   Maria Someşan şi Mircea Iosifescu, „Legile din 1948 pentru reforma învăţământului", in *Analele Sighet*, No. 6, 1998, pp. 439–444; Teresia B. Tătaru, *„Liceu, cimitir al tinereţii mele". Sovietizarea învăţământului românesc (1946–1952)*, Baia Mare, 1998; Nicoleta Ionescu-Gură, *Stalinizarea României*, pp. 324–356; Eugen Denize, „Învăţământul în sistemul de propagandă comunist din România (1948–1953)", in *Studii şi materiale de istorie contemporană*, No. 5, 2006, pp. 151–174.

9.   The first time this system was implemented was in the Soviet part of Germany, the future GDR, in 1945, when 28,000 professors, former members of the National Socialist Party, were fired (from a total of 40,000), see Hermann Weber, *op. cit.*, pp. 90-91. See also Dinu C. Giurescu, *Istoria românilor*, vol. X, *România în anii 1948–1989*, Editura Enciclopedică, Bucharest, 2013, p. 582 and the following.

10.   In this case as well, they used the methods of Soviet pedagogue Makarenko, which replaced all pedagogical experiences from the last few centuries, experiences meant to shape the child's personality and character. Makarenko's aim was adapting to communal life and anihilating uniqueness, both in students and in teachers, cf. Anne Applebaum, *op. cit.*, p. 386 and the following.

11. Or theoretical high schools throughout the country, cf. Nicoleta Ionescu-Gură, *Stalinizarea României,* p. 332.

12. Through the Ministry of Public Education's decree from January 1948, cf. Nicoleta Ionescu-Gură in *Stalinizarea României,* p. 332. This is how the affair is described by a former student of "Gheorghe Lazăr" high school from that time: "The educational reform was fast approaching and it's purpose was to destroy those high schools thought to be reactionary nests. The destruction went as follows: professors were dispersed, buildings were changed, traditional names of schools were dropped and their profiles were changed. Boys high schools turned into girls schools and the other way around. As for names, they became L.B. 1, L.B. 9 (Boys' High Schools no. 9), this had been called "Lazăr". It had been moved to the building formerly occupied by "Spiru Haret", and "Spiru Haret" had been closed. "Mihai Viteazul" high school (I don't remember what name it had) was moved to where the former commercial high school had been on Traian Street, and so on (...), the former location, turned into "Ştefan Gheorghiu" Academy, or rather the Higher Party School. (...) Law, together with the autonomy of these institutions, forbade high schools' uniforms and colors as such. (...) I think that we moved into "Spiru Haret"'s building quite late, in the Fall of 1948. The estrangement, the break couldn't be just spiritual, but also physical." (M. Gramatopol, *op. cit.,* vol. I, pp. 74-84).

13. "Liceul de băieți nr. 9" in Romanian.

14. December 30th, 1947, is the day when king Michael I of Romania was forced to abdicate.

15. May 1st, Labor Day. Parades were organized, so that the people could express their gratitude to the country's "brave leader".

16. Some years later I discussed this subject again in over 100 pages published in 1964, in a journal subversively called Glasul Bisericii (*The Voice of the Church). The Official Journal of the Holy Metropolitan Church of UngroWallachia,* issue XXIII (1964), pp. 777-802. I named my father co-author, who was a priest at Batiştei Church and Cabinet Chief to patriarch Justinian, to speed its publication, although he hadn't contributed at all. He'd even confiscated my royalties to mend the church's fence and do various repairwork.

17. In this neighborhood, only Batiştei Street, Blanduziei Street, Dianei Street, Italiană Street, Oțetari Street and Dr. Bacaloglu Street kept their names. Here

are the others: C.A. Rosetti was first Clemenței and then Grației; Vasile Lascăr was first Teilor (now only a section of the old street that began near Colțea Hospital), and then Galați under Ceaușescu; Nicolae Filipescu was originally called Scaune, and under Ceaușescu, Snagov; Alexandru Sahia was originally called Polonă (the name remained for the northern section, after Gogu Cantacuzino Square), then Gogu Cantacuzino (whose statue made by Ernest Dubois was erected in 1904 in Icoanei Park), and now a part of it is called Doctor Gerota and the other, Jean-Louis Calderon, after a French reporter who died in the 1989 Revolution (crushed by an army tank that, instead of going forward, as normal, went backwards); Dionisie Lupu was originally called Drumul Herăstrăului (a name kept by the street that comes after, Calea Dorobanți, renamed thus after 1877), and now Tudor Arghezi (part of it); Eremia Grigorescu was called Armașului (hence the access point Intrarea Armașului), and Pictor Verona was called Mercur until the intersection with Pitar Moș, and the open part up to Dionise Lupu and Sahia was called Memorei; Maria Rosetti was called Sfântul Spiridon; Iulius Fucik was originally Sălciilor, then Thomas Masaryk, a name that came back; Icoanei was called General Al. Lahovary; Hristo Botev was called Domniței; Radu Cristian in Rosetti Square was called Melodiei; Dumbrava Roșie was Strada Nouă; General Praporgescu was first Crinului, then Gheorghe Chițu; I.L. Caragiale was originally Rotarilor; Aron Florian was originally Ermitului, and a neighboring street, Martirul (I think it is now Marin Serghiescu); Logofătul Luca Stroici was first Surorilor, then Robert de Flers; Alexandru Donici was Popa Chițu; Dianei had an extension called Prudenței; Traian Vuia was first called Gloriei, then Eugen Stătescu; Vasile Conta was called Minervei; Ion Vidu, former Vasile Boerescu, near Rosetti Square, was called Pensionatului; Bălcescu Boulevard was first Colței Street, then I.C. Brătianu; Republicii Boulevard was originally Carol I and Protopopescu-Pache, then Mareșal Tolbuhin and then Carol I again. Clemenței and Mercur began on the other side of the boulevard, to the West, because the boulevard only came this way in the 20th century.

18. Neighborhood in Paris, around Saint-Germain-des-Près, where the greatest french aristocratic families lived.

19. Ulysse de Marsillac, *De Pesth à Bucarest. Notes de voyage*, Bucarest, [1869], in Romanian by Elena Rădulescu, *Bucureștiul în veacul al XIX-lea*, Meridiane,

Bucharest, 1999, p. 79; fragment quoted *ad litteram*, but for the last paragraph, in *Guide du voyageur à Bucarest*, Bucarest, [1877], by the same author, the same translation in Romanian, p. 111.

20. Constantin C. Giurescu, *Istoria Bucureștilor*, 2nd edition, Sport-Turism Pub, Bucharest, 1979, p. 337.

21. Cuckoo's Pond

22. The oldest house in Bucharest is Melik House at no. 22, Spătarului Street, dating back to 1760, rebuilt in 1820 and turned into the Theodor Pallady Museum in 1971.

23. "scaune" in Romanian

24. "săpunari" in Romanian

25. My colleague and friend Ştefan Andreescu spoke about it in an article, „Contribuții la istoricul bisericilor Scaune şi Săpunari", in *Glasul Bisericii*, 23, 1964, pp. 105–119.

26. I could never understand the phrase: "Dâmbovița, sweet thy water,/ Who shall drink will never wander!" Knowing the chronic levels of pollution in the river, I think those lines are rather ironic.

27. In 1828 the first sewer was installed to collect water from Colțea, Batiştei and Biserica Enei, and it spilled into Dâmbovița.

28. Alexandru Tzigara-Samurcaş, *Memorii, I (1872-1910)*, Grai şi Suflet-Cultura națională Pub, Bucharest, 1991, p. 18. Al. Samurcaş' house was built in 1894 by architect Joseph I. Exner, see Cezara Mucenic, *Bucureşti. Un veac de arhitectură civilă. Secolul al XIX-lea*, Silex, Bucharest, 1997.

29. George Potra, „Bucureştioara, un pârâu dispărut", in idem, *Din Bucureştii de ieri*, I, Editura Ştiinţifică şi Enciclopedică, Bucharest, 1990, pp. 198–205 şi 312–313. Now the garden is called Ion Voicu with impiety, because the violinist's house originally belonged to his father-in-law, a businessman who made his fortune during the war in Transnistria and other occupied territories (information from Professor Edith Ilovici, Voicu's neighbor). For more on Ioanid Park, see Cristina Woinaroski's incredible monograph, *Istorie urbană. Lotizarea şi Parcul Ioanid din Bucureşti în context european*, Simetria, Bucharest, 2013.

30. The writer I.A. Basarabescu (1870-1952) has a short story, *La casa din Batişte*, the area being described as "an aristocratic neighborhood" (*Nuvele*, 1903).

For different aspects of the neighborhood's past, see Mrs. Victoria Dragu Dimitriu's works, *Povești ale doamnelor din București*, Vremea Pub, Bucharest, 2004, pp. 69–97, 105–109, 183–217; eadem, *Povești ale domnilor din București*, Vremea Pub, Bucharest, 2005, p. 121 and the following; eadem, *Doamne și domni la răspântii bucureștene*, Vremea Pub, Bucharest, 2008, pp. 106–135, 377–454, 474–523; eadem, *A zecea carte cu povești din București*, Vremea Pub, Bucharest, 2015, pp. 295–297; Andreea Deciu (ed.), *Povestea caselor*, Simetria, Bucharest, 1999, pp. 13–22.

31. Back to Jules Michelet Street before 1914 (the former Dreaptă Street), a little to the North. On a piece of land ceded by the state in 1902, the Anglican Church near Grădina Icoanei was built in 1922.

32. Emanoil Hagi-Mosco, „O casă veche boierească în mahalaua Colții: fosta primărie", in idem, *București. Amintirile unui oraș*, Fundația Culturală Română, Bucharest, 1995, pp. 108–112.

33. Bucharest Phonebooks from 1939, 1941 and 1945. In 1950, the Popular Council was at no. 16, Republicii Boulevard.

34. His history, as well as that of the Geanelloni boarding-school, was recorded by George Potra, *Din Bucureștii de ieri*, vol. II, pp. 45-65.

35. Mater Consolata Bachmeyer, *Pitar Moș*, Dorul Pub, Aalborg, 2000; Gheorghe Parusi, *op. cit.*, pp. 245–246, 267–268, 655. The last mother superior, Clementina Mayer, was arrested together with the school secretary and died in Văcărești in July 195.

36. Emanoil Hagi-Mosco, *"art. cit."*, pp. 178-179, who mentiones that in the past there was a clock on the building's front.

37. Or Mărăscu, see a student's memories, Constantin Kirițescu, *O viață, o lume, o epocă. Memorii*, Sport Turism Pub, Bucharest, 1979, pp. 54–61.

38. "Associated professors"

39. Built in the same place as general Ioan Odobescu's house, buried in a luxurious monument in the Icoanei Church yard across the street. Another house in the neighborhood built in 1889, designed by Mincu, belonged to general Constantin Robescu at no. 12, Caragiale Street. It was sold to the state and offered in 1931 to marshal Prezan (now the Diabetes Institute "Dr. Nicolae Paulescu"). In 1889, Ion Mincu designed Șt. Vlădoianu House at no. 1, Sălciilor Street (Cezara Mucenic, *op. cit.*, p. CIX, photo 37).

40. a Romanian sport similar to baseball
41. Alexandru Ciorănescu, *Amintiri fără memorie*, I, 1911–1934, Editura Fundației Culturale Române, Bucharest, 1995, pp. 65 and 70.
42. *Katholische Schulanstalten in der Erzdiözese Bukarest, Bericht über das Schuljahr 1917/18*, Staatsdruckerei Bukarest, Bucharest, 1918; Nikolaus Netzhammer and Christa Zach (editors), Raymund Netzhammer, *Bischof in Rumänien im Spannungsfeld zwischen Staat und Vatikan*, 2 vol., Verlag Südostdeutsches Kulturwerk, Munich, 1996. The headmistress was Miss Paula Pucho, and the deputy was Rozsa Balint.
43. Zoltan Rostas, *op. cit.*, p. 122.
44. The house was built in 1884 by architect Ioan Roznoveanu, cf. Andrei Pippidi, *Case și oameni din București*, vol. II, Humanitas, Bucharest, 2012, pp. 268–270. There you can read more about the house at no. 4, Tudor Arghezi Street ("building suppression") and the mathematician Gheorghe Țițeica's house at no. 80, Dionisie Lupu Street.
45. Further down Dionisie Lupu Street, this is how Emanoil Hagi-Mosco (born in 1880), who spent his childhood around here, describes it: "the house on the corner of Clemența Street and Dionisie Lupu Street. A simple building, of moderate size, two-storied, a third one added later. This was once the Anton Altân Drugstore. I don't know who built it, but it is as old as its neighbor. I remember an accident caused by an explosion of flammable substances deposited in the building's cellar. The floor caved in just as a woman walked into the drugstore and as she fell into the cellar, she burned to death. Upstairs lived general Constantin Budișteanu, before moving to the street that was named after him. General Budișteanu had a lovely career. Born in 1838, Colonel Brigadier, he took part in the Plevna attack in 1877 where he was gravely injured. As War Minister, he created Militia batallions. As President of the Senate, he died in 1911. He was nicknamed general Bludgeon because in the Parliament, when discussing the introduction of the Manlicher rifle in the military, he spoke against it, comparing it to a bludgeon" (Emanoil Hagi-Mosco, „O veche stradă din București: ulița Clemenței", in idem, *București. Amintirile unui oraș vechi*, p. 180).
46. The photograph showing the inside of such a pub in the 1930s in Radu Oltean (ed.), *București. 550 de ani de la prima atestare documentară (1459–2009)*,

Bucharest, 2009, p. 230, with a poster that reads: "I am moving to N. Filipescu Street... Gogu Cantacuzino Street".

47. Buried in the churchyard of Oțetari, a neighborhood where two of his nephews lived as prominent businessmen, Niculae, the son of Voicu the skinner, known in Vienna as Nicolae Woikozitz (1803-1858) and Ilie Zamfirescu (d. 1862), see Adrian Majuru, *București. Istoria unei geografii umane*, Bucharest, ICR, 2007, pp. 58–63.

48. A description of these houses in Alex. Tzigara-Samurcaș, *op. cit.*, pp. 18 and 31-39. Scarlat Rosetti left money and 6,000 tomes for the Athenaeum library (D.R. Rosetti, *Dicționarul contemporanilor*, Bucharest, 1898, p. 163). The house numbers almost never reflect today's reality, they have changed constantly due to the emergence of new buildings. Photographs of the most beautiful ones can be found in Frédéric Damé, *Bucarest en 1906*, Bucharest, 1907; see Narcis Dorin Ion, *București. În căutarea micului Paris*, Tritonic Pub, Bucharest, 2003. The neighboring house at no. 23 belonged to doctor Kremnitz, writer Mita Kremnitz' husband and Titu Maiorescu's sister-in-law, cf. Alex. Tzigara-Samurcaș, *op.cit.*, p. 38.

49. Emanoil Hagi-Mosco, *București*, p. 126.

50. The street was numbered in 1891.

51. Th. Cornel, *Figuri contimporane din România*, București, 1909– 1913, p. 310.

52. Historical monument, architect Louis Pierre Blanc (1860-1903), see Cezara Mucenic, *București. Un veac de arhitectură civilă. Secolul al XIX-lea*, Silex, Bucharest, 1997.

53. Dates back to 1915, architect Ion D. Berindei.

54. Cf. Cezara Mucenic, *op. cit.*

55. Architects Ion D. Berindei and G. Ciogolea.

56. Andrei Pippidi, *Case și oameni din București*, vol. II, Humanitas, Bucharest, 2012, pp. 263–264; Cezara Mucenic, *op. cit.* Built in 1894–1895 by F. Bohacker and Ludwig Schindl, architect R. Quick (back then it was at no. 33).

57. Entrepreneur Aurel Ioanovici, see George Jurgea-Negrilești, *Troica amintirilor. Sub patru regi*, Cartea Românească, Bucharest, 2002, pp. 286–287, 397. A description of the interior ("a magnificent home of marble and inlaid woods") in Robert Bishop and E.S. Crayfield, *op. cit.*, pp. 101–103. In 1944, this is where the American Task Force took up residence, discovering

countless surprises in the former minister's home: over 500 suits, over 300 pairs of shoes, around 1,000 ties and a 6.5 ft by 5 ft crate full of French perfumes, Chanel 5 in 34 fl oz bottles. In the attic, an anti-aircraft shelter with a 23 in thick layer of sand, there were gold coins, bullions and Swiss franks that were worth 12 million dollars (handed over to the capital's mayor, general Victor Dombrovski). All rooms and phones were bugged, so the Task Force moved at no. 3, Oţetari Street. Still, in 1950, this was the American Military Attachés Office. The perfume was meant for Ică's mistress, the beautiful Ileana Kerciu Pociovălişteanu, to whom the minister offered a house – the future Zambaccian Museum – and in 1943 he sent her to Switzerland, where she met Constantin Argetoianu, see Stelian Neagoe, *Politică şi destin. Constantin Argetoianu*, Machiavelli, Bucharest, 2012, pp. 54–55. Radu Lecca affirms that the minister had his heart set on a Belgian's house on Batiştei Street from 1941, cf. *Eu i-am salvat pe evreii din România*, Roza vânturilor, Bucharest, 1994, p. 174

58. Architect Lous Blanc in Louis XVI style, with monumental horse stables designed by Ion I. Berindei, who also designed the apartment building at no. 3, Xenopol Street.

59. "A secluded house, with a pleasant appearance. A high ground floor and a rather exaggerated turret. It belonged to Nicolae Butculescu, who died in 1925, a member of the large family who owned several houses in this part of town. General Socec, the one blamed for having deserted during battle near Bucharest in 1916, tried and demoted, had bought the house. Socec, married to an Englishwoman, was a rather arrogant man" (Emanoil Hagi-Mosco, *"art. cit."*, pp. 179-180). In 1891, Alexandru Socec had already moved to no. 29, Clemenţei Street; in 1887 I find him at no. 5, Italiană Street, so in the same neighborhood. Another Butculescu, Dimitrie (Mitică), 1845-1916, lived at no. 13, Clemenţei Street in a neo-Romanian style house built by architect I.N. Socolescu. His heirs sold the house to dr. Constantin Angelescu (1869-1948), Liberal Minister and politician, and now in its place we find Hotel Lido, built in 1930, architect E. Doneaud.

60. This is how Emanoil Hagi-Mosco describes it: "It was built before 1900 by architect Maimarolu (who also designed the Military Circle Palace, former CCA. for the wealthy agricultural landowner Sava Şomănescu. He died in

1916, leaving most of his estate (a few thousand hectares), to the detriment of his sons, to his second wife. The widow sold the house in 1927 to the Agronomic Society. The Agricultural Mortgage Loan had its office there, before getting its own place in 1937, the large building on the corner of Academiei Street and Calea Victoriei." (Emanoil Hagi-Mosco, "O veche stradă din Bucureşti...", p. 179). In 1937 it was bought by former Prime Minister G.G. Mironescu (nicknamed Bonbon, 1874-1949), one of the richest people in Romania, President of the Bragadiru Corporation, who died in squalor in October 1949 and was found on a bench in Gradia Icoanei with a note bearing his name. Despite this, he was posthumously sentenced to 12 years in prison, on November 3rd. He also had a house at no. 5, Pitar Moş Street.

61. In 1886, architect Anton Anderlof built a house at this address for D.G. Cavadia (Cezara Mucenic, *op. cit.*, p. CI, photo 18). "Doctor Cantacuzino, seeing the size of Şomănescu's house, added another story to his house, saying he felt crushed by its vicinity" (Emanoil Hagi-Mosco, *"art. cit."*, p. 179). Architect: Paul Gottereau, author of the CEC building (1895) and of the University Foundation King Carol I (1898), who also built Prof. D. Stoicescu's house (no. 2bis, Batiştei Street), the house at no. 16, Dionisie Lupu Street (1883) and Ion D. Cantacuzino's house at no. 62, Dionisie Lupu Street (1884). See Cezara Mucenic, *op. cit.*, p. LXXVIII, photo 23. After 1920, the Liberal Club used by the Reserve Officers Association and the house then.

62. *"Art. cit."*, p. 180. There you can find a description of the Rioşanu house, where Cezar Bolliac, the famous publicist, lived. Other memories of this area before 1914 in Zoe Cămărăşescu (1895–1987), *Amintiri*, Vitruviu Pub, Bucharest, n.d.

63. In 1934-1935 architect Rudolf Fraenkel builds the Scala office building and cinema, and in 1936-1937 architect Emil Nădejde built the Scala apartment building and sweetshop at no. 36-38, Magheru Boulevard. Both collapsed during the 1977 earthquake and were rebuilt. *See Bucureşti, anii 1920–1940: între avangardă şi modernism*, Simetria, Bucharest, 1994. On Bălcescu Boulevard, no. 22, on the corner of Eugen Stătescu Street (Traian Vuia Street), architect Herman Clejan built in 1935 the apartment and office building owned by the Sun-Assurance ensurance company. In 1884, this was Anton Ladori's house, designed by Richard Kraft.

64. Constantin Argetoianu, *Pentru cei de mâine. Amintiri din vremea celor de ieri, I/1. Până la 1888*, Humanitas, Bucharest, 1991, pp. 68–71. The Athenaeum library opened for the public in 1930 and had 21,000 books.

65. Emanoil Hagi-Mosco, *"art. cit."*, p. 179. In 1910, her daughter, Elisa Cartian Leontie, also a midwife, lived at no. 10, Italiană Street.

66. Cezara Mucenic, *op. cit.*, p. LXXXI, photos 31 and 32.

67. Horia Creanga (1892-1943) also designed, in 1932, Dr. Constantinescu's villa at no. 3, Corneliu Botez Street.

68. The names of Bucharest's suburbs was generally given by the name of the church in the incorporated village at different times, about which we know very little, while some names cannot be located on a map. Batiştei Church is the oldest one in the neighborhood, built in 1627-1629 by a rich Cretan merchant, Baptista Vevelli (it is mentioned in 1660 as "Batişte's Church"). It was rebuilt with stone in 1763 by the butcher bailiff Manciu, whose heirs founded the Mănciulescu family, at no. 26, Batiştei Street. Oțetari Church and Icoanei Church date back to 1680-1682, Pitar Moş from before 1690 and Popa Chiţu and Popa Rusu fom the 18th century. The neighborhood was called Batiştei, a more elegant name, so we find aristocrats (especially Zinca Bălcescu, the revolutionary's mother) who lived around 1829-1830 near the Italiană Church on Bălcescu Boulevard, while their official address was in Batiştei Suburbs, which in turn was divided into two "colors" – red (the border was Colţei Street, renamed Brătianu Boulevard, then Bălcescu and Magheru) and yellow – a name given by the Russian administration in 1829 to administrative sectors in town.

69. One of our neighbors was a nurse here, Mrs. Oşanu, one of my brother's classmates' mother, doctor Mircea Oşanu from Elias Hospital.

70. This street was one of the most elegant in Bucharest during the fist half of the 20th century: at almost every number you could find people registered in the *High-Life Almanach* from 1910 and 1924: Minister Vintilă Brătianu, Ionel's brother (at no. 6), banker Aristide Blank (at no. 14, a house from 1891, architect Ioan Roznoveanu), dramatic artist Petre Sturdza, father of actress Lucia Sturdza-Bulandra, dr. Gheorghe Marinescu, who specialized in mental affection, a Professor (no. 29), later surgeon N. Hortolomei (at no. 34) and other engineers, officers, high magistrates and lawyers.

71. Let's not forget his good friend Caragiale lived on Rotarilor Street and they both met at Tănase Cantili's pub, then Sotir's Pub at no. 43, Scaune Street, now demolished, that Alexandru Teodoreanu evoked, "Un local de altădată" (1933) in *De re culinaria*, Sport-Turism Pub, Bucharest, 1977, pp. 210–213. Actually, Caragiale lived in many different houses in this neighborhood: no. 4, Pitar Moş Street, no. 23, Rotari Street, no. 5, Sf. Spiridon Street (Maria Rosetti), in front of which you can find his statue, and no. 90, Polonă Street (Burelly House). See Lelia Zamani, „Eminescu şi Caragiale la Bucureşti", in *Materiale de istorie şi muzeografie*, 24/2014, pp. 244–249.

72. Buried in the Oţetari churchyard, see Constantin Olariu, *Bucureştiul monden. Radiografia unei prăbuşiri (1940–1970)*, Paralela 45, Piteşti, 2006, pp. 35–36.

73. Lina "Warehouse" and Tincuţa "Birdcage"

74. Emanoil Hagi-Mosco, „*art. cit.*", p. 178.

75. Paul Constantin, *Arta 1900 în România*, Meridiane, Bucharest, 1972, p. 87 and fig. 117 on p. 95; p. 74, fig. 79 and 80. Architect Arghir Culina designed the apartment building of the Romanian Dacia Association on Gogu Cantacuzino.

76. Idem, *ibidem*, p. 86.

77. Radu Oltean (ed.), *Bucureşti*, p. 286. The house was illegally demolished in 2009.

78. *Ibidem*, pp. 82–83, fig. 93–95.

79. *Ibidem*, p. 82.

80. Accross the street there was Bazil G. Assan's beautiful house (1860-1918), the 1914 work of architect Ion D. Berindei in Louis XVI style.

81. Ion G. Duca, *Amintiri politice*, Ion Dumitru-Verlag, Munich, 1981, pp. 177, 255, 257.

82. Where Petrache Poenaru's house (1799-1875) had been, then Constantin C. Lecca's, see an image of this building in George Potra, *Petrache Poenaru, ctitor al învăţămîntului în ţara noastră*, Editura Ştiinţifică, Bucharest, 1973, p. 16, 22. Next to it, on the Boulevard, architect Horia Teodoru built in 1932 the "Ioan Dalles" Trust, where the philanthropist's house had been, built in 1874 by architect M. Caputineanu. In 1960, an eight-story apartment building incorporated the building's hall and former gound floor.

83. This is where the Tărtășescu family lived in the 19th century (they moved on Dumbrava Roșie Street later), direct descendants of skinner Ioan Dobrescu (177-c. 1832), a late chronicler and cantor in Batiștei Church. His chronicle, which had precious illustrations of the old Bucharest, was published by Ilie Corfus under the name „Cronica meșteșugarului Ioan Dobrescu (1802–1830)", in *Studii și article de istorie*, 8, 1966, pp. 309–403. The reserve colonel Alex. C. Tărtășescu was arrested in 1950 (he was 78) for frequenting the French library. Another victim of the American bombings in 1944 was the last house on Batiștei Street, on the corner of Vasile Lascăr Street, where an imposing block was built later.

84. This block's history in Dumitru Muster, „Imobilul din Piața Lahovary nr. 5A sau cutremurul de după cutremur", in Andreea Deciu, *op. cit.*, pp. 169–174. Here lived, among others, Geo Bogza and actor Ion Lucian. A few feet away, in the square between Dionisie Lupu Street and Pitar Moș Street, in 1934 there appeared a fountain called "Joc de copii", by Ion Iordănescu (1881-1949).

85. The name means "wicked" in Greek and was built in 1731. Torn down in 1890, when Carol Boulevard was extended, it is mentioned in an inscription on the wall of the house at no. 44. Here, in the monastery's yard, lived Eminescu for a while, who had previously been on Speranței Street, cf. Lelia Zamani, „ *art. cit.*", cf. Constantin Olariu, *op. cit.*, p. 248.

86. *București anii 1920-1940. Între avangardă și modernism*, Simetria, București, 1994, p. 175.

87. His History teacher (he had top grades in his class) from "Sfântul Gheorghe" high school, Tudor Seimeanu, lived back then at no. 4, Eugen Stătescu Street, then at no. 7, General Praporgescu Street. He was the grandfather of our colleague, Florin Seimeanu, his grandmother was probably Emilia Bălcescu, a niece of the revolutionary historian. Cf. Al. Oprea, *Mateiu I. Caragiale – un personaj. Dosar al existenței*, Muzeul Literaturii Române, Bucharest, 1979, pp. 186 and 306, note 43.

88. Andrei Pippidi, *op. cit.*, pp. 59–61 („De la Mateiu citire").

89. In the night shift, even, see Stelian Tănase, *Anatomia mistificării*, p. 367.

90. Gheorghe Jurgea-Negrilești, *Troica amintirilor*, 2nd edition, Bucharest, 2007, p. 364. That priest was my father, at Batiștei Church between 1935 and 1983.

He did have perfect teeth and got his first cavity when he was 70. Years later, Tutu Georgescu and Fatmé Magheru told me they came to church for the mass, but also to admire "the priest with nice teeth".

91. *Les communistes démasqués. D'après les comptes rendus sténographiques du procès contre „L'Internationale des traîtres"*, Société Roumaine d'Edition, Paris, 1953. See details in Mihai Dimitrie Sturdza, „Comuniștii demascați, dați în judecată la Paris de un grup din emigrație", in idem, *Rușii, masonii, Mareșalul și alte răspântii ale istoriografiei românești*, Compania, Bucharest, 2013, pp. 348–373.

92. Dorina Potârcă, *op. cit.*, p. 7 and 21. Note that Ana Pauker also lived on Maria Rosetti Street between 1944–1945, before moving to a villa owned by prince Jean Callimachi, cf. Lavinia Betea, *op. cit.*, pp. 102–103; Doina Tudorovici, *Amurgul nobililor*, p. 185.

93. She was arrested in 1951 as "dubious party" and sentenced to three years in a camp, as were two of her aunts, Stelian Popescu's sisters. The same thing happened to his son-in-law, Ion Lugoșianu (1890-1957, dead in Râmnicu Sărat), sentenced to forced labor for life, whose son was executed at 21 for spreading manifestos, cf. Dorina Potârcă, *op. cit.*, pp. 60, 71.

94. Stelian Popescu, *Memorii*, Majadahonda Pub, Bucharest, 1994, pp. 26–27.

95. Mihail Dimitri Sturdza, *Genealogiile familiilor boierești din Moldova și Țara Românească*, III, *Familia Cantacuzino*, Simetria, Bucharest, 2014, p. 572. She died in prison in 1955, see Ivor Porter, *Operation Autonomous*, pp. 236, 248. Under the name Ena Ralli, she is the heroine of Donald Dunham's book, Zone *of violence*, Belmont Books, New York, 1962. Dunham was USIS' manager in Bucharest between 1947 and 1950.

96. Victor Spinei, „Gheorghe I. Brătianu între vocația istoriei și tentațiile vieții politice", in idem, *Reprezentanți de seamă ai istoriogafiei și filologiei românești și mondiale*, Istros Pub, Brăila, 1996, pp. 91–267; Aurel Pentelescu and Liviu Țăranu (ed.), *Gheorghe I. Brătianu în dosarele Securității. Documente. Peri oada domiciliului obligatoriu. Arestarea. Detenția. Moartea*, Editura Enciclopedică, Bucharest, 2006.

97. George Potra, *Din Bucureștii de ieri*, vol II, pp. 291–292.

98.   And yet, in the last decade of the 19th century, Nicolae Grigorescu drew
      a few types of modest people in the neighborhood, as Alexandru Tzigara-
      Samurcaș, who knew the artist, pointed out: "Living for many years in the
      upstairs flat of the house on the corner of Batiștei Street and Polonă Street,
      Grigorescu captured in a series of pencil sketches the main types of peo-
      ple who happened to walk by his window. Thus we have the water bearer,
      mounted on his two-wheeled barrow, bringing Dâmbovița water to the sub-
      scribers, that had to be decanted with alum stone in porous stone vessels;
      the truck farmer bearing a yoke on his shoulders with baskets of vegetable,
      fruit, eggs and other supplies; the wood chopper with his buck, saw and
      axe; the *bragă* maker with his cap, selling cold bragă in Summer and warm
      salep in Winter; the cobbler sitting at his working bench at the church door.
      All these types, like many others, the cab driver, the chimney sweeper and
      others, make up the most precious illustration of life in Batiștei Suburb"
      (*Memorii*, vol. I, p. 37). It was mostly people from the poor neighborhoods
      of the city.

99.   In the 1950s and 1960s, the Batiștei Church congregation was made up of
      about 400 Orthodox families, more than in 1941, when there were only
      236 families with 754 people, cf. Anuarul *Arhiepiscopiei Bucureștilor cu date
      statistice pe anul 1941*, București, 1941, p. 155. Our neighborhood, as I said
      before, was much larger and went beyond these ecclesiastic limits.

100. Nicoleta Ionescu-Gură, *Nomenclatura*, p. 90, 148.

101. *Ibidem*, pp. 174–175 (in 1950) and 356–357 (in 1955, more detailed).

102. It was said that in 1948, this house held the Romanian Freemasonry
      archives.

103. In Bulgaria, there was a joke going around: "How's this or that movie? Is it
      good or is it Soviet?" (Georgi Markov, *op. cit.*, p. 49).

104. literally "small pepper"

105. Miss Holban, a student of Nicolae Iorga, was a researcher at the History
      Institute founded by the great historian, which was named after him. At
      the beginning of the 1960s, she went to Budapest and when asked by the
      passport service if she had ever been there before, she answered coldly: "Yes,
      I have, with my father, in 1919." Every year, before May 1st, August 23rd and
      November 7th, Miss Holban packed a suitcase for a few days: she was one

of the undesirables who were forced to leave Bucharest as not to disturb or endanger the great communist celebrations.

106. Around 1959-1960, when IDs were renewed, my mother had the unfortunate idea to indicate our address as being no. 1, General Praporgescu Street, our house being on the corner of Batiştei Street. The result: she was forced to go several times to an office at the edge of town where an illiterate clerk was unable to spell this name. Eventually she stayed on General Protopopescu, changed to General Praporgescu, but got her middle name misspelled from Georgeta to Gergieta. When she saw this, mother abandoned the fight and stayed Georgieta in papers. The house was demolished after 1989 together with those at no. 3 and no. 5, Praporgescu Street, replaced by a large apartment and office building with aluminum front and blue windows, a heresy placed a few feet away from a historical monument.

107. George Jurgea-Negrileşti, *op. cit.*, 2nd edition, pp. 446–449.

108. Dorin-Liviu Bîtfoi, *op. cit.*, pp. 329–330.

109. Around 1885, Suvenir Garden was here, visited by important people such as Prime Minister Ion C. Brătianu, for good music and excellent food, as well as for the charm of the bushes, appreciated by those seeking intimacy, see Vera Molea, *Hai, nene, la Iunion! Teatrele din grădinile de vară ale Bucureştilor de altădată*, Vremea Pub, 2014, Bucharest, p. 72. Another Summer garden, at no. 42, Teilor Street (Vasile Lascăr Street), was open around the same time. In 1914, the central store of Mercur Society had already been built here, a Co-op with branches on Calea Griviţei and Calea Moşilor.

110. Ion Paraschiv, Trandafir Iliescu, *De la hanul Şerban Vodă la hotel Intercontinental*, Sport-Turism Pub, Bucharest, 1979, pp. 254–255, with address and chronology errors; Zissu Garden still existed in 1953, the year of the Youth and Student World Fair, see above; Dorin-Liviu Bîtfoi, *op. cit.*, p. 327. The reopening of the Mercur Stakehouse, where you could admire piles of meats and all sorts of entrails, was a happy occasion for many enthusiasts in Bucharest, such as the art critic Petru Comarnescu. At a dinner with some of his friends and colleagues, Comarnescu couldn't stop praising the restaurant, proposing it should be turned into a meeting place for writers and artists. Amused and slightly irritated by the loud eloquence of his friend, Eugen Schileru put a wet blanket on him saying sharply: "Titel,

when you say the word Mercur, you sound like Goethe on his deathbed saying *Mehr Licht!*". The scene took place in Moldova Restaurant, near Grădina Icoanei, a meeting place for intellectuals where Păstorel Teodoreanu and many others would often be seen.

111.   literally "The Seven Legs"

112.   Annie Bentoiu, *op. cit.*, vol. II, p. 507.

113.   funeral wheat porridge

114.   Alexandru Paleologu, baptized by my grandfather on my mother's side but converted to Catholicism, like his brother, Andrei, told me that he came to Batiștei Church only on Easter, to listen to my father proclaim in a loud voice ("of cosmic proportions", said Conul Alecu) "Jesus is Resurrected!" Their mother, however, came to Batiștei Church mass regularly.

CHAPTER 5

"Spiru Haret" high school over the ages

———

BUT LET US GO BACK to our first school year, 1953-1954. We were around 50 students, all of us boys, split into two classes headed by two teachers, Mrs. Linte and comrade Renția (or Rențea), who didn't go by "madam". I evoked Mrs. Linte in my school memories (in the chapter called *Presentations*) and I maintain my belief that she was not a good pedagogue: for example, she gave me a 1 for the lesson with the letter "R", which I can't pronounce because I naturally say it in a guttural manner[1]. The teacher's verdict: I hadn't learned the lesson![2]

There were 20-30 children in my class, and only 9 of us graduated from high school in 1964: Ştefan Andreescu, Decebal Becea, myself, Petre Clar, Dragoş Duinea, Zamfir (Firu) Dumitrescu, Ladislau (Loți) Hajos, Nicolae-Andrei Popescu (Popică), Florin Scimeanu, and we saw each-other again, but for two of us (one absence was unaccounted for) after 50 years. The others moved and/or emigrated legally, many to Israel and other countries, because they were Jewish: Nicki Aronovici, Ivan Csendes, Kahane, Anton (Tonel) Laurian, Henri Löbel, Emilian Marcovici, Jack Mendesohn, Lucian Rosenblat, Jack (transcribed as "Giac") Rosenzweig, Alfred Scheffler, Schlesinger, Gerhard Simon (Coca), Robert Weidenfeld, Paul Vaininger. In our 3rd grade pictures there is also Tudor Cudalbu, Adrian Iuncu, Ştefan Orăşeanu, Dumitru Paloş, Octavian Şişman, Constantin Ştefănescu, Dumitru (?) Tobă, Ion Vârjan and another one I cannot identify. In comrade Renția's class there were Sergiu Aronovici, Dini Cernat and Sergiu Solomon, a boy called Peter Izsak, one of the first ones who went to Israel, in 1959-1960, the only ones I can remember[3].

A few of us knew each-other from the No. 1 Kindergarten on Vasile Lascăr Street, at no. 56A, now closed, where we were colleagues with the girls who came to "Spiru Haret" in 4th grade, in 1956-1957. We came from different families, each with its own history and troubles that I knew nothing about at that time. I don't have access to the data available in the 1953-1954 class-books for the 1st grade, but I can say that the majority of students came from bourgeois families - doctors, engineers, professors, civil servants and public officials. From the working class we had Ion Vârjan (his father was a school mechanic and he lived there as well) and one or two colleagues about whom I am not that certain. Most of us lived in the neighborhood, we walked to school, it only took a few minutes, and apart from Nicolae-Andrei Popescu, I can't remember any of us had to commute by streetcar for long distances.

Our communist education had begun since kindergarten: in the September 15th, 1948 issue of *Scînteia* newspaper, the Minister for Education, Gheorghe Vasilichi, wrote that "the state must pay special attention to the first steps in a child's life... By putting children together in kindergartens and daycare centers, we teach them... to discover the world around them, we discipline them and prepare them for living in a community". Like in factories or farmers' co-ops, the "labor plan" is specific to elementary schools as well. Here, too, there are "necessary activities" and every moment of your life is "organized". Instead of lullabies, children learn rhymed slogans. Fairyland is the Soviet Union. Instead of the Tale of the Three Bears, they learn the story of the Great Bear and Stalin was everyone's godfather[4].

Like other classmates, I remember a song and a riddle that I learned in kindergarten, both centered around the new myth of the tractor, communism's invincible weapon against the kulaks (this memory is strange because we didn't have any kulaks in our family and I didn't know any other kulak families either). My parents made fun of them, probably so they wouldn't disturb me: I don't think this was a good thing, because it was only later that I learned to distinguish between what you said at home and what you couldn't repeat at school[5].

The song went like this: "Rumble, rumble, goes the tractor/Rumble, rumble, rumble,/ Those who plow using a motor,/ Rumble, rumble, rumble,/

Make it all look like a game,/ Rumble, rumble, rumble,/ Putting the old plow to shame/ Rumble, rumble, rumble". The riddle was even more explicit: "Who lies in the field all heavy,/ Looking sad and full of envy?/ Close to tears he starts to mumble/ When he hears the tractor rumble." The answer was: "the kulak"! Aside from that, in kindergarten we made castles out of building blocks, shaped figurines out of play dough, and danced folk dances in pairs (my partner was Ana Zsoldos) or in a group. We all wore white uniforms with little aprons and a photograph reproduced by Loți Hajos shows those in our class sitting quietly at three long tables, giving a flower to our teacher, probably on March 8th, the International Women's Day. Another photograph shows us standing in three neat rows, singing heartily with our mouths opened. When the weather was nice, we would play in the kindergarten's graveled back yard.

The only thing of note about my years in kindergarten is something I did outside of it. On the corner of Batiştei Street and Vasile Lascăr Street, there was a neighborhood bulletin board on a wall, set in a wooden case, behind glass. I don't know what came over me, I couldn't even read, but I started flinging rocks to break it, alone or together with a colleague, and then we'd run as fast as we could. It worked the first couple of times, until a militiaman came to our door, the one who kept watch from the red-and-white striped jar-shaped cabin at the same intersection (they appeared in 1949, especially at city entry and exit points, in order to monitor suspicious cars and trucks). He was nice and explained to my parents that our vandalism had grown suspicious and that he would be held accountable for lack of vigilance on the job. Thus, my parents paid for the damage and I got a beating, after which I never broke the glass on the bulletin board ever again.

I said before that every family had its history and troubles that I didn't know about until much later. The record-holder was undoubtedly Tudor Cudalbu, a blond boy with an upturned nose, whose grandfather, also called Tudor, a great landowner from Tutova, senator and minister, died in January 1954 in the Sighet prison after three and a half years of detention, aged 86 (he was born in 1863), without having been tried or sentenced. He was "guilty" of having been the Minister for Agriculture and Domains during the great land reform (1920-1921) and the Minister for Justice in

1926-1927[6]. Our colleague's father, Ion Cudalbu, was sentenced to death in 1950, during colonel Serge Parisot's trial, a French military attaché in Bucharest, accused of running an espionage network. Pericle Martinescu, our witness from that time, wrote in his diary that all the accused plead guilty for their "crimes" and said they were sorry, asking the Court for mercy. "Only one of the accused, Ion Cudalbu, said: "I confess to what I did and I realize how serious it was. The punishment demanded by the prosecutor is well-deserved". I remember with admiration the confession of this downright man, who did not bow and scrape before his opponent, even in the hour of his death"[7].

Around the same time, Mr. Matei Oroveanu was arrested and accused of spying for the United States of America, the father of our colleague, Mihai, who came to "Spiru Haret" in 6th grade. Moreover, Dan Frangopol's uncle, engineer Nicolae Frangopol, head of the Production Planning Division, was arrested and sentenced to forced labor for life in the Danube-Black Sea Canal "saboteur" trial (September-October 1952). Accused in the same trial, engineer Aurel Rozei-Rozemberg, head of the Planning Sector, was sentenced to death and executed on October 13th, 1952, together with two of his colleagues: he was the uncle of our classmate, Adrian Rozei[8]. Other parents, grandparents or uncles and aunts of our classmates were persecuted and imprisoned between 1958-1964, like Ioana Casasovici and Ivan Csendes, the only ones I have information about.

The runner-up in the family drama top was Dini Cernat, the great-grandson of general Alexandru Cernat (1828-1893), a War Minister between 1877-1878, commander-in-chief of the Romanian army in the War of Independence. The general's son, Constantin Cernat, our classmate's grandfather, was a royal prosecutor and director of Siguranta until 1937, when the great trials against the communists took place, starting with the one at Dealul Spirii in 1921[9] and culminating in the ones between 1936-1937, which played a decisive role. Arrested and sentenced to forced labor for life, he died in Gherla in dramatic circumstances (he was assassinated) after 14 years of imprisonment, in 1962[10]. After his grandfather, Dini Cernat saw "all the men in my family... arrested. I lived in our house at no. 25, Italiană Street... [there were] 22 people, sisters, aunts, grandmothers, all left without their men". After being released, Dini's father was a worker at Decorativa co-op, the only job he was allowed to hold.

In 1953, when we were just starting school, both of Nicolae-Andrei Popescu's parents, experienced and well-trained professors, fell victim to the policy of "purging society of the old bourgeois elements" and were sentenced to forced residence[11].

Another dramatic case is the father of our colleague from 5th grade onward, Sonia Dulgheru. Mihail Dulgheru (born Mişu Dulberger, 1909-2002), an underground communist fighter[12], a character we've come across before, former chief of the Fifth Division (Criminal Inquiries) of the Securitate, Chief Cabinet Secretary of the Minister for Internal Affairs (MIA), Teohari Georgescu, a general since 1951 and a member of the Organizational Division of the CC of the PMR between 1949 and 1952. In 1952, he was arrested together with his direct boss, investigated and removed from all office, even thrown out of the army, demoted to the rank of rough soldier. In 1954, he was released and he found a job at the equivalent of wate Management in Bucharest, without losing his secret phone number and his beautiful house at no. 12, Armenească Street[13].

In the same field of repression worked the parents of some of our older colleagues, such as the two Brătucu brothers (who lived at no. 11A, Batiştei Street, in a very elegant apartment building), the sons of comrade Mircea Brătucu, secretary of the Police Prefecture in 1947, who later held a high office within the Ministry of Internal Affairs[14]. Another colleague, one year older than me, was Viorel Ţirli (now deceased); his father, Grigore Ţirli, was chief of staff within the MIA and had taken residence at no. 28, Snagov Street (Nicolae Filipescu), in an old house belonging to one of Nicolae Iorga's students, Miss Maria (Maricel) Holban, a distinguished lady and a great historian. The Ţirli family gave her a rough time during their forced cohabitation, going as far as to sequester her before the December 1989 revolution.

The fathers of at least two of our colleagues were Securitate field officers. The first was Gustav (Gusti) Bodor, a nice, blond boy, with an upturned nose, very quiet and polite. I was very surprised to learn recently that his father was a lieutenant-colonel for the Securitate between 1962-1963 and used to recruit agents and informants from the ranks of Romanian lecturers sent abroad[15], especially to Vienna, where Gusti, who'd graduated from the Faculty of Foreign Commerce (reserved for the communist elite, some of whom would be recruited as spies, see the case of Matei (Moțu) Haiduc), worked in the 1980s at the subsidiary run by the dictator's brother, Marin Ceaușescu, found hanging dead from a radiator in the building's basement. After the revolution in December 1989, Gustav Bodor, together with a few "colleagues", founded an import/export business that was successful for several years. This is how he met with a mutual friend at the Otopeni Airport, where he received and sent various goods. A short while after, Gusti had a heat attack and it seems he died.

The second colleague with a similar background was Hida (Gheorghe, I think). He was a lean and restless boy, with an unfortunate physique - his face was covered in freckles that were more like brownish blotches. I remember he told me once about "comrade Gheorghiu (Dej)", a way of speaking he'd picked up from his parents that was typical of party officers or members of the Securitate. He also mentioned comrade Petre Lupu, who probably worked with his father, which makes me think that he must have been Tibor/Tiberiu Hida (born Mayer Hirsch), an underground communist fighter, colonel in 1948 and vice-chief of the 7th Technical Department of the DGSP (the ones who bugged people's homes, tapped their phones, filmed them and generally dealt with spies and agents' gadgets), then he became chief and later was the head of the 12th Service within the 2nd Department of the Securitate. Relieved of his position, he became an economist for the Rocar Factory in Bucharest[16].

In 1953, our high school was an unfinished building, situated in the center of a reasonably large space and flanked on the right side, towards the street, by the beautiful gymnasium, and on the left by a few small buildings, one of which housed the doctor's office. I forgot his name, but I remember him being tall, elegantly dressed and very skilled, and his nurse, Scharf, was always smiling and kind-hearted. The next house belonged to the janitor, Dumitru (Buliftru), a nice man, and the intendent, or something like that, the vicious Eugen (nicknamed Oxygen), who was cross-eyed and always gave us a hard time. Behind them there were the two sports fields, one covered in asphalt (the basketball court) and the other in red clay, and between them there was an old, dilapidated house - the crafts workshops and home of the school mechanic, Vârjan, our classmate's father. Between the high school building and the gymnasium there was a large yard with asphalt, where the school festivities were held, and towards the back there was a stall where the school choir would perform, conducted by the music teacher, Mr. Dumitru Ionescu, also known as Mache or Măcelaru. Finally, in the school basement there was a large library, with books hid behind curtained bookcases (it was the old library, it probably hadn't been purged), with the amiable Mrs. Zugrăvescu ruling over it.

The headmistress was comrade Teodorescu (nicknamed Țuchi), a woman about whom we learn more from a former "Lazăr" student's memories, the philologist Mihail Gramatopol (born in 1937):

At one point, the elegant history teacher, Mrs. Manolescu[17], goes on maternity leave and is replaced by a young alumnus who distinguished herself by frequently bringing up King Michael I, whom she wouldn't stop heaping praises on. Mrs. or Miss Teodorescu's fervor went beyond the sober school festivities that paid homage to the King, whose portrait hung in every classroom. She wore pastels and has a slight deviation of the eye, meaning she was a little cross-eyed. After the King was exiled, Mrs. Teodorescu stripped her lessons of any political excursions, and the dominating color of her remarkable outfits reddened. Her eyes started to cross even more. From 2nd grade onward, I never saw her around the high school again...

I would meet the "ultra-royalist" history teacher again, a few years later, in "Spiru Haret", where the "Lazăr" high school had been moved (late, in the Fall of 1948); her clothes were redder, her cheeks were redder and she was more boss-eyed. She'd grown to be more of a communist. Andrei Pleșu, who also went to "Spiru Haret", knew her as the red, boss-eyed headmistress as well, and of course she was still a hard-line communist. I was "denounced" to her in 9th grade by my desk-mate, Brana Codruț, a Union of Young Workers (UTM) secretary for having mentioned "Borba", the name of the paper run by "Judas Tito". Mrs. Teodorescu and Brana (...) wanted me expelled for saying that one word. In front of Brana, I started saying how I remembered her from 1ˢᵗ grade in "Lazăr", when she would talk for hours on end about someone alto-gether different from "comrade Stalin". Brana was asked to leave the teacher's room and I kept reminding her how much she used to love "our beloved King, his Highness, Michael I". She turned even more boss-eyed and red than the communist face makeup. She told me to leave and keep my mouth shut if I wanted to stay in high school. Who knows, maybe her father had been a legionary. On top of that, she was an idiot if she thought her past had remained hidden from the communists. They knew it all too well, that's why they had promoted her and were using her, like so many others who'd been "green"[18]![19]

As for the students and the atmosphere between 1948/1949-1952/1953, let us see what Gramatopol has to say:

L.B. No. 9 had become a ridiculous copy of the "Lazăr" high school. Most students had a sort of upbringing and manners that were simply unimaginable to me. Churlish, every other thing that came out of their mouths was a curse word, they directed their phys-ical violence towards those who were not like them. In fact, this had been the purpose of the "reform". Some pretended to be like that, in an abject gesture of schizophrenia. I welcomed the physical moles-tation with outward tranquility. I was bruised all over from their blows and pinches. Classes were a total ruckus most of the time; we learned almost nothing. Only some Math and a little less Physics (both quite rudimentary at that time). Nothing sparked my interest anymore. I decided to escape from that Inferno, which was nothing more than one of the tiny *bolgias* of the great Inferno "under the open sky", when I heard that at "Mihai Viteazu", things were far from being so terrible.[20]

The recollections of this somewhat pretentious but very well polished intel-lectual with impeccable manners may seem like an overstatement. "Spiru

Haret" had been an elite school with very knowledgeable teachers (such as Dan Barbilian for Math, also known as Ion Barbu[21] for his poetry) and students like Mircea Eliade, Constantin Noica, Nicolae Steinhardt, Alexandru Paleologu, Barbu Brezianu, brothers Haig and Arşavir Acterian, brothers Alexandru and George Cioranescu, Alexandru Elian, most of whom were the sons of wealthy bourgeois[22]. My maternal uncle (born in 1915) also went here, as well as Ion Iliescu (born in 1930), a good student by all accounts, but with a selective kind of memory which made him state that under the bourgeois regime, the children of communist underground fighters were not allowed to attend schools or universities, himself being the living proof of this lie. And in 1953, my brother (born in 1939) was in the 8th grade. His classmates, the ones I remember - Mircea Axente[23], Florin Benea, Bugheanu, Gyuri Csendes, Georgel Dănulescu[24], Tomi Dinischiotu, Costică Dorobănţescu, Costache Erbiceanu, Ion Gerota, Mihai Grigorăşcuţă, Mirel Iliescu, Matei Mirică, Mircea Oşanu - were nothing like the students described by Gramatopol, who, admittedly, were a few years older, born before 1937. That is not to sat that they weren't rambunctious, even somewhat savage, but that is how things were back then. To this day, I still remember an unpleasant incident: around 1954-1955, I was in conflict with an older boy called Şafran, who was lanky, red-headed and had freckles on his face. I don't know what I said or did to him, and I can't remember what he'd said or did to me either, but I complained to my brother, who immediately set out to punish him. During recess, my brother's classmates came at Şafran, sat him on a drinking fountain in the school yard and started punching him, saying as one "If you believe in God, punch him!". I confess that after the initial moment of satisfaction, I was overcome by fear and I fled. It was the first and last anti-Semitic display I've ever witnessed, I was outraged and disgusted and I decided that from there on out, I would solve my conflicts with others by myself.

In a Class Roster from 1st grade (I was still in L.B. No. 9) I find the letters of the alphabet and little cane shapes[25], and on the second page, there is a poem called *The National Emblem* ("Stema Ţării"), written in an older spelling, despite the fact that the Spelling Reform dated back from September 13th, 1953. What is even more strange is that, although the Class

Roster is from the 1953-1954 school year, is the missing last stanza of the poem, written after September 24th, 1952, when he new constitution had added an extra star above the emblem. Here is this stanza that is stuck in my head: "And the star that's up above,/ What could she be thinking of?/ Socialism, she says loudly,/ Rises in my country proudly!"

On the third page, there is another interesting text: "Our classroom. Mircea has come back from school and says: "How big and beautiful is our classroom! And what beautiful pictures hang on the walls!" "Here is the great Stalin's portrait. And here is our beloved leader, Gheorghe Gheorghiu-Dej"."

I notice that "Our Ana" and "comrade Vasile Luca" had disappeared from our spelling books after their "fall" in 1952, and Stalin no longer had any other attributes except for "the great".

From my 2nd grade (I was now at L.B. No. 12), I kept a Math notebook full of problems and exercises with pioneer detachments, canteens and state groceries where you could by salami with 7 lei per kilogram, marmalade and canned food for 5 lei apiece, with brigades monitoring the agricultural co-ops, with students who watched 36 movies over the course of a single winter (?!), the Popular Council that sent 81 carts of wood to a school, knowing they used 9 carts per month etc. Unfortunately, I misplaced a written exam from my 3rd or 4th grade, on which Mrs. Linte had written in thick red pencil: "You get a 1 for stealing!" (Had this grade because I cheated?).

A special occasion was the end-of-year festivities. I don't know who the author of those extravaganzas we used to stage was (the first was *Little Red Riding Hood*), but in 2nd and 3rd grade I was invariably cast as the "Old Woman", in the company of Firu Dumitrescu (who played "Old Man"), or alone, in 3rd grade. The main character was Ghiocel himself, who went on a journey of self-discovery from the land of snow to the greed land of earthly paradise. We all knew each other's lines by heart and would mumble them during the show, akin to a Greek chorus. I was very unhappy with my part - I was swaddled in a large black shawl and wore my mother or my grandmother's traditional black skirt; you could barely see my face. But I remember my lines perfectly, they were words of encouragement for Ghiocel, who rested in my cabin: "As the spindle spins, behold,/ Grandma spins a tale of old,/ Of a tiny dwarf like you,/ Just as strong and just as true./ Gently putting you to sleep/ Comes a princess in your keep,/ And then a majestic bird/ Trills a song you've never heard."

In 3rd grade we were all made pioneers! It was an emotional moment of great pride for the happy people in the first group, and a matter of great teary-eyed sorrow for me, because I was not deemed fit to receive this honor (it was only at the end of the school year that the rest of us were allowed into this august fellowship). A photograph belonging to Ştefan Andreescu captured the moment when the first group - the conscientious students - proudly showed off their red scarves: there were 12 pioneers and 15 underdogs.

In 4th grade we began to study Russian with a series of teachers, the first being comrade Moşneanu, a worthy successor to the previous two whom Mihail Gramatopol described in his memoirs[26]. She was followed by another, mediocre and with no authority, and finally, by comrade Filofteia Stoian, petite and very fair, her hair pinned up in a bun, the wife of communist poet Nicolae Stoian, about whom she would talk with the first-row girls. This was the case for students in humanist classes, while those in science classes had one of the most despicable monsters as their teacher, called Grosu, who was an absolute terror. I don't know if my colleagues in science classes learned any Russian, but for those of us in humanist classes, it didn't really catch on, despite our eight years of studying this language that is quite beautiful in its own way, when it is spoken by aristocrats and intellectuals, but not in the way that it was taught to us. From this point of view, Mihai Gramatopol's conclusions apply to us as well.

In 4th grade, the school went co-ed and so we were reunited with many of the girls I had gone to kindergarten with, as well as new ones, who came later, between 1958-1959, when the second glaciation of the Romanian communist regime came about. For us, it meant that the higher-ups decided to "improve" the social makeup of the student body, therefore many boys and girls were forced to enroll at "Spiru Haret", coming from the suburbs of the I.V. Stalin district, namely Tei neighborhood and other such picturesque places. Most of them disappeared during the last few years of school for various reasons, but most likely because high schools had been built in these underprivileged areas or simply because people were moving to the apartment buildings on the outskirts of the city, where new neighborhoods had sprung up.

It can be said that the 1956 Hungarian revolution triggered not only the anxiety of the governing class[27], but also a fierce thirst for revenge on everyone who had dared to show their support, either overtly, in groups, or privately, for their Hungarian brothers, their social reforms, especially those in education[28]. But they were not the only ones. The strikes in Poland and the Hungarian revolution revealed the crisis of the Soviet Empire and that of Romanian society, the profound dissatisfaction of the working class which the communist party embodied in its discourse. In those years, the overall state of the economy was very poor, and the State Planning Committee, run by Miron Constantinescu, poisoned the Government with false data, as Gheorghiu-Dej admitted; thus, he was replaced by Alexandru Bârlădeanu (1955). A few years later, in a "strictly confidential" document "of utmost importance" sent out by the CSP, things are described as being very bleak. Between 1956-1960, Romania was basically the poorest communist country according to every economic indicator, a very long way from the more developed capitalist countries[29].

For that reason, after brutally putting down students, the regime began an extensive repression program, which made the 1958-1962 period feel like a second glaciation. At first - between 1956-1957 - they satisfied some of the more pressing needs of the peasantry and of the working class: suppressing mandatory taxes for most agricultural byproducts starting with January 1st, 1957, for the former, and a rise of minimal wages and child benefits, as well as a more versatile organization of labor in favor of the working class[30]. In doing so, the regime used the same methods as in 1945-1948, when it needed the support or at least the benevolent neutrality of those two social groups in view of the final battle against the bourgeois landlords.

The final turn came in 1957-1958 and was determined by two great international events. One of them was the first international conference (or counsel) of the communist and labor parties, in Moscow, in November 14th-16th, 1957, the first after the Comintern had been suppressed (in 1943) and the Cominform had been founded (1947, disbanded in 1956). The decisions made during this conference were kept secret, but an abstract - the rapport made by a delegate for the CC of the SED (German Socialist Party) - was published in the GDR.[31] In short, the conference set out to bring back the "class versus class" and "camp versus camp" strategy from 1947-1953, asserted the leading role of the USSR and the close cooperation based on brotherly help between countries within the communist block (this justified the soviets' intervention in Hungary), it condemned "dogmatism" (meaning Stalinism, a minor sin) and especially "revisionism", which meant trying to reform communism, the capital sin of Tito and Imre Nagy (who would be executed in June 1958), and it proposed "an ideological rearming of those communists who, during the 1956 crisis, had rather lost their way" (François Fejtö). In other words, "fighting against revisionism", thus "eliminating all attempts at reformation and liberalization, destroying any social and individual autonomy in relation to the state, annihilating independent thought[32], returning to Stalinist practices"[33]. The main victims of this fight were members of the former political parties, intellectuals, unruly peasants resisting the latest attack aiming to implement collective agriculture, and finally, the Orthodox Church. The ideal "new man" was captured in a famous joke from the USSR: "An appointment with a psychiatrist.

'Doctor, I have a split personality: I think one thing, I say another and I do something else entirely.' 'This proves you're absolutely normal!'"[34]

The second decisive event was the retreat of Soviet troops from Romania in June-July 1958, which had been in the works long before that time[35]. Related to this, there was a rumor that Molotov had personally told Gheorghiu-Dej in January 1954: "You have gotten used to living under the cozy wing of the Soviet army; if it weren't for the Soviet army, your people wouldn't last three days"[36]. Ana Pauker had said something along the same lines in the closed meeting with district party leaders from December 14th, 1944: "Dear comrades, put your hand on your chest and speak the truth. If, God forbid, the last red trooper left your district, be it Constanța, Galați or Iași, what would become of your party organization, what would happen to all prefects and policemen?" (Whom the communists had instated); and further: "We're lucky that the Red Army will remain here for a while longer"[37]. But now the Red Army was leaving and the Romanian communists decided to prove they had everything under control, even without the masters' help.

The preparations for the second wave of terror started as soon as the delegation for the communist party conference returned to Bucharest. In

December 1957, the Ministry of Internal Affairs compiled statistics of every-one in the country who was under surveillance: there were 323,207 "hate-ful individuals against whom we have compromising evidence", namely 84,621 former legionaries, 48,997 former PNȚ members, 32,346 former PNL members and so on. In March 1958, the Securitate once again reached the horrifying numbers from 1950-1953: 9,884 officers, 3,488 rehired ser-geants, 5,284 civilian employees, a total of 18,656 "workers". Aside from these, there were the Securitate troops with a total of 57,185 "fighters"[38].

At the same time, the number of informants had grown spectacularly: from 42,187 in 1951 to around 150,000 in 1958 and approximately 400,000 in 1965, making denouncement into "a state *virtue*"[39].

Once the secular arm was reorganized and strengthened, the regime went on to define the legal frame destined to legitimize the wave of terror: "The frame for this new repressive campaign is given by the Decree no. 89 from February 17th, 1958 and Decree no. 318 from July 21st, 1958, as well as the HCM no. 292/1958 and the amendment to the 209 article of the Penal Code (between 1958-1960)"[40].

The content of these laws and decrees is revealed to us by Stelian Tănase in his often-mentioned book: *"Decree no. 318/1958 greatly extends the num-ber of crimes punishable by death and it translates "the regime's concern regard-ing the people's political behavior and the possibility that they might show their displeasure more openly than before". The Budapest Effect transpires in article no. 9, where anyone who put together a group or collaborated with foreign pow-ers in order to declare Romania's neutrality was liable to receive the capital pun-ishment. Any offense brought to state symbols or to Romania's allies went in the same category. Economic crimes: sabotage, corruption, embezzlement, could also be punished by death. Decree no. 89 and HCM no. 282 adopted other punitive and restrictive measures. They related to forced labor and concentration in labor camps "for those individuals who, through their actions or attitudes, endanger or attempt to endanger the state order, if those do not constitute crimes". For what the Decision of the Counsel of Ministers (HCM) calls crimes, there was a frame between 1948-1950. There are two aspects of note here: the preventive nature of those laws, meant to intimidate, and the extension of the area beyond which public and private behavior could be sanctioned, even if it was not criminal, according to the Penal Code and to the Constitution. In fact, the line between guilt and innocence was being wiped away as society was suspected of treason and plot. (...) Those "hateful individuals" interpret economic failures and difficulties as acts of sabotage. The amendment to article no. 209 of the Penal Code in July 1959 stresses this fact. Undermining the national economy by means of state institutions and enterprises or sabotaging their usual activity for the benefit of former owners or interested capitalist organizations is punished by 5 to 25 years of forced labor and confiscation of property. In serious cases, the punishment was "death and confiscation of property". The same went for "destruction and defacement in order to undermine the national economy...", "the willing or negligent unfulfillment of certain obligations, in order to undermine the popular democratic regime, is counter-revolutionary sabotage and is punished by 5 to 25 years of forced labor and confiscation of property". (Buletinul Oficial, no. 27/July 21st, 1958). In 1960, further amendments are made to article no. 209 of the Penal Code, meant to annihilate any kind of civic or political activity. It was a crime to constitute or to participate in organizations that wish to "change the social order or the form of government". What this actually meant was that any group activity set up outside of official organizations could be punished, as long as any independent initiative triggered an accusation of "undermining the existing social order". The article set out to annihilate any public, civic or political activity, for fear of the old parties and organizations becoming active once more, as well as new ones surfacing to defy the communist regime and to threaten the power monopoly held by the political elite. The punishment was between 15 and 25 years of forced labor and civic degrading for 5 to 10 years, and in serious cases "the punishment is death". Constituting organizations was not the only thing being punished, but also "the act of spreading propaganda, panic or any action towards changing the existing social order or the form of government", "helping the above-mentioned organizations or associations in any way", as well as "acts of slander, libel or public defamation of the regime and any of its institutions and organizations made by one or more people". The attempt was punished the same as the fulfilled act".[41]*

Here is a commentary about article no. 209 made by an old acquaintance of communist prisons between 1948-1964: "Reading this article, you realize that it could very well include the entire Romanian population. (...)

After all, that's pretty much how things went, because for 15 years, according to communist numbers, over 99.01% of sentences were passed based on this article".[42]

The intensity of the new wave of terror can be measured by means of a few numbers form the Securitate archives: if between December 1955 and December 1957 a total of 6,211 people were accused of "acts against the state's Securitate", in December 1958 their number rose to 10,125, in January 1960 there were 17,613 people, and in May 1964 we had 8,875. More important are the statistics pertaining to those investigated under arrest: 47,643 in 1958, 37,893 in 1959, 21,176 in 1960, so over 100,000 arrests in just three years!

When he got to Jilava Prison in March 1962, Cicerone Ionițoiu was sent to room/cell 34, where he met with some of those sentenced in Constantin Noica's group, then he was moved to room 8 in the Reduit Wing, together with other 120 people who were waiting for their trial. "There," he wrote, "I learned news about the people who had been in Jilava and about those arrested all over the country. We realized that most of those who had been set free after 1954 were once again imprisoned for relapse. Another category was that of former prisoners who had been amnestied in the USSR and who were now once again placed under arrest after the Hungarian Revolution. (...) A third large category was that of peasants who had been against collectivization and many of them had received administrative sentences between 12 and 60 months and had been sent to extermination labor in the Danube marshes"[43].

Contemporaries and victims, historians and political analysts have tried to explain the meaning of this new glaciation, which followed after a few years of relaxation, of "recreation" (Cicerone Ionițoiu). The general consensus is that Gheorghiu-Dej and the party leaders were afraid of two threats: that those in command would be replaced by the Kremlin, as it had been the case in other communist countries between 1956 -1957, or that they would be overthrown through a revolution like the one in Hungary[44].

For Nicolae Steinhardt, sentenced in Constantin Noica's group, it was a mater of demented logic:

How does demented logic work perfectly? The premises: the bourgeois must die. Whoever is not with us, is against us. The conclusion: hack them off! Perhaps the 1947-1950 arrests were also a matter of political terror. Those between 1958-1959 are purely demented. The regime is consolidated, any political justification is gone. Now the wheels keep on rolling. The broom of the sorcerer's apprentice is twiddling its thumbs. The purpose is forgotten. *Swallow, chew.* The spiritualists, the bridge players, the choir singers are under arrest. There were many groups such as the bridge players' group, the spiritualists' group, the Patriarchy's group, the radio listeners' group, the commentators' group, the stamp collectors' group (they exchanged stamps, one had marshal Antonescu's face on it)[45].

Much colder and incisive is Barbu Cioculescu's opinion, the son of the literary critic who had been a leftist and even a communist supporter in the 1930s: asked "How do you feel about the regime's reiterated attack against the bourgeoisie, the intellectuals, the former elite?", he replied as follows: *"We had gotten used to the idea of prison. It was like a fatality, it could hit anyone at any time, not necessarily you or your family. It was like a plague: it touches you and you either get sick or you don't. But that moment after 1958 set us back terribly. It was very bad, because that was a time of great promise, not of freedom as such, but of an expansion of it, of relaxation. This relaxation or "liberalization" could be felt in all sectors. The years between 1958 to 1963-1964 are a significant chunk of someone's life. We were, at best, like plants kept in the dark. These trials took place when the brains of the Romanian society had already been laid bare. It was a way of gathering round the last people standing, of picking a fight with those who would have died peacefully at home in a short while.*

It was cruel. Communists have always been cruel. To arrest general Văitoianu who was 90 years old and senile, who said upon his arrest: "I will personally complain to his Majesty King Ferdinand"... To arrest Nicolae Batzaria, who was 88, because he'd been a municipal counselor once, meant there were no distinctions being made. It was a political move. It was part of their memory-wiping strategy. Had they lived, free, for a few more years, they would have merged with the young generation. Their greatest fear was that this merger should take place. It was like a second ploughing, after the one from 1948-1949. Meanwhile, they had destroyed the army, the political elite, the administration. All that was left was this area of interest, where they had only tried and sentenced the right-wing extremists who had previously been involved in politics. Gyr, Crainic, Vulcănescu etc., the stars of the first trials, who had received heavy sentences. Now they basically finished what they'd started, rounding up whoever was left. Note that the Securitate was an enterprise in need of working material. It had to have its own conspiracies".[46]

Finally, the trial of a convict from the ranks of the liberal politicians: "The phantom-Governments thought up in Cişmigiu Park or anywhere else during the euphoric relief period around the Geneva Conference [1955] were a pretext for the subsequent closed trials and the pre-established ritual to unfold: lawyers who acknowledged their clients' guilt, pleading at best for mitigating circumstances, witnesses who either weren't admitted in court or who didn't show up, standard interrogations that were irrelevant. These nuclei connected to a series of other people who may or may not have been involved directly. At the same time, there were other groups of convicts who had analyzed books published abroad or kept under wraps, accused of 'hate speech'".[47]

We learn about these trials from the memoirs of surviving victims or family members who were able to witness them, thanks to whom we are able to piece together detailed accounts of them, such as the trial of Constantin Noica's group (where Ioana Casassovici-Crețoiu's parents were investigated, while her grandparents and other relatives were arrested), or that of the Burning Pyre (Marius Oprea)[48].

Apart from the countless trials against the old party leaders and other "groups" put together for this occasion (apart from those mentioned by Nicu Steinhardt and Cicerone Ionițoiu, the ex-landowners, ex-kulaks, Zionists, embezzlers, saboteurs, extortioners, those who had gold or visas), another form of terror needs to be acknowledged. It is something specific to Romanian communism that sparked the admiration and even the envy of the soviet ambassador in Bucharest: "the unmasking", that is, the public trials of students and intellectuals organized by courts *sui generis* in front of the victims' colleagues, friends and admirers, assembled *en masse* and forced to witness that frightening and despicable show until the end. As in the case of the "reeducation" programs in Piteşti, Gherla, Canal etc., between 1949-1952, through these "unmaskings" Romanian communism brought a unique contribution to the horrors and crimes against humanity and dignity that define totalitarian regimes throughout history.

The great ringmaster of these new "blood-filled arenas" was, according to the general consensus, Leonte Răutu (1910-1993, nicknamed Leonte Malvolio by Petru Dumitru), the one who was ultimately in charge of culture and propaganda in the CC of the PMR[49]. A member of the Romanian delegation to the 40th anniversary of the October Revolution and to the communist parties counsel in Moscow in November 1957, he was injured in an accident on Vnukovo airport where Grigore Preoteasa died, while the other nine members of the Romanian communist delegation were only injured[50]. Back home after a few months spent recuperating, during which time he closely studied the counsel's decisions to intensify the fight against revisionism, that is, in communist jargon, against Western culture, Răutu organized a series of counsels between 1958 and 1958 "to debate some aspects of the fight against bourgeois influences in ideology"[51]. Armed with an ideological arsenal and with other "precious tips", Răutu's lackeys - Florian Dănălache, Gheorghe Pană, Tamara Dobrin and the party's rising star, Ion Iliescu (newly returned from his studies in the USSR, member of the CC of the UTM and President of the Romanian Student Association Union, a true *princeps juventutis*) and other *ejusdem farinae* zealously organized "unmasking" meetings with students (from the Spring of 1958 until the end of the 1958-1959 academic year)[52] and with intellectuals, workers and clerks, in Bucharest and throughout the country: 31 meetings on September 4th, 1959, 44 on the 5th and the 6th, 89 on the 7th and 8th, 36 on the 9th and 10th, and finally 15 between September 11th-13th.[53]

"They unmasked intellectuals, scientists, composers, painters, book editors," wrote Dorin-Liviu Bîtfoi. *"Those were seen as unworthy, their crimes cataloged as being more or less severe: composers Mihail Andricu, Leon Klepper and Sergiu Natra, conductor Sergiu Comissiona and the excellent pianist Mândru*

Katz; directors Sorana Coroamă and Malvina Ursianu, actress and director Marietta Sadova, entertainer Dan Demetrescu, opera singer Dora Massini, sculptor Milița Petrașcu, literary critic Cornel Regman, doctor Marius Nasta - and many others were added to the list. They were tried publicly, in large theaters and open spaces, at the Opera, at the Faculty of Law... But also in the Union Central Committee headquarters on Lipscani Street and in the Romanian Athenaeum, where an old man is brought to the stage, accompanied by a Securitate agent, and is forced to incriminate himself for his proposal to develop cultural relations with France and for lack of patriotism. He is composer Mihail Andricu, vice-president of the Composers' Union."[54]

In a rapport from April 29th, 1959 to Gheorghiu-Dej about the soviet ambassador's visit in Bucharest which also mentions these unmaskings, Leonte Răutu made the following comment: "Comrade Epishev... has expressed the opinion that our party has taken valuable action in this matter, which neither the Soviet Union, nor other countries have previously attempted and which is sure to yield wonderful results"[55].

A particularly hard blow was dealt to the Zionist movement in general and to the Jews who were set to move to Israel in 1958, when the emigration ban from 1952 was lifted. On July 28th, 1959, a National Bank van carrying 3 million LEI was robbed on Șoseaua Giulești by a group of five men and one woman, wearing masks and carrying guns, who disappeared in a taxi. A special investigation by the Securitate followed, and after a short while the perpetrators were identified, arrested, tried and sentenced to death, except for the woman who was pregnant and received a life sentence. The Securitate also made a (bad) movie re-enacting the attack and the investigation, which was screened in party organizations and other distinguished powerful circles. On this occasion, people found out that gangsters were all party members occupying high positions (two engineers, one lieutenant-colonel of the Militia and chief of the Judicial Militia Department, two reporters, one Assistant Professor), that they were Jews who had changed their names to sound Romanian - Ioanid, Mușat, Obedeanu, Sevianu - and that the purpose of the robbery was to help the Jews who had filed for emigration but lost their jobs waiting for a passport that wouldn't come[56]. The move was transparent and was quickly deciphered: they wished to focus public contempt against Zionists who were nothing more than lowly bandits, some gangsters operating the same way as those in Chicago. The daughter or granddaughter of Igor and Monica Sevianu (or Săveanu) made a movie about this in 2004, and another one premiered recently in Romania. The strange thing is that Edgar Reichman's testimony from his novel, *Denunțătorul* ("The Denouncer"), which was published in Paris in 1962 and was recently translated into Romanian, wasn't really taken into account. According to this former PCR activist, the Securitate set up the robbery with the help of a former NKVD and Romanian Secret Services agent called Sașa Mușat, Assistant Professor and Secretary of the party at the Faculty of History in Bucharest, where he had made himself known by organizing an unmasking trial against some brilliant students, including Răzvan Theodorescu and Alexandru Bogdan, who were expelled for two years and sentenced to forced labor[53]. Born Abraham (Abrașa) Glanzstein[57], he went to prison during Antonescu's regime for espionage in favor of the USSR. Released after August 23rd, 1944, he was a member of the UTC, and together with Barbu Câmpina, was one of the hooligans who broke the windows of the Romanian Athenaeum in 1946 during the celebration of the May 15th, 1948 gathering of Transylvanian Romanians at Blaj[58]. At the same time, he was officially a member of the Socialist Students Union where he acted as a crypto-communist agent[59]. On June 9th, 1946 he was elected, as a social democrat, to be the general secretary of the Student Communist Movement that would later become the National Romanian Students Union, a spawn of the National Congress of Democrat Students[60]. The following year, he was a delegate to the International Youth and Student Festival in Prague, together with G. Brătescu, Paul Cornea and Ion Solomon[61]. After this date he is out of the picture, and doctor Brătescu (Ana Pauker's son-in-law) finds him again in 1956, when his good friend tells him he hadn't gone to the West, as rumor had it, but "had worked as an informant for our party within the social-democrat circles in France. In danger of being exposed, he rushed home"[62]. Sașa Mușat was telling the truth, because during his stay in France, he met with Virgil Ierunca several times. The two met on August 30th, 1948 in a coffee shop and Sașa Mușat, "an interesting Trotskyst", told him he had recently arrived from Romania[63]. They meet infrequently over the following years, the last time being on August 31ˢᵗ, 1951, and then he disappeared[64].

In 1956, the man had grown and had new responsibilities: *"[Returned to Bucharest] he was appointed as Assistant Professor at the Faculty of History, receiving responsibilities regarding party education. However, he was very discontent with his situation, because his department colleagues, lead by Professor Oțetea, demanded he show proof of working on a PhD thesis in Paris, as he'd stated[65]. I often saw Sașa at the Academy Library, where he read about contemporary history. Although I found myself in the awkward position of being excluded from the party, he trusted me completely, sharing his inner turmoils and his reckless projects with me. Among other things, he told me that, unable to cope with the distrustful and threatening atmosphere maintained by his increasingly aggressive enemies, he had decided to leave the country. He'd thought to file for emigration under his real name - Glanzstein, but he was afraid that if they figured out he was actually Sașa Mușat, he would receive a negative response. Another time he told me he saw no other way out but to leave clandestinely. As his good friend, engineer Gugu Sevianu (whom I also knew from when we were UTC students), had once learned how to fly a plane, the two had planned to bribe a pilot to let them take off without authorization".*[66] It can be easily seen that "his good friend" was testing the waters with Gheorghe Brătescu, excluded from the party on account of being Ana Pauker's son-in-law, with a Jewish wife, so likely to flee the country, in order to bring him on board with the plot he was devising[67].

Florin Constantiniu was a student at the Faculty of History at that time (1951-1956) and he remembers Sașa Mușat as being "a very intelligent adventurer, sure of himself regarding his upswing and success". Here are some details:

At the Faculty of History he'd become party organizer (the equivalent of a party secretary), and making use of his abilities and authority, he did everything over the Dean's head, Mrs. Florența Rusu, a female sergeant by the looks of her, but lacking the pugnacity of the heroine in Vsevolod Ivanov's play. Andrei Oțetea, who was neither impressed, nor afraid of Sașa Mușat's achievements, blocked her career as a professor. He asked to see documents to attest that the candidate up for promotion had completed his studies in the chosen field, but in this case the cunning Saşa found no way to prove he had graduated from University. As a listener, I can tell you that his lessons were by far superior to those taught by his more esteemed colleagues.[68]

In light of all that is known about this man, Edgar Reichman's theory appears to be more plausible, so Saşa Muşat may have organized and instigated the operation and his mission may have been given by the KGB, most likely without the Securitate knowing about it[69]. Indeed, we know that after around 20,000 Jews had received passports between September 1958 and February 1959, emigration was blocked with no explanation, leaving 14,000 people without Romanian citizenship, jobs or homes, members of the same family were separated etc. The decision was explained as being triggered by protests in the Arab countries, as well as the urging of the USSR, who had a large interest in the Near East and was against Jews immigrating to Israel. Soon after, Zionists were being arrested, accused of treason and espionage, while three Israeli diplomats were banished. Among those arrested was a group of economists and high officials within the Ministry of Foreign Commerce, accused of corruption and of having accounts in Swiss banks. Among them was Mr. Andrei Csendes, the father of our classmate Ivan, who was crushed by the investigation and died a short while after being released, and perhaps other family members of "Spiru Haret" students: the Securitate was preparing to take over foreign commerce, a plan that was implemented and developed during Ceauşescu's reign as well. In 1960, those arrested were released and emigration went on discreetly via Austria, the Jews receiving passports to other countries, except for Israel, which they could reach via Vienna. Until 1965, 35,000 people emigrated this way, among whom were many of our colleagues from primary school. Emigration was sped up by a 1959 decree, which suppressed private medical practices, a measure that affected many doctors in our neighborhood, some of whom were our colleagues' parents or grandparents, such as gynecologist Alex. Th. Seimeanu[70], doctor Tache Tanaşoca, our classmate Sandu's father, other general practitioners who had looked after our parents and even grandparents, like dentist Gerson on Dionisie Lupu Street, an excellent doctor who had one of the most modern dental practices, or pediatrician Alexandru Gerenday, our classmate Petre Clar's grandfather.

The repression couldn't spare the school, of course. On September 18th, 1958, in a progress report meeting with district chiefs of the Securitate, the Minister for Internal Affairs, Alexandru Drăghici, said to those present:

> ...we cannot stand idly by, as long as these organizations of hateful individuals exist throughout our country and they are not properly monitored... We must even get to work in schools, because even in schools there are hateful comments being made... It is impossible that an agent has nothing to report to Securitate agencies on their meeting.[71]

These orders were not without consequences and I believe some of the new things implemented in our school during that time are due to this. Firstly, it was decided that the social and professional makeup of students had to be "amended" and so we suddenly got many new students in 6th grade (1958-1959) who lived in distant neighborhoods within the V.I. Stalin District. Most of them were the children of workers, even farmers from the villages around the city, forced to cross long distances in order to make it to school at 7 am when class started[72]. Many, especially the girls, opted to go to a humanist class in high school, because they weren't good at Math and their families didn't support them enough to overcome this subject's difficulties. When we finished high school, in class 11C there were only a handful of boys, and the rest were girls.

I mentioned before how young people and students were arrested and sentenced for manifesting sympathy for and solidarity with the Hungarian Revolution, asking for reforms in our country as well. The rulers' reaction extended to all categories of non-conformist young people, following the soviet example, of course, where the campaign against "parasites" started in 1957 and rapidly extended to many social and professional categories: extortioners, alcoholics, hooligans who disrupted public order, members of the liberal professions, painters, poets, artists[73]. Meaning those who didn't have a job, arrested and taken to labor camps, especially to harvest reed (by virtue of the no. 89 Decree and of the HCM no. 282), but, what was worse, the Jews who were waiting for their passport for Israel (condemned for "Zionist activities" and "conspiring against social order"), then young jazz and rock&roll fans who wore floral shirts, tight pants or blue jeans, girls who wore miniskirts and bikinis etc. That is was a soviet initiative adopted by all communist countries can be proven by the fact that they all took action to persecute those above simultaneously, the Militia and young Komsomols cutting up girls' skirts and ripping the spikes from blue jeans: thus, in Poland, they were called *bikiniarze*, in Hungary *jampecek* (deadbeat), in the GDR (but also in West Germany) *Halbstarke*, in Czechoslovakia *potapka*, and in Romanian *malagambiști* and parasites, like in the USSR[74].

Another consequence of state and party orders was the obsession for discipline, which seemed to be lacking in "Spiru Haret" in those years. I clearly remember the novelty of the organizing a meeting with all students in the schoolyard, in 1959 (I was in 6th grade). We all ignored the cause for that serious meeting, as we had been forced to participate under threat of grave consequences. Once we all gathered round, some of us, about 10 or 12, chosen from all grades, were called out by the headmistress and asked to form a line in the middle of the yard. I was the smallest, in shorts and proudly wearing my red scarf over a crisp white shirt. The biggest and the oldest of us was Ion (Ionuț) Rizescu from the upper grades, and I cannot remember the others, although I think there were a couple of girls there as well. We were all sternly told off for our indiscipline and threatened with severe punishment if we failed to improve our behavior. Luckily, none of the bystanders offered to "unmask" us or demand our expulsion, and so the ceremony ended fairly quickly. It was clear that it had been an order from higher-up, meant to terrorize those disruptive individuals such as myself: had it not been recommended that I go to a reform school, a real prison for minors in 5th grade by a classmate's father who wouldn't tolerate his daughter being in the same class as someone like me? Now I was already an old offender, the youngest in the school. That it was a matter of circumstance can be seen from comparing it to an incident that happened a few years later, in 1962, at the end of 9th grade when we got to choose which of the two types of classes we wanted to go to next, humanist or science. On the last day of school, some of us decided to skip school, the weather was beautiful, sunny and warm, so we went to the cinema and then to Ioanid Garden, far from the eyes of our headmistress and teachers. We were surprised to learn that on that day, the students who'd gone to school had made absolute chaos of the place, climbing onto desks and yelling, singing and dancing, tearing textbooks apart, it was an "orgy", as the headmistress, comrade Teodorescu, called it at first. This was followed by a thorough investigation and, as per usual, identifying the suspicious individuals ("the ringleader"), and I was one of them. However, the headmistress was sorely disappointed to learn that some of the possible candidates for this title and I (the usual suspects, that is) were missing that day, and the class was exclusively made up of the "good kids", the top of the class and the nerds who had fought all year for the highest average and wouldn't have skipped school in a million years, even if it was the last day, as well as some students with a "healthy" social background. As such, the investigation was promptly dropped and the perpetrators only got a mild scolding.

I remember other stories from that time: the first was when our History teacher, Constantin Necșulescu ("The Beast") was sacked, got a disciplinary transfer to a school in Floreasca, from where he returned a few years later even more reactionary and upset by the injustice suffered by him, a teacher with a degree from Heidelberg University. The second one was more of a lesson: I don't know how many of our classmates remember that around the same time, two vaudeville peasants sold sunflower seeds and walnuts by the jar by the high school gate. One of them was blond, with a cunning, smiling air, looking every which way, and what was more, he had a couple of gold teeth, which was quite strange; the other was taller and broader, a brunet wearing a huge hat, less exuberant, who disappeared after a while, whereas his friend was "in business" for two or three years. A few years later, my barber, Mr. Gheorghe Alexe (Mr. Gică), a true artist who worked at the barber shop on the corner of no. 17, Batiștei Street and Dionisie Lupu Street, told me that the blond peasant was a Securitate officer! One night, Mr. Gică said, as he was coming back from work down Italiană street, passing by the high school, he saw the peasant in townsman's clothes, holding a camera and hiding in a bush, trying to photograph two people sitting on a bench. Mr. Gică politely said hello, but the fake peasant told him something along the lines of "Quiet, I'm photographing these spies!" It's clear that him selling sunflower seeds by the high school gate meant he was listening in on our conversations in hopes of exposing a spy or a saboteur.

Finally, around the same time there was another meeting in the school yard, this time it was about a single "disciplinary case": our classmate Constantin Ştefănescu (aka "The Gipsy") who was paraded around in handcuffs and taken by a militiaman. We were told he'd attacked a taxi driver (the new Getax had appeared in May-June 1955) in order to rob him. After this, he went away from school and didn't return after serving out his sentence.

In 1960 we finished the first seven mandatory grades and there was the question - purely theoretical for most - if we should go on to high school or go to a trade school, like some of our classmates did, like Ion Vârjan, the only one I remember. Before the end of the school year, we were visited by a group of comrades from the district education board or something like that, who oversaw a homeroom class we had with comrade Nicolau, our Geography and homeroom teacher. I don't remember how the meeting went - because it was indeed a meeting - as those comrades told us about the importance of training engineers and foremen for the good of our economy and asked us what we wanted to do, should we fair the entrance examination for the 8th grade. Our homeroom teacher had told us what this was about in advance, and had suggested we say that we wanted to go to a trade school. When it was my turn to answer this question in public - or was I the only one being interrogated? - a red veil fell over my eyes and I answered in a shaky voice that if I should fail the exam, I would kill myself! I can still picture the stricken faces of the committee, of my teacher and of a gentle and beautiful classmate, Mona Toma, who still remembers this incident. The result of my bravado was that I failed the exam for getting very low marks in Math, despite having a very good average, and my mother was desperate, accusing my father of not caring about his children because he took no part in the chorus of lamentations on this subject. On top of this, professor Necșulescu came over and revealed that the lists with our results had gone to the district education board (or whatever it was called) three times before I was crossed out from the list of those who had passed the exam. I don't know if I was the only one who received this special treatment, but I found out that headmistress Teodorescu was known for playing favorites and other underhanded scheming. But what is certain is that there was a general directive that limited the access to high school for children with an "unhealthy" social background: it happened to Adrian Rozei from "Spiru Haret" and Ioana Casassovici from "Școala Centrală" (called "Zoia Kosmodemianskaia" back then) as well, and Dorina Potârcă (who used to live on Maria Rosetti Street before being thrown out) has a similar story about her son[75]. It is also known that the Ministry of Public Education limited access to middle schools and closed access to universities for "the children of slave-driving individuals"; they could only go to elementary schools, so grades 1 through 4. On July 28th, 1952, the Political Bureau of the CC PMR sent out an internal directive with the necessary measures to improve class makeup for pupils and students. On this occasion, Gheorghiu-Dej remarked that "hateful individuals have managed to infiltrate our schools and we are preparing them for becoming a part of our institutions". Thus, the criteria for admittance in middle schools and universities were defined as being the students' ability to learn and their social background, and students were sorted into three categories: 1) the children of industrial workers[76], agricultural workers, collective farmers, peasants with small and medium farms, soldiers, engineers, officials and retired people, co-op craftsmen; 2) the children of small-time non-co-op craftsmen, those with liberal professions and small-time merchants; 3) the children of kulaks, businessmen, industrialists and other exploiters[77]. As a consequence of the same directive, starting with the 1952-1953 school year, "the children of all war criminals, traitors, spies, political convicts, saboteurs, those who have fled abroad, the children of former ministers or other members of the bourgeois-landlord ruling class" were excluded from any form of education. The children of these social outcasts were only allowed to attend elementary schools (grades 1 through 4), which were mandatory and free[78]. This is how Tudor Cudalbu, Dini Cernat and others got to be in school. But as mandatory education had been extended to seven years in the meantime, when we sat for the high school entrance examination, the directive was still in effect, despite being eight years old, hence our failure in the Summer session. Our luck was that there was another session in September, when we all passed without any trouble[79].

One last measure to strengthen discipline and politicize our school was the appearance, during our last years (1961-1962) of a deputy, comrade Doina Tirea, the kind of female sergeant with a black leather coat who was our homeroom teacher and who only taught Chemistry to us, the class 11C. Her appearance coincided with a more accentuated vigilance about students' "decadent" manifestations, especially "tea parties", with all that implied - American dances -, but also about going to church for the Easter Vigil, when schools organized festivities meant to keep students away from churches. The stupidity of these measures was the fact that festivities ended at midnight, which allowed the interested parties to go straight to church where the Easter Vigil sermon was just getting started.

I remember a lesson told to us by comrade Tirea during a homeroom class in 1963-1964. Here's how this modern fable went: a comrade who holds an important position went to England on a mission. One day, he left to do some shopping, went into a store and asked for the best pair of shoes. The salesman brought the goods, the client bought them, and taking a closer look, he noticed they were made in... Romania. The moral of this story was that our country made top-quality goods, appreciated in the West, but which you couldn't find in our stores because they were made for export in order to pay for industrialization. When it is completed, you will be able to buy good shoes here. Not only goods that were "rejected for export". This story, made up by some bureaucrat from Planning or by the Securitate, to be used by party activists who spun the yarn for us, the underprivileged, was meant to explain away why state shops usually sold ugly, mediocre goods, especially "dead man's shoes" footwear, of an exceptionally poor quality. This was how the regime and the people communicated during that time: another push and we shall reach socialism, communism' bright future.

But 1962, when the last political trials took place (that of Cicerone Ionițoiu and other seven related convicts was held on February 26th), is the turning point when Gheorghiu-Dej and the party leaders noted that the agricultural collectivization had been successful, proclaiming this officially on April 25th, that all those who opposed them within the party had been eliminated, and they concluded that intellectuals and former politicians had learned the hard "lesson" taught to them starting with 1958[80]. The conflict with the COMECOM (same as CAER) and especially that with Khrushchev, the GDR and Czechoslovakia, despite only becoming notorious in 1963, could be felt even in the years prior to that, when Romania, where the forced industrialization program was in full swing, turned to capitalist countries for help in order to obtain the necessary factories, plants and technology to overcome underdevelopment. This went against Khrushchev's new doctrine of "socialist division of labor", according to which Romania and Bulgaria should specialize in agriculture and exporting raw materials, while industrialized countries - namely the GDR and Czechoslovakia - should buy them cheap in exchange for machines and technology[81]. It was clearly a callback to Hitler's Reich, when the entire South-Eastern Europe (including Hungary, Yugoslavia, Turkey and Greece) served as a base for agricultural and mineral raw materials and as a market for German industry[82]. The political, technical and scientific elites of Romania saw their positions, which they'd earned by making great sacrifices in the 1950s[83], as being under threat. But this was only one side of the economic diptych, the other being that pre-war facilities and factories were becoming obsolete, despite being the height of technology in their heyday, and needed to be replaced with new, Western ones, because communist countries were far from offering equivalent products.

The loans for these purchases were obtained, on the one hand, by selling the gold and jewelry confiscated from "the bourgeois landlords" (see above), by "selling out" Saxons, Swabians and Jews who emigrated in large numbers to West Germany, Israel and other countries, but also any Romanian citizen who paid, through relatives abroad, to be released from slavery in exchange for tens of thousands of dollars (this had been a practice between 1948-1950 as well), and finally, because the above-mentioned states vouched for those loans on the international market[84]. We notice that Romania normalized its relations with Western countries through agreements and treaties, visits made by economic delegations (of the Government, of course), and, on the side, through economic espionage, balancing out the compensation demanded by French, Belgian, Dutch, German, Italian and American companies that were confiscated after 1944 and nationalized in 1948[85]. Politically, braking away from Moscow as the soviet-Chinese conflict worsened and Khrushchev's fantasies grew more ludicrous (especially the Cuban Missile Crisis in 1962) lead to a tentative rapprochement with the USA, discreetly manifested by the Romanian Minister for Foreign Affairs, Corneliu Mănescu, during a talk with Secretary of State Dean Rusk, to whom he related Romania's intent to remain neutral in the case of a new international crisis like the one in Cuba[86].

Internally, in order to stop being dependent on Moscow's "overlord elite", communist leaders needed the support of Romanian society, the social peace that everyone aspired to after 1948.[87] The first measure was to recruit new party members, 600,000 between 1962 and 1965, a growth comparable to that at the end of the 1940s: in December 1965, PMR, now called PCR, had 1,518,000 members, 7,6% of the total population. From 551,000 in 1952, its numbers had almost tripled and some of those were great intellectuals such as Tudor Vianu and George Călinescu[88].

The second measure was to empty prisons and labor camps continuously, starting in February 1960: "From 1960 onward, however, the 17,613 prisoners who appear in the January logs of that year start are beginning to be set free. The following are pardoned from executing the rest of their sentence: 820 convicts, peasants arrested for resisting collectivization, on February 24th, 1960; 87 convicts on March 14th; 58 people convicted of "Zionist activities", on September 5th, and 31 others on September 16th; 199 people convicted of "counter-revolutionary acts" on November 9th, 1960; 65 people convicted of "conspiring against social order" (most of them Jewish) on December 14th, 1961; 773 people on April 21st, 1962; 1,462 people convicted of "conspiring against social order" and for common law offenses on September 27th, 1962; 2,543 convicts on January 3rd, 1963; 2,920 convicts for "conspiring against social order", treason and other crimes on April 9th, 1964; 84 convicts for economic crimes on April 17th; 3,244 convicts, out of whom 3,205 for crimes against the "state Securitate", on April 24th; 3,467 convicts, out of whom 2,500 for crimes "against the state Securitate", the others being common law offenders, on June 16th, 1964."[89] For "political ones", the Securitate had already begun the soft version of their "reeduca-tion" program since 1962, but the last prisoners, the most unruly ones, were only released at the end of July 1964[90].

A spectacular effect of the "thawing" was the de-russification and de-sovietization of Romanian society, which started with the disappearance of Stalin's statue in Bucharest, the changing of street names and even that of our district, I.V. Stalin, renamed December 30th, the disappearance of the Russian Book Publishing house, the Romanian-Russian Museum, the "Maxim Gorki" Russian Institute in Pitar Moș Street, the turning of Russian into an optional course in schools starting with 1963-1964, the Western radio stations (Radio Free Europe, BBC etc.) were no longer jammed. In 1964, an explosive book was published, *Karl Marks. On the Romanian People*, edited by historian Andrei Oțetea and Professor Stanislas Schwann based on the unpublished manuscripts in the Social History Institute in Amsterdam. The book was censored for three years (from 1961 it was already circulating among the party's higher-ups) and it was only pub-lished in October 1964, six months after the famous *April Declaration*, in which the PMR placed itself squarely between the PCUS and the Chinese Communist Party. I said explosive because Marx's comments and notes about some books from his time were extremely hostile towards Russia and its imperialist politics regarding Romania, a direction followed by commu-nists as well. The raping of Bessarabia was shown in total contrast with "the communist Vulgate" as textbooks showed Roller's History treatise to be[91]. My friend Mihai Oroveanu (back then he went to the "elite" high school "Petru Groza") told me that that year, he went to History class holding the textbook in one hand and Marx's book in the other, reading the conflicting passages out loud. Exasperated, the teacher asked him: "Whose side are you on, the Turks'?!" No comment.

The last two years of high school were the greatest of our school life. Each of us had chosen the preferred type of class - science or humanist -, many of us loved doing sports, most of us did gymnastics with Anton Ionescu ("Mr. Cane"), others did basketball, a subject our teacher hated but was forced to encourage because our older colleagues who were ahead of us by two or three years had won the Bucharest championship or had made it to the final. Some, very few, went to the "Gheorghe Lazăr" literary society meetings, supervised by Simion Vărzaru, a Romanian teacher, who put me in for president in 11th grade. I was following in Petru Popescu's footsteps, who was a little older than us and was already inclined to becoming a writer, having connections in the literary world[92], and had invited Radu Tudoran to one of our sessions where he fascinated and enchanted us all. In the year when I was president, I had the pleasure of launching a young poet who read some of his works, confirming the truth of Corneille's verse, *la valeur n'attend point le nombre des années*: he was the nephew of a distinguished French teacher, Mr. Vladimir Niculescu (truly a gentleman!), and his name was Andrei Pleşu...

The Baccalaureate went quickly by, without any great dramas or obstacles, despite having some very strict examiners in Physics and Chemistry, at least in our panel for humanist classes. I personally got a 9 in Physics and a 6 in Romanian, to Vărzaru's dismay, who had sent me to a national (or local) competition where I had to discuss the Romanian contemporary novel: a subject I knew close to nothing about, because I refused to read that realist-socialist trash[93] and I only discusses those writers I knew something about, such as Sadoveanu, George Călinescu, Titus Popovici, and... that was about it, because Petru Dumitriu had chosen freedom and his name was taboo.

A poor mark, but in Physics, was obtained by our classmate Mihaela Andrei, a shy, very nice girl who was my neighbor[94]. She was top of the class in 11C, together with other very smart and cultured girls, Ioana Borş, Georgiana Gălăţeanu and Daniela Pamfil. After the Baccalaureate, in the summer of 1964, I heard that she had killed herself without leaving a note, with no explanation (or none that we knew of) for her desperate act. A few days after this tragedy, Costin Chioralia, the colleague she was supposed to marry, hanged himself. They were buried separately, but after a while Costin's parents agreed to bring the two lovers together in the same grave. This tragedy remained unexplainable: Mihaela's parents invited us, me and some other classmates, to a meal (a funeral feast) in the memory of their daughter, but we didn't find out anything more concrete. It was only a few years later that a university colleague told me that Mihaela had been the victim of a collective rape in an unknown house where she had gone to a tea party with one of our colleagues. Costin was busy preparing for a trip to Austria, he was a guide for the ONT, and he couldn't go. When he got home, Mihaela called him on the phone, but he couldn't meet her then either, and so, in the depths of her despair, she chose death. With this "Romeo and Juliet"-like tragedy, we said goodbye to school and to our classmates. We each looked to the future, to our professional future: at 18, suffering is easily forgotten and life reclaims its rights. We each went our separate ways, bearing the memory of those great years, filled with happiness and sorrow, which shall never return.

April 2015

---

1. in a manner similar to French pronounciation, because of rhotacism; in Romanian, the "R" sound is a dental trill.
2. In my *Presentation*, I mentioned other "pedagogical" methods used by Mrs. Linte. Every time I tell my French friends about them, I see them grow indignant and they probably think we were a country of savages. All this did not deter my former teacher from requesting my father's assistance in priestly matters; she even came into our house and made herself at home while he was out. I remember her as resembling Mrs. Geltruda, the headmistress of the "Pierpaoli" reformatory school in Montaguzzo where Ionică Furtună (Gian Burrasca), the hero of Italian writer Luigi Bertelli (penname Vamba) was sent: "She is very short and very fat, with a red nose; she always declaims and gives half-baked speeches about petty things, she's always restless, running around, talking to everyone and finding fault with everything" (*Jurnalul năzbâtiilor lui Ionică Furtună. Tradus din limba italiană de Susana G. Boteanu. Desenele sunt făcute de Afane I. Teodoreanu*, 2nd edition, Cartea Românească, Bucharest, 1942, p. 214 and the portrait on p. 215: Mrs. Linte had two large warts on her face). The Italian original was published in 1920.
3. I have a copy of a photograph from 3rd grade of comrade Renția's students, given to me by Sergiu Solomon, in which I only recognize those I mentioned.
4. Emil Ciurea, "Education", in Alexandre Cretzianu (ed.), *Captive Rumania. A Decade of Soviet Rule*, Praeger, New York, 1956, pp. 211–212.

5. See examples of this from Poland, Hungary and the GDR, in Anne Applebaum, *op. cit.*, p. 496ff.

6. *Politics and political Parties in Roumania*, London, 1935, p. 432; Constantin C. Giurescu, *Amintiri*, Bucharest, 2000, pp. 463 and 486.

7. Pericle Martinescu, *op. cit.*, pp. 164–165. For the trial, see Gavin Bowd, *La France et la Roumanie communiste*, L'Harmattan, Paris, 2008, pp. 113–121. Luckily, the family was not thrown out of their home at no. 5, Eugen Stătescu Street, where Tudor Cudalbu lived in a single room with his brother, Călin, and their mother.

8. Petre Kovaceff, *Totul a început la Cernavodă*, Ex Ponto, Constanța, 2014.

9. Nicolae Iorga, who was called as a witness for the defense, describes the royal commissioner "Major Cernat, a cruel, cold, yet amiable man" (*Memorii*, vol. III, „Naționala" S. Ciornei Pub., Bucharest, n.d., p. 297).

10. Florin Șinca, *Martirii poliției române. Distrugerea poliției sub regimul comunist*, Bucharest, 2014, pp. 374–378.

11. The "purging" policy implemented by the teachers began in the Soviet half of Germany as early as 1946, through the educational reform which served as an example for all the other communist countries. 28.000 teachers out of 40,000 were purged and replaced with the "new teachers" (*Neulehrer*) who were usually poorly qualified, cf. Hermann Weber, *op. cit.*, pp. 90-91. In Romania, all teachers had their contracts annulled on October 1st, 1948, see Nicoleta Ionescu-Gură, *Stalinizarea României*, pp. 336–339.

12. a term used to refer to those who had been communist activists during the time when the Communist Party was illegal. After communism was reinstated, the underground communist fighters were honored by the new state and some of them held major positions within the new party's organisations.

13. Doina Jelea, *Lexiconul negru. Unelte ale represiunii comuniste*, Humanitas, Bucharest, 2001, pp. 106–108; Marius Oprea, *Banalitatea răului*, pp. 551–553; Iulian Apostu, *Zydocomuna. Evreii și comunismul. Cazul românesc (1944-1965)*, ed. April 2013, pp. 190–191. His wife, Liza Marcusohn, a political prisoner between 1941-1944, was, in 1964, had a FIAP pension (she was the only retired mother of a student in 1964). See also Horia Nestorescu-Bălcești, „Epurarea lui Teohari Georgescu, 1952", in *Arhivele Totalitarismului*, 6/4, 1998, pp. 189–214.

14. "The true leader of the Bucharest police is general secretary of the prefecture, Mircea Brătucu, a trustworthy communist"; see Testis Dacicus (prof. George Manu), *În spatele Cortinei de fier. România sub ocupație rusească*, Kullusys, Bucharest, 2004, p. 273.

15. Alexandru Niculescu, *Peregrinări universitare europene și nu numai*, Logos, Bucharest, 2010, pp. 65–69, 72, note 4.

16. Iulian Apostu, *op. cit.*, no. 1933, pp. 204–205.

17. The wife of a Math teacher from "Lazăr" and then "Spiru Haret", who made an excellent impression to many generations of students, particularly those in science classes.

18. right-wing extremists or sympathizers.

19. Mihai Gramatopol, *Gustul eternității*, vol. I, pp. 70–73

20. Mihai Gramatopol, *op. cit.*, vol. I, p. 81.

21. Gerda Barbilian, *Ion Barbu. Amintiri*, Cartea Românească, Bucharest, 1979, pp. 171–176; N. Acterian, „Ion Barbu profesor de liceu în amintirile unui fost elev", in *Almanahul Literar*, Bucharest, 1971.

22. The phrase belongs to Alexandru Ciorănescu, *Amintiri fără memorie*, I, 1911–1934, Editura Fundației Culturale Române, Bucharest, 1994, p. 58ff.; see also Mircea Eliade's recollections, *Mémoires*, I, *1907-1937. Les promesses de l'équinoxe*, Gallimard, Paris, 1980, p. 56ff.

23. A great basketball player, he was the son of a famous legionary, Paul Costin Deleanu, former diplomat in Berlin who fled to France, where he died. His wife, Jenica Axente, a chemist and a remarkable woman, stayed in Romania and raised her son on her own. Deleanu, a philosopher who specialized in splitting hairs, served as Ionesco's inspiration for the logician in *Rhinoceros*.

24. Georgel (Jurjel) was the son of doctor Constantin Dănulescu, a former State undersecretary within the Ministry of Labor in Antonescu's cabinet, tried in contumacy during the "great national treason" trial (May 1046) and he lived at no. 17-19, Jules Michelet Street. (*Procesul mareșalului Antonescu. Documente*, 2 volumes, ed. Marcel-Dumitru Ciucă, Saeculum I.O. Pub. – Europa Nova, Bucharest, 1996, vol. I, pp. 151–154, and vol. II, pp. 257–259, 293). His father lived in hiding for several years with some friends in Bucharest, where he died and was buried in his home village (or somewhere he used to own land). The Securitate found out, unearthed the body and found a notebook in his

pocket with the names and addresses of his friends and acquaintances, who were all arrested and investigated. The only ones who got away were the good Samaritans who had sheltered him and who were fortunately missing from the notebook. During his school years, Georgel was summoned by the Securitate on a regular basis, beaten and threatened to divulge his father's hideout. Fortunately, he didn't know it.

25. a shape similar to the letter "J" that children practice when learning cursive writing.

26. Mihai Gramatopol, *op. cit.*, vol. I, p. 79. The first (in 1950) was "a relic of the Bolshevik revolution... Ancient, unpalatable, dressed by the 1920s fashion, she looked like one of Goya's caprices... And when she would yell in that shrill voice "I'm telling you to be quiet!" you can imagine the silence that followed." The second taught at "Lazăr" ever since it was in the old building, in 1947-1948, and she was terrorized by her students, so she left teaching for good. The author's conclusion: "How can you learn a language with such teachers? I deduce that the Russians didn't intend to Russify the Romanians, but to make them dumb, showing once more that the Empire could not extend its borders and that the people in Kremlin were aware of this handicap, beyond cultural differences and a relatable civilization". We must mention Mr. Feuerwerger (nicknamed Foaieverde, or Foaie), who complained that a student "*laffed* all the time" during Russian class.

27. See the colorful testimony (about the party Nomenklatura's children who studied at the "Maxim Gorki" Institute) made by Constantin Turturică, *Nu ești obligat să mori tâmpit (mărturia informatorului)*, vol. I, Eminescu Pub., Bucharest, 2000, pp. 67–95.

28. Ioana Boca, *1956, un an de ruptură. România între internaționalismul proletar și stalinismul antisovietic*, Fundația Academia Civică, Bucharest, 2001; Doina Jela, Vladimir Tismăneanu (coord.), *Ungaria 1956: revolta minților și sfârșitul mitului comunist*, Curtea Veche, Bucharest, 2006.

29. Dorin-Liviu Bâtfoi, *op. cit.*, pp. 452–455.

30. Ghiță Ionescu, *op. cit.*, pp. 259–278.

31. François Fejtö, *Histoire des démocraties populaires*, II, *Après Staline*, Seuil, Paris, 1968, p. 151ff.

32. General Walter Krivitsky gave a good definition of the way in which communists saw conflicting opinions in society: those who criticized were the

"enemies", political adversaries were "traitors" and honest, active opposition was seen as "collusion" (*op. cit.*, p. 234).

33. Stelian Tănase, *Anatomia mistificării*, p. 148.

34. Dana Maria Niculescu Grasso, *Bancurile politice în țările socialismului real. Studiu demologic*, Fundația Culturală Română, Bucharest, 1999, p. 126.

35. Sergiu Verona, *Military Occupation and Diplomacy: Soviet Troops in Romania, 1944-1958*, Duke University Press, 1991, quotes an American report from Bucharest, 1955, which already spoke about those troops retreating; Alina Tudor and Dan Cătănuș, *op. cit.*, pp. 58, 116.

36. Stelian Tănase, *Elite și societate*, p. 106; another version by the same author in *Anatomia mistificării*, pp. 156 and 157.

37. *Stenogramele ședințelor conducerii PCR*, INST and Romania's National Archives, Bucharest, 2003, pp. 190–191, in Florin Constantiniu, *De la Răutu și Roller la Mușat și Ardeleanu*, Editura Enciclopedică, Bucharest, 2007, pp. 126–127.

38. Marius Oprea, *Bastionul cruzimii. O istorie a Securitatii (1948-1964)*, Polirom, Iasi, 2008, an important synthesis valuable for the following events ; Stelian Tănase, *Elite și societate*, pp. 175–176. However, browsing through the file of her father-in-law, lawyer Aurelian Bentoiu (imprisoned between 1948-1956, then again in 1958, died in Jilava Prison in 1962), Mrs. Annie Bentoiu came to the conclusion that everyone who was sentenced in the PNL group in 1958 had been followed and spied on as early as 1955 (*op. cit.*, vol. II, p. 543). "Workers" and "fighters" joined the torturers in labor camps, at the Canal, in Pitești and in Gherla, being arrested in 1963-1954 and released in 1957, over 70 officers and non-commissioned officers, see Cicerone Ionițoiu, *Memorii*, p. 196.

39. Cicerone Ionitoiu, *Memorii. Din țara sârmelor ghimpate*, Polirom, Iași, 2009, p. 207.

40. Stelian Tănase, *Elite și societate*, p. 175.

41. Stelian Tănase, *Elite și societate*, pp. 176–179; idem, *Anatomia mistificării*, pp. 146–148, 370.

42. Cicerone Ionițoiu, *Memorii*, pp. 144 and 204 for the other decrees and HCM.

43. Cicerone Ionițoiu, *Memorii*, pp. 228–229. For the agricultural collectivization process, see Dan Cătănuș and Octavian Roske, *Colectivizarea agriculturii*

în România. Represiunea, I (1949–1953), Institutul Naţional pentru Studiul Totalitarismului, Bucharest, 2000; vol. II, *Cadrul legislativ (1949–1962)*, Institutul Naţional pentru Studiul Totalitarismului, Bucharest, 2007; Dorin Dobrincu and Constantin Iordachi, *Ţărănimea şi puterea. Procesul de colectivizare a agriculturii în România (1949–1962)*, Polirom, Iaşi, 2005. A chilling testimony about the party activists' methods of coercing peasants to adhere to the collectivization belongs to Constantin Turturică, *Nu eşti obligat să mori tâmpit (Mărturia informatorului)*, Eminescu Pub., Bucharest, 2000, pp. 51–58. The collectivization actually meant that all peasants became members of the proletariat, because private property owned by peasants dropped from 88% of the total (in 1949) to 3.5% in 1962, cf. Stelian Tănase, *Elite şi societate*, pp. 185–186.

44. Ghiţă Ionescu, *op. cit.,* p. 255ff.; Stelian Tănase, *Elite şi societate*, p. 170ff.; idem, *Anatomia mistificării*, pp. 315–317, Paul Dimitriu's letter to the author in 1996.

45. Nicolae Steinhardt, *Jurnalul fericirii*, Dacia Pub., Cluj, 1991, p. 228.

46. Recorded by Stelian Tănase, *Anatomia mistificării*, pp. 150–151.

47. Paul Dimitriu, in Stelian Tănase, *Anatomia mistificării*, p. 315.

48. I myself knew two people who were arrested and convicted during those years for ridiculous "crimes": Georgel Mavrocordat, our neighbor on Dionisie Lupu Street (he lived in the basement of the house built by his father, diplomat Edgar Mavrocordat), he did personalized horoscopes and even did them for entire countries. He was arrested and sentenced to I don't know how many years for claiming, according to the prosecution, that "the Soviet Union's border is the Dniester River". Georgel denied this and explained, to the audience's dismay: "I meant to say that Bessarabia is Romanian land!" (A neighbor, bibliographer Alexandru "Toto" Rally had ratted him on). The second case is that of Vlad Stolojan, sentenced to 8 years for "hooliganism, political instigation and cosmopolitanism". His mistake: he had read the American magazine *Life*, with photographs from the 1956 revolution from Budapest, and had discussed the state of the world, at home, with his friends. See Sanda and Vlad Stolojan, *Să nu plecăm toţi odată. Amintiri din România anilor '50*, Humanitas, Bucharest, 2009. For the communists, anyone who criticized the regime was an enemy, see Hal Lehrman, *op. cit.,* p. 190. I must add my father to the list, who was

summoned to give a testimony on Uranus Street, where he was detained for a whole week, in March 1960, with no official explanation, leaving my mother and brother in a desperate situation: a great void surrounded us all of a sudden, the telephone stopped ringing, people would cross the street when they saw my mother, who went from ministry to ministry and from prison to prison, trying to find some information about my father, no-one knew anything, everyone was hostile in their silence. Father came back suddenly on a warm summer afternoon and he told us he'd been summoned to be confronted with a strange character, a pathological liar and a visionary, who claimed to have seen him at the Patriarchy. My father's luck had been that on that day, he was not in his office so the man couldn't have recognized him. For this five-minute confrontation, my father was put in a cell with a rat and left to toss and turn for a week! In his CNSAS file, I found a pile of reports about this pathological liar who went around Bucharest telling all sorts of things to everyone he saw. In a normal society, such a man would have been ignored, even marginalized, but we didn't live in a normal society. It is certain that the Securitate officers wanted to get my father involved in the Patriarchy case, that of Bartolomeu Anania and a few others, who were judged in the Burning Pyre trial. However, it seems that patriarch Justinian violently protested because he had noticed that around him, there was a void, all his closest collaborators having been arrested (a work colleague claimed that my father's arrest was "a check to the Patriarch"!). And my father was his closest collaborator, his chief of staff and they had been working together for 12 years, a collaboration which would end after 30 years, when Justinian died in 1977. See Valeriu Anania, *Memorii*, Editura Polirom, Iași, 2008.

49. See his biography by Vladimir Tismăneanu, *Perfectul acrobat. Leonte Răutu, măștile răului*, Humanitas, Bucharest, 2008; see also the testimonies of Mihai Șora and Pavel Țugui in Stelian Tănase, *Anatomia mistificării*, p. 168ff., especially his instructions given on September 2nd, 1959, for how to organize unmaskings, pp. 171–173.

50. Although he was mourned throughout the country, Grigore Preoteasa was accused by the jesting "reactionaries" that he lacked group spirit, because he had acted on his own and didn't die in a collective way! (Dorin-Liviu Bîtfoi, *op. cit.*, p. 482). In 1949, Virgil Ierunca said the following about him: "Rarely

have I been confronted with the image of a more narrow-minded communist than this Preoteasa, whom I met briefly in the newsroom of the communist publication *România liberă*. "The Imbecile" (as I called him, with a capital "I")" (Virgil Ierunca, *Trecut-au anii... Fragmente de jurnal*, Humanitas, Bucharest, 2000, pp. 17–18).

51. Vladimir Tismăneanu, *Perfectul acrobat*, pp. 349–380; Stelian Tănase, *Anatomia mistificării*, pp. 171–173. Leonte Răutu had shown himself as "High Inquisitor" as early as 1947, when he presented the "social realism" method in a conference at Sala Dalles, and especially in 1949, when he published an article in *Lupta de clasă* called "Împotriva cosmopolitismului și obiectivismului burghez în științele sociale", an idea taken from Andrei A. Jdanov's gospel, a sign that the ideological struggle had reached its peak. See, more recently, Dorin-Liviu Bîtfoi, *op. cit.*, p. 177–181.

52. Dorin-Liviu Bîtfoi, *op. cit.*, pp. 482–48: "The unmaskings stopped only at the end of the academic year [1958-1959], the percentage of expelled students being 15-20%". Along with the accounts given by some people who witnessed these "executions" quoted by the author, we may add those of Constantin Turturică, *Nu ești obligat să mori tâmpit*, pp. 97–127, and that of historian Florin Constantiniu, *op. cit.*, pp. 197–201.

53. Dorin-Liviu Bîtfoi, *op. cit.*, pp. 486–487; Stelian Tănase, *Anatomia mistificării*, pp. 173–180. My brother was a student at University Politehnica back then and he witnessed the famous meeting held in dorm 303 in Grozăvești. He thought he was as good as expelled, when a miracle happened: the first one in alphabetical order from his group was a Greek or Albanian student, a former partisan in the mountains. Accused of being reactionary, he unbuttoned his shirt to reveal bullet scars, shouted that he had fought valiantly against reactionaries. As such, Florian Dănălache stopped questioning him and moved on to the next group...

54. Dorin-Liviu Bîtfoi, *op. cit.*, p. 486. Art critic Petru Comarnescu told me a few years later that he had witnessed the "unmasking" of opera singers Șerban Tassian and his wife, Valentina Crețoiu, friends of my parents who lived at no. 20, Dionisie Lupu Street. The session was presided by Leonte Răutu himself, who had invited general Alexandru (Bubi) Ghica, our neighbor at no. 7, Praporgescu Street. The former World War I officer was a little senile and

didn't really know why he was there, until he heard Răutu preaching against "reactionaries like Alexandru Ghica, the former chief of legionary Siguranta, who"... Hearing this, Ghica got up a few times, saying it wasn't him, but someone with the same name, and each time the chairman told to "Sit down!" A veritable *opera bouffe*. I was not able to refer to Ioana Bentoiu's book, *Dragoste și viață de femeie – Valentina Crețoiu*, Editura Muzicală, Bucharest, 2003.

55. Stelian Tănase, *Anatomia mistificării*, p. 180. More about general A. A. Epishev, who became head of the Political High Department within the Soviet army, in a characterization made by Czech general Jan Senja ("a sinister man", "the most frightening Russian" he'd ever met) in Florin Constantiniu, *De la Răutu și Roller la Mușat și Ardeleanu*, Editura Enciclopedică, Bucharest, 2007, p. 406.

56. A hypothesis not shared by everyone, because here is what Simina Mezincescu says about it, a woman who was detained together with Monica Sevianu at Jilava and Văcărești: "she was a smart girl, a little older than me (we had both gone to "Regina Maria" high school). I asked her: "Well, what did you plan to do with the money?" "Buy jewelry and leave the country". "And where did you want to go?" "In a Western country". I said: " But, forgive me, I don't understand. You are Stalinists and believe that the actual communists strayed from the Stalinist path, that they practice a nationalist sort of communism. Why not go to Albania, then ? Or China ? Stalinism is rife there!" Which proves that, apart from a few exceptions where communists remain faithful to communism until the end, the others support it because it suits their own end, they don't actually believe in communism" (Stelian Tănase, *Anatomia mistificării*, p. 412).

57. A few biographical details in Iulian Apostu, *op. cit.*, pp. 294–295, only he was Florica's cousin, the wife of Emil Bodnăraș (himself a Soviet spy), and he was allegedly involved in Mihail Sebastian's assassination in 1945.

58. Cicerone Ionițoiu, *op. cit.*, p. 64.

59. G. Brătescu, *Ce-a fost să fie. Notații autobiografice*, Humanitas, Bucharest, 2003, pp. 158–159.

60. *Ibidem*, pp. 162–163. See the memories of Monica Lovinescu, *La apa Vavilonului*, Humanitas, Bucharest, 1999, pp. 41–42.

61. G. Brătescu, *op. cit.*, p. 193.

62. *Ibidem*, pp. 286–287.

63. Virgil Ierunca, *Trecut-au anii*, p. 82.

64. *Ibidem*, pp. 113, 119, 155–156, 227–228.

65. For his ignorance about History, see Răzvan Theodorescu's article quoted above.

66. G. Brătescu, *op. cit.*, p. 287.

67. Another argument would be that Brătescu doesn't seem to have suffered on account of his friend's action, he was not interrogated or persecuted as was usually the case with relatives and close friends of political prisoners.

68. Florin Constantiniu, *De la Răutu și Roller la Mușat și Ardeleanu*, Editura Enciclopedică, Bucharest, 2007, p. 115. His friends and colleagues from the Faculty of History, Barbu Câmpina and Eugen Stănescu, were in the same situation, both teaching in the University without having a PhD, a Baccalaureate or a Bachelor's Degree, who could only teach Party doctrines but who were old PCR members.

69. In his memoirs, an actor from the Giulești Theatre whose name I have forgotten wrote that Sașa Mușat was not executed, but that he was seen in Israel a few years after those events. This would be another piece of evidence in support of our hypothesis.

70. Born in 1900, chief at Brâncovenesc Hospital, he was the son of History professor Tudor Seimeanu. See Lucian Predescu, *Enciclopedia Cugetarea*, Cugetarea-Georgescu-Delafras Pub., Bucharest, [1940–1941], s.v.

71. Quoted by Cicerone Ionițoiu, *op. cit.*, p. 206.

72. This was the case, among others, for Antoniu (Bubuleț) Petrescu, whose father was written in the register as being a "collectivist" peasant, because he lived at the edge of the city, where he had inherited a house in the middle of an orchard from his father, the venerable priest of Visarion church, Ioan (Iancu) Petrescu, a world-class specialist in Byzantine music paleography. Antoniu studied at the Politehnica University, which explains, I think, why he sold his grandfather's library to the antiquarian near Enei Church: I had the pleasure of buying several books from this library, stored, in 1990, in a warehouse belonging to Mr. Enescu, the antiquarian, who had recently privatized his business and was friends with high school students who came to sell their inheritance.

73. Dorin-Liviu Bîtfoi, *op. cit.*, p. 490ff.

74. Michel Heller and Aleksandr Nekrich, *op. cit.*, pp. 465–466; Anne Applebaum, *op. cit.*, pp. 516–522.

75. Dorina Potârcă, *op. cit.*, pp. 50, 136, 138–139. The boy, born in 1939, whose parents were both arrested, was persecuted by his teacher at "Clemența" school and was forced to work when he was only 13 years old; later, in order to sit the Bacalaureate exam, he needed a "petit bourgeois" certificate from the Popular Council, although his mother had divorced her husband, who died in Sighet without trial; her daughter, born in 1943, a student at "Lazăr" high school, was expelled in 1960, before the Bacalaureate, even though she had a right to sit the exam. See Lăcrămioara Stoenescu, *Copiii-dușmani ai poporului*, Curtea Veche Pub., Bucharest, 2007.

76. This first category included children whose parents belonged to the Nomenklatura of the regime, named, as we saw above, "workers"!

77. This category included children of priests and prostitutes, the worst social classes of the age, as my uncle told me. He was a solicitor for a Ministry, the son of a priest himself, so he knew what he was talking about.

78. Nicoleta Ionescu-Gură, *Stalinizarea României*, p. 348ff.

79. It is true that, as far as I'm concerned, I solved Math problems and exercises all summer, so I did alright on this subject, too. The funny thing is that the person who gave me the good news (the results had not been posted yet) was nurse Scharf from the school doctor's office. One more reason for me to remember her with gratitude.

80. See for example Dan Ciachir, *Derusificarea și „dezghețul"*, Timpul Pub., Iași, 2009.

81. Ghiță Ionescu, *op. cit.*, pp. 337–344; Stelian Tănase, *Elite și societate*, pp. 209–216.

82. An American journalist who cannot be suspected of being a Nazi sympathizer wrote in 1947: "Even the Nazis gave Middle Europe better economic treatment than the liberating Russians who succeeded them – a shocking assertion but a true one. Whatever else their iniquities, the Germans did understand the economic interdependence between the Reich and the satellite states. Germany was a necessary market for them – and also a necessary source of supply. But the economies of Russia and her new satellites were competitive,

not complementary. Both were normally exporters of food, agricultural produce and semi-processed industrial goods. A new deal for the border economies could come only through industrialization and free markets, and such possibility lay only in the Westerly direction. Instead, the Soviets prescribed uneven barter pacts, autarchy, and a narrow economy one step removed from Middle's Europe ruin". (Hal Lehrman, *op. cit.*, pp. 302–303).

83. I have already mentioned that Romania was the worst country within the Soviet block, according to all economic indicators, cf. Stelian Tănase, *Elite și societate*, pp. 207–209; Dorin-Liviu Bîtfoi, *op. cit.*, pp. 452–455.

84. Ion Mihai Pacepa, *op. cit.*, p. 72ff., who quotes one of Ceaușescu's phrases: "Oil, Jews, and Germans, our best export commodities".

85. See their chronology in Mircea Babeș et al., *Politica externă a României. Dicționar cronologic*, Editura Științifică și Enciclopedică, București, 1986, pp. 267–274 (The agreement with France on February 9th, 1958 and in July 1954, with the US on March 30th and December 9th, 1960, with Japan in September 1962, with West Germany in June 1963, with Austria in July 1963, with Great Britain in September 1963 etc.).

86. Raymond L. Garthoff, „When and why Romania distanced itself from Warsaw Pact", in *Bulletin*, no. 5, 1995, p. 111 (Cold War International History Project), quoted by Florin Constantiniu, *De la Răutu și Roller*, p. 271.

87. A more detailed discussion in Stelian Tănase, *Elite și societate*, p. 222ff.

88. R.R. King, *History of the Romanian Communist Party*, Hoover Institution Press, Stanford, pp. 64–65; Stelian Tănase, *Elite și societate*, p. 218ff. The process went on during Ceaușescu's reign, in order to neutralize, in the name of "party discipline", any attempts to protest against the regime.

89. Dorin-Liviu Bîtfoi, *op. cit.*, p. 514.

90. Cicerone Ionițoiu, *op. cit.*, pp. 230–268.

91. Stelian Tănase, *Elite și societate*, p. 224ff. Something that was more overlooked by the public was a letter on the same subject written by Engels to Romanian socialist Ion Nădejde on January 16th, 1888, a note said to be "a true "high-caliber bomb" for "the fortified positions" of Soviet historiography" (Florin Constantiniu, *De la Răutu și Roller*, pp. 280–281). The letter was published in a book about labor and Socialist press that came out in 1964 as well.

92. His father was literary critic Radu Popescu, a communist underground fighter, who made a terrible impression as a person, cf. Pericle Martinescu, *op. cit.*, pp. 352–355; Stelian Tănase, *Anatomia mistificării*, pp. 360, 363. He lived on Thomas Masaryk Street.

93. A good account of this bewildering fact in Anne Applebaum, *op. cit.*, pp. 422–456, who quotes a joke on this subject ("What is Socialist realism?") that was going around in Warsaw in 1949: a great sculpting competition organized here in Pushkin's memory was won by an artist with a piece depicting a Stalin of gargantuan proportions holding a small book whose cover read, in tiny letters: Pushkin – Poems.

94. She lived at no. 27 on Alexandru Sahia Street (Calderon) in an apartment building, where another building once stood before being bombed in 1944 and left in ruins up until 1960-1961. People found the body of a newborn there, and soon after, when some relatively young people died, the tenants said it had been the work of a poltergeist, a child-vampire, who brought misfortune upon those who lived inside the building. As such, my father was asked by the doorman to bless the place, to exorcize the demon by going into every apartment and blessing it with Holy Water. The funny thing is that the building belonged to the CFR, I believe, or another state institution, reserved for higher officials, all of them party members, all atheists on paper, and some Jews. They all left their doors open and the service was performed one morning when they were away. This is how the "Balkanization of communism" worked in Romania, and after this operation there were no more violent deaths in that building.

Part Two - Memories from School

———

High School Memories - Stefan Andreescu

———

I AM ONE OF THE "Spiru Haret" veterans... More precisely, I spent the first three years of primary school there as well, starting with 1953. The iconic figure of that time – how long it's been! – remains our teacher, Mrs. Linte. Two of my most vivid memories are of her. First, there were the calligraphy notebooks, in which she made us draw "sticks" and other such abstract shapes. Nowadays, as you know, having beautiful writing is no longer important. Those kinds of notebooks have disappeared long ago, and it seems that handwriting itself is no longer a requirement in many parts of the world. We have computers now, don't we? The second memory is about her painful punishment: those who sinned, one way or the other, and were caught by Mrs. Linte, were dragged from their desks... by their sideburns or by their ears!

Finally, I should probably mention school festivities, held at the end of the year, with the famous "raffles" in which the scrumptious, unforgettable cake made by Mrs. Seimeanu, Florin's mother, was somehow always won by... Mrs. Linte! I should mention here that I went to school at the age of six, whereas the rule said children should go to school at the age of seven. My parents actually had to procure a pass for me, because I had insisted on going to school. My reason? All the boys on my street had already gone to school, I was the only one left and had no-one to play with.

Another "veteran", Decebal Becea, found the program of the first school festivity, from May 30th, 1954, in his personal archive. I, myself, featured among those who recited poetry, with the poem *Summer* by George Coşbuc. Others, however, had been forced to recite "works" such as *Comrade*

Gheorghiu-Dej, In the Coal Mines, The Fruit of Labor, The Tractor and so on. The entire list is actually a brilliant mix of poetry appropriate for our age and slogans in verse, which goes to show how we started our intellectual growth. It's a good thing we had our families...

When we got to 4th grade, schools and high schools were "mixed" together. And, on the other hand, they checked to see if you were enrolled at the right school for your district. In my case, they saw that, even though I lived very close to "Spiru Haret" – back then it was called L.B. 12 (Boys' High School no. 12) –, I belonged to a different school, on Moșilor Street (I think it became the "Coșbuc" high school). As such, I – temporarily! – went to a school that used to be exclusively for girls. So there were only three or four boys in my class, and the absolute majority were girls. Thus, in "crafts" classes we has to do what the girls were doing, which meant learning to... knit. This is how, by the end of that school year, I managed to produce... the back of a sweater.

Clearly, the following year, when I started middle school, I quickly went back to "Spiru" – I had grown very fond of it – and I continued my education there until the "maturity exam" (the Baccalaureate). In those years, when I first saw teachers being changed from one class to the next, based on the subject they taught, I stated to notice the difference in training between teachers from the older generations and those who had become teachers in the "glorious years"... Of course, what I loved most were the History classes taught by Constantin Necșulescu, about whom I would learn that he had published two remarkable studies in his chosen field before the war. He wasn't actually the only one to have such exceptional training. For Math, the late Mr. Cernica – like professor Manolescu (who didn't teach my class) – had written textbooks that were very much appreciated and reprinted. The second favorite subject was Romanian. And speaking of Romanian classes, I can't help but mention that one day, in 7th grade, we were told that we were going to skip the textbook lesson about Petru Dumitriu. He had just fled to the West...

In middle school, at the beginning of every school day – sometimes, in winter, it was dark at 7:30 in the morning – we had to sing the national anthem, *Te slăvim Românie*, together with our first teacher of the day, or, from time to time – on a whim – *Internaţionala*. They even tried to make us end the day with such a performance, once or twice. The experiment was short-lived, discouraged by the ruckus at the end of the day that broke out as soon as the last bell rang.

I won't forget to mention a "detail" that plagued my entire generation: the compulsory study of Russian. In my final high school years, I had a Mr. Grosu as my Russian teacher, a beast of a Bessarabian who flunked me. In order to pass, I had to learn *Jurământul Tinerei Gărzi* by heart, a text which spread over almost two textbook pages! I hold the same view as many others: it's a pity that learning Russian was compulsory, that we had an instinctual aversion to it because it was the language of our rulers. Otherwise, we would have picked it up much better.

For our final two high school years, we had to choose between being in a humanist class or a science class. I went for the humanist class, because I wanted to continue studying History. But my family said otherwise. If, by the time I finished high school, I still wanted to go to the Faculty of History, I would be free to do so. Until then, I had to go to a science class, hopefully to change my mind... This is why my older sister, on behalf of my family, went to the high school secretary and signed me up for science class. I don't regret it, because the two years of "positive" training in such a good high school like "Spiru Haret" went a long way to discipline my mind, a thing that helped me later, working as a researcher in History.

I heard that the officials of that time, probably someone within the Ministry of Education, said about my high school, after an inspection, that it wasn't "labor-oriented". It was true, most students at that time were the children of doctors, lawyers or engineers. A good deal were Jewish and they emigrated, especially after graduating from University.

The PCR proclamation from April 1964, the so-called "Proclamation of Independence", came on the eve of our Baccalaureate exam. All of us who were in 11th grade were called at once, one afternoon, to go to a meeting at the former "Zoia Kosmodemianskaia" Girls' School, near Grădina Icoanei Park. Thus, we sat through an "explanation" session, like so many others that took place throughout the country. I don't remember who the speaker was. It was probably a party activist. Anyway, we listened to an avalanche of attacks against the Soviet Union, many of which were not included in the official proclamation. This was the beginning of the so-called "liberaliza-tion" period during the Communist era in Bucharest.

———

"The liberalization years"... It was, as people have said, a partial liberaliza-tion. Here I give a personal account, from my time as a University student. I was at the end of my second year, so it was 1967. We were summoned to take part in the May 1ˢᵗ festivities and had to give our signature to acknowl-edge that we had been informed. I didn't go. After all, I didn't think it mattered. I was busy working on a fascinating paper and didn't want to stop. Surprisingly enough, there was a UTC meeting – I, myself, was a member, and I continued to be... into my old age, where various members were sanctioned. It was a way of showing that the regime was still in control. I protested, when my turn came, and so, instead of receiving a "blame vote" like all the other members who had been absent from the festivities, I got a "blame vote with a warning". This sanction was lifted only in my final year. It hanged over me like a sort of "Damocles' Sword", because I was actually being warned to keep my mouth shut, to stay in line, or I would be kicked out of University...

Apart from religious journals, where I had started publishing papers during my final years of high school, as a University student I started print-ing some articles in the student journals *Amfiteatru* and *Viața studențească*. That was when I realized once more how important it is for the author to edit his text at least once: when, in a short article of mine, I found that instead of Antim Ivireanu, I had written... Anton Mireanu!

At the same time, I had started writing a series of notes of no great importance for *Contemporanul*, a prestigious weekly journal. My first meaningful collaboration was related to the events of August 1968. More precisely, after Czechoslovakia was invaded, that is, at the beginning of September if I'm not mistaken, we were going to host an international con-ference about "Archeological Sources of European Civilization". We didn't know, however, if we would have foreign scientists as our invited speakers or not, due to the tension and rumors about a possible repeat of that invasion in Romania. For that reason, I was sent on my own to Mamaia, where, at Hotel "Internațional", the conference papers were going to be presented. Here I must applaud the professional manner of *Contemporanul* editors. As I announced the arrival of our foreign guests – including archeologist Dinu Adameșteanu, from Italy –, I was sent "backup". First, another collaborator, then a photographer. This is how I managed to get a full page of interviews, complete with my signature.

As my University graduation grew near, and the sad, pathetic workplace "assignment" along with it – where you had to show up, no matter the circumstances, for three whole years – I started thinking seriously about a solution. In 1969, I started collaborating with the *Magazin Istoric* journal. And, at some point, I asked the editor-in-chief, Cristian Popișteanu, if he could offer me a job. The answer was positive and so, in Iași, in July 1970, when the national "assignment" took place, I was called out from a separate list of people with "government assignments" or something like that. On an unrelated note, on this occasion, due to my negligence, my wallet was stolen, in which I had not only my identity card, but also the free boarding pass for the Bucharest train... Anyway, I was an intern editor for *Magazin Istoric*! But not for long...

————

I go back to "Spiru Haret". Recently I went up the main staircase, the old one, while attending a ceremony. I was impressed by how worn the front steps were, compared to how I remembered them. Then I though: why am I surprised? It's been fifty years...

Things I Didn't Write in My Autobiography
– Ioana Crețoiu (Casassovici)

———

Last name: CASASSOVICI
First name: IOANA MARIA ELISABETA
Date of birth: May 9th, 1946
Place of birth: Bucharest
Address: No. 35, I.L. Caragiale Street, district 1 Mai, Bucharest
School: No. 12 High School
Class: 8B
Pioneer: yes UTM
Father's full name: CASASSOVICI MIRCEA
Mother's full name: CASASSOVICI ELENA
Father's workplace: plumbing engineer, IMI 2
Member of the PCR: no
Mother's workplace: Tricotextil worker
Member of the PCR: no
Social background:
I hear myself asking: *Mother, what do I write under social background?*
After a while, my mother replies: *Write petty bourgeois, it's for the best.*

I HAVE FILLED OUT MANY autobiographies during my years as a student. When I was in University, I used to say *intellectual* under social background. It wasn't a lie anymore: the working class, the working peasants and the intellectuals were shaping a happy society in our beloved country. Landlords, industrialists and the bourgeois had disappeared altogether.

My Family

In 1948, after being evicted from the house built by grandpa Casassovici, at no. 4, Varşovia Street, our family took what they hoped was a "temporary" residence at no. 35, I.L. Caragiale Street, until the long-awaited Americans would come. Our clan was made up of: my grandpa and grandma from my father's side, grandma Iliescu, who was a widow, from my mother's side, my parents and their three children (my older brother, Dan, myself and my younger sister, Ştefana), our *teta*[1] Grete, the brother of my paternal grandmother with his wife and two children, who were older than us, an orphaned granddaughter of grandma Casassovici, whom she raised together with her old *"teta"* or housekeeper, Mitzi, as well as Marioara, our servant (today she would be called a maid). The house had been built to generously accommodate one family. It easy to occupy every room for the 15 members of our large family, Grandpa even had a study, the piano that had belonged to grandma's sister, who died of typhus during World War I, was placed in the drawing room, the living room and kitchen were used by everyone, the grandparents lived on the ground floor, while the children lived on the first floor (we, the three siblings, shared the same room for many years) and all parents lived in the loft. Soon enough, the Popular Council decided that we had extra space, so we had to house a young couple in grandpa's study and our living room was taken over by a Marxism teacher and her daughter. So we had to squeeze together even more, doors were boarded shut and covered with drapes. At the same time, we no longer had access to the ground floor bathrooms, the piano was sold and the drawing room became our living room. At our long table, everyone had their place, with different tablecloths for each family. Later, in a small room in the attic that heated up like a stove in summer, our cousins' cousin, the future director Tudor Mărăscu, took up residence clandestinely, and then their grandmother, Maman Paulette, the daughter of landlord Aurel Drugă, came from Craiova. After our older cousins got married and left to live somewhere else, their room was given to Commander Pop and his wife, two very nice cohabitants. Once they came, the kitchen had four cooking stoves: my grandma's, my mother's, my aunt's and the lady Commander's. Later, I read that communal kitchens were "fashionable" in the Soviet Union as well, the lodgers using pots with locked lids, so that their food would not go bad or get stolen. In our kitchen, pots had normal lids and I never heard any arguments. There was only the occasional fuss about the bathroom queue.

At no. 35, Caragiale Street, we lived as though we were in a play and an unknown director unexpectedly changed the fates of several characters, as well as the decor. Doors opened all the time, people went in or out, there were shouts and conversations on the stairs, you could hear the crackling sound of the Voice of America radio station, and on the ground floor, the only telephone in the house kept ringing. From time to time, things would disappear: a piece of furniture, a carpet, a crystal chandelier or a statue would be sold so that we could survive. My grandparents' generation went offstage; others moved somewhere close or further away. The curtain fell for good only after 1989.

Our parents, especially after Marioara Cantacuzino's students were arrested[2] (in 1952), tried to protect us, shrouding us "in silence". My father's first cousin, who had been imprisoned at Pitești, the teenager Ioan Lugoșianu, was executed at Jilava for being "a criminal accused of ruining the country"[3], every day people disappeared or were thrown out of their homes. Being helpless witnesses to these tragedies made many parents who had been dubbed enemies of the working class overnight be quiet around their children, hide the family's history from them, believing that not knowing would protect them from the looming, widespread and unpredictable evil.

I knew, even as a child, that some of the adult conversations that I couldn't understand, about "the Americans coming" or "the turning of the screw", how someone was "taken" in the middle of the night and sent to "the Canal", weren't meant to leave the house.

I confess that I am that little girl, who, when her mother started telling a story that began with "Once upon a time, there was an Emperor and an Empress...", went to close the window, lest people in the street hear anything about the royals.[4]

This is why no-one ever told me that my great-grandfather, Haralambie Casassovici, born in a merchant family from Alexandria, was part of Carol Davila's second generation of students. He was an army doctor during the

War of Independence in 1877, received countless medals and, towards the end of his life, wrote his memoirs[5]. Nowadays we would say he was a brave and tenacious man who became a colonel doctor, the first man in our family to have a higher education, 150 years ago.

I didn't know that my grandfather, Corneliu Casassovici, having completed his studies in engineering in Dresden, Germany, came home and was employed by the sugar factory in Roman. There, he founded the first bookstore in the city, a milk co-op, and even starred in a theatre production! Living in Dresden, he had expanded his horizons and had tried to change and develop the community at home, following the example he'd seen during his time as a student. Like him there were many others, who, returning from studying abroad (usually France or Germany), build a modern Romania! Then, he was named manager of the "Stan Rizescu" Textile Factory, became professor docent at the "Politehnica" University, laid the bases of higher education in the field of textile industry, built the first textile fibers research lab, initiated the first textile industry workers' association, built one of the most cutting-edge cotton mills in the country, together with a Czechoslovak company, was an editor and wrote a weekly economic column for the *Argus* newspaper, wrote lectures for textile engineering students and was a member of countless boards and committees. Nowadays, we would say he was an intelligent man who worked very diligently, created the first generation of learned textile engineers, made his fortune through hard work and climbed the social ladder naturally.

I didn't know that my father, having graduated from the Polytechnic University of Dresden *mit auszeichnung bestanden*[6], returned home to run his father's cotton mill without taking a single day off, was a member of the Romanian Alpine Club and wrote a book with his friend about their travels, going down the Bistrița river by raft and by kayak and reaching Constanța. I found the book, *În căutarea pelicanilor*[7], pages uncut, in the attic. After the factory was nationalized, he had a hard time finding work as a plumbing engineer on various construction sites around the country. The fact that he knew German so well helped him make technical translations every night, an activity which, despite being so poorly paid, added a little something to the family budget. It can be said that father was initially a young man destined to have a bright future, but political shifts changed the course of his life irrevocably.

But I didn't learn about all of this until much, much later. My mother was all about taking care of us, her three children, day after day, every waking moment. She let herself be suffocated by our presence, our love and by worrying about us all her life. My mother always found brave solutions for any situation. In our family, she was the minister of Finance – carefully pondering every dime, of Health, caring for us more expertly than a doctor, and last but not least, of Education. She wanted to teach us other things than what we were taught in school, and since she didn't have any teaching aids, she came up with very unique, original methods. Mother taught my sister and me French, and I am sorry I didn't keep the notebook she made with drawings and explanations in French, written in capital letters. Mother took us to her friend, Mariela Băbeanu, the daughter of architect Ion Mincu, who taught us about the life of Jesus Christ, in French. Mother taught us about art history, starting with Italian Renaissance, which she only spoke about, because she didn't have any illustrated books. She had made up a game with questions: Who painted the lady with the mysterious smile? Who is born from water, stands in a shell and was painted by Botticelli? In which painting does the angel bring a lily to Virgin Mary? What did Fra Filippo Lippi paint? What about Filippino Lippi? Who made the Florence Baptistery doors? And so on. The questions and answers made us curious and etched themselves in my memory.

Besides doing the usual and unusual chores around the house (electrical repairs, unclogging the sink), she had all sorts of jobs throughout the years: she sold things at the flea market, made *mărțișor*[1] charms, wove carpets at Mislea in prison, painted beads, worked at Tricotextil co-op (I raised the percentage of working mothers in my high school years!), painted icons, taught French privately.

Much later, I could even say it was too late, I discovered that my mother had written poetry in her youth, she'd been a member of various literary clubs, but repressed her talent when she had her first child.

---

1 a tallisman with a red and white string traditionally offered on March 1st in Romania.

All my friends' mothers had similar fates. I can't leave out the wife of a former diplomat who, while her husband was in prison and she was left home with four children, could only find work in landscaping, sweeping alleys in parks. The funny part is that the sweepers' boss was a former head of the Ministry for Foreign Affairs. He would wait until all the sweepers went to work and then he'd bring her a trash can, very politely, saying: "Your Excellence, here is your trash can!"

When I was a child, there was a polio outbreak in Bucharest, there were no vaccines, many children got sick, so we rarely went outside. We were four children living under the same roof, close in age, and if we counted our cousins from Columb Street, there were actually six of us. Later, this group split, by age, in two: my brother, cousin Ionuț Rizescu and cousin Ilinca Juvara (who both graduated from "Spiru Haret" when I was just starting 8th grade) and those closer in age to me: Ștefana and my cousin Alexandra Juvara, who went to the same middle school and high school as me, "Spiru Haret", of course, and we were one year apart. We were very close and still are, to this day.

From my paternal grandmother's side, who had six brothers, I had many other cousins who lived in different neighborhoods and whom I only saw when my grandmother took me on a visit or at different family events, such as my great-grandmother's 80th birthday.

At one time, I had a very special relationship with the family of one of my grandmother's sisters. Aunt Elena, who had remarried with Ion Vinea[8], lived in a beautiful house, in an elegant neighborhood, on Braziliei Street. I was sent there during winter, when no. 35, Caragiale Street would run out of burning oil and the heaters would stop working. My sister was sent to our cousins', Ilinca and Alexandra, my brother stayed home, in the cold, be cause he was a boy, he was older and needed to grow strong. In those winter days, at Aunt Elena's house, where we had gas and the stove was always warm, I grew close to my cousin Voica, and I met another part of society made up of poets and writers who I only knew from my school books. Ion Vinea, in those years, was to me the most charming, interesting and generous man. When he had money, he took us by the arm and went out with his two nieces to "Nestor", to the cake store! The novel *Lunatecii* and his poetry were published some time later.

Perhaps it would be fun to tell you about his wife's temper. Aunt Elena had first been married to a Colonel, and she was famous in our family on account of this story: *The family was gathered around the dinner table and a young lieutenant, in love with their daughter, had been invited. The main course was fried chicken, which everyone at the table ate with their hands, except for the lieutenant who struggled with a fork and knife. Being very observant, Aunt Elena asked him: "Lieutenant, why don't you eat with your hands, like the rest of us?" He replied: "Madam, I only eat chicken with my hands if I am at a picnic, on the grass". Hearing this, Aunt Elena called the maid: "Marghioala, hurry up and bring some grass from the garden and put it on the Lieutenant's seat, so he can eat chicken like the rest of us!"*

THE FIRST YEARS OF SCHOOL

In my 1st grade, we had moved to Beiuș, because my father had found work on the Ştei construction site. We lived there with two other families in a one-story house that stretched over a yard. We had two rooms, a hallway turned into a kitchen and a tiny bathroom. Since we had experience from living at no. 35, Caragiale Street, we managed to fit 6 people in that space. The parents had their bedroom in the smaller room, and us, the three children and Aunt Grete, took over the larger room, where we slept, ate and did our homework.

Beiuș, a small town on the banks of a river that flows into Crișul Negru River, nestled between the hills, with a forest nearby, was a place of absolute freedom for us. I even went strolling around the town's centre by myself. After learning to read in school, I read all the shop signs. This is how I discovered the word "Alimentara"[2] written above one door. This was a great mystery for me. I had never heard this word in our home before, but I was too ashamed to ask what it meant. I came up with all sorts of theories: "Ali" was a Turkish name, "menta"[3] was a plant, but what did "RA" mean? What did they mean together? One day, I plucked up my courage and went inside.

---

2 A type of state-owned food store chain in Communist Romania.

3 mint

It was dark, rank and I saw an oil barrel, some wooden crates, boxes of marmalade and people with bags standing in a queue. I had never seen anything like that before! It was nothing like the stores in Bucharest, where we went shopping at "Furnica", "Leonida", "Glodeanu", "Pantazi"! Slowly but surely, all those Bucharest stores were turned into "Alimentara" groceries, which made them get a bad reputation! In Beiuș, I went to the cinema for the first time and I saw the Soviet movie *Maximka*, the story of a colored kid, a shoe-shiner on an American ship. Saved from drowning by the crew of a Soviet ship, he stays with them, forgets about his past humiliation and lives a happy life. When I told my mother about the movie, she said right away that it was "a line movie". It was much later that I understood the coded meaning of the word, when I discovered that many other movies and books went along the line imposed by the party.

My brother entered 5th grade at a boys' school, while I went to a primary school in 1st grade, in a 1922 building that had been a pedagogical high school. It was situated in a park and the building even had a tower, like a fairytale castle. I went to school by myself, because it was very close to our house. In Beiuș, there were mixed classes for primary schools, so some of my classmates were boys, one of whom came to school barefoot. During recess, the boys were busy playing marbles, spitting or scuffling, while us girls huddled together like geese, far away from them. Some children had poor families, came to school with their spelling books in their knapsacks and didn't have any warm clothes or thick boots for winter. We didn't have uniforms. Some of my classmates were not very interested in learning, since they had other things to do around the house, and I don't think they did more than finish primary school. That year, I wrote my first letter to my grandparents in Bucharest and received a postcard from them on my birthday.

The following year, my father's construction site was closed and at the end of the summer, we went back to Bucharest. I went to Școala Centrală in 2nd grade, which was later named after Zoya Kozmodemyanskaya, on the occasion of her mother's visit. My teacher here was Mrs. Themo, who was very good at her job and made me eager to learn new things. It was a girls only class, and my classmates lived around Icoanie Park, Ioanid Park, Maria Rosetti Street, Polonă Street, Dacia Boulevard, Piața Gemeni and

Piața Amzei. I wore a black uniform with a white collar and a red ribbon tied around my neck. Some girls wore pigtails with white ribbons, like butterflies, embroidered collars, and the ribbons around their necks were plumped up like carnations. A doctor's daughter even had a fur coat that fastened with three buttons like little fluffy balls, and she had fur-lined boots. Her mother took her to and from school, and she also had an ankle-length fur coat. In those years, you could only get clothes "for points" (that you bought with cards), my mother wore loden, the hats had been hidden away and replaced with headscarves. In winter, I wore my brother's hand-me-down boots that I would later pass on to Ștefana. Our backpacks were made of cardboard with brown fabric glued on top, our pencil cases were made out of wood, we made jackets for our textbooks and notebooks out of blue paper and we wrote with pen and ink.

I remember that in my 2nd grade, coming back from school, I told my grandfather the poem *Stema țării* (The National Emblem) by Mihai Beniuc:

...Crops, hills, woods and scaffolds measure
My great country's largest treasure.
And the star that's up above,
What could she be thinking of?
Socialism, she says loudly,
Rises in my country proudly!...

My grandfather congratulated me and when Mr. Mott (the owner of the wine and champagne brand Mott), Mr. Mardan (his University classmate from Dresden), Mr. Culina (the renowned Aromanian architect Arghir Culina, who designed Ambasaor Hotel, Cișmigiu Hotel and so on) and Mr. Prager (the great construction engineer Emil Prager) came to visit him one afternoon, he asked me to come and tell them this poem. My grandfather was proud of his granddaughter, who (unfortunately) had learned a poem about Socialist Romania's emblem!

In 3rd grade, we were surprised to find a few scattered boys towards the back of the class. They were clearly a minority and they stayed that way. In our crafts classes, Mrs. Themo taught us how to sew buttons and mend holes in stockings. The boys were quite unwilling, thinking this activity was only meant for girls. Finally, one of them mended his father's sock better than any of us.

I got a certificate for outstanding achievements every year. I was made a pioneer. I took the streetcar to Palatul Pionierilor and, together with my classmate Ruji Weissman, was a member of the Natural Sciences Club. After an uninspired teacher made us dissect live frogs, we stopped going to Palatul Pionierilor. Meanwhile, Ruji had left the country. No one told us who built that palace or who had lived in it before being taken over by the red scarves.

We graduated from primary school knowing how to read, do Math, spell properly and keep those pesky "their", "they're" and "there" straight. All my life I let the elderly take my place on the streetcar (it's a reflex that I still have, even though it should be the other way around now!), I never pulled dogs' tails, never picked flowers from parks, never littered the streets, like our teacher taught us. We said our teary good-byes to the one who called herself "mother hen", sheltering us, "the little chicks" under her protective wing. We sat an exam to go into 5th grade, which we all passed, except for one sickly girl whose mother sold sunflower seeds at the school gate. It's true, that little girl with sad eyes was never welcome under our teacher's wing. I haven't seen her around the neighborhood since then.

GRADES 5 THROUGH 7

It was much later that I realized how fortunate I'd been to study in the beautiful Şcoala Centrală, built by architect Ion Mincu in 1851. On the front of the building you could make out the names Elena Doamna, Clara Doamna, Domniţa Bălaşa, Doamna Chiajna, only that of Carmen Sylva had been wiped off[4]. The inner courtyard was stunning; its beautiful columns impressed me, the corridor that surrounded it, leading to the classrooms, the colorful ceramic tile decorations. The school had an auditorium with a real stage, red velvet curtains and wings, a laboratory for Natural Sciences, one for Geography, one for Romanian, one for Chemistry, one

---

4 Romanian noblewomen, wives and daughters of important Romanian monarchs.

for Physics, boarding rooms upstairs, a dining hall and a kitchen in the basement.

I had the same classmates, our friendships were the same. For the first and last time in my life I loved my teachers with a passion, especially Mrs. Ciocârlie, the History teacher. I had the great fortune of having teachers that had finished their studies before Communism, who loved their job and who were an example to us. I was diligent and loved learning.

In those years there was a student competition about a building on our street. On Caragiale Street, across the road from us, there was an elegant building unlike the others, with an imposing ground floor, very large windows, a high roof whose framing highlighted the main entrance, with a beautiful garden and a chestnut tree extending its branches across the street. This house was an orphanage. From my window I could see the orphans standing in line, singing or playing in the yard, children with very short hair, wearing blue aprons, brown shoes but no socks, and I couldn't tell the girls and the boys apart. To me, it was the most beautiful and important building on the street, so I signed up for the competition. It so happened that I won an honorable mention. It was much later that I discovered the building had once belonged to the royal family, and I thought it ironic that I should win a prize in a school competition, in those times, with a story about a house of such poor social background. But stranger things had happened. After 1989, the royal family got that building back. And a few years ago, I went inside, as a guest to a wedding and a baptism. The building had been turned into a restaurant.

In the spring of 1959, everything changed. On Easter Eve, they came to arrest my grandfather. He was paralyzed in bed, couldn't move or talk after having suffered a stroke. They got my grandmother that night, the next they came after my father, my aunt, Adina Juvara, then my mother, my uncle, the surgeon Ion Juvara, and his cousin. They were arrested for owning gold coins and initially received sentences of 90 years in prison, later reduced to 30 years by the Supreme Court, and finally, after receiving an amnesty in the fall of 1960, my father and grandmother were the last to come back home.

We were a bunch of frightened children, our parents were gone and we were forced to go through rough times. My sister Ștefana was home when they came for our mother. So that Ştefana wouldn't witness her leaving, mother asked her to go upstairs and fetch a tablecloth. When Ştefana came back, mother was gone, she'd been taken away. Ştefana and I were all alone in the house one morning when they came with our father in stripes and chains to search the house. I remember them throwing things from our cabinets and wardrobes on the floor. There are other images that I can't forget, even though I wish I could erase them from my memory: the three children's attempt to see their parents at Văcăreşti, after they'd been sentenced, when I wasn't allowed to see them because each had the right to only one visitor and we were three children! To console me, an aunt took me to Mislea to see my mother in the visitation room. We were all alone in the house at no. 35, Caragiale Street, where you were never really alone in an XXL-sized family.

I kept going to school, I never even told my best friend about it, but all my teachers, the whole city knew how the Casassovici and Juvara children were all alone, their parents in prison and their grandfather paralyzed in bed. There were many people around us who helped. We were placed in an extreme situation, but I learned that, in life, when you are on the edge of a cliff, there's always hope!

In the summer of 1959 I finished 6th grade. At the end of the school year festivities, Ştefania's class put on a ballet performance, in which my sister was "prima ballerina", but mother wasn't there to see her and cheer her on, which still upsets her to this day. In the fall, our mother, aunt and uncle Ion Juvara came back home after their sentences were commuted.

After that, I was in 7th grade, preparing for the high school entrance exam, while my brother Dan sat his Baccalaureate exam and then the University entrance exam. He tried to get into the Faculty of Constructions, but didn't, on account of his unhealthy social background[9]. He got a very good grade in his written exam, but in his oral exam, despite having solved the problem correctly, his examiner said his answer was wrong. My brother proved to him that he was right. However, he got a very low grade and was flunked. In fall, he got into the Faculty of Constructions in Iaşi.

My mother was firmly told that I stood no chance of getting into the No. 10 high school, which had become very political after Liuba

Kozmodemyanskaya's visit, the mother of Zoya and Suhra, post-mortem heroes of the Soviet Union. I remember spending days on end with my mother, traveling to the end of some streetcar lines, on the outskirts of Bucharest, so she could enroll me in one of those trade schools (high schools?). I was so horrified by what I saw that my mother decided I should try and sit the exam at my former school after all. Of course, I was not granted admission[10]. This is when I saw with my own eyes what it meant to have an unhealthy social background. Nowadays, in academic terms, it would be said that I'd been a victim of social discrimination.

In the fall of 1960, I sat the entrance exam again, this time for No. 12 "Spiru Haret" high school. I remember the high school secretary, Mr. Diaconu, looking at my school records, feigning surprise at my not having gotten in on the first try with my high grades, despite knowing our situation very well, since my brother had graduated from the same high school.

After the start of the school year, in 1960, as a result of an amnesty, my father and my grandmother got out of prison. As fate would have it, they took the same train to Bucharest. Father told us how, in the Arad train station, he helped an old lady carry her ragbag up the train car steps. Mother and son didn't recognize each other at first!

My High School Years

So that fall I got into No. 12 high school, formerly "Spiru Haret", formerly a boys' high school, in class 8B, where I didn't know my classmates. Despite having been a boys' high school, there weren't that many more boys than girls. Girls always had other girls as their desk mate, and the same went for boys. The supreme gesture of tenderness from boys was when they tripped you or hit you with snowballs in winter. I had become very quiet and cautious, observing my new classmates, with whom I graduated high school four years later.

We were all at a difficult age. We were forced to wear horrible uniforms. Luckily for us, our youth overcame the ugliness of those uniforms! Us girls had navy blue dresses, fastened with buttons at the back, with a belted waist and white, detachable pique collars. Navy blue skirts with white blouses were also allowed, and in our last months of high school, some girls had turned their dresses into pinafores. Boys had navy blue suits with white shirts and dark colored ties. The fabrics of these uniforms was so horrible that the places where it touched our desks quickly became shiny, the boys' pants took the shape of drain pipes and the knees and elbows stood out. Girls tried to make their uniforms shorter, since mini skirts were becoming fashionable, or make them prettier by adding a nicer belt. Girls were also required to pull their hair back with a white headband that they put in their pocket during recess. The most horrible thing was that we had to sew a school registration patch on our left sleeve, with the high school number, namely NO. 12 HIGH SCHOOL. Some wore custom made patches, others sewed their own at home. I had made myself one no larger than a post stamp! I hated that patch, I figured we weren't cattle to be branded, so I usually pinned it in place and took it off as soon as I set foot outside the school gate. This trick stopped working when a monstrous Russian teacher came into our school, comrade Grosu, who indeed made our lives a living hell. In the morning, we entered the school building one after the other, in a queue. Grosu was posted at the entrance and pulled on our patches to see if they were sewn properly or not. Today, the thought that such a person, cursed by so many students, is surely boiling in the pits of Hell gives me a measure of satisfaction, but this is, of course, just a figure of speech.

Except for the one mentioned above, I only had good teachers, some of them former University professors sent to teach high school students for reasons unknown to us. I had grown up, I didn't love my teachers as I used to in middle school, but I respected them. I admired those who practiced their profession honestly, making us curious about the subject they taught, who were not absurdly severe, who understood us and helped us without question in difficult situations. Every student must have his list, but on mine there is Mrs. Atanasiu (the Romanian teacher), Mrs. Voinea (who taught English), Mr. Voiculescu (for Natural Sciences), and Mr. Manolescu (the Math teacher).

Our teachers had nicknames that we used at home when speaking about them: The Cane, The Tantrum, The Celeste, Cati, Hiroshima, The Beast, The Cell and so on. When my mother went to a parent-teacher conference for my brother, she asked the first man she saw where she could find Professor Cane. As it happened, it was actually him! Of course, Mr. Cane was not upset! For me, my parents never went to a parent-teacher conference. My father was sent, for once in his life, to go to Ștefania's class. When he was asked, he could say what grade she was in, but didn't know if she was in class A, B or C, so he came home, to our amusement! I remember how, during recess, the boys' mothers would come and speak to our head teacher. I always wondered why their mothers came to school, but mine never did.

Education was 100% political and none of the teachers ever strayed from the "party line", not necessarily out of conviction, but because they were helpless, unable to express a point of view that differed from the official one. They followed textbooks to the letter. The Ministry of Education was the author of every textbook, that, in high school, were no longer translated from Russian. History was the most butchered subject, turned into an endless class struggle between the oppressors and the oppressed, because the struggle was the yeast of progress. The history I learned was presented as a result of the nation's actions with the help of our great eastern brother who would, from time to time, give us a nudge or a pat on the back. I can't forget a caricature from our History textbook depicting a ragged peasant pulling a plough being whipped by king Charles I. Under the picture there was the following message: "Now that Charles I is king, we have a head!"

I remember the thrill of reading these words in our Latin textbook: *"Patria nostra est terra Europae. In patria nostra multe silvae sunt quae bestiae abundant..."* I felt like I was reading a political manifesto that made us aware of being European and not part of the Asian Steppe. In other subjects we were also told to pay attention to the merits of various Soviet scientists, who had invented absolutely everything, according to our textbooks! Natural sciences were influenced by Michurin and Lysenko, chemistry was hidden beneath Mendeleev's table, red flags flapped in drawing books and the sound of horns and drums could be heard during Music classes. Only Math and PE were neutral classes. Thus, Cane the Brave, our PE teacher, having nothing to do with politics, could organize the high school's basket team, sports camps and he was one of the most beloved teacher for generations of students. A proof of this is his statue that greets you on a school corridor, the work of sculptor Dinu Rădulescu, one of his former students.

Another absurd thing was that we were forced to go to a factory every week and work in production. Our class went to a hall with many lathes, which smelled like oil, and the workers in greasy overalls were rather bored by our presence. If this activity was meant to make us become more interested in getting a job in a factory or a plant, I must admit it didn't fulfill its goal. It rather made us more determined to go to University so that we could build socialism by sitting at a desk or in front of a drawing board.

Through the years, I heard people say regretfully "They don't teach kids like they used to do back in my day!" Unfortunately, in the past, as well as the present, the system only required the student to learn things by heart, to memorize. The teacher asks a question and the student has to give the answer like it is in the book. The school curriculum doesn't seek to develop logical and critical thinking, raise interest or encourage the exchange of ideas. The public system for mandatory education, of the type "shut up and swallow it", was and, unfortunately, still remains the same dull glop.

The High School Students

"Spiru Haret" students were famous, in my day, for their male and female basketball teams. Since I wasn't interested in basketball (unlike my siblings), this renown never impressed me. I liked to swim, to dive into the sea, to climb mountains, but back then these was not considered sports. Sports meant doing flips on cue, vaulting, hanging onto espaliers, relay racing, reacting to a referee's whistle, changing in cold and smelly locker rooms and many other activities that my rebellious nature thoroughly despised. Basketball players were never my heroes.

Among the older students, I admired Petru Popescu, the future author of the novel *Dulce ca mierea e glonțul patriei*, and Ioana Nestor, a model student, a member of the literature club who wore velvet dresses with ecru silk collars so naturally. There were also the school's "it girls", and I use the term honorably, who wore the horrible school uniforms as if they were dresses made by the greatest fashion houses: Goanga (Domnița Bârzotescu), Dina (Brătianu), Anda (Vasilescu), who turned all the boys' heads.

During those four years of high school, us classmates only got to know each other to the extent that we allowed it. I never spoke about my family's past or present, and I didn't ask anyone else about his or hers, either. My parents always had complete faith in how we chose our friends; we were three siblings and three cousins, forming a secure filter.

My classmates, broadly speaking, were: desk mates, more like conjoined twins, always together throughout the years; classmates who lived in the same area and went to school and home together; study buddies: for solving Math problems, prepare for exams, share cheat sheets; classmates you skipped class with; classmates you borrowed books from; classmates you danced or played card games with; classmates you smoked a cigarette with (we smoked in bathrooms); classmates you listened to music and went to concerts with; classmates who were in love; classmates who were an inexhaustible source of jokes, classmates you made discoveries with; classmates you spent your holidays with...

After graduation, we quietly parted ways, some moved to other places, in different periods. In the meantime, some of them have returned. It was only later that we saw each-other again and rediscovered one-another.

I can't help but remember a moment, 24 years ago, when a stranger who asked her if she was Ioana Casassovici's daughter stopped her in the street. Soon after, Irina came into my house with Ion Berindei. It was one of my first encounters with one of my former classmates who had left the country.

Back then, no one told us about the famous people who had been students of this high school between the two World Wars. Once again, I found out about them much later, much too late: Mircea Eliade, Victor Papahagi, Constantin Noica (my father's first cousin, who, in 1964, got out of prison), Barbu Brezianu, Adrian Gheorghiu (the future architect, who was my Perspective Drawing professor at the "Ion Mincu" Architecture Institute), Alexandru Ciorănescu, Haig Acterian and many others.

I recently went to an antiques shop and bought three issues of the "SPIRU C. HARET" high school magazine, *Vlăstarul*, from 1927 and 1928, where the above-mentioned students were published, along with the headmaster, Mr. St.V. Nanul, but also students from other high schools, such as Eugen Ionescu, who went to "Sf. Sava" high school. The magazine was founded in 1923 and the issue 1-2 from 1927 contains an article called "The Inauguration of our New High School Building", written by Ramis, that features the speeches held on October 16th, 1927, the day our building was inaugurated, by headmaster St.V. Nanul, lawyer Vlădescu-Olt on behalf of the high school's Committee, and finally, C. Angelescu, MD, the Minister for Culture. The author informs us that what followed was a great performance by the high school choir, conducted by professor Vasile Socoleanu. The festivities ended at 11 a.m. Ramis finishes the article with this statement: "What is *Spiru Haret* high school, with its building and Mr. St.V. Nanul? A creation and a name that shall go down to posterity".

Posterity remembers the names of many students who went to "Spiru C. Haret" high school. At that time, education sought to nourish a student's personality, and I quote from the magazine: "In high school, education is not focused on specific subjects, because we are not offering specialized courses. By means of these school subjects, we try to perfect the children's intelligence, sensibility and willpower for all their endeavors".[11] How clearly the high school's role is stated here, but unfortunately, no-one reads *Vlăstarul* anymore!

FREE TIME

For me, much more interesting than school, where my most burning questions went unanswered, was free time. Since it was mine, I spent it however I saw fit at that age, I chose my own activities and heroes, who lived in books. The first was the Count of Monte Cristo, who managed to employ a brilliant survival and revenge strategy, followed by many others.

I read day and night, in school, at the table, in the park, with a flashlight under the bedspread. Unfortunately, I didn't have a library at home. My parents left their books in the house they were forced to vacate quickly. Mother only managed to save a few poetry books that I read again and again through the years, discovering their true value with time: Baudelaire, Verlaine, Rilke.

The price of books back then, a joke by today's standards, was not cheap for everyone, much less for my family. The most beautiful gift was, indeed, a book! I still have books from the "Biblioteca pentru toți" collection, the one with pale blue covers, whose pages have since turned yellow and become brittle. But in those years, books truly had wings and were passed around freely among classmates and friends. Even grandma borrowed all of Mazo de la Roche's books from the "Yalna" series from a friend. The pages were coming apart, from the hundreds of hands that had turned them, they were held together by glue and tape, wrapped in paper that had once been white. But they were passed around, were lent and borrowed; there were deadlines for returning them... Of course, in our XXL-sized family, books would stay for much longer, as everyone on every floor, in every room, was reading them.

My readings, unfortunately, was not very organized. I read an author's works depending on whether the books happened to come my way, today *The Idiot*, a year later, *Crime and Punishment*, another couple of years after that, *The Brothers Karamazov*, *Demons* who knows when, and so on.

In Bucharest, there were French book fairs, and I never wanted to leave from those. At one point, they even sold books printed in France. Oh, the divine smell of the French language! A *livre de poche*, what a joy! How elegant those Skira edition tomes were! These were the greatest celebrations! Ever since then, I have a chronic hunger for books.

When I was a child, I would sometimes go on Sunday morning with my mother and my sister Ștefana to the Art Museum of the People's Republic of Romania, this is what was written at the entrance, but mother always said "we're going to the Palace!" It was, indeed, an imposing building, and later I found out it had actually been the palace of our kings. That is where I first saw an exhibition with Brâncuși's works. It was 1957. There was a black cloth above Constantin Brânuși's name, meaning that the artist had died. Mother was very emotional and she made us feel the same way. Among the pieces on display there were two heads of children, one bronze, the other stone. The bronze one was the head of a boy with eyes, nose, mouth and flap-ears, while the stone one was more like an egg. Mother explained the value of the stone one, which, despite not having a nose or a mouth, was the pure shape of a child's head! I didn't understand back then, but I did later. In school, our teacher asked what we did in our free time. "I went to the Brâncuși exhibition with my mother," I answered, and the teacher congratulated me. From there on I went to the museum many times, at first with my mother and sister, then by myself. I went to visit my friends: "The man with the blue hat"[12], the El Greco paintings[13], take a walk through the jade statue collection aquarium, see Grigorescu's soldiers who fought at Plevna in 1877, only to find out decades later that my own great-grandfather had been there as well.

I went to the Minovici Museum many times with my cousin Alexandra Juvara, when the cherries were ripe, that is, to Uncle Bobi, who was a good friend of her parents. First we ate cherries straight from the tree, then we visited the peacocks, the red fish in their tank, and finally, we went inside the museum, the red brick house built in 1930 in Tudor style. Uncle Bobi and his wife, Aunt Ligia, would show us an old book, a statue, a photograph. At one point, I heard whispers in the family: "Poor Bobi is desperate, they want to take his house and he doesn't know what's going to happen to the peacocks..." So that he wouldn't be thrown out of his house, his work of art, built only after he'd been to antique shops abroad to find every door, every window pane, every piece of stained glass, down to the very last doorknob, he was forced to donate it to the Communist state, and the Minovici family managed to stay in their home as custodians of the museum.

UTOPIAS

I took drawing and painting classes with Mrs. Laetitia Steriadi[14], but I stopped at one point, after it was decided at a family meeting that I was never going to get into the Belle Arte school, where there were very few spots available, and since I had such a bad social background, I stood no chance to make it. For me, studying art was a utopia! I couldn't risk becoming a "social parasite". My sister, who loved dancing, wanted to become a ballerina. For her, this wish was also a utopia!

Advised by a friend of my parents to learn a trade, since getting into University with my unhealthy social background was out of the question, I went to the local arts centre in Piața Kuibâșev (nowadays Piața Alexandru Lahovari) and took up a puppeteering class held by artists from the Țăndărică Theatre. It was a good experience, I learned a few things about how the shows at Țăndărică were staged, I met people devoted to puppeteering, I created and manufactured a few puppets myself for the show at the end of the class. I worked with great pleasure and interest.

SHINDIGS

Of course, on Saturdays I went to tea parties or "shindigs", as our little dance parties held in someone's house were called back then. The size of the "dance hall" didn't matter too much, we rolled the carpets, prepared refreshments to go with the times, we brought out the worst glasses, because there was a good chance they might break, and we called the neighbors. The music was very important, whoever owned a record player was invited everywhere, especially if they had "good music". For me, good music meant French music (Edith Piaf, Aznavour Bécaud, Brassens, later Adamo), and I still enjoy humming to it.

I went to parties with my sister who was a great rock and roll dancer, whereas I had two left feet. In high school I can't say I was a big fan of those parties, I dreamt of balls like the ones in Tolstoy's *War and Peace*, the one held by the Salina prince for his nephew, Tancredi, in Giuseppe di Lampedusa's novel, *The Leopard*, of dancing like Scarlett O'Harra in Rhett Butler's arms!

SCHOOL BREAKS

Us girls would only go on holiday in summer, my brother sometimes went in winter as well, to ski camps, but these camps were far too expensive for all three children. In summer, we went with our parents to the seaside, at Tataia, a neighborhood on the outskirts of Constanța, later to Costinești with our cousins and their mother, or we were left in the care of someone else we knew. It was not unusual for our parents to go on vacation with their children's friends. This is how, in summer, at the seaside, the locals' yards were full of people we knew, a habit that our generation also perpetuated, in the village 2 Mai.

I spent some lovely vacations with my cousin Alexandra and her parents in Retezat, in Maramureș and in the north of Moldavia. My aunt would give us a map and ask where we were, what the river we crossed was called, what the next city was. This is how I learned our country's geography and how to read a map. Today, I don't go anywhere without a map!

THE END OF HIGH SCHOOL

I spent my school years roughly between two historical events: the death of Stalin in 1953 and that of J.F. Kennedy in 1963. From Stalin's death I only remember the silence that paralyzed the entire city, the funeral music sounding from the speakers and the joy disguised as sorrow of those around me. The television broadcasts following the American president's assassination featured clips from his life and that of his family, which depicted a different world, the free world. The scene in which the First Lady bends over J.F.K. after he'd been shot and her pink suit is suddenly stained with blood is still very sharp in my memory.

My school years spanned between the death of a Soviet tyrant and that of a democratic president of the United States of America, between the frost and the long-awaited thaw that was short-lived. I swung between two worlds, the inner world (of thoughts and utopias) and the outer world (of various traumas), forever scared of taking one wrong step that, like walking a tightrope, was potentially fatal. My real role models, my heroes from the books I read at home, were the complete opposite of those in *Tânăra gardă*, positive heroes in textbooks, young people who had built the Bumbești-Livezeni railroad. The artists I admired didn't paint field engines, furnaces, plant chimneys. The role models put forward by Communist propaganda were fake: workers who exceeded their quota, female tractor drivers, intellectuals who praised the regime's achievements. *Mademoiselle Pogany* didn't fit in the Communist pantheon.

In those years there was a period of liberalization that gave us hope. In 1964, political prisoners started being released. That was when I realized my parents had had friends too, but they had been imprisoned. They were like shadows when they got out, but being people with exceptional morals, they started over. Since then, every Christmas, my parents invited Dinu Noica for dinner, and he told my mother, to her great delight, that he could "read her fortune in *sarmale*[5]"! After 1989, I read many books written by prison martyrs and I realized we had true heroes, unfortunately not so widely known. Today, many of them have left us.

I decided to sit the entrance exam for Architecture, it seemed a compromise between a technical University and an arts University, and there were obviously more spots available. I took private drawing lessons every week. In Bucharest, there were private schools dedicated to preparing future University students.

Most of my classmates knew what they wanted to be. In our last year of high school, we had grown more mature. In that time, social background lost its relevance.

After taking the Baccalaureate exam and getting my diploma, I never set foot in my high school again. I didn't go to the alumni meeting in December; I didn't see any of my former teachers. I had finished a chapter of my life and I never looked back.

---

5 Traditional dish made of cabbage leaves or vine leaves stuffed with ground meat.

Der Weg ist das Ziel or The Journey is a destination – Roland Filippi

———

WE ALL REMEMBER THINGS WE did for the first time in our lives: the time we first saw X or Y, our first love, our first time travelling, our first car, and so on and so forth. It is very natural that these memories awaken various feelings in us, such as pride, satisfaction, or even tenderness. The list can go on forever. Most certainly, all these memories come with a feeling of nostalgia, every time we revisit them.

I too feel nostalgia for the years I spent in Spiru Haret! The decision to go to this particular high school was the first independent decision I ever took for my future.

I spent my first seven years of school in Elementary School no. 23 (Silvestru) and at the Dimitrie Cantemir high school. Both schools had been chosen by my mother, who had a very dominant personality and whose central desire in life was to do her best for her children. I ended up in Silvestru because my sister, who is 2 years older than me, attended the same school. Back then; Silvestru was split in two, a school for boys and one for girls. Both schools had the same headmistress and the same teachers. Because the headmistress was a friend of mother's, it was self-evident that I was to also attend Silvestru. I quickly found out that it is not a good idea to attend a school where the headmistress knows your parents well, especially if your older sister also attends the same school. More so if she is a better student and the best behaved student in her class. Someone like me would only have to lose in such a situation. Any misdemeanor was immediately reported to my parents and I was always second to my sister, who was an exemplary student. The single positive aspect that came out from the time spent in Silvestru was that it was there that I first met Mircea Sebastian and we became life-long friends.

In my fifth grade, I moved to Cantemir. We lived on Gemeni Street and we were only 20-30 meters away from the school. I soon discovered that this closeness was also very detrimental to me. All my teachers would pass by my house on their way to catch the tramway or the bus. It often happened that they met my mother on the street and they would fill her in on the latest news regarding my activity as a not so nice student.

These negative experiences led me to the conclusion that a school as far away from home as possible is, in my case, a necessity. Thus, at the end of seventh grade, I came to my parents with the proposition of taking the admission exam at another high school, more precisely Spiru Haret. My mother didn't think it was a very good idea and expressed her wish that, if I insisted on changing schools, I should instead go to Centrala School (it was named "Zoia Kosmodemianskaia" back then), where my sister had gone. I objected vehemently. Centrala was back then a school mostly populated by girls, with only 20-25% of students being boys, didn't have any good sports teams and, another disadvantage, I would again be compared to my sister, which was not favorable, as I mentioned earlier. It took me a few months to convince my mother. Her discussion with Mrs. Filip, the mother of Kuki Filip, a colleague of mine from Cantemir, worked to my advantage, as he also wanted to attend Spiru. He fought a similar battle. Like me, he also didn't register in the "good student" category and his older sister, who also attended Cantemir, was a veritable "star". Zincuta – may God rest her soul – was terribly good at school, she was the brightest in her class and, unlike Kuki, she was appreciated by all teachers. The similarities in our situations led us to form an alliance and we ultimately convinced our mothers.

We took the exam in the summer of 1960 and in September, we began our career as Spiru high school students. Almost every morning, for four years, I would leave my house at 7 o'clock in the morning, cross the Gemeni Street, and turn right on Viitorului Street. The Vasile Alecsandri Elementary School was right on the corner, and right next to it was the old, decrepit boyar manor which housed the neighborhood library. The Demetrescu sisters lived on the other side of the street: Noni, Anca and Pupe. Noni was older, Anca was a colleague of my sister's and Pupe was Zincuta's colleague. After about 100 meters, I would reach the intersection of Viitorului with Salcamilor. The intersection is a small plaza that has been one of our most beloved places to hang out in our spare time. I played football on the street here for as long as I lived in Romania, even during my college years. It was naturally understood that Kuki and Mircea would play with me every time. A few steps away, on 37 Viitorului Street, I would enter the yard, walk up to the back and gently knock on the windowpane. Kuki would come out with his case in his hand and still chewing on the last bites of breakfast. We would hurry out of the yard and down Viitorului Street. Before the intersection with Vasile Lascar Street we would make a left on Luca Stroici and walk up to Popa Chitu Church. This section of our journey was not very spectacular, aside from the part when we would pass by Dan Davidescu's house, a former colleague of mine from Cantemir, whose mother sold borsch, and we often bought it from her. We didn't know anyone else on this street. But we would get to Popa Chitu, where the street formed a circle around the church, which was an ideal spot for bicycle racing. It was our neighborhood velodrome. Cars passed by very rarely, so we organized timed races. Mircea Sebastian once had an accident there and banged his eye on the bicycle bell. There was another attraction in the church roundabout: the Embassy of Indonesia. We would always stop in front of it and look at the pictures posted on the glass display. They were pictures from the games of the national badminton team, a sport that was not very well known in Romania at the time. The intersection with Maria Rosetti Street was a few steps away from the church. Mircea would come from the left and, after crossing the street, we would also meet up with Serban Manolescu. The four of us would walk down Logofat Luca Stroici Street to the intersection with Alexandru Donici. On the corner there was a state institution, and although I don't know what its role was, it must have been important, because there was a small glass box with a policeman placed near its entrance. Whenever he was not dosing off on his chair or talking on the telephone, the policeman would stand erect on the sidewalk and watch us pass by. After the policeman's booth, our good mood would start withering away. We would start talking about school and about the day's schedule. After a short round of questions, we would survey our group's standing in regards to homework. We would feel relieved to find out that the others haven't done much as well. I must confess that there were days when one or more of us would admit that they haven't done any of their homework. The situation would be assessed; we would evaluate how intensive preparation for school had been, if we still had some writing to do. When the majority would admit that they had indeed prepared very little for the test at hand, the whole group would rest assured. Nobody felt alone. It was comforting to know that others would later face the same hardship: a blank page before them and little inspiration. What could they write on it? Starting from early on in the morning, we were already confronting some problems for which we lacked the necessary preparations.

We would keep discussing until we would reach the intersection with Vasile Lascar. This was the point in which a decision had to be made. We could make a left on Vasile Lascar and a right at Piata Italiana in order to go to school or cross the street, go down Batistei Street and make a left on Otetari, which would take us directly to school. Deciding on the exact route rested upon how prepared we felt for the day at hand. If while on the way there the idea of skipping class that day would come up, we would choose this option. On the corner of Otetari with Italiana, there was a little park with two benches, and we could rest there, to once again evaluate our situation and reach the final conclusion. More often than not, we would lose heart and ultimately decide to go to school, like lambs to the slaughter; other times, we could not reach a unanimous opinion and we would split the group. It also happened sometimes that we all felt like skipping school and we would be joined by other colleagues with similar intentions. A decision would be made.

If we would decide against going to school, the day's schedule had to be put in order. With mothers at home, going home was not a feasible option. It differed on every occasion, but we would sometimes propose spending the first part of the day at one of our colleague's place, while both his parents were at work. There, unhindered by any parental supervision, we could deepen our knowledge in the field of poker. We also liked going to the cinema. Back then; almost all movie theatrs had matinees programs. From

April until June, and then from September until October, starting times for matinees varied. We would spend the time until we could go and see the movie in Ioanid or Icoanei Park.

Things were more difficult during the cold months, when the possibilities of killing time from 7:30 to 10:00 were drastically limited. The only alternative for these early hours was the I.C. Frimu Cinema, on 6 Martie Boulevard. This cinema had two advantages: the first matinee started at 8:30 and movies played on continuously. When it rained, snowed or it got extremely cold, the cinema guaranteed 3 or 4 hours of heating to its customers. As life goes, all good things must have a downside. The great downside of the cinema was that their program mainly consisted of communist films, and often enough, not only were they communist, but they were also Russian. Sometimes, during the film, I would regret having skipped class. *Ceapaev* or *Poemul pedagogic* twice in a row were a hard punishment to bear. Not to speak of *Eruptia*, *Avalansa* or *Lupeni 29*, Romanian productions, which were a veritable torture to sit through.

As it can be seen, I have gone through hard times during high school as well!

Thanks to Google Earth, I still can, from 1,600 km away, make the trip from my old house to my high school. I do this often and take great pleasure in it, because it is a part of my life I remember with joy!

Defeating the Communist System
– Ladislau G. Hajos*
Provided in English by Ladislau G. Hanjos

––––

FOR 35 YEARS THREE MONTHS and 20 days I lived in Romania, under a ruling monarchy, socialism and communism. I was not allowed to speak freely, without reprisals, about any topics. In fact, whenever I wanted to speak with my father about any sensitive subject we had to take long walks in the park. We did this because we knew that our two-room apartment (not two bedrooms) was bugged via the telephone by the secret police (securitate in Romania). What a relief to speak, read, write and walk freely as a Hungarian Jew born in Romania.

The story of my generation is the history of postwar Romania. Most of those who passed the exam of Baccalaureate at the "Spiru Haret" high school in 1964 were born in 1946. We represent what the West calls the baby boomer generation. We are the children that came to the world in large numbers after the war as a natural reaction to life, the joy of living after the massacres, the immense fighting and death camps. We are the first generation of children of the Cold War.

I started first grade in September 1953. I was seven years old. Nineteen fifty-three was a tumultuous year for me. This was the year I learned I was Jewish. My parents kept this a secret because the war recently ended and my father wanted us to assimilate for protection. My mother's tongue is Hungarian and I spoke very little Romanian. My parents were born in Transylvania in 1911, yes that Transylvania as popularized by Dracula. Transylvania was part of Hungary at the time of their birth. They left

Hungary and moved to Romania because Jews in Hungary were deported and Romania did not yet deport Jews.

My full name is Laszlo Hajos. Ladislau is the Romanian translation of Laszlo. Laci or Loţi is the abbreviation for Ladislau. In the early years of communism, my father believed in assimilation into the new regime as a form of protection. Therefore, I was given a typical Romanian middle name Gheorghe. No matter where I was, I was a foreigner. Hungary is the only country where my names can be pronounced correctly.

In first grade I spoke very little Romanian, because at home we only spoke Hungarian. My mother never learned to speak Romanian well. I now speak Hungarian, Romanian, French and English.

I had very good teachers who definitely contributed to my training. I will share some memories about these teachers:

Constatin Necşulescu was nicknamed "the Beast". The reason is understandable. If somebody did something he did not like he started screaming angrily with a particularly strong voice, "Ordinary Beast! Beast!" But the Beast was an excellent history teacher. He was well educated and thought well. I liked history, especially ancient Greek history. When Beast called me, or any of the boys, to the blackboard, he would ask us to put our nose between his fingers. When our nose was placed firmly between his two fingers, he would squeeze. During winters if I had cold, and the Beast's fingers became wet, he said laughing: "I am not disgusted." I was guaranteed the highest grade, even though I did not know the lesson that well. Later I found out he was gay, but at that time I knew nothing about this. This is also why the girls got lower grades even thought they knew the lesson well.

Radulescu was a Romanian language teacher. He was very good, but very severe. He was very elegant. Every day came to school wearing a different outfit. At that time everyone was modestly dressed. Good fabric for a suit was difficult to find. I always wondered how he was able to find and afford some many nice things. After a year or two of teaching, he disappeared. At the time his disappearance was a mystery.

Years later, when I was in college, my father asked; "Do you know Radulescu?"

I was surprised to hear his name. My father replied that he was working at his place of business. He was arrested for homosexuality in the trial of Gabriel Popescu and other ballet dancers.

When he was released from a three year prison sentence, he could not find employment. He was prohibited from working in the field of education. My father felt sorry for him and hired him. My father was chief engineer of the Enterprise 3 Insulation, a construction company that he founded in 1948.

Grosu was a very strict teacher of Russian. Russian language for him was the most important subject matter in school. He gave very low grades. I could not suffer this subject, but I learned everything by heart. At that time, I had a very good memory. For example, I learned a poem in Russian, which I can recite even today, although I am not sure I know what it means. Because we were all terrorized by Grosu we decided to pull a prank. Propane tanks were difficult to find in the 1960s. I do not know who had the idea to advertise that Grosu had a large supply to sell. We posted, throughout the whole neighborhood, announcements on the walls stating: " I sell affordable propane tanks. Call this number between the hours of 12am and 4am." The phone number posted on the advertisement was Grosu's. The next day a very angry Russian teacher came to class, thundering and screaming. He was very sleepy. Grosu never had the satisfaction of discovering the authors of the advertisement.

We were under scrutiny by the Securitate (secret police) and/or the government. By the way, the Securitate was one of the largest in the Eastern Bloc. It was the main suppressor of popular dissension. The Securitate frequently and violently quashed political disagreement. Once I picked up our phone to make a call. I could hear a short click signaling that the recording device had started. As I always liked to take things apart, I did that with the old-fashioned rotary type phone. Yes, there was a little device present. I left it there untouched. As a result of the device being present, we needed to be very careful about what we said over the phone. From time to time some telephone repairman stopped by. I had the firm belief that he was installing or replacing devices in our phone.

My mother had a brother, in Arad, and my father, a brother in Timisoara. Those are two towns in Transylvania. Telephoning was expensive so they wrote letters to each other. Once my father got a letter from his brother Iosif. Iosif addressed the envelope but the content started with "Dear Mary" in someone else's handwriting. I guess the contents of the letters were switched during inspection. Although we did not do or say anything wrong we had to be very careful with our discussions.

With all of these impediments we were able to survive. We lived relatively well mainly due to the effort of my parents. They worked extremely hard to protect and shield me. All I had to do was study. Life in Communist Romania teaches one lesson very well: how to beat the system! I carry this lesson with me to the present day.

Monologue - Ioan Ioardachescu

———

... A FEW MONTHS AGO, before the wonderful meeting celebrating half a century, I had written a few in order to remind my colleagues of who I am, and of course I have changed since then! The idea of writing a book about US is wonderful, but complicated. Why? We were little and it's difficult to accurately portray times back then, at least, in my opinion...

I will begin putting my presentation on paper – I don't know how interesting it might be, but I didn't come up with the idea to write this book, so you must bear with me...

I was born during the heavy winter of 1946, in a town in Moldova called Focsani (which I call *Focsani le Deux Eglises* jokingly), a town, which would soon plunge into starvation, like most of Moldova. Luckily for us, grandpa, who was an officer in the cavalry, had some money saved and took my father to travel to Transylvania, where they bought corn, wheat, and other foods, which allowed us to struggle through these hard times... but this was later on... for the moment, I was born – I was the first living child to be born in my family after the war, and they weren't sure I would survive (I was so very small and fragile at birth), and, after an old ritual, they had to sell me by passing me through the window to a mother whose children had all survived. And so I was sold to a neighbor, Mrs. Mischi, who had four children, all of them alive and well. I must diverge in order to say a few words about this Mrs. Mischi: she was an old lady, who during summer, found it impossible to sleep inside the house, due to her being overweight and having smoked from early on. So she would sit on the porch and doze off on a chair all night long, sighing deeply and panting. My father would come home from the restaurant where he sang, early at dawn, and, when he would pass by Madame Mischi, he would jokingly cough loudly. Madame Mischi would jump out of her chair startled and thus their conversation would begin:

"Good day to you, Madame Mischi…"
"*Moi* Gheorghe, damn you, you scared *moi*…"
"Oh, were you sleeping? How are you, Madame Mischi?"
"How could I be? I'm sleeping on *di* air…"
They would chat about this or that, after which father would furtively produce a small bottle of liqueur from his pocket, especially set aside for her.
"Very well, Madame Mischi, I'm off to bed, good day." And he would then add, while turning back to her:
"Oh, I almost forgot, this is for you!"
"You shouldn't have, Gica!"
"I know, Madame, but I insist… good day!"

This was my adopted "mother", however I only know her from stories I was told, as she died when I was very little.

I do remember one of the four brothers, Heim – I saw him coming to Bucharest for several years in a row, to celebrate grandpa and my birthdays on the 7th of January, on Saint Joan – Heim, my "brother", called this saint Johanan… He came to Bucharest a few times more and they left for Israel afterwards: he would always come in January to see us, especially grandpa, and he called me "brother Puiu". There was a life-long friendship between them, as Madame Mischi had been the same age as my grandma. I remember Heim: as short guy, with a bald spot centered on his head and surrounded by tuffs of hair; he had a wide smile that covered his entire face, and would always bring me something when he came to see us, and he used to hoist me up and sit me on his knees, caressing my hair and saying: "brother Puiu".

… This was the town where I was born. My father sang at the "Steiner", a large restaurant, famous before the war and a little while after, until…

I also can't forget my neighbor, who was the same age as me, Eitel – mother said we were so alike! Famine had settled in and she would pop her head from behind the fence:

"Puiuuu, do you want to play?"

"Mother, Etica is here, let her in!"

"No, you'll fight again!" mother would say.

"No, we won't!"

"Alright then."

The story would go like this: Etica was poor and she was always hungry – there were hard times! Eitel would come to see me, we would play some, and after a while she would inevitably ask:

"Puiu, let's play 'kitchen'!"

"Mother, give us something to play 'kitchen' with!"

Mother understood and would bring us some food, and we would both start eating. Mother was happy, because I was a bit of a picky eater – Eitel on the other hand would eat ravenously; I would sit and look at her in surprise, afterwards I would grab a spoon and hit her over the head with it, telling her to eat nicely. Etica would cry, mother would take her gently by the hand and out of the year, with her plate in her hands. The scene went on daily, until one day, when mother told my brother and I that we are leaving to Bucharest.

Of course, I didn't know what that meant, not even that I had to say goodbye to Eitel. Sometimes I wonder where she is now.

This was what childhood was like for us, those born in 1946!

I cannot forget the winter we spent in Focsani. My grandfather had a sort of brother-in-law, who still had ten coachmen, with carriages during the summer and sleighs in winter. Grandfather would advise him on horses, he knew a lot on this subject because he had been in the Rosiori division. I still remember the voice of the coachman who came to us, a bit harsh, strong, but warm, and his build, towering like a mountain: "Come on, Miss Chief, this boy has to get a tad of fresh air, just like the house! (That is how he called mother, "Miss Chief", because grandpa had been chief of the division)

And make it quick, it's going to get dark soon!" If the coachman said so, we would definitely go to a village near Focsani, where we had sons-in-law and the coachman had relatives! We would go, my mother would tell us that we would first go to our sons-in-law and then we would see the coachman's relatives, and come evening, red in our cheeks and wrapped in furs, we would return to our home to sit around the white terracotta fireplace… and grandpapa with his arms and his twisted moustache … and the piano at which mother would sit and play some little thing or the other, who knows what? But it was all-good, the war was over and they, the elders, had nephews, their eldest son had come back in one piece from being imprisoned…

And we left Focsani, and arrived to a place that wasn't mine, but bit by bit…

I remember there were still carriages around in Bucharest in the winter of 1954. During that heavy winter, the army, on sleighs, brought the food supplies for my neighborhood, between Chirigiu and Academia Militara! They brought warm bread…

See, we are the generation which came immediately after the war, I don't know if I can say much about the atmosphere in Bucharest back then, a city I discovered bit by bit, later and which, I can declare with joy, belongs to me now (I can say that this is partly due to my job!).

As Toparceanu would say:

I lived for a while …
… on Izvor, down from 2 by the Arsenal,
My neighbors were a tailor, an old lady and a baggage man!

The tailor and the old lady are real, the baggage man was not, but he was added to keep the rhyme! The building was diagonally opposite to Bulandra Theater, over the river (Dambovita), and so, during the evening, my parents would walk with me through the city center!

Times were peculiar! Rumors circulated later, towards the stabilization, about various odd things happening, we were small and our parents would always say: "Darlings, never tell anyone what we talk about in our home!" And I lived with this for my entire life! Until the zavera[6]! But let us come back to the first years of our generation and the atmosphere of our Bucharest...

A city that had recently gone through a war, the ravages of which I saw throughout my youth: an immense number of crippled men, men walking in crotches, a city full of gaping holes between houses, the results of bombings...

We walked down Magheru Boulevard, Victoriei and on the 6 Martie boulevard and my grandfather and father would say: "Look, there used to be a hotel here, look, this is where a good friend of mine lived, he was killed in..." and he would tell me the name of a battlefront on the East.

I remember that on the 6 Martie Boulevard, where an apartment building was built, situated diagonally opposite to the City Hall, where Cismigiu Restaurant had been, during my childhood, there was a large hole, where a sort of improvised sweets shop was erected, and it is where I had whipped cream topped ice cream for the first time! Across the street from the Athenee Palace Hotel, another hole after the bombing! And this was the state in which Bucharest found itself after the war...

One day grandpa dressed me up nicely, took my hand and said: "We will go to a place and please don't ask me anything there, we will come back home and have a talk afterwards." We visited the Throne Room, we saw the thrones and other rooms of the palace, which I do not remember... but I remember the Throne Room!

Grandfather had tears in his eyes, but that was not something to impress me or unsettle me, but the fact that at one point he squeezed my hand so firmly... I still remember it. Grandfather had been a member of the Royal Guard, I only discovered this later on... Another time he took me on Campineanu Street. Here I would meet my friends when we went downtown. How was I to know that it had once been the headquarters of a Lodge? I only found out after the revolution!

The Bucharest of my childhood...

---

6 Name given to the Revolution of 1821

Afterwards we lived more uptown, on Dealul Spirii. We used to catch tramway no. 7, and go towards Puisor, in Bragadiru, to the beer factory.

It wasn't very comfortable, we didn't have a bathroom, the toilet was shared, and it was an outhouse... When I grew up, I was already in high school, it was there, near the beer factory, where I bought my first pair of black socks! Back there, you could find all arrays of worker's colors, except for black!

But how fragrant Bucharest was!

I will never forget autumns with their smell of smoke from the dry leaves, I will never forget the first theater show I saw in Bulandra, with the maestro Cazaban, the father of our colleague.

Neither will I forget the Army Theater, up on the firefighters' hill, on 13 Septembrie, face to face with today's Comanduirea, where my father sang and where I met the famous actors, on the knees of which I grew up: Mircea Crisan, Ion Porsila, Igorov, Horia Serbanescu and Radu Zaharescu.

I also cannot forget the wonderful ballet maestro, who later worked for the Savoy Theater, an extraordinarily beautiful woman, and a Mrs. Teo Covaly, in the arms of whom I stood all the way from Focsani to Bucharest, when I left on the train of the Army Theater in a tour across the country, as well as the ballet maestro Sandu Feyer, who could step dance and taught me how to dance, and Mr. Fogel, the conductor of the orchestra. The latter was conductor of the Army Ensemble for nine years, and afterwards for the UTC Ensemble and had a daughter my age, with which I used to run around through the theater... Does anybody remember them? Does anybody remember the people who enchanted us with their presence, with their beauty? Mircea Crisan died in a clinic in Germany, poor and alone...

I would like to only remember the beautiful Bucharest, not the city where my mother used to say: "Darlings, please, never tell anybody about what we talk in our house!" And, thank God, they had what to talk about! The times were hard, but I was lucky to have a wonderful family, a mother and father who cared for us, who spun a web of infinite warmth around me, like a silk cocoon, which never allowed us to come into contact with the strife they were going through, the daily struggle, the deep sigh at the end of the day: "Thank God this day is happily over!". I wonder how many sacrifices they made.

I remember that one autumn; I went with Toni, my brother, father and uncle Grigore, mother's eldest brother, in order to buy boots: winter was coming! All went well, we entered a shop in the 6 Martie boulevard, we try them on, we buy them, and we stop at the bar to drink to make them last long! The boys drank a beer, we children had lemonade, we stood at while at Gambrinus, near Cismigiu and it was raining when we went outside to go home! Uncle set towards Colentina, we went down the boulevard to take the tramway towards Chirigiu, behind the Military Academy. Heavy rain poured down on us! When we got home, Toni raised one foot and cried: "Father, look!" the soles were swollen, they were full of water. The soles were made out of cardboard! I looked at mine and they were the same! My father was livid: the money was spent, we were barefoot, and winter was knocking at the door. The boots had two Russian letters on their labels. They were the aid sent by the Big Brother in the East, the future of Red Europe!

I would better remember the beautiful moments of the time, in that city of Bucharest, the city of my childhood and our childhood, as the poet said: *we are all chained together, on the obscure streets of Byzantium!* As a good friend of mine who sadly passed away, God rest his soul, the actor Coti Praida, who lived near the Athenaeum once said. We saw each other often, as I passed by on my way towards the Meeting, and he sat on the "La Mamma" Terrace in the yard of the Jockey Club, looking at the legs of the ladies who walked by, with an unbridled thirst in his eyes. When he would see me, he would cry: "Come on in, and remember, LIFE IS BEAUTIFUL, DON'T SQUANDER IT!"

... Mister Coti! He would pass by "Casa Universitarilor", where we would meet the actor Eusebiu Stefanescu, we would drink water and sparkling wine, reminiscing times at the theater in Ploiesti, or how they met Petrache Tutea. This was how he liked to call him, Petrache. Or the mischief he made with Lupu Buznea, or Teica, at the theater, or Caragiu, or how rehearsals with Hary Eliad went and how funny they were on the train to Bucharest, when they were commuting. This is how I met Cavuri, I met Ciupercescu again, who was also an actor at the Ploiesti Theater.

When Mr. Hary became director of the Jewish Theater, he took everybody with him to his theater, even if they weren't Jewish, even if they didn't speak a word of Yiddish, but they had been friends since they were young! I knew this Bucharest, later on in all honesty, but it is nonetheless our Bucharest, the Bucharest of our generation! Yes, life is beautiful, so why should I remember the less beautiful things from my years in high school?

You were talking about Matei, Tuchi, the high school headmistress. I didn't even remember she was named Teodorescu, and I probably didn't saw her more than two times in my whole life, and so her existence means nothing to me! She could have been a "comrade", doubtless, but who didn't try to hide or save themselves during those times?

I want to return to the Bucharest of my childhood years, of my pre-adolescence, because back then there were still wonderful people around, of a certain bohemian conviction, people who still gave Bucharest a "reminiscence of fragrance"!

Of course, I look at it now, through a slightly gray film of nostalgia, because it was a city I saw and which got imprinted into my memory as full of the holes of the bombings, and who never managed to recover, as Prague did, for example, because we were imbeciles, kneeling, obedient or cowardly…

I will never forget the city that became mine, with autumns smelling of the smoke of burning leaves, with the wine factory across Krateyl Circus, where the National Theater is now, with the Cartea Romaneasca Library on Calea Victoriei, across Tanase Theater, which they torched because it belonged to the bourgeois-boyar past, running through the city with father in order to get the Winter Celebration tree, standing in an immense line, raising ourselves to the tip of our toes, over other "queuers" in order to get some tree decorations, but also with the summer vacations with the theater! Sweet mother, what delights! A train leaves…

Or the pavilions in Carol Park, in the shape of letters C and E, standing for Carol and Elena, torched for reminding them of the monarchy!

But how can I forget my colleagues, my dear neighbors and colleagues, Liviu Lustman, from doctor Lustman's family, all from Focsani, about which I was to discover a short while before their final departure that they had a daughter who Liviu had named Papina. One day mother told me all about Papina, not the girl in the Lustman family, but the real Papina. In Focsani, there lived a slightly odd fiddler named Stefan, and everybody knew him for the madman he was, hence the saying: "Why do you take it this way, like Stefan the Mad?" Stefan had named his kobza Papina. Nothing special, until one day, the other fiddlers wanted to make a more serious joke on Stefan, who was a poor fiddler, and not a very good musician, and who would always go hungry. They put a sum of money together, and went to a more highly regarded restaurant and asked the owner to prepare some fried cabbage. One of them stole Stefan's kobza, and they went to the restaurant, broke his instrument and put it in the cabbage. Stefan, upset that he had lost his kobza, was walking through the city, when he met one of the accomplices. He listened to the misfortune of his colleague and, to make him somewhat forget his sorrows, invites him to a drink at the restaurant. They have some wine and he invites Stefan to have some cabbage with him… to his great surprise, they serve him splinters in his dish! Laughs and snickers all around, until they finally told him: "Hey, that's your Papina on the cabbage!" The whole business ended with a party among friends and a new Papina for Stefan. This is how I found out about the story and, as soon as I saw Liviu, I asked him about his Papina and he confirmed the story.

How could I forget Bibi Strutinschi who, after high school, went to Constanta and became a ship captain; I also met his grandfather: he was a huge Ukrainian, a former hunter and owner of forests, who went on bear hunts sporting only a knife! I even saw the knife! It was a kind of sword, albeit a bit short, but a sword nonetheless! I cannot forget him: he drank entire kilograms of tea every day and the most impressive thing about it was that he drank it right after he would take the kettle off the stove! Hot! Boiling hot!

Or the Slabacu neighbors, three brothers, younger than I was, but with whom I played in front of the houses, on Tudor Vladimirescu Boulevard. Mr. Slabacu was a citizen of Bucharest who had perhaps owned a small business in the city, which was taken away from him. He had not, for one moment, given up on his "freedom", on his revolt towards socialist integration, and so he engaged in various businesses, he had a small stand in Obor, and in the yard of his house he would produce concrete tubes for sewage, and concrete fences.

I will never forget the sumacs in our yard, neither will I forget the mulberry tree which we used to climb, and from which we came back home covered in smears up to our ears, with black mulberry prints on our shirts, a sort of violet dye which never came off. Does this color name still exist: mulberry black? I know of pitch black, cinema black, but mulberry black? When I see our colleague Firu, I will ask him!

I will also never forget our two colleagues Armine and the future Mrs. Architect Daniela Catanescu (how blue her eyes are!), or the Mitropolit Something-something Street we walked to for one kilometer in order to slide down the slope with our sleighs, a street close to the State Foundry, from which we came back home frozen and soaked to the skin! Or evenings when I would come home with father from the theater, after we crossed the Dambovita River on the Izvor Bridge, we would sometimes stop at the corner bar, were they grilled some formidable minced meat rolls, the best in all of Bucharest. The small pub was like "La Cocosatul" today, where father would meet and talk to his friends and I would listen carefully to all their discussions and jokes.

It was the postwar Bucharest of our generation, and of others, it was the Bucharest of our parents and our friends.

Or, for instance, Bucharest in summer (I was more grown up then), when I would go with my parents to the Cina Garden, where father would sing sometimes, and where we would go to listen to Ionci Korosi (I don't remember how to write his name!), Bebe Prisada or the famous Sergiu Malagamba, who dressed in such a peculiar manner! They always came to our table whenever they took a break and they would chat with my parents, exchange music sheets, or share news in the musical industry.

At the same restaurant, there was a restaurant for artists, a closed circle, only for them, were one of the serious clients (I mean permanent clients) was maestro Calboreanu, a wine professional, not a mere amateur. On one occasion, towards the end of the evening, he calls the waiter for the check: "Of course, maestro, two steaks, three water bottles and seven wine bottles" "No, six wine bottles!" "Why, Heaven Forbid, maestro, here are the bottles, there are seven of them! Would I ever dare to do such a thing to you?" "Six, here are the corks!" Laughter followed from all the colleagues present and the moment became history for the people in the trade – my good friend actor Eusebiu Stefanescu told it to me.

It is not less true that tragedies were unfolding in the same Bucharest – families left without a father. 100 kilometers away from us was Pitesti, with its tragedies about which I found later, to my utter horror. Four years ago, I was in Pitesti, building a house and I asked the person who was in the car with me to tell me where the sinister prison had been: "Right there!" This is how I found out that the horrible prison had been erected in the middle of the city, between apartment buildings!

There was also the tragedy of some families who would be suddenly left without jobs – parents who would wait for their paycheck at the end of the month or the letter informing them they had been fired.

I remember a song that was in fashion during those times, *Pleaca-un tren...* (A train is leaving...), do you remember it?

Leaving at dawn,
A train sets out towards the blue sea
And you leave with it, my love
Even now, I see your white handkerchief
Blowing in the wind...

Romantic, isn't it? Actually, the words hid great sadness behind them, a tragedy – not a grave one, but still, a tragedy – of several families who were relocated from Bucharest, forced to move to Constanta, without any prior notice, with all relatives, carrying all their possessions or none at all, as fast as they could. This is how the Fantasio Theater in Constanta came to be, when half of the Army Theater's actors had to leave Bucharest.

Sasa, Diadia Vania, and the entire balalaika ensemble left then, people on whose knees I had spent my childhood.

Or the tragedy of a lady who lived on the corner of the street, who had to teach French to make ends meet and who had a son who was older than, I and who was not permitted to apply to University due to his unhealthy origin and sold lottery tickets. One day, I witnessed a funny scene: I was queued for some thing or another, and it was a considerably long queue, and the French lady finally reaches her turn and the store clerk starts a conversation with her. Shortly after, cries from the public are heard: "Come on, quit your yapping, we've been sitting here for hours!" to which the store clerk replied: "Shut it! I'm talking to a lady, the only lady among you lot!" Complete silence. I will never forget this!

Or the tragedy of my teacher's daughter; he had been a high school teacher before the war. She was taken out of the exam room in college – the reason was that her father was already an intellectual; they didn't need another in the family! She got a job in a factory and later, following the recommendations of the party and the youth organization, she took evening classes to finish college.

Years passed and it was finally time for me to apply to high school. But where to apply? Father discussed this in the family and, probably following the advice of Horia Serbanescu or Zaharescu, they decided I should go to Spiru, although there were many other high schools closer to home. This is how I met all of you, my colleauges!

It was "wonderful", especially during winter; during the years we started school early in the morning. I left home while it was still dark outside, through the snow, and I had to walk up to the corner of T Vladimirescu Boulevard, wait for the no. 15 tramway, and, backpack in hand, I would catch on to a rail together with the working men and women who, like me, would crowd into the tramway which took them off to another day of work for the development of the socialist motherland, the one that had recently abolished the bread and meet ration card!

Speaking of ration cards! Let me tell you a story from back when almost everything was rationed using a card: bread, meat, clothes, anything… One day, a group of architects from the Bucuresti Project leave work; among them, a guy who had a great sense of humor and who was always full of ideas: Popescu nicknamed "Lac". And so, Popescu-Lac, together with his colleagues, on their way to Carul cu Bere Pub, since they had just gotten their paychecks, were walking down Lipscani Street, chatting about this or that. While going around a sea of people who had gathered in front of a shop, Lac says:

"Will you buy me a beer if, in all this commotion, I manage to get the clerk to follow me outside the shop?"

"Are you crazy? Can't you see how many people are waiting?"

Finally, they agreed. Popescu walks inside the shop, makes his way through the ladies sitting in queue, and after a lot of trouble to get to the front of the line, cries to the clerk:

"Mister, I want a lilac colored shirt, no. 46!"

"I'm sorry, young man, we don't have them in lilac!"

"But I saw them in the window!"

"We don't have them, next!"

"But you do! Why won't you sell me one?"

I must describe Lac: nearsighted, tall as a telegraph post, a bit hunchback, and very thin.

"Where did you see them?"

"In the window!"

Visibly out of his wits, the clerk gives in:

"Come on then, show me!"

The clerk follows Lac, and he shows him a shirt.

"But that one is WHITE!"

"Well, have you never seen white lilac before?"

Luckily for Lac, he could run fast!

But, I diverge. In the tramway, I would go down the hill of the Rahova beer factory (how was I to knw that I was a neighbor of the nephew of the former owner of the factory?), I would reach the Mitropolie, and then the Brancovenesc Hospital, a historical monument which he who had among his ideals the care for his fellow man tore it down with the carelessness worthy of a pasha. The tramway would then make a slight left, going past the Unirii Marketplace and reached Magheru. I would get off near Batistei Street. I would go around, behind the shop for Diplomats, another wonder of our adolescent years, and I would reach the high school yard. Here, a little before 8, I would have to face Grosu, our Russian teacher, who might not have taught us much Russian, but he was certainly the most hated teacher. Grosu would sort us by classroom and make us stand with our hands to our back, our feet apart, and would then proceed to verify our passes, the girls hairbands, the beige stockings or thick brown ones, like in the countryside, and would see whether the girls in the eleventh grade had any nail polish.

I remember well… and what of it? All in all, they were the best years!

With all the evenings we would gather for tea and dance until we were spent, we felt a little further away from our families' problems. I would talk with Ioana Casassovici and we would be thankful, a little bit late perhaps, but we thanked God that we had wonderful parents who kept us far away from the horrors of the time, who taught us not to hate, but to help each other, and to grow up with dignity. I have to add that the school and high school also had a major role in this. We also had good teachers, who behaved with dignity.

My God, the silly things we did! I was sitting in the first row, with Popica, the future doctor, and during history classes with Pipa, who used to sit with his hands on our desk when he lost himself in his discourse while teaching – we used to paint his nails in red with a red crayon!

Another time, P.E. with Baston, who made us run a lot and made us jump high (I almost broke my ribs once). Andrei "Craiova" and I were both late for history class. I was almost dressed, and Andrei was still in his jumpsuit. I must say that Andrei had an awful pair of snickers, who looked like they had been worn by two generations of a whole team instead of a single person, and they also smelled! Andrei tells me: "Listen carefully, take me in your arms, and when he opens the door, you say…" Andrei is a bit taller than I am, but just as thin. I take him in my arms, I open the door, I enter the classroom with his feet dangling about, announcing: "I am late, Mr., Andrei died!"

Pipa's eyes widened and before he could say anything, I release Andrei and he falls on the floor. All our colleagues start laughing. Pipa yells: "Get out!" Hooray! We were out of History class, scot-free.

But let me come back to Baston, who was not just a sports teacher, as he was also a lawyer. Let me explain: I was a good friend of Kuky Filip, and I would go to his place almost every day, where Mrs. Zincuta, may God rest her soul, would always pamper us with sweet words or who knows what else, as she was always immensely kind. This is where I also met little Zincuta, my colleague's sister, a good friend, and later a distinguished cardiologist who cared for my mother with a lot of devotion. A Mr. Filip was never with them. I wondered about this but never asked them about their father.

One day, a comrade comes to our class during P.E. on inspection. Baston lines us up and tells us to make our own presentations to the inspector comrade. When Kuky, who was in front of me, says his name, I heard Baston with my own ears, whispering to the inspector: "He is the boy of the Filip lawyer" followed by a gesture of his head sideways. The inspector nodded, as if saying he understood. Right then, I didn't understand their gestures, or what Baston had said. Much later on I met Kuky's wonderful father, an extremely well known lawyer among the specialists of the time. This made me think in regards to our teachers, as many where more than they seemed!

In order to know that the father of one of your students (we were approximately 400 in Spiru) is a lawyer, and moreover, has been imprisoned, and in order for the inspector to also immediately know who you are talking about, you had to have more than the knowledge imposed on you by the socialist system.

I met Kuky's father, Mr. N – he let me call him that – after he returned home suddenly one night. He himself had no idea how he had managed to get home; they had been let go from a truck at night. It was pitch black outside, in the middle of the road, and they had been released and told that they were free to go! I got to know him well, later, after Kuky left the country, we became friends and one day he asked me if I knew anything about the Masonry. I knew a thing or two, because I had a French dictionary of symbols at home, which I perused often. In 1992, after two years of trials, Mr. N and I signed the papers for the creation of the Great National Lodge in Romania! And this is also how I was elected in the Great Council of this Order, a title I pride myself in!

Back to school! One year, I think I was in the tenth grade, I remember that the film *Lupeni 29*, Ciubotarasu's last film, had come to the cinema – it was a film nobody wanted to see. People were fed up with stupid plots about workers battling exploiters and wanted new films, real films. And so, the school would send us to see the movie in the morning, at the Patria Cinema, with a 1 leu ticket, and afterwards we had to come back to school. One of the classes was History, taught by "the Beast", a very good teacher, who was also not very lenient. The lesson was about Alexander the Great, and his conquering campaign in Europe and Asia, the cities he had conquered. "The Beast" started roll call, want through the list of students and said: "I will now see what, followed by the long pause full of suspense, Iordachescu in front of the class!"

During recess, I had flipped to the map at the end of our book and I had underlined the cities with my pen. The sentence of the teacher follows: "Cities conquered by Alexander the Great!"

I opened the book carelessly and started enumerating the cities. "The Beast" looks at me in shock, turns back to the class, especially towards Matei and "Pendulum", well-known for their passion for history, and asks: "Did I say you should underline the cities? Did anybody else do this?"

The two, like all the others, were silent, but not because they had caught on and realized what I had done, but because they were also shocked by my progress. "The Beast" asks again: "Is he the only one?" Silence. "Good." Again, silence.

"The Beast" opens the class book, my heart had sank, thinking about how much effort I will have to put in in order to fix my average, study for finals, because "the Beast" and Varzaru (the Romanian Language teacher) seemed to know no grade above 2. But he opens his fountain pen and breaks the silence announcing: "10!". Oh my God! "The Beast" had awarded me a 10! I could not believe my ears: TEN! From then on, at the end of class, when we would talk about what we learned that day, "the Beast" would ask me, he never asked me again to come in front of the class and I had that 10 secured!

I remember the reunions or the balls, I don't remember how they called them, on the night before Easter, during the Resurrection, when we were forced, threatened to come to school and dance. I would employ a trick: I would go to the opera and buy a ticket for any show during that night, I would then go to the head teacher and show him the ticket, saying I cannot come to the ball! He knew my father played the violin and would accept the excuse. And so, I would go to the Opera, the performance would be over before midnight, I would then go to the Elefterie Church and light my candle, and finally go to the school reunion!

I remember that in my tenth grade I did the same, I came to school and danced with a colleague of mine who was older than I was, from eleventh grade, a member of the school's gymnastics team, a fine young lady, with wavy chestnut hair, big eyes, and warm sparks in her look – I had had an eye on her for a long time. During these reunions, we had to dance a manner of waltz: one hand extended, the other grasping the girl's waist, and the girl had an arm on the partner's shoulder! Otherwise, we would be considered decadent! Oh well, we danced rock that night! A tragedy! That night, the chaperons were the math teacher, that lady with a limp, and the inevitable Grosu! After the dance, we went out on the hallway, satisfied with ourselves, both with a satisfied smile on our faces – it made my partner wonderful! Our victory was short lived, as we immediately hear a colleague's voice behind me: "Hey, take her by the hand and go to Grosu, the both of you!" We knew what we had done! Mechanically, I grabbed her hand and with my heart sinking, but my head held high (come what may), we were approaching Grosu, when I heard his voice: "Look at that! He's also holding her hand!"

It was then that I realized that I really was holding her hand! I squeezed it harder: yes, I am holding her hand! We stood in front of him as he started rambling on, but we did not understand a word he was saying. We were somewhere up above, above it all: "You can yell to your heart's desire, can't you see I'm holding her hand and she hasn't pulled it back? Can't you feel how warm it is?"

Today I ask myself; I wonder where that girl with big eyes and warm looks is now.

I said earlier that I went to the Opera: I went often and I had the pleasure of seeing shows with Irinel Liciu, Gheorghe Cotovelea, to lisen to Stefanescu Goanga, they were the headliners of our time, of Bucharest during those years. I would buy a 2 lei ticket and go to the gallery, where I knew almost everybody, because we were always the same people there: students from music school or ballet school.

We would go to the theater, to Comedia, where we would get in free, because we were students. We would wait until the show was about to start, when Beligan, the director of the theater, would come on stage. He would see us, go to the usher closest to him, whisper something to her (we held our breath) after which he would leave without saying anything. The usher would come to us with a wide smile on her face and welcome us in! These were our victories. Now, after many years, I made a small scenography project for the Maestro Beligan, Eusebiu Stefanescu and Rodica Mandache. On this occasion, I remembered those times and I thanked him: we could not afford to go so often to the theater.

I knew full plays by heart, performed at the Comedia Theater by Caragiu, Marinus Moraru, Titi Cheza, Titi Rucareanu, Gheorghe Dinica, Ion Vulpe, whom I had befriended and with whom I would often go to "their" bar at the Tower, to listen to their stories about the theater! I was just a kid, but they accepted me, and I was very proud of it!

After this came the eleventh grade, with the final exam, and after that, countless other exams! I used to skip classes and get on the train without paying a ticket, to get to the mountainside. During summers, I always went to 2 Mai, I would eat what I could, pitch my tent on the sand, next to the sea, in order to feel its smell and hear its roar.

Also during these years, I met Ivonne Bertola (an actress), the niece of Clodi Bertola, and Sanda Ulmeni, two wonderful girls, so full of hope...

... and one day, next to my tent, I saw another, a wonderful, orange, and much larger tent than mine. I got closer, I lingered about, I started talking with the owner of the object and we became friends. When we left 2 Mai, I bought her tent, we exchanged addresses and after 9 months, in Prague, our son Ian was born, now a doctor in Prague!

In 1984, I managed to woo a nice lady, an art critic and historian, a talented portraitist, with a big sense of humor: Crenguta Munteanu, the niece of Argintescu Amza. After two years, also during summer, Ilinca Ioana was born, now an architect.

The year of graduation, 1964! Half a century has passed; the century changed in the meantime, and moreover, the millennium changed as well! Our Bucharest also changed, the Bucharest of our childhood and adolescence.

From 1970 to this day, I have designed factories throughout the country, I staged a play by Jean Genet (*Cameristele*), two or three plays by Caragiale, a Brecht, a Goldoni, I was awarded for interpretation two times, to be fair, in the amateur category (but as *amateur* comes from the Latin *amo-amare*, to love honestly…) Afterwards came two by Sofocles: *Iphigenia* and *Medeea*, a Mozart, *the flute*, at the Opera…

In 1994, my friend Vonny Bertola, said to me: "Puiu, I would like to redo this big house." Bertola and Mario live in a house that belonged to Lascar Catargiu, on Popa Rusu Street. Said and done, it was a restoration of which I am proud, as the project appeared in the magazine for historical monuments.

One day, more recently, I get a phone call: "Hello, is this Mr. Iordachescu?" "Yes." They say: "I am the Academy member. And I would like to have a suit…" In 2006, I designed the gala costume for the Romanian Academy, and in 2008 for the Royal Academy in Barcelona – and so the request did not take me by surprise. I said: "Professor, you only need to tell me your address, and I will be there with a tailor to take your measurements…"

He lives in that Bauhaus building in front of the statue of Vasile Lascar, a building with a façade facing the street. We arrive, take the measurements, and, to make time pass more pleasurably, I begin a conversation by telling the professor I studied near his house at the Spiru high school and that one of my colleagues who was one year younger than I, Alina, a beautiful girl with wonderful legs lived in the same building as he. The professor remains silent and fixes me with his lively eyes, after which his glance changes and becomes nostalgic, same as his voice. He asks me: "But have you met her mother?" This is how I found out that Alina had left for Paris long ago… Autumnal nostalgia!

The years in Spiru… they were beautiful years, but I also had days when I wish they had not existed!

I saw a film last year: the action takes place in England, during the war. It is autumn, the start of the school year, and London has been bombed the previous night. A grandfather drives his nephew to school and leaves him off at the corner of the street, near the school. The grandfather is sad because of the state of the destroyed city, and the nephew is sad because school is starting. The kid enters the schoolyard and freezes in amazement: the teachers are gathered in the center of the yard and all the students around them are running, playing, making a lot of noise. School was out: a bomb had fallen over the school. The kid comes to his senses, raises his eyes towards the sky and smiling wide he cries: *Yes! Thank you, Dolfy!*

The Motley Memories of an Atypical Adolescent - Adrian Irvin Rozei*

* Reviewed, corrected and modified by Adrian Irvin Rozei

———

"I have known that which those born now
Shall never in their lifetimes know… "

Mihai Beniuc

Sacha Guitry, the well-known French playwright, director and film-maker, wrote in his memoirs entitled *"Si j'ai bonne mémoire"* (If I remember well):

> *I won't pretend to have been a model student. Here is why. I am not one of those students who have remained at the same school for ten years – no, and, in actuality, I passed through no less than eleven institutions, high schools, colleges, and schools to reach the age of the baccalaureate.*

And, reflecting back on the consequences of these numerous changes in teaching institutions, Sacha Guitry concludes, decades after his adventures, that, all in all, it was a good thing! Because, at the age of adulthood, he has the opportunity to celebrate the anniversaries many more times over, and with many more friends.

I didn't have the chance, like Sacha Guitry, of passing through eleven institutions in the thirteen years from kindergarten to the baccalaureate! I have, however, managed to pass through eight such places of learning.

296

One by one, I was a pupil in the kindergarten on 52 Vasile Lascăr Street, then in the one in Alexandru Sahia Square (today called J. L. Calderon), a student in Dimitrie Cantemir High School and in Vasile Alecsandri School, located near Gemeni Market Place, and afterwards I went to Clemenţa School on C.A. Rosetti Street, to Centrală School on Icoanei Street, to Spiru Haret High School on Italiană Street and finally, to Mihail Sadoveanu High School, on Dacia Boulevard. Truly a long enumeration of addresses, just like in George Topârceanu's poem!

I only spent a few days in several of the aforementioned institutions, either because the administrative organization changed, or because I didn't like the school, or the school didn't like me – better put it, the leadership back then didn't like me. This was because, having "an unhealthy social origin", I was often found to be "a surplus"!

For example, from the very first try, with the kindergarten on Vasile Lascăr Street[15], I was kicked out after only three days, because I tore the blue paper off the glass window that separated the "boys" and "girls" sections! It was a quick decision, as I was certainly beginning to shape up as an "antisocial element", yet I was sent to the kindergarten in Al. Sahia Square.

In Dimitrie Cantemir High School, I wasn't permitted to attend one single class! Between the time when I was admitted, in spring, and the time when classes began, in September, the decision had been taken that all elementary class students be "unloaded" across the street, in Vasile Alecsandri.

In V. Alecsandri Elementary School, the circumstances were the most surrealist possible. The teacher in my class was an overweight woman, who tried to lose weight by all means. One of my fellow students was the son of a baker (back then, private businesses still existed). As the boy had noticed our comrade teacher's weakness for baked goods, he would come to school every day carrying a tray of sweet cakes, which he offered to her. She would desperately try to refuse, but our colleague would chase her with the tray throughout the classroom, insisting, and, finally, forcing her to take two or three. Of course, in these conditions, her authority and objectivity had become nonexistent!

In this condition, my parents began searching for a new school, with an authoritarian teacher, and this is how I got to study in Clemenţa, under the famous "professor" Borcea, where I met a lot of students I would later reunite with at Spiru and Sadoveanu.

Several years later, after the introduction of mixed schools, I was distributed to Centrală School, formerly known as "Girls' School" (Back then, it was called Zoia Kosmodemianskaia). Seeing as I was in a class of 27 out of which only … three were boys, and teachers would start their lessons by saying: "Girls, today we will learn about…", I concluded I had to get out of there quickly! My mother resorted to stalking about Spiru Haret High School – a place where the situation was reversed – until she found a girl willing to exchange places with me!

As for me leaving Spiru Haret High School, it was a painful affair, yet I was forced into it! When the time came for me to take the exam for admission into the eighth grade, I was brilliantly flunked, although I had had good grades in all previous years: when I asked for my grades, I saw that they were consistently good, with the sole exception of my last oral exam, where I had scored a 1 out of 10! That was just enough to make me fail the admission exam, in which I was already less than privileged, being "the son of a bourgeois" and being permitted to only compete for 30% of total available places.

When my father went to see comrade Teodorescu, the headmistress of the school, she told him: "Never mind this, Adrian, is a good student! He can retake the exam next autumn and he will be admitted."

We decided that the risk of a new "adventure" similar to what had just happened in the spring was too high! And so, we all decided that it was preferable for me to try and get admitted to Mihail Sadoveanu, a newly constructed high school on Dacia Boulevard, where the directors knew none of the students. And, deeply regretting the fact that I had to leave my friends behind, I was admitted to the new high school.

However, today, 50 years after finishing high school, I see these changes as being a positive element. Not only do they allow me, as in the case of Sacha Guitry, to celebrate the same event multiple times, but, more importantly, it has given me the opportunity to make the acquaintance of many more people from my generation. I left behind some of these people, only to find them again in another school, where we were colleagues once again.

Or, even more surprisingly, after decades, I found them in some distant corner of the world, by chance or intentionally, but always with the pleasure found in getting in touch with an old acquaintance. Maybe this is one of the reasons for which my school years seem to me more like an ensemble, from which I can hardly isolate one period, the intertwining events being too numerous. This is why I planed to not only detail the brief period between fifth and eighth grade (1957-1960), which I spent in Spiru Haret High School, but the entire period of my school years in the 50's and 60's. This was a period we all lived through, under one form or another and which shaped Generation '64.

———

A few decades ago, at the end of the meeting to evaluate my yearly results, the manager concluded by telling me: "You sir, are a atypical case!"

What he said shocked me at first. Afterwards, when I came to realize the more profound sense of his words, I became proud of his description of me. Not only did it emphasize the fact that I was out of the ordinary, just as my colleagues, but it also accounted for my experiences and the education I had received in a far corner of Europe, a place mostly ignored by the western world. It is true that we, the members of Generation '64, lived through the experiences, sometimes painful but other times joyful, of a society marked by constant changes. Its existence, during the 50's and 60's of the 20th Century, was never *"un long fleuve tranquille"*.

My other colleagues will describe the historical context of our childhood and adolescence. I prefer to remember the cultural context. This is perhaps because, while political events represent a "momentum" that must not be forgotten, cultural events are, more often than not, of international and timeless significance. They are able to serve as a reference in different areas, even decades after they have passed. As we shall see soon, one of these events is still mentioned by the press today, more than half a century after it took place.

Of course, this text does not seek to become an all-encompassing study of cultural life in the 50's and 60's of the last century. More likely, it reproduces the memories of one who lived in that period, together with occasional lapses and moments of enchantment that have survived the passing of years, in the hopes that some contemporaries will thus find their own memories within.

———

The oldest cultural event of some importance I can remember is the "Fourth Edition of the World Youth and Student Festival", which took place in Bucharest in the summer of 1953.

After previously being empty for several months, in order to stockpile goods, stores were now abundant in food, clothing and electronics during the two weeks of the Festival. The purpose of this was to show foreigners our superior quality of life and to underline the success of the "wise leadership of the Party and the Government of The Peoples' Republic of Romania"!

However, the festival allowed us for the first time to leave the overbearing shadow of soviet culture for a brief moment and achieve some manner of contact with the western world. Even if the participants in such manner of manifestations were, most of all, sympathizers of soviet ideology, the simple fact of being able to hear languages such as French, English or German being spoken freely on the streets gave us a feeling of freedom, one that we hadn't known for a long time.

We fully took advantage of these privileged moments, although I was only 6 years old – I was witness to the closing ceremony of the Festival, held on the 23rd of August Stadium, and watched the march of the participating foreign delegations and a massive spectacle the likes of which you can nowadays only see in North Korea or ... at the Olympic Games!

Actually, I didn't realize back then that, being only a few months after the death of Stalin, things were about to change and evolve until, three years later, we would enter a period of "defrosting", as a result of the anti-Stalinist discourse held by Nichita Sergheievici Hrusciov during the 20th Edition of the PCUS Congress in 1956.

Meanwhile, the period of "proletkult" was in full bloom! This term, first coined in Russia in 1917, encompassed three distinct categories of writers in postwar Romania.

Some, belonging to older generations, had begun writing before the war; they generally exhibited a more diversified experience and culture, but, under the pressure of soviet-communist dictatorship and sometimes in order to have their past "sins" forgotten, they had turned to the language and style imposed by Moscow by means of local loyal subjects. This is the case with writers such as Mihail Sadoveanu, Mihai Beniuc, Maria Banuș, Dan Deșliu, Zaharia Stancu, Petru Dumitriu, Eugen Jebeleanu... In some cases, by consistently lying to themselves, they had come under the impression that they were on the right path and had become the creators of a "new syle".

Others were plain opportunistic, lacking any talent, and would take advantage of the chance to benefit off honors and exercise their power within the art world. This is the case with Alexandru Toma and Eugen Frunză.

The third category was comprised of young talents, who had neither the time nor the opportunity to come into contact with universal education, who had not known anything aside the toll of the communist bell and who has been thus used by the system. Examples of such writers are Nicolae Labiș, Nina Cassian, and Veronica Porumbacu.

Finally, a not at all negligible category of writers who refused to fall "in line with the party" or due to having a compromising historical or artistic past, were eliminated from literary life, left without "the right to sign", or, simply left to rot in prison. This was the case with names such as Tudor Arghezi, Ionel Teodoreanu, Lucian Blaga, George Silviu, Radu Gyr, Nichifor Crainic, Ion Pillat and especially Octavian Goga, over which "post mortem" revenge was set in motion!

Of course, these categories are oversimplifying matters, because some writers, over the years, have passed from one to another, sometimes paying the price of pitiful consequences. Even the famous epigram writer of the time, Păstorel Teodoreanu, wrote:

At the Writers' Union Restaurant,
Are boys who drink with joy
From sundown to sunrise.
One could be a cupbearer
And others could be informers (in romanian, double
meaning for "cupbearer")

The best example is Petru Dumitriu, who had studied philosophy in Germany between 1941 and 1944, and who had for 15 years become the "adored son" of the communist regime, an ideology which he spoke of very highly in his novels. He ran away to the West despite the princely life he lived back in Romania.

As it happens, in 1960, while studying at Spiru Haret High School, I found out about Petru Dumitru's desertion. Fear grasped me, as I had just submitted my Romanian Literature thesis on his novel called "Pasărea Furtunii"(Bird of the Storm). Seeing as escaped writers were not only forbidden from being published, but it was dangerous to even pronounce their names, I was convinced that my thesis will be rejected and we would be forced to present a new one. Actually, following the indescribable system of generalized lies, nothing was officially said about the incident, we were graded as if nothing had ever happened, but our papers were never given back to us! However, the very next year, Petru Dumitriu disappeared from our Romanian Literature schoolbooks!

During the 90's, I saw Petru Dumitriu in Paris, at the Romanian Culture Center, where he told us that his greatest regret in life was having written the novel "Drum fără pulbere"(Path without Dust), celebrating the achievements in the construction of the Danube-Black Sea Canal, a symbol of the Romanian Gulag. Several months later however, this did not keep him from supporting the authorities back in Bucharest, who were the direct heirs of the people he had served back in the 50's.

I have had the pleasure of personally meeting some of the writers of the era. This was the case with Marcel Breslașu, poet, fable writer, composer and translator, whom I would often meet at concerts at the Athenaeum. After he had studied law and music in Bucharest, Marcel had been given the title of doctor in law in Paris, following his studies at the Schola Cantorum with Vincent d'Indy. At the end of his life, he had become the chief of the Party Organization for the Writers' Union of RPR. He had also studied in Spiru Haret high school, so we were, in a way, colleagues!

By the same means, I had come to know Horia Liman, journalist and writer from the prewar generation, and who became the editor in chief of Contemporanul magazine in 1946, holding the position for 11 years. There, he left the mark of an intransigent procommunist, almost giving himself away because of it. This, however, did not stop him from remaining in Geneva in 1970 and becoming a successful Swiss writer; he was even given a national award for his novel "Les bottes", considered to be an autobiography describing life in Romania during the 30's and 70's.

Many years after I had left Romania, I met Florica Jebeleanu (the daughter of poet Eugen Jebeleanu and painter, graphic artist, and sketch artist Florica Codrescu) in Paris who confirmed, from her own memory, the details of Pablo Neruda's visit to Bucharest in the 50's[16].

Upon reading the novel "Toate pânzele sus!" (Hoist the Sails!) during adolescence, which of us has not dreamed of visiting Tierra del Fuego? For me, this dream determined me to sell 3000 tons of PVC in Ushuaia, an action that justified visiting my client there during the 80's.

However, I never personally met Radu Tudoran, with whom I briefly crossed paths back in the 60's, until the beginning of the 90's in Paris. Less able politically speaking than his brother, the poet Geo Bogza, Radu Tudoran briefly passed through a "cone of shadow" in between 1947 and 1954, when his adventure novel mentioned before brought him back into the spotlight.

At the end of the 50's, I would impatiently wait in front of the newspaper stand for the arrival of the bimonthly issue of the collection called "Povestiri ştiinţifico-fantastice" (Sci-fi Stories). Among the successful authors of the time, I recall the two collaborating writers I. M. Ştefan and Radu Nor, with "future" novels such as "Drum printre aştrii" (Voyage among the Planets) and "Robinson pe planeta oceanelor" (Robinson on the planet of oceans).

I would latter meet Radu Nor's son, Raul Rudel, as we would both study at the Polytechnic Institute. We both suffered greatly when we failed the "Mathematical Analysis" exam during our first year. Back then, his father worked at the Meteorological Institute, and we had news about the weather even before the radio forecast[17].

One of the creators of sci-fi literature in Romania, Oscar Lemnaru, I would meet every week at the Philharmonic concerts; back then, my father would converse with him, because they had known each other for decades. The author of two remarkable fiction novels, "Omul și umbra" (The Man and the Shadow) and "Ceasul din turn" (The Clock Tower), Oscar Lemnaru passed through his own contradictory periods within the Romanian post-war writers' community.

Firstly, he was a communist Roberspierre, followed by his several years of being put to "the common work" of translation, he regained his place on the firmament during the 60's, when he was authorized to publish ten aphorisms or puns on the first page of the weekly political-social-cultural "Contemporanul" magazine. It was then that I began to meet him regularly, on Sundays after lunch, at the Athene Palace Hotel brasserie, where a part of the Romanian intellectual class gathered to purchase the famous "fixed menu" which cost 10 lei.

I cannot help but recall the famous building on 74 Dionisie Lupu Street, where, as mentioned by a plaque recently installed on its façade: "During various stages of their lives, numerous personalities have lived and created their works within these walls: Al. Andrițoiu, Anda Boldur, Ov. S. Crohmălniceanu, Dana Dumitriu, Valeriu Munteanu, Marin Preda, Catinca Ralea, Nicolae Stoian, Al. I. Ștefănescu, Nicolae Tăutu, Mihnea Gheorghiu". Along with each name, the dates indicating the period spent in this building are written. However, some names such, as Toma George Maiorescu, Mihai Stoian and Emanoil Petruț are not mentioned – why, I wonder. And most importantly, in regards to my concerns, there is no mention of Mioara Cremene, writer and journalist, poet and essay writer, who, after having studied at the University of Music in the class of Victor Ion Popa, had made her debut at the beginning of the 1950's as a journalist. Her "withdrawal of the right to sign" a few years later led her towards children's literature, a far less exposed domain. Which of us has never seen her play called "Mălina și cei trei ursuleți" (Mălina and the three bears) being performed at the Țăndărică Marionette Theater, directed by ... Liviu Ciulei and signed by Renee George Silviu?

Mioara Cremene fled to France in 1969 with her husband filmmaker Sergiu Huzum. I met her in Paris, many years later, and through our conversations I incidentally found out we are distantly related!

In 2000, Mioara Cremene published her memories, along with Mariana Sipoș, called "La ce folosește Parisul?" (What is Paris good for?) in which she names all the people in the artistic world in Romania.

The poet and actress Aurora Cornu and her husband Marin Preda were also living in this building. She played latter on in two of Erich Romer's "cult" movies of the 70's, one of them being the famous "Le genou de Claire" (Claire's Knee), along with French movie stars Jean-Claude Brialy and Fabrice Luchini. I still see Aurora Cornu, one of Mioara Cremene's great friends, during regular receptions and conferences at the Romanian Embassy in Paris.

Mihail Sadoveanu lived on a street parallel with Dionisie Lupu, called Pitar Moș. In 1960, when I was forced to leave Spiru Haret high school, I was admitted to Mihail Sadoveanu high school on Dacia Boulevard, a short walk away from the house owned by the bearer of its name.

Mihail Sadoveanu came to our high school to meet us during the last year of his life. Only, he had previously suffered a stroke and was unable to speak. We shall never know what he truly thought about this honor, which piled up with all the rest of the titles and functions he had accumulated throughout his life!

However, while never quite appreciating his proletkult novel "Mitrea Cocor", written on command, as well as his opportunistic political views, I have admired numerous works of his, both famous and obscure. About ten years ago, I was desperately in search for a copy of "Soarele în baltă sau aventurile șahului" (Sun in the Pond or the Adventures of Chess), translated into an international language, because I had promised the book to the famous Spanish writer Francesco Arrabal, a fanatic of the game and a friend and fighter against communism, along with E. Ionesco.

Similarly to Mioara Cremene and Radu Tudoran, many writers found refuge from ideological pressure in the 50's by writing literature for children, a field less scrutinized by censors. I cannot resist the temptation of mentioning the collection of novellas entitled "Complotul de la Piatra Verde" (The Green Stone Plot), written by my aunt, a reputable translator, under the pseudonym Elisabeta Gălățeanu.

Perhaps this is the place where I should mention at least one of the writers who refused to compromise themselves by siding with the communists back in the 50's. I am talking about the forgotten poet, journalist, writer, lawyer and politician George Silviu, an apt wielder of the Romanian language, who, by rejecting the "Anschluss" which the Communist Party made with the Social-Democratic Party of which he was a member of (the Titel Petrescu side), spent 18 months in prison, with no accusation and no due trial!

In 1961, I was a colleague with one of his daughters, Ioana George Macker. We met again in France in 1994, and I could thus peruse the five volumes of "Poezii, snoave, vorbe cu tâlc, piese de teatru sau romane" (Poems, anecdotes, words of wisdom, plays or novels) published by his daughters in the 90's, following the author's death.

———

Romanian Theater in the 50's and 60's also reflected the contradictions of a period of "passing from capitalism to socialism", as it was called back then.

Nine theaters functioned in Bucharest during this period:

- I. L. Caragiale National Theater
- The Municipal Theater (*Sala Splai*, later to become *Sala Studio* and finally *Lucia Sturdza Bulandra*)
- The Youth Theater
- C. Nottara Film Actor Theater, later known as The Theater for Children and Youth, today the Small Theater
- The Army Theater, renamed C. Nottara Theater after 1960
- The Giuleşti C.F.R. Workers Theater
- The State Jewish Theater

* Ţăndărică Marionette Theater
* The Central Council of Syndicates Theater

As well as various musical theaters:

* The State Opera House
* The State OperettaTheater
* The Estrada Humour Ensemble
* The State Philharmonic Orchestra (renamed George Enescu after 1955)

A new theater was inaugurated in 1961, called The Comedy Theater, under the initiative of Radu Beligan.

The theater programs were relatively specialized: thus, the National Theater had the objective of "promoting national theater literature" (by this, they meant recent Romanian playwrights: Mihail Davidoglu, Mircea Ştefănescu, A. Rogoz), as well as the plays of Caragiale; The Army Theater dedicated its programs to historical plays (Ion Vodă cel Cumplit). However, all theaters gave the "lion's share" (or rather, the bear's share) to Russian and Soviet plays (N. Gogol, C. Simonov, A. Ostrovski, C. Tremov, M. Gorki and B. Cirkov). Sometimes, a few plays from universal literature were selected (Lope de Vega or Shakespeare), but mostly nothing from recent western creation was ever shown. The period of "defrosting" had to come in order to see any Arthur Miller, Frederic Durenmatt, Steinbeck or Ionesco...

And yet, all things considered, this was the period in which I made my most powerful memories! Not only because it was the period of my childhood and adolescence, when one is much like a sponge ready to absorb any and all information one is passionate about, but also because I had the grand opportunity of meeting countless personalities belonging to the cultural life of the time, and, most of all, belonging to the world of theater.

In 1953, beginning first grade in Clemenţa School, I made the acquaintance of Costin Cazaban, with whom I remained colleagues for four years. We were later reunited for three years in Spiru Haret High School. A very tight bond of friendship formed between us, so tight that when I left for

Sadoveanu and began my technical career at the Polytechnic Institute, while he began his art studies at the University of Music, we kept seeing each other, often on a daily basis, while having friends in common and belonging to the same social groups.

He was the son of Jules Cazaban, "Emeritus artist", later "Artist of the People", and of Irina Nădejde Cazaban, who was an actress till after the war, with which I had certain family ties. Due to the fact that he lived in the Wilson building in the heart of Bucharest, and his family was very welcoming, their house was an important gathering point for all Romanian intellectuals back then, especially for those from the world of theater. Because Jules Cazaban was constantly playing on the stage of the Municipal Theater, and had also been second-in-command there since back in the days of Lucia Sturdza Bulandra, I mainly made the acquaintance of actors playing in that particular theater. We went to see all their plays, and we would even sometimes go to see the Sunday morning matinee, staying for just 10 or 15 minutes, in order to see this or that actor performing our favorite scenes from plays we had previously seen, or actors we had heard this or that anecdote about during our visits to the Cazaban house.

This is how I learned about the caprices of Bulandra, a *"monstre sacré"* of Romanian theater, and I saw her play the titular role in *Profesiunea d-nei Warren* (Mrs. Warren's Profession), *Vassa Jeleznova* (Vassa Zheleznova), *Mamouret, Nebuna din Chaillot* (The Madwoman of Chaillot), or the main role in *Pădurea* (The Forest) by Ostrovski. Her talent, her didactic capacity, and her directing initiatives were honored through numerous awards and titles, between which *Steaua Republicii* (Star of the Republic) and *Artist al Poporului* (Artist of the People).

During those times, I was also witness, as a spectator, to the competition for first place in "the new Romanian theater", held between Aurel Baranga, the author of the play *Arcul de Triumf* in which Jules Cazaban was an actor, and Al. Mirodan with his *Celebrul 702* (The Famous 702), interpreted by Radu Beligan at the newly inaugurated Comedy Theater. The play was later adapted for a movie, in which Jules also had a role.

Many years later, after he had left the country in 1977, I met Alexandru Mirodan in Israel, where he kept publishing the Romanian *Minimum* magazine until his death. To him I owe my nickname, given to me by our high school professor of mathematics: The chief of the soul sector, after Mirodan's play.

I cannot help but remember Mihail Sebastian, a man for which I feel intense admiration and nostalgia. Since I was a teenager, I would pass by Filantropia cemetery to lay a flower on his grave. I could not, for the life of me, choose between "*Steaua fără nume*"(The Star Without a Name) and "*Jocul de-a vacanta*"(Vacation Play Pretend)!

During the 60's and the 70's, a few Romanians that had sought refuge in Paris would meet at "*Le Colisée*" café on Champs-Elysées on every Wednesday afternoon – my mother would always join them. Among the people you would often find sitting with them were the wife of Victor Brauner and the brother of Mihail Sebastian, Bruno Hechter, who had been colleagues with my uncle on my mother's side. However, all this while I had refused to meet him! Was it the fear of being disillusioned? Was it the fear of getting close to the brother of my idol? These are questions that demand some analysis of the subconscious!

Even so, it happened that in 1996, thanks to the atypical writer Alexandru Vona, I had the chance of meeting an Aesthetics professor named Reutersvard in Stockholm. He told me, among many other memories from the time of the war, during which his father was the Swedish ambassador in Bucharest, about the reception organized by Martha Bibescu in the halls of the Mogoșoaia Palace. This was the same invitation described by Mihail Sebastian in his Journal!

Another remarkable moment was my meeting with Titus Popovici in 1960. He was the author of a theater play called "Passacaglia", in which Jules played the role of an elderly music professor. This gave him the occasion to showcase his musical talent – each evening, he would play a piece by Bach on his cello. It was rather strange for me to meet the author of novels such as "*Setea*"(The Thirst) and "*Străinul*"(The Stranger) which I had studied in school. It was like meeting Caragiale on the street or in a pub. By the way, the pub was no foreign place for Titus Popovici!

It was from Irina Cazaban that I first heard of Stanislavski's theater theories or about the interpretation given by actress Helene Weigel in the play *Mutter Courage* by Bertolt Brecht, which made theater history on the stage with the famous *Berliner Ensemble*, who had also visited Bucharest on their tour. French newspapers were all delighted with this interpretation. On this occasion, I remember that Miss Weigel, who lived next door to me in Bucharest, was related to the wife of Bertolt Brecht[18].

I also admired the staging done by Roger Planchon from Villeurbanne Theatre National Populaire in *The Three Musketeers* – they were on tour and had performed at Sala Palatului. And, if I had had enough money, I would have also gone to see *Georges Dandin*. What shocked me back then was that in the foyer, all spectators spoke French! But, this happened later on, during the mid-60.

However, I have to admit that the predominance of Russian theater in Romania during the 50's gave me the opportunity to discover the great authors of this grand culture (Chekov, Gorki, Ostrovski, Pushkin and Gogol), and even the works of less famous writers such as C. Treniov (with his *Liubov Iarovaia,* in which Jules played) or *Nunta lui Krecinski* (Krecinski's Wedding) by A. V. Suhovo-Kobîlin (staring actors Alexandru Giugaru and Grigore Vasiliu-Birlic)

What I would later notice about my contemporaries in France was that they would utterly ignore their vast knowledge of Russian theater – at most, they would mention *Trei surori* (Three Sisters) or *Unchiul Vania* (Uncle Vania), plays which I had seen in Bucharest, in the interpretation of Moscow's Vahtangov Theater[19].

Following the same line, I would remark how western authorities in theater would pride themselves with the discovery of translating plays (especially the opera or operetta) by displaying subtitles on a screen above the sage, ignoring the fact that in Bucharest you could go and see the plays performed at the State Jewish Theater and hear the translation in an earpiece as far back as 1950! Back then, it is how I saw a play called *Tevie lăptarul* (Tevie the Milkman), an adaptation of Salom Alehem's novella, which would two decades later become the world famous film *Fiddler on the Roof* and a musical comedy in France under the name *Un violon sur le toit*, performed by the now deceased Yvan Rebroff.

Among the countless Romanian theater personalities I met back then, I must mention the following:

* Septimiu Sever, a man I admired for his wonderful skill in handling the rapier.

    We often went to see him in *Marchizul de Possa* (The Marquis of Possa) from *Don Carlos* by Schiller, because it was a play in which he had to perform a duel in one of the scenes. One day, during one of his visits to the Cazaban house, Septimiu offered to duel with Costin and I, just to humor us. Seeing how unskilled we were, he proposed a supplementary handicap to even up the fight: between crossing swords with us, he had to strike the armoire in Costin's room in which the duel was taking place. After only a couple of such strikes, Irina Cazaban appeared and forbade us from continuing such a dangerous game … for the armoire!

    Tall and handsome as he was, we saw him as being much older; in reality, he was about 30 or 35 years old. Today, aged 90, Septimiu Sever continues his activity in Canada, where he fled in 1971, starting a career as an actor, performing both in English and French.

* Fory Etterle, a close friend of Jules, who, despite his uncontrolled movments and wrinkles, was still all the rage among high school girls.

* Paul Sava: I knew him as the host of the *Varietăți* (Varieties) television show, and especially as an actor at the Bulandra Theater. He played the role of two twin brothers in a Shakespeare play and, following the playful advice of Jules, would appear after the fall of the curtain with his own twin brother (who was a doctor), donning identical outfits, in order to confuse the audience. During the 80's, I saw him again in Paris, where he had fled. A while before his death, in 1995, I happened to meet him in the Louvre and we shared memories about the 60's.

* Sorin Popa, graphic artist and theater décor designer of great talents, sculptor and scenographer, artisan (he worked in wood and leather) and the son of writer Victor Ion Popa.

    As Jules and Irina Cazaban had been close friends with V. I. Popa and his wife Maria Mohor, Sorin Popa, imprisoned for political reasons for 16 years and freed in 1964, came to see them immediately. Jules, who had played the part of Ilie during the first performance of *Take, Ianke și Cadâr* in 1933, was no longer with us, but Sorin Popa kept seeing his family several times per week.

In 1981, he sought me in Paris and, after innumerable and bizarre adventures, including an exchange of letters with Mircea Eliade in which I played the role of mailbox for them, he disappeared into the crowd! After a few years, in 1984, I saw him again in New York where, as hotheaded as he was when he was 20, he had just gotten into a fight with some Romanians who didn't agree with his political views!

I don't know what happened with Sorin Popa from then on. But every day, my eyes pass over the Japanese woodblock prints and the painting of a Spanish nobleman, which I have hung around my house, as well as drawings, leather sacks and engraved works which he left me back then, saying he would come back to take them! I am still waiting for him today!

- Beate Fredanov, whom I saw at the Municipal Theater in many roles. I remember her most remarkably performance in *Dragă mincinosule* (Dear Liar) by Jerome Kilty in 1964, with Fory Etterle. One of the founding members of the famous *Barașeum*, a grand moment in the history of theater in Romania, she has remained an icon in the memory of theater artists through her talents in teaching, exercised for decades, until her death. Beate was, along with Jules Cazaban and A. Pop Marțian, one of the three professors to the '64 Golden Generation, at the Theater and Cinematography Art Institute (IATC).

- Octavian Cotescu, assistant at the IATC, so called Casandra, after the name of the hall where young actors would cut their teeth in acting from 1957 and on. After Jules's three years in teaching, Octavian, who was only 32 years old at the time, took up his class until their graduation. Afterwards, he continued on the path of an illustrious career in teaching.

The film *O dragoste lungă de-o seară* (A love lasting one evening) also reminds me of Octavian Cotescu. The film was shot in

1963 in Stremţ, a village in Alba County that has been in my heart for the last 16 years.

In 1969, when Bulandra Theater participated in the *Theatres des Nations* Festival in Paris, I had the joy of inviting him and Valeria Seciu, his wife, out for drinks, after they had been the hosts for the play *D'ale Carnavalului* (At the Carnival), directed by Lucian Pintilie. It was then that I met this great Romanian director, along with Iulian Negulescu, a young graduate from IATC, who had recently decided to remain in France, where he became actor *Julian Negulesco*.

* Gheorghe Storin, who lived in my neighborhood. I frequently saw him stopping passers-by who were running in order to catch the tramway by crying out loud in his thundering voice: *"Dear sir! You should never run after the tramway or after a woman. Another one will come by in a few minutes!"*

* George Măruţă, an actor at the Municipal Theater and a good friend of Jules, whose family I joined on vacation in Tuşnad and who had … a daughter …!

* *The young generation*, Jules' students from his classes in IATC, among which were Virgil Ogăşanu, Mariana Cercel and Ovidiu Moldovan.

Much about what I know of French history, I owe to Ilinca Tomoroveanu, whom I hadn't even met back then. Her mother, who was a colleague of my father's, lent me about 20 volumes of Alexandre Dumas novels, edited by Bibliotheque Rose, which I read voraciously during one summer in 1965.

I saw this artistic world again in 2004, when they celebrated their 40 years since graduation in Casandra and I took the occasion to write an article about it, which was published in Romanian magazines around the world.

* Ina Don, another actress at the Municipal Theater, maybe less famous because she primarily played secondary roles, with the exception of the titular role in *Don Gil de ciorap verde* (Don Gil of the Green Sock) by Tirso de Molina, a play which has apparently

faded from memory! I would have probably forgotten about her if she wasn't my neighbor when I lived on Donici Street, and a friend of my mother. Many years later, in France, I discovered that she was the niece of the renowned "French" cartoonist Don!

* Many other actors such as Nicolae and Ruxandra Sireteanu, George Manu, the *Ramadan actor* (called so after the plaque which was installed under his bust), Clody Bertola ... but my encounters with them were more sporadic, and thus less remarkable for me.

In conclusion, I realize that, although I have mentioned his name countless times, I haven't spoken about the life and trajectory of Jules Cazaban, one which I have followed step by step, for decades, from Ostrovski's *Pădurea* (The Forest), to *Visita bătrânei doamne* (The Visit), F. Durenmatt's play with which he ended his career. Sadly, this career, which unfolded on the theater stage as well as on screen and on air, has now faded into obscurity, even if some creations of his, such as Ianke from I. V. Popa's play, have become invaluable references in Romanian theater. His life's work deserves to be reevaluated[20]. In my opinion, I cannot say more than this, as the French say it: *"L'amitié d'un grand homme est un bienfait des dieux!"*.

————

In the spring of year 1958, the "World Festival of Puppets and Marionettes" took place in Bucharest. It was an excellent occasion to showcase the accomplishments of Romanian puppeteers and, for the public, to discover an artistic activity deemed by many to belong solely to children oriented plays.

During the festival, many accomplishments of internationally famous puppeteers such as Obrazțov, Trînka, Malik or Philippe Genty were showcased on the stage or on the screen – they in turn had the opportunity to discover the vivacity of the art of puppeteers in Romania, where this "specialty" had a history reaching back for over a century, in fares and markets.

The presence of foreign actors and the lively atmosphere thus created encouraged the appearance of associations, courses, amateur shows, conferences, lessons on puppeteering technique and the fabrication of marionettes and puppets. This is how I came to participate in several free lessons on the subject. I then discovered the world history of marionettes, as well as the existence of Pehlivan and Karaghioz, in Central Asia, or Guignol in Lyon.

A part of these classes were given by Renee George Silviu, the creator of the marionette theater, from the prewar period, who was the stage director at Țăndărică Theater but was forbidden to sign her work back then due to the activities of her husband, George Silviu.

We must also mention the accomplishments of Margareta Nicolescu, who was the director of Țăndărică Theater back then and who, along with Jacques Felix, created the International Festival of Marionettes, in Charleville-Mezieres, a finalization of their activities regarding this field that started in France in 1972.

We must draw attention to the fact that Țăndărică Theater, in its form today, as a result of the fusion of different puppeteer troupes, exists in Bucharest since 1949, whereas in Paris, a permanent stage for such puppet shows did not exist until 2003!

This fun activity, (a puppet play always has to have a happy ending, as a famous puppeteer would say) guides us to the animation film, an activity in which Romania excelled during the 50's and the 60's, mostly due to the efforts of the truly talented and unforgettable director Ion Popescu-Gopo. Starting with his first color animation film *Doi epurași* (Two Bunnies), and continuing with *Rățoiul neascultător* (The Naughty Duck) and *Poveste cu trei ursuleți* (A Tale of Three Bears) and culminating with *Scurtă Istorie* (A Short History) which won the *Palme d'Or* award in Cannes in 1957, he knew how to create symbolic characters, simplified to the maximum, playfully repre-senting timeless human traits and situations. Talented graphic artists, such as Matty Aslan, and genius humorists, such as Mircea Crișan, helped him. Gopo also collaborated with talented musicians, named Nicolae Kirculescu and Henry Mălineanu, who happily composed the scores for his animation films. Who hasn't joyfully hummed the tune of *Marinică, Marinică*, along with Dorina Drăghici, at that time?

Seen through the ages, these accomplishments seem ridiculous due to the proletkult comments of the tunes, such as the following lines, written about *Marinică, Marinică*: "*The critique done by his fellow colleagues and his love help him transform into a new man, with a healthy mentality and attitude."*

Not even Krateyl Circus, named the State Circus in 1954, was safe from the same treatment by the communists, who had nothing to do with the artistic activities but imposed the doctrine "from higher up": *"It is about the incessant perfecting of man, through pushing his boundaries in power, prowess, flexibility, ability and courage"* (Emil Krateyl)

Few people know that in fact Emil Krateyl, who was a talented horse trainer and the descendant of a numerous family of circus artists, had to donate all his equipment to the State Circus. He only kept his animals, with which he was then employed at the State Circus!

Back then, before the construction of the concrete building near Tonola park which would later house the circus in 1961, shows took place in a tent, installed in front of the University, on a land where the National Theater sits today.

There I went to see the *Parisul pe gheață* (Paris on Ice) show, with French ice skating stars, such as Nadine Damien, the French ice skating campion in 1953. Later, I gathered around, among other thousands of people from Bucharest, to see the famous Moby Dick whale kept in ice!

The Revue Theater in Romania also had numerous avatars during the 50's and the 60's! After the bizarre disappearance of Constantin Tănase, the uncontested maestro of the genre, in 1945, the authorities of the era sought to quickly forget his name, changing the name of the theater to The Estrada Humour Ensemble. Its function was defined thus, in the words of composer and director Ion Vasilescu:

"Although young and burdened by many responsibilities, the Estrada Ensemble is on the right path, graced with the help of the Party, the government and all people of the arts with whom it collaborates. The attention of the masses is sympathetically turned towards what constitutes an impulse towards even greater accomplishments in this domain, after the model of the Estrada Ensemble in the USSR."

In fact, the satirical character and critique of society was less of a focus for the program. Instead, it insisted more on folklore and proletariat centered ballet (with themes such as life in the countryside or bringing culture into the factories). Later, it became the State Estrada Theater and, starting with 1962, the C. Tănase Satirical and Musical Theater.

All this time, the C. Tănase Revue Theater (which regained its name after 1990), had a long list of strong personalities to grace its stage, such as: Maria Tănase, Ion Antonescu Cărăbuş, Dan Demetrescu, Vasile Tomazian, Horia Căciulescu, Radu Zaharescu, Horia Şerbănescu, Elena Burmaz, Zizi Şerban, Alexandru Arşinel, Stela Popescu, Nicu Constantin, Alexandru Lulescu, Gică Petrescu, Nicolae Niţescu, Luigi Ionescu, Nicuşor Constantinescu, Nicolae Frunzetti, Biţu Fălticineanu, Nicolae Dinescu, Ion Vasilescu, Gherase Dendrino, Henry Mălineanu, Gelu Solomonescu, Nicolae Patrichi, Sergiu Malagamba, George Voinescu and Oleg Danovski. But the most loved and admired actor of them all during this period was Mircea Crişan. The public who hoped to notice, beyond the puns and the feigned naiveté of the interpreter, the vitriol filled arrows launched towards the rulers of the day, eagerly awaited his sketches. It was a slight satisfaction for each of them, a manner of saying loud something that they all thought! This was up until 1968, when Mircea Crişan remained in Paris and later settled in Germany, where he started a new career in German theater, filled with tours through Israel where he played in Romanian. He also had comical interventions on the Free Europe Radio. In 1990, he was able to return on the stage in Romania.

Many Revue actors from the times continued the style they had created before the war, such as N. Stroe, with his famous: *"Hello, this is Stroe, and he asks you to allow him to cheer you up for a while, to joke again with you!"*

At the beginning of 60's I saw the show entitled *Vitamina M este muzica* (Music is Vitamin M) at the Boema Garden, on the land where we find the Central University Library (B.C.U.) today. Speaking of B.C.U., in 1958 I went to a conference held in the library's theatre celebrating one hundred years since the birth of the Jewish humorist Shalom Alechem. Various humorous texts belonging to the famous Yiddish writer where then interpreted by a few renowned actors. The height of the evening was the reading of a short story by Jules Cazaban, born in Fălticeni where he had lived among the Jewish population, and had thus the ability to masterfully mimic their accent. The most humorous moment was achieved when he interpreted the key formula, in the words of the main character: *"Moses, bring the bomb!"*, which raised the whole theatre to their feet and caused rounds upon rounds of applause. The formula stuck and was heard around the city for weeks on end!

I find it impossible to enumerate all singers and humorists who left their mark on Revue shows and, later, in TV during the times.

I found many of them to be ridiculous back then, especially because of the proletkult texts they were forced to sing (Trio Grigoriu with *"Cranes, silvery laughing in the sun, cranes..."*) or due to the parodies that circulated throughout the city (*At the "Trei Brazi" Cabin, we lack water and stove fuel*). Yet today, after so many years, without the context of the lidded era, we realize that the melody of such compositions by artists such as Ion Vasilescu, Henry Mălineanu, Gherase Dendrino, Marius Mihail, Temistocle Popa, Edmond Deda and Elly Roman were prime quality.

Even some of the texts were remarkable! If one listens closely to the song *Broscuța Oac* (The Ribbit Frog) written by the Grigoriu brothers, one cannot help but remark the multitude of words rhyming with *"ac"* they managed to find, which reminds me of a contemporary song by Serge Gainsbourg, with rhymes ending in *"ex"*!

And not to speak of the modernity of jazz we owe to Sergiu Malagamba, the creator of the "malagambist" fashion trend, a form of harmless revolt against the regime, which was nothing more than the continuation of the Ultra Swing (Zazou) movement in France in the 40's or the "gaga" in Mussolini's Italy. Half a century later, I would discover that our malagambists in Romania had their equivalent in the "stilyagas" in the USSR.

The Romanian groups "Kosak Sisters" or "Trio Armonia" were a variant of the famous "Andrews Sisters" in USA or the "Trio Lescano" in Italy.

Out of the tens of singers who were then admired on the stage of the Revue Theater, I will mention a few names: Aida Moga, Lavinia Slăveanu, Dorina Drăghici, Doina Badea, Pompilia Stoian, Gigi Marga, Mara Ianoli, Roxana Matei, Constantin Drăghici, Ștefan Bănică, Aurelian Andreescu, Dan Spătaru, Luigi Ionescu, George Bunea and Dorel Livianu.

I must mention Margareta Pâslaru and Marina Voica, who are still present on the stages and screens in Bucharest!

I have a duty of honor towards Gică Petrescu. For years, I have considered him to be "a mummy of the history of pop music", same as Charles Trenet!

In recent years, after this singer, poet and French composer – he himself a member of the Ultra Swing (Zazou) movement – became a "classic" in France or, as it is said today, "a cult musician", I began to listen once again to Gică Petrescu's songs and I noticed the similarities in style, energy and scenic features between the two artists.

But before that, at the beginning of the 2000's I happened to meet him by chance, at … the Bellu Cemetery! In front of me, I saw this elderly man, a bit untidy in appearance, wearing an enormous pair of sunglasses, who had brought a picture and wished for it to be put on his gravestone. This is how I remarked he was Gică Petrescu!

When I told him I am coming from Paris, he took off his glasses and surprised me with a nostalgic smile that brightened his face. He began remembering the concerts he had in Olympia, before and after the war, and he would not stop talking.

I had the chance to see Gigi Marga a few years ago at the Romanian restaurant in Brooklyn, where, on Easter, she sang for three or four hours to the delight of the audience, in five or six languages, like a true American crooner. And she is now 88 years old!

I saw George Brunea more than a decade ago, in Haifa in Israel, during a tour of the Revue Theater with the same *Trei Mărioare* (Three Maries) or *Lalele* (Tulips) (Which he shared with Luigi Ionescu in the 60's). But then, at the entrance of the Israeli theater, all the spectators spoke … Romanian!

As a consequence of global warming, I was recently reminded of the song *E primăvară în ianuarie* (It's Spring in January) which he sang along with Luigi Ionescu, accompanied by the Trio Armonia.

Maybe all these Estrada shows from the 60's would have not stayed with me if they wouldn't have represented the preparation needed in order to passionately fall in love with American musical comedy. From here came my desire to see *Mamma Mia, Les Miserables, Cats, A Chorus Line, 42nd Street, The King and I,* and *The Rink* – and so on, almost all musicals in

New York, a wish I had had for more than 35 years. The same goes for the tango shows in Argentina, the fado shows in Portugal, the Revues in Brazil and Columbia, and the list could go on. Because, finally, the Revue world is the same in C. Tănase Theater as in Caesar's Palace, in Las Vegas, or in the Casino of Beirut!

Just as well, a comic opera play can be just as good … or as bad at the Ion Dacian Operetta Theater in Bucharest as at the Reduta in Budapest or at the Theater an der Wien and Volksoper in Vienna!

I however had the chance to see prime quality shows on the stage of the Bucharest Operetta Theater during the 50's and the 60's, with remarkable actors, sometimes with stage set that was a bit obsolete, but corresponded to the style of performance, which is itself quite antique.

Let's briefly mention the unforgettable artists that played such shows during the era: Ion Dacian, Sile Popescu, Maria Wauvrina, Constanța Câmpeanu, Toni Buiacici, Virginica Romanovski and many more. Even a few classical actors briefly passed through this world, such as Radu Beligan, Jules Cazaban, Ion Lucian and Nicolae Gărdescu.

Even more interesting are the two distinct aspects of musical theater back then, today inexplicably overlooked:

*   National creation: Gherase Dendrino (*Lăsați-mă să cânt! – Let Me Sing!, Lisystrata*), Filaret Barbu, and Elly Roman. Even if the entire comic opera cannot reach the level of Strauss, countless arias are worth noticing. The success of duets by Angela Gheorghiu and Roberto Alagna with arias by Gherase Dendrino, in Romanian, on several stages around the world is the best proof of this!
*   Soviet operas, which we listened to during our adolescence, such as Dunaievski's *Vânt de libertate* (The Wind of Liberty) which had excellent music, despite the ideology filled libretto which was characteristic of the period.

As far as I am concerned, I cannot forget the communicative joy of musical shows from my childhood and I have tried to transmit it to the actors in the Operetta Festival which takes place two times per year in Lamalou-les-Bains, in the Languedoc region of Southern France.

———

As passionate about this genre as one can be, one cannot go to the theater or to the opera every day! However, you can watch TV or listen to the radio on a daily basis. In the 50's, the choice was easy! The radio had two stations, "Program 1" and "Program 2", and television started broadcasting in 1956. It was however, as I would later discover in Rome in 2014, during an anniversary exposition, only two years after the Italian television started broadcasting!

At the beginning, radio programs alternated between the news and folklore music. Moreover, their broadcast schedule would fit on half a page in the newspaper, under the initials "SuMoTueWedThuFriSat", meaning "Sunday/Monday ...".

Later came the musical programs entitled *"Din folclorul popoarelor"* (From the peoples' folklore), from which we would occasionally fish out an Italian song or one from the Far West. Bit by bit, interesting programs started popping up, especially during Sundays, such as *"De toate pentru toți"* (A Bit of Everything for Everybody), during which we eagerly awaited for Ioan Grigorescu's segment, called *"De pe alte meridiane"* (Across Other Meridians).

Just as awaited were the trivia game shows such as *"Cine știe câștigă"* (Answer and Win), during which I would closely follow each stage up to the grand prize. One of our family friends, the endocrinologist Frederic Watts, who had created a bit of fame for himself in Bucharest high society due to his famous diet (already!), won the grand prize with the subject "The life and works of Rubens". He was a man with an extraordinary memory, and, a few years later, he managed to learn Russian by watching soviet films with Romanian subtitles on the TV. However, despite the small selection of programs, many people berated all activities on the small screen, calling it "idiotvision".

In my last two years of high school, classes started at 2 o'clock in the afternoon, and I would spend my mornings listening to the radio while doing homework. This is how I came to discover the work of mural artists from Mexico such as Orozco, Siqueros and Diego Ribera, the tropical rhythms of Ernesto Lecuona and the comparison between Carlos Gardel and Ionel Fernic's tangos. I had the opportunity to verify this knowledge, some 30 years later, in Mexico, Guadalajara, Havana, Siboney and Buenos-Aires.

The first television broadcast I ever saw was the Yves Montand's recital, in Floreasca Hall. The tour of the famous French singer through Eastern countries, accompanied by his wife Simone Signoret, rised then a lot of controversy, because it was a short while after the occupation of Budapest by soviet tanks. His visit to Moscow was seen as silently supporting this invasion. Yves Montand later stated his reasons, but I will not reproduce them here. What shocked the entire Romanian public back then was that he appeared dressed in a smoking in Moscow and wearing overalls in Bucharest!

Even if Romanian Television had its humble beginnings, with hosts selected on political criteria, it evolved rapidly, changing into a more attractive medium, with hosts such as Cleo Stieber and Florin Brătescu. Cultural programs multiplied: the broadcasting of Sunday concerts at the Athenaeum Philharmonic, opera and ballet shows, theater plays and adaptations made exclusively for the TV in which the same admired actors played. I, for example, remember George Constantin in *Doisprezece oameni furioși* (Twelve Angry Men), who played just as magnificently as Henry Fonda did in the American original, or F. Durenmatt's *Pană de automobil* (A Dangerous Game), starring Mircea Albulescu.

A moment of "defrosting", greatly appreciated by spectators, was the appearance of the Sunday program *Varietăți* (Varieties), hosted by Paul Sava, which emptied the streets of Bucharest. Apart from the usual folkloric dances and songs, of questionable authenticity, you could see the true stars of the opera Nicolae Herlea, Niculescu-Basu, Ștefănescu-Goangă, Dan Iordăchescu, Magda Ianculescu and Iolanda Mărculescu) and operetta (Ion Dacian, Constanța Câmpeanu, Toni Buiacici…).

The more surprising part was Ion Fintești anu's cabaret number, in which he sang: "*Tempted I was/ To have her in my paws/ A demi-goddess spawned/ A fair nymph so blonde"*. Or the apparition of Elena Zamora, in a powdered wig, looking like she just came from the Court of Louis, King of France, singing Charles Tenet's song *Le menuet c'est la polka du roi!*. Only a few years later, in 1968, Michel Simon, during a veritable marriage in the presence of Tenet, would sing the same song – it was a moment that made history on French television!

The first out of a long list of successful series, which have now been aired on televisions across the world, was *Sfântul* (The Saint) with Simon Templar (Roger Moore), which fascinated us, as it fascinated all Romanian viewers.

I had the opportunity, back in 1953, when the building of the Romanian Radio Broadcast was newly inaugurated, to walk through its studios and down its hallways. A very talented photographer named Ferester thought I was photogenic and took me there to take pictures of me. The yellow wood padded studios and the hectic yet silent atmosphere impressed me. I find the same atmosphere lately, three or four times a year when I come by to record for RRI. Nothing has changed in 60 years! Even the door handles and the white marble of the stairs are still there, with the signs of usage acquired over the years. What shocked and disappointed me back then was the fact that Silvia Chicoş, the young 10 year old voice which I had adored in her radio programs for "children and pioneers", was in reality a 40 year old lady who had a limp. Of course, back then I did not know any of the drama in the life of the radiophonic idol of children in Romania.

———

I do not know why, but cinematographic production in Romania during the '50's and 60's always gave me a feeling of being "unfinished".

Of course, the proletkult subjects from the scenarios such as *Mitrea Cocor, Răsună valea* (The Valley Echoes), *In sat la noi* (In Our Village), *Nepoţii gornistului* (The Nephews of the Bugler), *Viaţa învinge* (Life Conquers) had nothing to be enthusiastic about. Less so were the historical "fabrications" in the style of *Lupeni 29*, produced in order to emphasize *the glorious struggle of PCR during the illegality times*. Even if the actors playing in these films

(George Vraca, Ion Talianu, Septimiu Sever, Irina Răchițeanu-Șirianu, Fory Etterle, Geo Barton, C. Ramadan, Marcel Anghelescu and Ghe. Ciprian) were the best actors the Romanian scene had to offer! Despite the musical score signed by talented composers (Paul Constantinescu, Sabin Drăgoi, Ion Dumitrescu and Radu Paladi), it all sounded false. Not to mention the mandatory presence of Lica Gheorghiu, daughter of PCR leader, who, despite having a pretty face, was utterly bad at acting. All of Bucharest was in stitches when they aired a short film called *Lica și leul* (Lica and the Lion)!

The only achievements that somehow managed to slip through the claws of the party where the adaptations of great Romanian classical novels as *Lanțul slăbiciunilor* (The Chain of Weaknesses) with Radu Beligan and Marcel Anghelescu, or *Vizita* (The Visit) with Gr. Gion and C. Ramadan, directed by Jean Georgescu. Maybe this is the reason why the first "consistent" Romanian film I can remember is *Moara cu noroc* (The Lucky Mill), produced in 1955 by Victor Iliu, a true Romanian western, starring Geo Barton, Ioana Bulcă and Constantin Codrescu. This film was nominated for the *Palme d'Or* award in Cannes in 1957.

A satirical film entitled *Directorul nostru* (Our Director) also came out in 1955. It was a critique of the prevailing bureaucracy, and its roles fit like a glove to actors Al. Giugaru and Gr. Vasiliu-Birlic. The theme was not to the authorities' liking, who took Jean Georgescu's right to sign his work until 1962. This film stuck in my memory because of one scene, which was filmed in Drobeta Square (today called Spain Square), near where I lived.

The male star of the era, the pretty boy of Romanian cinematography was Iurie Darie, back then. A strange example, a true classic, without the common spelling of "comrades", and which even included a fashion show (!) was Paul Călinescu's 1956 film *Pe răspunderea mea* (It's On Me), starring Iurie Darie and Ileana Iordache, with Liliana Tomescu and Ion Talianu in the main roles. If I am not mistaken, Iurie Darie also starred in *Alo? Ați greșit numărul!* (Hello? Wrong number!), filmed by Andrei Călărașu in 1958, with the famous exchange between Iurie's character and his beloved, played by Rodica Tapalagă: *Volens? Nolens!* The title of the film was mocked by the humorous voices back then and became: *Alo? Ați băgat degetul într-o gaură străină!* (Hello? You put the finger in the wrong hole!).

Other accomplishments in this medium followed, varying in scale, but I will only mention *Darclée* in 1961, starring Silvia Popovici and Victor Rebengiuc, in which Jules played a secondary role. The film was also nominated for an award in Cannes. It was filmed entirely in Romania, and the grand theaters around the world (Milano, Buenos-Aires, Montevideo, Paris and Rio) were replaced with postcards. After I saw the film at the Cinemateca in Bucharest early 90's, I followed the itinerary of the great singer and I travelled to Montevideo (Teatro Solis), Buenos-Aires (Teatro Colon), Rio (Teatro Municipal) and Milano (La Scala Theater).

Another noteworthy film was Gh. Turcu and Andrei Călărașu's 1960 film *Portretul unui necunoscut* (Portrait of an anonymous). The detective plot centered on a Van Dyck painting was an excellent pretext to visit the collections of the National Museum of Art and especially the recently renovated Stirbey Vodă wing of the Royal Palace (called The RPR Palace back then).

Earlier, I had seen Aurel Mihales and Gh. Naghi's 1959 film *Telegrame* (Telegrams), after I. L. Caragiale's short novel with the same title. The film had had a great casting, including resounding names, among which Gr. Vasiliu-Birlic, Șt. Ciubotărașu, M. Anghelescu, Jules Cazaban, Nicky Atanasiu, Costache Antoniu, and Vasilica Tastaman, and was also nominated for an award in Cannes.

I could now mention the role of Caragiale, played by Jules Cazaban in 1962, on the stage of the Comedy Theater, in the play called *Procesul D-lui Caragiale* (The Trial of Mr. Caragiale) by Mircea Ștefănescu, accompanied by Radu Beligan, Șt. Ciubotărașu, Dem Savu and Ion Lucian.

Jules created an extraordinary role back then, helped by such convincing makeup, that he would be stopped on the street and asked if he was indeed the famous playwright.

Remembering the Cinemateca of my adolescent years, I cannot forget the evenings I spent in the company of Jean Gabin, Erich von Stroheim, Michelle Morgan, Emmanuelle Riva, Jean Pierre Leaud, and Robert Lamoureux in the cinema in Cosmonauților Plaza (called Lahovary today) and, afterwards, on Magheru Boulevard. I saw countless old films from the Cinematography Archives, with Ch. Chaplin, Stan Laurel and Oliver

Hardy, Harold Lloyd, Malec, Mary Pickford, Buster Keaton and many other stars, some of them forgotten. The Cinemateca also created a prize (a free pass that lasted one year) for the spectator who could recognize this or that actor from the silent movies!

Unforgettable was the night of the presentation of "Intolerance: Love's Struggle throughout the Ages" by D. W. Griffith. Two and a half hours without any kind of musical score, in complete silence, apart from the occasional cough or dropping of one's keys on the floor!

At the same cinema in Lahovary Plaza I must have seen "The Young Ones" with Cliff Richard about ten times or Gianni Morandi singing "In ginocchio da te". The documentary about the Moiseiev Ballet tour in the United States also had an unexpected success when it showed in that cinema. It wasn't due to the long scenes depicting Russian folkloric dances, but rather to the two minutes in which Harry Belafonte sang *Matilda* in a bar in Los Angeles. We occasionally stopped by right at the moment of this scene and after it was finished, we would get up and carry on with our daily lives!

This unforgettable couple of minutes made me choose, from a variety of Las Vegas shows in 1973, Belafonte's show in Caesar's Palace and his show in Dusseldorf in 1986.

Other successful films were historical reenactments, in which Jean Marais and Jean-Paul Belmondo excelled (*Contele de Monte Cristo, Cocoșatul* (The Hunchback), *Cei trei mușchetari* (The Three Musketeers), and *Cartouche*). In the same genre, Gerard Barray excelled in *Căpitanul Fracasse* (Captain Fracasse) and *Cavalerul Pardaillan* (The Pardaillan Knight). These divertissement films were ideal for hot summer evenings in the capital city, and they would fill stadiums and outdoor theaters, where they were shown on Cinemascope wide screens. Sometimes the attention of the spectators would divert towards the sky, when they would notice the shifting light of a satellite, a rare sight back then!

At that time, I saw Alberto Sordi's Italian musicals like *Veneția, luna și tu!* (*Venice, the Moon and you!*) and the Austrian films with ski champion Toni Seilers. On a note, not less serious because it is about comedy, but much more consistent due to the quality of the actors Vittorio Gassman and Jean-Louis Trintignant, the anthology film seen in Volga cinema, named *Il sorpasso* (The Surpassing) by Dino Rissi, gave me the opportunity of recognizing the Italian actor, whom I met about four years later in Milano.

And of course, everybody remembers Michelangelo Antonioni's films with Monica Vitti, Fellini's films with Giulietta Massina and Anthony Quinn, *Vikings* with Kirk Douglas and the long introduction accompanied by Cesar Franck's symphony or *Fun in Acapulco* where Elvis Presley starred and sang!

I would like to mention two special moments at the beginning of the 60's:

* The American Film Festival, in the presence of Shirley MacLaine and Jack Lemmon, who starred in *The Flat*. Many people who had been to the premiere at Patria (I mean ARO!-the name of this cinema before the war) or to the cocktail after party at the United States Embassy would occasionally stop me on the street to tell me of the striking resemblance between the American actor and ... my father! I would see Shirley MacLaine again on Broadway in 1984. It was perhaps the greatest one woman show I have ever seen, one which celebrated her 50 years anniversary. I bought a bootleg cassette of the recording in Dubai, a few months later.
* The French Film Festival, also screening in ARO, where Marina Vlady assisted at the premiere of *La Princesse de Clèves*.

   We all remember the steps that followed in her artistic and personal life, as well as her French-Romanian cinematographic collaboration: the film *Mona* by Henry Colpi, with Claude Rich and Cristea Avram, her liaison with the Romanian actor. She talks of these moments with utter sincerity in her memoir book called *24 images/seconde*.

To Anthony Quinn, I owe *une fiere chandelle*, as the French say! In 1966, when I had failed the Special Mathematics exam twice in my second year, I already saw myself failing the entire year and having to present all the 12 exams again. My moral was down to 0! While waiting on the committee to issue their decision, I went to see Kakoyanis' *Zorba the Greek*. I came out of the cinema with my moral back up and the will to move mountains! After only a few hours, I found out that another exam session was to be organized, during which I successfully passed and avoided failing the entire year. I must confess that the extra exam session was not put in place for my personal comfort, but rather because the son of Gogu Rădulescu, Central Comitee member of the PCR was in the same situation as I was!

Was it Anthony Quinn who interceded in our favor? Or where we, so to speak, laureates in the circumstance competition?

Of course, no one can ever forget Hentri Colpi, who gave Romanian films international dimensions through his art and talent:

- *Codin,* an adaptation of a novel with the same name by Panait Istrati, brought him on the podium in Cannes, with a *Prix pour le scenario* award in 1963.
- *Mona, l'etoile sans nom*, an adaptation of Mihail Sebastian's *Steaua fără nume*, a film filled with subtlety but which, sadly, did not achieve the success it deserved. Marina Vlady writes in her memoirs: "*...this film, which will always be one of my favorites, even if unfortunately it wasn't as successful as it could have been in France. I think Henri Colpi is somewhere outside of time, outside of fashion, and in this case, he managed to create one of the most beautiful cinematographic works. Was it too early or was it too atypical?*".

Once again, atypical! Maybe this is why I loved it so much!

Soviet cinematography was also present on the screens of Bucharest. Even if countless proletkult productions left me with no remarkable memories – perhaps I didn't even go to see them! – a few films really stayed with me from my adolescence.

Of course, one of them is *Zboară Cocorii* (The Cranes Are Flying), winner of the *Palme d'Or* award in 1958 – it made an impression on all of us. Beyond the wonderful acting by Tatiana Samoilova and Aleksei Batalov, beyond the universal intrigue that differed from the usual themes of soviet movies, the long period of "defrosting" echoed as a cry of hope in change coming soon. A dream we all had!

Naturally, Einstein's masterpiece films could be seen at the Cinemateca. Two of them were especially remarkable for me: *Steaguri pe turnuri* (Flags on Towers), a 1958 adaptation of a book by "the genius soviet educator Makarenko", who explained "the importance of the influence of the collective in the task of reeducating asocial elements". The second film, rather different in theme, was the 1956 *Noapte de carnival* (Carnival Night), a true American musical comedy, doubled by a satirical take on communist bureaucracy, all illuminated by Ludmila Gurşenko's charming smile.

There is so much more to talk about regarding Romanian cinematographic art during the half of the last century! However, I would rather mention a few less known people from this world.

I only met Pavel Constantinescu during the 70's. In the paper entitled *1234 Cineaşti Români – Ghid bibliofilmografic* (1234 Romanian Filmmakers – A Bibliofilmographic Guide), Cristina Orciovescu and Bujor T. Rîpeanu published the following biographical note:

Constantinescu, Pavel
(Josefson, Pavel)
Documentary film director (Odobeşti the 10ᵗʰ of April 1933)
Studies: The Union Institute of Cinematography, Moscow, 1961, enlisted in the Soviet Army. 1945-1950: UTC CC activist. Vicepresident and general director of the Cinematography Committee (1950-1953), general director of the Buftea Studio (1954-1955). From 1960, at the Al. Sahia Studio. Lives in Israel from 1971.
Awards: Praga 1967 (Romanian art treasures); Leipzig 1967 (Stolen Childhood).

A list follows, detailing 16 documentary films produced in Bucharest between 1959 and 1971. The most important are a series of four films on the work of Brâncuşi, filmed in 1970 and 1971 in the great museums around the world, locations where the sculptor's works are found.

A complex character, contradictory yet charming, Pavel was impressive through his optimism, his thirst for knowledge and his talent as a narrator. He passed away in Tel-Aviv in 1997, he left behind not just the above quoted films, bought at a hefty price from the Alexandru Sahia Studio, but also numerous production notes, memoirs of his voyages and several scenarios intended for future films.

In all my school years, I also met a talented cinematographer named Gyuri Hershdorfer, who worked in Romania during the 50's and the 60's with director Paul Barbăneagră (Barba-Negra in France!). I remember one of the films, a black and white motion picture, without text, about the life of fishermen in the Danube Delta. The artistic documentary film was accompanied by music inspired off Carl Orff's *Carmina Burana*. After 1964, after he had fled to France, Paul produced tens of documentary films, all under a common theme: *"Géographie – Architecture et Sacré"*. During his last years, Paul would host literary gatherings at his house, where he would invite top Romanian intellectuals who were in exile in Paris.

Few still remember Nina Behar, a talented documentary film director (approximately 30 titles between 1958 and 1974) as well as her dramatic destiny. After winning international awards in Paris (1965), Lausanne(1966) and Venice(1969), she fled to France, where she lived the last of her days (1989) working as an usher.

Elisabeta Bostan was a Romanian film maker, specializing in films for children (more than 25 films between 1956 and 1991, among which *Amintiri din Copilărie, Pupăza din tei* and *Fram*).

In 1962, in my daily passing by Ioanid Park on my way towards Sadoveanu high school, I saw the filming of a scene from the movie *Puștiul* (The Kid). I stopped to admire not only how the director worked with the young actor in the main role, but also the art of the scenographer who had managed to create, with few means but by artfully using the natural surroundings, the frightening atmosphere needed in the scene.

Documentary enthusiasts remember the Timpuri Noi cinema on the 6th of March boulevard (renamed Gh. Gheorghiu-Dej after 1964, today called Regina Elisabeta, as it was before 1948), where short documentary films were shown all day, from morning to evening. This would allow us to skip only one class at school (incidentally, it was the Russian Language class!) and to come back for the rest of the day.

There I saw the famous Italian film *Mondo Cane* in 1962, which shocked the world when it came out and gave birth to a new style of reporting, and later an entire branch of the "7th art", the "shockumentary". Moreover, Jacopetti's next film in 1966, *Africa addio!*, rose numerous discussions regarding the authenticity of its footage. However, *Mondo Cane* also made the song *Ti guardero nel cuore* famous – its translation in English was entitled *More* and recorded by the great American stars of the 60's.

But first of all, I sat in queue in front of Timpuri Noi cinema to see Jacques-Yves Cousteau's film entitled *Lumea tăcerii* (The Silent World), directed by Louis Malle and awarded *Palme d'Or* in 1956 and an Oscar for the best documentary feature in 1957.

In 1993 I would meat Cousteau's team in the Bucegi Mountains (!), as they had come to Romania to film a documentary on the Danube Delta! Jacques Cousteau was also named a member of the Romanian Academy and Doctor Honoris Causa of the Bucharest University in 1990 and 1993, respectively.

———

Opportunities to meet with the people of the arts were not at all rare during the 60's – they were, in fact, available for anybody.

The People's Art University held its classes in Sala Dalles and it sufficed to acquire its schedule in order to choose the subjects or professor you wished to attend.

I remember a series of conferences held by Petru Comarnescu about "The history of Western art" in which he made an extensive comparison between Rubens and Rembrandt, expressing his preference for the former. This was an occasion for me to go back to the National Museum of Art, in order to more accurately get my own opinion on the subject. Beauty is in the eye of the beholder! *De gustibus...!*

What amazed me back then in his talk was the freedom with which he spoke about his studies in the United States and his friendship with Mircea Eliade (they had both been awarded the *Cartea Românească* scholarship before the war, but he had chosen to study in the USA, while Eliade had left for India).

This observation holds for other high-ranking intellectuals who, at some point, had agreed to countless compromises with the communist system, going further than their own left wing convictions. I am referring to men such as Matei Socor or Alexandru Graur, with whom I had loose family ties. Some of them, such as Jules Perahim or Victor Mașek, had the opportunity, while fleeing to the west or living past the 90's to "turn coats". I will always have this question regarding some of them: When where they honest and when where they just opportunistic?

Coming back to the conferences in the 60's, it was then when I attended some in Sala Dalles held by Eugen Schileru and by Viorel Cosma at the University of Music. I was excited about the series called "Friendship of the Arts", in which Viorel Cosma followed a common philosophical or literary theme through different art mediums, as it had been touched upon by composers, writers, painters and so on. This idea stuck with me even after I went to France and I pitched it in 1968 to the organizers of the *Maison de la Culture* (House of culture) in Saint Etienne, where I studied at Ecole des Mines.

Everything was ready! A round hall seating 200 people, I even chose the jingle that would start and end the program (*J'ai rendez-vous avec vous!* by Georges Brassens).

At that time, I realized that I had to choose between Ecole des Mines and my artistic career. Being the realist I am, I chose the former, without giving up the idea of occasionally flirting with the latter!

I should mention that all the cultural activities I was engaged in during the 60's were done in the company of Costin Cazaban – we were always up to date with the artistic life of the Capital and the latest news on the stage and screen, of the quill pen or paintbrush. He had a preference for the world of music, to which he dedicated his life and career.

———

The press during the 50's was more than dull! The daily newspapers (*Scînteia, Scînteia tineretului, România Liberă, Munca* and, later, *Informația Bucureștiului*) were only four pages long and usually most of them were dedicated to the propaganda in favor of the activities of PMR, while the last page contained a closely selected and highly interpreted version of the international news. Even " *Contemporanul, weekly newspaper dedicated to political, social and cultural matters*" would publish extensive polemic pro-communist articles, signed by the same educators of the Party: Radu Lupan, Horia Liman, Ion Vitner and Ion N. Bălănescu. Only the last pages contained true artistic or literary chronicles written by authors such as Mioara Cremene, Nina Cassian, Ovid S. Cohmălniceanu and Emil Suter – however, they all had the same ideology substrate. Even *Sportul popular* "The Peoples' Sport"'s first page was filed with propagandist articles or "visits of Party and State leaders in friendly countries"!

Only at the beginning of the 60's, *Contemporanul* became a true cultural magazine in which, skipping the first pages of propaganda, one could find information about the cultural life around the world, even the western part. At this point, the cartoons drawn by Rik or Nell Cobar depicting fat American imperialists with cigars at the corner of their mouths and sporting top hats disappeared! George Călinescu, distinguished intellectual who had formerly published *Cronica mizantropului* (The Misanthropist's Chronicle), would reappear in 1956 with a column called *Cronica optimistului* (The Optimist's Chronicle)!

Secolul XX, revistă de sinteză (The 20th Century, a synthesis magazine), edited by the Writers' Union starting 1961, with Dan Hăulică as editor-in-chief and issued with the help of Şt. Augustin Doinaş, represented a cornerstone for our national and international culture. Within its pages I read extracts from the writings of the great American novelists (Faulkner, Steinbeck), chronicles regarding French authors ("*La Nouvelle Vague*", Alain Robbe-Grillet, Francoise Sagan) and I even discovered Romanian artists that had been forbidden for years (Eugen Ionesco, Ion Barbu and Ion Ţuculescu).

Western press was forbidden for almost two decades! The sole exceptions were the few newspapers owned by the communist Party, such as *Lettres francaises*. However, even their circulation was restricted! Some acquaintances of mine, ladies born in France and married to Romanian men during the war who became "people with important functions" during the 50's, told me they had to go to their husbands' office in order to read a French newspaper! They did not have the permission to take it out of the Ministry!

In 1962, my father met a group of French people on the street, members of the PCF. Sure that we shared his political views, one of them offered to subscribe us to the French communist newspaper *L'Humanite*. This is how, for three years, I had the chance of reading a French newspaper out of which, apart from the traditionally communist formulas it used, I could also learn information that I wouldn't have otherwise discovered unless I were to listen to the programs on Radio Free Europe, when they were not jammed! Maybe this is why, to this day, I read daily both a right wing journal (*Le Figaro*) and a left wing journal (*Le Monde*), in my efforts to uncover the objective truth.

In *L'Humanite* I followed the daily columns: *Mais,… dit Andre Wurmser* or Maurice Thorez's funerals, worthy of a Roman Emperor. However, between 1960 and 1963, Jules Cazaban would receive *L'Avant-scene* monthly magazine, and so I would know what was playing in Parisian theaters.

The situation was changed in 1965 when I met and befriended a French family in Mamaia. They promised to send me every month the four or five weekly issues of *l'Express*, which I received regularly until I left Romania in 1967.

This is how I discovered the great French journalists of the 60's: Jean-Jacques Servan-Schreiber, Françoise Giroud, François Mauriac, Catherine Ney, Ivan Levai, Claude Imbert and many, many others. Of course we all eagerly awaited every end of the month to receive the package coming from France, and which, after it was read by all the family, it would be happily exchanged for *Paris Match* or *Le Nouvel Obs* that other friends received.

A matter that intrigued me in regards to my *l'Express* magazines was that some quarters on several pages where always missing and it seemed they had been neatly cut out with scissors. Was it censorship? I later found out that these missing areas where the free TAMPAX coupons, kept by my French friend for his three daughters!

As I read all the magazines I received with gripping curiosity, I discovered, outside of political and cultural life in France, the small matters concerning daily life, through commercials for "*la pile Wonder, qui ne s'use si l'on s'en sert*", the *Petrole Hahn* shampoo, or the *Schick Injector* shaving kit. All these commercials, apparently useless, helped me, a few years later, to more easily adapt to life in France. This is also one of the vital purposes of the press!

———

My connections with classical music started in a strange manner!

As my father played the violin every day for two or three hours in the afternoon, I "floated" through a musical ambiance since I was young. I cannot say that he was a virtuoso of the violin. However, passionate as my father was about classical music, he "rewrote" the main violin concerts, removing the parts, which were hard for a talented amateur to play, but keeping the main themes and the melody of his favorite pieces.

In the beginning, he only had the famous classical concerts for the violin (Tchaikovsky, Beethoven, Paganini, Mendelssohn-Bartholdi and Lalo), and later he added themes from opera arias (Verdi, Gounod, Offenbach), famous works for violin (Kreisler and Vieuxtemps), transcriptions after piano pieces (Debussy, Schumann, Rubinstein and Chopin), even some ballad (*Mai am un singur dor, Steluța, Ce te legeni codrule*), the songs in fashion at the time (composed by N. Kirculescu, Soloviov-Sedoi and A. Giroveanu). He also played a selection of Romanian folkloric themes (*Trandafir de la Moldova, Pe Mureș și pe Târnave*), Italian music (*Torna Surriento, Santa Lucia, Bella ciao*), Spanish music (*Amapola, Ay, ay, ay*) and even soviet music (*Suliko, Nopțile în împrejurimile Moscovei*). This is how he created a repertoire for himself of over 100 themes I heard repeated with regularity, under his violin bow. As I write these lines, I glance at his five notebooks, bearing the RPR coat of arms on their cover, "saved from the fire" by some colleagues from Ecole des Mines de St. Etienne and brought back to us during a voyage in Romania in 1968.

In 1957, Mendi Rodan, my mother's cousin, a "wonder child" of the violin and brilliant conductor at the young age of 28, invited us to attend his concert at the Romanian Athenaeum. He would later succeed in having a career as a conductor overseas, in front of the most prestigious orchestras in the world in Vienna, Brussels, London, Paris, Jerusalem and Oslo. However, at the age of ten, the idea of spending two hours locked in a room listening to classical music was not a very enchanting prospect. Moreover, I wanted to finish a volume of stories I was reading back then. My father had an excellent idea: *You can take the book with you and read it during the concert.* I don't know how, but I didn't even read two pages, this is how passionate I became about what I heard there.

The next year, the first edition of the George Enescu Festival and International Competition took place. I passionately attended and saw the Festival's concerts on TV, and next year, we acquired a yearly subscription for the concerts held by the George Enescu Philharmonic Orchestra, subscription we renewed every year until we left Romania, six years later. As a pupil and later a student, the price for such a subscription was ridiculously low – between 2 and 4 lei, if I remember well. Throughout this period, I kept my seat in the Athenaeum, a seat I strive to obtain today when I attend a concert!

Of course, in all these years I also saw concerts in Sala Palatului, in Sala Radio, in Sala Mică on Stribey Voda, at open air events, but the Sunday morning concerts at the Athenaeum stayed with me throughout my life.

Back then, for seven years, I saw the greatest musicians play and conduct music on these stages. To list them all here would be much too fastidious, maybe even impossible. However, I cannot help but remember David and Igor Oistrah, Yehudi Menuhin, Sviatoslav Richter, Isaac Stern, Nathan Milstein, John Barbiroli, Herbert von Karajan, Roberto Benzi, Ivry Gitlis, Ghenadi Rojdensvenski, André Cluytens, Lola Bobescu, Henri Szering, Magda Tagliaferro, Monique de la Bruchollerie, Lorin Maazel… and many, many others. Of course, I also saw the work of talented Romanian conductors such as George Georgescu, Mircea Basarab, Iosif Conta, soloists like Ion Voicu, Valentin and Ștefan Gheorghiu, Șt. Ruha, Alexandru Demetriad, Daniel Podlovschi… I also appreciated those who later escaped outside the country, such as Sergiu Comissiona, Mândru Katz, Constantin Silvestri and Radu Aldulescu.

I also met countless Romanian composers in these concert halls (Anatol Vieru, Ion Dumitrescu, Tiberiu Olah and Miriam Marbé) as well as foreign composers (Haciaturian).

With Ludovic Feldman I often conversed during intermissions – or rather, my father did, as they were friends since childhood.

After 1964, when Costin Cazaban was accepted into the University of Music, many of these musicians became his professors, another occasion to better get acquainted with them.

I already mentioned the tradition we had in the 60's: after the Sunday concert, we often went to the Athenée Palace brasserie, where we would have the same "Menu fixe" which cost 10 lei: cauliflower soup, pike soufflé and marmalade rolls! It didn't matter what we ate! The most important for us was the atmosphere, the quality of service and the habit we had formed to frequent such places. As I said back then: "Noble you are, noble you live!". This is another unexected consequence of the musical life we led back then!

By coming back every week for seven years to attend the concerts of the Philharmonic orchestra, I made a close circle of friends and acquaintances.

I cannot forget a picturesque character named professor Faion. He taught mathematics in a high school in Bucharest and earned additional income through private tutoring in his home. Professor Faion always attended Sunday concerts, where he sat in the first rows, right behind the conductor. However, aside from his 130 kg and his rather oily costume, he dragged a kind of noisy slippers through the whole hall. As he had the habit of running late, conductors would always wait for professor Faion to be seated before beginning the concert.

After the concert, you could meet them at the Athenée Palace brasserie, where, after a hearty meal, he would invariably order a "combed one": in a soup bowl, a layer of "Mascots" (chocolate cakes), with a layer of whipped cream on top, followed by a layer of "Joffres" (another kind of chocolate cakes with cream) and again whipped cream! He would mix them well with a fork, until they became "a homogenous mixture", which he then ate with satisfaction.

On one Sunday morning in 1966, when I came to the concert hall, something seemed different. Only when I raised my eyes, I realized that the strip of red velvet, which had covered the fresco for so long, had disappeared over night! I didn't understand why it was called "From the She-Wolf[7] to

---

7 Referring to the she-wolf, which fed Romulus and Remus in the mythical founding of the Roman Empire.

the Lupească (sweethart of the king)", because Carol the Second did not appear! Later I would find out that Carol the Second and the Great Voivode Mihai had been "eliminated" from the fresco during Marshall Antonescu's time. Other versions claim that the last scene, depicting the Great Union, was painted during the communist regime. Available data is contradictory, especially due to documents from that era (post stamps, photographs and drawings).

From then on, I had vast opportunities to admire the fresco, especially during the mandatory interpretation of compositions by contemporary Romanian composers.

Matei Socor was among the composers appreciated by the communist regime; he was the author of two succesives State Hymns of RPR, the director and later president of the Romanian Radio Broadcast between 1946 and 1952, the ultimate judge in the musical world during the period. Although we were related, I never met him. However, I recently discovered a letter written during the war, signed by the most reputable Romanian musicians (G. Enescu, M. Jora, M. Andricu, E. Ciolan and C. Brăiloiu) and addressed to the Ministry of Internal Affairs, asking for the release of Matei Socor from the concentration camp in which he had been held for two and a half years, because of his communist activities. He probably forgot about this incident in the 50's!

Among the young musicians I met back then, and who went on to attain international fame, I would like to mention the following:

* Silvia Marcovici, many times award winning violinist, with which I traveled on the 86 bus, full to the brim as she went to Music School and I went to the Polytechnic Institute. She held her violin in her arms and I held her, so she wouldn't fall of the stairs of the bus!
* Christian Badea, violinist and conductor of international fame, who conducted symphonic orchestras and operas in the United States, Amsterdam, Spoleto, Vienna, Sidney and Bucharest.
* Silvian Iţicovici, violinist, the student of Yehudi Menuhin, today the first violin in the Saint Louis Stmphony Orchestra in Missouri, USA.

* Daniel Podlovischi, violinist awarded by the Enescu Festival in 1961 who taught me violin...

In the 60's, not just reputable performers of classical music graced the cultural world of Bucharest.

Through the opening made by Yves Montand in 1956, many more stars belonging to the pop or folkloric genre came to Romania.

The first was Raj Kapoor in 1957, the star of films *Vagabondul* (Awara) and *Articolul 420* (Shree 420). A descendant of a dynasty of Indian cinema artists, which still continues with his sons and nephews, Raj Kapoor was the indirect exponent of the group of *"non-aligned countries"*, very favorably seen by Moscow. Because of this, he was given a grand welcome in the USSR and its satellite countries.

Completely ignored in the west during the period, (the films I mentioned earlier were not introduced in the French film library until seven years ago!) he left an unforgettable mark on the Romanian public, offering opportunities to other Bollywood production, as well as an atypical phenomenon, unique in the world: the singer Naarghita. And so, in the 70's, when I used to come to Romania, I would go and see an Indian film as well, despite the fact that subjects were very repetitive.

During the same period, Arkadi Raikin from USSR came to Bucharest. He was the "alter ego" of Mircea Crişan, who produced a show in both Russian and Romanian. The line *"What will it be? Let there be cold beer!"* echoed down the streets of Bucharest for quite some time!

Numerous western singers followed. Meanwhile, while Sala Palatului was built in 1960, they had a stage for their shows during winter, as during the summer, such shows would generally be held in open-air venues.

Among the Italian singers known to the public through the San Remo Festival, transmitted on TV in Romania, I had the opportunity of seeing Remo Germani, Marino Marini and, of course, Domenico Modugno, whom I still admire today. They were, for me, my first steps in understanding and learning Dante's language. Apart from the widely known hits (*Come prima, Il vecchio frak, Volare*), he also sang *Donna riccia* (the woman with curly hair), in Neapolitan dialect. This song reminded me of our Romanian

Language teacher at Spiru Haret, Rădulescu's theory, which said that each curl was a question mark – *Are you still in love with me?* – and that they only multiply with age.

It was the case of Bulgarian singer Antonova, who released *Mambo, mambo* and *C'est si bon!* in Bucharest. The latter soon became "*C'est si bon/ I'm Popescu Ion/ I came from the Raion* (Party authorities)…"

It was during this period that South American music came into fashion. Among the singers who came to Bucharest was Luis Alberto del Parana, accompanied by *Trio Los Paraguayos*. Luis Albert, the national glory of Paraguay, recorded five albums in Bucharest; he died suddenly at only 48 years of age, in 1974. After only a few months, I spent a memorable evening, dining with the members of *Los Paraguayos,* after one of their shows in Dublin. Their trio had since become a quartet, and even a quintet, due to the Reynaldo Meza, the brother of Luis Alberto, joining them!

Yma Sumac, the famous Peruvian singer, dubbed the Inca princess, made an impression on Bucharest through her exceptional ambitus (4 octaves!), as well as the quality of her songs, written by her husband, Moises Vivanco.

The most peculiar phenomenon is that the only European recording of Yma, who spent more than 6 months in the Soviet Union in 1961, is the one made by Electrecord in Bucharest, entitled *Live in Russia*, with the orchestra conducted by Moises Vivanco and Sile Dinicu!

Another grand star who shined over the Bucharest firmament was Sara Montiel. Made famous by her success in Mexico, Spain, Cuba and the United States, as well as the world of theater, film and recording, with openly left wing ideas, she came to Romania with the certainty of an absolute success. It was the case, from an artistic and media perspective, although rumors circulated throughout the city regarding her real age, despite her being little over 30 years of age back then!

I had the chance to see Sara Montiel again in Paris in 1982, during an unforgettable evening organized by Frederic Mitterrand, during which her films were shown … from evening till dawn!

I reminded her of her royal tour through Romania and she gave me an autograph, which I still keep today.

A few years later, I saw her again on stage in a theater of Buenos-Aires, close to *Corrientes 348*, an address she charmingly sang about in her song *A media luz*. A plaque is set to remind passersby of this torrid tango[21].

I intentionally left the French artists last – so numerous, I am sure I will forget to mention some of them. Additionally, many of them participated at the Cerbul de Aur Festival in Brașov, after I left the country in 1967 (Gerard Lenormand, Barbara, Rika Zarai, Guy Mardel, Frida Boccara). I could not, of course, attend their shows.

Among the ones who left a strong impression, I will mention the following:

- Gilbert Becaud, *Mr. 100,000 Volts*, wearing his blue tie with white spots and jumping like a kid goat on the stage of Sala Palatului.
- Petula Clark, with her success in mixing French with English (*D'antan – Down Town, Le chariot – I will follow him*).
- Orlando, the brother of French/Italian/Egiptian Dalida, during the few years of his singing career, on the stage of the State Circus, accompanied by the *Les Rocamboles* band.
- *Les Surfs*, the group of brothers and sisters who sang all the *ye-ye* successes of the age, along with Sacha Distel, Sylvie Vartan and Claude Francois.

  After a concert at Sala Palatului, I accompanied them to the Ambassador Hotel, where they were staying. On the way there, I tried to convince one of the girls who was of my age (was it Moniquie or Nicole?) to visit Bucharest with me. Maybe I could have convinced her to do so, if it wouldn't have started snowing … like in a fairytale!

- Jean-Claude Pascal, who had won the Eurovision award in 1961, passed through Bucharest for one single show at Sala Palatului. Sadly, my parents, who didn't think he was a very important artist, didn't give me the funds necessary to buy a ticket, so I didn't get to see him perform. However, several years later, I discovered him in Sacha Guitry's film *Si Versailles m'etait conté* (<u>Royal Affairs in Versailles</u>) in which he played the role of Axel de Fersen, while

Romanian actress Lana Marconi played the queen of France, Marie-Antoinette.

I came into contact with countless pop music and music hall stars thanks to the discs and cassettes brought from the West or illegally recorded and copied.

All members of the *ye-ye* group in France (Johnny Hallyday, Sylvie Vartan, Françoise Hardy, Claude François, *Les chaussettes noires,* Patricia Carli...) or Italian singers (Rita Pavone, Gianni Morandi, Mina, Renato Carossone, Marino Marini, Connie Francis...) were in fashion at "tea parties" organized by this friend or the other. From this came the utmost importance of one character in our adolescent lives: "the man with the mag", the person who had the best music (western music), "recorded" on magnetic tape. The *Mag* was, broadly speaking, a Czechoslovakian mobile *Tesla.*

Because of this, if one was missing the latest music, one could find, on a Saturday evening, "by the clock at University Square", *Mag* owners, eager to get invited to parties with strangers!

Thanks to a few friends who had connections to the West or who had visited, I discovered other aspects of western music.

Through Mihai Oroveanu, whose grandfather, the sculptor Ion Jalea, had visited Paris, I found out about the existence of a few French music-hall stars (Francis Lemarque, Juliette Greco, Alain Barierre).

But first of all, I passed through the phase of *Patephone* discs: those who still had ebonite discs from before the war and all necessary machinery, they would carefully extract them from the furniture in which they were tucked (they were very fragile and could break at any moment) so we could listen to Maurice Chevallier or Josephine Backer, Charles Trenet or Rina Ketty.

When the *Electrecord* discs became available, some Romanian singers belonging to the few minorities who had chosen to stay within the country, were allowed to sing in their native languages. Who still remembers Gianni Spinelli with *Picolissima serenata* or *Domani*, which were in fact Italian songs by Toni Renis or Minucci? After 1960, Marina Voica began singing all "standards" of Spanish and South American music.

Then came Charles Aznavour's discs (*Il faut savoir, Les comédiens* and *La bohème*), which were passed from person to person.

Other friends brought us famous books from Paris (*Aimez-vous Brahms?* by Francoise Sagan or *Paroles* by Jacques Prevert). I would copy Prevert's poems in my notebook, to remember them after I had returned the book, oftenly edited in *Livres de poche*, to its happy owner, who had only borrowed it to me for a few days. Some of these poems, which I had copied and learned by heart, I would later encounter as one of Yves Montand's hit songs, with the music written by Francis Lemarque or Joseph Kosma. The same Francis Lemarque who wrote the lyrics for Edith Piaf's *Johnny tu n'es pas un ange*, which was in fact *Sanie cu zurgălăi*, its music and text originally composed and written in Romania!

In the 60's, the Universal Literature Press published a series of vital reads from around the world, translated into Romanian. We discovered our passion for *Forsyth Saga* by John Galsworthy, as well as *Lust for Life* and *Agony and Ecstasy* by Irving Stone, the latter written in 1961, shortly before it being published in Romania.

I was greatly surprised when, a few years ago, I discovered that the novel *Proud destiny, Foxes in the Vineyard* by Lion Feuchtwanger, published in the United States in 1946 and which we read in 1966, was not published in French until 1977!

It is true that an important book written for children, *Cuore* by Edmondo de Amicis, published in over 12 languages since it was first edited in Italy in 1886, and which we read in Romanian when we were young, was not fully translated in French until 1968!

Not to mention Mario Appelius, an Italian writer who was probably rather minor and somehow peculiar because of his political views. Traveller, journalist and author of 19 travel books, out of which I own two volumes translated in Romanian before the war, he is completely unknown in French and English.

During a cultural program on French television, a renowned actor from *Comédie Francaise*, while discussing the project of adapting Ostrovski's *Pădurea* (The Forest) on the Parisian stage, complained that it could not be made due to the lack of funding!

In the same manner, Asafiev's ballet with its libretto inspired by Pushkin's poetry *The Fountain of Bakhchisarai* was first presented on a stage in France a few years ago. The French ballerina Marie-Agnes Gillot was made to go all the way to Perm in Siberia or to Tokyo, in order to interpret the main role in this masterpiece of universal ballet!

Reading this text again, I realize I forgot to mention a major element of our cultural life during our childhood. Of course, there are other such memories that only now come to me, but, at some point, I must end this nostalgia which risks extending over other dozens of pages! I cannot, however, leave *Pif le Chien* aside!

I don't know how and when my passion for comics began. This genre is named *fumetti* in Italian and *tira comica* in Spanish.

However, it would be natural for me to name it by its French name because everything began with *Placid et Muzo*. I clearly remember that, one morning in June 1957, when I had to show up to the exam to pass my fourth grade, instead of passing through my schoolbooks, I would amuse myself by copying Placid cartoons from a journal for children! I would adapt them to our world, by replacing the French flag with the Romanian one!

Next came *Vaillant, le journal le plus captivant*, with its star character: Pif le chien. It was through those comics that I learned the basics of the French language, as well as some of France's history (Jean et Jeanette, Guy Môquet, Robin des Bois) and the history of other countries (Nasdine Hodja, Davy Crockett, Ragnar the Viking), I discovered French humor (*Arthur le fantôme justicier, A. Bâbord et Père O.K., La pension Radicelle*) or adventure novels (Bob Mallard) and later, when Moliere's language became familiar to me, I read about scientific experiments available to adolescents at the beginning of the space age...

I didn't know back then that the French Communist Party issued this journal, but its values of justice, courage, and even "ecology" ideas were universal and perfectly suited to our age. It is not like we had a choice, anyway...![22]

After I left Romania, I forgot about this "specialty" practiced regularly by my colleagues in the Ecole des Mines. Several decades had to pass before I would again find the pleasure in reading comics books, with the help of Hugo Pratt and his famous *Corto Maltese*, and, more recently, Hermann, who, at the beginning of the 21st Century, illustrated three volumes of comics books, depicting the entire adventure of *Count Dracula*, in space and time. An important Romanian presence, unfolding across over one hundred pages!

———

While trying to maintain a relatively objective perspective over the cultural life in which I participated during my childhood and adolescence, feelings of pride and gratefulness envelop me.

Pride because, in spite of the hardship of that epoch, I had the opportunity to grow up in an exceptional cultural medium, of rare variety and quality.

And gratefulness for all who gave me the possibility of fully taking advantage of this medium and due to whom I am who I am today.

I am sorry to discover that all these names, anecdotes, events and meetings have a common denominator: double language. The unwritten obligation to use one kind of language within the family and another in public, differing from the written word and what flies away as mere spoken word!

It is painful and it leaves a person scarred for life. Or, as Julien Clerc and Maxime Le Forestier said in the song called *Double enfance* (Double childhood):

A plonger dans les eaux troubles
De mes souvenirs lointains
Si quelquefois je vois double
C'est que l'enfance me revient!

Jumping in the troubled water
Of my remote souvenirs
If, sometimes, I see a double image
Means that my childhood is coming back!

Adrian Irvin ROZEI
Boulogne, April 2017

1. The word "teta" is found in Lithuanian, Slovenian, Czech and it means "distant aunt". In Aromanian it means "aunt". In Romania, between the two Wars, it was used to refer to young Saxon women who spoke German and studied infant care in Sighișoara, and wealthy families hired them to take care of their new-born babies until their education, according to their age, was entrusted to someone else. After the Communists took over, many of these "teta" women became members of the families that had hired them, until they left for Germany.

2. See the book "Cantacuzino, ia-ți boarfele și mișcă", Oana Orlea, an interview by Mariana Marin, Compania Press, Bucharest, 2008.

3. Elena Popescu-Lugoșianu, „Jerfele mele: tatăl, soțul și fiul", testimony featured in *Ioan Lugoșianu. Omul. Avocatul și universitarul. Omul poltic și diplomatul. Ziaristul. Martirul*, Ioan Spătan, ed., p. XVII, TIPARG Press, Pitești, 2008.

4. See Stelian Tănase, Anatomia mistificării, 1944–1989, Humanitas, Bucharest, 1997, p. 290.

5. H. Casassovici, I.M.E. Crețoiu, „Povestea vieții mele", in *Magazin Istoric*, September-November 2013.

6. Graduated with honors, translation from German.

7. *În căutarea pelicanilor*, eng. Mircea Casassovici, eng. Vasile Ciuchină, Cartea Românească, Bucharest, 1947.

8. Ion Vinea (1895-1964), the literary penname of Ion Eugen Iovanaki, a symbolist poet who was close to the avant-garde movement.

9. A good, healthy social background was that of workers, collectivist peasants and their children. Former landowners, industrialists, political figures, intellectuals who didn't praise the achievements made after August 23rd, 1944, together with their families were of bad, unhealthy social backgrounds. The worst social background was that of those with a political prisoner in their family.

10. 50 years later, I found out from my classmate Cristina Bulgaru that for those with unhealthy social backgrounds, at the No. 10 High School, there had been only 3 available spots that year. She managed to secure one of them. Our classmate Ioana George was also rejected and that fall she was enrolled at the "Sadoveanu" high school. There she was the classmate of Adrian Rozei, a former "Spiru Haret" student who, on account of his unhealthy social

background, sat the entrance exam for "Sadoveanu" instead. What twisted paths we took on the educational chessboard!

11. V.V. Haneș, „Personalitatea elevilor", in *Vlăstarul*, year IV, no. 7–8, May-June 1928, p. 3.

12. A portrait painted by Jan van Eyck (1395-1441) – Flemish painter, founder of the Northern Renaissance art movement. In 1948, this painting (from a lot of 19 paintings from the collection of the Brukenthal Museum from Sibiu) was confiscated and brought to Bucharest, in line with the Communist centralization policy. Nowadays, the paintings have returned to the Brukenthal Museum.

13. The paintings by El Greco (1541-1614), a Spanish Renaissance painter, were a part of the art collection owned by king Charles I that was confiscated by the Communist regime.

14. The wife of painter Jean Alexandru Steriadi (1880-1956), Romanian painter and illustrator, a University professor at the School of Fine Arts in Bucharest, a honorary member of the Romanian Academy since 1948.

15. After reading my colleagues' presentations, I discovered that some of them had also attended this kindergarten. However, in just three days, I didn't have the chance to meet them!

16. The period following Neruda's visit in Romania was illustrated in the 1994 remarkable film *Il postino*, with actors Philippe Noiret and Massimo Troisi.

17. In recent years, after reuniting with my former Polytechnic Institute colleague, I found out that Radu Nor also wrote memoirs, and prose in German, Romanian and Hebrew.

18. I was asked by some of my friends to justify my claim. I recently found a volume, published in Bucharest, in which Theo Weigl is mentioned having lived on 25 Donici Street (*Avangarda românească în arhivele Siguranței*, Editura Polirom, 2008)

19. I also saw a play entitled *Terrorism* by the Presniakov brothers on the stage of the National Theater in Bucharest in 2015. These authors, famous around the world, have never had any of their plays performed in France! However, the French contemporary playwright Eric-Emmanuel Schmitt is often times played in Bucharest!

20. Happily, while the art of the theater actor is transient, the film actor can survive his own demise!

    Film enthusiasts can periodically see films in which Jules Cazaban played in theaters throughout the country. We can only hope that one day his radio plays will also be reedited, in the same manner that the volume entitled *Jules Cazaban, a professionist* by Constantin Paraschivesc has been edited in 2010.

21. In the last couple of years, my meetings with Sara Montiel have multiplied considerably! After reading Ion Dichiseanu's book *Am fost rivalul regelui* (I was the King's Rival) and meeting him in Bucharest, I ran across Sarita's photograph in a famous restaurant in Madrid. In Rome, retracing the journey of the famous pair led me to the *Alfredo alla Scroffa* restaurant and the *Excelsior* hotel. However, the greatest surprise was waiting for me in Havana, on December 2016. Not only did I find the picture of Sarita in famed *National* and *Havana Libre* (former Hilton) hotels, dating back from 1958 when, in full glory, she sang in Cuba only three months before the Castro regime began, but I also found her portrait and songs in an antiquary's shop. Some years later, Sarita came back to Havan and went to see the concert hall where she had sung. She was surprised to find out that the name of the hall had now been changed to… Karl Marx!

22. A year ago, in Bucharest, I came across a volume of *Vaillant* magazine issues from 1958 in an antiquities shop. Six months' worth of issues, in hardcover, sold for the ridiculous sum of 20 Euros. I hesitated for a couple of hours, because of the approximately two kilograms of extra luggage such a volume entailed. When I came back, it had been sold. I searched for a similar volume in France: I discovered that it cost at least 100 Euro, depending on its condition. It was an unexpected opportunity that made me run across a similar volume in St. Etienne. I bought it and read it from cover to cover. I realized that the memory I had of it, from over half a grandchildren, I would encourage them to read it: it is more relevant than ever!

Photos

——

School Year End Show, „Story Book", year1956. Upper row, from left to right: Peter Clar, Decebal Becea, Adrian Brighidău, **Robert Weidenfeld**, Matei Cazacu, Zamfir Dumitrescu, Florin Seimeanu, Paul Vaininger, Nicky Aronovici. Bottom row, from left to right: unidentified, Dragoş Duinea, Ladislau G. Hajos, Tudor Cudalbu, unidentified.

3rd grade (1955/1956), with our teacher Mrs. Maria Linte, 1956. Left side seats, left to right. 1st row: Adrian Iuncu; 2nd row: Ivan Csendes and Lucian Rosenblatt; 3rd row: Henri Löebel and Jack Mendelson; 4the row: Jack Rosenzwerg and Ion Vârjan; 5th row: Emil Marcovici and Anton Laurian; 6th row: Nicky Aronovici, Dumitru Paloş, Simon Gerhard, Mrs. Linte in back between the row of banches. Right side seats din dreapta, from left to right: 1st row, alone Dragoş Duinea; 2nd row: Ladislau G. Hajos, Paul Vaininger, Decebal Becea; 3rd row: Florin Seimeanu, Nicolae Popescu; 4th row: Matei Cazacu and Constantin Ştefănescu; 5th row: **Robert Weidenfeld** and Zamfir Dumitrescu; 6th row: Ştefan Andreescu and Alexandru Popovschi; 7th row: Octavian Cişman and **Tudor Cudalbu**.

4th grade. Young pioneers with our teacher, Mrs. Linte, 1958.

Top row left to right: Dragos Duinea, Henri Loebel, Adrian Brighidau, Nicolae Popescu, Constantin Stefanescu, Florin Seimeanu, Anton Laurian, Peter Clar, Decebal Becea, unidentified, unidentified

Middle row from left to right: Ion Varjan, Adrian Iuncu, Adrian Stoica, Jack Mendelson, Nicky Aronovici, Dana Cristescu, Paul Vaininger, Ladislau G. Hajos, Dna Linte, Sofica Schwartz, Lucian Rosenblatt, Zamfir Dumitrescu, Ivan Csendes,

Bottom row from left to right: Maria Rada, Cornelia Bauer unidentified, unidentified **Elena Moisuc**, unidentified, Patricia Filip, Marilena Lazar, Michaela Valentin, Ana Zsoldos, Viorica Minea, Liliana Balutescu

Winter of 1957. Bottom row: Peter Clar, Adrian Rozei,
Florin Seimeanu, unidentified, Ladislau G. Hajos, Silviu
Schlesinger, Valentin Cristescu, Dan Frangolop.
Second row left to right: Michaela Feldstein, **Englentina
Vlasie**, Adrian Gavrilescu, Matei Cazacu, Sergiu Solomon,
Tudor Cudalbu, Ana Zsoldos, Irina Pascu (in the back), Dana
Cristescu, Ileana Alexandrescu, Cornelia Bauer, Mia Dinca

9th grade, 1961. Bottom row: Mihail Andreev, Emil Bărbulescu, Constantin Gherghel, Adrian Stoica. Middle row: **Costin Cazaban, Andrei Drogeanu**, Florin Seimeanu, Ladislau G. Hajos. Upper row: Niculae Ene, Zamfir Dumitrescu, Constantin Cernat.

11ᵗʰ grade with Mr. Niculescu: Cantemir Ionescu, Constantin Gherghel, Roland Filippi, Șerban Manolescu, Nicolae Filip, Valeriu Aldea, Rodica Peligrad, prof. Niculescu, Petre Rusu, Viorel Duncan, Mircea Sebastian, Gabriela Vasilescu, Mihail Andreev, **Domnica Sufană** (1964).

**11ᵗʰ grade (1964) cu teachers Anton Ionescu ("Baston"), Atanasiu ("Criza")
and Grosu.** 1st row, sitting Mircea Țilenschi, Constantin Gherghel, Adrian
Stoica, Ladislau G. Hajos, Viorica Setii, Petre Rusu, Rodica Peligrad, **Felicia
Bădescu**. 2nd row standing: Valeriu Aldea, Roland Filippi, **Englentina
Vlasie**, Constantin Cernat, Mircea Sebastian, Florin Seimeanu, prof. Grosu
(Russian language), Florin Seimeanu, prof. Atanasiu (Romanian language),
Șerban Manolescu, prof. Anton Ionescu (gym), Gabriela Vasilescu, Monica
Diaconu, Beatrice-Alexandra Nicolaide, Viorel Duncan, Ioana Casassovici,
Maria Matei, Ana Zsoldos, **Ion Berindei**, Niculae Ene, Rita Tessler

11th grade, with Mrs Atanasiu Atanasiu ("Criza"). Back row: Adrian Stoica, Mircea Țilenschi, Ladislau G. Hajos, Virgil Duncan, Florin Seimeanu, Șerban Manolescu, Petre Rusu, Neagu, **Mircea Sebastian**, Roland Filippi, Mihail Andreev. Middle row: Gabriela Vasilescu, Georgeta Dumitrescu, Silvia Daneliuc, Maria Matei, **Felicia Bădescu**, Vasilica Setti, Monica Diaconu. In center: prof. Atanasiu, Patricia Filip, Mona Toma, **Englentina Vlasie**. Bottom row: Ana Zsoldos, Alexandra Beatrice Nicolaide, Rodica Peligrad, Constantin Cernat, **Ion Berindei**, Constantin Gherghel (1964).

9th grade, at the gym. Upper row, left to right: Viorel Duncan, Roland Filippi, prof. Anton Ionescu („Baston"), **Ion Berindei**, prof. Atanasiu („Criza"), Ladislau G. Hajos, Adrian Gavrilescu, Mircea Țilenschi. Rândul din mijloc, de la stânga la dreapta: Adrian Stoica, Cantemir Ionescu, Lucian Moldoveanu, Ioan Jelev, Sergiu Aronovici, Valeriu Aldea. Bottom row, left to right: Constantin Gherghel, Petre Rusu (1964).

50ᵗʰ high school reunion (colleagues from kindergarten)
From left to right: Ștefan Andreescu, Peter Clar, Ivan Csendes,
Zamfir Dumitrescu, Decebal Becea, Adrian Stoica, Florin
Seimeanu, Ladislau G. Hajos, Constantin Cernat (2014).

50th Highschool reunion 2014. Bottom row left to right: Ioan Iordăchescu, Mona Toma, Miki Feldstein, and Alexandra Beatrice Nicolaide. 2nd row: Mrs. Sorina Ionescu, Maria Matei, Monica Diaconu, Florina Mârşu, Mia Dincă, Ioan Jelev, Sergiu Aronovici with spouse. 3rd row: Adrian Gavrilescu, Cantemir Ionescu, with spouse, Mrs. Ţilenschi, Mrs. Jeni Filippi, Mircea Sebastian, Mr. Popescu – Nicolaide's husband, Roland Filippi, Mrs. Otilia Russu. Top row: Constantin Gherghel with spouse, Niculae Ene, Andrei Popovici, Decebal Becea, Mircea Ţilenschi, Mrs. Christiane Becea, Dini Cernat, Roxana Lazarevic, Mrs. Popovici, Dani Andrei, Ileana Alexandrescu, Peter Clar, Florin Russu, Ioana Casassovici.

School yard 1964

From left to right: Monica Diaconu, Patricia Filip, Ioana
Casassovici, Decebal Becea, Ladislau G. Hajos

Playing 1964

From left to right: Florin Seimeanu, Zamfir Dumitrescu,
Şerban Manolescu, Ladislau G. Hajos, Adrian Stoica

Part Three – The last 50 years

—

Ioana Crețoiu (Casassovici) - Wandering through the Class Roster

———

IN THE WINTER OF 2014, when the idea to organize the 50 year anniversary of the graduation from Spiru Haret, was born, our colleague Ladislau G. Hajos (Loți) spontaneously became the logistics coordinator of this action, managing to accomplish true performance from where he lives, in the United States of America.

First of all, he took on the role of international detective, managing to find half of our colleagues who had spread across the world, and to identify the ones who had, sadly, gone too soon from this world. Out of the total of colleagues who had gone out into the world, he found the address of 54 people, and sent them invitations to see each other in May.

Aside from the various spreadsheets he made, with our names, the names we acquired through marriage, our email addresses, countries we live in, phone numbers, high school nicknames, classroom (A, B or C), Loți had an absolutely genius idea: we should write about what we had done in the past 50 years!

Not only did he have this idea, but also he had the tenacity to see it implemented. Each of us received countless messages to warn us of the impending deadline for submitting our "autobiographies". The autobiographical content was to be accompanied by two photographs: one taken during high school and another, more recent one. In order to motivate us, Loți invented another method: only those who sent their "autobiography" would receive the others' work. In the end, Loți received 44 presentations, which made it possible for us to see and recognize each other before actually meeting. All this documentation, regarding the 119 graduates of the Spiru Haret High School in 1964, was given to each of us on a memory stick and was also printed (through the generosity of Decebal Becea), when we met on the 24th of May 2014, an event which was perfectly organized by dr. Florin Julian Russu, in Săftica.

The result of this idea represents the present section in this book, which illustrates the path we took after we finished high school. I think that perhaps, without the "autobiographies" requested by our colleague Ladislau G. Hajos, this book would not have existed. We thank you, dear Loți!

In order to more fully illustrate this group formed by the 1964 graduates, we considered that the following short statistics are welcome, as they try to illustrate who these graduates were according to the "personal data" page in the Class Roster (See "Our Classl Roster" below) and who they are today according to their presentation (See "The Paths of Our Lives").

OUR CLASS ROSTER
High School no. 12 (The Spiru Haret National College), 17 Italiană Street, Sector 2, Bucharest.

The Class Rosters of classes XI A, XI B, XI C – school year 1963-1964, "personal data" page contains a table with eight columns:

- First and Last name
- Date and Place of birth
- Last name of parents
- Parents' profession and current work place
- Parents' address (City, street, number)
- If the student is a Pioneer or UTM member
- Page of the Class Roster where student is registered (completed only in the case of XI C)
- Volume and page of registration (completed only in the case of XI C)

Performing an analysis of the columns, we observe the following:

First and last name: we observe that in the three classrooms (A, B, and C), we find 119 (40 + 41 + 38) students, out of which 71 are boys (over 60%) and 48 are girls (under 40%). The number of students is evenly distributed among the classrooms. In classroom XI C, studying humanities, we see that the number of girls is two times higher than that of the boys. By name, 81% of students are Romanian ethnics, 21% of names ending in "escu".

Etymologically, 52% of boys' names come from the Christian calendar (Nicolae, Gheorghe, Mihai), history (Mircea, Cantemir, Decebal), literature (Virgiliu, Răzvan, Antoniu) or are of foreign origin (Roland, Ladislau, Robert). For boys, the name of Nicolae is the most common, found in 8 instances.

38% of girls' names have biblical origins (Maria, Ana, Ecaterina, Veronica), traditional (Smaranda, Domnica, Ileana, Rodica, Doina), from literature (Virginia, Felicia, Beatrice), foreign origin (Janeta, Patricia, Sonia, Zoia), or names of flowers (Margareta, Viorica).

The year of birth was: 1943 (one student), 1944 (6 students), 1945 (14 students), 1946 (75 students) and1947 (24 students). The age at which they went to school differs (6, 7, and 8 years of age). 63% of students started school at the age of 7, 11.7% of students started school at the age of 6 and 80% at the age of 8. 7 students had to repeat school years during high school or Middle/primary School.

Place of birth: was Bucharest for 77.8% of students. 22.2% of families moved to Bucharest after the birth of their child.

Parents' profession and workplace: There are 7 fathers and 3 mothers with this section crossed out without any further explanation. We noticed that to the 119 students correspond 238 parents mentioned in the document, 116 mothers and 112 fathers. Out of the 116 mothers: 50 are housewives (43.1%), 64 are working mothers (55.17%) and two are pensioners. Out of the total of working mothers: 7 (11%) are unqualified workers, caretakers; 8 (12.5%) have higher education: 2 are engineers, 3 are professors (1 university lecturer), 3 are doctors; 49 (76.5%) work as clerks, 20 as nurses, 3 as typists,

2 as librarians, 2 as school teachers, 1 as kindergarten teacher, 1 as editor, 1 as literary secretary, 1 as model creator and 1 as painter. Out of the 112 fathers, 111 worked and 1 was a retired. Out of the total of 111 working fathers: 24 (21.4%) work as unqualified workers, artisans assimilated into workers; for 40 people (35.7%) the profession matches their workplace: 14 engineers, 10 doctors, 9 professors (out of which 6 teaching at university), 3 lawyers, 3 economists, 1 architect; 41 people (36.9%) are: clerks, accountants, quality control workers, controllers, inspectors, directors (3), violinist (1), 4.5% are in the army or work in Securitate: one army (MFA) officer and 2 MAI officers.

- *Parents' addresses (city, street, no.)* is the city of Bucharest, over 50% live in the May 1st District (nowadays Sector 2) where the high school is located.
- From the column *"If the student is a pioneer or young workers' party (UTM) member"* we find out that 17 students are not UTM members (14.2%)

In conclusion, in 1964, the distribution of students was uniform throughout the three classrooms. As a former high school for boys, we see that the difference between the number of boys and girls is maintained in the favor of the boys. The exception is the humanities class, where girls are twice as numerous as boys. After their name, the vast majority of students (82%) are of Romanian origin. The names of students are common: the majority of names come from Christian saints, history, or literature. The majority of students (77.8%) have been born in Bucharest. The age at which they started school is between 6-8 years of age, depending on the parents' decision, the health and intellect of the child, as well as other social factors. A number of 7 students have repeated school years throughout the education process. Thus, the age of graduation varies: 21 years (one student), 20 years (6 students), 19 years (14 students), 18 (75 students) and 17 years (24 students).

The information pertaining to "parents' profession and workplace" have been primarily presented without regards for the distinction between the two. For example, for directors, the literary secretary, the model creators, the accountants, quality control workers, and inspectors, their profession is not mentioned. Moreover, the title of "clerks" included during that period, people with different professions, and sometimes higher education, who had not received, due to social discrimination, a post to reflect their professional level.

We notice the high number of housewives, who had dedicated their entire lives to raising children, after the traditional family model in the interwar period. Starting with the next generation, housewives disappear from the urban landscape. The social profile of mothers differs from fathers, as there is less who is employed as workers or has jobs that demand higher studies, the rest being employed as clerks in a bureaucratic administration that is in the making. Many of the mothers' professions are stereotypically feminine (nurses, teachers, and other similar professions), associated with the traditional role of the female as a caregiver, but we also see two female engineers, a sign of the emancipation that had begun in the interwar period.

Over half of the students live within the May 1st District, in which the high school is situated (in the center of the capital) or in the proximity of this district. Students walk to their school, rarely using public transport. We must mention the fact that public transport was not yet developed in Bucharest, and that students generally studied in schools located in the proximity of their homes.

The percentage of students who are not UTM members (14.2%) is high, considering the importance this membership had on the future prospects of students. The lack of UTM membership does not seem to follow any kind of social discrimination. Nonmembers include the children of workers, as well as doctors, Ministry of the Interior (MAI) officers and pensioners.

The Paths of Our Lives

The present attempt at an analysis is based on the information received in the year 2014 from 58 colleagues, on the occasion of the 50 years anniversary of graduating from the Spiru Haret high school (1964). Out of the 119 students in classrooms A, B, and C, 72 people were identified, over 60% of the total of students. Out of these 72 people, 14 are sadly no longer with us.

Out of the 72 people, 37 (over 50%) left Romania, sometimes passing through emigration camps or transit countries (9 people), to finally seek permanent refuge in: The United States of America (19 people), The Federal Republic of Germany (5 people), France (4 people), Israel (4 people), Great Britain (3 people), Canada (3 people), Switzerland (2 people), and Spain (1 person).

The vast majority left Romania before 1989 and only two people after this year. For three people, the attempt to leave the country resulted in their expulsion from the University they were attending, arrest, and even fleeing from the bullets fired by border patrol. After 1989, three colleagues came back and settled in Romania, starting various companies and businesses.

Out of the total of 58 graduates, 55 (over 94%) obtained thier higher education in Romania or the countries in which they settled. Three students were not able to finish the studies they began in Romania, due to the fact that they left the country before finishing them, one even being expelled. They continued their studies in other countries. Other two students left before finishing high school, and managed to graduate in the countries they settled in.

We observe that 33% opted for the Polytechnic Institution of Bucharest, preferences reaching towards new specializations offering jobs in new branches of industry, vital for the economy: telecommunications, electrical engineering, power engineering, aerospace engineering, and industrial chemistry.

Over 22% opted for The University of Bucharest which, apart from a teaching career, also offered the possibility of working with various institutions as researchers, translators, literary secretaries and so on.

Out of the total of Spiru Haret graduates, while approximately 67% of boys opted for the Polytechnic Institute, the majority of girls (88%) went to the University of Bucharest.

For approximately for 13% of graduates, architecture represented the illusion of a special profession and a means to express their creative talents, due to the quality postwar architecture present in Romania in 1960-1970. After 1970 however, graduates from the Architecture Institute were confronted with "prefabricated" architecture, as their activity would mainly entail adapting already existing type projects.

Table no.1: Higher education studies

Institution	Faculty	No.	Graduate M	Graduate F
The Polytechnic Institute of Bucharest	Electronics, Telecommunications and Information Technology	18	4	-
	Power Engineering		4	1
	Electrical Engineering		2	-
	Mechanical Engineering		-	3
	Aerospace Engineering		2	
	Applied Chemistry and Materials Science		-	1
	Unspecified		1	-
The University of Bucharest	History	12	2	-
	English		-	4
	German		-	1
	French		-	1
	Philosophy – the department of sociology		-	1
	Physics		-	1
	Chemistry		1	1
Ion Mincu Institute of Architecture		7	4	3
The University of Construction	Civil		1	1
	Installations		2	
	Electronics		-	1
	Roads and Bridges		1	-
The University of Medicine		3	2	1
The University of Pharmaceutics		1	-	1
The Fine Arts Institute of Bucharest	Painting	1	1	-
The National University of Music	Composition	1	1	-
The Institute of Petroleum and Gas		1	1	
The Academy of International Commerce (Paris)		1	1	
The Institute of Mathematics (Argentina)		1		1
Stomatology (Israel)			1	
Minnesota Univ. of Architecture			1	
Univ Constr. Mun (München)			1	

Four colleagues chose the University of Medicine, where competition was always fierce; one single graduate came from a family of doctors.

No one chose to study law, due to the heavy involvement of politics in this domain during the period and because one needed a spotless background in order to apply.

In order to apply to institutes regarding the arts (painting, music, theater), one needed to have a lot of talent and be determined as well as lucky, as places were very limited.

We must mention the fact that beginning with 1964, access to higher education was officially provided without regards for the social origins of candidates.

After finishing their studies in Romania, five people went study abroad, in the countries in which they settled: in France, the so-called "prestigious schools" École Supérieure des Mines Saint-Etienne, École Nationale des Chartres Paris, and the Orsay Technological University Institute – the computer science department; in Australia, civil engineering; in Germany, in München: international commerce.

At the end of their studies, depending on their results, all graduates were distributed and received a workplace – it was mandatory that they accept it and work there for three years. There were limited workplaces available in Bucharest. Part of the graduates, especially medical school graduates, would receive workplaces in the countryside.

The Spiru Haret graduates who finished their studies at the Polytechnic Institute in Bucharest were privileged, as they were placed in Bucharest: in data centers, research institutes, in learning institutes, factories, and one single person was appointed to an important factory outside the capital, in the main city of a county.

More than half of the polytechnic graduates, a few years after finishing their studies, began leaving the country, many building their careers from the ground up, climbing up to managerial positions in important companies or starting their own businesses.

The eight polytechnic graduates who remained in Romania either sought academic careers, or were promoted in conformity with the standards of the time and had a new chance after 1989, when new opportunities opened up for them.

After 50 years, we learn that, after finishing college, 3 people suffered the pressures of recruitment as informers. Attempts were made to recruit informers during their studies as well.

Over 29% of graduates from institutes of higher education went on to PhD or master's degrees in Romania as well as abroad. Out of the 13 graduates with PhD studies, 5 are female and 8 are male.

Table no.2: Postgraduate education

Institution of higher education	Postgraduate study	PhD	Master's Degree	M	F
University of Sorbonne	PhD in Composition and Musical Analysis	1	-	1	-
The Bucharest Faculty of Pharmaceutics	PhD	2	-	-	1
University of Bucharest, History	PhD	1	-	1	-
University of Bucharest, FSP	Master of Public Administration	-	1	-	1
University of Sorbonne 1, Paris	PhD in History	1		1	
University of Bucharest, Faculty of English	PhD	2	-	-	2
The Bucharest University of Fine Arts	PhD	1	-	1	-
University of Liege, Belgium	PhD	1	-	1	
Drexel University, Philadelphia	Master of Sciences and Electrical Engineering	-	1	1	
USA	Master of Engineering	-	1	1	
University of Bucharest	PhD in psychology	1			1
Bucharest Faculty of Dentistry	PhD	1	-	1	
Faculty of Chemistry	PhD	1	-	-	1
Polytechnic Institute of Bucharest	PhD	2	-	2	-
	TOTAL	13	3	0	6

* *Teaching careers:* 18% of Spiru Haret graduates chose teaching careers: 2 became high school teachers (physics and French) and 8 became university professors as follows: 1 professor at the Political Sciences Faculty of the University of Bucharest, 1 Associate

Professor at Sorbonne (Paris IV) and at INALCO School for Oriental Languages, 1 Emeritus Professor at Colorado University and Distinguished Professor at Leight University in Pennsylvania, Doctor Honoris Causa at the Bucharest and Iasi University of Construction and the University of Liege, Belgium; 1 Assistant Professor at the University of California, Los Angeles (UCLA); 1 tenured professor on Environmental Management and Doctor Honoris Causa at the Oradea University; 1 Associate professor of the Hyperion and Bioterra private universities. It is not to be overlooked that 7 parents of the graduates of 1964 were also university professors. PhD supervisors: 1 professor at the University of Bucharest; 1 professor at the Polytechnic Institute of Bucharest; 1 professor at universities in the United States.

* *Ephemeral careers:* 1 member of the Romanian Parliament (The Chamber of Deputies), 1 state secretary, 1 deputy minister, 1 technical consultant for the ministry, 2 ministry directors.

* *Family life*: 99% of the 55 colleagues are married or have been married multiple times; 3 colleagues joined their husbands on diplomatic missions (2 before 1989 and 2 after 1989).

One colleague received the title of Lady in 2012, when Her Majesty Queen Elizabeth II of the United Kingdom of Great Britain and Northern Ireland knighted her husband, for "humanitarian, community and financial service".

The 55 colleagues have a total of 74 children (35% have one child whereas 6,5% have over 4 children). Some of them have become grandparents, with 38 grandchildren in total.

* *At the age of retirement*: What are they doing today, at the age of retirement? They are pensioners, naturally, and they all travel. The professors have kept teaching (some of them), supervising doctorates (others), publishing books and articles in their domains, offering consulting services and evaluating. The painter creates, shows his work in galleries and sells: artistry, glory, and money. The amateur

artist climbs on stage, others climb mountains. The ecologist plants pine seeds on his balcony, subsequently finding gardens to house his saplings. Some play bridge, others play poker, and many play with their grandchildren. Five of them have picked up writing; some even publish their works. Others study fields that have interested them in the past, for which they never had the time before. A couple of them are perfecting their French in Munchen. Many practice sports and play golf. Some are still in the process of getting back what the communists stole from them. Some do business and have even started medical companies. And they have no free time, no free time at all! God bless them!

❧ *Conclusions*: Our group, formed by 58 colleagues, had an exemplary trajectory in life, 94% finished university studies, 29% finished postgraduate studies, 18% chose careers in teaching. Both those who stayed in Romania, as well as those who left, mostly dedicated themselves to their chosen profession and managed exceptional careers both in Romania and outside the country. All of them have families. None of the mothers remained housewives, as all of them worked on par with their life partners, while also maintaining their main role within the household, a very demanding life in communism. Perhaps this is one of the reasons why their professional success (with a few exceptions) was moderate.

Today, at the age of retirement, many have kept working, at a slower rate, while engaging in sports, hobbies and relaxing with their grandchildren. But they only represent half of the Spiru Haret graduates from 1964. Where are the others? How was their life?

Presentations

———

LADISLAU G. HAJOS COORDINATED THE autobiography section. Ioana Poenaru translated the stories that were written in Romanian. There some who reviewed and corrected their translation. There are some that wrote their presentation directly in English.

PATRICIA FILIP AND VALERIU (BEBE) ALDEA*

*Translation reviewed and corrected by Patricia Filip & Val Aldea

Separate summaries of our last 50 years since we graduated the high school would have had too many elements in common, so we decided to write only one, "killing two birds with one stone," as the American proverb goes, or rather, as our grandson once said, turning the proverb on its head, "killing one bird with two stones." Indeed, our lives have been entwined since our last year of high school, when we were both part of a rather large group that was studying for the admission exam for the University of Architecture. We both passed the exam and ended up in the same workgroup, and then we both graduated in 1970 with a Masters in Architecture. Our romance seemed destined; our birthdays were a day and one year apart, and Bebe was born on Patricia's name day - March 17th - St. Patrick's. So we got married in February 1971, and in September 1972, our daughter Dana was born.

In 1976, as a result of Patricia's Jewish heritage, we were permitted to legally leave Romania for Israel, where Patricia's relatives took us in. Two months later, after lots of formalities, aided by Bebe's Christian religion, we were permitted to leave for Italy, where an agency helped us get our American Visas based on affidavits from Patricia's aunt, who lived in New York City. We arrived in New York on Thanksgiving Day in 1976, with few possessions, no money, and a four-year old child, all housed in Patricia's aunt's living room.

At that time, New York was in the middle of a major economic crisis, which affected the construction of new buildings to such an extent that a skyscraper in Midtown Manhattan, called the "Building of Architects," where we tried to apply for our first jobs, was practically abandoned, with dozens of once-bustling offices bolted shut, and piles of papers and blue prints littering the corridors. Nevertheless, we managed to get modest jobs as draftsmen, and were soon able to prove that we were actually skilled and knowledgeable architects, getting more advanced assignments for the same measly pay. In 1982, we both passed our official professional certification exams. By becoming Registered Architects, we now had the right to sign our projects, although we concomitantly risked being sued if anything went wrong. Bebe quickly rose through the ranks, becoming Vice President at the boutique Architectural and Design Firm where he worked, and he subsequently opened his own firm, designing numerous modern banks, retail stores, apartment buildings, and high-end residences in New York City and its suburbs. Patricia worked in a mid-sized company for over 20 years, where she was a Senior Associate and Chief Project Architect for numerous American hotels and casinos. Some of the buildings which Bebe and Patricia designed and/or coordinated the design and construction teams were published in major architectural magazines.

In the 1990's, a new construction crisis hit the United States. Bebe had to close his firm and was hired by large companies to work on major infrastructure projects, including airports and subway stations. A big architectural firm, mainly working on large office buildings, employed Patricia, after the bankruptcy of the firm in which she was Senior Associate. After the September 11, 2001 tragedy, construction in New York halted again, and we both took refuge by working for the City of New York, in two different government agencies, where we supervise, coordinate, and approve numerous projects, designed by an array of architects. Bebe, as Senior

Architect, is the Owner Representative for the construction and renovation of all Courthouses in the five boroughs of New York City, all City owned. Patricia, as Code and Zoning Specialist for the New York City Buildings Department, ensures that the design and construction of all buildings, new and renovated, complies with all urban zoning and local laws regulations. Although we are both 70, we are not in a hurry to retire from our jobs, because it is not bad at all to be listened to with respect (real or feigned) by people in the same profession - some of them of international fame.

We are very proud that our little Dana became a well-known lawyer, following in the footsteps of Patricia's father, receiving numerous professional awards, with many of her notable cases published on the front page of the *New York Law Journal* and receiving national media attention. Presently, she is a Partner at a law firm with a diversified practice, and also teaches Criminal Practice at the Law School from which she graduated.

We danced at her wedding in September 2000, when she married Tom, a computer expert, who has a great personality and dexterity at practical tasks and magical tricks, and is always eager to help and patiently share his encyclopedic knowledge, constantly expanded by surfing the Internet. We entered a new chapter of our lives, beginning the 21st century as grandparents for Lia, born in 2004, and Aidan, born in 2006. Luckily, we live within an hour of the kids, and are together at least once a week. We love playing games with them, going to museums and the zoo together, riding bikes with them, watching shows together, and taking them boating and horseback riding. Lia, now almost 13, is already a published poet, with several of her works printed in her school magazine and in a national anthology of young authors. Like Patricia's mother, she also loves the theatre, performing in all of her school plays and at a local Improvisational Theatre workshop. She is also a fearless adventurer, who loves wakeboarding, watersports, and zip-lining through the forest canopies. Aidan, now 11, is a budding mathematician, following in the steps of Bebe's mother. He is quick-witted, funny, very competitive and has a shocking memory for all the info he collects; but has a kind heart and a sensitive soul. He takes gymnastics and skateboarding lessons, and likes to thrill us with his flips and stunts; but also loves playing the clarinet, and serenades us with solo concerts every weekend. We hope that our health will allow us to dance at their weddings, too, and to see them grow and succeed in whatever fields they choose to pursue.

Stefan Andreescu

I graduated from the Faculty of History of the University of Bucharest in 1970. I applied for a PhD in 1973, under the supervision of professor Constantin C. Giurescu and I presented my thesis a short while after his death, in 1978.

From 1970 until 1972 I worked as an intern editor for the *Magazin Istoric* magazine. My internship there ended with a rather resounding resignation and a short period of inactivity, which fortunately only lasted for three months.

I began working at the *Nicolae Iorga* Institute of History in the summer of 1972, first as an editor, and then as a editing secretary for *Revue Roumaine d'Histoire*, an academic periodical paper written in various internationally circulating languages. I was invited several times, before 1989, to become a member of the PCR, but I declined the offer under various pretexts.

All I can say is that my entrance in the Iorga team had a positive influence on my evolution, due not only to the people I met while working there, but also the opportunity to study in an excellent library specialized in my field of study and initiated by great figures such as Nicolae Iorga and Georghe I. Bratianu. This is how, after I made my debut in one of the Patriarchy's Magazines – *Glasul Bisericii* – when I was still in Spiru Haret, I managed to publish my first volume at 29 *(Vlad Tepes – Dracula intre legenda si adevar istoric* – Vlad Tepes, Dracula between legend and historical truth*),* after which I kept publishing regularly. I received the Mihail Kogalniceanu award given to me by the Romanian Academy in 1997, for my third volume in the series *Restitutio Daciae*, dedicated to Mihai Viteazul.

In 1995 I was admitted into the institute's research department, and two years later I was promoted to Main Researcher I (today it is called Scientific Researcher I).

At the same time, from 1994 I obtained the title of Associate Professor teaching the political history of Romanians at the Faculty of Political

Sciences of the University of Bucharest. Afterwards, in 1998, the University Senate approved my advancement to Tenured Professor. I began teaching in 2008.

From 2001 I am the director of the *Europa Centrala, tarile romane si Marea Neagra* project, held by the N. Iorga Institute of History of the Romanian Academy. I am authorized to supervise Doctorates in the Institute.

I have been married since 1985, but unfortunately I do not have children, but I have two nieces, with which I am utterly in love...

Mihail Andreev

I was born in 1946 in Bucharest, and my first residence was in a house on Berzei Street, which has since been demolished. My father was a doctor in the military and afterwards a civilian doctor – he was a very talented diagnostician. As a military doctor, he worked for the air forces and the air defense forces, and afterwards he was the director of Bucur Hospital and the Ana Ipatescu Clinic. My mother was a functionary in the Ministry of Finances until 1940, and afterwards she became a housewife.

In my first school year I studied at the Cuibul cu Barza School. In 1954 we moved on Ion Ghica Street and from my second year of school until my graduation I studied at Spiru Haret. Ever since my high school years, I was fascinated by electricity and radio technology. Engineer Oscar Steinhardt, the father of famous Nicolae Steinhardt, who was old and would walk down the hallway on floor 2 and sometimes would enter my small room by the stairwell, fashioned into a sort of laboratory, would tell me: "you'll become a university professor!"

It didn't came true, but I did build a few variants of radio apparatus which worked, to my and my friends' joy, having a source for dancing music, from Monte Carlo Radio, BBC General Overseas Service, Antenna Program no. 2 and the Courier, which transmitted music from Rhodes from the VOA Arab program. Almost daily, I would visit the electronics shops in the evening with Vio Duncan and Doru Ene, in search of new things.

Afterwards, after intense training, I was admitted to the Faculty of Electronics, Telecommunications and Information Technology with a score of 9.07 out of 10, along with Sergiu Aronovici, Viorel Duncan, Cantemir Ionescu and Antoniu Petrescu. I graduated from university in 1969 with an average of 8 out of 10, passing all my exams. I could have done better, if it wasn't for my passion for western pop music, especially French music. I would thank my extraordinary professors from high school and university, if they could hear me!

I was assigned to the Calea Rahovei Electromagnetic Plant and I worked at the Institute for Telecommunications Research and Development (ICPT) until retirement. The institute was created by the technical services of the Electromagnetic Plant, on the 4th floor of the new building. We mainly designed, along with a group of colleagues, electronic circuits for telephone exchanges, the army and intercoms. I travelled in Greece, the USSR, Nigeria and other places with my work, sometimes staying more than one month. For a while, I worked in the evening at the Romanian-American company Link, where I learned of new and exciting technology.

In 1974, I married Cristina Vasiliu, an energetics engineer, and in 1975 our daughter Ioana was born. In 1977, after the earthquake, we fled from our apartment building in the center of Bucharest and we moved in the Drumul Taberei neighborhood.

Today I practice ecology and electronics on my own. I've grown dozens of pine trees and spread them throughout Bucharest and the country. Some have escaped the destruction of the elements and of "some people" and I rejoice when I visit them. I have a few coniferous trees in Cismigiu Garden and in Herastrau Park and I take great pleasure walking by them.

My passion for music was transferred to jazz and classical music, especially piano music. Soon I am to experience the great joy and amazement all grandparents go through when their grandchildren were born.

Sergiu Aronovici

I began studying at the Spiru Haret High School during the second trimester of my first year of school, after three months spent in Matei Basarab.

Until my seventh school year, Dini Cernat, Sergiu Solomon and myself were always together, and we were nicknamed "the three musketeers".

I remember the hours we spent playing football and rugby in front of Dini's apartment building. New friends started joining us as the years went by: Costin Cazaban, Valentin Cristescu and Radu Pfeiller. I played poker betting on a lot of money (for that period) with Radu and Valentin and I began learning bridge, which became a passion of mine that I still maintain today.

Years passed by fast, with college knocking at the door. I was admitted to the Faculty of Electronics, Telecommunications and Information Technology in the first 10% and I graduated in 1969 as the 16th, which is why I was offered a position in ASE at the Center for Economic Cybernetics and Calculus. It was an interesting career. The Center had the first IBM computer (after Internal Affairs), due to Manea Manescu, Prime minister and the director of the institution. My responsibilities were the development of application systems using Fortran, Cobol, Assembler, PLI and other programming languages from back then.

I was an assistant and I taught Monte Carlo simulations. At the same time, I was responsible for managing the time spent by external clients using the center of calculus. At the center I met Mariana Falkenflug, a mathematician, who became my wife in 1972. We both taught mathematics for the admission exams at the University and we begun playing bridge professionally at the CFR club, the only bridge club in Bucharest. We took 2nd place in the National Championship for mixed pairs in 1975. The first computer program to tally the results of these competitions was our idea. We developed it together and used it, managing to publish results in record time.

Our first daughter was born in August 1975. In February 1976 we left the country and came to New York in August, after spending 6 months in Rome, Italy, where I worked as a translator for the Italian doctor who made the medical examination of the emigrants.

Life in the United States of America began on the 26th of August 1976. As we landed in New York in the evening, there were 42 Degrees Celsius outside. HOT START! Both my wife and me began working in programming and operational research after only three weeks from arriving. In the beginning, we changed companies very often. In 1978, I started my career with Ciba Geigy (nowadays named Novartis) as a manager for systems, scientific applications used by chemists, biologists and toxicologists.

My entire career was in the pharmaceutical industry, as manager, director and executive director for vas departments (hundreds of programmers and analysts). I was in charge of the supply of information systems for the R&D Division for some of the largest pharmaceutical companies in the world: Ciba Geigy, Lederle Laboratories, Pfizer and Schering Plough (Merck). I initiated *Advisory Boards* in New Jersey for the Oracle Corporation as well as the Documentum Corporation, being a founder of the panel, which suggested strategic directions for software products such as Oracle and *Intelligent Business Systems*.

During my career, I travelled a lot to England, Japan, and France, developing a passion for seeing the world. My second daughter was born in 1983. Our home was always close to Manhattan, in the New York, New Jersey, Connecticut area. I pursued my passion for bridge, winning important victories on a local level, sometimes even regional and rarely on national level competitions. My desire to travel and play bridge more often influenced my decision to retire in 2003. We moved to Tuxedo Park and we spend a lot of time on interesting trips around the world and playing bridge on national championships in various cities across the USA.

I still occasionally work as a consultant in the Healthcare industry.

DECEBAL BECEA – IN SEARCH OF MY WAY*

*Translation reviewed and corrected by Decebal Becea

EYES ON THE TARGET

As an adolescent, I dreamed of becoming an architect and, during my ninth year in high school, I started preparing. My last school years were dedicated to intense study; I kept drawing for hours and hours in preparation for the admission exams where there were eight candidates per spot! Good God, how nerve wracking it was!

Finally, I was an Architecture student! Moreover, a good part of my colleagues from school had had the same dream. But I must first pause and go back into the past.

When I was about 9 or 10 years old, my friends and I (I definitely remember I went with Loți and perhaps Tudor Cudalbu) went to the Palace of the Pioneers to take fencing classes, thinking of "The Three Musketeers". But alas, there were no fencing classes being conducted that year, and there were instead shooting classes. Because we were there, we stayed for the presentation followed by a shooting exercise, with three bullets, and I had the best result. Afterwards, I became a member of the shooting club, and I practiced this sport until a while ago. I was a multiple champion in team and individual competitions, junior European champion, maestro of the sport and on the Olympic team for the 1972 Munchen Games.

Of course, these results came after long and arduous training to which hours of drawing practice were added, along with the curriculum for the baccalaureate. There wasn't much time for other activities, although I was passionate about my sport and happy to be with my colleagues, with which I tied lasting friendships, which still continue today.

THINKING OF THE WEST

The years spent at university where years where a lot of ingredients mixed. The permanent contact with the Aesthetic, which always carries you towards high dreams, life in the grey daily struggle, meeting my future wife, who came from France, and regarding this aspect, problems with the authorities. The most spectacular "action" took place on the Baneasa Airport, when I was on the plane with my shooting team, travelling to Budapest for a competition. A few moments before take off, the engines stopped, the ladder was brought back, the door opened and tow officers came in. In the dead silence, which had settled in the plane, they asked me to give them my passport and come along with them... My questions were curtly answered with: "Ask the Federation". I took a bus back to the city and arrived on Vasile Conta Street, in the building, which still houses the Ministry of Sport today. I took the elevator and with me, two acquaintances, colleagues from another club, went inside with us, achieving the performance of not seeing me at all. Down at the Romanian Federation, the same situation: I was see-through. Finally, one of the coaches present told me to go upstairs, where I was reprimanded for having relations with a foreign citizen. I asked if I have to wear a special tag, because I had submitted a special request for the approval of my marriage with a foreign girl, a request addressed to the First Secretary of the Central Committee, Nicolae Ceausescu!

Today, the situation seems tragically amusing. However, after that incident, I was not permitted to leave the country anymore. In 1968, on the occasion of De Gaulle's visit, the request was approved. After the approval of the marriage I requested to permanently leave the country.

A few years passed, I presented my thesis and I said to myself: the exams are over! However, the future would prove me wrong. In the meantime, in 1970, distributed to Bistrita Nasaud as a new architect, together with 5 colleagues and 2 other construction engineers, one of them being Mircea Sebastian or Sese, we discovered that we had been distributed to an institution that did not exist! Yes, you read correctly.

We were 8 people in a 20 square meters room, 5 chairs, 2 tables and a heater for which we were given 3 pieces of wood per day during the unforgiving winter and no work at all. I will write a novella about the things that happened there.

In the summer of 1971, a day before the 14th of July, I was taking off on my way to Paris.

Capitalism is defined by the exploitation of man by other men. In communism, it's the other way around.

Finally in France, Paris. The subway. Monuments known by heart. The Seine. The 14th of July, fireworks, public balls at the Firemen Department. My first trip to the produce filled market, so abundant, it became too much for me in ten minutes. Over all these, the impending thought – oh, so trivial! - of finding work. I entered the vicious circle of trying to obtain a working permit, which one only obtains if one has found a job, which can only be found if one has experience and references...

I worked as an architect for 12 years, in different workshops; small and medium in size, with long work hours and sometimes-intense labor. Not for me in particular, it is a matter of professional practice, however as a foreigner it is preferable to give more then the others in order to show your competences.

I had two grand satisfactions.

The first was my meeting an exceptional man, a great architect, doubled by his extraordinary capacity for working. We worked together a lot and this man allowed me, a rare thing I wish everybody could have, to see where I stand and to know exactly how much I am worth as an architect. The second was the projects I worked on: The Montreal Olympic Complex, the most expensive apartment building in Paris, on Foch Avenue, palaces for presidents Mobutu and Senghor in Africa, the construction site for West Africa's Economic Community Center in the Superior Volta and many other buildings in France. Schools, office buildings, houses.

And aside from work, work and work and back home? After nearly 2 years, I returned to practicing my sport. I climbed the podium in regional and departmental competitions, I even set a few records. At the national level I had a few victories with the team as well as individually and I was selected to be a member of the national French team.

1981: elections in France, the left wing came into power, with Mitterand, and in two years, the construction sector entered a crisis. I found myself unemployed.

MY SECOND LIFE.

As an irony of fate, my first day of unemployment was the 1st of May (Labor Day). I quickly found job offers, however, they were only short-term contracts, lasting a few weeks, during which you would be exploited to the fullest and then forced to repeat the cycle. In this context, the stork came with a baby boy. What do we do?

In this moment, my beloved friends came into action, to advise and support me. We were at the beginning of computer technology and junior programmers had the same salary as experienced architects. The offer was surpassing demand. And again my good friends advised me not to take a short course, and to apply to university.

They were right, but I had to pass an admission exam containing modern mathematics, apart from the ones I had learned about in high school, and high school was 18 years away. I spent a long summer with integrals, derivatives, and the like. I took the admission exam for two different universities and I was admitted to both. I chose the more prestigious one and I took over 30 exams during my studies, followed by 3 months of practice in a company. There were also funny moments during school.

One day when I had to take an exam, while waiting for the professor, a colleague of mine asked me a question, and I went to the blackboard to explain it to him. The door opens, I was turned away, the professor sees a young man next to an older man whose balding head suggested a considerable age gap suggesting a student and professor. Thinking he had entered the wrong room he closes the door behind him. We were studying in a campus, and buildings were quite far away from each other. He came back after a while and saw me behind my desk...

I had the opportunity of spending my months of practice in an important industrial group, Pechiney, which produced aluminum and aluminum products; after the three months there, I was offered a permanent job.

In computer science, everything moves rapidly, new products appear, the organization is changed, the material becomes obsolete in 8 or 9 months and so on. I spent more than 20 passionate years occupying different functions in factories in the group. I ended my career managing a department of the IT center of the group.

But my journey through the ocean of my second life, also had its share of storms. The storm, which rose in Romania in 1989, coincided with a storm within the family, which resulted in a shipwreck. And once again, admirable friends who actually represented an ideal family supported me.

Architecture is a wonderful profession, but the working conditions were utterly awful back then. Changing my profession brought a "normal" rhythm, with weekends, vacations and lunch breaks – another life.

In 1990 I organized fundraising campaigns and a few transports of goods for orphanages and retirement homes in and around Bucharest. Less than 10% reached their intended recipients. A printing shop created with sacrifices evaporated after just a few months of existence.

I travelled extensively, I came back to Romania more often, I hiked through the mountains, an old passion of mine and I involved myself in my sporting club beeing the treasurer. In 2007, I bid my farewells to the factory and my colleagues there.

Once again at school. My third life.

One of the advantages of life in the factory was my access to different "personal development" courses. If they are well made and led by competent people, the effects are positive. I took an NLP course, short for Neuro-Linguistic Programming, a few days per month, for one year. Between courses, we would practice on each other.

Of course psychiatrists refute NLP methods, because it's stealing their bread. With psychiatry, a phobia (the fear of flying or of rats, for example), is treated in months, with NLP, it takes a few hours.

I also took a massaging course, for more than one year. A type of relaxing massage, ideal for people who are stressed and tense. This came from a long trip to Asia where I discovered various techniques, with remarkable effects. So here I am, a professional in two other fields, and I practice them in close circles, family, friends, sporting colleagues. I have also studied, by myself, the bases of a healthy diet.

And so I detailed the situation of the mind, the body, and now the only one left is the soul.

Many years ago, I read an article on the pilgrimage to Compostela, (the Camino to Santiago) in Western Spain, to the remains of St. James, one of the three apostles who witnessed the Transfiguration on Mount Tabor. I was fascinated. In France, there are four historical routes, the first one dating back from 950 AC. I was still working back then, and even if this road can be made bit by bit, I felt the need to make it from one end to the other and so I waited for the appropriate moment to do so.

In 2009 I began my journey down the first road, the one in the middle, from Vezelay. It took almost three months, walking 25 km per day, and I can say that there was a before and an after. I met extraordinary people, from all around the world, I formed new friendships and I learned a lot of things, mostly about myself. There is much to be said, and many books have been written about it, some are very good; for those interested by this, I am at your disposal. Let us not forget that, biologically speaking, we have been programmed to walk on foot. The wonders one can discover during a day's walk can never be seen during a 20 minute drive.

In 2011 I left again, from Southern France, and last summer I set out a third time, from home, in Paris. Meanwhile, I managed to fulfill an old wish of mine, and I climbed twice up in the Himalayas, once around the Anapurna peaks, for three weeks, and once in the Mustang Kingdom, near the frontier between China and Nepal. I want to set out on the fourth pilgrimage towards Compostela, with the Good Lord's will.

MONICA BOTTEZ – BEFORE AND AFTER 1964*
* Provided in English by Monica Bottez

When I look back on my school years a gallery of portraits comes to my mind, associated with pleasant or unpleasant memories. From my middle school years Ion Rădulescu, the Romanian teacher, ironically smiles at the class under his thin moustache. The lame Mrs Nicolau, the geography teacher, tells us interesting things about orogenic movements. The music teacher, Mr Dumitru Ionescu (Măcelaru or the butcher) – a name that may have been real or a nickname (he was also called Mache [máke]), tries in vain to make a chorus out of us. The fair Mrs Galis, the English teacher, endeavours to make us pronounce the difficult sounds correctly. Constantin Necşulescu, the history teacher nicknamed the Beast (because he called us all beasts – a term that lost its insulting edge in his mouth, however) proved how much he cared for us as he gave some of us free coaching with a view to the coming exam.

From my high school years, the dark blue eyes of Mrs Atanasiu, the Romanian teacher, watched us intensely while illuminating our minds as to how a literary text and subtext work on our sensibility and intellect. She was also our class mistress, frequently having a hard time appeasing the anger of other less clement teachers. Ion Manolescu, the maths teacher, calmly explains to us complicated algebraic formulae or geometry problems, amused at our puzzled stares. The smiling face of Aurelia Voinea, our English teacher, brightens up when she wants to convey to us her enthusiasm for English literature (and with me she was quite successful). Mrs Celesta Luchian and Mrs Katy Şerbănescu patiently try to open our minds to the mysteries of organic and inorganic chemistry. Mr Voiculescu – Old Man Cell (a nickname probably derived from his diminutive stature), makes us excitedly understand biological phenomena, whereas Mr Cantar teaches us psychology with a remarkable sense of humour. Mr Berciu, the history teacher, is on the verge of tears because of the unruly class that he cannot control, although his presentations of historical figures and phenomena are vivid, well informed and worthy of attention. Grosu, the hateful Russian teacher, takes disgusting satisfaction in giving very low grades to an ever increasing number of pupils and in checking strictly that all the details of our uniforms should be in place and in accordance with the regulations. The deplorable geography teacher (whose name I do not even remember and whose uncouth appearance matches her ignorance of the subject she teaches) always reads out the lesson she is supposed to teach, unaware of inadvertently turning two pages at a time. She must have been admitted to the university without an entrance examination, in the quota of places reserved to candidates of "sound origin," that is, to those born into peasant or working class families.

But she was the singular exception. All our teachers had been trained before the establishment of the communist regime and I can realize now that most of them formed not only our minds by their knowledge, but also our character by their personal behaviour and dedication.

What have I done since I graduated from the Spiru Haret High School? I have made an academic career and have built a wonderful family – two most rewarding achievements.

In 1964 I chose to study English and Romanian at the University of Bucharest. There I met Sorin Bottez, whom I married at the age of twenty. He was my senior by sixteen years, fifteen of which he had spent in prison as a political detainee for his anti-communist activities. Arrested at the age of eighteen, he was subsequently sent to some of the most gruesome prisons in the system, among which the Gherla penitentiary, where he was submitted to the inconceivable tortures of the so called "Reeducation" programme for half a year. Sorin had a brilliant mind, was highly cultivated, and was a man of such strong character as you can probably find one in a million (in 2008 King Michael awarded him the Cross of the Royal House of Romania in acknowledgement). When he finally got out of prison in 1963, his father had passed away without having ever seen his son after his conviction and without knowing whether he was still alive or not!

For eight years my husband and I lived in the domestic's room that his mother's flat was provided with. This room measured 2x1.80 metres. That was all the space we could get, as two rooms of the apartment had been commandeered by the authorities, which had established a norm of eight square meters per person, so the members of the family had the lawful right to live in three of the rooms, while the other two were occupied by two families of imposed "tenants". An American lady who heard our story years later could not believe her ears. "And after living eight years in that room you were still friends?" she exclaimed in amazement.

Yes, we were still friends and became even happier when we could finally buy our own apartment and have our two children. We went on living in that socialist apartment (and I still live there), and after 1989 many people were quite surprised that we did not move into a villa, as my husband became a Member of Parliament (as a prominent founding member of the new National Liberal Party), then Romania's ambassador to South Africa, and then a minister of state.

Because he had been "an enemy of the people", my husband was not allowed to hold a university position, so he became a high school teacher, although he had been valedictorian (being the only one in the country to graduate with 100%, that is with the highest mark in all the forty-one exams he had taken in his five years of study). However, I was allowed to embark upon an academic career. But because I was the wife of a former political prisoner, I could never get a scholarship to the UK or the USA and, although I got my PhD in 1981, I was not promoted to a superior academic rank. Until the communist regime was overthrown in 1989, I was a teaching assistant (for twenty one years) and, had not communism collapsed, I would probably have retired from that position.

My doctorate was also a stressful event until it was validated, as my sister had recently defected to Germany, which was a very likely ground for invalidation if the Superior Commission knew about it. However I was lucky, they probably did not, but the suspenseful stress lasted for four months.

The 1980s were very difficult times for all Romanians, as the country was practically turned into a vast prison, from which you could get out (that is, visit foreign countries) only with the special approval of the Communist Party and that of the Secret Police (my husband and I were denied visas even for Bulgaria). And you were not supposed to talk to any foreigner in the country either.

But the most terrible thing was the shortage of food, the blackouts and the central heating outages. I remember my students taking notes wearing gloves and spectators sitting in concert or theatre halls in their winter coats (and thinking of the poor artists and actors who could not do the same). As regards food, sugar and cooking oil were rationed, but most articles could never be found in shops, and for those that could there were huge queues. As I had no time to queue and I have no gift for buying goods under the counter or for using back doors, there were months when I had no cheese or eggs in the fridge (and I had two young children to feed!). It was a terrible decade because of Ceaușescu's decision to pay off all the foreign debts of the Romanian state on the one hand, and on the other hand because of his project of building Casa Poporului/The People's House, which he ambitiously wanted to be the second largest and the most expensive building for administrative civil use in the world. It now houses the Romanian Parliament.

To us, the world of culture was a refuge from the dreariness and shortages surrounding us. My husband had a great love and remarkable knowledge of music, especially of opera, which was apparent in his highly appreciated radio programmes on opera singers and performances, over two hundred of them. As in 1986 we became the happy owners of a VCR, we invited our friends to share the joy of watching opera tapes that featured great contemporary singers. But after a few months we had to stop, as a neighbour told us that a man, obviously from the secret police, had come to inquire what he knew about the Sunday morning gatherings in the apartment of the Bottez family.

When the communist regime was overthrown in December 1989, I could finally compete for higher positions in the academic hierarchy until I became a full professor and was also authorised to supervise doctoral theses (twenty so far). I was also able to get scholarships and research grants in the UK, the U.S. (a Fulbright at Princeton), Canada and Germany, and give lectures in the U.S., South Africa and Germany. I have published four books (a monograph on Dickens, a book on the post-war American novel, a volume of studies in English Canadian literature, a book on analysing narrative fiction), co-authored *Postcolonialism – Postcommunism. A Dictionary of Key Cultural Terms* and written over eighty articles on English, Canadian and American authors, often from a comparative perspective with Romanian literature. I have also translated fiction by British, American and Canadian authors. Together with a colleague in the French Department I set up the Centre of Canadian Studies and a M. A. programme in Canadian Studies at the University of Bucharest in 1996. I became a very active Canadianist, the Central Association of Canadian Studies awarding me its Certificate of Merit in 2012. Upon my retirement in 2011 I also received a diploma of Honoured Professor from the University of Bucharest. But I am still very active, functioning as professor emeritus now.

But what I take the greatest pride in is my offspring. My daughter, ALINA-MONICA BOTTEZ, senior lecturer at the English Department of the University of Bucharest and opera performer (soprano), has written an outstanding doctoral thesis on the musical masterpieces inspired by Shakespeare's Falstaff plays; my son, VALENTIN-VICTOR BOTTEZ, associate professor at the Department of Ancient History (Faculty of History, University of Bucharest), has written a remarkable doctoral thesis on the imperial cult in Moesia Inferior and is an archaeologist committed to the study and research of the ancient Greek city of Histria, where excavations bring to light new discoveries every year.

My husband passed away in 2009, leaving us deeply bereaved, but privileged and grateful to have had him in our lives.

The years have passed. A lot has happened – good and bad. It is important to remember it all, to stay young at heart and pass our legacy further to the younger generation with the hope that the bad will never return and that the good will get even better!

MATEI CAZACU - MY TWO LIVES: ROMANIA AND FRANCE

I am part of the group of privileged people (or the less privileged, it depends on how you look at it) who spent all their school years in Spiru Haret, from the first grade until my baccalaureate. This privilege cost me rather dearly, as I was well-known by all professors and the administrative staff and I could not blend in the crowd: Dumitru (Buliftru) knew me, the venomous Eugen (Oxigen) knew me, Țuchi Teodorescu and the sinister Diaconu (apologies to Monica!) knew me, Voiculescu (Cell) and Catela and Fit and Cane knew me as well, but not mainly for my own merits or personal defects as much as for the bad memories left behind by my brother, Andrei, who was seven years my elder and who, after a spotless record lasting eight years, went through a crisis in his adolescence and finished his last two years with failed subjects and multiple misdemeanors (he was part of the experimental generation with only 10 years of school, with or without foreign languages and other proletkult nonsense). His misdemeanors came back to haunt me in full, after which I went through a crisis of my own during my fifth and sixth grade, which resulted in threats to send me to juvenile hall (a kind of penitentiary for youth) and other drastic measures. In addition to this, I was "the boy of the priest on Batiște" ("singer in the mystic bar" or "the People's opium dealer"), a rotten pedigree in the era of victorious socialism, a pedigree I had to bear unwillingly and through no fault of my own. In the seventh grade I failed the admission exam for eighth grade (although my average grade was high) because the district party decided that I was unfit to go to high school, after the admission lists travelled back and forth from the high school to the Communist party offices three times! (This was the punishment I received for my impertinent comment witnessed by Mona Toma).

I want to be understood, I do not wish to pose as a victim – I had my share of faults – I just want to rationally explain the cynicism and indifference with which I regarded our school and some of our professors. Starting with Mrs. Linte, the ruthless and venal shrew (she would accept expensive gifts from parents): do you remember how she used to pull us by our ears, slap us and knock our heads together, and afterwards knock them against the blackboard? I call it sadism. Our Russian Language teacher

Moşneanu, was an ignorant and a fanatic Bessarabian? Ţuchi Teodorescu, was an avid legionnaire since her youth, afterwards she became a passionate monarchist, trying to redeem her past sins, through her avid revolutionary vigilance! Not to mention Voiculescu, nicknamed "The Cell", who taught Darwin's theory, while telling the whole classroom that I was unable to understand such a concept? (I have the satisfaction of having cheated on the final exams without him catching me; he caught Ştefan Andreescu, (the poor guy). Rădulescu, who taught Romanian, and who grabbed us by the sideburns until he pulled us to our feet and tears ran down our cheeks, while he grinned (he was kicked out for being homosexual). Same happened with Catela and Fit who, as beautiful young women, had to bear the impertinence of my brother's hooligan classmates and had transferred their resentments to me, and so on. Same with "Cane" who didn't allow students to play basketball in the schoolyard and who persecuted my brother's classmates to such extent, that they took revenge by pissing on his beautiful Jawa (or MZ) Motorcycle.

On the other side, I have kept warm and excellent memories of true professors such as Robert Cantar, profound philosopher and modest savant, forced to teach plant biology (!) and how well he taught it: "three petals, three sepals, three stamen and a pistil! Five petals, etc., multi-petals etc." I remember them perfectly to this day. Luckily times changed and he was able to teach those extraordinary Logic lessons during eleventh grade. Or Constantin Necşulescu ("The Beast"), a good historian and passionate teacher, with all his oddities (he was a bastard child of King Ferdinand, from whom he had inherited a heavy load of genetic baggage, the cause for his failure to adapt to the new world; plus, he was a permanent "objective" for the Securitate police, who spied on him in his own home through one of his relatives): do you remember how he explained the mechanism of imperial elections by giving the role of Great Elector to some of us? Or his great ideas when he came after Cernica's class and would find the blackboard filled by formulas, he, who was obsessed with cleanliness? While one of the students was erasing the blackboard, Necşulescu would theorize: "Look at this: x plus y equals zero, x squared plus y squared divided by z squared equals zero; if everything is equal to zero, why even study about them?"

This and his other idiosyncrasies such as holding his nose using two fingers, to call the students "beasts" (the worst he would say was "lugubrious beast"), making thinly veiled allusions intended for the students who did not wash was off-putting for some of the students. However, he sparked my interest for history, which made him very happy and was one of the reasons he defended me in front of the council of professors many times. Did you know that they sent him to the Elementary School in Floreasca (it was during the second ideological ice age during 1958-1962). When he came to Spiru, he was furious with the injustice that was made to him, a professor who had studied at Heidelberg?

I have the same happy memories of Berciu ("Pipe", "Lip") who taught history, the sad clown who wore different colored socks; of Vărzaru, who taught Romanian Language, well read and helpful, hypertensive and with freshly washed, bushy hair; of Cernica and "Blinky", who didn't manage to make me love mathematics, but whom I treasure more as people and good teachers because they spared me from second examinations (of course, with the occult help of Sergiu Solomon, my friend and colleague), when they found out that I wanted to study history; comrade Eremia who studied gymnastics, with the body of a Grecian athlete, who taught in our school for too short a while and even "Pușpurică", a kind man, both kicked out as a result of the Baston-Țuchi Teodorescu intrigues; the superb Madam Galiș-Vasiliu, who was cross-eyed and taught English, as well as her successor, whom I met later in Paris, although sadly I do not remember her name (Mrs. Bibița Voinea); Vladimir Niculescu ("Fafone") who taught French, the uncle of Andrei Plesu, a true gentleman, elegant and even proud, who had black hairs covering his fingers, which were quite obscene although they somehow fascinated us; "Mache" (or "Măcelaru" – ""the Butcher") who taught music and choir lessons (I wonder what his real name was), who always wore wrinkly clothes and a filthy tie, yet he was a good man, with a speech impediment, from which he acquired his nickname "Macelo-Gaze" – "Butch-Gas"; Filofteia Stoian who taught Russian, the country girl with all her provincial candor and shyness, the wife of poet Nicolae S. who, she told the girls sitting in front, would read his poems to her first, adding the famous line: "My birth certificate is my Party Member Card"; Mrs. Nicolau

("Şchioapa" – "the Lame") who taught Geography, the class master who saved me from perdition in sixth grade and made me a UTM member during eighth grade, along with the last group (the same had happened when I was made a pioneer, because of my "bad" origins, see the photograph of Mrs. Linte's third grade class) in Doftana!

I say "perdition" and I am not exaggerating: during a parents' meeting, my mother who was ill at the time asked a friend of my father's to attend on her behalf, saying he was an uncle of mine. When he came back from school, Mr. Vasilescu, a Doctor in Law from Paris and former magistrate, was pale as if he had seen a ghost: the Securitate police Colonel who had brutally questioned him in 1948 (for an "illegal" attempt to cross the border), a feared man among all reactionaries, had shouted during the meeting that he wanted me to be sent to juvenile hall because he did not want his daughter to be in the same classroom, as such an "element" (a high achieving colleague who sat at the front of the class had accused me, sitting in the back, of playing poker in the classroom!) I won't mention his name, he knows who he is: I will only say that around 1958-1959 Colonel D. had already been demoted to the rank of soldier, kicked out from Securitate (the Secret Police) and worked as a laborer at ICAS (or ICAB, the shit scrubbers, as they were called). He still had the nerve to force Celesta Luchian to give passing grades to his daughter, who was failing, through a grotesque series of questions, which I will never forget: "Isn't it true that salt is made out of natrium and chlorine? Isn't it true that sulphuric acid is made out of … " To which the student would answer "Yes, yes", and this is how she was saved from failing, especially following the intervention of Ţuchi Teodorescu, the principal, because the Colonel had a considerable amount of dirt on her, having read her file.

My last years in high school were the most beautiful: I had opted for the modern profile, and only a few of my old colleagues had remained (Costin Cazaban, Lucică Moldoveanu, Popescu Niculae – Popică, Florin Rusu, Daniela Pamfil and Ioana Borş), the others were students who had come from peripheral neighborhoods (Tei) during sixth grade, following the initiative of terminating the high school's socio-professional profile: as in the PCR, there were too many of the bourgeois and too few of the proletariat.

I played basketball, I read a lot and I had lots of fun, so much so that I had half a mind to repeat the eleventh grade. Tuchi had lost her influence, but we had a commissary woman as an adjunct headmistress. She was comrade Tirea, loyal to the party; she wore a black leather short coat and she sparked fear in all our hearts. And so I passed the baccalaureate and I began studying hard for the admission exam for the Faculty of History. Something was happening in Romania, during 1963-1964, the regime had become somewhat less strict, and one of the signs of this mellowing down was the abolition of the political grade (or social grade, as it was called) when applying to the Polytechnic Institute in 1963. Later I found out that at the Faculty of History (and the whole "ideological front") had taken the same measures in 1964, exactly the year I applied. For those who have forgotten what this meant, I will mention that the grade obtained at the admission exam was averaged with a grade based on one's file, which included the social origins of one's parents, their fortune before the 23rd of August, their political activity from before, one's relatives who had been imprisoned and/or had fled the country, the so-called "What-what" form (what does your father do for a living? What does your mother do …). In my case, my grade was 0, as priests and prostitutes were on the bottom step of the socialist social ladder, even if my parents had not engaged in politics, had not owned land and proprieties, did not have any relatives outside the country, and the ones who had been imprisoned had begun to regain their freedom beginning with 1964. This is how my older sister and brother's files had not even been accepted back when they wanted to apply to Journalism and the Conservatory, respectively. In 1955 and 1956, thus my sister became a chemist and my brother an engineer, even though he wanted to become a pianist.

But let us come back to myself. During the summer of 1964, while I was arduously studying in order to try and apply to History, Țuchi Teodorescu sent word for me that I had no chance of getting admitted and that I risked being enrolled! To this day, I never found out if it had been one last poisonous arrow thrown by the exophthalmic headmistress or a well-meaning gesture sent through someone I trusted (Vladimir Niculescu). I replied that I thank her for the advice, but I insist on studying history, that it was my passion, passed down from my grandfather who had gathered a considerable collection of history books, and that me discovering them in 1959 had had a significant impact on my future. History was for me the only refuge from a word which I felt was hostile towards me, although I did not fully understand why – but who can truly understand bloody dictatorships?

I passed the admission exam (we were 11 competitors per place), I studied for five careless years that passed like a dream, and in 1969, upon graduation, I was hired as a researcher for the Nicolae Iorga Institute of History of the Academy. My dream had come true and I was prepared for great things to come. I knew the greatest historians who still lived, I had skilled colleagues, some of them quite exceptional, the schedule was relaxed, the atmosphere was good, the Party (meaning Ceauşescu) had no interest in history as of yet. I lived, as all Romanians did, the illusion of the 1964 mellowing of the regime, I had profited from it fully during my college years, when I began publishing articles in history magazines – I was considered a young man with a bright future.

However, in the summer of 1971 – the July thesis and Ceausescu's cultural mini-revolution – I felt the wind changing, as it blew once again towards the East, towards the nationalist mask bearing communism, or the national-communism which was about to balkanize Bolshevik type communism. I was not a party member, but I discovered I had an uncle (a cousin of my grandfather's) who was a founding member of the PCR in 1921, had disappeared after 1940 and had been restored to grace after 1968. I boasted this illustrious connection in order to make fun of it (in my autobiography I wrote "descending from an old family of communists") and I was subsequently noticed by the Base Organizational Bureau (B.O.B.) of the party and the secret police, which made me into an "objective" (they set up microphones throughout my house, all my conversations were transcribed, I was put under 24h surveillance, and all my friends and acquaintances were put on file) as early as 1966 (our conversations on the phone had been monitored from 1949 or 1950, same as the mail)! I also had a codename: "the Englishman". However, I had no intention of leaving the country, I felt good, I was, after all, privileged, at the institute I had colleagues and fine professors whom I admired, a few friends, some of which had passed away, poor fellows (Sandu Tanaşoca, Radu Otetelesanu, Mihai Oroveanu), I had money and my parents would let me do anything I wanted, even smoke the pipe. My decision to leave was taken in the summer of 1972, upon receiving an official invitation from France (EHESS and CNRS) with which the Academy and my Institute had signed a scientific cooperation accord, to which I had taken part. I went through six nightmarish months while my requests for a passport was denied on a variety of levels: the Institute's Communist Party Organization, then the Academy's, then the passport police. The secret police contributed to all this, as they tried to take advantage of my situation and recruit me as an informer – I flat out refused "comrade Costin" during our meeting for coffee at the "Albina" tea shop. In the end, I was able to obtain my passport through "priestly connections", as well as my French visa and even my plane ticket. In that moment I swore to myself I would not spend another day in this country run by monsters and I left, wiping the dust from under my feet, as the Bible says (a manner of speaking, as it was January 1973 and the ground was covered by snow) – a separation I believed and I still believe to be final.

In France I continued my studies, attending a *Grande Ecole*, obtaining diplomas, my PhD and docent rank and in 1978 I was hired as researcher for the Centre National de la Recherche Scientifique, in an institute dedicated to the study of history. It was exactly what I had worked as back in Bucharest, but at another level, without syndicate meetings, without days on the field, without a human resources manager who worked for the secret police, without microphones hidden in your home, without informants and salami made out of soy, but with a great deal of pluses, and an incomparable opening towards Europe. I taught at Sorbonne (Paris IV) and INALCO, the so-called School for Oriental Languages from 1975 to 2011.

I thought I was done with Romania and I avoided Romanians in exile or who had emigrated, as I did with the very few who rarely came from the country: it is a reaction common to all exiles, as is the recurring nightmare in which one sees oneself back in Bucharest, without knowing how one got there, and without any possibility of ever leaving. But in 1977, the Paul Goma business erupted – the writer's protest defending human rights and in solidarity of the Charta 77 from Czechoslovakia, the creation of the SLOMR free syndicate, the actions of Vasile Paraschiv and others. Together with a few friends and acquaintances, starting with Mihnea Berindei, I engaged in the battle, I collaborated with Radio Free Europe, the BBC and The Voice of America, I signed pleas, I protested in front of the Romanian Embassy in Paris – in short, I gave Ceausescu and his henchmen a rough time. Unlike Mihnea however, I continued my research activities. I got married and I have two children who now live in London and Montpellier.

From 1990, I began coming back to Romania, where I met with a few good friends and colleagues. Here, I published a multitude of books and articles, but the idea of settling back in Bucharest never concerned me. I kept my Romanian citizenship because I did not want to give Ceausescu the pleasure of depriving me of it as well as all the assets I had left in the country: those who have read the official form to renounce citizenship understand me perfectly, it is a veritable interrogation by the secret police (I kept it as an historical document). I was born before Ceausescu came into power, it was not he who gave me my Romanian citizenship, and I was not about to ask him such a thing.

My scientific activity amounts to 15 books, approximately one hundred articles, tens of conferences and talks, plus the classes I held for over 35 years. My doctorate thesis was about Dracula-Vlad Țepeș and was published in 1988 (three editions), followed by a biography of the character published in 2004 in Paris (awarded by the French Academy) and translated in seven languages. Following the same idea – the relations between myth and history – I published a book about Gilles de Rais (Bluebeard) and another one about Frankenstein, the character created by Mary Shelley (2005 and 2011). I also wrote two books about Bessarabia – The Republic of Moldavia, a state in search of a nation –, two about Romanian cuisine and gastronomy (published in Bucharest, ICR publishing house), a book about the wars between the Russians and the Chechens, another about women travelling in the Orient, a book about miracles, hallucinations and premonitions in the Romanian past, and finally a history of the Florescu family of boyars, written alongside professor Radu R. Florescu from Boston College, and old friend of mine who gave me a tremendous amount of help when I first came to Paris. My last book, published last year, is about Ioan Basarab, the founder of Țara Românească, written as a retort to the nonsense published by Neagu Djuvara on the subject. Another two books, which will be published in Romania, are under way.

At the end of four decades of exile – approximately twice the time I spent in Romania – the French think of me as being Romanian, and many Romanians consider me French. Personally, I persist in the belief that I have remained myself, no more, and no less, that I did no compromises with my conscience, and that, without being perfect, I consider myself to be a man who has fulfilled his aspirations in life.

Constatin Cernat

I am an architect by profession. After graduating, one passes through a gray period, during which one cannot practice their craft. Because I worked for the corporation, I was lucky and I designed a few houses. I went on to execution.

Within the corporation, you could be head of the construction site without being a party member. They asked me to become a party member once, and I told them that we should first go to the Bellu Cemetery to see if my grandfather is turning in his grave.

After that, they left me alone.

My grandfather, who was also named Constantin, was the chief of the Romanian Siguranta (the secret police at the time) until 1937. He was sentence to death and his sentence was changed to forced labor for life. He died in prison in Gherla after 14 years. All the men in my family were arrested. We were staying in the house on 25 Italiana Street (in which my sister Ioana, who also graduated from Spiru Haret, and her husband now live). 22 women, sisters, aunts, grandmothers, were left without men. I will carry a ferocious hatred for this horrible regime and all its descendants to my grave.

However, after 1989 I immediately quit as head of the site, I gathered good teams of people around me and I went into the private sector. Everything went smoothly, like a charm, we had projects, until I noticed that all my men were stealing from me. The socialist system had perverted them, nothing could be done!

Meanwhile I had started opening legal cases in order to take back the fortune of the family. At one moment, I had 82 ongoing trials. In numerous cases, I was my own lawyer. I had no money for lawyers and at first I managed to get back two buildings. Our apartment building on 25 Italiana Street was the first building to be given back to me in Bucharest, of course, with the aid of a very good lawyer.

24 years have passed and I still have open cases. It is amusing that we had a manor by the seaside in the 23 August town, where I've been suing the Ovidiu Worker's Cooperative for 15 years. 5 months ago, the town's mayor called me and told me to sit down, so as to not faint; the manor was gone, it was stolen and in its place lay a big hole: the townspeople had stolen it during the night. Such is life: from being an architect, I changed into a lawyer in order to take back what is mine, and my son (Constantin Vlad, 33 years old) is a pleading lawyer, and is now building a bunch of settlements: two hostels and a hotel for pets.

I had two marriages, which failed, and I only have one son from my first marriage. For 20 years I've been enjoying a beautiful relationship with my girlfriend, Roxana.

Life is a wonderful thing. All the while, I've been optimistic and confident in what I was doing. I went through hard times. In Paris, I had my failing aorta replaced.

IOANA CREȚOIU (CASASSOVICI) - HOW FAST 50 YEARS FLEW BY ...

After I graduated from the Ion Mincu Institute of Architecture, I "crash landed" into the "labor field", as jobs were named back then! It was called The Institute for Research and Development in the Wood Industry, although it was in the middle of the field, in Pipera ouskirt of Bucharest, the field wasn't really worked. It was a place where we pretended to be working and they pretended to pay us. Today, I often ask myself how I managed to work there until 1990, when I had the opportunity of changing my workplace. Changing jobs was a move I could not have considered until then, because even if it no longer mattered "what father and mother do for a living", my brother and sister had left the country, and nobody would hire a person with such a background and realtives. I admit I didn't get any satisfaction out of my job during that absurd period and I managed to go through the excruciating daily routine thanks to my colleagues, who were honest and humorous people.

During college, I married Serban Crețoiu, a sculptor, with which I navigated and sailed through all of life's waters, calm or stormy. With Serban, with our daughter, with the books, with our bookcases, with the statues in the workshop, with vacations spent at the village of 2 Mai, with trips to the mountains, trekking for mushrooms, with the 4 beehives we tended for a few years after taking a few classes about bee keeping, with the flowers in our garden, with our dogs and cats, with no television, and, last but not least, with our friends who stayed in Romania, we built our small corner, away from the real world. Family is very important to me and I thank my parents and grandparents daily, even if they are no longer with me, for the education they have given me during those hard times and I am happy to have been with them until the very end.

The end of the year 1989 was a new start for me! It was then that I believed everything was possible, and that is how I found myself singing and shouting during the protests that followed.

Between 1991 and 1996 I was one of the few volunteers (something regarded somewhat suspiciously back then) and, with the help of a friend of mine who moved to Greece, I founded the Romanian Girl Guides. Around me, everybody was starting companies, business ventures; we were the only ones doing voluntary work! Every week we visited an orphanage, where tried to engage the children in teamwork exercises, inspire honesty and courage! Holy naïveté! We had various endeavors: teaching courses, summer camps for girls in orphanages, support granted to the refugee children in the Gociu center, information and education for girls and young women, information about gender/role issues in society, democracy through education taught by playing (my favorite brainchild), all these done after projects we developed and which were financed by the United Nations, the Soros Foundation, the Ministry of Youth and Sports, The High Commissariat for Refugees, Phare Tacis, Phare for Democracy, FDSC, UNDP and many others. These were very interesting years, filled with searching, satisfaction, during which I learned many things by participating in various conferences, training courses, national and international meetings, meeting many people and getting the feeling that I was changing the word. The foundation survived through dire conditions: my home housed its headquarters, meetings took place in the living room, where I also set up beds for the volunteers come from outside the country, the papers were stacked in the bookcase, training sessions were conducted in the garden, evaluations in the kitchen, the house phone was also the foundation's phone… It finally got a proper headquarters, the new taught members elected a new leadership and my family finally had some peace.

I worked like a madwoman, I was very motivated, I applied all I learned from my trainings and previous projects to the Romanian Girl Guides. I sought the advice of service suppliers, I read, I collaborated with young journalists, and finally, I prepared normative acts. This is how financing began for services offered by social assistance foundations: by a process of selection, eliminating the corrupted system of influenced decisions. I organized meetings, I published clear guidelines regarding financing such endeavors, I periodically instructed personnel, I always consulted my partners, I was part of various committees, workgroups, I published articles in various magazines related to this subject, I had the opportunity of meeting a series of intelligent people, trustworthy and always, always on the side of decentralization, and who supported criteria and clear cut procedures in various areas of expertise, so as to maintain a constant and continuous application of the new laws.

In 2001, my granddaughter Alexandra was born and I finished my Master's Degree in Public Administration at the University of Bucharest, the Faculty of Political and Administrative Sciences. This was another extraordinary period in my life: a period of study, accumulating and discovering new things! I remember I was excited about Francis Fukuyama's theory on trust. I had the honor of being invited and meeting him at the conference he held in Bucharest.

Starting with 2002, after our country's leadership twisted and turned some more, I left the Ministry out of my own volition. I gave up the files, the suits, the heels, and I came back to jeans. I offered technical assistance in the Phare program for the Civil Society, working with people who were very young, and gave me new energy.

In 2003 and 2005 I was part of the University of Bucharest team – the political sciences department, along with prof. Georgeta Ghebrea and Marina Tataram, in the research project coordinated by the Queen's University in Belfast called "Enlargement, Gender and Governance: The Civic and Political Participation of Women in EU Candidate Countries", also published by Nemira.

In 2007 I decided the moment had come for me to calm down and retire! It is safe to say, but hard to put into practice.

I started travelling a lot, I even went to places I had long dreamed of visiting: Petra, Capadocia, Machu Picchu. In 2011, I travelled on foot the final 110 km of the journey made by Apostle Jacob to Compostela. I always have the fortune and joy of discovering new extraordinary places, as was the case in Bulgaria or the Buzau Mountains last year.

The year 2012 was the year in which I participated in the popular races of the marathons run in Bucharest. At "We run Bucharest", I came on the 3rd place for my age group, of over 55. Did I feel an Olympian or a Paralympian? Today I don't run anymore, but I kept trekking, taking long walks or climbing the Bucegi and Piatra Craiului Mountains. My most beautiful memory is on the Lancia peak in Bucegi, where I climbed on the trail made by a wild goat.

I almost forgot: in the autumn of 2013, I revolted once more and participated at the protests against using cyanide in the extraction process in Rosia Montana, rattling a plastic bottle filled with pebbles and carrying signs made in my moments of super-activism!

In 2013, I took a course on *creative writing* with writer Cristian Teodorescu and I began writing stories, when I find the time. I am one of the authors published in the collective volume coordinated by Ioana Parvulescu called *Si eu am trait in communism* published by Humanitas in 2015, and the short story book called *Alegeri dificile* was published in 2016 by Polirom, in the Ego proza collection. At the same time, I studied my family's history: I collaborated with Eng. Gherman for his article published in the Romanian Academy magazine NOEMA, no. 10/2010 about my grandfather: professor engineer Corneliu Casassovici, industrialist, the founder of higher studies regarding textiles in Romania. I published in the *Magazin Istoric* magazine (September, October and November 2013), memories from the 1877 War belonging to my grand grandfather, Colonel Doctor Haralambie Casassovici, who was part of Carol Davila's second generation of students.

I am still very aware of what is happening around me.

Ivan Csendes*

* Provided in English by Ivan Csendes

I was born in Timisoara. When I was 5 we moved to Bucuresti in an apartment on Batistei Street, in the same block where Ana Zsoldos lived.

I often played with Matei Cazacu and Florin Seimeanu in front of Matei's house. I went to kindergarten among others with Loți Hajos, who became my best friend, Peter Clar, Firu Dumitrescu. I attended Spiru Haret for the first 7 years of schooling. For the last of school I attended and graduated from C.A. Rosetti School in Floreasca, an outskirt of Bucharest. I move from one of the best schools, located in the center of the city to a school situated at the other end of the Bucharest for political reasons.

My father, who was a vice – director at Prodexport, was kicked out of office because of his bourgeois origin. He was later arrested and brought to a big show trial as an enemy of the state. He was sentenced to 15 years of prison and my mother was afraid that I might suffer negative consequences at school where many knew our family.

After graduation from high school in 1964, I managed, despite my "bad" origin, to pass the admission exams to the Manufacturing Engineering Technical University. I spent only a little over one semester there. The only thing I remember is that I had the biggest headache with the Teachings of Marxism-Leninism, a class rated higher than the engineering classes.

My father passed away in prison in May 1964. It was only after his death that my grandfather, who was living in Vienna, succeeded in buying free my mother, my older brother with his wife and me. In March 1965 we received the one page "passport" for leaving the country. My grandfather sent us airline tickets for a flight with Austrian Airlines. The date we left Romania was just one day after the funeral of the party leader, Gehorghiu Dej. After checking in at the airport we were separated from the other passengers and brought to a big empty room, where we waited for over one hour and became more and more concerned that we would not be allowed to leave. Finally we were led to the airplane and embarked ahead of the other passengers. After we were seated, an official delegation approached the airplane. Four people embarked the plane. It was the delegation of the Austrian communist party that had attended the funeral festivities. In front of the airplane representatives of the Rumanian Workers Party were waving them and us good-bye. Ironically one of them was Ceausescu. It was a big relief when we finally reached Vienna.

In the fall of 1965 I started to study chemistry at the Technical University. During summer vacations I worked at Sandoz in Basel. In 1969 I left Vienna and continued my studies at the University Basel. I graduated in 1972 and finished my PhD study in organic chemistry in 1976. In Basel, in 1974, I met a lovely young Swiss girl, who became (and still is) my wife. Our first son was born in Basel 1975. In 1976 we went to Berkeley California, where I worked for 2 years as a post-graduate research fellow at the University of California, School of Chemistry. In 1978 our second son was born in Berkeley, California. Our daughter was born in 1991. After returning to Basel in the fall of 1978 I was hired by Ciba-Geigy as an antibiotics research chemist. My scientific career ended in 1985 when I moved to the business development unit, a small group responsible for identifying and licensing in acquiring third party development and or marketing medical products which would complement Ciba-Geigy's portfolio. After merger of Ciba-Geigy with Sandoz I continued to work in the Business Development group of Novartis until my retirement in 2009. Besides my work at Novartis, I was a cofounder of the Swiss Pharma Licensing Group (PLG). In 2001 I was chairman of the European Pharma Licensing Council. I am still active as a consultant to young pharmaceutical companies. Besides consulting I enjoy family events with our children, our four granddaughters, and travelling with my wife to foreign countries.

ZAMFIR DUMITRESCU*

* This text was taken from the artist website www.zamfirdumitrescu.com

Zamfir Dumitrescu was dean of the Faculty of Fine Arts Bucharest and president of Artists Association of Romania. He wrote seven books, about perspective and Universal geometric painting composition.

Regarding family life, the painter Zamfir Dumitrescu. He has six daughters and three grandchildren.

Zamfir Dumitrescu was born on 15th April 1946 in Bucharest, Romania, to a family of intelectuals. His parents lived at the time on Caimatei Street, in an old part of the town, not far from the University of Bucharest. They later moved to Cotroceni, not far from the Opera House, where the artist lives to this day.

His mother, Margareta (born Eckert), was half austrian (by her father Francisc Eckert) and half swiss (by her mother Clara Filk). Margareta was trained in classical music and showed artistic talent and she later studied and graduated from the Academy of Physical Education and Sport in Bucharest.

His father, Dumitru Dumitrescu, was a true scholar. He graduated from the University of Bucharest, with degrees in Mathematics, Law, Literature and Philosophy and at the same time he obtained an engineering degree from the Polithechnics Institute in Bucharest. He then studied aeronautics and electrical engineering in Paris, graduating from the École Nationale Supérieure de l'Aéronautique et de l'Espace and also from École Supérieure d'Élcctricité. A PhD followed in Gottingen in the field of fluid mechanics. He was elected member of the Academy of Romania, where he served as General Secretary between 1963 and 1967, and was associate member of the Academy in Toulouse.

Zamfir Dumitrescu studied at the renowned "Spiru Haret" College in Bucharest and then chose to dedicate himself to the fine arts, in particular to painting. He recalls asking his father for advice choosing between engineering and painting; the great scholar let him choose for himself but added "an ordinary engineer, maybe even a stupid one will find work, whereas nobody has any need for an ordinary artist".

Studying at the Institute of Fine Arts "Nicolae Grigorescu", Zamfir Dumitrescu is part of the 'golden gencration' alongside Stefan Caltia, Sorin Ilfoveanu, Cornel Antonescu, Wanda Mihuleac, Victor Teodorov, Mihai

Buculei, Napoleon Tiron, Bata Marianov, Florin Codre, Ovidiu Buba and Tereza Panelli. This generation is already considered to be part of the history of arts in Romania.

It is during his years as student, as pupil of master Corneliu Baba, that Zamfir choses painting as his way of life, his tool for exploring and understanding life.

An important moment in the artistic development and personality of Zamfir is represented by the time spent in Norway over a period of 15 years and where he felt like home. In this period, he painted and exhibited in both Norway and Sweden. The honor of being chosen to paint the portraits of members of the Norwegian and Swedish royal families demonstrates that, in the homeland of Grieg and in the homeland of Strindberg, he was adopted without reserve and appreciated for his art.

Zamfir painted His Royal Highness King Olav the 5th, His Royal Highness King Harald the 5th and Her Royal Highness Queen Sonja from the royal family of Norway, His Royal Highness King Carl the 16th Gustaf and Her Royal Highness Queen Silvia from the Royal family of Sweden, but also Nicolae Ceausescu and his family. All were official commissions, which represented for the artist real challenges for his painting, for the art of portrait.

Artist, painter, university professor doctor, member of parliament, Zamfir Dumitrescu is above all one of the finest representatives of culture in Romania, a true intellectual - fifth generation as demonstrated by his family tree continuing in his quest for perfection.

Virgil (Vio aka "the Swan") Duncan – Biography[*]
[*] Provided in English by Virgil Duncan and edited by Georgiana Galateanu

Early Years
I was born in 1947 in a family of intellectuals. My father, a civil engineer, was a very good professional who worked long hours, so he advanced quickly in the hierarchy, even though of Jewish origin. He rose through the ranks to be appointed Chief Engineer of the capital city, Bucharest, and in that

capacity he was in charge of building almost everything in the city. My mother, the daughter of a very large farm owner, became an artist painter against her father's wish, who would have liked her to be an accountant and take over the family farm. But the communist regime came to power in 1945 and confiscated everything my parents owned: arable and forest land, animals, farm buildings, as well as their city house. (I should mention here that the city house was confiscated abusively, not even in accordance with the communist nationalization law! Therefore it was a double injustice, and I am still fighting the current Romanian authorities for some restitution, after 21 long years and spending thousands of dollars in lawyer's fees in corrupt Romanian courts.)

I remember myself as a kid who always asked questions. In kindergarten I saw the portraits of Politburo members hanging on buildings and among them one woman (Ana Pauker, probably at that time the highest position a woman held anywhere in the world). I asked my father loudly in the street "why only one woman and six men?" Immediately my father took me inside, punished me, and of course I wanted to know why – "just don't ask questions in the street" I was told. After a couple of months the woman's portrait disappeared and I asked again "why?" but not so loudly this time... Again I was taken inside and this time I learned my lesson, because it was very painful. Many years later I found out that if anybody had heard me, the authorities would have arrested my father and most likely sent him to a labor camp, if not worse. The reason? There were many thousands who were jailed or killed on fabricated accusations. Regime abuses in those times are well documented.

"SPIRU HARET" MIDDLE SCHOOL AND HIGH SCHOOL

I was admitted to Spiru Haret Middle School in fifth grade, after moving with my family to downtown Bucharest. The transition was not easy – leaving my old friends behind and not being an extrovert kid. About sixth grade I became friends with Miki Andreev and together we started a hobby that helped me a lot in my engineering career, years later: we were building and repairing AM/FM receivers, HiFi audio amplifiers, and later TV receivers.

In middle school I was also good at sports; our PhysEd teacher, Anton Ionescu, nicknamed "Baston," sent me many times to track-and-field inter-schools contests. One day my uncle Marcel Duncan (he was one of the Romanian national women's team gymnastics coaches who discovered Nadia Comaneci – later a famous Olympic champion – as a child in the town of Onesti – see "My own story" by Nadia Comaneci) sent me to one of his friends, a flatwater kayaking coach, for a tryout.

My parents agreed because I was skinny and shy, and they hoped that competing would give me a boost in self-confidence and toughness. Well, they did not know what they were bargaining for because I started training after school every day, winter or summer. Of course, it was much better than being on the street, but it meant less time for study. During summer vacations I spent at least four hours paddling on the Snagov Lake every day.

I also convinced my friends Bebe Filippi and Mircea Sebastian to join me. Firu Dumitrescu participated, too, but compared to us, he was much more successful when it came to girlfriends.

In competitions I was doing better and better – I earned second place twice in the National Junior Flatwater Single Kayaking Championships. Once I even competed in the Senior Nationals, in neighboring lanes with Aurel Vernescu, the World Champion at speed kayaking – he came up first and I was fifth out of nine racers. Following that I was selected in the National Team, but my father took me out after six months; I had to study for the more important College Admission exams. In the West everybody can get into college if they have the tuition funds. In Communist Romania failing the admission exam to college usually meant studying to become a technician vs. an engineer with an advanced degree.

Again I cannot forget the day when "Baston," our school PhysEd professor, mentioned my name in front of the whole school assembly after my first success in the Junior Nationals. I was pleasantly surprised because he had located my name in the brief article in the National Sports newspaper where the event was described.

My high school years went by very fast. I survived when it came to study because I was so busy with sports. My friends were Bebe Filippi, Mircea Sebastian, and Miki Andreev.

I had fun and smart classmates – besides the three names above I was impressed by Dini Cernat, Loţi Hajos, Decebal Becea, Monica Diaconu, EnglentinaVlasie, Ioana Cassasovici, Mariana Matei, Gaby Vasilescu, and many others.

We had first-class professors I will never forget: Ion Voiculescu (Natural Sciences), Robert Cantar (Psychology/Philosophy), Ion Manolescu (Math), Berciu (History), Georgeta Atanasiu and Simion Varzaru (Romanian Literature), Vladimir Niculescu (French Language and Literature). Most of them were overqualified as HS teachers and had probably held high government positions under the previous regime. The new regime demoted all of them for no reason. I am sorry I did not gain more from their knowledge and wisdom. I was too immature and busy with sports, almost to an obsession.

In college I continued my friendships with Sergiu Aronovici, Cantemir Ionescu, Adrian Stoica, Miki Andreev, Adrian Gavrilescu, and others.

COLLEGE YEARS AND PROFESSIONAL ACTIVITY IN ROMANIA
The next big step forward for me was when I was admitted to the Bucharest Polytechnic Institute, Electronics and Telecommunications Department. For me this represented not just studying for a degree that was popular at the time, but also developing expertise in a field I already had hands-on experience in. I remember the high stress during the admission exam. We were given a Physics exercise that had a strong engineering and less theoretical part.

I think I did well in that and that's why I found myself very high up on the admitted list, in very select company. After five years of hard study, graduation day came together with a workplace assignment. As opposed to the West, the government in any communist country assigned you to a job position, and you had to take it because they had invested in you (free college tuition). This workplace could be far away in the countryside. The best positions were in the Hi-Tech R&D Institutes, but my GPA was not that high, so I missed those. I remember getting the last place in Bucharest – I was to be a professor of Telecommunications and

Computers in a school-preparing technicians for industry. The Principal offered me the opportunity to swap my teaching assignment for a job in any R&D Institute because somebody very high up in the hierarchy wanted to place his daughter in the position assigned to me. I declined his offer because I knew I would not be allowed to emigrate if I worked in R&D. My luck was that I had hands-on technical knowledge in the subject I was about to teach, and the School Principal preferred me to anybody else.

After graduating from college I had to go through six months of compulsory military training, which I did together with the other male members of my class – we did basic training at a Reserve Air Force officer school. It was both interesting and useful – I believe very strongly that every young person should undergo some form of national service (even in the West) for a few months in order to mature and meet new people with different life experiences. This national service does not even have to be in the military – it can be in healthcare, teaching/tutoring the poor, etc.

When I was away in the military, one day I got a phone call from home with the sad news that my father had passed away. Getting home I found our apartment full – both family and people I had never met before. My father had been a perfect leader, appreciated both as a professional and a human being. I immediately realized two things: I had big shoes to fill and I was responsible for my family. There was something else, too, harder to explain. I felt I was next in line, so I had to live my life to the fullest. In the ambulance my father had told my brother hours before dying, "Prepare yourselves for the day you will have to leave for Israel." First I had to keep my family together and obviously that was too much for a 22-year-old. My mother felt a big void in her life and started to look for a friend to ease her loneliness. My younger brother got married very quickly. I, on the other hand, did not have a steady girlfriend, so I decided to submit an application to immigrate to Israel on my own. At the same time I hired a tutor to learn Hebrew and the history of the Jewish people. By the time I got my emigration visa I knew a thousand words in Hebrew and could understand, read, and speak the language on a basic level.

Life and Professional Activity in Israel

At the time we knew that the Romanian government had started to accept foreign currency for Jewish emigration, from both the Israeli government and private people. This had been done many times in Jewish history in order to save/protect Jewish lives and usually there had been no other options. However, the official authority that accepts the money has a problem when doing that at the end of the 20th century as opposed to the Middle Ages. But "the more things change, the more they stay the same." In conclusion, I was bought twice: once by the Israeli Government, and secondly by my aunt from Israel. I got my exit passport about six months after the money had been paid. At the other extreme, my future wife's family had waited twenty years for their exit visas, for obvious reasons (no money paid privately).

I landed in Israel one early morning in October 1973, during the Yom Kippur war, and through the airport windows I saw an impressive picture. Every 10 minutes a large American Galaxy military cargo plane landed, unloaded, and left. The State of Israel was at war. Military jet planes were up in the sky day and night. I had never known what real war was while in Romania. The years spent in Israel helped me understand the conflict in depth. This understanding was impossible to get in Romania just from books and the news. This conflict is active on two dimensions: religion and nationality/tribe multiplied by the hurt each group has suffered since the Middle Ages. There will not be peace there until each nationality and religion gets its own state and accepts to leave in peace with the neighboring countries.

The Immigration clerks sent me to a kibbutz. I did not stay long there because I knew Hebrew from Romania. After two nights I returned to the Tel Aviv area and started looking for work.

After the war the Israeli economy was in depression. Even though in ceasefire, many men were still active in the military – hostilities could start anytime even as governments were negotiating the temporary peace. There were still soldiers dying every day in front-line skirmishes. I was offered only low-level temporary jobs. I started as a technician fixing TV sets in a basement. After some time I found a position as Project Engineer for the Saba TV sets manufactured under license in Israel. The job was temporary too, and I was paid by the hour as an "intern student". I was fired after six months because I was about to be taken into the army – obviously the company did not want to give away a permanent position with benefits to a person going into the army and then have the position unstaffed for two years.

In 1976, after the Israeli compulsory military service, I got hired as Project Engineer in Medical Electronics. The product was one of the first CT-scanners in the world. It was amazing to see the difference between an X-ray picture and a CT-scanner picture – seeing all the detail inside the human body and being able to do advanced diagnoses not possible before. This was part of the technological revolution happening under my own eyes and I was fortunate to be there and learn it.

The engineers around me were all top notch. It was hard for me to keep pace since my technical knowledge from Romania was already obsolete. I decided to go for an advanced degree, if possible in the USA, because in this way I would also improve my English.

LIFE AND PROFESSIONAL ACTIVITY IN THE USA

I was accepted into a Master of Science program in Computer and Systems Engineering in 1977, in a prestigious Engineering School.

After one year I graduated and started to work again in Medical Electronics, in the Boston area.

My wife joined me a few months after graduating from Medical School in Israel, but the US laws did not allow her to work as a doctor for another two years. After she fulfilled all the requirements she was accredited to work in a prestigious hospital in Manhattan.

Because we had to move, I had to leave the Boston firm for a New York Metropolitan area company making Computer Angiography X-ray instrumentation. Things were quite difficult for us as a family; we had two small children and long distances to drive every day. We decided to move to New Jersey, in an area with good schools and closer to work.

In 1987 I applied and was accepted to a position with AT&T Bell Laboratories, working in the area of telephony switch development. This company was the place where the phone switching, the transistor, the cell phone, and the UNIX Operating System were invented among many other things. I attended seminars given by people whose names I knew from textbooks and who later won Nobel Prizes for their inventions.

Here I worked initially in phone systems design for performance, and then I moved into Internet dial-up network infrastructure design and deployment. When the company split, I continued to work (after 1997) for Lucent Technologies in cell phone networks System Engineering and Performance.

I retired in 2014 to have more time for hobbies that reflect my numerous interests: tennis, bridge, psychology, anthropology, and history of religions. I am active in Interfaith meetings where we discover how much we have in common and discuss the origins and sources of our religious differences.

In addition, I am looking to volunteer as a mentor and tutor for high school students who come from fatherless homes. I also have three grandsons, with a fourth one on the way, and they will definitely need an active grandfather in their lives.

FAMILY

In 1975 I met and got married in Israel to Eva, also born in Romania. We are happy together and I thank God for this quality lady He has sent my way. We have been together for the last 40 years and we have helped each other along the way. We raised two wonderful children (Diana and Sam), now successful adults in both their professional and private lives.

NICULAE ENE - SHORT PRESENTATION

After finishing school I was able to get into the Faculty of Mechanical Engineering of Iasi, and after a year I was transferred with my permission to Bucharest. Eating at home was far better. I graduated from the Faculty of Mechanical, Aerospace and Civil Engineering department board installations. At first I thought not to see it but the reality was different.

Meanwhile, being in Iasi, I practiced skydiving. The Students Association in Bucharest "suggested" finishing my studies first and then, if I have courage, to practice skydiving. Actually in Iasi was my last parachute jump.

First I was assigned to the aircraft-building factory in Brasov. I returned to Bucharest after some family events and Tarom hired me. Following two kidney surgeries I had to orient myself to something less physically demanding so I transferred to the Training Center and Professional Staff of Civil Aviation

(CAPPAC). I taught various employees licensed and we had a small piece of mechanical flight to IPB. I was part of the ICAO TRAINAIR initiated, during which we visited the cities of Amman, Manama, Bangkok, Cairo, Paris, Moscow and Warsaw. I managed to do a short flight program.

For five years I am retired and are happy to enjoy the tranquility of a continuation of the teaching program, which will be over eventually.

I am married, have two children and a grandchild.

I wish you all a long and happy life.

MICAELA FELDSTEIN

My maiden name is Michaela Feldstein, but everybody called me Micky. I was a colleague and a very close friend of Mia, Mirela and Mona. I remember many names, but I forgot the majority of them. I spoke Romanian in my home while my parents were still alive, but after that I only spoke it with a few of my Romanian acquaintances who lived in Argentina. Neither my husband, nor my daughters know Romanian, as it seemed for me that it was a language spoken only in one country in the world, which couldn't prove useful to them on another continent. I did not think of the possibility of ever meeting you again, because I kept no relations to my past. I would write to them at first, but one by one, they stopped writing back.

I left Romania in 1961, because I lived in a very beautiful apartment and people from the party had their eyes set on it – they gave us a first permit to leave, which they later revoked and after a while a second one was given to us and we were allowed to leave.

We left Bucharest by train and arrived in Trieste. From there we took another train to Rome. An institution in charge of people leaving communist countries helped us for the year we remained there, in order to obtain all necessary documents to go to Argentina. We visited a lot, we discovered as much as we could for our condition, with my parents telling me I should absorb all I can, as I was never ging back to Europe.

We took a ship from Genova and we spent 17 at sea. The Ocean was sometimes calm and sometimes tumultuous. We were third class, kept away from the other fine, elegant classes, stowed away like thieves. All things considered, we had a good time on board the ship, and many years later, I went on a cruise on the same ship, this time in the elegant first class, something I thought I was entitled to, considering my past.

In Argentina, I found the language to be easy to understand and I was on top of it within three months, but my studies back in Romania were not accepted here, and I had to start from scratch. This was a very difficult period, I started learning at a school for the illiterate, in order to master reading and writing, and after that I worked and worked for many years and managed to finish school. With tears in my eyes, I would take courses to finish some classes and go to exams for others, as my parents worked hard and had no time to take care of this aspect as well. Near the end of my school years, I met my husband and my best friend, my partner in the voyage of life, my greatest support through all hardship. He was a doctor in economics, while I studied mathematics. Later, after several other insignificant jobs, we decided to open our own company. This is how the Sacoma Computational Center was born, which grew and developed very well. We had over 180 workers and we offered informatics services to our clients, who were mainly banks, as well as selling computing machines, which we imported. During this time, we had two daughters, Karin and Alina, our joy, and we were able to provide them with all I couldn't have when I was little. Today, Karin is a doctor in Ibiza, and Alina is a lawyer in Madrid. Both of them have found their own way with a lot of talent and luck. Karin is married and has a 9 year old daughter, named Iliana, our pride. Alina is not married, but she has a very successful law firm.

Back in Romania, I could not understand I was living in a country occupied by the Russians, and I complied when I was told not to speak of anything I heard within the walls of our home and that I was not allowed to have a room for my own. Mother used to complain that she must share the kitchen with other people, but she never wanted anybody to know about this. Later, when I understood how things were in other countries, I hated communism and how much suffering it brought to my parents, and I had the joy to see the Berlin wall fall, and how one by one Russian occupied countries won their freedom. It was a great satisfaction for me. In the meantime, either military man who killed many people, or corrupted men, who stole from the country's wealth, ruled Argentina.

Although I had vowed never to leave for another country again, I saw that the situation was not favorable for my daughters, and I decided, for their well-being, to move to Spain, where we knew the language. I made this decision in an extraordinary moment, when my daughters had broken their engagements, and they thus accepted to move – it was once again hard, but this time we at least had some money.

In Spain, I again searched for our school, and I fortunately found it on the internet, complete with an address I could write too. I wrote that I was a former student of the school, and asked whether someone still remembered me and within 5 minutes, Mona Toma replied: "We used to sit at the same desk." It was a very intense moment. This is how I was able to reestablish contact with my old life, of which I knew nothing since I had left it behind.

Led by Florin Russu, we arranged for a general gathering, searching for our former colleagues throughout the world, and we had an extraordinary meeting, during which we all felt like 15-year-old friends, and we acted as if we had never been apart. This was one of the most emotional moments of my life, and, due to this reunion, this book was written, with the help of Matei Cazacu's great talent and many other contributors. The book was published in Romania, and now, again with the help of Matei Cazacu and Loți, it is translated and can be read in other languages, so that we can leave a page of our history and the history of our country to our children. I thank everyone for their effort; it could not have been possible without them.

Roland Filippi - Lebenslauf/ The Course of Life
I. Prologue

I have decided for a simpler system, with a clear structure. The reasons: the text is shorter and the danger of spelling errors is smaller. My years in pre-school and primary school will be left out, as they have not in fact been half as exciting as the ones to come.

II. High school years

During my eighth to eleventh grade, I studied at Spiru Haret. Baccalaureate: the 1964 generation. My high school years were happy, but I have to confess they were hard years as well. If one is mischievous and not too hard working, life as a high school student is not easy! And so, aside from all the splendid memories of these years, I do remember some days, which were filled with conflicts with teaching authorities. Today even those bear a manner of delight to remember.

III. Student in Romania

Between 1964 and 1969, I studied at the Faculty of Installations of the Institute of Construction. In May 1969, I was in my fourth year, when I was kicked out for having requested to leave the country with my family to Federal Germany.

IV. Emigration in Germany

Luckily for us, in August 1971 we received the authorization for the whole family to leave together: mother, father, sister, brother-in-law and their daughter. On the 20th of September we got on the plane for Frankfurt on Otopeni Airport. After a short hop we reached Munchen, where we settled. Almost all my relatives lived here. We sorted our documents out in Germany, requested the equivalence of my baccalaureate, and a place to study. And I don't want to leave out the 1972 Summer Olympics.

V. Student in Germany
In October 1972 I began my studies at the Technical University in Munchen, Faculty of Construction, which I graduated from in the autumn of 1977, when I received the title of *Diplomingenieur*. Today I can say that the "serious" part of my life began in Munchen, with my studies at the University. I began to harbor the interest and the pleasure of studying and obtaining high grades. I began having professional and career goals.

VI. Working years
Immediately after finishing my studies I began working at the Josef Hebel construction firm in Memmingen, an old city, with history dating back to the coming of the Romans in Germany. The city lies 110 km west of Munchen and approximately 60 km away from Constanta Lake. The firm is one of the big construction companies in Southern Germany and has a long and interesting tradition. This is where I spent my whole working life and I made a career for myself. At first I was a site engineer and I built bridges and buildings with various purposes. Starting with the summer of 1968 up to the summer of 1989 I ran the Munchen division. In 1989 I was called back to the headquarters, in Memmingen, where I led the department of civil, industrial and bridge construction as a member of the board, up to the end of 2003. In January 2004 until my "retirement" in December 2011 I lead the whole company. I wrote the word retirement in quotes because it doesn't truly reflect reality. The great energy I still have left and the pleasure I have for my job will not let me live my life as a pensioner. For two years now, I have been a member of the company's Counselling Committee and I am still in charge of Real Estate Development.

VII.   Other activities
Apart from my jobs in the company, I practice various other activities: I am a honorary judge for the work tribuna, a member of the control committee for AOK health insurance, a member of the control committee for the labor force and I occupy various functions within the Bavarian

Federation and the Federation of Construction Entrepreneurs; I am a member of the Wealth Administration Committee for my Catholic church. And, not to forget, I am a co-author of the book entitled *Hadnbuch fur Compliance – Management*, published in 2010, which analyzes ethical issues in business.

VIII. FAMILY

I have been married to Jeni from 1973. She is the small part from Spiru Haret, which I took to hold with me for all my life. Jeni (Her maiden name is Eugenia Danet) has also graduated from our high school, in the 1966 promotion. After many requests, interventions and audiences, in the summer of 1973 I received the approval of the Romanian State Council to marry her. I do not know if it is a consequence of this approval or, perhaps, it is because the functionary who married us was stuttering profusely, or maybe even due to the pitch black chimney sweep who crossed our path as we exited the building, but we have a very harmonious marriage for more than 40 years now! We have a 33 year old boy named Roland Andreas, who has been working as of last year, for the same company that I have been working and still work for.

IX. MY ACTIVITY AS A PENSIONER

Aside from the fact that we have been travelling more than before, I have a single other activity as a pensioner. On every Wednesday morning I take my wife and we go to Madame Silvie Joly, a French professor, who helps us with our French, building upon the foundation we both have from the honorable Mr. Fafone (this was the nickname of our French teacher during high school).

X. FRIENDSHIP FOR LIFE

I am proud of one thing in my life. I still have a friend today, who has been very close to me during my childhood, high school and college years.

I am talking about our colleague Mircea Sebastian. Despite the breakup, the distance, the former regime, who had no love for friendships between Romanian citizens and westerners, we never severed our ties and kept our friendship all these years. We spent many holidays together. Last Christmas Mircea visited me again with his wife. We hope to see each other more often in the future.

Note. Unfortunately Mircea passed away in December 2015. May he rest in peace.

P.S.: During my high school years, my father, also named Roland, was the "senior". Today I have inherited this title, because my son is also named Roland. Nowadays, he is the "junior"!

Dan Frangopol[*]

[*] Reviewed and corrected by Dan Frangopol

We parted ways in 1964. Since then, many things have happened and life sucked us fiercely into its whirlwind. In 1964, I was admitted as an undergraduate to the Institute of Civil Engineering located in Bucharest, on the Lacul Tei Boulevard, from which I graduated in June 1969. In July of the same year I married Irina, the daughter of our English teacher (Mrs. Ileana Galis Vasiliu). Upon graduating college, I became an Assistant Professor at the Institute of Civil Engineering. In January 1972, our first baby, a girl, Andrea Dana was born. Shortly thereafter, I won a nationwide competition to study for my doctor's degree in Liège, Belgium.

In 1974, Irina and I had the joy of also having a son, Radu Cristian. Meanwhile I finished the formalities needed to leave for Belgium, where I studied at the University of Liège from January 1974 to November 1976, with short trips back, during the summer, to be with my family. In December 1976 I resumed my teaching with the Faculty of Civil Engineering in Bucharest and was promoted as Lecturer.

In August 1979 a friend from the University of Liège invited me, and during that trip I decided to make my home in Belgium. From 1979 to 1983 I worked as a design engineer for an engineering company in Brussels. Meanwhile, my wife and children joined me. In 1982 I competed for a position of Associate Professor in the Department of Civil, Environmental, and Architectural Engineering of the University of Colorado at Boulder. In 1988, I became a full professor and taught at the University of Colorado at Boulder for 23 years, until 2006, when I retired as Emeritus Professor. From 2006 until present I continued my academic career at Lehigh University in Pennsylvania, as the Fazlur R. Khan Endowed Chair of Structural Engineering and Architecture, with a tenured position as Professor of Civil Engineering. Details about my academic career can be found in my homepage http://www.lehigh.edu/~dmf206.

Irina and I live near the city of Bethlehem, PA, about 100 km from Philadelphia. Andrea and Radu have both graduated from the University of Colorado at Boulder, studying respectively business and computer/electrical engineering, respectively. Radu is working in Fort Lauderdale (not far from Miami) in Florida, and Andrea, married with two daughters, Emma and Elisabeth, lives in Denver, Colorado. Irina's mother, our teacher of English, is 90 years old and lives in Boulder, Colorado.

In 2001 I came back to Bucharest to receive the title of Doctor Honoris Causa (DHC) from the Institute of Civil and Industrial Engineering, from which I had earned my bachelor degree in 1969. In 2008, I received the DHC title from the University of Liège, in Belgium. In 2014, I received the DHC title from the Gh. Asachi Unversity in Iasi.

I am genuinely sorry to be unable to attend the reunion in 2014 celebrating 50 years from our high school graduation. However, it so happens that I will be in Bucharest on the 9th, 10th and 11th of June, when I would be happy to get together with those of you who find the time to meet me during that period.

Best regards to you all, Dan Frangopol

Georgiana Gălățeanu-Fârnoagă - A Life Across worlds[*]
[*] Provided in English by Georgiana Gălățeanu-Fârnoagă

I attended Spiru Haret High School in my senior year. I wanted to specialize in English Language and Literature in college, but my command of the language was limited and private tutoring was out of the question – my father abhorred the concept. Pressed by my mother to do something, he had me transferred from Sfantu Sava, the high school I was attending, to Spiru Haret, where he had heard there was an excellent English teacher. Indeed, two of my classmates and I did pass the entrance exam for the English Department of Bucharest University with the help of Mrs. Voinea's competent teaching.

I think I could describe my entire life as a string of transfers.

My father's parents were farmers in a village near Iasi (English: *Jassy*), a city in northeastern Romania. My grandfather had fought in World War I, and that experience had broadened his view of the world. As a result, he wanted his oldest son to do more with his life than farm the family's land. When the time came, he had Father take the entrance exam for high school in Iasi. Upon graduation, Dad decided to pursue an engineering degree. Thus, he became the first person in his village to go to college, with both his secondary and higher education funded by scholarships from the "bourgeois regime".

"Fortunately," with eight children to inherit the family land, my grandparents couldn't be labelled as "wealthy land owners" in the Stalinist era (1948-53), and their lower economic status provided both Dad and his children (my brother and myself) with a "healthy social origin". This made it possible for him and later for the two of us to occupy professional positions commensurate with our education. First, Father was an engineer at the Nicolina Railway Works in Iasi. After working there for several years, he was interviewed by the manager of Grivita Rosie Plant in Bucharest, who needed a competent engineer with a "healthy origin" to run his steel production department.

Father accepted the position of chief engineer and we all joined him in the capital city, moving into the factory office that had been assigned to us as living quarters. Mother, who had studied Romanian and Italian at the

University of Iasi, became a full-time housewife because Dad was spending his days and nights beside the furnace. Any failure in steel making could be considered sabotage in those days, an offense punishable by a long term in prison. And with the rapid industrialization of the country, most of the workers were new at their jobs.

About a year later, Grivita Rosie rented Father a small one-bedroom apartment (with wood stoves) in a company-owned apartment building near Bucharest's main railway station. Our neighbors were all considered "trust-worthy citizens" – a railway union official, the conductor of the Romanian president's private train, and two engineering graduates who had returned from their studies in the USSR with Russian wives.

In September of 1953 I entered first grade. The children of railway station employees and former neighborhood merchants attended school no. 154, a six-minute walk from home. Every morning as I set off for school, Mother would urge me not to talk to the other children – with the Stalinist terror raging all around she was afraid that anything I might say could be interpreted as critical of the new regime. She needn't have worried. With my North-East Romanian (Moldavian) accent and vocabulary still intact, I was the butt of everyone's jokes. And my surname, Gălăţeanu, had generated the nickname *Galeata*, "Bucket"! I kept as quiet as a mouse.

In truth, however, my silence couldn't last long. I rapidly learned what I could and couldn't say, and the dialectal expressions that peppered my speech were soon replaced with words approved by the Romanian Academy and my first-grade teacher. After a short time I also befriended the union official's daughters.

My middle school years were a continuous source of joy. I developed a passion for learning languages – Russian and German at school, and French at home with a French lady who had married a Romanian (a graduate of a Paris engineering school in the 1930s). As a Pioneer (a member of the national children's organization during Communism), I participated in exciting adventures. Our leaders, two students of geography at the University of Bucharest, took us on outings in the forests around Bucharest and on guided tours at the Natural Science and History Museums. One Sunday morning we even visited Bellu Cemetery, the resting place of prominent

Romanians. We recited poems in front of the statue of our beloved Romantic poet, Mihai Eminescu, and stared into the crypt of Iulia Hasdeu, a talented 19th century poet who died at the age of 19.

By the time my brother and I entered high school, Mother had had enough of being a stay-at-home parent, so she found herself a job as a librarian at the Polytechnic Institute, Romania's premier engineering school. Father had also spent what seemed like a lifetime around Grivita Rosie's steel furnaces, so he now found himself a job as a superintendent in the Ministry of Education, coordinating the introduction of vocational subjects into the curriculum of high schools throughout the country. As a "perk" for me, I think, Dad introduced sewing as a vocational subject for girls at Sfantu Sava High School. Later, as an engineering undergraduate, my brother never had to stand in line at the library window to borrow his course readers: his librarian mother would bring them home for him.

Around 1960, my mother and her three siblings managed to sell their parents' beautiful house in Iasi. With her share of the proceeds, Mom was able to bring our tiny Bucharest kitchen up to 20th century standards. The icebox that my brother and I had filled with blocks of ice from the neighborhood market was replaced with a sleek white refrigerator; in similar fashion, the modest cooking oil lamp mother had used for years was discarded in favor of a grandiose gas stove with four burners and an oven.

When the time came for me to go to high school, Mom's cultural snobbishness led her to choose Sfantu Sava, which she considered to be the best high school in Bucharest. I don't know if it was the best, but it did seem like the largest, with hundreds of students from all over the city and dozens of teachers of all ages. I found refuge in the basketball team, which offered me a stable group of friends, the joy of practices, and excitement of games. At school I never found myself off the honor board, out of an instinctive need to stand out in the large student body.

At Spiru Haret, a small high school where many students had known each other since first grade, the atmosphere was different, but because of my shyness I found it hard to get close to my new classmates. Mihaela Andrei, a delicate and sensitive girl, was my only close friend. She passed away soon after being admitted to the university.

College was a time of intense intellectual growth for me. With a double specialization – English and Romanian – I enjoyed the immersion into two rich cultures and my growing confidence in switching from one language to the other. In my free time I continued to play basketball, this time for the University of Bucharest. Together with my team and coach, I travelled to other university cities for games, and to the Black Sea and Carpathian Mountains for training camps.

After graduation in 1969, I worked as a school teacher in Bucharest for five years, first in an elementary school and then in a high school with an intensive English language program. The experience that I accumulated teaching in those two schools influenced my entire professional life. Fresh out of college and with limited training in language teaching methodology, I found myself in classrooms full of students eager to learn English. With advice from the elementary students' teachers (I taught 3rd and 4th grades in 1969-71), with suggestions from more experienced language teachers, and ideas from extensive reading, I gradually learned how to teach both young children and adolescents. The consequence of this pedagogical enlightenment was an ardent desire to publish materials that could be useful for other language teachers and learners. Thus, I became the author or co-author of two series of English middle school textbooks, a pedagogical grammar, two grammar exercise books, conversation manuals, and works on foreign language pedagogy. From 1973 through the first decade of the 21st century, many students of English in Romania used one or several of the language learning materials that I had written.

In 1974 I was hired by the English Department at the University of Bucharest where I had been a student; later I also obtained my doctorate there. As a Teacher Educator involved in both pre-service and in-service teacher training, I was able to contribute to the modernization of English language teaching methods in Romanian schools.

Having a "healthy social origin" and no relatives abroad, I was periodically asked to serve as an interpreter for international events in Bucharest or for English-speaking delegations that met with Romanian representatives of various political or cultural organizations. From 1968 to 1989, this activity enabled me to meet and communicate with interesting people from around the world without fear of being accused of "selling state secrets" and without having to write reports to the secret police (the *politruk* accompanying the delegation was in charge of that). Just as when I first started school, I had to be careful not to say anything negative about Romania or the Romanian Communist Party.

Representatives of the Ministry of Internal Affairs who wanted me to join their ranks twice contacted me. Both times I managed to extricate myself from the situation by bursting into fits of crying and referring, between sobs, to my emotional instability, which was manifest in the noisiest way possible.

Each summer I spent several weeks as a guide for the national Youth Tourism Bureau. Listening and talking to my guests, I honed my colloquial English language skills since I mostly used academic vocabulary when teaching at the university. In Romania I accompanied groups of young people from English speaking countries. In European countries where the local guide, if not the entire population, spoke English, I served as an interpreter for the Romanian tourists.

Memorable events? When I met with my first group of British visitors, I left two of them behind at a small train station on the Black Sea Coast. This taught me to count my "clients" each time we were going somewhere together. In August 1968, the Soviet invasion of Czechoslovakia found me in the Danube Delta, in the company of four frightened Australians. We hurried back to Bucharest for fear we might get shot among the swans and pelicans. And on a Youth Tourism Bureau trip to the West, almost half of the group "forgot" to return to the train station in Vienna, where we had made our first stop. They had chosen to request political asylum…

During my tenure at Bucharest University, once every few years we had a Department meeting at which a colleague would be nominated for a Fulbright grant offered by the American government. Every time there would be an excellent nomination, but it would often get lost along the Romanian bureaucratic chain. In 1990 it was the first time that we could submit individual applications. I did submit one, I was awarded the grant, and in October of the same year I started teaching Romanian Language, Literature, and Civilization at the University of California, Los Angeles

(UCLA). In the post-1989 world, Romanian had become a strategic East European language, and a growing number of students were interested in taking my classes. The Department of Slavic, East European and Eurasian Studies, the academic host of Romanian Studies, hired me as a Lecturer.

Accomplishments? From 1994 to 2002 I organized an annual student colloquium (similar to those held at the University of Bucharest), where both undergraduate and graduate students made presentations on Romanian topics in front of their colleagues and an enthusiastic Romanian-American audience. In 1998 the Slavic Department broadened the scope of the event to all of Eastern Europe and the participation to undergraduate students from all over the US. By 2017 the Slavic colloquium had reached its twentieth year and my students had benefited from the exposure to a larger scholarly dialog and audience.

In 2006 I proposed a new academic specialization, Central and East European Studies, to include the two non-Slavic cultures and languages, Romanian and Hungarian, in the Department's list of Bachelor's degrees. The University Senate approved the new specialization, and I created and started teaching two new courses – *Society and Culture in Central and Eastern Europe* and *Women and Literature in Southeastern Europe*. During Summer Sessions I began teaching an Intensive Romanian Language course while continuing to train school teachers in Southern California through methodology courses offered by the Department of Continuing Education of UCLA Extension.

After 1990 I reduced the quantity of my publications, although – I hope – not their quality. In the 1990s I published new editions of my English language learning materials for Romanian students. In the 2000s I co-authored several Teacher's Manuals and Student Workbooks for English Language textbooks published by Oxford University Press. Throughout the years I have translated contemporary Romanian literature for my students and the general public. One of the prose translations, *The Phantom Church and other Stories from Romania* (Pittsburgh University Press, 1996) has been a source text for my course on Romanian literature (Co-translator: Sharon King; Preface and biographical notes: Florin Manolescu). Hippocrene Press, New York, slates my most recent work, Beginner's Romanian, an elementary-to-intermediate Romanian Language textbook for English speakers, for publication in 2018. And the anthology *A Balkan Tapestry: Women's Stories from Southeastern Europe,* co-edited with Professor Peter Cowe, is soon to be published by University Press of the South, New Orleans.

My brother, Lucian Gălățeanu, a graduate of the Electronics Department at the Polytechnic Institute of Bucharest (1970, PhD 1993), was – until he retired – a Senior Researcher at the Institute of Microtechnology (IMT) in Bucharest. Over the years he proposed and conducted important projects at the Institute, after 2007 also (co-)funded by the European Union. He has published over 100 articles in his field of specialization.

My husband, Dan Farnoaga, a geologist specializing in the Danube Delta, is no longer with us. Adrian Farnoaga, the little boy we adopted from a Romanian orphanage, is the dearest and most important person in my life. In September 2015 I became a mother-in-law, and Andreea, Adrian's girlfriend since his college years, became Mrs. Farnoaga and my second child.

ADRIAN GAVRILESCU

I left high school with a diversified culture that helped me in many circumstances throughout my entire life.

In 1969 I graduated the Polytechnic Institute of Bucharest, the Faculty of Electronics and Telecommunications, the department of Radio technology. Back then, this faculty was considered to be an elite school, which gave me the opportunity and the pleasure of having very knowledgeable colleagues. Among these colleagues I shall mention Cantemir Ionescu, Sergiu Aronovici, and Antoniu Petrescu. I was then hired in the television tuners engineering team at the Electronica Factory in Bucharest. In this team I participated in a part of the history of the Romanian television receivers, made under the baton of several "conductors" of this industry in Romania: the evolution from transistor tubes to integrated circuits, from the back and white TV to the color TV. At the same time, following the classes I took at the Institute for Physical Culture (ICF) in Bucharest, I obtained an instructor's and referee's license for bodybuilding, subsequently being included in the Central Committee for Bodybuilding, with the responsibility of being a referee for Romania. On the same line, I engaged in various activities with the Dinamo club and the Spiru Haret high school bodybuilding department.

Between 1978 and 1986 I was part of the first postwar dog training team in Bucharest, participating in numerous exhibitions and competitions in various cities throughout the country, with my German Boxer (the first true German Boxer in Bucharest). This is how I was qualified as a canine conductor.

Between 1985 and 1987 I engaged in several attempts of crossing the Iron Curtain. In 1987 I was arrested in the Budapest-Vienna train, on the board of which two friends of mine had managed to escape one month prior. After two weeks spent in arrest at Gyor, in the company of several German young men who had had the same endeavor, I was brought back to Romania and, as by an utter miracle, I was set free. Preparations for 1989 had begun...

In July 1990, after the so-called mineriades, I left for France and stopped in Switzerland. There I began working for the aviation, in the field of on board computers for small and medium aircraft. I fell in love with this small, beautiful country, full of hard-working and free people, whose motto in life is "tidiness and order".

In November 1993 I immigrated into Canada. After four months I managed to get hired in a high-tech company, which produced and sold emergency telecommunications systems. As a result of my activity there and a few courses on Management I took at the Carlton University in Ottawa, I was promoted to manager for the department of production technology. I was one of the first worldwide to engage in FMEA (Failure Modes and Effects Analysis) studies. I was granted Canadian citizenship and, for the first time in my life, I gained my dignity as a free man. During my free time I began studying alternative medicine practices, a study that I am still passionate about today.

In August 2000, I came back to Switzerland, where I found a job in a high-tech company. As a quality assurance director I remained in this company until my retirement, in 2011. I kept working 50% for this company for one more year, after which I switched to a similar company, as Quality Control System Manager. During this period I became specialized in legislation and regulations in the pharmaceutical and medical equipment industry. Today I am also a Swiss citizen. In 2010, I got my first degree in Reiki, in Bucharest, under the instruction of Mr. Gabriel Dutchievici.

Between 1968 and 1970 I had my first marriage, which was unsuccessful. In 1975 I remarried my present wife, who is an exceptional medical staff member, being one of the few Romanians who have obtained high functions within Swiss medical institutions.

I travelled extensively by car through Europe and North America. Twice a year I come back to Romania, to keep my sweet mother company (she is 89 years old).

CONSTANTIN GHERGHEL

I was born in Bucharest on August 24, 1946. I am married and have two children and three grandchildren.

From 1953 to 1960 I attended Elementary cursurileȘcolii no. 31 in Bucharest, then, between 1960 and 1964 High School "Spiru Haret", and during 1964-1969 Polytechnic Institute of Bucharest, Faculty of Mechanical Engineering - Department of Civil Aviation. I qualified in aircraft, engine BAC1-11, Boeing 707, Boeing 737 CL / NG. I worked as an engineer Trainee Transport Research Institute for Studies Bucharest Aero-Naval Laboratory (1969-1972), flight engineer BAC 1-11 Tarom Service Quality Technical Control (1973-1974), BAC 1-11 aircraft engineer Tarom – Service Technical (1974-1976), BAC 1-11 aircraft engineer for the Department Civil Aviation - Aeronautical Technical Service (1976-1989), inspector certification BAC 1-11, Boeing 707, Boeing 737 CL / NG Tarom - Technical Control Service Quality (1989-2004).

I retired from Tarom in 2004. Currently, since 2005, I am working on Blue Air, as a maintenance engineer on Technical Lines Boeing 737 CL / NG.

Ladislau G. Hajos - Both Sides of the Iron Curtain *

* Provided in English by Ladislau G. Hajos

After graduating high school, I enrolled in college. Acceptance into college was not easy. The year I applied, to the Polytechnic University engineering school, there were four to six candidates for each available position. Selection for admission was based on social classification, similar to the present American affirmative action (not color based though, but social origin). The first tier was for the children of the Communist Party members of the working or peasant class; the second tier was for the workers and peasant families, even if not Party members; the third tier was for the intellectuals, or white-collar individuals who were Party Members; and the fourth tier was for the non-Party intellectuals. Unfortunately, I barely made the last tier. My father was considered an intellectual but he was excluded from the Party. In the early 1950's the communist leadership purged the Jews who were in top party leadership positions. My father was not in a leadership role, but his connections were party leaders.

Based on this tier system, my only way to get into college was to study and beat the odds at the entry exam. Math and Physics were my best subjects and I was very good at them, but I still needed to spend a lot of time studying. If the tier system did not exist, I would have been in the top ten out of 200 admitted applicants. The tier system knocked me down to number 50.

A job in communist Romania is guaranteed by the constitution. There is no unemployment in communism. They do not pay much but then again you do not have to work much. While a job is guaranteed, the type and location of the job is not. Based on my grades, I was able to get a job in Bucharest at the Power Engineering Company.

At age 21 I received my right to vote. We all knew who would win the election with 98.97% of the vote and a participation of 99.99%. Voting was mandatory and by 3 PM forced volunteers would knock at doors to make sure people went out to vote. My mother told me:

"Never close the booth curtain. Make sure they see you as you vote to make sure there is no doubt who you are voting for."

I will always remember my father's story that at the first free election after the Russians occupied the country, they bused voters from one polling station to another. In 1948 my father voted at least 10 times at 10 different places. This is how to rig an election. Not surprisingly the communist won. After college, came compulsory 5.5 months of military service. As college graduates we went to an officers' school. After completing officers' school we earned the rank of sub-lieutenant

One morning the battalion captain took us out to the shooting range. We were given AK-47 Russian rifles. The captain told us to get in position on our bellies and shoot at the targets. I closed my eyes and pulled the trigger. My shot was the best.

"You will train these people," the captain said. I tried hard but of course they realized very fast that there was no way I could really shoot.

Successful completion of officers' training school consisted of completing an exercise at the Black Sea. I was in the anti-aircraft missile battallion. Everything was going well for me until one of the gun commanders broke his leg. A replacement for his position was needed. I was the only soldier with no assignment other than food delivery. I became the anti-aircraft gun commander. The gun was a huge 70mm Russian anti-aircraft gun. The mission was a live gun exercise. There were five soldiers on each gun. The target was a simulated American plane attacking Romania from Turkey. I was told that once all the soldiers on the gun said that they were ready, I was to raise my arm and scream fire. I know how to scream so I agreed. The exercise started. Each soldier said ready. I raised my arm and screamed FIRE! At that moment the missile was deployed. The noise was deafening. The gun jumped on the sand. I also jumped, and then I ran. The captain ran after me and tackled me on the sand. I told him "If the Romanian army needs me, they are in big trouble".

The training wasn't too difficult, but we were told that we would have to go on long walks with heavy backpacks to build up our resistance. Therefore, one day I volunteered to supervise the kitchen staff. I was in charge of both food delivery and managing the kitchen.

This was the best decision I made. As my friends were walking, I was coming with the food truck. Every night the kitchen staff would wake me up to eat a meal of steak and fries. This remains my present day food staple.

While I was in the army, the military party leader tried to convince me to join the communist party. I resisted as much as I could. Two years after completing mandatory military service, I was promoted to lieutenant. Fortunately, for the Romanian army, the military did not promote me again.

After the army I began to work. I was assigned a desk in a small room with eight other engineers and technicians/drafters. The room was small and the desks were attached. There was only one phone for the room. Of course there were also some cabinets because nothing was supposed to be left out overnight. The communist believed that American imperialists would come to steal the secrets. There were really no secrets because everything was already copied from the west. Also no one could come in and out of the building without permission.

A typical workday in Romania was long, eight hours, but productivity was short. The workweek was forty-eight hours, working Monday through Saturday. We did not work on Sunday. The office staff, where I worked, was comprised of eight employees: three draftsmen, two women and one man, and five engineers two men and three women. In the morning, the ladies did their hair and makeup. After the makeup was applied, the girls started calling husbands or boyfriends. Lunch followed. No one was working. They used to say, "… as long as they simulate payment we simulate work." I worked hard because I wanted to learn. Many days I was the only one working in the room. My starting salary was the equivalent of 50 US dollars per month.

I was sent on business trips. In communist Romania, a solo traveler could only rent a bed in a double room. When travelling with a member of the opposite sex a marriage certificate was required to rent a hotel room for two. I always tried to beat the system and pay for a full room, meaning both beds. I did not want to share with a stranger, although I was only reimbursed for one half of the cost of the hotel room. There is a story behind my not wanting to share a room.

I was on a business trip at the Danube Hydro Power plant in 1978. It was late and freezing. I was given a bed in a double room. The beds were attached. After dinner I returned to the room. The room was dark and I heard someone snoring. In the dark room I could see a leg at the door. I looked around trying to determine how can someone sleep in the bed and have a leg at the door. Mystery solved, my bedmate had a wooden leg that he left propped up against the door. There is no doubt that my roommate did not shower on a frequent basis.

The situation in Romania became more and more difficult. I was contacted by the Secret police. The police called me to their headquarters. I was told that I would be working as an informant for the Securitate. An informant was supposed to listen and report what certain people discussed. I had to agree. Refusal was not an option. I went through a terrible time for about six months. Informing on others was in stark opposition to my moral character.

They called me on a monthly basis. I met an officer in an empty apartment that had only one chair and one little table. It took me one hour to write a report. My reports were very simple and short. I heard nothing, saw nothing and knew nothing. I guess they thought I was dumb and after six months they stopped calling me. This experience helped me to decide to leave the country. There was no life for me in communist Romania.

Leaving Romania was no easy task. Disagreeing with communism or being a political refugee was not a good reason be granted a passport. Openly speaking against Communism got you sent to jail. The most acceptable and common reason for leaving Romania was family reunification. I had no family outside Romania. Since I had no living relatives, the Romanians saw no justifiable reason to approve my request for emigration.

My late wife had relatives in Israel. She also had a good friend that had connections at HIAS in Paris. HIAS is an American charitable organization founded in response to the late 19th and early 20th century exodus of Jewish emigrants. We decided to emigrate to Israel. We planned, upon receipt of our passports, to buy a one-way airline ticket from the Israeli Embassy travelling from Bucharest to Tel Aviv on TAROM, the Romanian airline. We would also purchase another set of one-way tickets for an earlier flight on Swissair from Bucharest to Zurich to Tel Aviv. For some reason we could only fly on Swissair. My friend Radu Breyer in Germany purchased and hand delivered the tickets to us. This transaction was done in total secrecy. Once in Zurich, we replaced the Zurich – Tel Aviv tickets with Zurich - Paris tickets. We had to go to Paris because that was the only visa we could obtain through HIAS.

After we applied to emigrate, I was excluded from the communist party. My late wife was fired from her job. One year later, on my 35ᵗʰ birthday, I was called back to the headquarters of the secret police. I was taken to a dark basement office. I was shaking. My first reaction was that I would never see the light of day again. I was told that my wife and I were approved to leave for Israel. The officer said he had only one demand. He mandated that when I became a soldier in the Israeli army, I was to send him pictures and military information. Of course I promised knowing very well that I was not going to Israel and I could not, would not, spy. Spying and reporting on others is against my internal moral code.

On January 13, 1982, we left Bucharest with Swissair to transfer to the other side of the Iron Curtain. This trip was the first time in my life that I travelled on a western airline. The plane was a Boeing 707. The carpet shampoo smelled great in comparison to the Romanian airlines, which stunk. We were six people on 150-seat airplane. I was dressed in a suite. In the bathroom I saw little soaps, which I had never seen before. As a result I filled my pockets with these little packets. Actually when I left the first Swissair flight I had lots of soaps and chocolates in my pockets. Once in Zurich, I went to exchange the tickets. All of a sudden I heard on the loud speaker someone calling my name. I was scared. I was wandering who in Switzerland would know my name. Could it be the airline looking to recuperate their soaps? I was sure that the Romanian secret police did not have such a long arm. I picked up one of the phones and my friend Radu from Germany was calling to welcome us to the west. Also he made me say " f… you" Ceausescu. I could not say it out loud, although no one would understand Romanian. I kept looking around me. The communist education was still in me and stayed with me for years.

We spent three months in Paris waiting for the American entrée visa. HIAS and the Paris Jewish community supported us with a little apartment in LeValois with minimum funds for food and metro. All we had to do was to visit Paris. The HIAS chief asked me if I want to remain in France. I said no. I loved Paris but again I was 35 years old, too old to emigrate again in case things did not work out in Paris. In my mind the USA, was and still is, the only place in the world where with hard work you can accomplish your dreams. I have the same opinion today.

We arrived in New York in April 1982 to begin our new life. It was not easy, by any means. We arrived with two suitcases. One had a comforter since, I was told it was cold in America and the other had clothes, mostly suits. Years later, my present wife, Linda, called them communist clothes and made me dispose of all of them. I had about $1000 USD in my possession. I had purchased the money illegally on the black market in Romania. Finding employment was difficult. President Reagan was working hard to rebuild the economy after the Carter fiasco had damaged the American economy. Furthermore, I did not know how to manage the task of seeking employment. I sent out more then 100 resumes. In one place I was told that if I were a black female engineer I could get a job immediately. This was my first encounter with equal opportunity employment and affirmative action.

Fortunately, I received help from my Romanian friends and former colleagues. I started as a designer at Devenco. I then moved up to working as an engineer at Public Service Power and Gas (PSE&G). I was promoted to Senior Engineer, Project Manager and finally Engineering Manager at PSEG. In 1988, I opened my own engineering consulting company. In 1985, three years after leaving communist Romania, I purchased my first house. The house had four bedrooms and three bathrooms. The house was in Cherry Hill, New Jersey with an interest rate of 14.75%. After approximately 10 years, my wife and son died of Muscular Dystrophy.

Also in 1995 on my 50th birthday I met a wonderful lady Linda who has been on my side ever since. Meeting Linda, my present wife, is the best thing that ever happened to me.

I have lived in the USA for over 34 years. We reside in Florida, Palm Beach County. Our home is in a gated Golf and Country Club community. There are only two seasons here, hot and very hot. Living in Romania, I could never imagine that I would learn to play golf. In the very hot season of Florida, we travel all over the word.

Only in America can a Hungarian Jew from Romania, living in a two room flat, wind up living in a golf and country club. What a country!

CANTEMIR IONESCU

In 1964 I finished the high school, the exact sciences specialization (classroom XI A), and afterwards I engaged in one of my hobbies – radio-electronics – and I was admitted to the Faculty of Electronics and Telecommunications (of the Polytechnic Institute of Bucharest), which I graduated in 1969, specialized in Radiocommunications. A job in a factory was not really attractive to me, so I decided to work in research and development (R&D) in such a dynamic domain, with a bright future, and I got a job at the Institute for Research in Telecommunications. I had to go through the six months of mandatory military service (which needed a quite high sense of humor in order to overcome many stupid and difficult situations), and then I got to work in my field of interest.

During my 20 years of R&D (until 1990) I was involved in many interesting projects, cutting edge back then, and I worked for them passionately: digital microwave links (the first prototypes in Romania for 2 Mb/s and 8 Mb/s microwave link equipment), UHF television transmitters and satellite television reception. I participated in the introduction of new technologies and I obtained two invention patents for original solutions for some devices. In 1974 I obtained a scholarship (Digital Microwave Radio-links, three months in Italy) from the International Telecommunications Union. It was my only trip to the West until the 90's (not for lack of wanting…), but what an experience it was! Many asked me why I didn't stay there… but I had my family back in my country, and apart from that, if you remember, during those few years we still thought (or hoped) Romania was heading in a good direction… At the Institute, I was promoted up to Main Scientific Researcher. 1989 saw many changes there as well and other opportunities became available.

In September 1990, I accepted to join the team of the new Minister of Communications (a good reformer and a very capable technocrat). I was technical advisor to the Minister, and afterwards the Director of the General Directorate for Regulations. Going from R&D to regulations and legislation was an interesting challenge, especially during a time when the communications domain, until then a state monopoly, needed to be liberalized and stimulated.

I was in charge of preparing the legal framework (the audio-visual law, the telecommunications law, the law of the radio spectrum usage, and so on) and regulations for the liberalization of radio, television and telecommunications, harmonizing them with the European Union policies (even before Romania entered the EU), and also of authorizing the equipment, networks and telecommunication services. The multitude of radio stations and TV programs, which appeared after 1992, the cable television, as well as the fast development and diversification of telecommunications in Romania were all possible due to this legislation.

During the same period, I represented the country in activities developed by the ITU and CEPT (The European Conference of Postal and Telecom Services), I attended a course on communications in the USA and I was a speaker at a series of European conferences. It was a busy time, from which I learned a lot.

However, in 1995, the minister I was collaborating with so well was replaced with a political one, from PUNR, who was more engaged in authorizing his businesses and the businesses of his people. After I argued with him vigorously on several occasions, I quit and I left for the private sector – it was a good decision to make. Between 1995 and 1997 I worked in purchasing and installing TV transmitters, satellite transmission equipment, and microwave radio links for a private TV broadcaster, and I enjoyed once again engaging with the technical side of my profession.

In 1997 started the first mobile telephony (GSM standard) company in our country, Connex (later bought by Vodafone), and I worked there from its beginnings to 2011, when I retired. It was the most beautiful and diversified period of my professional life, but it was the most demanding as well. I held different offices, from transmissions manager to senior network director to IT director. It was here that I developed further my technical and managerial skills, through multiple courses, including Executive Development at Wharton Business School, University of Pennsylvania.

In 1970 I married our high school colleague Domnica Sufana, who had been my friend since high school, and in 1975, our daughter Ilinca was born. Unfortunately, Domnica left this world in 1984, barely 38, after a severe illness.

In 1987 I remarried Sorina, my current wife, and we have also a boy, Alexandru. Of course, both children have now grown up, and have their own jobs and homes. They haven't left the country and it was their decision, I never attempted to influence them one way or the other.

Aside from my interest on electronics and radio, I love travelling and I visited many countries (of course, after 1989 – until then, I had nice holydays on the seaside in 2 Mai and treks on the mountains in Romania). I like listening to classical music, but I really love the mountains. I went (and still go) on beautiful hikes on our mountains, as well as in the Alps and especially in the Dolomites (Italy), including climbing many "vie ferrate" during the last several years.

Ioan Iordăchescu

After the wonderful summer of my graduation, I took the admission exam for the Institute of Architecture, and I successfully failed it! I graduated from the Technical School of Architecture and I was placed in Bucharest, where I worked ravenously "for the motherland and its people" for 25 years, building factories for the wood industry in Giurgiu, Arad, Rm. Valcea, Suceava, Galati, Tulcea, and Focsani. But I didn't forget my grand passion – theater – reason for which, I contributed to the construction of the Podul Theater. I thus received two international awards, and after, I made costumes and scenography at the Hyperion Faculty of Theater, and for two independent troupes, at the National Opera House.

I am married; I have a boy – Ian – who is a doctor in Prague (from a relationship with e Czech girl) and a daughter - Ilinca – who is a landscaping architect.

Ioan Jelev
STAGES IN MY PROFESSIONAL CAREER:

After my rather tumultuous high school years, during which I engaged in countless time consuming activities (for examples: during school, I also attended music school, where I had specific activities on daily basis, just as numerous as in any other school, although I was the only outside student, by means of a permission that was hard to get; I was the captain of the gymnastics school tea; I played polo at the *Steaua* club, a time and energy consuming activity, and many others), I was admitted to the Polytechnic Institute of Bucharest, the Faculty of Energetics, where, by giving up some of my extracurricular activities I managed to excel, benefitting from the republican scholarship and the so-called *Gheorghiu-Dej* scholarship during my last two years. During high school and college, I never even imagined that life would lead me through such extraordinary situations, and I would have the opportunity to occupy positions I thought intangible, meeting amazing people, both foreign and Romanian from the fields of culture, science, politics, while travelling and seeing the world (one of my greatest wishes to travel the world came true in this manner, although late in my career, after my 40th birthday). I will mention some of these accomplishments below:

* Scientific Researcher and Senior Scientific Researcher for the Bucharest Hydraulic Engineering Research Institute, the Environmental Engineering Research Institute (the former Hydraulic Engineering Research Institute) and the National Institute of Hydrology and Water Management.
* Laboratory Chief for the Department of *"Complex hydraulic systems"* at the Bucharest Hydraulic Engineering Research Institute.
* Head of the Department of *"Fluid Mechanics"* at the Bucharest Hydraulic Engineering Research Institute.
* Director and General Director for the Bucharest Institute of Research and Environmental Engineering.
* General Director for the Environmental Protection in the Ministry of Agriculture, Forestry, Environment and Water Management.

- Deputy Minister and Head of the Department of Water Management in the Ministry of Agriculture, Forestry, Environment and Water Management.
- State Secretary, Head of the Environmental Department in the Ministry of Environment.
- Associate Professor at the Faculty of Land Reclamation and Environmental Engineering in Bucharest and the Faculty for Environmental Protection in Oradea.
- Tenured Professor on Environmental Management at the University of Oradea from 1999. Doctor Honoris Causa at the University of Oradea.
- Tenured Member of the *Gheorghe Ionescu-Sisesti* Academy of Agricultural and Forestry Sciences.
- President of the Commission on Ecology, Environmental Protection and Water Management in the Consultative Committee for Scientific Research in Romania.
- President of the Sectoral Monitoring Committee for the accreditation of laboratories in Romania
- Advisor to the Director of the National Institute of Hydrology and Water Management.
- General Secretary to the Academy of Agricultural and Forestry Sciences *"Gheorghe Ionescu-Sisesti"*.

The moment that offered me the greatest satisfaction was the day I was chosen to be a tenured member of the *"Gheorghe Ionescu-Sisesti"* Academy of Agricultural and Forestry Sciences. I published books, scientific articles in magazines in Romania as well as outside the country (*"Studii și cercetări de mecanică aplicată"*, *"Hidrotehnica"*, *"Water Power&Dam Construction"*, *"Journal of Hydraulic Research"*, *"Révue de mécanique appliquée"*, *"Our Planet"*-UNEP, *"Kluwer Academic Publishers"* etc.), articles about the popularization of environmental protection in general and especially pertaining to water. At the Institute I participated in the development of mathematical models for hydraulic transients in pressurized pipes, the sizing and development of important hydro technical projects in Romania, as well as other countries, hydroelectric power plants, pumping stations, dams and water supply systems, as well as the homologation of systems and automated devices for flow and pressure adjustment in pressurized hydraulic systems. Among the more important works, I shall mention the development of 50 pumping stations and irrigation systems in the *Kirkuk – Adaim* system in Irak, the *Celei, Babadag, Sarichioi, Vadastra, Ighis, Petrosani-Arsache* pumping stations, hydraulic studies for *Golesti* and *Vidraru* dams on the Arges River, *Maneciu* on Telejean River, *Redea, Redisoara* and *Caracal*, the hydroelectric power plant with pumping accumulation on *Tarnita-Lapustesti* and *Arges* and many others. Between 1990 and 2005, I had the opportunity of participating to the development of legislative and institutional frameworks in environmental protection in Romania: the creation of the Environment Department, County and Regional Agencies for Environmental Protection, the National Agency for Environmental Protection, the National Environmental Guard, The Environment Fund Administration, The *Danube Delta* Biosphere Reservation, over 17 national and natural parks, the negotiation of environment related issues with the European Union. I was chosen to represent Romania as president or vice-president in numerous international organizations such as the *Basel Convention* regarding the trans-boundary movement of hazardous wastes – of which I was president for a considerable number of years (a convention that, at the time, had 168 member countries, including the European Commission) or vice-president of the World Forum of Environment Ministers, vice-president of the European Regional Reunion for the top reunion in Johannesburg for sustainable development, member in the Governor Council of the European Environment Agency in Copenhagen, member of the Commissions on limnology and technical terminology of the Romanian Academy, evaluator for the European Union research programs and the University of Hong Kong research programs. Currently I am a counselor of the president of the *Gheorghe Ionescu-Sisesti* Academy of Agricultural and Forestry Sciences and coordinator of the International Relations Department of the Academy. I am the president of the UNESCO *"Man and Biosphere"* Romanian National Committee.

AREAS OF EXPERTISE:

* Fluid mechanics;
* Hydraulic systems;
* The physical and mathematical flow modelling of steady and unsteady free surface water from rivers and canals, pressurized flows (hydroelectric power plants, pumping stations, pumped storage plants) as well as mixed flows (alternatively or simultaneously free level and pressurized flows);
* Environmental protection;
* Water management;

A FEW PERSONAL DETAILS:

I was born on the 7th of January 1947 in Oradea, Bihor County. My father made his career in the military, he was a war veteran, general, and had held high responsibility offices within the army. Mother was a journalist and editor for several newspapers. I came to *Spiru Haret* at the beginning of my third grade, in 1955.

Between 1964 and 1969 I studied Hydro-energetics at the Faculty of Energetics, where I was colleagues with Nicu Vasiliu. I married Viorica Jelev on the 28th of July 1978; she is an associate professor at the *Spiru Haret* University. Viorica was born in Bucharest, on the 11th of September 1957. Our godfathers were Domnica and Cantemir. We have a boy, Ioan-Alexandru Jelev, born on the 6th of October 1981 and who graduated from the Faculty of Journalism and Communication Sciences. Alexandru's godparents are also Domnica and Cantemir. It so happens that I was Ilinca's tutor, Domnica and Cantemir's daughter. Alexandru worked in television for quite some time as a sports editor and on technical issues. At present, he is getting a Master's Degree on Tourism in Copenhagen. He has not married yet. I hope he will do so soon. Viorica and Alexandru are the soul and joy of our family. I had the great opportunity of travelling a lot throughout the world, especially after 1989. It is true that the majority of the trips I made were in the interest of my work and I often didn't have the time to visit the places I wanted. I practiced swimming extensively, having Anton Ionescu, our sports teacher, as a trainer initially, and I played polo for the *Steaua* club, making the senior's team with which I participated in games from the first league. I was also the captain of the high school gymnastics team, and we also had our colleague Braileanu on the team. I remember that sometimes, apart from our trainers, Ileana Alexandrescu would offer us advice, because she also practiced gymnastics. Although he was a harsh teacher, Anton Ionescu appreciated me very much and would often praise me in front of other trainers, which made me very proud. I took joy during winter vacation when Anton Ionescu would take us to the mountains, to *Babele* and *Clabucet*. They were unforgettable moments, being with my colleagues amidst the wonderful landscape of winter. We often spent our evenings in front of the fireplace, telling stories in the mysterious atmosphere of those wood cabins. Another rare experience was my summer vacation at the end of my ninth grade, when we were taken to agricultural labor near Afumati. The work was hard and unpleasant, but the fact that we were together made for good memories. Often, down in the IAS headquarters, in an old mansion, they would organize dances. In fact, it was there that I learned how to dance with Domnica Sufana and Badescu Felicia, two of our beautiful colleagues, whom I liked very much. Sadly, they are no longer with us. I went to music school during high school, where I studied piano. During my last years in high school, and especially after I graduated, I started going skiing, and I often went to the mountains with Cantemir. I was very close to Cantemir, we shared the desk (last desk, middle row). Sometimes we pulled pranks together. At one point, the action of rubbing a pen against the floor by using the soles of your feet had come into fashion. This made a distant, yet irritant sound, and it was very hard to pin point its location, to the desperation of our Russian teacher, Mrs. Stoian, a nice lady. During this time, we stood still and gave no signs of mischief, looking away like two angels. In the end, she identified the source and kicked us both out of the classroom. Without any remorse, we started playing ping-pong on the teacher's desk in an empty classroom down the hallway. Unfortunately for us, the headmistress caught us and gave us a harsh scolding. When I was smaller, I was a friend with Sergiu Aronovici and Costin Cazaban, when we would duel with our hands, imitating Alexandre Dumas's three musketeers, due to the fact that his books were popular at the time, especially after a movie adaptation with famous French actors. For a while, until we were distributed in different classrooms, I was a friend with Firu (Zamfir Dumitrescu). We were impressed with his talents in painting and storytelling. These qualities were apparent since back when Firu was little. I, as well as my parents, was convinced that he would become a great writer, because he would create captivating stories that drew everybody around to listen. In the evening, we would often sit on the edge of a fence, with our friends on *Caimatei* Street, and we couldn't get enough of his stories and he could go on as long as we wanted to lend him our ears. First he would start by asking us if we wanted a funny story or an adventure. Then he would start and go on effortlessly, after the preference we would previously express. I was an avid story reader, and I admired the fact that his stories were entirely original, and had nothing to do with the children's stories published at the time. I remember that sometimes when the teacher had to leave the classroom, he would sit Firu in front of the class and we would all quietly listen to the stories he instantly "fabricated" for us. Although he had this amazing talent, he would later opt for his other great talent, painting, and he became a famous painter. I now pride in having a picture painted by him in my house. As I have mentioned before, I came to *Spiru Haret* in the middle of my third grade, from School no. 148 on *Cotroceni* Hill, *Panduri* Drive, near the Military Academy. We had a very kind teacher there, to which I am still thankful today, Mrs. Anitei, who taught us very well. I was a bit defiant back then. One time I started whistling during class, thinking it was normal for me to do so. It was one of the few instances when I got her so mad, that she turned to slap me, but I dodged her hand and she missed. After that she wanted to send me outside, and because I refused to leave, she grabbed me by my hands and started dragging me out. I locked my feet onto my desk and we dragged the desk through the classroom. In the end, she started laughing and let me go. In *Spiru Haret* I had Mrs. Linte as a teacher during third grade and Mrs. Rentea in my fourth grade. I don't have good memories of Mrs. Linte. I saw her as a mean woman and she seemed to have something against me. My parents were forced to move me to another class. Mrs. Rentea was sweet, kind, and knew how to talk to us, and so I finished fourth grade with a Diploma of Merit. Aside from Anton Ionescu, other teachers I remember of often and have good memories of are Botez and Varzaru who taught Romanian, Roiu and Mrs. Nicolescu who taught math, plant biology and zoology teachers Urbanschi and Cantar, our anatomy teacher Voiculescu (nicknamed Cell), Necsulescu and Berciu who taught History, Valentina Ionescu who taught physics, our geography teacher Stan, music teacher Falculete, French teachers Eugenia Lupu and Niculescu (nicknamed Fanfone), chemistry teacher Luchian (Celesta) and many others.

Years passed. I would gladly tell you more about my years in school, but the space is limited. With small exceptions, we are all pensioners today, and our years in school remained as vivid in our memories, as they were in our youth, and the present book offered us the unique occasion of reliving and reuniting these experiences, to feel as young, free and enthusiastic as we were back then.

MARIA MATEI

I was born on April 13 1946 and I attended Elementary School no. 31 in Bucharest, between 1953-1960. From 1960 to 1964 I was a student at the "Spiru Haret" high school and those years were the most beautiful memories.

We studied, but we also had fun, jokes, more jokes, I was young and carefree and we enjoyed every moment spent together.

I remember the excitement of our teachers, Georgeta Atanasiu (Romanian language), Manolescu (math), Serbanescu (chemistry) Anton Ionescu (Gym). The years went fast and I woke up at the end of high school, with many memories that haunted me all my life and whenever they I had the opportunity, I returned to school.

I participated at the 10 years reunion, in 1974. I saw how the teachers called aut the catalog.

In the following years I went, whenever I had time at our school anniversary date on December 12 each year. There I learned about the famous students of our school from other generations: Mircea Eliade, Constantin Noica, Victor Papahagi Alexander Cioranescu S.A.

I personally met the wife of Mircea Eliade, who told us about his life, with illustrious husband, or Andrei Plesu, two years younger than us who reminisce high school with his characteristic humor. Of course I met on December 12 of my colleagues with whom I tried to keep in touch, but only after 1998 we formed a group with which we meet regularly and spend a wonderful time.

The first meeting was held in Cornu, invited by Rodica Peligrad (Tinca) where we gathered about 15 colleagues. I attended the meeting in Voinesti, with the family of the late Lucian Moldoveanu.

We also met in smaller group at the home to Mona, Tuky, Florina and Monica. Then followed several meetings in "The Cherry Orchard" str. Grigore Alexandrescu, where Decebal, Ileana Alexandrescu, Ionescu Cantemir, Bubu Jelev an others, increased the group.

I remember with pleasure the anniversary of 40 years of high school in 2004, organized by Dini Cernat at the Bragadiru Palace, and spending the 45 years anniversary at Casa Universities organized by Florin Russu.

After school I attended the Faculty of Electrical Engineering, which I finished in 1970. I took three years of probation at the Institute of Design for Building Materials (IPMC). In April 1974 I started working in the foreign trade of the Ministry of Electricity (MEE), where I remained until 2000 when I retired.

On the personal side, I got married in 1971 with a graduate of the Faculty of Electronics and Telecommunications, who graduated in 1969. From this marriage I have 2 boys, Mihai Alexandru (born 1971) and Adrian Virgil (born 1976).

In March 1978 I left the whole family in Geneva, where my husband was assigned as an international civil servant at the International Telecommunications Union (ITU) for two years. I left with memories about this wonderful country, Switzerland, with beautiful landscapes, the people and civilized lake Leman, on the banks of which I used to walk with children.

After returning home it followed a tough time for my family with many problems and misunderstandings, so in 1984 I divorced and my children were entrusted to me. Unfortunately my husband had a heart attack in 1988 and died at age 43 years

Life continued and our children grew up and currently they live abroad.

- Mihai Alexandru graduated from the Faculty of Electrical Engineering, is married to a fellow student and in 2002 went to Montreal, where he lives at present time. He has a 9-year-old son.
- Virgil Adrian graduated in Computer Faculty in 2000, and married in 2001. He went to London, where he obtained a job at a computer company. He has two daughters 13 and 10 years.

After my children left I did not work, I took care of my elderly and sick parents. I always had an active life; I like to go on trips, to walk, to read, to go to shows, to browse the Internet, to take care of flowers and my kitty.

I remember the pleasure of meeting 50 years after graduation, "SH 50" as we called us, where we gathered about 40 colleagues, and with wives / husbands we were about 60 participants. The meeting lasted almost a weekend, the first day we met in a residential complex in Saftica organized by our colleague Florin Russu. The next day I was invited by another colleague, Andrei Popovici at his villa on Lake Snagov with a boat ride on Lake Snagov, followed by a festive meal special.

I hope I will continue to be healthy so I can spend pleasant moments and take care of my grandchildren.

Florina Mârșu

After finishing high school I took the entry exam to the Faculty of Biology together with Luiza Duducgian and Ana Ciolacu. By misfortune, after 10 years I learned from Louise, that there was that year a second session which I missed it. However, I did mot miss the admission to Health Technical School – Radiology section.

After two years I became a medical nurse at radiology and have advanced gradually. I retired on 19 July 2003. I have restarted work at various Medical Centers. Since the end of 2007, I work at Bio-Medica International Medical Center of Russu brothers. Up until now I happy moments, as well as mishaps, but the biggest regret is that I not have a child.

This is life. It is beautiful and the most important thing now is that we will see after each other after half a century.

BEATRICE-ALEXANDRA NICOLAIDE – POPESCU - BIOGRAPHY
Dear souvenirs - wonderful rose petals- spread over all my life

ORIGINS

I will start by saying I was lucky enough to be born in a family who loved me. I can even say that my family spoiled me, being an only child and having only one cousin.

I fondly remember my grandmother on my mother's side (with whom I spent my childhood), *Alexandrina Miulescu*, a dynamic, brave, tenacious and very talented teacher, the first woman inspector of primary schools in Romania. She personally met *Nicolae Iorga* from which she obtained and audience for the construction of a school in the Potârnicheşti village, in Buzău County. She was the headmistress of the girls' school on Popa Russu Street in Bucharest. With her students here, dressed in the national costumes, they greeted the Prime Minister of France, *Louis Barthou*, when he visited Bucharest, with *Nicolae Titulescu* (there are photographs of this event in the National Television Archives).

My grandmother on my father's side, *Eufrosina Nicolaide* (*Georgiade*) was a piano teacher, and at the age of 100, she could still play Chopin's *Grande Valse Brilliante*! Although she spoke Greek fluently, she preferred speaking French with her family. The copy of her Conservatoire Diploma (from 1899) is signed by *Ion Nonna Otescu*. She lived to be 104, and she died in the house on the former Georgiade Estate in Mogoşoaia. Her husband, *Gheorghe Nicolaide* (known by his family as... *Le Beau Georges*) who studied in Belgium (where he stayed for 15 years), taught French and violin at the High School in Caracal. Two brothers of hers, *Constantin Georgiade* (married to the Englishwoman, *Beatrice Cook*, who gave me the name of Beatrice when I was baptized) and *Gogu Georgiade* (married with the Frenchwoman, *Camille*) got their PhD in Law in Paris and were lawyers for the ASTRA Society. One of her sisters, *Elena* (*Lila*) *Georgiade* got her PhD in Philology at Sorbonne and was *Haricleia Darclee's* French teacher. She was married *Puricescu*, sister-in-law to *Jeana* (*Ioana Puricescu*) *Urseanu*, and the wife of Vice-Admiral *Vasile Urseanu*, who brought Brig (Bricul) Mircea in Romania. After the death of her husband, Jeana Urseanu donated the building on Lascăr Catargiu Street to the Municipality of Bucharest – it now houses the *Admiral Vasile Urseanu Astronomy Observatory*.

My grand grandfather, *Dumitru Nicolaide*, doctor in medicine in Padova, practiced medicine and was the primary doctor of the Buzău District. In 1891, he wrote the book: *Medicul de casă (the house physician)* or *Tratament elementar asupra diverselor maladii ale omului cu descrierea simptomelor boalelor și causa lor (Elementary treatment for various illnesses of man with the description of their symptoms and their cause)* (Tipografia Alessandru Georgescu, Calea Unirei, 703 pages), perhaps the first general medicine book in Romania addressed to the public. I mention that Dr. Nicolaide also lend his services for free, one day a week, for people in need who could not afford healthcare.

My mother, *Olga Cornelia*, who studied Philology and General Medicine, specialized in Dental Healthcare, was a pediatric doctor. She took pride in her professors at the Faculty of Medicine: the famous *Francisc Rainer* (Anatomy), *George Emil Palade* (a laureate of the Nobel Prize, which he got as an assistant), *Grigore T. Popa* (who, along with *Unna Fielding*, Australia, discovered the port system of the hypophysis) and others.

My father, *Dumitru Constantin Nicolaide*, had a military career and, fighting on the Eastern front against the Soviet Union (where his brother lost his life), received the Order of the Romanian Crown, class V and the Order of the Romanian Star, class V. He was kicked out of the army after 1946, when he was Major of Artillery. Without a job, for two years, night guard, fire fighter, humiliated as an unqualified worker, and finally, because of his knowledge in topometry, was hired as a sub-engineer for a research institute in Bucharest (ISPIF), where he took topometric measurements in the Danube Delta (Mila 23, Sulina, Sfântul Gheorghe). After 1989, he was restored as Colonel in Reserve, but he died chagrined by the fact that the new government had cut his military pension. However, in 2011, at the age of 100, he was decorated, as a former officer of the Royal Army and distinguished service on the Eastern Front with the *Regele Mihai I – 90 de ani Medal* by his Majesty, King Mihai I of Romania – this was most consoling for him, before he left us, at 101 years.

EDUCATION AND CAREER

I finished grades first to fifth in a General School (I can't remember its number!) on Olari Street. Grade sixth and seventh I spent them in *Spiru Haret* High School, where I had Mrs. *Enăchescu* as my physics teacher who showed us very interesting experiments. After finishing seventh grade I took the admission exam for the same high school and I became a colleague to you, the writers in this book, and to those who, unfortunately, are no longer with us. After graduating from high school in 1964, I applied to the Faculty of Physics of the University of Bucharest, specializing in Biophysics. I graduated in 1969. During the same year, I was distributed as a teacher, to my disappointment, to the "23 of August" Industrial High School in Bucharest where I taught physics, for 13 years, after which I transferred to the MihaiViteazul High School (now called Colegiul Național Mihai Viteazul) in Bucharest, from which I retired in 2014. However, I have not given up on being a teacher, and I still work part time at my school, and I do so with pleasure.

I was head of the Physics Department during the following periods: 1988-1992, 1995-2004 and a physics methodologist in Sector II during: 1993-2006, 2001-2006, as well as professor for the Excellence Center for Performance Capable Youths in Bucharest (2002-present).

I am the president of the Vice-Admiral Vasile Urseanu Scientific and Cultural Foundation. One of the foundation's objectives is preparing talented students who participate in scientific Olympics at the Mihai Viteazul National College. On Saturdays, with the help of other physics teachers, I lead the Excellence Center mentioned earlier, where students of grades fourth through twelfth from Bucharest (chosen by means of an exam) attend additional physics lessons.

My entire didactic activity, which I exercised with immense pleasure and dedication, I encouraged gifted students to make the best out of their talent and to keep feeding it through perseverant exercise and work. I will only mention that numerous students of mine have had extraordinary results at the Olympiads, National and International Physics Competitions: First place, *Iacutia*, Siberia (1996); Silver Medal, *Toronto*, Canada (1997); Honorable Mention, *Taipei*, Taiwan (2003); Bronze Medal, *Kazakhstan* (2006); Silver Medal, *Singapore* (2006); Silver Medal, Infometrix, *Bucharest* (2008).

Additionally, I also supported students who were less inclined to the study of Physics to make the best out of their other talents in other areas of expertise, without forcing them to focus exclusively on Physics – I believe that each person has their own path and that we are fortunately different, which is very good and comforting. I told everybody that the most important things in life, more important than knowledge (which can be completed and enlarged later on), in any area of expertise are: *attitude, continuity of work, perseverance, optimism* and *the pleasure of interacting and collaborating with others.*

My family

My husband, *Aurel Popescu*, a professor in Biophysics at the Faculty of Physics at the University of Bucharest (former Dean between 1992-1996 and Head of the Department between 2000-2012), a colleague of mine during university studies, also continues his activity, as a doctorate supervisor for the Doctoral School of Physics (the Department of Biophysics and Medical Physics). With him, I had the opportunity to visit (several times) universities and scientific research centers outside Romania: *Université Paris-Sud* (XI), Orsay; *Université Paul Sabatier*, Toulouse, France; *Bielefeld University,*

Germany; *Coimbra University*, Portugal; *Wisconsin University*, Milwaukee, USA; *Abdus Salam International Center for Theoretical Physics*, Trieste, Italy.

I have two sons, *Răzvan-Alexandru* and *Dragoș-Mihail*. The first of them followed the family tradition and graduated from the Faculty of Physics (specializing in Biophysics) of the University of Bucharest, a Master's Degree at Université Paris VI (Pierre et Marie Curie) and a PhD in Biophysics at Université Paris XI and Unité de Biophysique Moléculaire, Institut Curie, Orsay, France. My second son graduated from the Carol Davila University of Medicine in Bucharest (specialized in Dental Hygiene) and, currently, he and his brother own the *DentalMed-Luxury Dental Clinic* near Marriott Hotel. DentalMed-Luxury Dental Clinic was chosen to serve the Royal House of Romania. Dragoș is the promoter of *one stage surgery concept* in dental healthcare in Romania and he successfully applies this method as an implant specialist.

I have two very well raised grandchildren (I cannot but be subjective in this matter!) from Dragoș: *Diana-Andreea*, tenth grade student at the Gheorghe Lazăr National College and *Stefan-Alexandru*, middle school pupil in the eighth grade. My daughter-in-law, *Daniela (Dana) Popescu*, is also a dentist at the DentalMed-Luxury Dental Clinic.

MEMORIES FROM HIGH SCHOOL

Regarding the beautiful years I spent in Spiru Haret High School, look back on them with immense pleasure mixed with nostalgia, I remember our teachers, some of them I could even name illustrious, such as: Mathematics (*Nicolae Manolescu* and *Nicolae Cernica*), Physics (*Liliana Barbici* and *Valentina Anastasescu*), Chemistry (*Ecaterina Serbănescu* and *Celesta Luchian*), Biology (*Ion Voiculescu* nicknamed *Celula*), Geography (*Aurelia Nicolau*), History (Mr. *Berciu*), French (*Vladimir Niculescu*). To all of them, I keep a most pious memory and I am very grateful, even if, back when I was a student, I didn't appreciate them enough and I only sympathized some of them.

I also dearly remember the sky camps at the Babele Cabin, organized by the brave and distinguished gentleman *Anton Ionescu*, nicknamed by so many generations *Mr. Baston (Cane)* who was our Sports "prof". When we were in the eighth grade, my mother, who was very prudent and who would worry about me, didn't want to let me go skiing in the Bucegi Mountains. However, Mr. Baston insisted with utmost diplomacy with both my parents for me to go and, finally, managed to convince them! Because I loved camp so much and especially skiing, although I wasn't very talented at it, I also convinced my husband to give it a try. And so, we are still skiing today, even at our… young age, and I took my children on the ski track since they were only 2 years old and they have now become really addicted to skiing, as have my two grandchildren, and they often go to Poiana Brașov, at 2,000 m Height, Predeal or in the Alps in Austria, France or Italy to ski. Moreover, although I was a Physics teacher and not a Sports teacher, all skiing camps at the Mihai Viteazul College were organized by me. Thus, many students of this school have fallen in love with this sport and practice skiing due to me.

In Spiru Haret College, I had many warm friendship ties with many colleagues, girls and boys, from which I only remember some: *Monica Diaconu (Bottez)* who lived in the same neighborhood, one street away from me, *Rodica Peligrad (Tinca), Cantemir Ionescu, Ioan Jelev* (nicknamed *Bubuș*), *Constantin (Dini) Cernat, Mona Toma (Ionescu), Ladislau G. Hajos (Loți), Mircea Tilenschi, Michaela (Miky) Feldstein, Virgil Duncan, Sergiu Aronovici*.

From time to time, with a lot of love but also a lot of sadness, I think of my colleagues who are now in a more enigmatic world, maybe a better world than ours, out of which I shall remember: *Felicia Bădescu (Ursu)*, who I shared a desk with and my best friend, a very talented mathematician (she later graduated from the Faculty of Mathematics), *Ionică Berindei*, who had real artistic talent, which allowed him, after graduating from the Institute of Architecture, to become a remarkable architect, *Domnica Sufană (Ionescu)*, who was a professor for the Faculty of Chemistry at the University of Bucharest.

The colleagues I evoked, as well as the ones I did not mention here and our professors *may God grant them eternal peace*!

To you, my dear colleagues, who appear in this book, I wish you all the good in the world, a long and peaceful life, away from worries, full of joy from your children and grandchildren!

Amintiri, dragi amintiri…petale de trandafiri
Sute, mii înmiresmate…peste-o viață presărate!

Finally, I would especially like to thank *Loți Hajos* for the effort, commitment and time he put into making this revised and completed edition possible.

IRINA PASCU - IRINA'S STORY – 50 YEARS OF LIFE (1964-2014)

My story took place over five decades spreading over two different centuries. This is how my story unfolded….

I successfully graduated from Spiru Haret High School at the beginning of summer of year 1964 receiving my High School Diploma as an official proof that I acquired all the general knowledge taught during my 11 years of schooling. At the same time my Diploma proved that I was now ready to join the ranks of the Romanian adults.

Like many of my colleagues and friends, I continued my studies at the Polytechnic University in Bucharest, the Faculty of Electrical Engineering, graduating in 1969 with a degree in electrical engineering. Shortly after graduating I started working for a consulting engineering firm in Bucharest - IPIU (The Institute for design and engineering of Light Industrial Projects).

While still in high school I met Sandu Vescan, my current husband, he was also a high school student at the Petru Groza High School. We were married in 1969, after we both graduated from the Polytechnic Institute. We have been together for 45 years, a rare thing these days.

In 1974 our family of three, the two of us together with our two years old daughter Alexandra (Andra), left Romania, immigrating to Israel. We left Bucharest on July 23, 1974 on the same flight as Ana Zsoldos and her family. In Romania, we left behind our parents overrun with grief.

Although, we were received with open arms by all our family and friends in Israel, and in spite of having Ana, my best friend and her family with us, starting life in a new country where we were practically illiterate was very difficult. We didn't manage to make ourselves at home and in 1975 we left

Israel, alone this time, to go to Canada. Andra (our daughter) was almost 3 years old and I was five months pregnant with our second child. Our second immigration was radically different from our first. This time we were alone. No one was waiting for us; we didn't know anybody in this foreign country, very different from what we were accustomed to.

We arrived in Toronto, Canada, in June and in September our son Allan was born.

This is how we started our new life in Canada. We settled in Toronto. Everything got gradually better. We both started working and had good jobs. The education received in Romania paid off and we managed to occupy good positions at senior management level. After 31 years of service I retired from the Canadian Standards Association in May 2008.

Ana (Zsoldos) and her family followed us to Canada in 1980 and my parents joined us shortly after that. Our two children grew up, got married, and each of them has two children of their own. Andra has an 9 year old son and a 6 year old daughter, and Allan has a 4 year old daughter and a three months old son. We are happy grandparents and we try to help when we are needed. We are lucky to live only 15 km apart from each other. Allan is a surgeon specialized in the neck and head (everything above the shoulders, apart from the brain, he says). Andra is an authorized accountant and has her own accounting firm We are proud of them and we somehow consider that their accomplishments are in part our merit.

Now we are both retired, and, thank God, healthy. We travel, are staying active and are trying to find joy during the years we have left. These were "50 years in retrospective.

Rodica Peligrad Tinca[*]

[*] Provided in English by Rodica Peligrad Tinca

After graduating the fifth year in the Central School, my mother, herself a principal in one of the schools from the same District (1 Mai), opted for changing the school for Spiru Haret (and it was a wise decision, since my memories are very much alive and pleasant, much more so than the ones as a student).

Hence, I arrived in the new school in the class 6B and throughout high school I was seated only next to the window, somewhere in the second or the third row, alongside my beloved Tucky (Englentina) Vlasie – may her soul rest in peace, the tiny and joyful girl with dimples in her cheeks, with Alexandra Nicolaide, Monica Diaconu, Mona Toma, Patricia Filip (she was nearby, in the middle row), Dini Cernat or Andrei Popovici behind us.

I also remember our wonderful teachers (as well as others not so wonderful) which, despite that some of them were severe or even tough with us when we were not behaving, deserve even today our full respect: Manolescu in Math, Atanasiu in Romanian classes who was also our homeroom teacher (and her famous Literature Circle, first chaired by Petru Popescu, followed by Matei Cazacu and Andrei Pleşu), then Celesta in Chemistry, with her beautiful face, but cold as a husky, Mrs. Atanasiu in Physics, with her astonishing blue eyes, Ionescu Baston and Lenke in Sports (and indeed, back then we were having real gym classes).

Years have passed, so did the baccalaureate with its many oral exams, including the Constitution, but I remember particularly our graduation party at the Herastrău Restaurant, on the shore of the lake with the same name. After that, almost all of us have made it to the university, to various faculties. I chose Electrical Engineering, together with Irina Pascu and Mariana Matei.

I graduated the Polytechnic Institute after five years, I got married and I gave birth to two children, Ştefan and Ioana who, on their turn, gave us two grand-daughters, Mara, 14, and Teodora, 12, and a grandson, Matei, 8, whom I love wholeheartedly. I am sure that they also love me, although we all know how kids-grandparents relations are…

Here I am, in the early 70s, with my own family and my own job. However, life took me on a different path. I lived many years abroad, six years in Geneva and other six in New York (where the main UN institutions and headquarters are located). More recently I have spent five years in Prague. But everywhere I lived, I kept running into someone who in a way or another reminded me of my years in Spiru Haret. For instance, in Geneva I have met in the same environment with Mariana Matei. In Prague I once met Firu (Zamfir Dumitrescu), who helped us organizing a wonderful paint exhibition. I also met in the Czech capital a young soprano from Iași, who was living in Greece. I've got acquainted with her at a concert, I recall it was *Tosca*, where she was starring, and again at the dinner after the show. She was explaining me how she started her career and how tough it was for her at the beginning, until she met an exceptional manager, a Romanian lady living in Paris. After signing with this manager, her career changed dramatically. Out of female curiosity, I enquired who this lady was: her name was Luiza Laxer.

Does anyone recall who used to be our sexiest colleague back then? (And nowadays, when I read a novel by Petru Popescu, I keep on remembering her!). Therefore, it so happens that so many years have passed since high school and sometimes at many kilometers away from Km O in Bucharest, memories always took me to my years in Spiru Haret.

In Bucharest, upon the initiative of some enthusiastic colleagues, we've kept on meeting among some of ourselves, either at Florina Mârșu, at Țucky, at Monica, at Andrei Popovici in Snagov or at Lucică Moldovan in Voinești. I have hosted myself one such gathering at our country house in Cornu. But the greatest event was of course our 50-year gathering organized marvelously by Florin Rusu.

I honestly hope that we shall keep on meeting each other and keep close among ourselves because every time we do, I find something new to add to my memories and I discover that going back to my roots makes me young again.

RADU PFEILLER[*]

[*] Provided in English by Mircea Tilenschi

After graduating from Spiru Haret, I studied Electroenergetics at the Polytechnic College Bucharest. Following college graduation, I worked as a Design Engineer for ISPE Bucharest (Institute for Energetic Studies and Design). In the fall of 1984 I immigrated to Germany with my family, settling down in Munich, where I still live.

1974 I married my officemate Delia, a graduate of the French Faculty. We have a son, Christian, born in 1981, who studied tourism in Munich. In 2008 he moved to Zurich for working in the tourism area, activity which he enjoys a lot.

I worked in Munich for different companies and organizations, retiring in 2012 at the age of 65

Doina Pinca

For technical and personal reasons, Doina asked me (Decebal) to write her story of the past 50 years. Without the experience and handiness of a secretary, I wrote a few lines during our conversation over the telephone. I must confess that right now I cannot recall how Doina looks...

D.P.C. graduated from the Faculty of Philosophy in Bucharest and was distributed to the Institute of Reasarch in the Transportation Industry. She was promoted in the institute from Research degree I to the post of chief of the "Human factor and the Psychology of Labor in Transportation" Department. She is a specialist in the safety of traffic in the four main types of transportation: land, air, sea and railway. She retired in 2007.

She participated in 75 research projects on safety, observing ship captains, locomotive conductors, drivers and aviators. Among her projects, I will mention:

- An experiment involving a mixed crew on sea (we can now pause our reading and imagine a story like in the film *Mutiny on the Bounty...*) with much hesitance and halts;
- The psychological evaluation of seafaring personnel during long periods at sea (more than 1 year) for ocean fishing;
- The evaluation and selection of seafaring personnel;
- Expertise in accidentology in transportation;

She took part in various committees for the scientific referral of research projects, the licensing of navigators from instruction centers and doctorates on human resources. She was the president of the Human Factor Committee in the Road Safety Council.

She got her PhD in 2003 and has various books published on the running, authority and conflict on board ships; the audit of working conditions for locomotive conductors.

She was editor for various magazines in the branch, and wrote articles on road safety, she was an associate professor for the Hyperion and Bioterra Universities.

After retiring, she opened an office for psychological counselling and assistance. She is married, has two boys, aged 33 and 37.

Nicolae Andrei Popescu[*]

[*] Provided in English by Nicolae Andrei Popescu

I was enrolled at Spiru Haret School in the first grade, due to the fact that my mother was a teacher there. She and I went to the school at the beginning of the first class year, and half way toward the entrance to the building, she told me to continue alone. She then turned back toward the exit from the schoolyard. I ran after her and asked her why she did not go to her classroom instead. She told me that we will discuss this when I arrive home. When I came home, I found out that both my parents had been fired that same day, and that our family was left with no resources to survive. Furthermore, I found out that my parents were given a restricted area of residence and they could not travel out of town without notifying the police. My family was victimized under the communist doctrine of "cleaning of the society of old bourgeois members". My family was considered to be a part of the bourgeoisie and of the exploiters of the working class. Most likely, I did not discuss this with anyone at that time, but now I must confess that since the age of 14, I firmly decided that I would not continue living in Romania.

In 1964 I was admitted to the Faculty of Medicine of Bucharest, after a very restrictive examination session at the class of General Medicine. It was one of the most beautiful periods of my life. I studied medicine avidly and for the first time in my life, I had the feeling that I had found real direction. I graduated in 1970 and ranked in the first 10% of my class. I was not able to obtain an internship position, due to the fact that were only very few positions and, of course, those positions were reserved for "tovarasi" or comrads.

As a result I was sent as a doctor of General Medicine to a village on the Olt riverbank.

After one year I married Adriana Silvia Catilina, a classmate at the Pediatric section of the School of Medicine. She had been my girlfriend since my fifth year of faculty. I can state without any hesitation that this was the happiest and important moment of my life. We had the best marriage two people could hope to have.

My wife and I worked for one more year in a village in Teleorman County. Afterwards, we prepared for the examination of specialization in medicine, which we both passed and, as a result, we were able to return to Bucharest. After three years of studies, I was granted the title of Specialist in Dermatological Diseases and obtained a position at the Railway Workers' Hospital Number 2 (CFR No. 2) in the vicinity of "Casa Scinteii". I continued to work there in that capacity until my departure from Romania in 1983. My wife Silvia, worked at the same hospital in the Pediatrics section.

I alone, without my wife, was approved for a visit to Israel, where I was invited by former students of my wife and me, who were enrolled in the Romanian School of Dentistry of Bucharest. I remain friends with them to this day. I was in Tel Aviv for only four days, during which time I interviewed with the USA Consul, who advised me to go to an emigration facility in Europe, because I could not emigrate from Israel due to the fact that I was not Jewish. As a result I arrived at a facility in Traiskirchen, Austria. After four months, I was accepted to travel to the USA with the status of "political refugee". I was granted political refugee status due to the hardship to that my family endured under the Communist Regime.

In the USA, it is mandatory to take and pass a variety of medical tests, irrespective of status in one's country of origin, if one desires to practice clinical medicine. In brief, I became an Assistant Professor of Medicine and Allergy/Clinical Immunology at the University of Rochester, in Rochester

New York. In 1997 I left academic medicine for private practice and relocated to Syracuse, New York, where I practiced until late 2012, when I retired.

My wife Silvia passed away in 2006 with metastatic breast cancer. I have a son, Andrei Alexandru Popescu, an attorney at law, who lives and practice in New York City. He recently married his girlfriend of many years, Alexandra McGuiness.

My primary interest at this point in life is to write several books. One will be about my professional history as a doctor, and as an advocate for universal health care, which will provide health care for every citizen in the USA. A second book will be about the history of my family, starting with the period between the two World Wars, discussing my maternal grandfather, who was a mayor and a politician, and ending at the time of my retirement.

Finally, I have some beautiful memories from my time at Spiru Haret. I wish good health and much happiness to all of you who may remember me. Whoever wishes to communicate with me is welcome to do so. I have never returned to Romania since leaving and I do not have any plans to return in future, but who knows where life will take me?!

ANDREI POPOVICI*

* Provided in English by Andrei Popovici

Now here we are, after all these years, after all this time?

Whatever was difficult went away.... Many times, I don't even want to remember. It was difficult so many times, more difficult than I would have imagined.

What was bad has been forgotten in the mists of time, it's been nearly 50 years,.

What's the point digging up memories now?

After we graduated from high school, a lot changed. A lot and I regret high school years so much. I have to confess it was the best period of my life. Since then, I have dear friends whom I love and see every time I get a chance: Dini, Firu, Florina, Lucian Moldoveanu who unfortunately left us too soon.

I went to Veterinary Medicine, after two years I managed to leave for France (as most of you know, my mother was French and my family was in Strasbourg). It was difficult to leave, all who took that path will tell the same. I don't advise anybody. It was difficult, sad, heartbreaking, many sleepless nights, many nights crying and screaming with pain.

In Paris, I studied at the Academy of International Trade (ACI) rue de Torqueville 17, after which I worked in tourism for many years.

In 1976, I opened my own travelling agency in Brussels TRANSUNIVERS –ROMANIA TOUTS and I organized trips to the Romanian seaside or to the famous GEROVITAL treatments, to regain one's youth. I was working in Paris and in Brussels and I was commuting.

In 1979 I was declared Persona non grata in Romania. This happened on November 29, 1979, the day Nixon landed in Bucharest. What an ordeal for 10 years, i was lucky to have met vio my current wife. God helped me, He was good to me M.

Another difficult period began for me because everything was connected to Romania. During those years, nobody was foreseeing the events from December 1989.

I married Ioana Aderca in 1971, we got divorced, and in 1982 I remarried a young Belgian girl, then we divorced. We didn't have any children, so it was without too much trouble.

I came back to Romania on December 23, 1989 with aids sent by the Belgian state and never returned to Belgium. I started small businesses in Romania, I remarried and I have a handsome big boy whose name is Andrei Ioan. He studies in Switzerland at the Faculty of Tourism Management from Montreaux.

Carpeting business went well; from carpeting I started making road markings, street rehabilitation and national roads.

I currently run a company together with my wife who is my most precious help, a company with 52 employees that provides services for municipalities in Romania. Returning to Romania has brightened me, I am happy to be home, I regularly see my childhood and high school friends, I can leave when I want and where I want without being responsible to any-one, without having to fear I cannot leave the country.

Life is beautiful home!!!

I can't wait to see you because I miss all of you, especially those who left us too soon.

Love you all!!!

Adrian Irvin Rozei[*]
* Reviewd and corrected by Andrian Irvin Rozei

Adrian Irvin Rozei was born in Bucharest in 1947. He studied first at the Polytechnic Institute in Bucharest and, after moving to France in 1967, completed his studies at the "Ecole Supérieure des Mines de Saint-Etienne". He graduated with the title of Ingénieur Civil des Mines. For 35 years he worked in various companies in France and Germany, including the oil groups ELF and TOTAL, where he managed the export business of various chemicals in Europe, America and Middle East. He dealt for 14 years with the export of mining products. He was awarded with the "ELF Foundation prize" for the restoration of an historical monument in the department of Hérault.

Since year 2000, he collaborated with reports, interviews and press reviews in various Romanian cultural magazines in Denmark, Canada, Australia, New Zealand, Switzerland and Romania.

For over 10 years, he provided a bimonthly column in a newspaper published on the Internet. He took part regularly in the organization of "Rencontres Franco-Roumaines en Méditerranée" held every year in south-ern France or Romania. He was appointed honorary ambassador for the city of Capestang (Hérault department) as recognition of relational activities developed between Languedoc and Romanian communities in the world. He is a member of the "Société Archéologique, Scientifique et Littéraire" a bicentennial artistic society in Béziers. Collaborate to broadcasts at "Radio

Romania International" with reports and interviews in Romanian and French. He speaks eight languages.

He is married and has two children, Laurent Aurel, born in 1988, and Olivier Florian, in 1990.

Hobbies: travel, photography, cultural news, gastronomy.

In 2011 "Publishing House Duran's" in Oradea, edited his bilingual volume "Secante Româneşti / Sécantes roumaines" with articles published in around ten countries in Romanian or French. They highlight Romanian artistic, scientific and literary less known or forgotten presences all over the world and connect France and Romania, in particular with the Languedoc area, the adoptive region of the writer.

FLORIAN IULIAN RUSSU

Motto: *Old age is not for the faint-hearted!*

If you carry your childhood within you, you will never grow old!

I will break up my life into several parts, depending on how the destiny of my life and family changed over the time.

I was born in Bucharest, on the 3rd of February 1947. I come from a very interesting family: my father is Dr. Iulian G. Russu (renowned surgeon) who worked for the Grigore Alexandrescu Hospital and my mother is Dr. Maria Magdalena Russu (Angelescu). Father had four brothers, all of them doctors, who got married to partners who also studied medicine. A single brother is still alive in Washington. I went to German kindergarten and primary school in Brasov. When I finished my fourth grade a new law was issued – one had to have both parents of German origin in order to study at the German high school. This is how I became your colleague in Spiru Haret.

I will never know why my parents chose a school so far away from our house (the Casata building on 26 Magheru Boulevard). During school, nothing out of the ordinary happened. However, I did do a notable thing all this time: I practiced fencing, a reason for which I was selected into the national team. Even if many people complain about that period, we children had a wonderful time, with summer vacations by the seaside and winters spent in the mountains. My favorite resort was Predeal, and Neptun by the sea.

As you all know, I think I am the youngest colleague in our school – I really rushed in to start school. Like you, I finished high school in 1964. Meanwhile, my friendship with Mia Dinca, of a particular kind, and my friendship with Florina Mârsu of another kind, allowed me to live through beautiful moments in a world without TV or iPhones. I read a lot. During vacations (in Arad), I used to read through entire works of Balzac, Jules Verne and other interesting books. I think it was during that period that I discovered my passion for travelling, although I had a single handicap, that of being unable to fly (an ear infection caused me intense pain that could last for up to three days).

Budapest, Prague, Vienna, Warsaw, and Sofia were pretty familiar to me. I wasn't allowed to visit other countries. In 1956, mother's sister, mother and the aunt from Brasov found themselves caught in the Magyar Revolution in Budapest. Mother came back (my brother Lucian was barely one year old), but that date changed our destiny. Mother's sister and her husband emigrated to the USA. That is how I found myself having relatives in capitalist countries.

Upon finishing high school, the fight started in order to become intellectuals in a country where they had to work more and much harder. I chose and prepared myself for External Commerce (my wish to run away was very powerful). Due to practicing my sport on a professional level I had seen all communist countries save for the USSR (to which I had an aversion I now regret, because the trips organized then cannot be taken now).

And so I applied for the Faculty of External Commerce and my file failed exceptionally, due to the fact that I had relatives who had fled to the USA. I had no time to study vigorously in order to apply to medicine school and I failed, with modest grades, as we were 8 candidates per place. With the advice from my parents and Florina's support, I applied to the Sanitary Technical School on Pitar Mos (behind Patria Cinema).

I was convinced I did not do very well on my exam (I had only had one month to prepare) and I was subsequently not very interested with the results. Florina calls me and tells me I was admitted, and that I was on the lists. I went to see the lists, and as many had been admitted, I started searching for my name from bottom to top. I got bored half way and I returned home. I phoned Florina and asked her if this was her idea of a food joke, to make me go all the way downtown and hold me back from leaving to the seaside, where I was an ONT guide.

She asked me if I had actually read the lists and I told her the story; she suggested I should read it from top to bottom. To my surprise, I was on the second place.

I finished this school as well, and I got the most sought after distribution, the Dental Healthcare Faculty, but I became a student in the autumn, and I signed my first resignation. I continued fencing as a semi-professional up until my second hepatitis in 1967, type B this time, which definitely took me out of the game. My career in sports was over.

I dedicated myself fully to medicine (I could not bring the Russu name to shame).

In my second year, I married my colleague Anca Stanescu (the daughter of Dr. Puiu Stanescu, the chief of the Ophthalmological Hospital in Bucharest). Everybody thought this was a "smart" move, because he was Ceausescu's eye doctor. It wasn't so. Anca remained my best friend, and our marriage was as modern as one could be during those times. Fair enough, we had our own car, our own apartment, but we ate at her mothers' and at my mothers', alternatively. Due to Anca's tenacity, we both graduated on very good positions, but due to my wish to be near a large body of water, we moved to Galati in 1973.

Here we realized that our paths in life will part (let us say that one of the reasons was that I wanted to have children), and so I went through my first divorce. I didn't waste any time and I married Silvia Pavel in Galati, with which I have three boys: Demis, born in 1975, Lucci, born in 1984 and Julian, born in 1988.

I don't know how many of my colleagues know that I lived in the Casata building for 18 years. On the 4th of March 1977 I was on call, my brother as well, and my mother had left 20 minutes earlier in order to buy an icon of St. Nicholas. We survived, but we lost everything!

Mother immediately requested permission to join her sister and she left for the United States in December 1977. Until 1980 I worked in different places around Galati county (Pechea, Vladesti, Oancea) and then I got a post in Galati city. This entire time mother struggled for us all to leave (legally). On the 25th of April 1981 we managed to leave to New York. We arrived on JFK (the international airport) right when president Reagan was shot, and the airport was closed until the perpetrator was caught. This is how our American experience began. I say us because I was joined by my brother, Lucian, his wife, and my son, Demis. When everybody was scattered around Europe, with the money sent by my father (20,000 dollars) we made our down payment for our house in Shirley, NY.

When the family started gathering up, we had a four-bedroom house, near a pine forest, down a cul-de-sac (our Paradise!). We had to work hard to pay off our house, so we went job hunting. I discovered, unfortunately, that the equivalency of our diplomas would cost us an enormous amount of money, and we decided to join the army (we were the first RSR Romanian citizens to join the US Army). It was something new for them, as it was for us.

The basic training was not quite a vacation in the state of Missouri (Fort Leonard Wood is a barracks of the USA Army in Missouri Ozarks). Two months of labor, and I, at the venerable age of 35, was competing with 18-19 year olds. But I had a positive outlook on things (they were young Americans who paid good money for survival training, who were learning how to fend for themselves in any situation, and I had a house and food and a salary). I succeeded (I was awarded a medal, as only 80% of those admitted pass basic training) and I set out to Fort Sam Houston, TX. Out of the Missouri cold and into the Texas heat, it was as if I was going to paradise. After 6 weeks of instruction, things changed and I was sent to Fort Jackson, South Carolina (Columbia).

I stayed here for almost two years and among the more interesting things I did was train the fencing team of the South Carolina University. It should be observed that all active military staff would receive, after basic training, a panoramic X-ray of their denture in order for them to be identifiable upon death. I first had them made on microfilm, which was deposited in the desert in order to better preserve it. Nowadays they burn them on glass CDs, invented by a Romanian.

Meanwhile I took English classes, for four months, on the Lackland Air Force Base, near San Antonio TX. This is where I met the Shah (the Shah of Iran) and his family, exiled in the USA. From San Antonio was close to Laredo (the border with Mexico), and Rio Grande is a myth, it is not grand at all, and so I would visit the neighboring country two times a month, where it felt "like home". I finished my 2 year training (active) and I got in the ready reserve, with 2 weekends of training and 2 weeks in the summer. I was r.r. for 11 years. During this time I could travel the world on board the US Air Force, from Delaware to Germany (Frankfurt) or Spain (Madrid). Meanwhile, the children came to Shirley with their mother. We lived in the house in Shirley: mother, my brother, Luci, with Viorica, my three sons and my wife and me, Florin.

After I finished the civil army, I returned to New York and, following the advice of a good friend of mine, I rented a car from the UTOG Corporate Car Services and I started working 16 hours a day, from 17:00 to 08:00, in three states (New York, Connecticut and New Jersey); I knew New York City very well. The work was hard, but the money was good and I was my own boss. I got three traffic tickets and 2 extraordinary stories.

Usually, I would leave for work at 17:00 and at about 8:00 to 9:00 I would finish my shift (back then I would sleep at my friend's place in Jackson Heights, who would leave for work by 8:00 and would come back after 17:00). That day, the night had been pretty quiet and I wasn't really in a hurry to get home, so I was listening to the radio and paying attention to jobs being offered. At one point, a job for Teterboro Airfield NJ (an airport for small private aircraft) popped up. I didn't wait for the announcer to finish and I pressed the bid button. They announced me as the winner of the bid and I hurried to New Jersey (we would sit around 50th Street in NYC).

I got there in time, the airport staff conducted me to the 8 people aircraft from which two men and a woman descended. They were about 40, the woman was about 30. They tell me they have to go to the Pepsi-Cola headquarters in Manhattan and I head to the (former) Pepsi-Cola Building, 500 Park Avenue, 62 East 59th Street, Manhattan, NYC. Here they tell me that the husband, the vice-president, and his secretary will remain at the headquarters, while the lady wishes to visit a shop, The Cartier, on 653 Fifth Avenue, New York, NY.

I left her at the shop for about two hours, while I slept profoundly in the parking lot. She came back carrying several boxes, and asked whether I could recommend her someplace to eat. I tell her I am Romanian and I don't really know where the fancy restaurants are, but that I've driven various couples to a few places. She tells me that unfortunately she cannot dine with me in a fancy restaurant, but if I know a place that has takeout she will happily eat with me in the car (do not forget – these cars had a bar). We ordered something that was not too messy and we spent two wonderful hours, after which she asked me to take her to their hotel reservation. She apologized again for not being able to take me to her suite. She went up, and I once again slept for three hours in the car. Around 17:00 I left for Pepsi-Co, I picked up the two gentlemen and we went to the airport in New York. On departure, they shook hands with me and put my voucher in a nicely scented envelope.

The three boarded the plane and they were gone (it was then that I found out that King Mihai had appeared at a dinner party in Florida). When I got back to the office, I took out my vouchers from the envelope. When I took the voucher out, I saw they had also left me 200 dollars (with 100 dollars I could buy a basket of food to feed the entire family for a week), scented with the perfume of a beautiful lady.

And now for the second story: a trip from Manhattan to La Guardia Airport is announced (it suited me, as I would go home from Queens). I place my bid and I win Mr. Frank Lorenzo who was going to work. The passenger gets in the car and all the way I keep thinking where I've seen this person before. When I reach the airport I see a Continental plane and it all makes sense to me! (In 1981, Texas Air Corporation, the aircraft company holding controlled by the United States of America aviation, managed by Frank Lorenzo, bought Continental after long battles with its leadership, who was set on resisting Lorenzo).

I immediately started telling him how after my first year in America I had a girlfriend in California, how I bought a round-trip ticket with People

Express for 200 dollars, how I during the meeting I had lost the ticket, and so on and so forth and how now, when Continental bought People Express, I lost 100 dollars! Mr. Lorenzo gave me his business card and told me to write my story to him. I did as he told me. I sent it to the address and I waited. One month, two months, three months passed, and nothing. I had given up. Upon coming home one weekend, I found a thick envelope with Continental written on it. I thought they had sent me their fly schedule by mail, and I was ready to throw it away, but there was a very beautiful lady down at the travel agency in Shirley and I decided to go there now that I had a reason to talk to her. I gave her the envelope and I waited, looking at the beautiful and tempting posters plastered all around the room from different parts of the world. When my idol comes back, I see that she was having a hard time with the contents of the envelope. Worried, I ask her what was going on and she tells me she has never seen anything like what she saw in the envelope. What was it? It was a night ticket, first class, valid for one year on all continental USA routes. What did this mean for me? After 20:00 I would go to any USA airport and ask for available seats. They gave me the boarding pass and while waiting to reach my destination I would eat, drink and sleep. I would arrive somewhere (I only did this during the weekend, remember I still had a job!), I would visit the place and by 18:00, hungry and tired like a workhorse, I would wait for departure, after which came the "pampering"! This is how I visited all major cities, and there are a lot of them in America. God bless America and Frank Lorenzo!

After this phase was finished, I made some money and I started seriously thinking about my career. Following the advice of the Polish immigration service (because the Romanian one did not exist), I applied to New York University (NYU) for a master's degree in Management and Dental Materials. I managed to get away with only paying 7,000 dollars because they hired me as an assistant professor considering my former training. I worked in research for two years and I participated in three very interesting projects. Meanwhile, with the team here, I produced hydroxyapatite (a material with a chemical formula similar to bone). This material had begun to be successfully used in Europe in the treatment of cists on the mandibular and sold for 30 dollars per gram.

Mixed with silica and heated in a dental ceramic oven, hydroxyapatite transforms in a colorless, glass-like substance, the first step to obtaining synthetic bone. This is the manner in which mandibular implants and reconstruction could be made, immediately after its removal (for various reasons). Unfortunately, the formula was lost. Prof. Dr. Mila Smith, who knew the necessary quantity of silica, passed away, and apart from me, no one knows the temperature where the two powders start turning into "glass".

I finished this course with an important diploma, and I applied for a job as a professor in Singapore. Out of three candidates, I came out second, and so I was unable to pursue a teaching career, although I would have liked it very much. I managed two medical clinics in Bronx, and I would drive two hours to get there and two hours to get back home and I had to leave at precisely 17:00, because after that time the street became a veritable battlefield between gangs of drug dealers.

During this time, I met Sharon, and I thought she would become my American wife, but the formalities of my divorce lasted over 5 years. Because of this, we were never able to get married. We have a 18 year old son named Andre. Because of a rare condition of hers and fearing our healthcare system, Sharon never dared move to Romania and our relationship faded away. Only our son is left, and he is the Weingarten's favorite boy.

In 1987, while returning to Romania to visit my father, I stopped by some dentist friends in Vienna, Dan and Cristina Gataiantu. They had a dentist's office in a very good location and they asked me if I wanted to stay and work with them; they offered me very tempting conditions, two weeks of operating in Vienna and two weeks of staying in Marbella, a city on the shore of the Mediterranean Sea in the south of Spain. Because the offer was so generous, I stayed until the "revolution" started in Romania. Meanwhile, being very close, I started my PhD in Romania at the BMF with prof. Burlibasa. The thesis was about the treatment of mandibles with bone cavities. By using classical methods, they could be repaired within 6 to 12 months, but with the hydroxyapatite I brought, I managed to repair them within 3 months, without the risk of fractures.

When tensions started growing in Timisoara and Bucharest, we wanted to take the RSR Embassy in Vienna by assault, but he Austrian army stopped us. In order to keep the "rats", led by Marin Ceausescu, from escaping the embassy, we barricaded the door, but we didn't know they also had a secret exit. However, Marin was found dead! (The circumstances of his death were rather suspicious).

Together with our friends in Vienna, we started gathering humanitarian aid for Romania, and with the aid of a truck convoy, we brought the supplies in March 1990 and distributed them to orphanages that were not on the government's list, where Michael Jackson and Brigitte Bardot were brought to visit.

For a week we stayed in Bucharest and we saw that every child received his portion of fresh food we had brought for it. Upon discussing the subject extensively with father and Lucian, we came to the conclusion that it wouldn't be bad if we moved back to Romania and put our experience to good use. This is how the Bio-Medica International idea came to be – it was one of the first five privately owned clinics in the country, founded on the National Day of America, the 4th of July 1992.

My father gave us his villa on 42 Eminescu Street and wished us good luck, but saw our endeavor with a dose of skepticism. Two days after opening and having no clients at all, a heavy lady shouted from the door: "Is this the address of the clinic?" We answered yes and we ran to the door (the lady was trying to get a dog into the building). She was our first client.

We started with general medicine and dental healthcare. We talked with all our patients, and, based on their feedback, we diversified our services. Nowadays, Bio-Medica has four locations, which it shares with BIODERM laser center and One to One (Saftica, www.nursing.ro).

Until 2010 we were on the rise. Now we are starting to scale down, as the prices have grown exponentially, and purchasing power has decreased spectacularly. For example, back in the good days we used I have 15 ambulances with 3 complete teams, 24/24, 7 days a week.

All this time, I was the director for external relations. I had direct relations with the most renowned medicine professors in Austria, Germany and the USA.

Through the BioTop International medical management company, I advised over 400 patients from Romania, Belarus, Bulgaria, Moldava and

Greece. Through the three medical airlines we made more than 100 medical flights from Romania to Europe and back.

Between 1996 and 1997 I worked for USAID, and I was manager of the Romanian branch for the American department on Health.

I struggled for 2 years to change the Semansko Russian system with a more European approach. The most suitable for us was the Portuguese one, but I am ashamed to say I was not successful in this endeavor. I introduced the DRG (diagnostic related group) and a few other modern investigation methods, as well as computers, in many hospitals. In 1997 I quit my position out of frustration.

In 1998, together with a few important businessmen, I became a founding member of the ROTARY Continental Club. For many years, I kept my post as treasury keeper, but nowadays I'm relatively inactive. (the Rotary Bucharest Continental Club is part of Rotary International, the biggest private organization in the world. The rotarians' reason to be is that of service to the community they are a part of. In Romania, the first club appeared in 1929 in Bucharest, followed by others throughout the country. After a period when it suspended its activity due to political conjectures, the rotary movement was revived in 1992 in Bucharest. The Rotary Bucharest Continental Club was created in 1998, and now there are 5 such clubs in Bucharest. Some of the most important projects were the aid of flood victims, the donations of medical equipment to hospitals in Bucharest, programs seeking the prevention of infantile abandonment, the donation of computers for laboratories in schools, the modernization of classrooms for primary schools, the restauration of the Amman Museum, and program for social accommodation of orphan children).

In 2002, with the help of the Tennessee Rotary Club, I founded the first privately owned orphanage NOVA 2002 in Galati. From 2002, the NOVA 2002 Association helps children and their poor families. Our activities and support centered on small children, new-born at risk of abandonment, and their mothers and families. Our mission is the formation, maintenance and strengthening of family bonds, supporting the family to assume their parental responsibilities, the instruction of mothers and adult family members for social and professional integration, in order to prevent the abandonment of children.

The NOVA 2002 Association, through its maternal Center, offers support to single, adolescent mothers, who have no support, together with their newborn and infants. The support they offer is temporary shelter for the mother and her children, protection and care (food, clothing, toys, and care products), informing and supporting the mother in resolving social, sanitary, education and professional problems, mediation with institutions, emotional support, support for the reestablishment of family ties, familial and social integration.

After a law regulating the statute of orphanages was issued – those were to be dissolved and the children were to be put into foster care – I gave up the orphanage to the authority charged with children surveillance.

I came back to Bucharest and together with Otilia Palade, now Russu, I created two companies: Biotop International and Sirene Blue. Despite all the hardships, we managed to maintain the quality of our services and I was an ARC representative for Romania (member of ARC Europe, whose primary goal is road assistance). Now, I am only left with *HTH Worldwide*. What does this mean? Any medical problem a patient who was ensured by them has in Romania, becomes my problem, and I have to resolve the issue to the best of my abilities and as fast as I can.

On the 11th of August 2008, Marie Rose was born, the long awaited daughter, who started German school in 2013. In June 2012 I finished work on the Lascar Clinic (750 square meters), turning it from a bank into the Bioderm Laser Center. From then until now, I have been working here five days a week full-time and I do Medical Escorts (with medical or commercial aircraft) and international ambulance transport. Also, a strong point of mine is medical management, for all those in need of advice. Advice costs nothing with us!

Day by day I practice pain therapy (for any kind of pain), as our team finds the most efficient methods of relieving acute and chronic pains.

My daughter Marie Rose was born on 08.11.2008. My wife Otilia has made me a joy and an invitation to live for another 20 years.

Romania disappoints me politically and economically. This is not what we wanted when we came back from the USA. Therefore we decided to move to a better climate. There I will do what I know best, a recovery and maintenance center for the elderly and the obese. I still want to live 20 more years.

We are moving to Tenerife this fall.

Mircea Sebastian*
*Mircea Sebastian passed away on December 2, 2015.

After completing high school, I attended the Faculty of Installations at the Institute of Civil Engineering. After graduation, I was forced to so three years of probation in the countryside (as was the rule at that time). During this time I worked as a design engineer and installer both in the execution of industrial and civil engineering projects.

In 1973 I returned to Bucharest and worked at Polytechnic University in Technical Services. Since 1975 I have been working on industrial sites in the Group sites-assembly plants in Bucharest belonging to the Ministry of Industry and Wood Materials for Construction. I went through various stages from ordinary engineer to chief Engineer. There have been years with many difficulties, with hard work and many site trips. The work I had was both in Bucharest and in the cities of the south of Romania, from Craiova to Constanta. I led the implementation of installations and installation of equipment for: Furniture factories; Plant materials; Synthetic Fibers; Gravel; Pits and many other projects.

In the period 1986-1988, as all construction companies were obligated to work on the People's House and yard, and participated in the execution of works in several objectives. It was a period with more accumulation of professional knowledge and with many unforgettable memories. In 1993 I made the step to the private sector, establishing my own company. One of the main activities of the company was to trade in old art objects or antiques. For this purpose I have set up an antique shop (4th of its kind in Bucharest at the time).

This new activity involved the accumulation of much new and varied knowledge and study of many special documents. Here I must mention the important support I received from my best friend, Bebe Filippi in purchase catalogues, books, dictionaries, etc. with whom I kept in touch, regardless of time period.

Our daughter graduated from the Institute of Architecture and for five years she is the mother of a daughter named Ana. As a result we are grandparents. After the revolution, also thanks to my good friend Bebe Filippi, we visited together many wonderful places in Europe, spending unforgettable holidays. Our friendship goes back over 60 years and I am very proud of it.

The years came and went and in 2009 I retired and this year we stopped all activities of firm. This is how 50 years of working and living, look like in summary.

Florin Seimeanu

My first social step was enrolling in kindergarten. At first it was not easy, but little by little, I used to it and there I met some of mine future schoolmates. Kindergarten lasted three years from ages 4 to 7 years. It was not far from our house and from the second year I walked there alone. This were good memories...

From 7 years I went to "Spiru Haret" highs chool. In the four years in the primary school my teacher was Madam Lentils. Bully by nature we were bullied every day. With and without reason we her students were her punching. She had many family problems and her nerves were discharged on us. At the age 7-10 we were innocent. After the passing 5th grade things have changed. I was now accustomed to school.

A school tradition "Spiru Haret" was a well known and highly regarded in Bucharest. Many renowned intellectuals of the country studied here, such as the great Romanian philosopher Emil Cioran. According to school rules we were boys and girls in the classroom. Following puberty at13-14 our eyes looked girls. I "loved" a colleague Daniela Pamfil. I was in a group of colleagues with Dini Cernat Andrei Drogeanu and Firu Dumitrescu. After school we came to my house and played "Poker". We played for money and earnings could "climbed" to 1-2 lei. One could buy a cake with that amount. Weekends we organized parties among each of us and play "the darkroom".

After a year or two began I stated studying for entry into the university. Intense studying started. If not in college immediately after high school, you must go the army for two years, which for me means a torment. I studied seriously – doing 20.000 exercises to math and I joined the faculty of "Equipment for Buildings" in 1964 at the age of 18 years.

I was never inclined to figure orders, I had not had anyone in the family with military tradition, and my father stories about War I, were horrible. My father was awarded the Order of "Mihai Viteazul", but I fear that I do not banish army. In my family history of over 400 years, beginning first representatives were military mentioned in historical records from the time of Mihai Viteazul. The name "Seimeni" was actually soldiers, paid officers, which defended the King. They were recruited from the free people. After 1720, the Turks had no confidence in the Romanian royal family: Brâncoveanu and Cantacuzino and brought to power the "fanariote princes" (Greek). Based on my father's stories Dr. Dr. Seimeanu "Seimenii" were disappointed left the army and purchased land. My grandfather's estate is near Ploiesti and was called "Bereasca - Ploiestiori".

Between 1964 and 1969, I attended the Faculty of Building Bucharest and I had a wonderful student life. So I graduated in five years, except that only 1/3 of my group of students 20 in number at first succeeded in over five years to finish college and I found myself among them. Saturdays and Sundays I went to "teas" = parties with girls and boys. It was the most fun for whole my life without responsibility.

In 1969, after graduation I worked at establishing design for light industry Bucharest IPIU., There I worked on many projects for textile industry. We also studied the thermodynamic efficiency of thermal supply and facilities (machines) technological, which was a novelty at the time.

From 1975 started differences with the regime in power and the authorities always baffled me. In1978 I started with a friend back in London first group in Romania of "Amnesty International". In 1979 I joined the "Free

Union SLOMR" and 18 Aprilie1979 my name was read in "Free Europe" as a new member of this union. After this action retaliatory actions of security at the highest level began. I was arrested 26 times, beaten, spit on, isolated, no longer being able to get any connection to my knowledge in Bucharest, and my phone was constantly listened to by Securitate. In my room, in the partition wall of the neighboring apartment, Securitate installed a microphone. The work was of such a poor quality that it could be seen with the naked eye. I should note the lack of solidarity of my schoolmate Matei Cazacu – which I saved you from drowning at age four. He could have supported me by making a call to "free Eupopa" in Paris, where he was in a very comfortable position. But he did not! Spineless! Times were very hard for me, but I kept my patience and temper after a year and a half in June 1980, I received a passport for family reunification in Germany, where there were relatives of my mother's German descent, born in the former Austrian empire. My mother came from a noble family Rosalia Seimeanu Austrian Cernowitz. BALCESCU name of my grandmother contributed to obtaining the passport. My father's mother's grandfather was brother of Nicolae Bălcescu, a national hero and Communists wanted to avoid a scandal, which had been reported in the international press.

In Munich I was surrounded with joy by my uncle and cousins of my mother. At the end of April 1981 my first son was born in Munich, when my parents arrived. After studying marine biology he is in Brisbane, Australia to research reefs. In terms of freedom from Munich I traveled a lot, the passion of my life. After I met my future wife in 1994, who was then a law student in Bucharest, we were married and together we have 3 children 21, 17, 14 years old. Eldest daughter is a law student in 2nd year.

All my children have studies or still studying at a Franco – Italian high school. They speak five languages with Romanian and their Latin names, in the spirit of respect and admiration our family to Rome and the Roman Empire. We speak Romanian in the house. Together with family I visited many countries. In the professional field I worked in several design offices and between 1988-1992 studied "International Trade" in Munich, where I obtained the Diplom Kaufmann with top marks.

Since 1990, after the fall of the communist regime in the Alianza Civic in Munich, where I became its vice-president, we have collected medicines, clothes and computers to help center - Batistei Street - of needy people.

I never cared for high positions, although I had many opportunities. I always wanted to be a free man; as it was my father, grandfather and their ancestors. I have conservative principles like my ancestors, and I transfer these principles to my children. I am happy that I have not gone to anyone; I was and am a dignified and free. I realized what I wanted. For several years I am writing short TV stories, and I am interested in art especially Neoclassical style (Biedermeier) Jugendstil and Art Deco. As a result of living among the antiques, which I had in the house in Bucharest, I collected and filled my home with old collections of these objects. I am proud that my children show an interest in art and antiques. Julia, eldest daughter, is painting very beautifully, and I painted more modern, aiming to eventually spend more time with my family.

Florin Seimeanu, Munich

MIRCEA ȚILENSCHI (ȚILI) *

* Provided in English by Mircea Tilenschi

Confucius: Talking of experienced troubles, would only prolong them…
I was born in Brasov, but as a young boy moved to Bucharest with my family. I arrived at Spiru Haret in grade 9 (B), coming from St. Sava, where I had been a student in grades 5-8. At St. Sava there had been 2 other future colleagues from Spiru Haret: Mihaela Andrei (deceased during school years) and Radu Pfeiller. I finished high school at Spiru Haret in 1964. I remember my classmates of the class XI B, but also a few of the other ones. I was and still am friends with Adrian Stoica ("38"), at school also having friendly relationships with Petre Rusu, Miky Andreev ("The Horse"), Nicolae Ene ("The Cat"), Serban Manolescu (Manole), Mona Toma, Bebe Filippi, Mircea Sebastian (Sese), Bebe Aldea, Patricia Filip (Picci), Ladislau G. Hajos (Loți), Zamfir Dumitrescu (Firu), Nicolae Filip (Cuky), Constantin Cernat (Dini), Ion Berindei, Decebal Becea (Deciu), Andrei Popescu, Nicoleta Nedelescu, etc. In my first year at the University, the father of our schoolmate Domnica

Sufana, an eminent surgeon, operated on my rather protruding ears, sticking them to my head. Thus, the source of a strong inferiority complex, of which I had suffered throughout school, was removed.

I grew up and lived in a family of chemists with tradition. My grandfather, Michael Tilenschi, was a professor emeritus in Iasi, an author of Chemistry school textbooks and for a few years the mayor of that city. My father, Silviu Tilenschi was a Department Head professor at the Chemistry Faculty in Bucharest. As for myself, I studied at the University of Bucharest, getting a BS in Chemistry and an MS in Physical Chemistry. I worked in the area of semiconductors almost for my entire professional life, first being involved in research, development and manufacturing of integrated circuits and later selling highly performing equipment for this industry. At the same time I started developing strategic partnerships between semiconductor and equipment manufacturers.

After graduation I married my college classmate Sanda Simulescu (another chemist in the family!!!), and we had two daughters, of whom only one is still alive. My wife and I are still in love with each other, this being the reason for young generations to tease us by considering us some sort of dinosaurs who survived the meteorite impact!

Having German ethnic origin, I immigrated in 1976 to Germany with my wife and our daughter (who has given us 2 grandchildren so far), settling down in Munich. After some difficulties, inherent to starting anew in a foreign country, I began by working for a company, which was the world leader in chip manufacturing for digital clocks. Among our customers there were best-known brands: Swatch, Timex, Omega, etc. There, I was involved in the R&D and the manufacturing of semiconductors. Later I held different management positions with leading US semiconductor manufacturers (including 14 years with MOTOROLA).

After several years of self-employment, when I sold hi-tech equipment for semiconductor manufacturing companies, a headhunter recruited me to join a leading company in the area of manufacturing leading edge electronic microscopes and other similar instruments (these microscopes were the first in the world to make visible the atoms in a crystalline material lattice). In the position of a Strategic Customer Manager (in which I worked until my retirement in 2011), I succeeded to reinforce and further develop significant cooperation ties between our company and some of the strategic world leaders in microelectronics, such as INFINEON and AMD. As a result, the company I was working for has strengthened its position in Central Europe and was able to develop new high-end equipment, perfectly suited to the requirements of the Microelectronics Nano Research.¯

———

Some retired people are aiming to have a walk on The Moon or to learn the Maya Language by singing. We still haven't decided on that. What we for sure do is trying to help our daughter Chris as much as possible in raising Kim and Tom, her adorable children. This is because Chris is an extremely busy professional, being involved in real estate projects. We do this with dedication; it makes our lives meaningful and helps us forget the various aches and diseases that have not spared us. We have a solid friendship with former Spiru Haret classmates like Adrian Stoica, Bebe Filippi and Radu Pfeiller and started new ones to other colleagues we met at the **"50ᵗʰ Anniversary of Spiru Haret Graduation"** reunion.

———

Mihaela Toma

I came to Spiru Haret at the beginning of my sixth grade (with a tail!); I lived behind the Coltea Hospital, near Scaunei Church, with mother, father and my grandparents.

I was a bit shy, but I think I fit in pretty quickly. From those years, I remember the face of Botez, who taught Romanian, Roiu, who taught math, and my colleagues Matei Cazacu, Tuky, Feldstein, and Ana Zsoldos.

Afterwards I got into high school, new students, new professors: Mrs. Atanasiu, our head professor who taught Romanian, Manolescu who taught math, Cati Serbanescu, our chemistry professor, and many others. Years flew by fast and I found myself finishing high school, full of memories I carried with me all my life!

Upon finishing high school in 1964, we parted ways, each of us setting out on their own path, full of enthusiasm, curiosity, as well as a lot of hope. Until 1989 I have numerous beautiful memories with Monica and Tuky! After 1998, we started forming a group of former colleagues, and we used to meet and have an extraordinary time! Our first meeting was at Cornu, invited by Rodica Peligrad, and 12-14 of us got together, out of which I had not seen some since we graduated from high schoo: Florin Russu, Andrei Popovici and Lucian Moldovan. I must admit that it was Florina Mârsu who motivated us! Afterwards, we met again in Voinesti (at Vio's parents, the wife of the late Lucian Moldovan). We then met at Andrei Popovici's place, my place, then Tuky's, Florina's, Monica's (when Bebe Fillipi, his wife and Mihail Sebastian also joined us). Next, we had innumerable gatherings at "Livada cu visini" down on Grigore Alexandrescu Street; the group got bigger, Decebal, Stefan Andreescu, Ileana Alexandrescu, and Ioana Casassovici joined us. Dini was always the heart of the gathering! I take pleasure in remembering the 40 year anniversary from our graduation, in 2001, organized by Dini at the Bragadiru Palace, the party celebrating 45 years held at the Casa Universitarilor, organized by Florin! I cannot leave out my meeting with Adrian Rozei, when we shared a multitude of memories (he more than I!), the emotional moment when I saw Miky Feldstein again, strolling through Bucharest, down the streets, remembering places wc uscd to go back during high school…

I think perhaps I should tell you something about me as well! They aren't absolutely fantastic things to be said, but they are part of me, of my life.

I studied organic chemistry, at the Faculty of Industrial Chemistry at the Polytechnic Institute in Bucharest. I worked in research from the beginning: at the Institute for Chemical Research (ICECHIM), and from 1990 to present at the Centre for Medical-Military Scientific Research. I got my PhD in chemistry, bordering on medicine and I still find pleasure in working on "the least walked paths" in science. I travelled to Italy, Slovakia, Greece, Austria and England for various congresses and specializations.

I married in 1971 and I have two children, a boy and a girl, both with accomplished lives, beautiful families and I have three lively grandchildren!

I am not happy with myself for spending so little time with them (especially since they live in Otopeni). I hope that from 2015 on, when I will retire, I will be able to make up for lost time!

My mother is 94 years old and lives by herself; she is blind (glaucoma) and has tremor esentiale (Minor's disease); she finds difficulty in raising her glass, holding cutlery, and her whole body is shaking, with the exception of her head. Her mind is however intact and agile! I go to see her about 2-3 times a week: I do groceries for her, cook and do anything she needs. My brother also helps her.

I have a great joy: my house in the countryside, bought in 2001, in the Tohani area (Prahova county), complete with flowers, orchard and vine-yard! We haven't finished it yet, due to lack of funds, but every year we build a little more, "brick by brick", giving it as much as we can! I go there every weekend and I always find something to do, but I come back satisfied and energized! I envy my husband, who is a pensioner and can spend more time "on the propriety" but from next year on, I will join him as well, as a "young" pensioner!

As you can see, I am an active person and I try to stay positive!

Gavril Trandafilov (Gâlă)

Gala is busy and doesn't feel like writing. This is why, upon my insisting, he agreed to an interview (Ladislau G. Hajos is the journalist taking this interview with Gala Trandafilov, who now calls himself Gavril Trand). As they say in our parts, I put on my journalist hat and we agreed to meet at the La Vendetta Romanian restaurant in Hollywood, FL. Gala lives in Miami and Hollywood is approximately half way between Miami and West Palm Beach. We met and we both shared memories. I listened as closely as I could, and I hope I can put all the important parts on paper. I interrogated him as much as I could!

Gala was kicked out from a school in Floreasca and this is how he ended up in Spiru Haret with us. He finished school in 1965 and got admitted to the Institute of Petroleum, Gas and Geology (IPGG). As usual, he went through the adventures common to the age and to his style. He borrowed money from an Algerian who got mad with him and asked for the money back early, so he shattered a Borsec bottle over his head, fracturing his skull. Gala was kicked out, of course, unfairly. He was taken back and he finally graduated. He wanted to leave the country and never come back.

That is why, before his final exam, he got a passport to visit Bulgaria, his homeland. He is of Bulgarian origins.

In 1971 he left for Bulgaria, but his plan was to go further. This is where his adventures, worthy of a movie, begin. From Bulgaria, he took the train t Greece. It was winter, and it was right between Christmas and New Year's. At the border, the Bulgarians did not want to let him cross into Greece, but he ran and the frontier officers shot their rifle. Gala, who was an athlete, ran after the train and caught it. He arrived in Greece in Salonic and stayed with relatives, and it was there that his life in the West began.

He could not ask for political asylum in Greece, out of fear that his two brothers and his parents would have to suffer back in Romania. This, of course, speaks volumes of the kind of man he is!

From Greece he ended up in Israel, with 3 dollars in his pocket. He told me how surprised the bank teller was when he went to change them into shekels. He had the address of an ex-girlfriend from Romania, but she didn't recognize him. Now he was in Israel, with no money, no girlfriend, utterly alone.

At first, he worked in the Tel Aviv market, where he would clean during the day and sleep in a shack on newspapers during the night. As time passed, he began to settle in. Along with a partner, he started a handyman business. It went reasonably well, until he started having problems with the IRS. In the end, this business was over as well and he had to move on. His final goal was Australia, and, in the end, he arrived there in 1972.

He applied to the University in Melbourne and he graduated from the School of Civil Engineering. The government hired him until he decided to go on his own. From then on, he has been a technical consultant. This business took him from Australia to Papua New Guinee, Zambia, Somalia, Indonesia and many others.

At the present, he lives in the south of Florida. He seems to be content and well off. He went through four marriages. He has two kids: a boy and a girl in Australia "as far as he knows". He cannot come to the reunion, although he is sorry, because he is waiting for a contract. He is now a technical consultant and does engineering management.

Nicolae Vasiliu[*]

[*] Reviewed and corrected by Nicole Vasiliu

Nicolae VASILIU was born in Buzau in 1946. In 1964 he graduated from "SPIRU HARET" high school in Bucharest as valedictorian. He continued his studies at the Polytechnic University of Bucharest, Faculty of Power Engineering, which he graduated in 1969 as valedictorian.

In 1973 he completed a period of specialization at the STATE UNIVERSITY OF GAND and VON KARMAN INSTITUTE from Bruxelles. In 1977 he defended his doctoral thesis at the Polytechnic University of Bucharest, with the specialty "Theoretical FLUID MECHANICS".

He attended several trainings of specialization courses: ROMANIAN AEROSPACE INSTITUTE (INCREST), NATIONAL INSTITUTE FOR APPLIED SCIENCES from TOULOUSE (I.N.S.A.T.) and reputable firms: FESTO, IMAGINE, LMS, AUTODESK, BUDERUS, and SIEMENS PLM SOFTWARE etc.

Upon graduation he became assistant to Hydraulics and Hydraulic Machines Department of U.P.B. reaching professor in 1994. The same year he became Associated Professor at NATIONAL INSTITUTE OF APPLIED SCIENCES from Toulouse. Currently he teaches in Romania and abroad courses in "Modeling and Simulation of the Fluid Power Systems". He accomplished numerous teaching laboratories, research and certification electrohydraulic system performance.

Nicolae Vasiliu conducted theoretical and experimental research in the fields of FLUID MECHANICS and FLUID POWER SYSTEMS. He published 29 technical books, 8 patents applied in industry, 202 articles in 10 countries, 67 papers at congresses and over 250 technical reports prepared under contract for industrial research.

The original scientific researches were validated by the design of the greatest industrial hydropower turbines set up in RÂUL MARE-RETEZAT hydropower plant (PNUD PROJECT) and in CLĂBUCET-DÂMBOVIȚA hydropower plant, by the design of a patented DIGITAL SPEED ELECTROHYDRAULIC GOVERNORS for RM. VÂLCEA hydropower plant, and by many others patented electrohydraulic digital servo systems.

His technical contributions have been recognized by numerous medals and awards: gold medal at the International Exhibition of Inventions in Moscow (1985), prize Best Patented Applied Project in NATIONAL PROGRAM INVENT (2006), Diploma of Honor and Gold Medal at TIB 2003. He obtained gold medal at the International Exhibition of Inventions Eureka from Bruxelles (2008) and Prize Tehnopol MOSCOW (2008), gold medal at the International Exhibition of Inventions in GENEVA (2009). He also was awarded the Best Paper Award of the conference ANSYS WORLD CONFERENCE Pittsburgh, U.S.A. in 2002.

As a result of his accomplishments he was elected in the ROMANIAN TECHNICAL SCIENCE ACADEMY in 2012 and continues to work as a full professor at the same university. She works also as an expert in Fluid Control Systems for SIEMENS PLM SOFTWARE, with headquarters in LEUVEN (Belgium).

Since 1990 he is the Head of the Doctoral School of "FLUID POWER SYSTEMS", where he completed 43 theses. Dr. Vasiliu meets or continues to meet numerous public duties of great responsibility:

- Scientific director and general manager of the MANGEMENT RESEARCH AND DEVELOPMENT AGENCY "POLYTECHNIC" in the period 2000-2010;
- General Director of ENERGY AND ENVIRONMENTAL PROTECTION Research Center of U.P.B. from 1996;
- Responsible for International Research Network for Romania of the FLUID POWER INTERNATIONAL NET and member of the

Editorial Board of the International Journal of Fluid Power edited by CRC TAYLOR & FRANCIS in the U.S.A;

* Marie Curie project director - VIRTUAL POWERTRAIN - Host Fellowships for the Transfer of Knowledge (TOK) Industry - Academia Partnership;

* Director of the European FP7 project ENVINPACT;

* Director of projects in the R & D ROMANIAN AUTOMOTIVE ASSOCIATION.

He is married for 30 years with Daniela Vasiliu, full professor at the same university. They have two married children, many grandchildren and two great-granddaughters born in Brazil. They live in Bucharest and Saftica (near Bucharest), where they own a weekend home.

Ana Zsoldos - Then (1964) and now (2014)
The history of Ana Adari (Ana-Veronica Zsodos) in the last 50 years (1964-2014)

We reunite in order to celebrate 50 years of my life and my family's life during two different centuries and on 3 different continents. We begin, as everybody, in 1964 when I graduated – successfully – from the Spiru Haret high school. I got a diploma with my photo and name on it proving the fact that I went to school for 11 years and I am ready for… nothing special, just that I have the ambition to keep going on and learn something more useful.

I went further to the Institute of Construction – I specialized in Electrical Power Systems. After the final exam, in 1969, I got a diploma with a more recent picture of a more mature me at my first engineering position at the ISPA in Bucharest, where I worked on electrical systems for the next 5 years.

During my last two years at University I was very impressed with the sense of humor and blue eyes of a thin and blond young man who told jokes, which were almost funny. We got married after same day graduation and we celebrated 45 years of marriage this Canada Day.

During the 5 years of working and starting a family I realized that my dream of travelling and seeing the world was not about to come true. In

1974 we left for immigrated to Israel. We were on the same airplane with my first grade friend (Irina Vescan Pascu), Sandu Vescan and her daughter (very good friend of our daughter's Andreea).

Life in Israel was nice and we were happy to be free. Now I could finally travel wherever I wanted, I said to myself. But the warm climate, which was almost year-round, and the endless beaches of the Mediterranean Sea kept me in Israel all these years. I never left once. For 6 years, I studied Hebrew and I had my second daughter, Tali. I worked in the same field as before. Life got a little bit more complex and we decided to immigrate to Canada. Irina and Sandu encouraged us and supported us with starting out again. They keep giving us their whole support and encourage me when I cannot keep up with them (as they are running too fast).

And so we went through a new emigration, a new language, and I once again began to work in industrial electrical systems for the Canadian Standard Association. I hope I have helped many to prevent being electrocuted or catching fire! Here, we finally made our dream of travelling come true. I worked in Europe (Italy, Austria, Germany, Finland, with the must stop to see my uncle in Paris), in Japan, Hong Kong and in a lot of parts of the USA.

We also vacationed in USA, Europe and Israel.

Everything must come to an end, and in 2011, after 30 years of working in Canada, on the day of my 65th birthday, I retired. The total years of my engineering career on 3 continents were 42. Good enough!

Daughter no. 1 – Andreea – is now a lawyer, she is married and has an 8 year old boy and a 5 year old girl. They live 5 minutes away from us.

Daughter no. 2 – Tali – is a high school teacher and has three daughters: 4 years, 2 years and 6 months old. They live 35 minutes away from us.

We are very proud of their success and we think that the good example of their parents helped them to some degree. With our 5 grandchildren we are very, very busy.

Among other distractions we vacation a lot and I also play Texas Hold'em poker at various charity clubs.

I don't know how I spent all my time working before retiring. And this is how the last 50 years went by.

After 50 years…- Andrian Irvin Rozei[*]
[*] Reviewed and corrected by Adrian Irvin Rozei

One of the main reasons behind my visit to Bucharest in May 2014 was the celebration of 50 years since the baccalaureate.

As I was a student in two high schools (fifth to eighth grade in "Spiru Haret " and eighth to twelfth grade in "Mihail Sadoveanu"), I had the opportunity to attend two separate meetings. I was impressed to see, as I was crossing through Bucharest, many groups of people, both old and young, pouring out of their schools and faculties, after celebrating 10, 20 or 30 years since graduation.

Indeed, if the "Sadoveanu" reunion was certainly emotional (about 45 people attended), the one in "Spiru" was truly unforgettable!

Preparations for the event started back on the 15th of February and took place on three continents. This was because, aside from our colleagues who still live in Romania, we made efforts to gather the ones who had gone away, in the great big world! It was especially hard to get hold of our female colleagues, who had married and changed their last name, and of all who have adapted their names to suit the spelling of the country they had moved to.

However, for the "S.H. 50" – the name we gave to our meeting – we managed to get hold of 54 colleagues, out of which more than half live today outside the borders of Romania (in the USA, Canada, France, Germany, Switzerland, Israel, Spain, Great Britain, even Australia!). Forty colleagues participated, along with their spouses. We totalled approximately 60 participants. Of course, such a massive participation, for colleagues that had not seen each other for half a century entailed exceptional logistics. It wasn't a mere reunion at dinner, for a barbecue and a few beers!

In practice, the reunion lasted for one weekend: on the first day, between 12 AM to 12 PM on a residential complex near Săftica Lake, and on the second day, honoring the invitation of one of our former colleagues, in his house near the Snagov Lake.

The description of "activities" carried out during these couple of days would be much too fastidious to be presented in detail! I will, however, mention, during the first day, apart from the welcoming discourse and the moment of silence held for those who were no longer with us, the projection of a presentation made by one of our colleague containing "old timey" photographs, the distribution of an individual badge, hand painted by another former colleague, a memory stick, we all received, containing individual presentations along with "then" and "now" photographs of everybody, as well as a biographical folder and even the school books from back then. On the second day, we took a two hour trip on Snagov Lake, followed by a monumental barbeque.

Despite this impressive schedule, the time we spent together seemed too short for all of us! Although we had all read from the presentations we shared between us before the meeting, there were so many things left untold, the memories of yesterday and the events in each of our present life, so as, at our departure, we agreed to meet next year as well.

However, we suggested that next time we would meet in another country, perhaps somewhere in Western Europe, the "centre of gravity" for our presence around the world. And, eventually, we would also extend our stay to a few days, in order to also visit the region we have chosen.

Of course, the emotional moments during such a reunion have been countless! Moreover, a faint feeling of awkwardness prevented us from fully expressing our emotion for each and every moment. More so, for those of us who had left the country, and who were now revisiting the places and recordings of our adolescence, common to all present people.

I will mention two moments in particular.

While I was packing my bags for this journey, I found the shirt with which I left Romania, almost 50 years ago. It was, more than ever, the perfect occasion to wear it again for our reunion, even if it was a bit worn around the collar and cuffs!

One of our colleagues found the letter she had sent to her best friend, before leaving Romania. Each of us understood the emotion behind these findings at the S.H. 50 reunion.

Here is the story of this letter:

La memoria es un espejo deformante!

("Memory is a warping mirror", in the words of my friend Alina Diaconu, a well-known Argentinean writer, who left Romania a few years before myself and who is currently still living in Buenos Aires).

I'm not sure things are quite like this, but I realize that this is how I experienced them back then, how I still feel they were, after over half a century.

We lived in Bucharest in a very beautiful apartment in a building on Dianei Street, just behind Spiru Haret high school.

In 1954, I began studying in this high school, after it had recently become a boys and girls school. Among my classmates I befriended many girls, but my best friend was Maria Dincă or Mia, as everybody called her.

Actually, my family had a very special situation during this time. For quite some time, we had requested permission to leave Romania, but we were still waiting on a decision.

This was until 1959, when we found out that our passports would be issued because a General in the Ministry for Internal Affairs had set his eyes on our house and had obtained permission to move into it after our departure. Moreover, the General, who was about 35 years old, and his pregnant wife who was about 18, had arrived and moved into our apartment with us, while waiting for us to move out.

The only dumb thing was that right about then, the issuing of our passports was cancelled.

Meanwhile, Loly, the General's wife, gave birth to a baby, and mother helped her a lot during this period. Living with them had contradictory facets: I quite fancied being driven around with the General's car – he even had a chauffeur! On the other hand, my parents were not so happy about the constant smell of spicy alcohol which filled the house, especially because they discovered that this concoction was being made in our silver tea boiler!

Seeing that nothing was moving, the General left our apartment, but other military staff members took his place. Meanwhile, in order to be able to immediately leave after our passports would be issued, we sold most of our furniture.

Finally, in 1961, we received our authorization to leave and we began filling the necessary forms to all authorities doing all formalities needed in order to leave the country. During all that time, the military staff members with whom we shared the apartment were afraid that someone might occupy the house illegally, and forbade us from receiving any guests – we had to meet our friends in our neighbours' house!

Fulfilling the requirements back then, we had to renovate the house and leave it as new when we left. While this was being done, we moved in with some friends.

Only at that time, I told Mia that we were going to leave the country. Naturally, she was surprised, as, despite our close relationship, we had never touched this subject before. She then started crying incessantly, saying that I was the second friend who left forever.

On the day of our departure by train, all sorts of friends of ours came to say goodbye and cried as they saw us go. In the same way, at the train station, many friends came and cried as they said their farewells, although, back then it was quite dangerous to manifest such feelings for the traitors leaving "the communist paradise".

In the train, on our way towards the frontier, I was reading a very interesting book, but before we reached the border, my parents made me toss it out the window, because we were not allowed to take it with us. Years passed before I could get a hold of that book to find out how the story ended!

At the border, when the security checks began, they discovered that my mother had accidentally taken a silver spoon with her; they took us off the train and declared that we were forbidden from leaving. I remember my father, begging them to let us go, my mother in tears and me, utterly scared. They didn't let us get back on the train until, in a moment of madness, father broke the spoon in two.

The train started moving again and I remember a soldier saluting with his hand on his hat, us waving goodbye and myself, thinking we would never return again.

It was then that I wrote a farewell postcard to Mia and my colleagues, with tears streaming down my cheeks, in which I told her:

Dear Mia,

I find myself on the train and I have about one hour left until I reach the border. I glance out the window, as it is perhaps the last time I see the wonderful landscapes of Romania. Best greetings to all my colleagues. To you, many kisses and I will never forget you.

Micky

I came back to Bucharest after 52 years and I was reunited with a group of my friends, among which was Mia.

I was surprised when Mia brought me all the letters I had written her during two or three years and, of course, the postcard I had sent from the train.

I had carried her with me in my heart, for all these years, and she had kept all the letters that had united us.

Never in your entire lifetime will you find friendships quite like the ones you make during your adolescence!

(Michaela Feldstein, the 27th of April 2014

EPILOGUE – LADISLAU G. HAJOS

————

THE STUDENTS OF THE SPIRU Haret High School class of 1964 were all born into a communist society. The graduates, born in the middle to late 1940's were educated in communism. This book offers an historical overview of the era in which they lived, from King Michael to democracy. While many facts are presented, there remain a number of important questions about the individual lives that grew up during these tumultuous times.

Approximately 40% of the graduating class left communist Romanian to live in countries where democracy rules. Does a change in location and government really change the communist education that was impregnated at an early age? Does living in democracy modify our desires to succeed? Can an individual learn to adapt and embrace freedom?

As soon as we began our formal education in school, we had to learn and admire the communist leaders both Romanian and Russian. The education in high school was narrowly defined by the tenets of communism. For example, many discoveries, in every field, were attributed to the Russians. The world knows that in 1895, Guglielmo Marconi invented the radio. The students attending Spiru Haret were taught that Popov, the Russian, was the inventor. Similarly our education was misdirected in the field of physics. Antoine Laurent Lavoisier, not the Russian Mikhail Lomonosov, discovered the law of conservation of mass or matter. Learning the Russian language was mandatory. Scientific Socialism, the study of Marx, Engels, Lenin and Stalin, was a mandatory course of study.

Boy Scouts or Girl Scouts did not exist. There were no groups for children to gather for the sake of enjoyment or free spirited camaraderie. We all

501

had to be pioneers and young communist. Being a pioneer meant participating in demonstrations and attending party meetings. Young pioneers were also forced to "volunteer" and work the fields by picking corn and potatoes.

If we were hungry after all the forced "volunteerism," there was little or no food available in any of the stores. If there was food, it consisted mainly of chicken beaks and chicken feet. Gasoline and food were rationed. Each family member received two coupons, per month, to be used for the purchase of oil and sugar. It was hard to believe in the superiority of the socialist/communist society. Our parents shielded us, to the best of their ability, from the harsh realities of communism. The role of protector created tremendous stress in the household and sometimes in the marriage.

The teenage years were particularly difficult. Typical teens enjoy listening to music, watching TV and wearing the latest fashions. We weren't allowed to listen to the Beatles or Elvis Prestley. We could not wear blue jeans, or if by a miracle you got a pair from the west and tried to wear them, some policeman would cut them with scissors. Television programing ran from four pm to 10 pm. The TV station dedicated a large part of the programming to speeches, meetings, activities and political functions to Nicolaie Ceausescu.

Growing up in turmoil impacts an individual and a generation that has similar experiences. Some rise to the occasion and others falter. Some give in to the unpredictability of life and lose their will to perform. Others rise to the occasion and gain control where there is control to be had.

The impact of growing up in a country where there was constant change couched in secrecy, is isolation. With isolation, there is paralysis. Each of us thought that we were alone in the trauma that we experienced. As a result, there was little chance to change the system. We lived in fear. We lived in secrecy. We lived with chaos. We lived with the belief that we were unable to effect revolution.

I am one of those survivors. I came to America with little money and few language skills. I possessed a strong will to succeed. A sense of purpose mixed with the right amount of Romanian savvy formed the basis for my life. This book is the story of a generation that like me grew up in chaos. It chronicles the lives of my classmates from birth to the present.

This book is an excellent description of communism from 1946 to 1989. The younger generation can learn a great deal about a time period, which continues to hang over the young Romanians like a dark cloud. Our experiences of living under communism and chaos have shaped the lives of all of us. Though many of our class travelled far and wide, we carried with us the impressions of a regime, which did not value or promote freethinking, individualism or free enterprise. Perhaps future generations we will see that communism no longer has a hold on their new society. It is unclear how much time must pass before the effects of communism no longer shapes a generation of students. With any luck, those of us that graduated from Spiru Haret High School and successfully transitioned from communism to embracing independence will pass on those skills to the next generations. Hopefully, future readers of this book will look back on our struggles and see them for what they are-historical memories.

IN MEMORIAM

––––

Mihaela Andrei 1946 - 1965
Felicia Badescu 1946 - 2014
Ion Berindei 1947 -2009
Adrian Brighidau 1946 -?
Costin Cazaban 1946 – 2009
Constantin Chioralia 1946 - 1965
Tudor Cudalbu 1946 -?
Andrei Drogeanu 1946 - 1997
Elena Moisuc 1946 – 1975
Lucian Moldoveanu 1946 - 2013
Mircea Sebastian 1946 – 2015
Domnica Sufana – Ionescu 1946 – 1983
Petre Rusu 1946 - 2009
Alexandru Tanasoca 1947 - 2008
Englentina Vlasie 1947 - 2014
Robert Weidenfeld 1946 – 1967

ABOUT THE AUTHORS

———

Matei Cazacu was born in Sinaia, Romania, and currently lives in Paris, France. He received his master's degree from the University of Bucharest and his doctorate from the University of Paris 1–Panthéon.

Ioana Crețoiu was born in Bucharest, Romania, and still lives there to this day. She became politically active after the events of 1989 and was deeply involved with the rebuilding of the country. Crețoiu received a degree in political science from the University of Bucharest and has campaigned for the political participation of women in the EU.

Ladislau G. Hajos has seen both sides of the Iron Curtain. Hajos studied electrical engineering at both the Polytechnic University in Bucharest and Drexel University in Philadelphia, Pennsylvania. He has since retired to West Palm Beach, Florida.

Made in the USA
Lexington, KY
21 April 2018